Arab-Israeli Military Forces in an Era of Asymmetric Wars

_____

Arab-Israeli Military Forces in an Era of Asymmetric Wars

Anthony H. Cordesman

Published in cooperation with the Center for Strategic and International Studies, Washington, D.C.

Praeger Security International
Westport, Connecticut · London

Library of Congress Cataloging-in-Publication Data

Cordesman, Anthony H.
    Arab-Israeli military forces in an era of asymmetric wars / Anthony H. Cordesman.
        p. cm.
    "Published in cooperation with the Center for Strategic and International Studies, Washington, D.C."
    Includes bibliographical references and index.
    ISBN 0–275–99186–5 (alk. paper)
    1. Israel—Armed Forces. 2. Arab countries—Armed Forces. 3. Middle East—Armed Forces. 4.
    Asymmetric warfare—Middle East. I. Title.
    UA832.C665 2006
    355.00956—dc22   2006018359

British Library Cataloguing in Publication Data is available.

Library of Congress Catalog Card Number: 2006018359
ISBN: 0–275–99186–5

First published in 2006

Praeger Security International, 88 Post Road West, Westport, CT 06881
An imprint of Greenwood Publishing Group, Inc.
www.praeger.com

Printed in the United States of America

The paper used in this book complies with the
Permanent Paper Standard issued by the National
Information Standards Organization (Z39.48–1984).

10 9 8 7 6 5 4 3 2 1

Contents

Illustrations

Acknowledgments

The author would like to thank Anna Wittman for her assistance in researching and editing the chapters of this book. This book also would not have been possible without the suggestions of many regional experts, US, Arab, Israeli, and European officials that cannot be mentioned by name.

1

Introduction

Fundamental changes are occurring in the Arab-Israeli military balance. The advances in joint warfare, strategy and tactics, human factors, and technology that make up what some Western analysts call the "revolution in military affairs" (or RMA) have decisively shifted the military balance from one based on force quantity to one based on force quality. At the same time, most nations in the region cannot afford to convert their forces to provide the new mix of manpower and technology required to respond to the RMA and lack the leadership skills to do so. In some cases, the inability to properly modernize conventional forces has led to a steady decline in their war-fighting capability, and even the most advanced nations must struggle to keep up.

The role of military forces is also changing. The conventional military balance is shifting from one based on conventional war fighting between Israel and its Arab neighbors to a balance based on peace and deterrence. There is little near-term prospect that Israel will fight a major war against all or most of its Arab neighbors.

Yet, there is little prospect of a full peace. Israel and the Palestinians are involved in a war of attrition. What once was a "peace process" became a "war process" where sporadic peace efforts at best lead to temporary pauses in an enduring, low-level war of attrition. The victory of Hamas, a militant group dedicated to Israel's destruction, in the Palestinian elections of January 25, 2006, threatens to make this conflict more intense for at least several years to come. So does Israel's continuing expansion of its settlements, its erection of major new security barriers to separate Israelis and Palestinians, and its movement to unilaterally adjust the boundaries separating a greater Israel from the Gaza Strip, Jerusalem, and the West Bank.

This Israeli-Palestinian war of attrition creates the risk that Israel's Arab neighbors could become involved in either direct support of the Palestinian cause or some form of asymmetric war with Israel. Syria has long manipulated Palestinian and Lebanese militants as proxies, and Iran is increasingly a player in such efforts. There is still a risk of civil conflict in Lebanon or that the Lebanese Hezbollah could become involved in another round of asymmetric conflict with Israel.

These risks are increased by the impact of Islamic extremism, divisions within Islam and the Arab world, and the war in Iraq. Neo-Salafi Islamic extremist movements have become a serious force in the regional balance. Movements like Al Qa'ida have cells in Egypt, Jordan, and Lebanon and raise a growing internal security problem. Islamist extremists tied to the Zarqawi-led branch of Al Qa'ida in Iraq have conducted terrorist attacks in Jordan, and Egypt's most violent Islamist movements have links to Al Qa'ida and other Islamist extremist movements throughout the world. There is a serious risk that Palestinian movements like Hamas and the Palestinian Islamic Jihad will become affiliated with such movements.

More broadly, all of the countries that make up the Arab-Israeli balance face serious internal security problems and a threat from Islamist extremists and terrorists. This threat results from both internal problems and external threats and is forcing each nation to give new priority to internal security missions.

The Iraq War is having a broader impact. Arab anger over the U.S.–led invasion of Iraq is spilling over to interact with Arab anger at U.S. support for Israel, creating problems for Arab regimes with ties to the United States and who are committed to peace with Israel. Many Arabs and Muslims perceive U.S. counterterrorist activities since "9/11" as hostile to all Arabs and Islam. In the case of Europe, this anger is also directed at those nations who have supported the United States in Iraq, but anger at U.S. ties to Israel is far more broadly directed at the feeling that Arab and Muslim immigrants and workers are seen as inferior and denied the right to practice their religion and culture.

At a different level, Iran is also changing the Arab-Israeli balance. Neo-Salafi Sunni Islamic Extremism attacks all Shi'ites and other sects of Islam as the equivalent of apostates or nonbelievers. The emergence of such Islamists as a major force in the Iraqi insurgency and throughout the Arab world has led Iran to react. Coupled with the U.S. presence in Iraq, it has led Iran to strengthen its presence in Iraq and ties to Iraq's now dominant Shi'ite majority. At the same time, Iran has strengthened its ties to the Alawite-controlled regime in Syria and Shi'ite movements like Hezbollah in Lebanon. This has led Arab Sunni leaders like King Abdullah of Jordan, President Mubarak of Egypt, and Prince Saud, the Foreign Minister of Saudi Arabia, to warn of a "Shi'ite crescent" of Iran, Iraq, Lebanon, and Syria becoming a new threat to the region.

Iraq is also blamed for supporting Hezbollah with massive shipments of long-range rockets that can strike deep into Israel and for being a major force behind smuggling arms to antipeace Palestinian factions like Hamas and Hezbollah. Some see Iran as truly hostile to Israel, an impression reinforced by calls by Iran's President for Israel to be driven into the sea and his qualified denials of the Holocaust. Some see it as Iranian posturing to make Israel a common enemy and assert its status as an Islamic state and supporter of Arab causes. Both explanations may be correct, but Iran's hostility takes on new meaning because of its commitment to deploying long-range missiles and acquiring nuclear weapons.

U.S. intelligence still estimates that Iran will not have nuclear weapons until well after 2010, and the threat new forms of proliferation pose in the Arab-Israeli balance is still limited. It does, however, continue to increase and could shift dramatically over the coming years if Iran succeeds in acquiring long-range missiles and nuclear weapons. The end result could shift the balance from a largely passive Israeli nuclear monopoly to a war-fighting posture based on a risk of an Israeli-Iranian exchange.

The end result is that the Arab-Israel military balance must be addressed in very different terms than in the past. The conventional military balance is still of major importance, and the risk of another conventional war cannot totally be ignored. At the same time, the details of force quality have become steadily more important and must be analyzed in terms of the ability to fight joint warfare.

It is issues like the Israeli-Palestinian war of attrition, Islamic extremism, and capabilities for asymmetric warfare, however, that are emerging as critical aspects of the changing balance. Nonstate actors have emerged as key players. Internal security and counterterrorism have become as important as conventional forces. Proliferation is still more a specter of the future than a major current risk, but Iran has made potential changes in the nuclear balance, and the use of other weapons of mass destruction, another critical shift in the balance.

PEACE AGREEMENTS AND THEIR IMPACT ON CONVENTIONAL WAR FIGHTING

The breakdown in the Israeli-Palestinian peace process does not mean that other peace agreements are not critical factors in the balance. The core geography of the Arab-Israeli balance has always been determined by five "Arab-Israeli" states—including Egypt, Israel, Jordan, Lebanon, and Syria—and a Palestinian entity or proto-state. Three of these nations have borders with other subregions. Syria borders on Turkey and Iraq, Jordan on Iraq and Saudi Arabia, and Egypt has borders with the Sudan and Libya. The military forces of all six nations have, however, been shaped primarily by their participation in six Arab-Israeli wars, which took place in 1948, in 1956, in 1967, in 1970, in 1973, and in 1982.

Past conventional conflicts have had some elements of a broader regional conflict, and some Gulf countries have sent forces to such conflicts in addition to the North African states. They have also been shaped by major changes in the potential role of Arab states outside the immediate Arab-Israeli "confrontation" or "ring" states. Iraq, however, has been the only nation outside the Arab-Israeli subregion that ever sent significant military forces into an Arab-Israeli conflict, and it sent significant forces only during the 1973 war. Iraq has also been the only outside Middle Eastern military power to conduct long-range air or missile strikes against Israel. It fired Scud missiles at Israel during the Gulf War in 1991. (Israel used its long-range strike fighters to destroy Iraq's Osirak reactor a decade earlier.)

The political dynamics of the region have changed more quickly than its nations' military forces. The Arab-Israeli wars of the past have been followed by peace agreements between Israel and two of its neighbors. Egypt and Israel—the two most important military powers in the region—have been at peace since the late 1970s, and Jordan reached a peace treaty with Israel on October 26, 1994. Lebanon had never been a significant conventional military power or threat to Israel, although various Lebanese and Palestinian groups have launched attacks from Southern Lebanon, and Israel perceives groups like Hezbollah as a serious unconventional threat.

The fall of Saddam Hussein's regime in 2003 has eliminated Iraq as both a conventional and a missile threat to Israel or any other power for at least the next half-decade. At the same time, the peace proposal advanced by Crown Prince Abdullah of Saudi Arabia in 2002 received support from virtually every outside Arab power. Even former radical Arab opponents of Israel like Libya seem to have abandoned any interest in serious military options, and Syria at least talks of peace. Iran is now the only nation whose leader still calls for Israel to be removed from the face of the earth and raises hostile conspiracy theories such as Europe creating the illusion of the Holocaust in World War II.

Peace treaties and negotiations have made the military aspects of the "Arab-Israeli balance" into a largely Israeli-Syrian balance in terms of conventional war fighting, although it is still possible that Egypt and/or Jordan could become hostile to Israel in the future. Jordan no longer plans and structures its forces around such a contingency as the primary basis for force planning. The Egyptian-Israeli peace agreement has now been tested for a quarter of a century without a major crisis or incident.

Peace must, however, be kept in perspective. Neither Egypt nor Israel deploys and readies its forces for even the prospect of a defensive conflict; both have cooperated in efforts to secure a broader peace. Egypt, for example, agreed to deploy its forces to secure its border with the Gaza Strip after the Israeli withdrawal from the Gaza Strip in 2005. Nevertheless, each state competes with the other in upgrading its conventional forces and still prepares for the contingency that the other might attack it. The risk of such a conflict is also a major reason for Egypt's concern over Israel's monopoly of nuclear weapons. Ironically, their "arms race" has been fueled by massive U.S. military aid and transfers of advanced weapons and technology to Egypt and Israel—aid and transfers that originated out of efforts to give both states an incentive to ensure they keep their peace agreement.

Jordan lacks the resources to maintain and modernize anything like the forces it needs for war with Israel, even for a multifront war in which it cooperated with Egypt and/or Syria. It is too vulnerable to Israel air and missile strikes to contemplate such a conflict even if it had the prospect of winning a significant land battle. Jordan does, however, structure its forces to deter and defend against an unexpected Israeli military attack as well as an attack from Syria. It also cannot be certain that it might not be dragged into some future Israeli-Palestinian struggle. Peace is "secure," but "relative."

Syria is not at peace, and the Golan area remains a potential area for a major conventional conflict. Syria has become a weak and ineffective military power and at best can only hope to fight Israel on a defensive basis and limit the scale of an Israel victory. Neither Egypt nor Jordan is likely to risk war on Syria's behalf, particularly in the face of Israeli air power and strike capabilities. War, however, is not usually the choice of rational bargainers. It is often the result of the unanticipated and mistakes. Syria may still fight a war even though it is virtually certain to lose one.

In short, the conventional balance may have diminished importance, but it is still all too relevant. If one considers all of the risks involved for all of the nations involved, peace is "important," but scarcely secure or "decisive."

A SHIFT TOWARD ASYMMETRIC WARFARE AND WARS OF ATTRITION

Asymmetric war is more than a risk, it is an ongoing reality. Formal wars between the Arab-Israeli states have been followed by a continuing pattern of asymmetric warfare between states, in the form of civil conflicts, and wars between states and nonstate actors. These wars have normally been relatively low-level struggles but have generally lasted years, rather than days, and most have been political and military wars of attrition.

There have been three significant asymmetric Arab-Israeli conflicts in recent years. The first was the "First Intifada" between Israel and the Palestinians of the Gaza Strip and the West Bank between 1988 and 1993. The second was a struggle between Israel and an allied Christian-led Lebanese force, and Shi'ite factions in Southern Lebanon led primarily by Hezbollah with Iranian and Syrian support. This war grew out of the Israeli occupation of Southern Lebanon in 1982 and lasted until Israel withdrew from Southern Lebanon in 2000. The third is the Israeli-Palestinian War that began in September 2000, led to the collapse of the Arab-Israeli peace process, and which has gone on ever since.

The Israeli-Palestinian War is one of the most bitter and polarizing sources of tension in the Middle East. It is a war of political and military attrition that has led to a brutal struggle in which Israel has exploited its vast superiority in conventional forces to attack Palestinian insurgents and "terrorists" in ways that have often produced significant civilian casualties and collateral damage. The Arab media is filled with the images of such Israeli military activity, and the Arab world has grown steadily more angry and hostile toward Israel. This same hostility has spilled over toward the United States, as Israel's only major ally and main weapons supplier.

At the same time, the Palestinian side has used terrorist attacks against Israeli civilians and "soft" targets as its principal form of military action and has shown little ability to control its extremist and terrorist movements. Neither Israel nor the Palestinians have leadership that seems capable of moving toward peace unless it is forced to do so through sheer military exhaustion, and both peoples have become steadily more distrustful of the other side and less able to understand the other side's motives and needs. It is also harder and harder to predict whether the changes in Palestinian and Israeli leadership are moving toward enduring conflict or the prospect of peace.

The Palestinian presidential elections held on January 9, 2005, after the death of Yasser Arafat in November 2004, brought about the election of Mahmoud Abbas. Abbas, considered a moderate, is opposed to continued violence and believes in renewing negotiations and talks with the Israelis. This brought about a renewed hope within Israeli politics that now there was a partner to negotiate with on the other side.[1]

Since that time, however, elections for the Palestinian national assembly have led to a radical shift in Palestinian politics. On January 25, 2006, Hamas, an Islamist faction committed to struggle with Israel and regaining all Palestinian territory and Israel proper, emerged as the dominant political party in the Gaza Strip and the West Bank. The future of Palestinian politics, the role of the Palestinians in the peace process, and the role various Palestinian security forces, militias, and terrorist groups will play in the future have become totally uncertain.

The political changes on the Israeli side have been less dramatic, but they have not affected the tensions caused by Israel's ongoing expansion of its settlements and development of East Jerusalem and territory east of the 1967 boundary between Israel and Jordan. Even Israel's unilateral withdrawals may do as much to maintain the Israeli-Palestinian conflict as to end it.

Although Prime Minister Ariel Sharon was elected in February 2001 as what many saw as a prosettlement and an antipeace candidate, he changed his policy over time. In 2003, he began to advance the idea of a unilateral Israeli withdrawal and creating security barriers in the greater Jerusalem and West Bank areas to supplement the barriers that already existed in the Gaza Strip. In a speech at a conference in Herzliya on December 18, 2003, Sharon outlined a highly controversial "Disengagement Plan" to withdraw all Israeli forces and settlers from the Gaza Strip and small settlements in the West Bank.

This plan was so controversial that Sharon almost lost to a vote of no confidence in the Knesset over the issue in 2005. He narrowly passed this vote when five of six members of the opposition group Yahad voted to uphold the government because of Sharon's disengagement plan.[2] Sharon established a coalition government with Likud, Labor, and the ultraorthodox United Torah Judaism party and passed his Gaza Strip disengagement plan in the Knesset by a margin of 58 to 56 with 13 members of his own party—Likud—opposing the plan.[3] Israel went through with the Gaza Strip disengagement on August 16–30, 2005, clearing the Gaza Strip of Israeli settlers. The Israeli military presence was fully withdrawn by September 11, 2005.

This unilateral withdrawal from the Gaza Strip, and some small exposed settlements on the West Bank, established a new status quo and a new situation from which both sides began renewed negotiations. It was, however, as much an Israeli strategic choice to end a pointless and an expensive commitment, and enhance the separation of Israelis and Palestinians, as a move toward peace and did not make major progress toward ending the Israeli-Palestinian conflict.

Israel still wants far more security than the Palestinians can or are willing to provide, and the Palestinians want the return of more territory and other demands that Israel is not willing to provide. Israel's expansion of its security zones and walls is a subject of major contention, as is the status of greater Jerusalem and Israeli settlements on the West Bank. The control Abbas and secular Palestinians once exercised over Palestinian politics has become tenuous to the point of vanishing, and the strength of Hamas and other militant movements with violent antipeace elements has grown to the point where Hamas scored a decisive victory in the January 2006 legislative elections. Israeli politics are equally uncertain; it is far from clear that even propeace Israelis are willing to make concessions Palestinians will accept. Violence has diminished, but scarcely ended.

The Israeli-Palestinian War has not involved direct intervention by outside powers, but there have been continuing political efforts from the United Nations, the West, and the Arab world. A UN–U.S.–EU–Russian peace plan exists in the form of a "road map" for peace, and the United States has been notably more active since the Israeli disengagement from the Gaza Strip.

U.S. Secretary of State Condoleezza Rice, who visited the region often in the months following the Gaza Strip disengagement, applied pressure on the Palestinians to crack down on militant groups and on the Israelis to ease up on restrictions to Palestinian movement between the Gaza Strip and Egypt and the Gaza Strip and the West Bank.[4] The peace proposals advanced by King Abdullah of Saudi Arabia remain the position of the Arab League, and Egypt has played an active role in both encouraging the peace process and in providing security for its border on the Gaza Strip.

At the same time, Syria and Iran have provided extensive support to Hezbollah, some support to Hamas, the Palestinian Islamic Jihad (PIJ), and other anti-Israeli forces in all of these conflicts. Whether one labels such movements as terrorists, freedom fighters, or nonstate combatants is a matter of perspective. What is clear is that nonstate actors are beginning to play a steadily more significant role in the Arab-Israeli balance and that states like Syria and Iran increasingly use them as proxies. Israel has struck at Syrian targets in retaliation for Syrian support of Hezbollah (and tacitly for Syrian support of Hamas and the PIJ).

In fact, the struggle between Israel and Syria is another enduring asymmetric war of attrition. Syria has long used Hezbollah and its presence in Lebanon to put pressure on Israel and has done so with active Iranian support. Syria has been forced to largely withdraw its military forces from Lebanon and has made political gestures toward new negotiations over the Golan. Neither Syria nor Iran, however, has abandoned their support of Hezbollah or violent Islamic Palestinian movements. While a serious conflict between Israel and Syria seems unlikely, an escalation to a Syrian proxy war coupled with repeated Israeli retaliation is all too possible.

There is also the risk that this pattern of asymmetric warfare can broaden if the Israeli-Palestinian conflict deepens and violence escalates. It is unclear whether nations like Egypt and Jordan can continue to ignore the steady escalation of fighting and the anger their populations have toward Israel and the United States. The war has been particularly destabilizing for Jordan, which had a Palestinian majority, while virtually every faction in Egypt has expressed anger at Israel or attacked it politically. Even low-level or proxy war between Israel and Egypt and Jordan still seems unlikely, but it is possible. It could also become much more likely if Israel should take any action that leads to massive Palestinian civil casualties or a massive expulsion or flight of Palestinians from the West Bank.

THE PROBLEM OF PROLIFERATION

Since the 1960s, the Arab-Israeli balance has been shaped by the fact that Israelis have had a nuclear monopoly and the fact that the Arab states around it at most have a limited capability to chemical warfare. Israel has been a major nuclear power for more than three decades, has long-range missiles and strike aircraft, and may have acquired chemical and biological weapons. Israel has the air and missile power to use such weapons to strike at targets anywhere in the greater Middle East. Syria has extensive chemical weapons and missiles with chemical warheads and may have biological weapons. Egypt ceased its nuclear weapons research program in the 1970s, but has continued with chemical and biological weapons research and may have small, aging stockpiles of chemical weapons.

Iran is a very different story. Iran is acquiring long-range missiles, as well as weapons of mass destruction. It has declared that it has chemical weapons as part of its compliance with the Chemical Weapons Convention, but has not declared the kind, how many, or where they are deployed. Iran's efforts to develop biological weapons are unknown, but it has the necessary technology and may have active efforts to acquire such weapons. It has denied it has nuclear weapons and has repeatedly pledged to fully comply with the Nuclear Non-Proliferation Treaty and to allow inspections by the International Atomic Energy Agency. Iran, however, has repeatedly asserted its right to continue to pursue nuclear technologies on multiple occasions, and the following chapters strongly indicate that Iran has active efforts to produce nuclear weapons.

The political tensions between Iran and Israel have steadily escalated in recent years, and it is clear that Israel has at least developed contingency plans to strike at Iranian nuclear facilities. Iran has made threats to retaliate. At present Iran's forces are still in development, but there is a risk that it could give chemical and possibly biological/radiological weapons to a proxy like Hezbollah or PIJ. Iranian efforts at proliferation cannot be divorced from those of Syria, and it is unclear that either Israeli or U.S. strikes on Iran could end its efforts to proliferate, as distinguished from driving them underground.

THE GROWING IMPORTANCE OF INTERNAL SECURITY THREATS

Like the rest of the Middle East and North Africa region, the Arab-Israel countries face internal security threats that in some cases are at least as serious as external threats. These vary by country, but all are affected by the threat posed by Islamist extremism and movements like Al Qa'ida and the violent offshoots of neo-Salafi groups, many of which have some past association with the Muslim Brotherhood in Egypt:

- Egypt has long faced a low-level threat from such movements, particularly the Gama'a al-Islamiyya, or Islamic Group. It is fighting a constant struggle to suppress such movements, which have attacked the regime, Egyptian moderates, and tourists. These

Israel and Neighboring States

Map 1.1   The Arab-Israeli Ring States   (University of Texas Library)

problems have been compounded by Egyptian government efforts to suppress or weaken opposition movements, which have had the effect of driving some Egyptians toward extremism.

- Israel faces problems with antipeace/anti-Arab extremist groups like Hamas. These groups lack anything approaching Israel's military strength and have been able to do little more than carry out bombings, suicide attacks, and low-level ambushes, but they present a continuing threat. Furthermore, the Israeli-Palestinian War and the creation of security walls and other measures have alienated Israeli-Arabs and have given extremist movements a strong incentive to find ways to use asymmetric/terrorist attacks in Israel proper.

- Jordan has played a strong role in supporting both the peace process with Israel and the U.S. intervention in Iraq. A large number of Jordanians oppose these, however, and express sympathy with Al Qa'ida and Islamist extremist groups. Such groups have made major attempts to attack Jordanian and U.S. targets in Jordan and successfully carried out a terrorist attack on three hotels in Jordan in the fall of 2005. Jordan faces further divisions because so much of its population is Palestinian or mixed. While many Jordanians support the peace process to some degree, even most supporters of peace express anger at Israel and the United States over the Palestinian issue. Some Jordanians and Palestinians in Jordan support violent Palestinian movements like Hamas and the PIJ, and controlling them requires constant intervention by the Jordanian security services.

- Lebanon remains deeply divided by sect. National unity remains tenuous, political violence is a serious problem, and the situation is further complicated by Syrian efforts to maintain political control and influence that include the support of assassination, intimidation, and bribery. Hezbollah and Amal remain relatively well-armed militias, supported by Iran and Syria. Other sects are also armed. Lebanon's military forces remain weak and unwilling to confront Hezbollah, and the Lebanese security forces are divided, corrupt, and subject to Syrian influence. Sometimes violent Lebanese action against Palestinian refugees adds a further complication.

- The Palestinian movement is increasingly divided among the "secular" Palestinian Authority, rival Islamic movements like Hamas and the PIJ, and a variety of other antipeace/anti-Palestinian Authority groups. The Palestinian Authority is itself deeply divided and has been unable to create unified and effective security forces. Strong elements within the Palestinian Authority want new political leadership and/or to take a more hostile position toward Israel. Internal Palestinian violence is a constant problem.

- Syria remains a de facto dictatorship under Ba'ath and Alawite control. Its intelligence services directly support internal violence and terrorism in Lebanon, Israel, and Iraq. At the same time, Syria faces internal threats from its Sunni population and elements of the "Muslim Brotherhood." There were an increasing number of violent confrontations in 2005. While little is known about the structure and depth of internal opposition, the Syrian internal security services have become steadily more repressive.

Major Trends in Force Strength

The Arab-Israel "ring states" differ sharply in both force quality and force quantity, and the differences between Arab states are as striking as the differences between Israeli and Arab forces. It is also clear that the time when Israeli force strength could be compared to some total for all Arab forces is long over. Such a contingency is possible, but now seems extremely improbable unless massive changes take place in both the political and military conditions in the region. Even some form of catastrophic political event that did unite the Arab states would catch the forces of key nations like Egypt and Jordan unprepared to devote more than limited amounts of the forces to a struggle with Israel.

Any summary overview of the military balance must recognize these facts and the reality that the Arab-Israeli balance now consists of two subordinate balances: Israel vs. Syria and Israel vs. the Palestinians. In the first case, Syria has become so weak and isolated relative to Israel that such a war could still be bloody and costly to both sides, but would almost certainly be won by Israel both quickly and decisively. In the second case, the normal measures of force quality and force quantity are both relatively meaningless. The war is asymmetric and is a political and a military war of attrition where the Palestinians are forced to fight by unconventional means.

THE IMPORTANCE OF FORCE QUALITY VS. FORCE QUANTITY

Any assessment of the Arab-Israeli balance must also address the fact that force numbers and force quality can be very different. Modern military equipment is far more sophisticated and capable than equipment made a decade or more ago. This is especially true when such equipment is supported by the most modern precision-guided weapons and area ordnance and supported by modern intelligence, surveillance, and reconnaissance systems. In other cases, the ability to modernize and modify older equipment is equally important, as is adequate maintenance. Each one can be far more effective in one country, or in a given combat unit, than in another.

As is discussed in detail throughout this analysis, Egypt and Israel have benefited from high levels of military aid from the United States and from the transfer of modern American weaponry. Israel has further benefited from the fact that it is the only country in the Arab-Israeli ring states to create a world-class defense industry, although Egypt and Jordan have had some success in this area. Jordan has had some access to modern U.S. weapons, but has faced decades of serious financial constraints.

All three powers retain significant amounts of low- and medium-quality systems, but Israel has far fewer numbers of such systems and has done a better job of modification and modernization. Egypt retains large amounts of obsolete Soviet-bloc systems that have been poorly modernized and modified—when updated at all. It also retains aging European systems that compound its standardization and interoperability problems. Jordan has done a reasonably good job of updating and modernizing much of its equipment, but has faced acute financial resource constraints and has had only erratic access to modern Western weapons.

Syria lost access to massive transfers of cheap or free Soviet-bloc weapons in the late 1980s. It has had some major weapons transfers since 1990, but has become something of a military museum—a problem compounded by poorly organized technical and maintenance support and the failure to modify and update much of its equipment. Lebanon has had only erratic access to modern weapons since the late 1970s. It lacks modern forces. The Palestinians have had only legal access to light arms and token numbers of light armored vehicles. They have smuggled in large numbers of additional light arms, mortars and rocket propelled grenades (RPGs), and explosives. They have also made or smuggled in rockets. They are not, however, equipped to play a role as more than light security or guerrilla forces.

While many other problems are exposed in the country analyses that follow, there is another major qualitative disparity that deserves close attention. All of the countries in the Arab-Israeli subregion focus primarily on their neighbors and immediate area of operations. Only limited elements are designed for any kind of power projection in which the country can move and sustain the forces involved. In general, these are strike elements in the air force (Israel) and Special Forces/ranger units (Israel, Egypt, and Jordan). Egypt and Syria, however, have the additional problem that large elements of their forces have become garrison units with little recent practice in moving and operating outside of their bases and casernes in anything approaching demanding and realistic ways. These "garrison" forces have little real-world mobility and sustainability once they leave their main base area.

LOOKING AT A SNAPSHOT OF TOTAL FORCES

Arab-Israeli forces differ as much in force size as in force quality, and there are significant uncertainties in the force counts available from unclassified sources. Figure 2.1 does, however, provide a broadly accurate "snapshot" of the forces of each

Figure 2.1   The Arab-Israeli Balance: Forces in the Arab-Israeli "Ring" States in 2006

Category/Weapon	Israel	Syria	Jordan	Egypt	Lebanon
Defense Budget					
(In 2000, $Current Billions)	7.87	1.72	0.956	2.5	0.53
Arms Imports: 1997–2000 ($M)					
New Orders	5,000	600	600	6,300	0
Deliveries	5,000	500	500	3,800	200
Arms Imports: 2001–2004 ($M)					
New Orders	4,800	300	1,100	6,500	0
Deliveries	3,400	300	500	5,900	0
Mobilization Base (% of total population)					
People aged 0–14	27	37	35	33	27
People aged 15–64	64	58	62	62	66
People aged 65+	10	4	4	5	7
Manpower					
Total Active	168,300	307,600	100,500	468,500	72,100
(Conscript)	107,500	–	–	–	–
Total Reserve	408,000	354,000	35,000	479,000	–
Total	576,300	661,600	135,500	947,500	85,100
Paramilitary	8,050	108,000	10,000	330,000	13,000
Land Forces					
Active Manpower	125,000	200,000	85,000	340,000	70,000
(Conscripts)	105,000	–	–	–	–
Reserve Manpower	380,000	280,000	30,000	375,000	–
Total Active & Reserve Manpower	505,000	480,000	145,500	715,000	70,000
Main Battle Tanks	3,657	4,600 (1200)	1,120 (168)	3,855	310
AIFVs/Armored Cars/Lt. Tanks	408(?)?	2,200	226	520	?
APCs/RECCE/Scouts	10,419+/408 (4,300)	2,400	1,350	5,162	1,335
WWII Half-Tracks	500(3,500) (?)?	0	0	0	0
ATGM Launchers	1,225	4,190+	670	2,672	130
SP Artillery	620	430	399	489	0
Towed Artillery	456	1,530	94	526	147
MRLs	224	480	0	498	25
Mortars	4,132	710	740	2,415	369

SSM Launchers	100(7)	72	0	42	0
AA Guns	0	2,060	395	674+	10+
Lt. SAM Launchers	1250	4,335+	992+	2,096	20
Air & Air Defense Forces					
Active Air Force Manpower	35,000	40,000	15,000	20,000	1,000
Active Air Defense Command	3,000	60,000	3,400	80,000	0
Air Force Reserve Manpower	24,500	70,000	–	10,000	–
Air Defense Command Reserve Manpower	15,000	–	0	70,000	0
Aircraft					
Total Fighter/FGA/RECCE	381	534	100	485	6
Fighter	199	390	85	334	0
FGA/Fighter	376	0	0	0	0
FGA	177+	136	15	131	6
RECCE	5	8	0	20	0
Airborne Early Warning (AEW)	2	0	0	4	0
Electronic Warfare (EW)	31	10(?)	0	7	0
Fixed Wing	?	0	0	3	–
Helicopter	0?	10	0	4	–
Maritime Reconnaissance (MR)	3	0	0	2	0
Combat Capable Trainer	26	96+	0	73	8
Tanker	5	0	0	0	0
Transport	63	22	14	41	2
Helicopters					
Attack/Armed	96	71	40	110	2
SAR/ASW	6(?)?	–	–	20	–
Transport & Other	186	?	71	110	35
Total	281	?	?	251	35
SAM Forces					
Batteries	25	150	0?	702	0
Heavy Launchers	79?	848	992?	628	0
Medium Launchers	0?	60	0	36–54	0
AA Guns	850	0	–	2,000	–
Naval Forces					
Active Manpower	5,500	7,600	500	8,500	1,100
Reserve Manpower	3,500	4,000	–	20,500	0
Total Manpower	11,500	11,600	500	29,000	1,100
Naval Commandos/Marines	300	0	0	0	0
Submarines	3	0	0	4	0

Destroyers/Frigates/ Corvettes	3	2	0	11	0
Missile	3	2	1	10	0
Other	0	0	0	1	0
Missile Patrol	12	10	0	25	0
Coastal/Inshore Patrol	32	20	20	48	32
Mine	0	5	0	15	0
Amphibious Ships	2	3	0	12	2
Landing Craft/Light Support	4(?)	4	0	?	–
Fixed-Wing Combat Aircraft	0	0	0	0	0
MR/MPA	0	0	0	0	0
ASW/Combat Helicopter	0	25	0	27	0
Other Helicopters	–	–	–	–	–

Note: Figures in parentheses show additional equipment known to be in long-term storage. Some Syrian
   tanks shown in parentheses are used as fire points in fixed positions.
Source: Adapted by Anthony H. Cordesman from data provided by various editions of the International
   Institute for Strategic Studies (IISS), *Military Balance.*

state in 2006. Egypt and Syria clearly have the largest forces, with Israel ranking
third. Jordan has much smaller forces, and Lebanon has only token military strength.
Palestinian forces are all paramilitary or irregular and cannot be compared on the
same basis.

Figure 2.1 reveals several other important aspects of Arab-Israeli forces. First, even
a cursory examination shows that each country has adopted a different approach to
mixing active and reserve forces and to choosing its equipment mix in each service.
Israel has strikingly low ratios of active manpower to equipment, although this is
largely a function of the fact that it is highly dependent on its reserves and is the only
country to have an effective reserve system.

Second, such an examination also shows that each country has a very different mix
of arms within each service, particularly because of its history of combat and partly
because of the different emphasis each country places on force quality vs. force
quantity.

There are many different ways these numbers can be assembled to show different
kinds of Arab-Israeli military balances. Figure 2.2 takes a "traditional" approach to
measuring the balance and compares Israel's *operational* military strength to that of
all of the Arab countries around it. As might be expected, the Arab countries have
a major lead.

This comparison, however, ignores the fact that Egypt and Jordan have peace
agreements with Israel and that the Lebanese armed forces have token defensive
and virtually no offensive capabilities. It also ignores mass qualitative differences that
generally favor Israel and the fact that no country shown can now mass and sustain
all of its forces in a war with another. Nevertheless, while it is a highly improbable

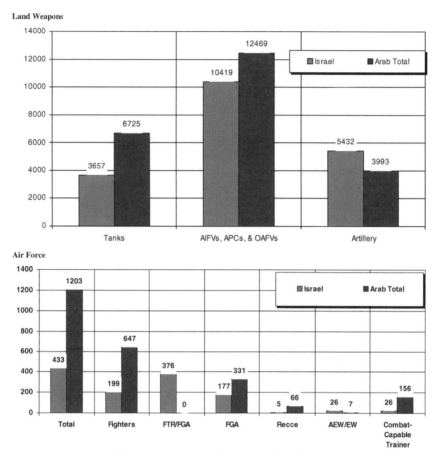

Land Weapons

Air Force

Note: Israel had 3 Gulfstream V ELINT aircraft on order, Egypt had 100 M-1A1 tanks, 179 M-109A2/3 artillery and 1 E-2C AEW aircraft on order, Jordan is awaiting delivery of 47 Challenger 1 tanks. AEW/EW Arab totals include 4 Commando 2E ECM helicopters. Total Artillery includes towed and self-propelled tube artillery and multiple rocket launchers. Total air forces include operational fixed-wing combat and combat-capable aircraft, including fighters, attack, fighter-attack, and combat-capable reconnaissance and training aircraft. IISS now labels all Israeli aircraft as FGA/FTR.
Source: Adapted by Anthony H. Cordesman from data provided by US experts, and the IISS, The Military Balance, various editions.

Figure 2.2   Israel vs. Egypt, Syria, Jordan, and Lebanon in 2006

model of the military balance, it is not impossible. Some kind of Israeli-Palestinian crises, or series of political upheavals in Egypt, Jordan, and Syria, *might* create a war-fighting balance somewhat similar to the one shown in Figure 2.1.

Figure 2.3 reflects what may be a more "realistic" picture of the balance. It compares *operational* Israeli and Syrian forces, and the ratios are reversed in Israel's favor. This comparison may do more, however, to explain why Syria is deterred from military adventures than portray what might happen in war. Israel's quantitative lead is matched by a similar qualitative lead.

As Figure 2.4 shows, this lead is almost certain to grow in the near term. Israel has had a truly massive lead in arms imports for more than a decade, and Israel has vastly

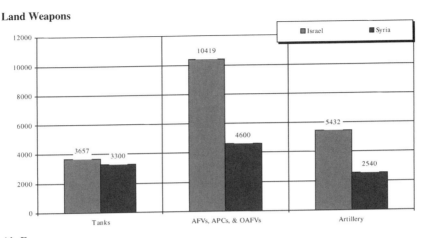

Figure 2.3   Israeli vs. Syrian Operational Force Strength in 2006

Note: Israel had 3 Gulfstream V ELINT aircraft on order. Total Artillery includes towed and self-propelled tube artillery and multiple rocket launchers. Total air forces include operational fixed-wing combat and combat-capable aircraft, including fighters, attack, fighter-attack, and combat-capable reconnaissance and training aircraft.
Source: Adapted by Anthony H. Cordesman from data provided by US experts, and the IISS, The Military Balance, various editions.

superior defense industries. Moreover, Israel not only leads in actual deliveries, but in new orders—which normally take from three years up to a decade to deliver. This more than 12:1 lead in new agreements is particularly important because so many advances have taken place in precision-guided munitions, munitions lethality, sensor systems, and the "netcentric" integration of battle management, intelligence, targeting, tracking, and communications systems during the years involved. Syria has had to fall far behind in force quality.

One important caveat that must be kept in mind, however, is that Israel is a comparatively small country surrounded on three sides by Arab nations. These nations have never fought tightly coordinated wars, but Egypt and Syria did achieve a major degree of surprise in their attack on Israel in 1973 and attacked before Israel

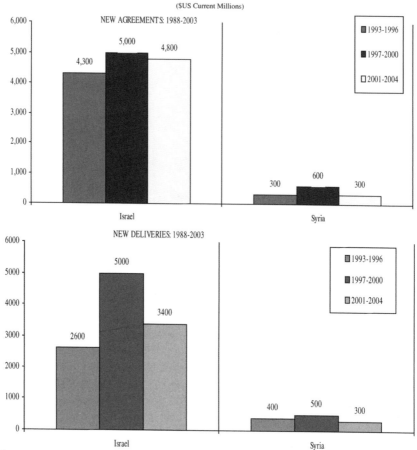

Source: Adapted by Anthony H. Cordesman, from Richard F. Grimmett, Conventional Arms Transfers to Developing Nations, Washington, Congressional Research Service, various editions.

Figure 2.4   Syrian-Israeli Arms Agreements and Deliveries: 1993–2004

mobilized. As Figure 2.5 shows, borders are an issue, and so is territory. Israel is a country with only 20,330 square kilometers of land territory vs. 990,450 square kilometers for Egypt, 91,971 for Jordan, 10,230 for Lebanon, and 184,050 for Syria. The strategic center is an area where history has repeatedly shown that flight times are measured in minutes, long-range artillery can reach deeply into enemy territory, rapid armored maneuver can be critical, and warning and reaction times can present existential threats.

COMPARATIVE MANPOWER QUANTITY AND QUALITY

Total manpower is an uncertain measure of force strength at the best of times, and it is a particularly poor measure when countries set such different standards as Israel,

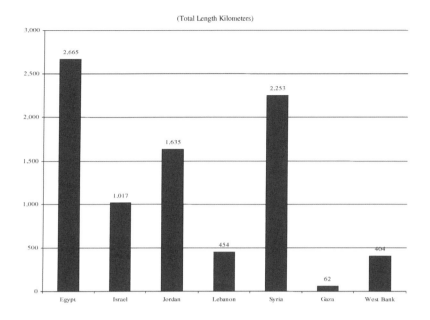

(Total Length Kilometers)

	Land Boundaries in Kilometers						
	Egypt	Israel	Jordan	Lebanon	Syria	The Gaza Strip	West Bank
Egypt	–	266	–	–	–	11	–
The Gaza Strip	11	51	–	–	–	–	–
Israel	266	–	238	79	76	51	307
Iraq	–	–	181	–	605	–	–
Jordan	–	238	–	–	375	–	97
Lebanon	–	79	–	–	375	–	–
Libya	1,115	–	–	–	–	–	–
Saudi Arabia	–	–	744	–	–	–	–
Sudan	1,273	–	–	–	–	–	–
Syria	–	76	375	375	82–	–	–
Turkey	–	–	–	–	822	–	–
West Bank	–	307	97	–	–	–	–
Total	2,665	1,017	1,635	454	2,253	62	404
Coastline	2,450	273	26	225	193	40	–
Maritime Claims in Kilometers							
Contiguous	38.4	–	–	–	41	–	–
Territorial	15.2	15.2	4.8	15.2	35	–	–

Source: Adapted by Anthony H. Cordesman from CIA, *World Factbook, 2005*.

Figure 2.5   Arab-Israeli Borders

Egypt, Jordan, Lebanon, and Syria. Figures 2.6 and 2.7 do, however, provide a rough measure of total force strength and show the trends in the forces concerned.

- Israel's active manpower has not changed radically over time, but has fluctuated according to fiscal and security pressures. A comparison of Figures 2.6 and 2.7 show just how dependent Israel is on reserve vs. active manpower. Israel has a very small active force, but if its high-quality reserves are added to its total actives, its force strength is far more competitive with its Arab neighbors.

- Egypt's manpower has been relatively static since the early 1980s, and its high numbers reflect civil pressures to use conscription as a means of "nation building" and employment as well as efforts to maintain a large force structure for military purposes.

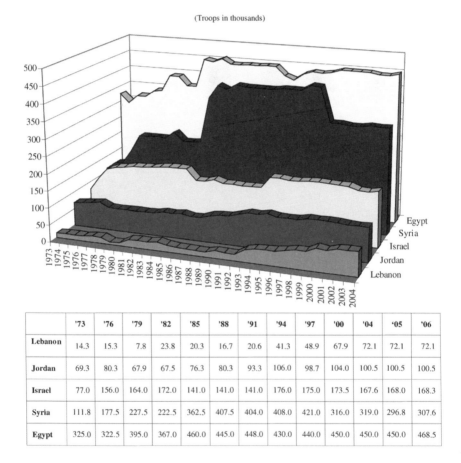

(Troops in thousands)

	'73	'76	'79	'82	'85	'88	'91	'94	'97	'00	'04	'05	'06
Lebanon	14.3	15.3	7.8	23.8	20.3	16.7	20.6	41.3	48.9	67.9	72.1	72.1	72.1
Jordan	69.3	80.3	67.9	67.5	76.3	80.3	93.3	106.0	98.7	104.0	100.5	100.5	100.5
Israel	77.0	156.0	164.0	172.0	141.0	141.0	141.0	176.0	175.0	173.5	167.6	168.0	168.3
Syria	111.8	177.5	227.5	222.5	362.5	407.5	404.0	408.0	421.0	316.0	319.0	296.8	307.6
Egypt	325.0	322.5	395.0	367.0	460.0	445.0	448.0	430.0	440.0	450.0	450.0	450.0	468.5

Source: Adapted by Anthony H. Cordesman from the IISS, The Military Balance, various editions. Some data adjusted or estimated by the author.

Figure 2.6   Total Arab-Israeli Active Military Manpower: 1973–2006

(Troops in thousands)

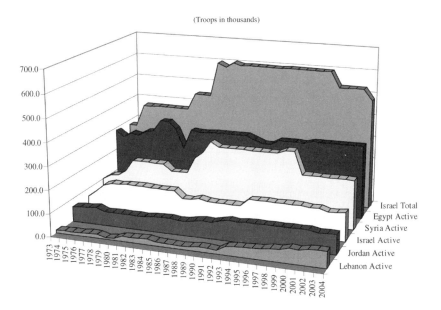

	'73	'76	'79	'82	'85	'88	'91	'94	'97	'00	'04	'05	'06
Lebanon Active	13.0	14.0	7.0	22.3	19.0	15.0	19.3	40.0	47.5	65.0	72.1	72.1	72.1
Jordan Active	65.0	75.0	61.0	60.0	68.0	70.0	82.0	90.0	90.0	90.0	100.5	100.5	100.5
Israel Active	65.0	135.0	138.0	135.0	104.0	104.0	104.0	134.0	134.0	130.0	167.6	168.0	168.3
Syria Active	100.0	150.0	200.0	170.0	240.0	300.0	300.0	300.0	315.0	215.0	319.0	296.8	307.6
Egypt Active	285.0	275.0	350.0	235.0	315.0	320.0	305.0	310.0	310.0	320.0	450.0	450.0	468.5
Israel Total	275.0	375.0	375.0	450.0	600.0	598.0	598.0	598.0	598.0	530.0	525.6	576.0	576.3

Source: Adapted by Anthony H. Cordesman from the IISS, The Military Balance, various editions. Some data adjusted or estimated by the author.

Figure 2.7 Arab Active vs. Israeli Mobilized Army Manpower: 1973–2005

• Jordan slowly raised its manpower from the early 1970s to mid-1990s in ways that reflected the increase in its population and draft-age manpower as much as out of any military necessity. Its manpower has since been relatively constant, in part because Jordan has given priority to professionalism, modernization, and readiness.

• Syria maintained extremely high manpower levels after its 1982 war with Israel, but then cut them back in the late 1990s, partly because of their cost and partly because it could not properly equip, train, and support such forces.

• Lebanon has slowly increased its force strength since the end of its civil war, which shattered its military forces, but has built up to a moderate manpower total over the last decade.

Once again, however, numbers tell only part of the story. Human factors are at least as important as equipment. Training, experience, and personnel management development are critical "intangibles" that are hard to compare and virtually impossible to quantify, and which again can differ radically from country to country and unit to unit. Countries differ strikingly in the demands they put on personnel for promotion and the trust and initiative given to junior officers. In some countries, given forces have highly effective cadres of noncommissioned officers (NCOs) and technicians. In others, a major gap exists between officer and other ranks that degrades every aspect of operations.

Israel, for example, has achieved or surpassed most Western powers in giving human factors the emphasis needed in modern military operations, and its only major problem is a high degree of dependence on conscripts and reserves, which limits the size of its fully trained, experienced, and combat-ready cadres. Egypt is slowly improving personnel management and has some good units, but still has large numbers of low-quality personnel, an inadequate NCO core, limited initiative for junior officers, and inadequate career development and personnel management. Jordan now has a mix of good professional forces and conscripts and high levels of personnel quality in areas like Special Forces. Money remains a problem, as does technical training and merit-based promotion.

The lack of recent combat experience and political and cultural factors have tended to create problems with military bureaucracy and a garrison mentality in all of the Arab forces in this region. Syria, however, has compounded these problems with corruption, nepotism, and an occupation of Lebanon that further politicized and corrupted its forces. There are pockets of excellence, but they exist in spite of —not because of—Syria's overall approach to manpower quality. Lebanon has some excellent officers, but has not been able to fund a high level of effectiveness in any aspect of its military personnel system, and is still affected by serious sectarian divisions and rivalries. Personnel quality is improving, but slowly. The Palestinians have learned asymmetric warfare by fighting it, but their trained security forces are hopelesly divided, are corrupt, and have been crippled by Israeli attacks. The training of extremist forces, militias, and similar informal forces is poor and often more a showpiece than anything meaningful.

The net result is a gap between Israel and its Arab neighbors that is bridged only to a moderate degree in Egypt and Jordan. Israel has a greatly superior unit and exercise training at the field (FTX) and command post (CPX) levels—although this has been weakened since 2000 by the need to fight the Palestinians. Egyptian FTX- and CPX-level exercises are sometimes good, but are often showpiece efforts that are undemanding and unrealistic. Jordan has moderate FTX and CPX capability, emphasizing Special Forces and some elements of its armor. Syrian FTX and CPX exercises are limited and unrealistic. Lebanon and the Palestinians have little experience, although Lebanon has made a few attempts at such efforts.

As the following country-by-country analysis shows, similar disparities exist in the key elements of military organization, systems, and training that underpin what some experts have called the "revolution" in military affairs. Israel is the only country to develop a modern mix of "jointness" between its military services: integration or netting of its command, sensor, communications, information and intelligence systems; and integrated or "combined operations" within its individual services. Egypt and Jordan are making slow progress: Egypt is limited by a sometimes stultifying military bureaucracy and Jordan by resources. Syria is a rigid and outdated military structure lagging several decades behind modern standards. Lebanon and the Palestinians have not had the opportunity or means to modernize in these areas.

These problems are compounded in the case of most reserve forces. Israel does have modern and relatively well-trained reserves, many of which have had extensive practical experience in asymmetric warfare since 2000. Jordan has some good reserve elements. In general, however, Arab reserve military forces are little more than "paper" forces with no real refresher or modern training, little or no exercise experience, poor equipment and readiness support, and little or no experience in mobility and sustainability. These forces are often given low-grade or failed officers and NCOs. They do little more than pointlessly consume military resources that would be better spent on active forces.

COMPARATIVE LAND FORCE STRENGTH

There is no easy way to analyze the comparative strength of land forces. Various war games and equipment weighting systems can help provide insights into some aspects of military capability, but they also disguise many of the qualitative differences involved. War games can test only certain aspects of force capability in given scenarios, and equipment weighting systems present major problems because there are so many types of equipment that come in so many different force mixes, levels of modernization, and levels of readiness.

There are, however, some trends that are useful, and comparing equipment holdings by type and quality provides at least some insights into the qualitative differences between land forces.

Comparative Land Force Manpower

Figure 2.8 shows that the trends in army manpower largely mirror image the trends in total manpower in all four services. Figure 2.8 compares mobilized Israel manpower with active Arab country manpower because Israel organizes its forces to rely on its reserves as a substitute for active manpower.

Figure 2.9 displays the full diversity of Arab-Israeli land force manpower, including paramilitary forces. Data are lacking on the number of conscripts in several countries, but such dependence is a critical factor affecting manpower quality in Israel, Egypt, and Syria. As has been noted earlier, the large numbers of reserves in the Arab countries are largely meaningless. The same is true of the large numbers of paramilitary forces. The vast majority have no war-fighting capability, and most lack more than minimal capability even in their main mission.

(Troops in thousands)

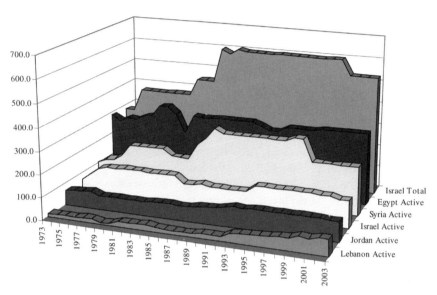

	'73	'76	'79	'82	'85	'88	'91	'94	'97	'00	'03
Lebanon Active	13.0	14.0	7.0	22.3	19.0	15.0	19.3	40.0	47.5	65.0	70.0
Jordan Active	65.0	75.0	61.0	60.0	68.0	70.0	82.0	90.0	90.0	90.0	84.7
Israel Active	65.0	135.0	138.0	135.0	104.0	104.0	104.0	134.0	134.0	130.0	120.0
Syria Active	100.0	150.0	200.0	170.0	240.0	300.0	300.0	300.0	315.0	215.0	215.0
Egypt Active	285.0	275.0	350.0	235.0	315.0	320.0	305.0	310.0	310.0	320.0	320.0
Israel Total	275.0	375.0	375.0	450.0	600.0	598.0	598.0	598.0	598.0	530.0	530.0

Source: Adapted by Anthony H. Cordesman from the IISS, The Military Balance, various editions. Some data adjusted or estimated by the author.

Figure 2.8   Arab Active vs. Israeli Mobilized Army Manpower: 1973–2003

As has been touched upon earlier, such figures disguise the major differences in manpower quality between countries. They also disguise the major differences between units. Israel and Jordan do maintain a rough consistency in the quality of the manpower in their major combat units, but even these countries give some units significantly higher priority in terms of officer and NCO quality, realistic training, and cadres of professional full-time soldiers. The quality of combat support units is often higher than that of service support and logistic units.

Egypt is still split between units with modern U.S. equipment, units with older Soviet-bloc equipment and reserve units. Overall personnel management is erratic, but the better-equipped units also get the better manpower in terms of officers,

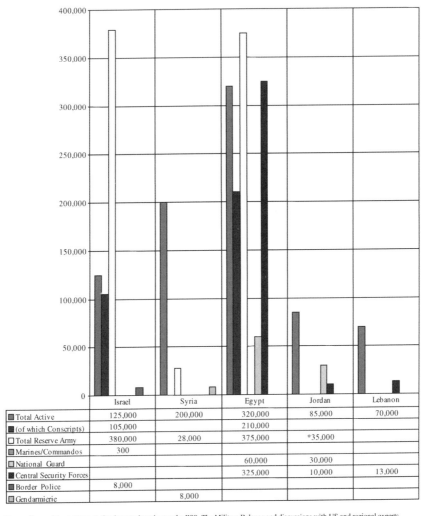

	Israel	Syria	Egypt	Jordan	Lebanon
■ Total Active	125,000	200,000	320,000	85,000	70,000
■ (of which Conscripts)	105,000		210,000		
□ Total Reserve Army	380,000	28,000	375,000	*35,000	
■ Marines/Commandos	300				
□ National Guard			60,000	30,000	
■ Central Security Forces			325,000	10,000	13,000
■ Border Police	8,000				
□ Gendarmerie		8,000			

Source: Prepared by Anthony H. Cordesman, based upon the IISS, The Military Balance and discussions with US and regional experts.

Figure 2.9   Arab-Israeli Land Force Manpower in 2006

NCO, and professional cadres. Soviet-bloc units often have substantially lower manpower quality, and reserve units are often little more than "placeholder units" to park less competent officers and NCOs. Support and logistic units have very mixed manpower quality. A vast military bureaucracy also consumes large amounts of trained manpower with limited practical benefit.

Syria has seen a steady drop in army manpower quality since the early 1990s and has become more and more a bureaucratic garrison force. Some Special Forces and armored units are exceptions, but promotion is highly dependent on favoritism and nepotism. The NCO corps and technical specialists in other ranks lag badly in both quality and status. The occupation of Lebanon has also encouraged a pattern of corruption, compounded by relatively poor salaries and a slow loss of social status.

Lebanese forces are still in transition to a true national force both in terms of integrating an army that will not divide once it comes under sectarian pressure and one with manpower that has the proper training and capability to take the initiative. Individual levels of training are often good, but this is not a cohesive force or one with exercise experience that compensates for its lack of recent practical combat experience.

One key lesson that emerges out of these differences, and the many other differences that follow, is that fully adequate force comparisons would have to look far beyond the totals and examine the differences between each major combat unit in each army's order of battle, and in the relevant combat support, service support, logistic, and other units. There is no way to validly generalize about entire force structures, and assessments and simulations based on the thesis that the major combat units in given countries are similar—or in country-to-country comparisons—are simply wrong. The qualitative and quantitative differences between units are often so great that a fully valid analysis of war-fighting effectiveness can be done only on a unit-by-unit level.

Varying Mixes of Armor and Antitank Weapons

Figures 2.10–2.15 show the trend in Arab-Israeli armor. They show that every country except Lebanon is "tank heavy" and places a major emphasis on heavy armor—partly because the outcome of past wars has been so heavily shaped by armored maneuver warfare. These figures also show, however, that the mix of combined arms within each army is, however, strikingly different.

Figure 2.10 shows that Israel has emphasized main battle tanks (MBTs) and armored personnel carriers (APCs). Syria has supported its tanks with large numbers of other armored fighting vehicles (OAFVs), but has much less overall armored mobility and far fewer armored personnel carriers. Jordan has a somewhat similar mix of armored vehicles to Israel, although far fewer numbers. Egypt too emphasizes main battle tanks and armored personnel carriers over other armored fighting vehicles. Lebanon has limited tank strength, but an adequate number of APCs for its relatively small force.

Figures 2.11 and 2.12 show the relative quality of the main battle tanks in each country. Israel and Egypt have a distinct lead, Israel with its Merkavas and Egypt with its M-1s. The M-60 series is still a good tank by regional standards, as is the T-72, but even the best upgraded M-60s are technically inferior to the Merkava. The export versions of the T-72s in Syria have competent armor and drive trains, but poor ergonomics and inferior fire control, targeting, and night vision systems. The Jordanian Challengers are roughly equivalent to upgraded M-60s, with better armor and worse fire-control systems. Even upgraded T-62s are now obsolescent.

(Numbers of major combat weapons)

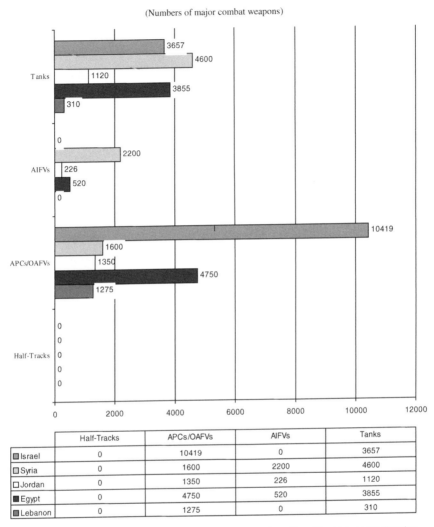

	Half-Tracks	APCs/OAFVs	AIFVs	Tanks
▣ Israel	0	10419	0	3657
▢ Syria	0	1600	2200	4600
☐ Jordan	0	1350	226	1120
■ Egypt	0	4750	520	3855
▣ Lebanon	0	1275	0	310

Source: Adapted by Anthony H. Cordesman from the IISS, The Military Balance, various editions. Other data based upon discussions with US experts.

Figure 2.10   Arab-Israeli Armored Forces in 2006

The older T-54s, T-55s, M-47s, M-48s, Ramses, and Chieftains shown in Figure 2.11 can still play an effective role in armored infantry combat, and sheer numbers can be important. They are all obsolete, however, in engaging truly modern main battle tanks.

Figures 2.13–2.15 show the relative strength and quality of Arab-Israel other armored vehicles, including armored infantry fighting vehicles (AIFVs) and APCs. Figure 2.13 shows that Israel has a major lead in sheer numbers, but the totals shown

(Numbers of major combat weapons)

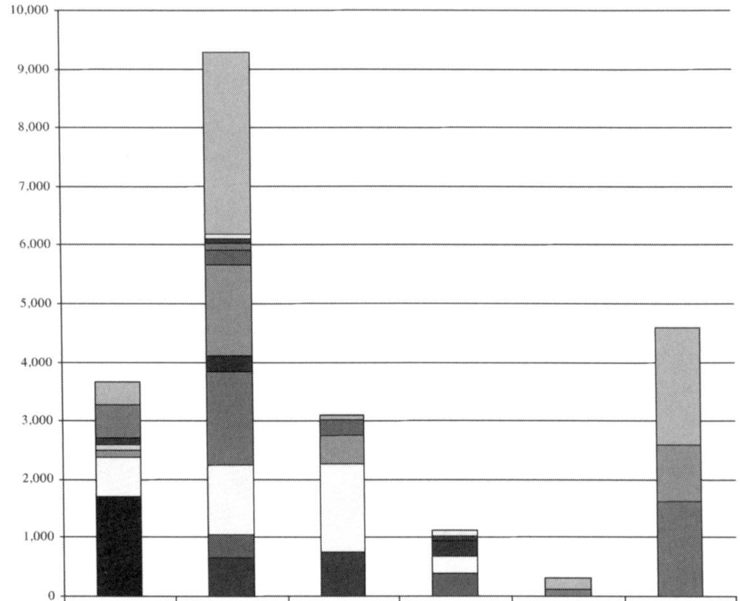

	Israel	Total Arab	Egypt	Jordan	Lebanon	Syria
▨ T-54/T-55	387	3,095	80		200	2,000
▢ Centurion/Tariq	0	90		90		
▣ M-47/M-48		78		78		
▨ M-48A5	561	110			110	
▨ Ramses II		260	260			
▣ Ti-67(T-54/55)	114					
▢ Magach 7	111					
▨ T-62	100	1,550	500			1,000
▣ Chieftan/Khalid		274		274		
▨ T-72		1,600				1,600
▢ M-60A1/A3	711	1,188	1,500	288		
▣ Challenger 1/Al Hussein		390		390		
▣ Merkava	1,681					
▣ M-1		650	755			

Note: The totals include large numbers of vehicles that are in storage or are fixed in place. In 2000, these included 300 M-47/M-48A5s for Jordan, 1,200 tanks for Syria and an unknown number for Egypt, Israel, and Lebanon.
Source: Adapted from the IISS, The Military Balance, various editions. Some data adjusted or estimated by the author. Data differ significantly from estimated by US experts.

Figure 2.11   Israel vs. Egypt, Syria, Jordan, and Lebanon: Operational Tanks by Type 2006

include significant numbers of obsolete half-tracks that are more useful for transportation across rough terrain than armored combat.

Figure 2.14 shows the relative strength in true armored fighting vehicles, and it is clear that Egypt and Syria have a major quantitative lead. Many of these systems, however, are worn and obsolete or obsolescent. The Ramtas, BMPs, and YPR-765s are limited exceptions, but are lightly armored by modern standards. They cannot engage in tank warfare except in the support role or in defensive positions where

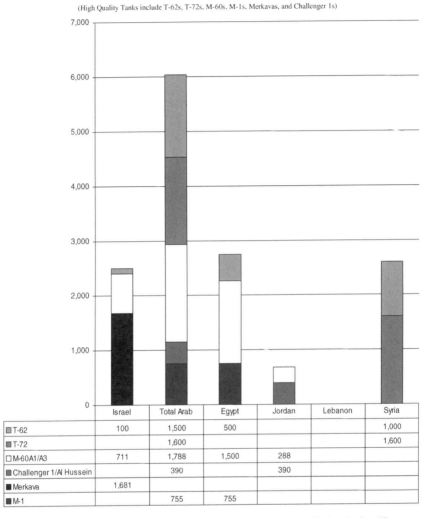

(High Quality Tanks include T-62s, T-72s, M-60s, M-1s, Merkavas, and Challenger 1s)

	Israel	Total Arab	Egypt	Jordan	Lebanon	Syria
▨ T-62	100	1,500	500			1,000
▨ T-72		1,600				1,600
☐ M-60A1/A3	711	1,788	1,500	288		
▨ Challenger 1/Al Hussein		390		390		
■ Merkava	1,681					
▨ M-1		755	755			

Source: Adapted from the IISS, The Military Balance, various editions. Some data adjusted or estimated by the author. Data differ significantly from estimated by US experts.

Figure 2.12   Israel vs. Egypt, Syria, Jordan, and Lebanon: High-Quality Tanks by Type 2006

those equipped with modern antitank guided weapons can be far more effective. Almost all, however, can play an important role in bringing infantry and weapons squads into the forward area and in providing some fire support role. This "battle-field taxi" role can be critical in ensuring tanks have suitable combined arms support in combat.

Figure 2.15 shows holdings of conventional APCs. It shows Israel has excellent combat mobility even without its half-tracks being in the count. Egypt and Syria

(Numbers of major combat weapons)

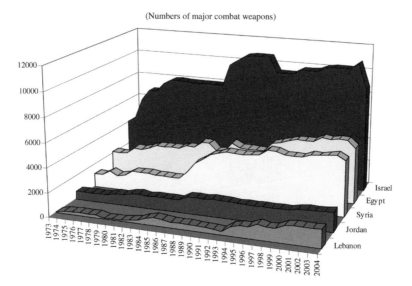

Country	'73	'75	'77	'79	'81	'83	'85	'91	'93	'95	'99	'01	'04	'05
Lebanon	80	204	239	80	80	245	658	402	312	915	1085	1463	1463	1463
Jordan	670	670	680	860	1102	1022	1022	1403	1324	1304	1324	1501	1595	1595
Syria	1100	1470	1300	1700	1600	1600	2200	4275	4250	4800	4510	4785	4600	4600
Egypt	2100	2100	2630	3080	3130	3330	3830	3660	3660	4501	4886	5172	4682	4752
Israel	4015	6100	6965	8080	8065	8000	8000	10780	8488	9488	10188	10308	8770	13078

Note: Includes APCs, scout cars, half-tracks, mechanized infantry fighting vehicles, reconnaissance vehicles and other armored vehicles other than tanks. The totals include large numbers of vehicles that are in storage or not operational. In 2003, they included 3,000-3,500 half tracks for Israel, 220 BMP-1s and 1,075 BTR-60/OT-62s for Egypt, and an unknown number for Lebanon, and Syria.
Source: Adapted by Anthony H. Cordesman from the IISS, The Military Balance, various years. Some data adjusted or estimated by the author

Figure 2.13   Arab-Israeli Other Armored Fighting Vehicles (Light Tanks, AFVs, APCs, Scouts, RECCE, OAFVs): 1973–2005

have good mobility, but many systems are worn, wheeled vehicles and hard to sustain in maneuver warfare. Jordan and Lebanon have adequate numbers of APCs for forces of their size.

One key point about these figures is that they show total numbers before combat. Armor, artillery, and aircraft numbers in combat depend heavily on support, maintenance, and repair capabilities.

Israel and Jordan have significant numbers of antitank guided missiles (ATGMs) and other antitank weapons. Egypt and Syria, however, have exceptionally large numbers of ATGMs, in part because Israel has forced them to fight defensively against Israeli tank attacks. Many of these ATGMs are now mounted on APCs and AIFVs, but each country has a different force mix.

It is important to note that Israel, like the United States in Iraq, has learned the hard way that irregular forces like Hezbollah and the Palestinians have learned how

(AFVs include Light Tanks, MICVs, AIFVs, and Reconnaissance)

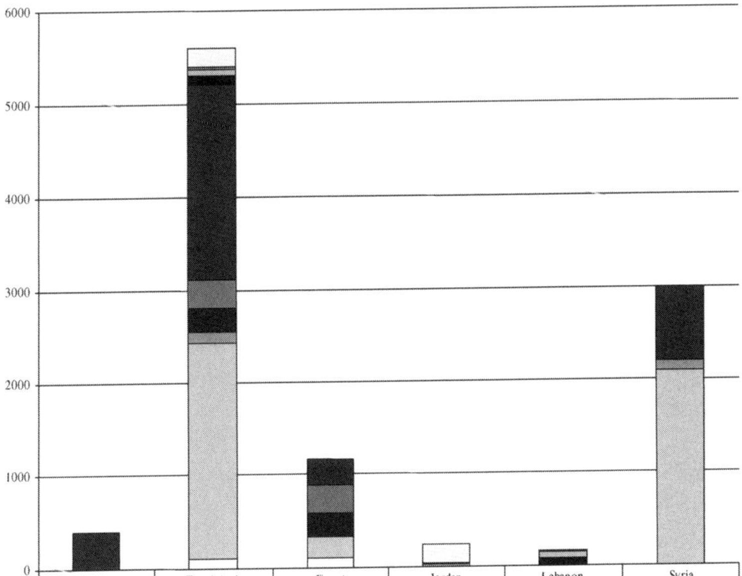

	Israel	Total Arab	Egypt	Jordan	Lebanon	Syria
☐ Ratel-20		200		200		
▣ Saladin		25			25	
☐ AML-90		60			60	
■ AMX-13		81			81	
▣ Scorpion		19		19		
■ BRDM-2 Rkh						
■ BRDM-2		2100	300			800
▣ YPR-765		300	300			
■ BMR-600P		250	250			
■ BMP-3						
▣ BMP-2		126		26		100
☐ BMP-1		2320	220			2100
☐ Commando Scout		112	112			
■ Ramta, RBY, BDRM	400					

Source: Adapted by Anthony H. Cordesman from the IISS, The Military Balance. Some data adjusted or estimated by the author on the basis of comments by US experts.

Figure 2.14   Israel vs. Egypt, Syria, Jordan, and Lebanon: "True AFVs" 2006

to carry out sophisticated ambushes with light antiarmored weapons like RPGs and improvised explosive devices and that such attacks can be effective in urban warfare, against exposed patrols. The depth and the nature of armored warfare are changing, and Israel has increasingly found that only main battle tanks and heavily armored tanks to AFV conversions can safely engage in close combat in urban and built-up areas. Israel has not as yet, however, encountered the kind of systematic ambushes and improvised explosive device attacks on soft support and logistic vehicles that have forced the United States to up-armor many of its support and logistic vehicles in Iraq.

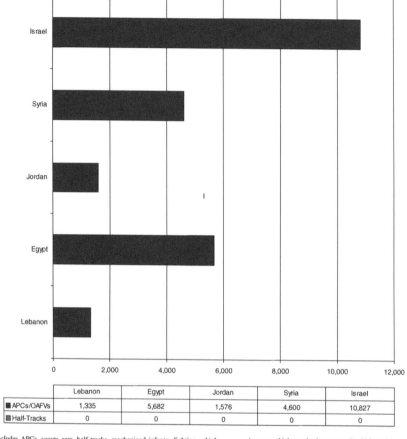

	Lebanon	Egypt	Jordan	Syria	Israel
■ APCs/OAFVs	1,335	5,682	1,576	4,600	10,827
▨ Half-Tracks	0	0	0	0	0

Includes APCs, scouts cars, half-tracks, mechanized infantry fighting vehicles, reconnaissance vehicles and other armored vehicles other than tanks. The totals do not include large numbers of vehicles that are in storage or not operational. In 2000, they included 3,000-3,500 half tracks for Israel, 1,075 BTR-60/OT-62s for Egypt, and an unknown number for Lebanon, and Syria
Source: Adapted by Anthony H. Cordesman from the IISS, The Military Balance. Some data adjusted or estimated by the author on the basis of comments by US experts.

Figure 2.15 Operational Arab-Israeli Armored Personnel Carriers in 2006

Varying Mixes of Artillery and Antiaircraft Weapons

As might be expected from armies that have fought several major wars of maneuver, Israel, Egypt, Jordan, and Syria all have large numbers of self-propelled artillery weapons—although the ratios differ and there are major differences in equipment quality. All of the armies also retain large numbers of towed weapons, although Syria has a very large pool of such weapons compared to its neighbors. This reflects a long-standing Syrian emphasis on artillery, growing out of its past dependence on French doctrine from the 1950s and 1960s, and Soviet doctrine thereafter. It also, however,

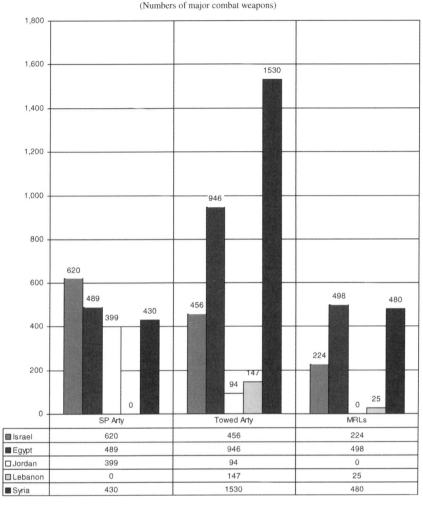

(Numbers of major combat weapons)

	SP Arty	Towed Arty	MRLs
■ Israel	620	456	224
■ Egypt	489	946	498
☐ Jordan	399	94	0
☐ Lebanon	0	147	25
■ Syria	430	1530	480

Source: Adopted by Anthony H. Cordesman, based upon the IISS, The Military Balance and discussions with US experts.

Figure 2.16   Arab-Israeli Artillery Forces by Category of Weapon in 2006

reflects Syria's heavy dependence on mass fires and the use of towed artillery in defensive positions.

Figure 2.16 shows the overall mix of artillery weapons in each country. Figure 2.17 highlights relative strength in self-propelled weapons and reflects the Israeli emphasis on self-propelled weapons over towed weapons. These systems are broken out by weapons type in Figure 2.18. In theory, the weapons in Egyptian and Syrian hands should have a range advantage over those in Israeli forces.

In practice, Egypt and especially Syria have lagged badly behind Israel in long-range targeting capability, the ability to shift and rapidly retarget fires, other artillery

(Numbers of major combat weapons)

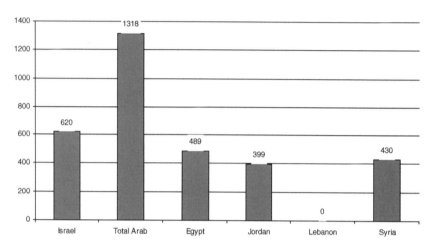

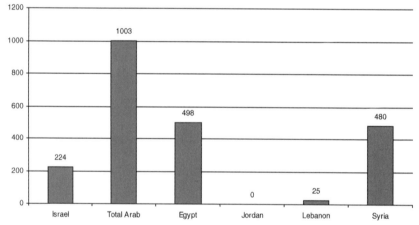

Source: Prepared by Anthony H. Cordesman, based upon the IISS, The Military Balance and discussions with US and regional experts.

Figure 2.17   Israel vs. Egypt, Syria, Jordan, and Lebanon: High-Performance Artillery in 2006

battlement systems, the use of counterbattery and other radars, use of unmanned aerial vehicles (UAVs) as targeting and reconnaissance systems, and mobile ammunition support. Jordan has good artillery numbers for a force its size, but faces financial limitations in providing adequate numbers of targeting and battle management systems.

Figure 2.19 shows that Israel, Syria, and Egypt also have significant numbers of multiple rocket launchers (MRLs) and surface-to-surface missiles. The numbers of MRLs are misleading, however, since Israel has developed a family of highly

(Numbers of major combat weapons)

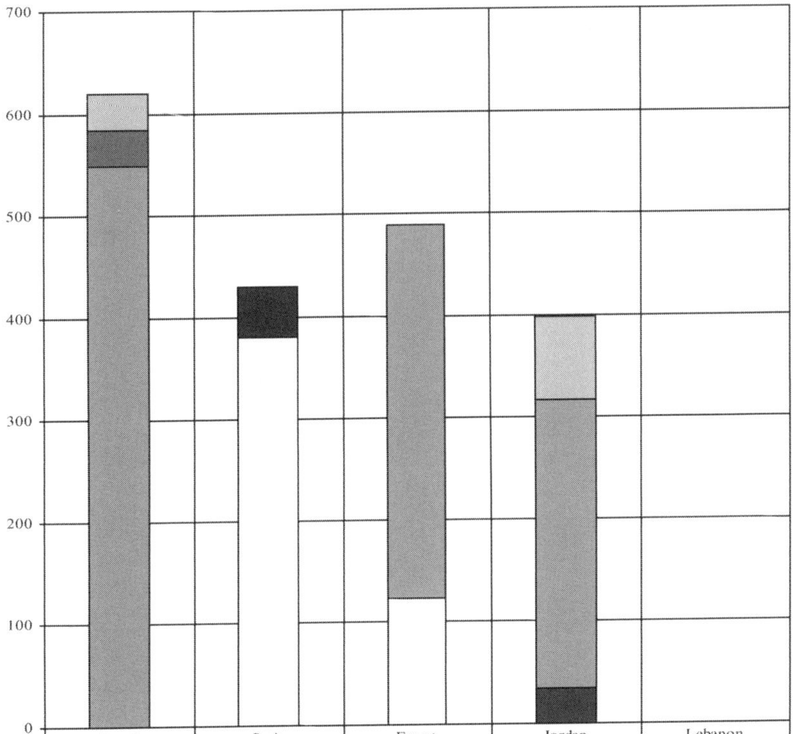

	Israel	Syria	Egypt	Jordan	Lebanon
☐ 203 mm	36			82	
■ 175 mm	36				
■ 155 mm	548		365	282	
■ 152 mm		50			
☐ 130 mm					
☐ 122 mm		380	124		
■ 105 mm				35	
■ 100 mm					

Note: Israel is phasing out its 175-mm weapons.
Source: Prepared by Anthony H. Cordesman, based upon the IISS, The Military Balance and discussions with US and regional experts.

Figure 2.18   Arab-Israeli Self-Propelled Artillery by Caliber in 2006

sophisticated rockets for its MRLs, and Syria and Egypt are dependent on conventional Soviet-bloc rounds with limited accuracy and lethality. These figures are also somewhat misleading because some irregular forces like Hezbollah have large numbers of rockets that can be fired from single round launchers or improvised vehicle launchers and various Palestinian groups have started manufacturing crude single round rockets. All of the countries involved have significant numbers of mortars, many mounted in armored vehicles, for close combat.

(Numbers of major combat weapons)

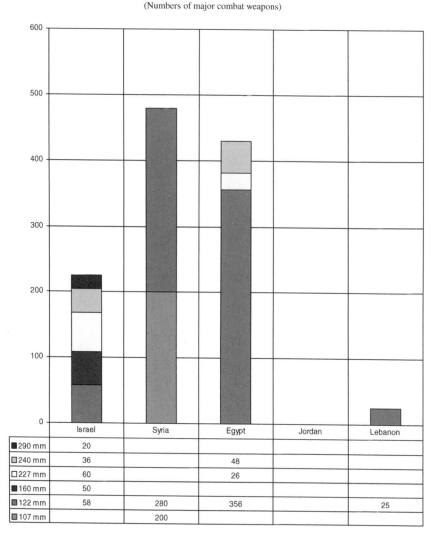

	Israel	Syria	Egypt	Jordan	Lebanon
■ 290 mm	20				
▫ 240 mm	36		48		
☐ 227 mm	60		26		
■ 160 mm	50				
■ 122 mm	58	280	356		25
▫ 107 mm		200			

Source: Prepared by Anthony H. Cordesman, based upon the IISS, The Military Balance and discussions with US and regional experts.

Figure 2.19   Arab-Israeli Multiple Rocket Launchers by Caliber in 2006

The figures for surface-to-surface missile launchers almost certainly sharply under-state Israeli, Egyptian, and Syrian holdings. These weapons generally have operation-al conventional warheads, but lack the accuracy and lethality to be useful as much more than terror weapons. Israel has had conventional cluster warheads, but it is unclear that these are still in service. It is widely assumed to have tactical nuclear war-heads with variable yields. Egypt is believed to have chemical warheads. It is unclear what agents it has stockpiled and whether it has cluster chemical munitions. Syria is believed to have mustard and nerve gas warheads, probably including persistent nerve agents, and chemical cluster munitions. It may have experimental biological devices. Jordan and Lebanon do not have such weapons.

Two additional points need to be made about interpreting the data in Figures 2.16–2.19. Israel is the only country to have really moved to develop "precision artillery" capabilities in terms of training and doctrine for rapid maneuver, the ability to target and register the effect of individual fires in near real or real time, and the ability to shift fires to strike at a mix of individual targets. Egypt and Jordan have made some progress in these areas, but have only limited equipment assets and training and doctrine remain dated, with weak actual field experience in the most modern techniques for combined arms maneuver warfare. Syria has an obsolete artillery arm that is still heavily oriented toward mass fires, lacks the equipment needed to support its massive artillery holdings effectively, and does a poor job of conducting meaningful training for an artillery doctrine that is weak on precision fire, rapid maneuver, and rapid changes in well-targeted fire. Lebanon is still in the process of developing effective artillery forces.

As is the case with tanks, Israel retains a lead in battlefield recovery and repair capability and in overall maintenance, readiness, and armored support vehicle capability. Jordan is making significant progress in these areas, and Egypt is making progress with its best units, but both countries lag badly behind Israel. This is a critical capability in combat. It takes only days of maneuver, or minutes of intensive combat, for the ability to recover major weapons and make rapid repairs to be at least as critical as the initial force ratios of weapons committed to combat.

All of the armies, except Lebanon, have extensive numbers of land-based air defense weapons. Egypt, Jordan, and Syria have large numbers of antiaircraft guns (AA), some radar guided and mounted on armored vehicles. Israel, Egypt, Jordan, and Syria all have large numbers of man-portable and vehicle-mounted light surface-to-air missiles with a variety of infrared and radar-guided missiles. These differ sharply in quality and range. In general, most such short-range air defense systems are more a way of pushing attack helicopters and strike fighters back to longer attack ranges than a means of killing large numbers of aircraft in combat. These capabilities are discussed later, in more depth, in the broader analysis of air defense systems.

COMPARATIVE AIR STRENGTH: QUALITY OVER QUANTITY

As has been discussed earlier, air force quality is generally more important than air force quantity. Nevertheless, even simple numerical comparisons do provide important insights into the Arab-Israeli balance. This is particularly true when basic comparisons of force numbers are supplemented by comparisons of the quality of the equipment involved.

Comparative Air Force Strength

The total number of combat aircraft each country has in inventory has little real meaning. It is the quality of modern combat aircraft, their associated munitions, their targeting and sensor systems, and their battle management that is critical. Syria, with the largest numbers, has one of the least capable air forces. Certainly, it is the worst air force per plane in service. (Lebanon has no real air force.) Israel and Egypt are the only two air forces with large numbers of "enablers" like airborne warning and control, intelligence, battle management, and electronic countermeasure capabilities. Israel has a distinct lead in its ability to use these systems and its tankers in long-range strike missions

Figure 2.20 compares air force manpower. The amount of active manning in each force is roughly in proportion to the size of the air force involved. Once again,

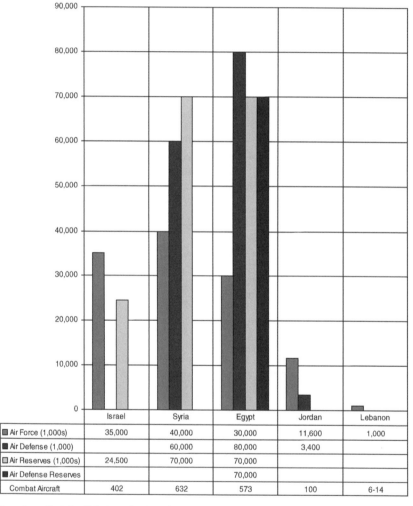

	Israel	Syria	Egypt	Jordan	Lebanon
■ Air Force (1,000s)	35,000	40,000	30,000	11,600	1,000
■ Air Defense (1,000)		60,000	80,000	3,400	
☐ Air Reserves (1,000s)	24,500	70,000	70,000		
■ Air Defense Reserves			70,000		
Combat Aircraft	402	632	573	100	6-14

Source: Prepared by Anthony H. Cordesman, based upon the IISS, The Military Balance and discussions with US and regional experts.

Figure 2.20   Arab-Israeli Air Force and Air Defense Manpower in 2006

however, Israel is the only country to make really effective use of reserves—although some small elements of the Egyptian reserves have value in special purpose functions. The active and reserve manpower for the land-based air defense forces in Egypt and Syria is vastly out of proportion to the need, at best reflecting an emphasis on manning unguided, obsolescent antiaircraft guns that makes little sense in modern military operations.

Figure 2.21 shows the trend in total combat air strength. Oddly enough, it is the downward trend in Israeli numbers that is the best indication of effectiveness. It is Israel that has done the best job of emphasizing overall force quality over numbers and full mission capability with all of the necessary munitions, force enablers, and

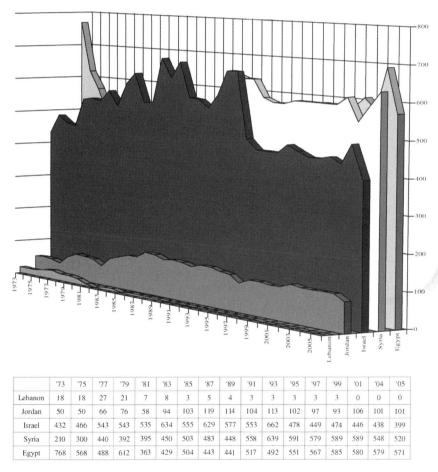

	'73	'75	'77	'79	'81	'83	'85	'87	'89	'91	'93	'95	'97	'99	'01	'04	'05
Lebanon	18	18	27	21	7	8	3	5	4	3	3	3	3	3	0	0	0
Jordan	50	50	66	76	58	94	103	119	114	104	113	102	97	93	106	101	101
Israel	432	466	543	543	535	634	555	629	577	553	662	478	449	474	446	438	399
Syria	210	300	440	392	395	450	503	483	448	558	639	591	579	589	589	548	520
Egypt	768	568	488	612	363	429	504	443	441	517	492	551	567	585	580	579	571

Source: Prepared by Anthony H. Cordesman, based upon the IISS, The Military Balance and discussions with US and regional experts.

Figure 2.21   Trends in Total Arab-Israeli Combat Aircraft: 1973–2006

sustainability. Egypt and Syria maintain larger forces than they can properly support —in effect, disarming by overarming.

Figures 2.22 and 2.23 show total aircraft by type and the number of high-quality aircraft on each side. In war-fighting terms, it is the aircraft in Figure 2.23 that really count, and the contrast between the two figures is striking.

If one looks only at the total aircraft numbers shown in Figure 2.22, Arab forces have a massive lead in low-quality aircraft, driven in part by the large number of

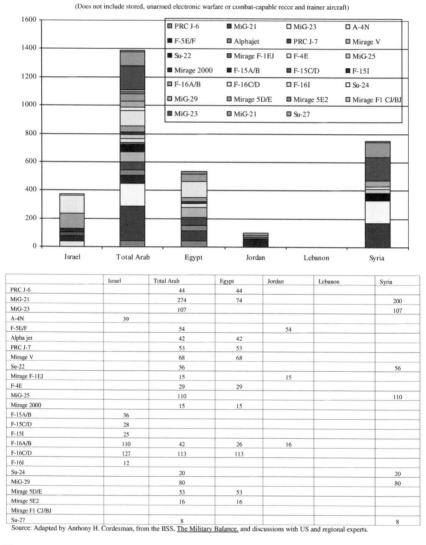

(Does not include stored, unarmed electronic warfare or combat-capable recce and trainer aircraft)

	Israel	Total Arab	Egypt	Jordan	Lebanon	Syria
PRC J-6		44	44			
MiG-21		274	74			200
MiG-23		107				107
A-4N	39					
F-5E/F		54		54		
Alpha jet		42	42			
PRC J-7		53	53			
Mirage V		68	68			
Su-22		56				56
Mirage F-1EJ		15		15		
F-4E		29	29			
MiG-25		110				110
Mirage 2000		15	15			
F-15A/B	36					
F-15C/D	28					
F-15I	25					
F-16A/B	110	42	26	16		
F-16C/D	127	113	113			
F-16I	12					
Su-24		20				20
MiG-29		80				80
Mirage 5D/E		53	53			
Mirage 5E2		16	16			
Mirage F1 CJ/BJ						
Su-27		8				8

Source: Adapted by Anthony H. Cordesman, from the IISS, The Military Balance, and discussions with US and regional experts.

Figure 2.22   Total Operational Arab-Israeli Combat Fighter, Attack, Bomber by Type in 2006

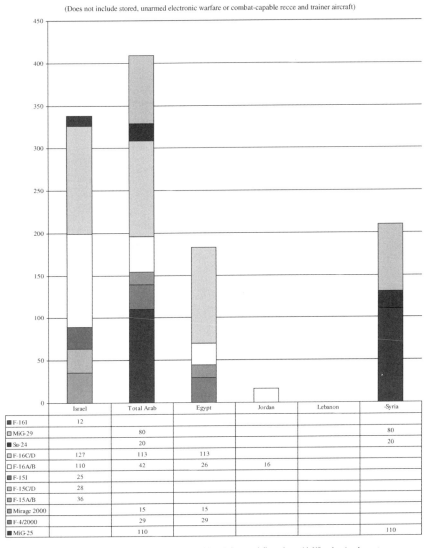

(Does not include stored, unarmed electronic warfare or combat-capable recce and trainer aircraft)

	Israel	Total Arab	Egypt	Jordan	Lebanon	-Syria
■ F-16I	12					
▢ MiG-29		80				80
■ Su-24		20				20
▢ F-16C/D	127	113	113			
▢ F-16A/B	110	42	26	16		
■ F-15I	25					
▢ F-15C/D	28					
▢ F-15A/B	36					
▢ Mirage 2000		15	15			
■ F-4/2000		29	29			
■ MiG-25		110				110

Source: Adapted by Anthony H. Cordesman, from the IISS, The Military Balance and discussions with US and regional experts.

Figure 2.23   High-Quality Operational Arab-Israeli Combat Aircraft in 2006

obsolete and obsolescent aircraft in Syrian forces and Egyptian retention of obsolescent European aircraft and obsolete Soviet-bloc types that serve little war-fighting
purpose. Furthermore, it is clear that Egypt and Syria are trying to train for, maintain, arm, and sustain far too many different types of aircraft. This puts a major—
and costly—burden on the air forces and dilutes manpower quality to little, if any,
war-fighting purpose.

If one looks at the high-quality aircraft shown in Figure 2.23, however, Israel has near parity to the Arab total and a vast superiority over Syria, whose MiG-29s and Su-24s now at best have obsolescent avionics and cannot compete with Israeli types on a one-on-one basis. Egypt and Jordan's F-16s are highly capable aircraft, but do not have avionics that have air-to-air combat and precision air-to-ground and electronic warfare capabilities equal to the Israeli-modified F-15s and F-16s. Egypt's Mirage 2000s are moderately capable aircraft, but need updating.

Figure 2.24 provides a rough picture of the "enabling" aircraft in each force. It shows that Israel has a major lead in both the quantity and quality of the air battle

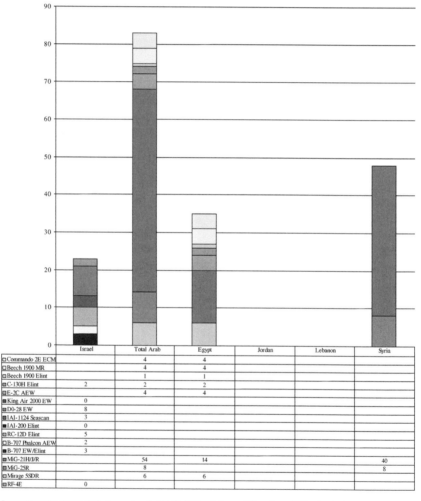

	Israel	Total Arab	Egypt	Jordan	Lebanon	Syria
Commando 2E ECM		4	4			
Beech 1900 MR		4	4			
Beech 1900 Elint		1	1			
C-130H Elint	2	2	2			
E-2C AEW		4	4			
King Air 2000 EW	0					
DO-28 EW	8					
IAI-1124 Seascan	3					
IAI-200 Elint	0					
RC-12D Elint	5					
B-707 Phalcon AEW	2					
B-707 EW/Elint	3					
MiG-21H/J/R		54	14			40
MiG-25R		8				8
Mirage 5SDR		6	6			
RF-4E	0					

Source: Adapted by Anthony H. Cordesman, from the IISS, The Military Balance and discussions with US and regional experts.

Figure 2.24 Unarmed Fixed and Rotary Wing (RECCE), Electronic Warfare, and Intelligence Aircraft in 2006

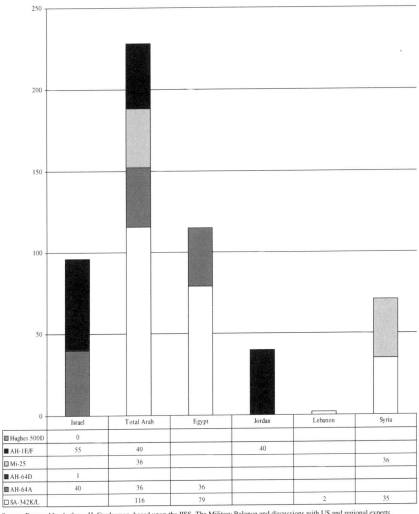

(Does not include ASW or anti-ship helicopters)

	Israel	Total Arab	Egypt	Jordan	Lebanon	Syria
▣ Hughes 500D	0					
■ AH-1E/F	55	40		40		
▢ Mi-25		36				36
■ AH-64D	1					
■ AH-64A	40	36	36			
▢ SA-342K/L		116	79		2	35

Source: Prepared by Anthony H. Cordesman, based upon the IISS, The Military Balance and discussions with US and regional experts.

Figure 2.25   Operational Arab-Israeli Attack and Armed Helicopters in 2006

management, intelligence, warning, and targeting systems critical to making use of modern air power and precision weapons, and this advantage is greatly enhanced by superior Israel tactics, overall training, and the use of other technologies like UAVs. Israel has its own intelligence satellites for surveillance and targeting purposes and much more advanced "netting" of its communications, battle management and intelligence systems, plus world-class electronic intelligence and electronic warfare capabilities. Egypt, along with Saudi Arabia, has acquired some of these capabilities,

Figure 2.26 Arab-Israeli Land-Based Air Defense Systems in 2005

Country	Major SAM	Light SAM	AA Guns
Egypt	702+ launchers *282 SA-2* *212 SA-3A* *56 SA-6* *78 IHawk*	2000 SA-7 Ayn as Saqr 20 SA-9 50 Avengers Stinger <u>26 M-54 Chaparral SP</u> *24 Crotale* *72 Amoun Skyguard/* *RIM-7F* *36 quad SAM* *Ayn as Saqr*	200 ZPU-2/4 14.5 mm 280 ZU-23-2 23 mm 118 ZSU-23-4 SP 23 mm 36 Sinai SP 23 mm 200 M-1939 37 mm some S-60 57 mm <u>40 ZSU-57-2 SP 57 mm</u> *14/- Chaparral* *2,000 20 mm, 23 mm, 37 mm,* *57 mm, 85 mm, 100 mm* *36 twin radar-guided 35-mm* *guns* *Sinai-23 radar-guided 23-mm* *guns*
Israel	*3 Patriot Bty.* *17 IHawk Bty./* *51 fire units* *2 Bty. Arrow/* *18 launchers* *3 Bty. PAC-2/* *48 launchers*	250 Stinger 1,000 Redeye *35 M-163 Vulcan/*	*850 20 mm: including 20 mm,* *Vulcan, TCM-20, M-167* *Chaparral* *150 ZU-23 23 mm* *60 ZSU-23-4 SP* *M-39 37 mm* *150 L-70 40 mm*
Jordan	*2 bde/14 Bty./80 I* *Hawk* *3 PAC-2 Bty.*	50 SA-7B2 60 SA-8 92 SA-13 300 SA-14 240 SA-16 250 Redeye	395 guns 139 M-163 SP 20 mm 40 ZSU-23-4 SP 216 M-42 SP 40 mm
Lebanon	None	20 SA-7/B	20 mm ZU-23 23 mm 10 M-42A1 40 mm
Syria	*25 Ad Brigades* *150 SAM Bty.* *560 SA-2/3* *220 SA-6* *48 SA-5*	35 SA-13 20 SA-9 <u>4,000 SA-7</u> *160 SA-8* 20 SA-11 100 SA-14	2,050 Guns 650 ZU-23-2 400 ZSU-23-4 SP 300 M-1938 37 mm 675 S-60 57 mm 25 KS-19 100 mm <u>10 ZSU-5-2 SP</u> *Some 4,000 AD arty*

Note: Syria has S-300 SAMs on order from Russia. Figures in italics are systems operated by the Air Force or Air Defense commands.

Source: Adapted by Anthony H. Cordesman from the IISS, *The Military Balance*. Some data adjusted or estimated by the author.

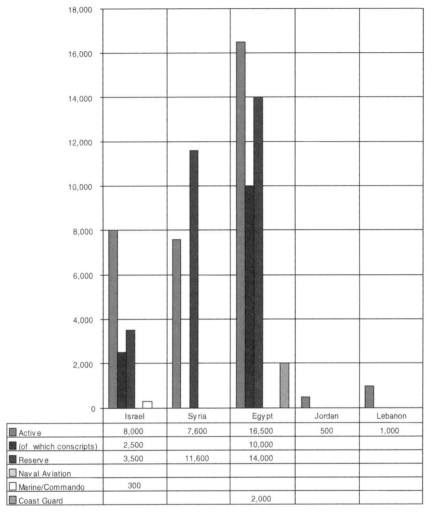

	Israel	Syria	Egypt	Jordan	Lebanon
Active	8,000	7,600	16,500	500	1,000
(of which conscripts)	2,500		10,000		
Reserve	3,500	11,600	14,000		
Naval Aviation					
Marine/Commando	300				
Coast Guard			2,000		

Source: Prepared by Anthony H. Cordesman, based upon the IISS, The Military Balance and discussions with US and regional experts.

Figure 2.27   Arab-Israeli Naval Manpower in 2006

but cannot truly compete. Syria has little or no meaningful capability. Jordan is severely resource limited, and Lebanon has no real air force.

Figure 2.25 shows the total strength each air force and army have in rotary wing combat aircraft, less naval assets. Israel and Egypt are the only countries with truly advanced attack helicopters like the Apache or AH-64. Israel is also now in the process of taking delivery on 18 highly advanced AH-64Ds, with extremely advanced avionics and "fire and forget" capabilities that do not require the aircraft to wait and track the missile to its target. The AH-1 has moderate capability. Syrian attack helicopter units are elite units, but Syria has not been able to modernize its rotary wing combat forces, and its training and tactics have not been fully updated over the last decade.

Comparative Land-Based Air Defense Forces

Figure 2.26 shows the strength of each country's land-based air defenses. As Figure 2.20 has shown, some countries integrate their major air defenses into their air forces and some have a dedicated air defense force. Most countries also deploy a separate mix of short-range air defenses in their land forces.

Egypt, Israel, and Syria all have large forces, but only the forces of Egypt and Israel are relatively modern, and Egypt dilutes its force capability by retaining large numbers of obsolete Soviet-bloc systems. It also has a weak command-and-control system and training and readiness problems. Syria's system is obsolete in weapons, sensors, and command and control capability. Jordan has improved a cost-effective system with reasonable readiness and proficiency, but has never had the resources to compete with the larger Arab-Israeli powers.

The effectiveness of some of the systems in Figure 2.26 is increasingly uncertain. Advances in air targeting and long-range, air-to-ground precision combat capability —coupled with steady advances in the long-range strike capabilities of rockets and missiles—have reduced the effectiveness of many air short-range air defense systems. Some have limited or no effectiveness against low-flying helicopters unless the pilots cannot avoid overflying the defenses, and many others lack the range, lethality, and energy of maneuver to attack fighters that can use long-range air-to-surface missiles.

Many of the longer-range systems—particularly the SA-2, SA-3, SA-5, and SA-6—are now so old that electronic and other countermeasures, including antiradiation missiles, can deprive them of much of their effectiveness. If they use their radars persistently they can be located, characterized, and jammed or killed. If they make sudden use of their radars, or remote radars further to the rear, reaction times are slow and lethality is low. If they attempt to use optical means, they generally fail to hit a target. The Improved Hawk or IHawk missile is considerably better if it has been fully updated, but has some of the same vulnerabilities. The Patriots in Israeli forces, and which Egyptian forces have on order, are the only fully modern long-range air defense missiles in Arab-Israeli hands, although Syria has long sought Soviet-designed S-300 and S-400 surface-to-air missiles, which have many of the advantages of the Patriot.

Israel's Arrow II missiles are the only antiballistic missile defenses in the region with significant area coverage, although the Patriot has meaningful point defense capability and the IHawk has limited value as a point defense system.

At present, no country has a fully modern and properly integrated mix of sensors and battle management systems to tie together its surface-to-air defenses. Israel and Egypt do have moderate capability in such operations, and Jordan has limited

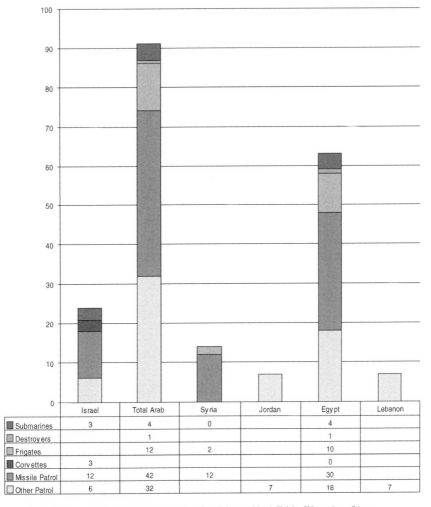

	Israel	Total Arab	Syria	Jordan	Egypt	Lebanon
◼ Submarines	3	4	0		4	
◻ Destroyers		1			1	
◻ Frigates		12	2		10	
◼ Corvettes	3				0	
◼ Missile Patrol	12	42	12		30	
◻ Other Patrol	6	32		7	18	7

Source: Adapted by Anthony H. Cordesman from the IISS, The Military Balance and Jane's Fighting Ships, various editions.

Figure 2.28   Arab-Israeli Major Combat Ships by Category in 2005

capability. The Syrian system has decayed over time and is increasingly vulnerable, but still has some capability.

COMPARATIVE NAVAL STRENGTH: PERIPHERAL MISSIONS

The Arab-Israeli countries still maintain significant naval forces, but only Israel and Egypt retain significant operational capability, and naval forces are now seen as useful largely in peripheral missions. The one major exception is the possibility that

Figure 2.29   Other Arab-Israeli Naval Capabilities in 2006

Israel

Smaller Combat Vessels:	32 PFI under 100 tons, 1 support craft. Other small craft.
Amphibious Lift:	1 landing craft tank (LCT); 1 Landing craft medium (LCM).
Naval Aviation:	5 ASW helicopters; 3 IAI-1124 maritime reconnaissance in IAF.
Marine and Commando:	300-man commando force.
Coast Guard and Paramilitary:	50-man coast guard with 4 patrol craft and small craft.

Egypt

Smaller Combat Vessels:	15 mine warfare craft (6 oceangoing and 7 coastal).
Amphibious Lift:	3 Landing ship medium (LSM), and 9 Landing craft utility (LCU).
Naval Aviation:	12 air-to-surface missiles and 15 ASW helicopters, and some UAVs.
Marine and Commando:	Coast defense force manned by army under naval command, with SSC-2b Samlet and 3/3 Ootomat 1 launchers, and some 100-mm, 130-mm, and 152-mm guns.
Coast Guard and Paramilitary:	2,000-man coast guard with 60 small boats, including 14 PCIs, 18 PFI less than 100 tons, and 7 Bertram patrol boats.

Jordan

Smaller Combat Vessels:	13 light patrol craft of less than 100 tons.
Amphibious Lift:	None
Naval Aviation:	None
Marine and Commando:	None
Coast Guard and Paramilitary:	None

Lebanon

Smaller Combat Vessels:	25 armed boats.
Amphibious Lift:	None
Naval Aviation:	None
Marine and Commando:	None
Coast Guard and Paramilitary:	Customs force with 7 small patrol craft of less than 100 tons.

Syria

Smaller Combat Vessels:	8 light patrol craft of less than 100 tons; 5 minecraft (1 ocean and 1 coastal).
Amphibious Lift:	3 LSM, some landing craft.
Naval Aviation:	25 ASW helicopters, some with antiship missiles.
Marine and Commando:	Some shore-based antiship missiles and guns operated by army.
Coast Guard and Paramilitary:	None

Source: Adapted by Anthony H. Cordesman from the IISS, *The Military Balance,* and *Jane's Fighting Ships,* various editions.

Israel may react to increasing missile threats by seabasing some of its nuclear armed missiles on its new submarines.

Figure 2.27 again shows how disparate national manning levels are. The naval forces shown reflect significant Egyptian overmanning and comparatively large Egyptian and Syrian naval reserves with little or no current war-fighting capability.

Figure 2.28 compares the major combat ship strength in Arab-Israeli forces. The qualitative issues affecting these forces have been described earlier. Israel has relatively modern and effective submarines and surface forces, backed by effective air power. Egypt is less proficient and again dilutes force quality by maintaining too many obsolete and ineffective ships. Nevertheless, it has some effective force elements.

Both Israel and Egypt have effective antiship missiles, although Israel has superior systems and targeting/electronic warfare capabilities. Egypt has a mix of effective European and obsolescent Chinese and Former Soviet Union designs. Israel and Egypt have relatively modern, operational submarines. Syria's navy is obsolete, ineffective, and dependent on obsolete antiship missiles. Jordan and Lebanon have only token navies.

Figure 2.29 compares the smaller forces and other elements of each navy. Mine warfare capability exists, but is limited. Amphibious lift is more useful for Special Operations than conventional warfare. Naval aviation is limited, and largely focused on antisubmarine warfare capability.

Total Resources: Recapitalization, Force Modernization, and Impact on Effectiveness

The data on Arab-Israeli security efforts have many limits and uncertainties. These problems are compounded by the fact that the U.S. State Department and the International Institute for Strategic Studies (IISS) have failed to update much of the reporting on such expenditures that they used to provide in the past. There are data, however, that have enough broad accuracy to provide a useful picture of the trends in the balances and the resources behind the force numbers that have just been discussed. In broad terms, these data show that several Arab states now have much larger force postures than they can properly modernize and support.

This is particularly true of Syria, which ceased to get concessional arms sales and loans from the Former Soviet Union and the Warsaw Pact when they collapsed, after years of trying to rival Israel in military power. Much of Syria's conventional force posture is now obsolescent or obsolete, and its failure to properly modernize and "recapitalize" its forces has reached the crisis level.

Egypt and Israel have benefited from massive U.S. military assistance. Egypt, however, is still attempting to maintain a far larger inventory of its aging Soviet-bloc and non–U.S. equipment than it can afford to maintain, modernize, and sustain. Roughly one-third of its force posture is an obsolete and largely hollow shell that wastes resources that would be better spent on force quality than on force quantity.

Israel's forces are better modernized, but even Israel is forced to maintain a "high-low" force mix with substantial numbers of obsolete systems. It also is still heavily reliant on conscript and reserve manpower to free resources for arms imports and its heavily subsidized military industries, and it is unclear if this gives it the manpower quality and readiness it needs to take maximum advantage of its high-technology systems.

Jordan has made a series of painful trade-offs between force quantity and force quality, reducing numbers to pay for modernization, readiness, and training. Even so, Jordan simply has not been able to compete with Egypt and Israel in developing high-technology forces.

Lebanon has never had particularly effective military forces and continues to recover from the impact of years of civil war. Syrian occupation forces still occupy the country (although they have been reducing in number), and the rise of independent forces like Hezbollah have replaced the old militias that were largely disbanded at the end of the civil war. The Lebanese forces are badly undercapitalized and are likely to remain more of an internal security force than forces capable of sustained conventional warfare.

COMPARATIVE TRENDS IN MILITARY EXPENDITURES

One key aspect of the Arab-Israeli military balance is that there is almost no correlation between force size and national military spending. This is reflected all too clearly in Figures 3.1 and 3.2. The first figure shows estimates by the IISS, and the second figure shows declassified U.S. intelligence estimates as reported by the U.S. State Department.

Figure 3.1 Estimate of Military Spending and Manpower Trends: 1985–2000

Trend: 1985 vs. 1999 and 2000* ($U.S. are in Constant 1999 prices)

Country	Military Spending in $U.S. Millions			Military Spending Per Capita ($U.S.)			Military Spending as a % of GDP		
	'85	'99	'00	'85	'99	'00	'85	'99	'00
Israel	7,486	8,846	9,373	1,768	1,465	1,512	21.2	8.9	8.9
Egypt	3,827	2,988	2,821	79	45	45	13.0	3.4	3.2
Jordan	891	588	510	255	95	76	15.9	7.7	6.9
Lebanon	296	563	553	111	164	468	9.0	3.4	3.5
Syria	5,161	989	760	491	63	47	16.4	5.6	5.6

Trend: 1985 vs. 2001 and 2002* ($U.S. are in Constant 2000 prices)

Country	Military Spending in $U.S. Millions			Military Spending Per Capita ($U.S.)			Military Spending as a % of GDP		
	'85	'01	'02	'85	'01	'02	'85	'01	'02
Israel	11,498	9,857	9,437	2,709	1,590	1,499	21.2	9.2	9.7
Egypt	4,617	3,111	3,121	95	45	44	13.0	4.0	3.0
Jordan	915	767	844	261	150	162	15.9	8.9	9.3
Lebanon	173	572	509	65	159	144	9.0	3.5	3.2
Syria	8,014	1,869	1,819	763	113	107	16.4	10.9	10.3

Source: International Institute for Strategic Studies (IISS), *Military Balance*, various editions.

(Military Expenditures in Constant $US 1999 Millions)

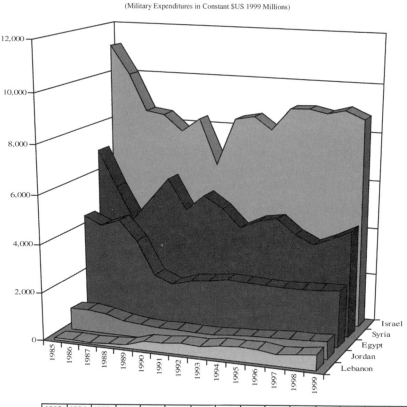

	1985	1986	1987	1988	1989	1990	1991	1992	1993	1994	1995	1996	1997	1998	1999
Lebanon	100	75	75	120	150	382	413	486	445	572	589	594	495	559	653
Jordan	889	941	825	635	554	503	513	491	499	538	589	617	651	685	725
Egypt	4,490	4,168	4,443	3,652	2,270	1,940	2,180	2,260	2,350	2,300	2,260	2,280	2,290	2,330	2,390
Syria	6,976	5,508	4,168	5,094	6,020	4,728	5,420	4,920	4,190	4,550	4,690	4,100	3,750	4,080	4,450
Israel	11,14	10,00	8,521	8,399	7,760	8,290	6,420	8,400	8,540	8,020	8,940	9,000	8,840	9,020	8,700

Source: Adapted by Anthony H. Cordesman from US State Department, World Military Expenditures and Arms Transfers, various editions.

Figure 3.2 National Trends in Arab-Israeli Military Spending in Constant Dollars: The Decline in Arab Forces as a Share of Total Spending: 1985–1999

Both figures convey the same message. Israel has spent far more on its forces over time than any Arab state. In fact, Israel has consistently spent more than all of the Arab states combined. This disparity partly reflects higher Israeli manpower and maintenance costs, but Israel has also spent more efficiently in terms of procurement, the ability to draw upon an advanced mix of military industries, and virtually free access to advanced U.S. military technology. At the same time, Israel must still plan for a larger Arab-Israeli conflict in spite of its peace treaties with Egypt and Jordan, and Israel has been fighting a prolonged series of asymmetric wars while its Arab neighbors have not.

Figure 3.2 shows the annual trend in military expenditures in constant 1999 dollars. Once again, Israel has a clear lead in military spending over any of its neighbors, which does much to explain its consistent qualitative lead over its neighbors. A comparison of Figures 3.1 and 3.2 also shows, however, just how serious the resource pressures are on Syria. Insufficient data are available to provide directly comparable figures, but it is clear that Syria has fallen further and further behind Israel, while the earlier figures have shown it has tried to compete in force size.

While Figure 3.2 shows that Syria outspent Egypt during the late 1980s to late 1990s, Figure 3.1 shows it has since fallen far behind Egypt, in spite of spending a much higher percentage of its gross domestic product (GDP) on military forces than Egypt and more than Israel. In broad terms, these resource data help explain why Syria's overall force management and readiness is so bad. Syria has effectively created hollow forces. It is trying to compete with Israel at levels it simply cannot afford.

The data also show that Egypt obtained a substantial "peace dividend" in terms of military spending during the mid to late 1980s and reduced military domestic spending. It is important to note, however, that the data in Figures 3.1 and 3.2 do not seem to include U.S. grant aid to Egypt—which would raise the total for Egyptian spending.

The data for Jordan show that its spending has been consistently smaller relative to Israel, Egypt, and Syria than its forces. This has occurred in spite of the fact that Jordan is spending a relatively high percentage of its GDP on its forces. The data for Lebanon show a steady increase in spending since the late 1980s, but its spending levels remain far too low to support effective forces.

Figure 3.3 shows more recent trends in military expenditures in current U.S. dollars. These data are considerably more uncertain than the previous data because they include estimates for some countries for 2004 and 2005 rather than actual data. Israel's edge in military resources remains clear, although its spending efforts have dropped in spite of the Israeli-Palestinian War, while other security-related spending has increased to pay for civil programs like roads and settlements that Israel funds for security reasons.

Egypt and Jordan have benefited from both peace and U.S. aid, although it is clear that Jordan faces serious resource limitations and Egypt is funding its forces only at about 30 percent of the level of Israel. Syria's military expenditures continue to decline and are less than one-third of the level needed to pay for the mix of manpower quality, readiness, and modernization it would need to compete with Israel in overall conventional force quality.

Figure 3.4 shows the long-term trend in military effort as a percent of GNP. As Figure 2.29 has already indicated, the regional burden has been cut sharply since the mid-1980s, but is still one of the highest of any region in the world.

COMPARATIVE TRENDS IN ARMS IMPORTS

The trends in arms imports provide another important measure of military effort and one that shows how well given countries are modernizing and recapitalizing their

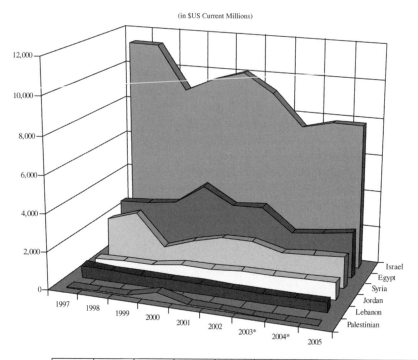

(in $US Current Millions)

	1997	1998	1999	2000	2001	2002	2003*	2004*	2005
▨ Palestinian	75	85	100	485	85	75	-		
■ Lebanon	676	594	563	578	588	536	512	528	530
▢ Jordan	496	548	569	792	789	893	886	919	956
▨ Syria	2,200	2,700	989	1,500	1,900	1,900	1,500	1,640	1,720
■ Egypt	2,700	2,800	3,000	4,100	3,200	3,300	2,050	2,240	2,500
▨ Israel	11,300	11,300	8,900	9,600	10,100	9,100	7,400	7,800	7,820

Source: Adapted by Anthony H. Cordesman, the IISS, The Military Balance, various editions. Palestinian total is rough estimate based on FMA.
* Number reflects amounts budgeted as opposed to expenditures as the IISS no longer reports expenditures.

Figure 3.3   Arab-Israeli Military Expenditures by Country: 1997–2005

forces. The data are more uncertain than those for military spending, and almost all come from declassified U.S. intelligence estimates provided to the State Department and to the IISS. Once again, however, they are useful in providing a picture of broad trends.

Figure 3.5 compares the national trends in deliveries of Arab-Israeli arms imports during 1985–1999, as measured in constant U.S. dollars. These figures show a major drop in such deliveries to Lebanon, Jordan, and Syria over time. The drop in deliveries to Syria is so precipitous as to have had a crippling effect.

Figure 3.5 also indicates that Egypt and Israel both received roughly similar average levels of arms imports during the period shown. While technically true, such figures ignore the facts that Israel is the only state in the region with a relative efficient defense industry capable of producing modern military weapons and equipment and

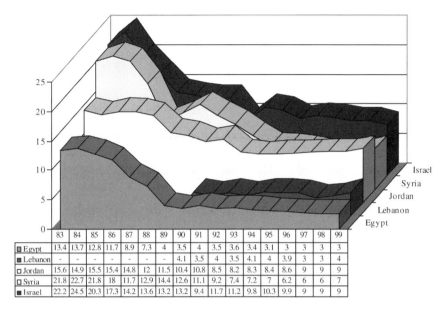

	83	84	85	86	87	88	89	90	91	92	93	94	95	96	97	98	99
▣ Egypt	13.4	13.7	12.8	11.7	8.9	7.3	4	3.5	4	3.5	3.6	3.4	3.1	3	3	3	3
■ Lebanon	-	-	-	-	-	-	-	4.1	3.5	4	3.5	4.1	4	3.9	3	3	4
▢ Jordan	15.6	14.9	15.5	15.4	14.8	12	11.5	10.4	10.8	8.5	8.2	8.3	8.4	8.6	9	9	9
▢ Syria	21.8	22.7	21.8	18	11.7	12.9	14.4	12.6	11.1	9.2	7.4	7.2	7	6.2	6	6	7
■ Israel	22.2	24.5	20.3	17.3	14.2	13.6	13.2	13.2	9.4	11.7	11.2	9.8	10.3	9.9	9	9	9

Figure 3.4   Trend in Percent of GNP Spent on Military Forces: 1983–1999: Half the Burden of the Early 1980s

that it imports large amounts of U.S. technology and equipment that it includes in its weapons systems, but which are not classified as arms imports under the present definition of the term. This estimate shows a precipitous drop in Jordanian and Syrian arms imports that has had a crippling impact on both countries since the early 1990s. Lebanon has not had significant arms imports.

Figure 3.6 provides more current data on both new arms orders and arms deliveries, using a different source. It reflects the same general patterns for Israel, and Egypt, and shows that new arms orders have risen sharply in recent years. Jordan increased its arms orders in 2001–2004, largely as a result of increased U.S. aid resulting from its peace treaty with Israel and its support for the United States in dealing with Iraq. Syria shows no recovery in either new arms orders or deliveries, in spite of some reports of major agreements with Russia. Lebanon remained a minor player.

Figure 3.7 shows the source of Arab-Israeli arms imports. It shows that Israel clearly has had large-scale access to U.S. arms imports, including the most modern equipment, and these totals ignore massive imports of parts and subassemblies that are not classified as arms imports. Egypt has also had access to U.S. arms and technology, but has spent significant amounts on Russian, Chinese, and European arms to try to supplement what it can obtain with U.S. grant aid and to keep the Soviet-supplied portion of its forces operational.

Jordan has been heavily dependent on the United States since 1990, although it has obtained some European arms. Syria has lost Russia as a major supplier without

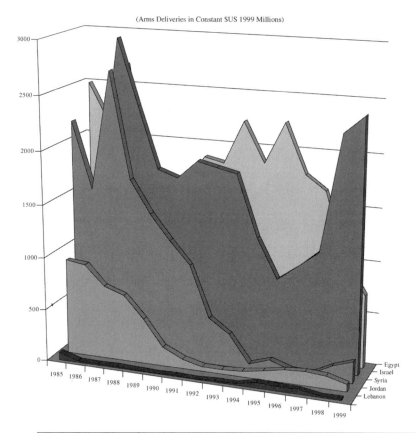

(Arms Deliveries in Constant $US 1999 Millions)

	1985	1986	1987	1988	1989	1990	1991	1992	1993	1994	1995	1996	1997	1998	1999
■ Lebanon	74	15	13	13	6	0	6	0	11	11	53	42	41	10	10
▣ Jordan	915	889	704	636	428	182	93	46	45	55	85	126	134	122	70
▨ Syria	2194	1565	2683	1687	1383	1150	934	445	312	55	117	52	41	142	210
■ Israel	1609	1565	2951	2336	1761	1695	1869	1825	1782	1200	827	969	1130	2233	2400
▣ Egypt	2486	2134	2683	1427	1258	1573	1869	1825	2227	1854	2242	1780	1644	1015	700

Source: Adapted by Anthony H. Cordesman from US State Department, World Military Expenditures and Arms Transfers, various editions.

Figure 3.5　National Trends in Arab-Israeli Arms Deliveries in Constant Dollars

finding any replacement—particularly one capable of selling advanced arms and technology. Lebanon's arms imports have been too small to be significant.

Figures 3.8 and 3.9 put the previous comparisons of Israeli and Arab arms imports in a broader perspective. They show that Israel has had far larger amounts of grant military assistance than Egypt and has been able to import far more equipment. These differ from the previous totals in that they include total funding for modernization, including the ability to import goods for military industry, while the other totals counted only deliveries classified as "arms."

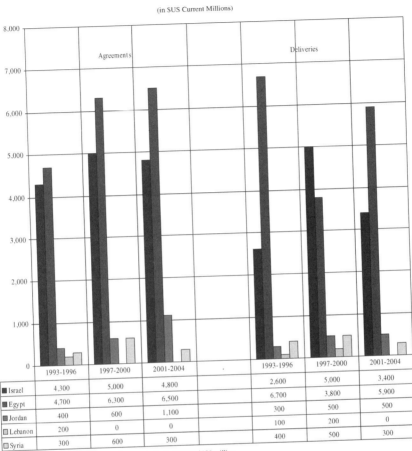

(in $US Current Millions)

	1993-1996	1997-2000	2001-2004		1993-1996	1997-2000	2001-2004
Israel	4,300	5,000	4,800		2,600	5,000	3,400
Egypt	4,700	6,300	6,500		6,700	3,800	5,900
Jordan	400	600	1,100		300	500	500
Lebanon	200	0	0		100	200	0
Syria	300	600	300		400	500	300

0 = Data less than $50 million or nil. All data rounded to the nearest $100 million.
Source: Richard F. Grimmett, Conventional Arms Transfers to the Developing Nations, Congressional Research Service, various editions.

Figure 3.6   Arab-Israeli New Arms Agreements and Deliveries by Country: 1993–2004

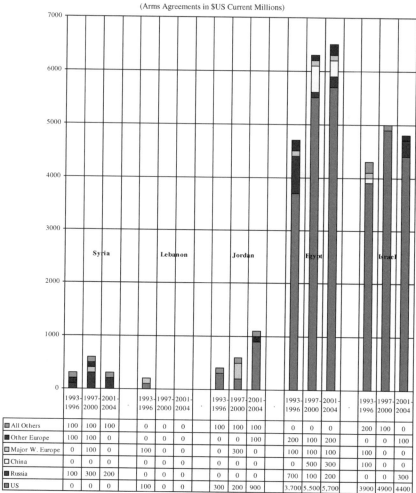

(Arms Agreements in $US Current Millions)

	1993-1996	1997-2000	2001-2004	1993-1996	1997-2000	2001-2004	1993-1996	1997-2000	2001-2004	1993-1996	1997-2000	2001-2004	1993-1996	1997-2000	2001-2004
▣ All Others	100	100	100	0	0	0	100	100	100	0	0	0	200	100	0
■ Other Europe	100	100	0	0	0	0	0	0	100	200	100	200	0	0	100
▢ Major W. Europe	0	100	0	100	0	0	0	300	0	100	100	100	100	0	0
▢ China	0	0	0	0	0	0	0	0	0	0	500	300	100	0	0
■ Russia	100	300	200	0	0	0	0	0	0	700	100	200	0	0	300
▣ US	0	0	0	100	0	0	300	200	900	3,700	5,500	5,700	3900	4900	4400

0 = less than $50 million or nil, and all data rounded to the nearest $100 million.

Source: Adapted by Anthony H. Cordesman, from Richard F. Grimmett, Conventional Arms Transfers to the Developing Nations, Congressional Research Service, various editions.

Figure 3.7 Arab-Israeli Arms Orders by Supplier Country: 1993–2004

Figure 3.8 The Comparative Size of U.S. Military Assistance and Commercial Arms Sales to the Arab-Israeli Ring States: 1986–1996

	1987	1988	1989	1990	1991	1992	1993	1994	1995	1996
Israel										
Foreign Military Financing Program	1,800	1,800	1,800	1,800	1,800	1,800	1,800	1,800	1,800	1,800
Payment Waived	1,800	1,800	1,800	1,800	1,800	1,800	1,800	1,800	1,800	1,800
FMS Agreements	100.5	130.9	327.7	376.7	361.4	96.5	161.0	2,142.9	631.3	828.7
Commercial Exports	1,024.8	474.8	997.2	387.3	169.1	27.9	41.8	34.0	34.7	13.1
FMS Construction Agreements	–	–	–	–	–	–	–	–	–	–
FMS Deliveries	1,229.6	754.1	230.3	146.3	239.0	718.7	773.9	409.2	327.0	385.8
MAP Program	–	–	–	74.0	43.0	47.0	491.0	165.9	80.0	22.0
MAP Deliveries	–	–	–	–	114.7	0.6	44.7	–	0.0	–
IMET Program/Deliveries	1.9(0)	1.7(0)	1.9(0)	2.1(0)	1.1(0.2)	0.6(0)	0.5(0)	0.8(0)	0.8(0)	–
Egypt										
Foreign Military Financing Program	1,300	1,300	1,300	1,300	1,300	1,300	1,300	1,300	1,300	1,300
Payment Waived	1,300	1,300	1,300	1,300	1,300	1,300	1,300	1,300	1,300	1,300
FMS Agreements	330.9	1,306.1	2,646.3	969.5	1,631.7	587.0	435.2	409.5	1,014.8	1,269.1
Commercial Exports	55.4	73.1	252.5	206.0	75.6	31.0	18.7	9.6	10.3	3.5
FMS Construction Agreements	112.4	118.8	65.1	48.2	269.7	66.9	124.0	139.2	83.0	57.0
FMS Deliveries	955.1	473.0	296.8	368.1	482.3	1,026.7	1,236.0	889.0	1,478.7	1,083.2
MAP Program	–	–	–	–	–	–	–	13.5	–	–
MAP Deliveries	–	–	–	–	–	–	–	1.4	1.6	–
IMET Program/Deliveries	1.7	1.5	1.5	1.5	1.8	1.5	1.7	0.8	1.0	1.0

Jordan

Foreign Military Financing Program	–	–	10.0	67.8	20.0	20.0	9.0	9.0	7.3	100.3
Payment Waived	–	–	10.0	67.8	20.0	20.0	9.0	9.0	7.3	100.3
DOD Guaranty	81.3	–	–	–	–	–	–	–	–	–
FMS Agreements	33.9	28.7	9.4	26.7	0.4	6.8	14.5	38.7	13.0	199.5
Commercial Exports	73.4	18.3	23.5	12.1	0.9	27.9	41.8	34.0	34.7	13.1
FMS Deliveries	49.7	55.4	59.5	42.1	22.9	19.5	24.9	31.5	47.0	15.7
MAP Deliveries	1.1	0.8	–	–	0.4	–	0.1	–	–	10.7
IMET Program/Deliveries	1.9	1.7	1.9	2.1	1.1	0.6	0.5	0.8	1.0	1.2

Lebanon

FMS Agreements	4.9	0.5	–	–	–	–	2.4	29.3	64.4	15.8
Commercial Exports	0.1	0.0	0.2	0.1	0.5	0.4	1.0	0.8	0.5	0.3
FMS Deliveries	12.1	11.9	3.9	2.0	0.3	1.3	4.9	3.6	40.9	31.7
IMET Program/Deliveries	–	0.3	0.3	0.1	–	–	0.6	0.3	0.4	0.5

Source: Adapted from U.S. Defense Security Assistance Agency (DSAA), *Foreign Military Sales, Foreign Military Construction Sales and Military Assistance Facts*, Department of Defense, Washington, DC, various editions. Syria received no U.S. aid or sales during the period shown.

Figure 3.9   The Comparative Size of U.S. Military Assistance and Commercial Arms Sales to the Arab-Israeli Ring States: 1997–2004

	1997	1998	1999	2000	2001	2002	2003	2004
Israel								
Foreign Military Financing Program	1,800	1,800	1,860	2,820	1,976	2,040	3,086.6	2,147.3
Payment Waived	1,800	1,800	1,860	2,820	1,976	2,040	3,086.6	2,147.3
FMS Agreements	506.4	654.6	2,430.7	782.6	2,882.1	674.9	663.6	606.9
Commercial Exports	12.8	11.5	4.2	26.3	4.0	1.4	16.5	418.9
FMS Construction Agreements	–	–	–	0.3	9.9	12.7	5.6	63.5
FMS Deliveries	497.2	1,202.7	1,224.4	570.8	759.8	632.2	824.6	891.4
MAP Program	–	–	–	–	–	–	–	–
MAP Deliveries	–	–	–	–	–	–	–	–
IMET Program/ Deliveries	–	–	–	–	–	–	–	–
Egypt								
Foreign Military Financing Program	1,300	1,300	1,300	1,300	1,297	1,300	1,291.6	1,291.6
Payment Waived	1,300	1,300	1,300	1,300	1,297	1,300	1,291.6	1,291.6
FMS Agreements	961.0	978.5	2,058.7	1,612.2	1,720.5	1,020.1	927.9	2,063.9
Commercial Exports	5.0	2.4	0.6	3.8	0.9	0.04	15.9	166.8
FMS Construction Agreements	45.6	27.3	61.9	93.3	48.9	33.4	10.4	55.5
FMS Deliveries	896.8	570.7	450.4	805.3	881.9	1,832.8	877.9	1,328.2
MAP Program	–	–	–	–	–	–	–	–
MAP Deliveries	–	–	–	–	–	–	–	–
IMET Program/ Deliveries	1.0	1.0	1.0	1.0	1.1	1.2	1.2	1.4
Jordan								
Foreign Military Financing Program	30.0	50.0	95.9	124.9	74.8	100	604	204.8
Payment Waived	30.0	50.0	95.9	124.9	74.8	100	604	204.8
DOD Guaranty	–	–	–	–	–			
FMS Agreements	17.5	17.9	14.7	120.5	122.3	111.3	146.5	533.8
Commercial Exports	12.8	11.5	4.2	26.3	4.0	0.24	0.71	19.1
FMS Deliveries	41.7	47.0	48.7	52.7	80.4	57.2	69.5	106.7

MAP Deliveries	16.3	50.2	7.5	8.2	11.5	8.0	0.6	–
IMET Program/ Deliveries	1.7	1.6	1.7	1.7	1.7	2.0	2.4	3.2

Lebanon

FMS Agreements	16.7	12.3	1.6	6.9	5.5	1.3	0.7	2.0
Commercial Exports	0.8	0.8	0.1	0.1	0.1	–	0.144	0.09
FMS Deliveries	33.0	8.0	7.0	4.9	6.1	3.1	3.1	2.0
IMET Program/ Deliveries	0.5	0.6	0.6	0.6	0.5	0.57	0.7	0.7

Source: Adapted from U.S. DSAA, *Foreign Military Sales, Foreign Military Construction Sales and Military Assistance Facts,* Department of Defense, Washington, DC, various editions. Syria received no U.S. aid or sales during the period shown.

_____

The Military Forces of Israel

Israel is threatened by both its geography and its demography. It is a small country surrounded on all its land borders by Arab and predominantly Muslim powers. It has a total area of 20,700 square kilometers. It has borders with Egypt (266 kilometers), the Gaza Strip (51 kilometers), Jordan (238 kilometers), Lebanon (79 kilometers), Syria (27 kilometers), and the West Bank (307 kilometers). It has a 273-kilometer-long coastline on the Mediterranean and a small coastline on the Gulf of Aqaba. Like its Arab neighbors, Israel also faces serious challenges in terms of water and agriculture. Only 16.4 percent of its land is arable and only another 4.2 percent can grow permanent crops.

Its population was over 6.3 million in 2006, including some 200,000 settlers in the West Bank, 178,000 in east Jerusalem, and 20,000 in the Israeli-occupied Golan Heights. Its population was roughly 80 percent Jewish, and 20 percent non-Jewish, largely Arab. About 16 percent of the non-Jewish population was Muslim and the rest was Christian, Druze, and other.[1] The non-Jewish population of Israel continues to have a higher birthrate than Israelis, but the main demographic challenge comes from the Gaza Strip and the West Bank.

As Figure 4.1 shows, the total Palestinian population in Israel, the Gaza Strip, the West Bank, and Greater Jerusalem will be much larger than the Jewish population well into the 2000s, although declines in the Palestinian birthrate are projected to eventually reduce this disparity. The Israeli fear of being in a minority in a "greater Israel" is both a reason for advocating separation and for arguments that Israel should unilaterally withdraw to territory it can ensure is a truly Jewish state.

The immediate security threats Israel faces, however, are military. Few nations have faced as many "existential" military crises in modern times. Ever since the mid-1950s, conventional military forces have shaped the Arab-Israeli balance and the outcome of regional conflicts. This has led to a continuing arms race where Israel

(In Thousands)

UN Estimate

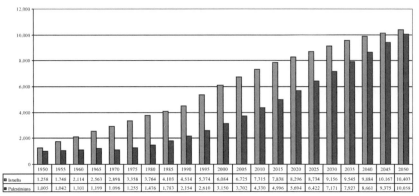

	1950	1955	1960	1965	1970	1975	1980	1985	1990	1995	2000	2005	2010	2015	2020	2025	2030	2035	2040	2045	2050
Israelis	1,258	1,748	2,114	2,563	2,898	3,358	3,764	4,103	4,514	5,374	6,084	6,725	7,315	7,838	8,296	8,734	9,156	9,545	9,884	10,167	10,403
Palestinians	1,005	1,042	1,101	1,199	1,096	1,255	1,476	1,783	2,154	2,610	3,150	3,702	4,330	4,996	5,694	6,422	7,171	7,923	8,661	9,375	10,058

Notes: i) Palestinian population is that of the occupied territories. It does not include refugees. ii) These projections are based on medium variant.
Source: Population Division of the Department of Economic and Social Affairs of the United Nations Secretariat, World Population Prospects: The 2004 Revision and World Urbanization Prospects: The 2003 Revision. http://esa.un.org/unpp, January 31, 2006.

US Census Bureau Estimate

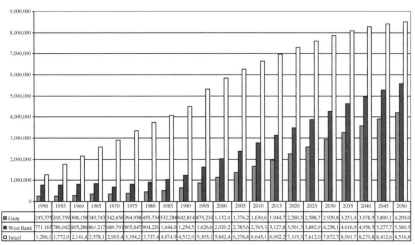

	1950	1955	1960	1965	1970	1975	1980	1985	1990	1995	2000	2005	2010	2015	2020	2025	2030	2035	2040	2045	2050
Gaza	245,375	265,759	308,158	349,743	342,656	394,958	455,734	532,288	642,814	875,231	1,132,0	1,376,2	1,650,6	1,944,7	2,260,3	2,588,7	2,920,8	3,251,4	3,578,5	3,899,1	4,209,0
West Bank	771,165	788,042	805,288	861,217	689,791	805,847	904,220	1,044,0	1,254,5	1,626,6	2,020,2	2,385,6	2,765,3	3,127,8	3,501,3	3,882,9	4,258,1	4,616,9	4,956,5	5,277,7	5,580,3
Israel	1,286,1	1,772,0	2,141,4	2,578,1	2,903,4	3,354,2	3,737,4	4,074,9	4,512,0	5,305,1	5,842,4	6,276,8	6,645,1	6,992,2	7,315,3	7,612,0	7,872,7	8,091,7	8,270,8	8,412,6	8,516,8

Source: U.S. Census Bureau, International Data Base, online.

Figure 4.1   Palestinians and Israelis: Total Population in Israel, the Gaza Strip, the West Bank, and Greater Jerusalem: 1950–2050

has struggled to develop and maintain a decisive qualitative "edge" over its Arab neighbors.

Israel has largely won this struggle in conventional war-fighting terms. Syria, its primary current threat, has fallen far behind in force quality. Egypt had made impressive progress in conventional military modernization, but is at peace with Israel and has emphasized the search for a broader peace—taking on difficult missions such as securing the Gaza Strip's southern border in the process. Jordan was a reluctant participant in the 1967 war, stood aside in 1973, and is also currently at peace with Israel. Its forces are defensive and do not post a major threat. Lebanon has never had significant war-fighting capabilities.

This Israeli conventional superiority or edge is a major factor in securing peace with its Arab neighbors and is critical to deterring Syria. Maintaining Israel's conventional edge, however, is anything but cheap. The burden of security expenditures is far lower than during the periods when Arab armies could pose a major threat, but Israel is forced to spend some 9 percent of its gross domestic product on military and security efforts. Israel's ability to maintain its conventional edge has also been complicated since 2000 by the costs of the Israeli-Palestinian War and the need to devote much of Israel's forces to low-intensity combat missions.

ASYMMETRIC WARS OF ATTRITION

Israel also faces asymmetric threats of a very different kind. The first such threat is the asymmetric war of attrition it has fought with the Palestinians since Israel's founding and which became serious warfare in September 2000. This is a war where Israel's vast conventional superiority to the Palestinian security forces, and groups like Hamas and the Palestinian Islamic Jihad (PIJ), has given Israel almost total freedom of action in the air and the ability to send ground forces into areas in the Gaza Strip and the West Bank with only limited casualties.

At the same time, the Israeli-Palestinian conflict is a war that is extraordinarily difficult to win and whose political dimension is one where Israel has lost support in Europe and many other parts of the world. Israel has found many countermeasures to Palestinian irregular forces and terrorist attacks, but the Palestinians have learned to adapt their tactics as well. Moreover, the Israeli-Palestinian conflict has seriously undermined and divided the secular Palestinian Authority and strengthened hardline Islamist opponents of peace like Hamas and the PIJ.

The struggle between Israel and the Palestinians has also become a "battle of separation" in which Israel seeks to create security, and physical barriers between the two peoples focus the struggle on defeating or penetrating Israel's security barriers. So far, Israel has had considerable success in establishing and maintaining such barriers, but the Palestinians have already begun to acquire rockets and mortars capable of firing across such barriers.

Israel faces serious threats from at least four Palestinian militant groups that are described in Chapter 8. Groups like Hamas and the PIJ have begun to change their tactics to focus on ways of penetrating through the security lines and by using Israel's Arab population. Other anti-Israeli groups like Hezbollah already have stocks of 10,000s of long-range artillery rockets on the Israeli-Lebanese border that present other problems.

Israel faces more than one set of asymmetric threats. It also faces a range of low-level asymmetric threats from both Hezbollah and Syria that are also described in detail in Chapters 6 and 9. These threats have not been particularly active since

Israel's withdrawal from Lebanon, and Syria has even made a new peace initiative. At the same time, Hezbollah has become steadily better armed with Syrian and Iranian support and by the fact that Syria tolerates or encourages the actions of some Palestinian militant groups.

Israel has dealt with these threats with reprisals, retaliation, and covert operations against Hezbollah. It entered Syrian airspace on several occasions in a campaign aimed at encouraging Syria to end its support of the Islamic Jihad terrorist group. In September 2003, Israeli jets intentionally flew over a palace owned by Syrian President Basher Asad's family. More forcefully, Israel bombed a suspected Islamic Jihad training camp outside of Damascus in October 2003. Israel had reportedly ruled out full air strikes or an invasion to remove the Islamic Jihad, but Israel remains committed to degrading Asad's influence.

It is unclear, however, whether such actions do much more than reinforce the level of deterrence created by Israel's military superiority. They do not seem to diminish Asad's power and may produce a rally-around-the-leader sentiment in the Syrian populace. Syria has so far refused to end its support of the Islamic Jihad, claiming that the group is not really a terrorist organization, has broken no Syrian laws, and does not hurt Syria.[2]

The Threat from Proliferation

The second threat is the prospect that Iran may acquire both nuclear weapons and long-range missiles to deliver them. Ever since it first acquired nuclear weapons and long-range missiles, Israel has had another decisive edge over its Arab neighbors. Jordan and Lebanon have never sought to compete in this aspect of the regional arms race. Egypt has sought to improve its missile forces and seems to maintain some form of chemical warfare capability, but seems to have abandoned any serious search for biological and nuclear weapons. It has focused more on efforts to create a nuclear-free zone than proliferation. Syria has missiles and chemical weapons and shows a continuing interest in biological and nuclear weapons, but seems to have made little serious progress.

There is a risk, however, that Iran may acquire both long-range missiles capable of striking any target in Israel and nuclear warheads for such missiles. Most estimates put such a development at least three to five years in the future, and Israel would almost certainly be able to deliver a devastating response. Israel already has some level of missile defense capability and could rapidly improve its long-range nuclear strike capability. By normal standards, it should have a decisive deterrent edge over Iran for the next decade.

The fact remains, however, that Iran's behavior may not be based on "normal standards." It may act out of ideology, make mistakes in threats and escalation, launch under attack if struck by the United States or Israel, or use such weapons for reasons that have little to do with the values of Western game theory. There is also the risk that Iran or other nations could give terrorists or hard-line Palestinian groups weapons of mass destruction or deliver weapons by covert means. The history of rational deterrence is the history of wars that did not occur; the history of modern war is the history of the failure of rational deterrence.

It is also possible that terrorist or hard-line movements could acquire chemical, biological, radiological, or nuclear weapons on their own, or without any clear tie to a state actor. Such attacks might well have limited lethality, although the risk of serious biological and nuclear attacks is likely to grow over time. Such attacks would, at a minimum, force Israel to change its strategic posture to focus on a global threat of terrorism and any nation where such movements were based or which might be the source of such weapons. It would change Palestinian and Arab perceptions of Israel's vulnerability and force Israel to adopt drastic new security and counterterrorist measures.

Israel has unique existential vulnerability. It may or may not be a "one bomb" country, but it is clear that any attack that killed or incapacitated a serious percentage of the population of the greater Tel Aviv area would have a devastating effect.

SHIFTING FROM A CONVENTIONAL TO AN ASYMMETRIC EDGE

These shifts have already had a major impact on the way Israel uses and structures both its military forces and its internal security and intelligence services. The fact that Israel has had to conduct more than half a decade of asymmetric warfare with the Palestinians had forced it to shift many of its conventional military resources to low-intensity conflict, raids and reoccupations of Palestinian territory, and internal security missions. There is no way to precisely quantify just how much of Israel's effort has been shifted to such missions, but they may consume nearly half of Israel's military resources in terms of self-financed security expenditures and some 25 percent of its active and mobilized reserve manpower.

The end result has been a steady expansion of the training and the equipment Israel Defense Forces (IDF) units have for low-intensity conflict and internal security missions, although few of the details are public. For example, Israel signed two separate security agreements, one with Russia and one with Turkey, promising to share information about terrorist groups.[3] Israel hopes that the added intelligence will boost the IDF's effectiveness in the low-intensity conflict.

Israel has utilized unorthodox strategies both domestically and internationally in an effort to enhance security. These have included aggressive diplomatic efforts, heavily targeted toward the United States, taking back Palestinian territory to defeat terrorists, isolating Yasser Arafat and the Palestinian leadership, use of forces and physical barriers to separate the Palestinians from Israel, economic warfare, and direct attacks on hostile Palestinian forces.

In the process, Israel has implemented a targeted assassination policy to try and destroy terrorist organizations by decapitating their leadership ranks. An extreme example of how this policy has been implemented is the assassination of Hamas's spiritual leader Ahmed Yassin in March 2004, and the assassination of Hamas's newly named leader Abdel Aziz Rantisi some three weeks later. Although the killings boosted Hamas's popularity within the Palestinian population, it appears that there

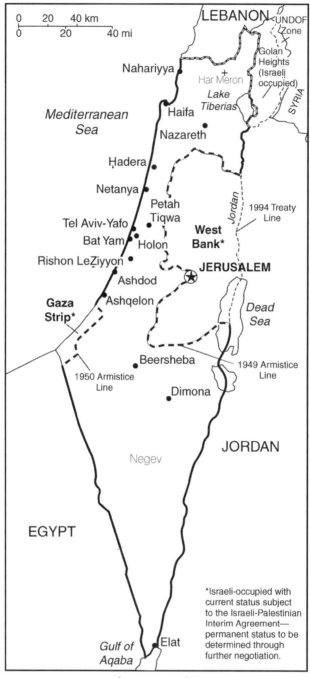

Map 4.1 Israel (Cartography by Bookcomp, Inc.)

was a serious leadership crisis within the movement because, even though it was promised, there was not any direct retaliation for the assassination of Yassin and Rantisi.[4]

Opinions differ over the effectiveness of such hard-line tactics. Some Israelis feel that any new leader that arises will first and foremost have to concentrate on staying alive and not on killing Israelis.[5] This policy has produced critics both abroad and at home. Many Arab nations, and obviously the Palestinians, opposed the policy, seeing it as counterproductive to the peace process while pointing out the strikes frequently incur bystander casualties.

Others disagree. Some reservists refuse to serve in either the Gaza Strip or the West Bank, and 27 Israeli Air Force pilots, including the most decorated pilot in Israel's history, refused to carry out further strikes. Four former heads of the Shin Bet security service declared that Israel's activities in the territories actually eroded national security instead of bolstering it.[6] A former deputy Chief of Staff of the IDF stated that Israel lacked a grand strategy and that the West Bank security fence that Israel is constructing at a cost of $450 million a year precludes the creation of a Palestinian state.[7]

Broadly speaking, however, the Israeli government and many Israelis feel Israel's asymmetric strategies and tactics are working. The IDF reports that gunfire attacks on Israelis in the West Bank decreased by 1,016 incidents in almost one year. Israelis and the IDF were bombed 578 times in 2002 compared to around 220 times in 2003. In 2004, only six suicide bombings occurred inside of Israel, with the number of attempts declining by 50 percent.[8] Israel touts these statistics as proof that the controversial strategies are successful. It should be noted, however, that the number of *attempts* to kill Israelis, especially by suicide bombers, have risen.[9]

Israeli Approaches to Asymmetric Warfare

The IDF has found a number of ways to use its forces to limit the scale of reoccupation and mix containment and isolation with targeted raids and precision strikes and assassinations in order to limit casualties and help reduce the number of tactical engagements in which IDF troops have had to fight in urban or built-up areas under conditions where their superior equipment and training could be offset by superior Palestinian knowledge of the ground and the short ranges imposed by street fighting.

The IDF's use of decisive force, shock, and tools such as tanks, bulldozers, and clearing of security perimeters has helped to provide protection and separation from Palestinian threats. These measures to reduce the risk of Israeli casualties have developed over the course of the war as part of a larger evolution in IDF tactics.

Israel has also relied heavily on air power, or "Environmental Air Control," a term coined by Major General Dan Haloutz, a former Israeli Air Force commander, who was appointed commander of the IDF in February 2005. Haloutz pushed for the Air Force to take over duties usually left to ground soldiers, such as preventing infiltration, enforcing curfews, destroying weapons caches, and attacking terrorist cells, as a means of reducing the IDF ground presence in and near the Gaza Strip and the West Bank.[10]

The IDF's tactical diversification and escalation have taken somewhat different forms in the Gaza Strip and the West Bank. The Gaza Strip is a compact, densely populated, urban area that is almost entirely Palestinian and thus relatively easy for the IDF to isolate and seal off. The Israelis began building a second fence in the spring of 2005 around the Gaza Strip to compliment the existing fence on Israeli territory to the east. The two fences, replete with sensors, created a security buffer zone between Israel and the Gaza Strip that is 100–300 meters wide and extends for 70 kilometers in advance of the settler evacuation.[11]

A similar fence or security barrier has since been under construction near the boundary between Israel and the West Bank and East Jerusalem, and "security barriers" are being created around some settlement areas deep in the West Bank. The West Bank is a much larger area with porous borders, extreme terrain, and a population where Israelis and Palestinians are far more intermingled. It cannot be isolated in its entirety, making it necessary for the IDF to operate within its confines to a greater degree and to isolate it piecemeal.

At the same time, the IDF's operations and techniques share many similar characteristics in both areas. It is difficult to provide a summary of such measures without oversimplifying the issues involved, or the complexity and sophistication of the IDF approach to asymmetric warfare. The following case examples do, however, provide a picture of some of the strengths and weaknesses in the Israeli approach and why Israel came to rely more and more on separation, barriers, and unilateral withdrawals as the war went on.

Rubber Bullets

Israel initially sought to minimize the use of force against ordinary Palestinians and adopted the following rules of engagement: Tear gas and stun grenades are used first. Should these fail to disperse a protest, rubber-coated metal bullets—which are supposed to be shot at the lower body from a distance of 25 meters or more—are then used. Live ammunition, shot at the lower body, is used in response to firebombs; and, finally, when encountering shooting and/or grenades, Israeli soldiers will shoot to kill.

Palestinian sources have claimed that Israeli forces have not abided by these rules and have made frequent use of lethal shots with rubber bullets aimed at the upper body or head.[12] Conversely, other Palestinian sources have argued that IDF troops deliberately aim at the legs of young men in order to cripple them quoting that as of November 12, 2001, approximately 21.4 percent of the 4,448 Palestinians admitted to hospitals were shot in the legs. Physicians for Human Rights claimed that the existence of such a pattern of injuries over time likely reflects an ongoing policy.[13]

War, however, is war. There are serious limits to what nonlethal force can accomplish, and the very term "nonlethal" is so misleading that most military experts call such weapons "less lethal." Weapons like CS gas (tear gas) and rubber bullets have limited range. They often are not effective in stopping large groups. At the same time, gas can be lethal in closed areas and with young children, the elderly, and the sick. Rubber bullets produce serious trauma in 5–20 percent of actual hits even when used within their proper range limits. They are much more lethal at very close ranges.

At the same time, a number of Israeli experts have pointed out that Israel's problems in minimizing Palestinian casualties were compounded by Israel's failure to develop large, well-trained, and well-equipped units dedicated to riot control and the nonlethal use of force before September 2000, and by the lack of joint training for such missions by both the IDF and Palestinian Security forces. The emphasis on peace negotiations before September 2000, coupled with a heavy emphasis on counterterrorism, left both sides poorly prepared to minimize violence during a war and to enforce efforts to halt the violence.

A report issued by the UN High Commissioner for Human Rights, based on a visit to the West Bank and the Gaza Strip in November 2000, though highly dependent on Palestinian sources, illustrates the real-world human cost of asymmetric warfare even at low levels of violence.[14] The report quotes figures provided by the Minister of Health of the Palestinian Authority claiming that approximately 6,958 people (3,366 in the West Bank and 3,592 in the Gaza Strip) had been wounded between September 29 and November 9, 2000, and that 1,016 Palestinians had been wounded in Israel during that time. It also reported that 13 Arab-Israelis were killed following street demonstrations in late September and early October, and over 1,000 were imprisoned.[15] According to these Palestinian figures, 40 percent of those wounded were under 18 years of age, and 41 percent of the wounds were caused by rubber bullets, 27 percent by regular ammunition, 27 percent by tear gas, and 11 percent by heavier weapons like rockets.

At the same time, this same report states that the IDF found that rubber (plastic coated) bullets, tear gas, and water cannons were not effective at ranges over 50–100 meters and that "the IDF have over the last few months tested dozens of weapons but have concluded that less than lethal weapons effective to range of 200 meters do not currently exist."[16]

House Demolitions

The IDF has used house demolitions to punish Palestinians suspected of resistance or attempting to commit violence as far back as 1987, except between 1998 and 2001. According to the IDF, this policy is based on the idea that the fear of demolition will prevent Palestinian militants from attacking Israelis. The former head of the Special Functions Division in the Israeli State's Attorney office, Shai Nitzan, has said that destroying houses is "intended, among other reasons, to deter potential terrorists, as it has been proven that the family is a central factor in Palestinian Society."[17]

According to United Nations Relief and Works Agency, as of September 2004, 2,370 housing units in the Gaza Strip had been destroyed and approximately 22,800 Palestinians were left homeless due to these particular military operations.[18] According to the Israeli Information Center for Human Rights in the Occupied Territories, B'Tselem, Israel destroyed approximately 4,170 Palestinian homes between September 2000 and November 2004.[19]

Most house demolitions have been considered "clearing operations"[20] and mainly take place to help protect Israeli settlers and soldiers in the Gaza Strip.

Another type of the house demolitions carried out by the IDF has been considered "administrative," meaning the destruction of Palestinian homes built without an Israeli permit. The Israeli government authorized the demolition of 768 Palestinian structures in Area C of the West Bank between 2001 and 2003, and 161 structures in East Jerusalem from 2001 to February 2004, because they were built without an Israeli permit.

The third type of house demolition involves houses of relatives and neighbors of Palestinians suspected of violent acts against Israelis civilians or soldiers. These "punitive" demolitions target the homes where the suspects live. Since 2001, the IDF has destroyed approximately 628 housing units of 3,983 people.[21]

The Israeli High Court has extensively reviewed and has generally upheld the IDF practice of destroying the homes of those individuals who are known to have either carried out suicide or other lethal attacks against Israelis or against those who are found to have been responsible for sending individuals on such attacks.[22] However, it is important to note that there have been numerous occasions when the High Court of Israel prohibited the destruction of Palestinian homes based on appeals. For example, on July 22, 2004, the court banned the demolition of ten Palestinian homes in the Gaza Strip in response to a petition filed by Adalah, the Legal Centre for the Rights of the Arab Minority in Israel.[23]

Israel has, however, received much international criticism over its house demolitions. It came under particularly intense scrutiny after an Israeli bulldozer killed American peace activist Rachel Corrie on March 16, 2003. According to witnesses, Corrie was trying to prevent the demolition of a Palestinian family's home in the Gaza Strip.[24] After this incident, the U.S. Department of State outlined its views on this incident and on the policy as a whole:

> Our policy on demolitions has been stated repeatedly and is well known. We have been very clear that we view demolitions as particularly troubling. They deprive a large number of Palestinians of their ability to peacefully earn a livelihood. They exacerbate the humanitarian situation inside Palestinian areas, undermine trust and confidence and make more difficult the critical challenge of bringing about an end to violence and restoring calm.[25]

While Israel initially alleged that Corrie was killed by falling debris, the Israeli National Center of Forensic Medicine performed an autopsy and found that her "death was caused by pressure on the chest from a mechanical apparatus."[26] The death of Rachel Corrie brought near immediate international attention to Israel's policy of demolition.[27] The lack of a widely regarded credible investigation, the fact that Corrie was an American, and the gruesome nature of her death cost Israel international support at the time. The publicity of Corrie's death was also effectively used by Palestinians to further their cause. In fact, one year after Corrie's death, Yasser Arafat even hosted her parents to thank them for "their daughter's sacrifice."[28]

Urban Warfare

The IDF has had some of its most serious problems in urban warfare. Israel has been forced to adjust its tactics and engage in urban warfare in spite of the risks and difficulties in such conflicts. This has led to long sieges in some cities like Bethlehem. In other cases, like Ramallah, Palestinian resistance was minimal, lacked organization, and was over within the first two days. Israeli forces were able to enter the city without fierce battle.[29] Palestinian resistance in Nablus, however, lasted for five days. Israeli F-16s, tanks, and bulldozers demolished buildings to clear "some 300 booby traps" for IDF ground troops.[30]

The IDF operation in the Jenin refugee camp April 4–15, 2002, was conducted nearly simultaneously with the operation in the old city of Nablus April 3–22, 2002. The IDF was forced to engage in over a week of urban warfare in April 2002, after conducting an incursion into the refugee camp in accordance with the IDF policy of containment. Although Israeli forces claim to have warned residents of Jenin before entering the camp, many remained in the camp and fought rather than evacuated.[31] A number of Palestinian fighters from outside Jenin also moved into the area to assist Jenin fighters in carrying out organized resistance to the IDF.

This resistance led to many Palestinian casualties, but was also costly to the IDF—which was not properly prepared or trained for urban warfare. In nine days of fighting in Jenin, 22 IDF soldiers were killed, including 13 in one attack.[32] During the fighting in Jenin, 22 Israeli soldiers were killed, including 13 in an ambush. On April 9 alone, 13 Israeli troops were killed. On that day, two squads of reservists had been maneuvering through narrow alleyways in Jenin when an explosion erupted and Palestinian gunmen seized the opportunity to open fire on the soldiers, killing 13.[33]

The IDF also had to make extensive use of combat engineering, a practice that now seems a standard tactic. D-9 bulldozers and a special unit of engineers proved essential in clearing mines and defending the front line in order for other special units and infantry to move forward into the dangerous urban area filled with booby-trapped passageways and buildings.[34]

Jenin became the first major example of urban warfare in the conflict and immediately raised major political issues over how such warfare should be conducted. Approximately 15,000 Palestinians resided in the 90-acre refugee camp, where the resistance fighters held out for nine days. According to Human Rights Watch, 22 Palestinian noncombatants were killed during the fighting. However, Human Rights Watch stated that Palestinian militants "endanger[ed] Palestinian civilians in the camp by using it as a base for planning and launching attacks, using indiscriminate tactics such as planting improvised explosive devices within the camp, and intermingling with the civilian population during armed conflict."[35]

This kind of fighting led the IDF to launch a multimillion-dollar program in June 2002 to upgrade the Army's national training center and provide Israeli soldiers with an "urban warfare" training facility.[36] This expansion built upon existing efforts. According to the upgrade program's manager, Israeli forces already practiced "abbreviated urban warfare operations at a few bases around the country."[37] An urban battlefield facility opened at the Lachish base in the Negev Desert in 2001, and "soldiers practice[d] approaches, surveillance techniques and maneuvers among loosely constructed facades of buildings, homes, and roadways."[38] This facility was equipped with laser identifying markers in addition to voice and data recording devices.

Targeted Assassinations

"Targeted killings" are another example of a tactic Israel developed to minimize the casualties and collateral damage caused by broader combat operations, but which can also be counterproductive and produce significant civilian casualties and/or produce negative media attention. The Israeli security forces have killed many Palestinians directly involved in attacks on Israelis, but they have killed others not directly involved as well. Such killings are not new. Israel has long fought its side of asymmetric warfare by engaging in the practice of political and antiterrorism assassinations.[39]

Israel markedly stepped up such attacks after the outbreak of the Israeli-Palestinian War, however, and adopted a policy of selectively assassinating Palestinians it held responsible for attacking or planning attacks on Israelis. It made increasing use of IDF Special Forces and attack helicopters in such attacks, although many killings were carried out by the intelligence and security services.[40]

The rate of Israeli targeted assassinations, and the rank and prominence of the targets they have struck, grew as the conflict progressed. The overall deterrent impact of this escalation in Israeli targeted assassinations, however, is uncertain. Palestinian militants view such tactical hits on their operatives and operations as provocations that require revenge. For instance, shortly after the Israeli assassination of Hamas founder and spiritual leader Sheik Ahmed Yassin on March 22, 2004, Abdel Aziz Rantisi, the newly appointed leader of Hamas in the Gaza Strip, promised vengeance: "Yassin is a man in a nation, and a nation in a man. And the retaliation of this nation will be of the size of this man."[41] And after Rantisi himself was assassinated in an Israeli missile strike less than a month later on April 17, 2004, Ismail Haniya, another senior Hamas political leader, proclaimed, "Israel will regret this—revenge is coming. This blood will not be wasted . . . The battle will not weaken our determination or break our will."[42]

Such Israeli action has provoked Palestinian reaction. Palestinian militant groups often attempted to strike in revenge and reprisal against Israeli targets to counter any suggestion that the Israeli attacks were impairing their ability to function by chipping away at their leadership. Yet, Israel's targeted assassination strategy had that effect, and Palestinian counterstrikes often failed to materialize.

For instance, Hamas and other militant groups were not able to fulfill their promises to rapidly avenge the assassinations of Yassin and Rantisi. In a late April 2004 interview with Iran's state controlled news agency, a leader of the Al Aqsa Martyrs Brigade admitted that "the Islamic and Arab world . . . expected . . . Palestinian Fatah and Hamas . . . combatants to take revenge for the bloodshed of martyr Sheikh

Ahmed Yassin immediately. But [they] are unaware of the limitations and [the] amount of pressure imposed against the Palestinian combatants."[43] The unnamed leader went on to cite Israel's recent successes in killing or capturing key leaders and members—particularly bomb makers—of Palestinian militant groups and the difficulties in replacing them as a primary reason why they have been unable to retaliate. The fact that Hamas did not disclose the name of Rantisi's successor in the Gaza Strip over concern for his physical protection also reflected the difficulties the group had experienced in operating under the continuous threat of Israeli targeted killings.

Although Israel's assassination policy has not reduced—and may actually have reinforced—the motivation or determination of Palestinian militant organizations such as Hamas, it did weaken their ability to carry out terrorist operations. Furthermore, successful retaliatory attacks by Palestinian militants often had the effect of increasing the level of Israeli countermeasures since they further shift Israeli public opinion to the right of the political spectrum and strengthen support for targeted killings and other Israeli military action.

Dealing with Roadside Attacks and Retaliation

Securing lines of communication is another example of the need to adjust to asymmetric warfare. At the start of the crisis, Palestinian tactics focused on limited violence, largely consisting of the use of rock-throwing teenage boys oftentimes encouraged to risk their lives by their peers, the Palestinian media, and a deep desire to assist in the liberation of Palestine. These groups primarily appeared to target military outposts and settlers creating tense situations in which the probability for errors in judgment and misassessment of threats was extraordinarily high for both sides. The stone throwers were also frequently accompanied by armed Fatah activists who increased the underlying tension and risk in already volatile and potentially tragic situations and increased the likelihood that the IDF would employ lethal ammunition. Most often this created a political and a media environment that easily influenced international public opinion through the martyrdom of Palestinian young men that served the interests of the Palestinian Authority. However, it also propelled both sides toward higher levels of violence.

Moreover, the use of roadside bombs and ambushes led to increased fears among the settlers that the IDF could not fully ensure their safety when traveling. For example, on November 13, 2000, in two separate incidents, unarmed Israeli female civilians were shot while driving. One week later, on November 20, a roadside bomb killed two Israeli adults and wounded seven children, dismembering some, on their way to school. And then on December 10, Palestinian gunmen ambushed a highly regarded rabbi—he, however, escaped unharmed. These incidents demonstrate how difficult it is for the IDF to control all of the access routes all of the time. It also helps explain why the IDF emphasizes the importance and even the necessity of barriers and physically secured routes, even at the cost of the local separation of Israelis and Palestinians.

Attacks on Settlements and the IDF Response

Israel has had to respond to attacks on the settlements. At the onset of the war, Palestinians began to conduct low-level attacks on Israeli settlements primarily at night. According to IDF officials, there were upward of 600 such incidents by December 5, 2000. These attacks did not pose any significant threat of actually overrunning Israeli settlements and did not inflict as many casualties on the settlers or the IDF as did attacks on the access routes.

However, Palestinian attacks became better coordinated as time went on. The IDF expressed its concern over a "very well coordinated and orchestrated attack" on December 4, 2000, against Rachel's Tomb that was the "most dangerous" event thus far in the conflict.[44] The attack involved a coordinated strike from three directions on an Israeli settlement from 1 A.M. to 4 A.M. It was conducted on such a large scale that the IDF forces solicited air support. Palestinians disputed the claim that any such attack was made and rather claimed that the gunfire was from an Israeli offensive attack against Palestinians in Bethlehem.[45]

One area particularly affected by such low-level attacks was the Gilo neighborhood on the southern edge of Jerusalem. Beginning in early October 2000, Palestinian gunmen regularly fired shots from the adjacent Arab village of Beit Jala, hitting targets inside the homes of Israeli families. In response to these attacks, Israel escalated its response. IDF troops increasingly fired back, frequently using helicopter gunships, machine-gun fire, and tank shells, as it did for the first time on October 22 and 23, 2000. In the process, the IDF unintentionally hit several private Palestinian homes in Beit Jala. After a week of shooting in mid-February 2001, Israeli shelling for the first time killed a Palestinian resident of Beit Jala.[46]

In early May 2001, the IDF conducted its first incursion into Beit Jala to battle Palestinian gunmen. Israeli troops killed one Palestinian militia officer and injured 20 others, qualifying that they pushed into the village in an attempt to stop Palestinian gunmen who were firing on Israeli army positions and on nearby roads used primarily by settlers. Fires and drive-by shootings had killed several settlers since the outbreak of the Israeli-Palestinian War. Another round of fierce fighting on the Gilo-Beit Jala flashpoint occurred May 14, 2001, when four residents of Gilo were wounded by shooting that originated in Beit Jala.[47]

Such attacks not only forced Israel to provide defense in depth, they were yet another factor leading to the IDF's increased emphasis on security barriers, walls, and physical separation.

Ground Raids by the IDF

Israel made only limited use of ground forces at the beginning of the war. In October 2000, the IDF deployed special antiguerrilla units that were designed to carry out aggressive penetration and counterguerrilla missions. Despite the inherent difficulties of such raids, Israel achieved a good success rate by November 2000 and combined such raids with the use of air power and standoff weapons. It also continued to use such tactics in spite of the fact that the IDF had to change the way it trained its soldiers during the height of the Intifada. In order to ease the pressure on the reserves, Israel abandoned the 17-week training prior to deployment and instead they received one month of training with half a year of actual operations, getting instructed in the field.[48]

Israel found the use of commando raids and selective attacks from the ground sometimes offered Israel advantages in public relations terms over attacks and killings using advanced weapons like the AH-64 and tanks. Such raids may not reduce civilian casualties and collateral damage, but they seem to have a lower profile, are easier to deny or to confuse with internal Palestinian conflicts, and a slipup involving an M-16 rifle leads to much less publicity than a mistracked missile.

Such raids depend heavily on good intelligence for their success, however, and put Israeli forces directly at risk.[49] Israel's ability to obtain human intelligence had diminished during the peace process as the territory under the control of the Palestinian Authority expanded. Fewer informers cooperated, while the dangers to such informers increased. It became more difficult for Israeli agents to disguise themselves as Palestinians and infiltrate Palestinian areas.

These problems increased after the outbreak of the fighting. The deep-seated anger that existed during the first Intifada and the peace process also increased as the war went on, and it made intelligence-gathering operations more risky. Even though Israel was still able to achieve significant successes, parts of its informer network weakened over time, infiltration became more difficult, and Israel was forced to rely more on signals intelligence and unmanned aerial vehicles (UAVs) as substitutes for human intelligence (HUMINT) sources on the ground.

The political impact of such raids also varied from raid to raid. The majority of raids were successful and did not result in many Israeli or Palestinian casualties or much collateral damage. However, others did produce more Palestinian casualties, resulted in serious collateral damage, and/or were later admitted to be mistakes. For example, on April 30, 2001, an explosion that targeted a member of Fatah accused of the entrapment and murder of an Israeli youth killed two nearby children. Less than a month later on May 14, Israeli troops shot and killed five Palestinian officers stationed at a West Bank roadblock at Beitunya. The IDF later admitted that it had killed the wrong persons as a result of an intelligence error.[50]

At the same time, it soon became apparent that limited use of ground forces could not defeat Hamas or the PIJ and that "decapitation" strikes had serious limitations. Each successful small raid or killing seemed to create martyrs and lead to new groups of volunteers. In many cases, the end result was revenge rather than success in deterring and defeating the enemy, and the loss of trained leaders and cadres oftentimes encouraged the recruitment and use of young Palestinians as suicide bombers. Moreover, Hamas, the PIJ, Fatah, and other such groups learned how to improve their security, create cells separate from known leaders, and shelter in civilian areas and facilities where it was harder to strike without creating additional casualties. As is the case in most forms of asymmetric warfare, there is always a counter tactic. Enemies always learn from experience if they are given the chance.

Drives into the Gaza Strip and the West Bank

Israeli ground tactics became increasingly aggressive as the war progressed. IDF forces began to enter, exit, and reenter Palestinian cities in the West Bank—extending the scale of operations and the length of their stays as the situation escalated. Prime Minister Ariel Sharon ordered an incursion into the Gaza Strip, shortly after taking office on March 7, 2001, signifying a new trend of entering Palestinian-controlled territory. In April 2001, bulldozers were used for the first time since the start of the Israeli-Palestinian War to level Palestinian civilian and security buildings and to clear trees to create "free-fire zones" nearby the Khan Younis and Rafah refugee camps in the Gaza Strip—areas determined to be the source of gunfire and mortar attacks on Israeli troops and settlements.

According to the *Washington Post,* the Israeli press criticized Sharon for ordering an invasion of the Gaza Strip and then pulling back "under U.S. pressure." The launching of mortar attacks on Israeli military posts and settlements continued well after the IDF withdrawal from the Gaza Strip.[51] As the months passed and the fighting on both sides intensified, the frequency of such ground incursions escalated, despite original disapproval from the international community. The first incursion into Palestinian-ruled territory led to "international outcry, including…criticism from U.S. Secretary of State Colin L. Powell. Over time, however, the incursions became routine."[52]

On August 27, 2001, Israeli forces employed both armored vehicles and helicopter gunships to enter the West Bank town of Beit Jalla in order to seize structures. These structures, according to the IDF, were sites where militants were launching mortars into the Israeli settlement of Gilo.[53] After entering Beit Jalla with a combination of armored units on the ground and helicopters in the air, the IDF withdrew on August 31.[54] On October 19, 2001, Israeli infantry forces and armored units again entered Beit Jalla after incidents of renewed launching of mortars on nearby Gilo. Israeli forces seized a number of buildings in the area and returned fire.[55]

On October 17, 2001, Israeli Tourism Minister Rehavam Zeevi was killed by four Popular Front for the Liberation of Palestine (PFLP) militants in revenge for Israel's assassination of PFLP leader Mustafa Ali Zibri in August of that year. Later that evening, the IDF responded by tightening its security around the West Bank cities of Ramallah, Nablus, and Jenin. Access routes to Jenin were closed and placed under the control of Israeli forces.[56] As the conflict escalated, IDF forces continued to enter, exit, and reenter Palestinian cities.

On the evening of February 27, 2002, Israeli Forces entered the Balata refugee camp near the city of Nablus in the north of the West Bank. Following the IDF incursion into Balata, the IDF entered other camps and Palestinian cities including Bethlehem and Beit Jalla in the West Bank, and Jabalya in the Gaza Strip.[57] Many of the Palestinians highest on Israel's most-wanted list escaped capture, yet the three-week operation that began on February 27, 2002, and ended on March 18 with the withdrawal of troops from Bethlehem and Beit Jalla, captured thousands of Palestinians.[58]

Such incursions were followed by steadily larger IDF ground force attacks, but did not represent a major shift in IDF strategy as much as a more intense implementation of tactics that were already in use. According to IDF Colonel Nitsan Alon, "targets were . . . prioritized to achieve as much as possible before international pressure culminated."[59] Israeli air, ground, and naval forces were used to conduct simultaneous operations in cities and camps across the West Bank. Several joint task forces based on infantry and armored units, and including Special Forces, engineer corps, and intelligence units moved into the areas. The IDF had already been moving in and out of Palestinian cities for months. Operation Defensive Shield did, however, involve an Israeli attack on six major Palestinian cities in the West Bank: Ramallah, Bethlehem, Tulkarem, Qalqilya, Nablus, and Jenin.

A report by the Washington Institute describes the impact of these encounters from an Israeli perspective:

> "It is estimated that several thousand troops took part in the operation, with two or three hundred tanks alongside the air and naval forces." In this escalation of force on the part of the IDF, Israeli forces attacked terrorist infrastructure, refugee camps perceived as safe-havens for terrorists, and facilities of the Palestinian Authority. In the camps and towns under attack, Israeli forces seized strategic locations—using armored vehicles to clear the tightly planned streets of refugee camps—and then began implementing curfews, gathering information, and conducting searches. The IDF seized a number of Kassam rockets, demolished about 10 factories where rockets were manufactured, destroyed and seized a number of other weapons and explosives, and arrested and killed several suspected militant activists. After collecting intelligence and damaging terrorist infrastructure, Israeli forces pulled out without accepting the task of overseeing civilian aspects of life. To avoid as much confrontation as possible, the IDF warned the Palestinian security forces in each area. Moreover, though many homes were destroyed in the attacks, the danger to Israeli troops—in addition to civilians—was limited as buildings were demolished to open the narrow streets.[60]

After about two weeks of restraint during mediation efforts, tensions escalated again in late March and early April 2002 following an escalation in suicide bombings during the month of March.[61] The IDF did not stop operating while Israel was practicing a policy of restraint; however, the IDF did refrain from responding to suicide bombings with air attacks.[62]

The problem with these drives was that each such escalation on the ground led to new Palestinian asymmetric attacks and escalation. The IDF showed it could achieve tactical victories, but soon learned it could not pacify or stabilize the areas where it operated. Its inability to give strategic value to its tactical successes was another reason it began to focus on security barriers and separation.

Use of Large-Scale Arrests

Israel has long made use of mass arrests and made this a more aggressive tactic beginning in early 2002. For example, the IDF took an increasingly large number of Palestinians into custody during Operation Defensive Shield—as a means of both gaining intelligence information and arresting those discovered to have connections with militant groups. Israeli forces also carried out its policy of confiscating weapons on a more expansive scale during Operation Defensive Shield. After three days in Ramallah, the IDF had "arrested 10 wanted men and seized 19 sniper rifles, two mortar shells, [and] four pipe bombs."[63]

In order to gather intelligence and arrest militant activists, Israeli forces took 700 Palestinians into custody in the first four days of the incursion in Ramallah.[64] Israeli forces strategically operated to isolate the Palestinian Authority and the Palestinian leader, Yasser Arafat. By the summer of 2002, over 8,000 Palestinians had been taken into custody as a result of Operation Defensive Shield and nearly 2,200 still remained.[65]

During this operation, the IDF also began major efforts to destroy civilian facilities of the Palestinian Authority in addition to its security institutions, targeting not only Arafat's compound and Palestinian police offices but the Legislative Council offices, the Chambers of Commerce, and the Ministries of Agriculture, Education, Trade, and Industry as well.[66] Moreover, the Palestinian headquarters for Preventive Security was targeted for the first time by the IDF.

Attacking and Isolating the Palestinian Leadership

Israel initially avoided attacks on Arafat and the Palestinian leadership. However, after more Palestinian suicide attacks in late November and early December, the IDF, on December 3, 2001, destroyed Arafat's three Mi8 helicopters in the Gaza Strip with air-to-land missiles.[67] On December 4, 2001, the IDF imposed a siege around Arafat's West Bank compound with armored vehicles and troops.[68] On December 4, Israelis also launched air strikes against offices of the Palestinian Authority in both the West Bank and the Gaza Strip—one missile was fired near an office where Arafat was working. In response to a question regarding whether Israel was targeting Arafat himself, U.S. Secretary of State Powell said, "Israel says they are not targeting Arafat."[69] Nonetheless, attacking targets close to Arafat and part of his administration's infrastructure indirectly made Arafat a target of Israeli military force. Israeli tanks positioned "only a few hundred meters from his office" confined Arafat to Ramallah.[70]

Israel held Arafat responsible for not keeping militant organizations under control and for the terrorism in Israel. The tactic of "isolation" marked a major shift in IDF strategy. Until December 2001, Israel still treated Arafat as a potential peace partner. After December 2001, Israel showed little interest in preserving the relationship Yitzhak Rabin had forged with Arafat when they cosigned the Oslo Accords. Israel publicly associated Arafat with the terrorist attacks and the armed struggle and, as a man so committed to armed struggle, that he could no longer be trusted in cease-fire negotiations or treated as a true partner in peace.

Demolishing Arafat's helicopters, and surrounding the leader's headquarters, confined Arafat by preventing him from traveling to places outside of Ramallah. By confining Arafat, the IDF hindered his ability to mobilize his forces, curtail extremist forces, and engage in dialogue with internal political opponents, as well as international political leaders.[71] In maintaining this policy, Israel aimed to weaken his power and diminish the legitimacy of his rule in the eyes of the international world, as well as in the eyes of the Palestinian people.

Prime Minister Sharon made a statement in the first week of December 2001, stating that the aim of attacking Arafat was to "forc[e] him to take responsibility."[72] The Israeli cabinet did not label Arafat a terrorist but, nonetheless, it did take steps to delegitimize his security forces. The Israeli cabinet also publicly "declared Force 17, one of Arafat's security units, and the Tanzim, the militia wing of his Fatah Party, 'terrorist organizations' that will be acted against accordingly."[73]

On December 12, 2001, the Israeli government announced its decision to cut off ties with Yasser Arafat.[74] Prime Minister Sharon declared, "Yasser Arafat is no longer relevant to the state of Israel, and there will be no more contact with him."[75] Sharon enforced Israeli military isolation of Arafat with this political statement, cutting him off from engaging in "normal" political relations with Israel and putting his political clout into question internationally.

These steps established a pattern of Israeli behavior that deprived Arafat and the Palestinian Authority of the ability to use their security forces effectively. It also led to a pattern of escalation that eventually destroyed the Palestinian Authority's infrastructure when Israel attempted to remove Arafat from power, and it prevented terrorist attacks with a series of barriers and forced separations of Israelis and Palestinians.

After 2001, Israeli forces steadily escalated the intensity of their attacks on the infrastructure of the Palestinian Authority. For example, the IDF demolished the runway at Gaza International Airport with bulldozers.[76] They also continued to scout out Palestinian militants with secret-service units.[77] In early December 2001, they fired missiles onto the headquarters of the Palestinian Military Intelligence in the West Bank town of Safit and attacked police stations in Jenin, as part of the trend to attack the Palestinian infrastructure.[78]

These attacks dealt significant blows to the security infrastructure of the Palestinian governing body that continued throughout the war. They also raised questions as to whether Israel's motive was to diminish the ability of Palestinian Security forces to operate effectively in order to weaken Arafat's regime, or if it was acting because Arafat clandestinely was promoting terrorist organizations and thus countering the effectiveness of his own security forces.

In any case, the Israeli cabinet stated that Arafat was "directly responsible for the terror attacks" on December 13, 2001, and began to take over much of the "policing" of Palestinian areas.[79]

Use of Air Power

The Israel Air Force's (IAF's) use of high-accuracy weapons from a distance has given the Israelis a technological edge in the conflict, while reducing the number of troops needed on the ground.[80] Increasing the use of air power to replace some of the tasks traditionally carried out by troops was consistent with IDF goals of reducing the visibility of soldiers and easing tensions between the Palestinians and Israelis, as well as reducing some of the burdens placed on Israeli troops. The IAF became involved in preventing infiltrations, enforcing curfews, attacking terror cells, and destroying weapons caches.

Israel's use of air power in urban combat has been impressive. "In the past six months or so, 60 percent to 80 percent of all armed Palestinian combatants targeted for liquidation by Israel's Shin Bet security service and intelligence arms were killed by air strikes. And that percentage rises to nearly 90 percent in the Gaza Strip, IDF sources here said."[81] Israel effectively used intelligence, technology, and tight command and control to achieve these results while driving collateral damage down as well. "This year [2005], in targeted killing operations, we are averaging 12 armed terrorists killed to every one innocent, whereas before, it was almost a ratio of one-to-one," an IDF official stated.[82]

The IDF has also turned to the use of UAVs, which have already killed senior members of Hamas. The UAVs came into full use during the Operation Days of Atonement incursion in September 2004. Israel's UAV arsenal includes the Hunter, the Harpy, and the Searcher.[83]

This shift toward more use of air power may have been a factor contributing to the choice of Major General Dan Haloutz, a former Air Force commander, to lead the IDF instead of Major General Gabi Ashkenazi, an infantryman. The use of air power in urban operations is also likely to be further tested in the evacuation and the pull-out from the Gaza Strip, which will most likely occur under fire. Israeli officials state that it will be up to the IAF to deter attacks on Israel during the operation.

Israeli Use of Helicopters and Aircraft

Israeli use of combat helicopters and aircraft has been a topic of debate since the beginning of the conflict. At the start of the war, Israeli forces generally entered Palestinian territory from the air, bypassing the problem of using IDF ground forces to drive through Palestinian areas. Since that time, they have continued to make use of helicopters, fighters, and standoff precision weapons, while IDF ground forces have increasingly acted to seize and destroy key Palestinian strongpoints and facilities that could be used to attack Israel. Caterpillar D-9 bulldozers and additional special ground forces also entered the combat scene as Israeli forces began to infiltrate Palestinian cities and increase their presence in areas of the West Bank and the Gaza Strip.[84]

Israel made its first extensive use of attack helicopters to strike targets in the Gaza Strip and the West Bank during October 2000. AH-64A Apaches were used to hit targets in Nablus and in the Gaza Strip, including Chairman Arafat's compound. The AH-64 was used instead of the AH-1G/S Cobra because of its superior range, sensors, and weapons and its ability to better distinguish between civilians and "combatants."[85] Between October 2000 and December 2001, Israeli forces used these weapons to assassinate at least 60 Palestinian militants.[86]

"Precision," however, is always relative and any attack on built-up and urban areas risks killing innocent civilians. Unfortunately, in some cases, AH-64 Apache attack helicopters failed to hit the desired targets and inflicted collateral damage. One example that occurred in the beginning of the war involved an AH-64 attack against the Fatah in El-Bireh in October 2000 that hit the house next door.[87] In another case, which occurred on October 20, 2003, an IDF AH-64 launched a first missile toward a vehicle in the Nuseirat refugee camp transporting several members of a terrorist cell. The missile hit the target and the militant's vehicle subsequently lost control and crashed into what was perceived by the IDF to be a tree. A second missile was launched as the car tried to escape. From the IDF video of the attack, it appeared that no civilian was near the car. However, according to Palestinian sources, before the AH-64 fired another missile, it waited until there were rescue workers and gatherers near the car—in fact, firing the missile deep into the streets of the refugee camp. This report was adamantly denied by the IDF.

Israeli use of such advanced weapons reduces Israeli casualties, but has also allowed the Palestinians to politically exploit the IDF's highly visible use of force—and Palestinian military weakness—by charging that the use of fighters and attack helicopters are "disproportionate." Such charges have uncertain value. The key issue in assessing such uses of force is the result, not the means. The careful use of advanced weapons such as precision-guided missiles can be far more humane than IDF ground force incursions or Palestinian suicide bombings in civilian areas. The use of systems like attack helicopters has also almost certainly allowed Israel to hit key targets with fewer civilian casualties and collateral damage than alternative means of attack in spite of occasional mistargeting and collateral damage.

In any case, the use of helicopters became part of a broader IDF effort to deal with extremist violence by attacking the leaders of the groups rather than conducting broad attacks on their members. Other examples include Hamas and Fatah leaders. Israel first implemented its policy of selective assassination of known terrorists on November 9, 2000. An Israeli helicopter attacked a truck carrying Hussein Abayat, a local Tanzim commander. Then on December 11, 2000, a PIJ bombing suspect, Anwar Hamran, was the target of an attack while he was waiting for a taxicab. Prime Minister Ehud Barak acknowledged Israel's responsibility for these and other such attacks and pledged to continue with similar operations if Israeli citizens continued to be attacked.[88] According to a report by *Agence France Press,* Israel killed approximately 31 Palestinians in the period between November 9, 2000 and May 5, 2001.[89]

In 2002, Israel assassinated 72 suspected militants, 37 more than the previous year. In 2003, one Tel Aviv lawyer asserted that "the main weapon the Israeli army has in its arsenal against terrorism is the assassination policy."[90] This has led to widespread international criticism and some domestic criticism. In October 2003, 27 Israeli active and reserve fighter pilots and instructors, including Brigadier General Yiftah Spector, one of the most decorated pilots in Israel's history, signed a letter that derided the targeted assassination policy in urban areas as "illegal and immoral."[91] The nine pilots who were active at the time were grounded, and the instructors, including Spector, were relieved of their duties. It is uncertain, however, that their actions will have much impact on the Israeli government's policy, on the public, or on the rest of the armed forces' perceptions.

Other changes have given the Israeli Air Force a wider role in antiterror operations, ranging from curfew enforcement to anti-infiltration missions. As mentioned
above, the IAF's use of high-accuracy weapons from a distance gives the Israelis a
technological edge in the conflict.[92] A tactic that Israel employed was to try to be less
visible by replacing tasks carried out by ground troops with other means, such as barriers, increased use of air power, and by turning over some security responsibilities to
the Palestinians. By reducing Israeli visibility, the Israelis hoped to ease tensions and
reduce the number of attacks on both Israel and Israeli troops while increasing their
security.

Countering Palestinian Arms Smuggling and Manufacturing

Israel has had considerable success in halting both Palestinian militant groups' and
the Palestinian Authority's arms smuggling operations and arms manufacturing
efforts. The IDF has had the advantage in terms of controlling all of the Palestinian
"borders" and coasts, intelligence support from the United States, a modern set of
intelligence sensors, and a significant HUMINT network. Under these conditions,
it is scarcely surprising that Israel has had more successes than it has had failures.

The most conspicuous success was when the Israeli Navy intercepted the *Karine-A*
in the Mediterranean Sea in 2002. The ship carried weapons "that have never before
been in the PA's possession." These included modern missiles carrying Tandem-
Charge warheads with the ability to penetrate heavy armor, and 122-mm Katyusha
rockets that have a range of 12 miles.[93] The *Karine-A* incident shows that control
of the sea is as important as control of the boarders and the coastline.

The Palestinians have been able to manufacture some arms, but relatively few. The
IDF has demolished many warehouses in Palestinian cities in addition to many factories where weapons are locally manufactured. The IDF has largely been able to
close off air, land, and sea passages granting access into the Palestinian territories.

There have also been some smuggling attempts across land boundaries from Iraq
through Jordan, and from Egypt. Most weapons, however, have been smuggled into
the Gaza Strip by tunnels or the Mediterranean Sea. On January 29, 2001, for example, Israeli forces came across two sealed barrels filled with weapons near Ashkelon,
and it is assumed that other barrels from the same shipment reached their destination
in the Gaza Strip. After inspecting the barrels, the IDF determined that the arms had
been carried from Hezbollah in Lebanon and were bound for the Gaza Strip where
the Palestinian Islamic Jihad was to pick up the shipment.

Israel has also had to deal with arms being smuggled in from Egypt through
underground tunnels. Since October 2000, the Israelis uncovered over 100 tunnels,
with lengths up to 800 meters and depths down to 15 meters long. The IDF has
found grenade rockets and launchers, hundreds of kilograms of explosives, assault
rifles, and thousands of bullets and ammunition. A combination of human intelligence, technology, and tactics has allowed the Israelis to shut down many of the
tunnels.[94]

WITHDRAWAL FROM THE GAZA STRIP AND THE WEST BANK

Barriers and separation have effectively become another form of asymmetric warfare and a means of achieving "separation." In February 2004, Ariel Sharon declared his plans to unilaterally withdraw from the Gaza Strip and some small settlements in the northern West Bank. This proposal became a reality in August 2005 when within one week the 25 settlements slated for evacuation, 21 from the Gaza Strip (all the Gaza Strip settlements) and 4 from the West Bank (the area around Jenin), were evacuated. Sharon reversed a position that such settlements were important to Israeli security that had been an official position for some 38 years.[95]

This disengagement from the Gaza Strip reduced a major burden on the IDF because securing the settlements in the Gaza Strip had been expensive in terms of both manpower and defense resources. It did not occur, however, without serious political infighting between the settlers, the religious, the leftists, and the seculars, but ultimately the majority of the population and the Knesset supported the move. When the time came on September 11, 2005, all the Israeli military forces within the Gaza Strip were completely withdrawn and responsibility was handed over to the Palestinian Authority in less than 12 hours.[96]

There was wide support for the disengagement within the Palestinian population, and even antipeace movements supported it: Hamas and Islamic Jihad claimed responsibility for the Israeli pullout. In practice, many Palestinians seem to have believed that the pullout was a result of their violent struggle against the Israelis. Mahmoud Abbas publicly agreed with this explanation for the Israeli pullout, although he had opposed the militarization of the Intifada from the start and continued to take this position once he replaced Arafat.[97]

The Palestinians got little initial material benefit from the withdrawal. Once the Israeli settlers were out of the Gaza Strip the Israeli army started demolishing the homes that some had lived in for as long as 38 years. The homes were demolished since it was agreed by both sides that the style of the homes in the settlement would not be appropriate for the 1.3 million Palestinians.

The withdrawal also produced separation without necessarily producing security. The cleared areas in the Gaza Strip soon became an area where Hamas and the PIJ began to operate. The border between the Gaza Strip and Egypt also became a crossing point for hard-line opponents of the peace and arms smuggling, in spite of the fact that the Egyptian military had redeployed to the border.[98]

Israel's unilateral withdrawal from the Gaza Strip and small West Bank settlements has so far done nothing to ease Palestinian resentment and anger at Israel. If anything, the combination of such action and Arafat's death have created a Palestinian political environment that has strengthened Hamas and the opponents of the senior leadership in the Palestinian Authority—the Tunisians—even among the younger party leaders and officials within the coalition that makes up the Palestinian Authority.

The advantage of Israeli "unilateralism" in setting Israeli-Palestinian boundaries is that it breaks the stalemate that has occurred since Oslo. The disadvantage is that there is no Palestinian agreement to the actions taking place, no peace process or climate of peace, and no basis for a stable Palestinian society or economy. All of the key divisive issues remain: the 1967 boundary, access to and control of Jerusalem, water and land issues, right of return, etc. This, in turn, ensures that the remaining mix of outlying Israeli settlements, security roads, and IDF position on the West Bank are both divisive and require Israeli security activity that makes it difficult to impossible to create a functioning Palestinian state and economy.

Israel does, however, face significant problems in containing such an asymmetric conflict. Israeli withdrawal from the Gaza Strip seems more likely to create an increasingly hostile Palestinian enclave with a troubled border with Egypt and security problems in controlling its coast and airspace than lead to peace. Its security barrier—or "Wall"—on the West Bank may provide physical security but has already alienated many Israeli Arabs, Arabs in other nations, non-Arab Muslims, as well as Palestinians. This, in turn, has helped violent Islamist extremist groups like Al Qa'ida exploit the Arab-Israeli conflict and hostile foreign leaders like the President of Iran.

Separation, Security Barriers, and the "Fence"

Perhaps the most serious shift in Israeli tactics and methods in dealing with the Israeli-Palestinian War has been a shift toward separation, walls and security barriers, and the creation of unilateral boundaries. Israel has not only exploited its conventional military and tactical superiority over the Palestinians, it has exploited its ability to largely isolate them.

The Israeli-Palestinian War, Palestinian demographic pressures, and Israeli settlements on the West Bank have all helped lead Israel to make separation, the creation of unilateral "boundaries," and physical separation of the two peoples a key element of its strategy. These developments have been accelerated by the election of a Hamas government in the Gaza Strip and West Bank in 2006, and by the later election of a new Israeli government committed to both creating a full sect of security barriers on the West Bank and around Jerusalem that would unilaterally define the "border" between Israel and the Palestinians.

Israel has already withdrawn from its small settlement in Hebron. Unlike the situation in the Gaza Strip, however, Israel is unprepared to accept a total withdrawal back to the 1967 green lines. There are far larger and more important Jewish settlements in the West Bank, and Israel has sought to maintain control of all of greater Jerusalem. Moreover, Israel would lose much of its present strategic depth if it returned all of the territories. It would then be a mere 14 kilometers wide from West to East in its narrowest area near Tel Aviv.

These factors helped lead the Israeli Defense Establishment to study comprehensive separation plans long before they became the formal policy of the government. According to a report in the *New York Times,* former Prime Minister Barak directed Ephraim Sneh, then Israeli Deputy Defense Minister, to develop contingency plans to deal with a total breakdown of the peace effort as early as October 2000. These plans were to be capable of being executed in the event of either a prolonged low-intensity war over months or years or in reaction to a unilateral Palestinian declaration of statehood under war or near-war conditions.[99]

According to the *New York Times* report, former Prime Minister Barak directed Avi Ben-Bassat, staff director for the Finance Ministry, to assemble an "interministerial task force and assess the feasibility and cost of a 'separation' strategy." This task force concluded that Israel could sharply reduce the need for Palestinian laborers in agriculture and construction and that this would in turn produce higher base wages and lower unemployment for unskilled Israeli workers.[100]

This plan did not win immediate acceptance after the start of serious fighting. Prime Minister Ariel Sharon was elected soon thereafter and stated that he did not find such a plan feasible. When answering a question on unilateral separation a *Washington Post* columnist posed in March 2001, Sharon said,

> one should look at realistic plans. Until 1967, the length of the border of Judea and Samaria was 309 kilometers, and we never managed to control it. If we were to make the separation Barak mentioned, the length of the border would be over 700 kilometers. Who could patrol this border? It is not realistic. There should be an interim agreement or a situation of non-belligerency. I know the Palestinians are suffering from lack of contiguity [between the areas under the Palestinian Authority's control]. They don't want Israeli check points.[101]

Nevertheless, the steady intensification of the Israeli-Palestinian War led the Sharon government to build a massive network of new and improved deployments, security roads, and perimeter barriers, which not only could be used to protect Israel proper and the settlers on the West Bank, but to divide the Palestinian population in the West Bank into three major areas. The idea of unilateral separation also became more popular with the Jewish population of Israel. A Peace Index Survey conducted on May 29 and 30, 2001, showed that approximately 60 percent of Israeli Jews supported unilateral separation, with another 34 percent of respondents opposing, and 6 percent having no opinion on the issue. Among Sharon voters, 53 percent supported a unilateral separation that would include a withdrawal from certain areas, while 42 percent of these voters were opposed. In contrast, slightly more than 76 percent of Barak's supporters backed such a solution and 17 percent opposed it.[102]

In June 2002, the Israeli government went further and began work on separation barriers between the West Bank and Israel proper. Prime Minister Sharon stated that he had reversed his opposition to the fence as the result of a series of suicide bombings during May 2002.[103] He also indicated that the Israeli government perceived its actions to be providing a long-term solution to the prevention of terrorist attacks in Israel.[104]

The Israeli Ministry of Defense (MOD) stated that the route of the main security barrier was determined based on topography, population density, and a threat assessment of each area the fence was to pass.[105] According to the Israeli MOD, the route was derived from taking the following six considerations into account:

1. **Continuity:** The Security Fence provides a response to the operational assignment requiring continuity. It is a continuous land-based obstacle stretching from Beit Shean (North) to Arad (South).

   - *Stage A,* running from Salem to Elkana and around Jerusalem (in the northern and southern sections), was approved in August 2002 and was completed by the end of July 2003.

   - *Stage B,* running from Salem toward Beit Shean, through the Jezreel Valley and the Gilboa Mountains, was approved in December 2002.

   - *Stage C,* which consists of 68 kilometers of fence circling Jerusalem, was approved in August 2003, but was revised after the June 30, 2004, ruling of Israel's Supreme Court.

   - *Stage D,* running from Elkana toward Carmel, was approved in October 2003.

2. **Command and Control:** Create an area that enables command and control through the usage of observation systems, as well as provision of space for pursuit after a suspect.

3. **Environmental Considerations:** Cause minimal damage to the landscape and its vegetation, as well as restoring the area, once work has been completed, to its former stage as much as possible.

4. **Avoidance:** Make every effort to avoid including any Palestinian villages in the area of the Security Fence. The Security Fence does not annex territories to the State of Israel, nor will it change the status of the residents of these areas.

5. **Minimum Disruption:** Cause minimal disruption to the daily life of the populations residing on both sides of the Security Fence along its course in several forms:

   - Narrow agriculture passageways, dozens of which will be located along the route, to enable farmers to continue cultivating their lands.

   - Passage for pedestrians and vehicles, at which inspections will take place to maintain security.

   - Crossing points, for transfer of goods across the central area and in the Jerusalem region.

6. **Simplicity of Maintenance:** Passage for pedestrians and vehicles, at which inspections will take place to maintain security. In terms of accessibility, cost, and time.[106]

Acting Israeli Prime Minister Ehud Olmert discussed such separation plan from the West Bank in February 2006, as a major feature of his campaign to replace Ariel Sharon in elected office. He claimed that existing barriers had helped reduced suicide bombings by 90 percent between September 2000 and April 2006. He insisted that "[w]e are going toward separation from the Palestinians... We are going toward determining a permanent border for the state of Israel." In an interview, he said that Israel would disengage from "most of the Palestinian population that lives" in the West Bank. He stated that Israel would keep Maaleh Adumin, with 32,000 settlers next to Jerusalem; Gush Etzion in Southern Jerusalem; some 14 settlements including Ariel and Immanuel with 20,000 settlers deep in the West Bank; and the Jordan valley. While Olmert did not offer details about other settlements, he asserted that "it is impossible to abandon control of the eastern border of Israel," and added that Israel would maintain "united Jerusalem."[107]

By the time a newly elected Prime Minister Olmert visited Washington in late May 2006, detailed maps were available of the proposed line of separation. The map showed the initial barriers were now roughly 50 percent complete and would include a total of some 222 square miles to the east of the 1967 lines. The barriers were said to be 456 miles long when completed, with 201 miles completed, 84 miles under construction, 138 miles under legal challenge, and 33 miles in the final planning stage. Unlike the Gaza Strip, which had only two official crossing points, the barriers on the West Bank were to have 15, with special sensors and detection devices to allow rapid screening of individuals and cargo.[108]

What the Barrier Seems to Mean

The maps showed the barrier did include a major new area around Maale Adumin to the east of Jerusalem, which was now planned to expand from 32,000 to 50,000 settlers. It also included the rest of the greater Jerusalem area, including the Gush Etzion bloc and Har Homa areas. It would provide homes for some 183,000 Israelis in the East Jerusalem area, but also cut off some 216,000 Palestinians from the West Bank. Another 40,000 Palestinians would be isolated by the barrier around Qalqilya in the north.

Some aspects of the barrier did involve major walls, with some 20 miles of 26-foot high concrete barriers in urban areas to provide separation using minimum amounts of territory and prevent firing across the barrier on a line of sight basis. In most areas, however, the barrier or "fence" uses a mix of chain link dividers, barbed wire barriers, loose soil that showed any crossing activity, 8-foot deep antivehicle trenches, relatively simple motion sensors mounted on a 10-foot fence, and paved patrol roads.

The design of the main security barrier or fence encompassed a mix of structures and included barriers such as walls, ditches, patrol roads, fenced portions, and electronic surveillance units.[109] These were tailored to the security problems in the area where the barrier was created. In most secure areas, there is a multilayered composite obstacle that made the fence difficult to penetrate without detection. For example, in one area, there was a ditch and a pyramid-shaped stack of six coils of barbed wire on the eastern side of the fence. However, there were gates that allow passage from one side to the other—secured by IDF troops.[110]

There was usually a path that enables the Israeli defense units to patrol on both sides of the fence. At the center, there was an intrusion detection unit with sensors to warn of any infiltration. There was also a smoothed strip of sand running parallel to the fence to make the detection of footprints easier.

In certain areas, such as Bat-Hater and Motan, the security fence turns into a security wall. The total length of these wall sections is approximately 8.5 kilometers, out of a planned fence route of approximately 400 kilometers.[111] As of late September 2003, 90 miles of the fence had been built and a second portion, estimated at 28 miles, was planned to be built farther east into the West Bank than the original plan, which followed the 1967 Green Line.

Other technological developments have enhanced Israel's ability to separate Israelis and Palestinians, control the territories, identify threats, and neutralize fence infiltrators. In 2005, two brigades were outfitted with an optical and an electromagnetic sensor system, dubbed the Massua'ah 20, that enabled the IDF patrol vehicles to rapidly receive geographic references while in the field.[112]

Israel continues to improve the mix of technologies it is deploying to support the barrier. Two systems were introduced or further developed in 2005 to try to prevent infiltration of Israeli territory from the West Bank and the Gaza Strip without sending out patrols that can be targeted by ambushes and land mines. The Stalker mobile reconnaissance and surveillance system was mounted on Humvees and utilized Doppler radar, forward-looking infrared, and an extensive command, control, communications, computers, and intelligence (C^4I) system to rapidly identify and target would-be infiltrators from between 10 and 24 kilometers away with artillery, snipers, or other means.[113] Originally deployed in 1997, the system was further developed and deployed in 2005. In addition, Israeli forces used the Spider detection system that consisted of sensors mounted on vehicles or stationary poles that automatically detected moving objects over a wide area using forward-looking infrared and laser range finders.[114]

Moreover, Israel is building a series of barriers, not simply a main barrier, and such barriers cover outlying settlement areas that normally are not shown in maps of the fence. These smaller barriers are allowing Israel to significantly expand its separation of Israelis and Palestinian areas like East Jerusalem without attracting the attention created by the construction of the main barrier system or fence. The Israeli road system is also designed to support the barrier system by providing secure access for Israelis and the IDF, and eventually a series of roads for Palestinians that have limited access and ensure they do not mix with Israelis. There also are sensors and security posts located to support the barrier in depth, and not simply at the barrier itself.

Israeli officials claim that the security barrier system is necessary in order to prevent terrorist attacks. They have cited the effectiveness of the security barrier that already encompasses the Gaza Strip. Since a security barrier system was erected around the Gaza Strip in February 1995, there have been few terrorist attacks in Israel that can be traced back to the Gaza Strip. Israel has asserted that it was this fence that prevented terrorists from infiltrating Israel.[115]

According to Israeli sources, the security barrier system in the West Bank area began to be effective even in its early stages, when many key sections were still incomplete. From April to December 2002, there were 17 suicide attacks directed from the northern part of the West Bank, referred to by some as Samaria. After the construction of this section of the security barrier system began, however, there were only five attacks originating from this region throughout all of 2003. In some other areas, where there was no security barrier system, suicide attacks slightly increased.[116] There was also a 50-percent decrease in fatalities from 2002 to 2003.[117] In contrast, there was no reported decrease in the number of attacks originating there as of May 2004 in the areas where the security barrier system had not yet been constructed.[118]

Israeli public opinion about the creation of such barriers has been divided. Nevertheless, a poll conducted by Tel Aviv University's Peace Project in October 2003 showed that, when Israelis were asked simply, "Do you support the fence as a way to improve security," 70 percent of Israelis did respond positively, with 63 percent believing that the security barrier system would significantly reduce terror.[119] Moreover, some were convinced that the security barrier system will probably stimulate the Palestinian community to take action against terrorist organizations since the barrier may be perceived as a "price to pay" for terrorism.[120]

While those who oppose the security barrier system are largely in the peace movement, there are other factors that divide Israeli opinion. Some who support the security barrier system base their support on both the security it provides and the potential boundaries it establishes. They want the security barrier system to incorporate all settlements into Israel proper. However, if settlements remain on the Palestinian side as a result of the security barrier system, many settlers oppose supporting the security barrier system, on the grounds it will leave them vulnerable to hostile Palestinians.[121]

The security barrier system has also received criticism from some Israeli hardliners who perceive it as establishing the borders of a Palestinian state, a compromise that they refuse to accept. They maintain that since the cost of the security barrier system is an estimated $1.3 billion,[122] it will likely not be destroyed after a final status agreement is reached. They see it as a permanent step.[123]

BARRIER, BOUNDARY, OR BORDER?

Serious questions do exist about the extent to which the security barrier system will become the de facto border between Israel and a future Palestinian state, its coverage of Israeli settlements, and the extent to which it minimizes Israeli suffering and casualties at the cost of Palestinian inconvenience and distress. Some Palestinians have said they are willing to accept the security barrier system, but only if it strictly follows the 1967 Green Line, which they believe should become the border of their future state. However, Palestinian opposition to the security barrier system has generally been unified and vocal.[124]

On June 11, 2004, the most senior Muslim cleric in Jerusalem and the Palestinian areas, Grand Mufti Ikrima Sabri, banned Palestinians (living in Israel, and Israeli citizens) from assisting Israel in building the security barrier system. He told reporters for Reuters that he had renewed a fatwa and that the fence was "banned religiously, and a sin" and that any Palestinians that contributed to the building of the security barrier system would be regarded as "traitors."[125] In addition, most Palestinians perceive the security barrier system as an Israeli attempt to unilaterally determine the borders of an eventual Palestinian state.[126]

Palestinian cabinet member Saeb Erekat estimated in June 2002 that the security barrier system could leave up to 30,000 Palestinians in the buffer zone between the West Bank and Israel.[127] In addition, up to 20,000 Palestinians living in East Jerusalem may become isolated from the rest of the city, thus moving them outside the city's borders. Another 300,000 Palestinians could be located on the Israeli side of the security barrier system, effectively cutting them off from their families who live on the other side of the barrier as well as possibly preventing their children from attending schools that could be on the other side of the security barrier system.[128] Palestinians argue that if the security barrier system makes their lives more difficult, by preventing them from seeing their families or preventing access to farmland, then more terrorism will be encouraged.[129] According to Israel, the land that the security barrier system is constructed on that is not a part of Israel proper was seized for "military purposes," not "confiscated," and it will continue to remain the property of the rightful owner.[130]

Bad Fences Make Bad Neighbors?

It seems almost certain that the security barrier and further Israel efforts to unilaterally define boundaries will have other effects. They will strengthen Hamas and anti-Israeli Palestinian movements and convince more Palestinians that any meaningful peace is impossible. They will lead to more efforts to acquire rockets and artillery, to find ways to counter the sensors and barriers in the system, and dig tunnels or find other ways to attack. Israeli withdrawal from the Gaza Strip has already shown that one reaction is to attack the crossing points as key areas of vulnerability, and that attackers see the resulting damage done to Palestinians and the Palestinian as something that helps them, by increasing hostility to Israel. At least some Al Qa'ida and other terrorist literature has also called for attacking Israelis and Jews outside Israel where they are more vulnerable.

Israeli officials tend to downplay the broader regional impact of such steps, but such impacts exist. The Egyptian and Jordanian governments may be at peace, but they have populations who are increasingly angry at Israel, and there is a possibility that more hostile regimes may evolve over time. Continued peace with Egypt and Jordan is a probability, but scarcely a certainty, particularly if Israel does not make more progress in peace with the Palestinians or a new set of Israeli attacks on the Palestinians capture support in the Arab world.

There is a growing risk of another kind of "second front." It is far from clear that a politically and militarily weak Syria can make effective use of antipeace Palestinian groups, and other proxies like the Lebanese Hezbollah, to put major pressure on Israel. This is, however, a possibility. The risk is compounded by Iran's hostility to Israel's very existence and its willingness to use Hezbollah and violent, radical Palestinian groups to attack Israel by proxy. This hostility from state actors is further compounded by the fact that violent Islamist terrorist movements like Al Qa'ida have increasing made the Palestinian cause part of their ideology and propaganda, although such movements continue to make the overthrow of moderate Arab and Muslim regimes their primary objective.

The success of the barrier around the Gaza Strip has also been relative. During the period before Hamas gained political power, serious efforts were being made to reduce the political impact of the barrier. The Israeli Ministry of Defense was managing a pilot program, funded largely by the United States, to replace IDF soldiers with civilian security inspectors at checkpoints. The goal is to turn over the security of these checkpoints to private Israeli security firms. In addition, according to the MOD, "Our huge challenge is to provide 100 percent security checks of all people, goods and equipment entering Israel in ways that preserve the quality of life of the Palestinians and contribute to the economic development of the Palestine Authority." This is due to U.S. pressure on Israel to ease the travel of Palestinians in and out of Israel as well as through Israel from the West Bank to the Gaza Strip and vice versa. In 1999, 700 Palestinian crossed a checkpoint in the Gaza Strip. This number is down by half, to 350, in 2006.[131] Under a U.S.–Israeli agreement, the United States was to finance $50 million in high-tech scanning devices and other inspection technologies to manage these checkpoints. The project will be managed by the USAID, but the Israeli government will manage these devices. According to MOD, these advanced detection systems will allow each checkpoint to inspect 500–700 people an hour.[132]

As Chapter 8 describes in detail, however, this effort has collapsed. Israel has been forced to nearly isolate the Gaza Strip, has left only one crossing point, and has triggered a potentially explosive decline in the Palestinian economy. It has experienced constant problems in securing the area against tunnels and has been forced to steadily expand the level and sophistication of the barrier around the Gaza Strip as well as improve defenses against infiltration by sea.

Israel also has found little or no support for such actions from states outside the region. The EU states almost universally oppose such actions. At least as of May 2006, the talks between President Bush and Prime Minister Olmert showed that the United States still had great reservations about the broader impact of Israeli policy and had not given a green light to the full barrier, providing all of the aid Israel requested, or replacing the "road map" with unilateral separation.

ADAPTING WHILE RETAINING CONVENTIONAL MILITARY STRENGTHS

Some analysts feel that Israel has been forced to sacrifice some of its conventional edge to adopt these asymmetric tactics. There is some truth in such comments, but they need to be kept in careful perspective. The conventional capabilities of key threats like Syria have continued to deteriorate far more quickly than those of Israel, and Egypt and Jordan have not made any significant gains. Moreover, transforming Israel's conventional war-fighting capabilities to include asymmetric capabilities provides real-world combat experience while expanding Israeli war-fighting capabilities to deal with the new military requirements of the twenty-first century.

At the same time, Israel continues to emphasize many of its classic conventional military strengths: leadership, demanding exercise training, promoting on the basis of competence, maintaining a relatively young and aggressive officer corps, and insisting on forward leadership. It uses training that develops battlefield initiative, and it allows flexibility in executing orders. In contrast, Arab forces often require highly detailed written orders and systems of accountability in order to ensure that

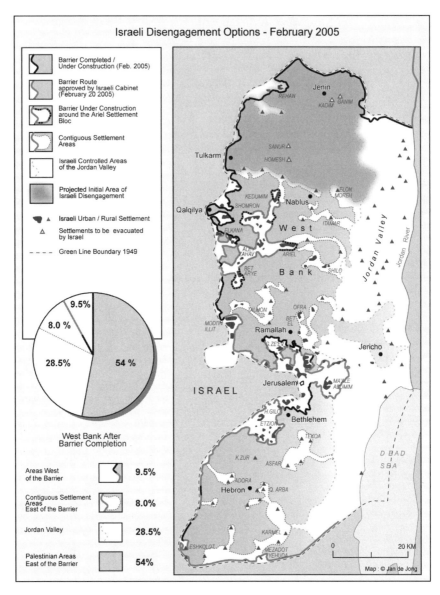

Map 4.2   Routes for the Israeli Security Barrier   (Foundation for Middle East Peace)

orders are obeyed, and commanders are taught not to deviate from orders when presented with new battlefield opportunities or unanticipated problems. Most exercises have predetermined outcomes that sharply limit the initiative of the officers involved and make it impossible to determine the relative effectiveness of the forces involved.

The IDF has adopted a new, radical training regimen for its soldiers. In the past, it assumed that soldiers needed to be trained for months prior to deployment. Largely

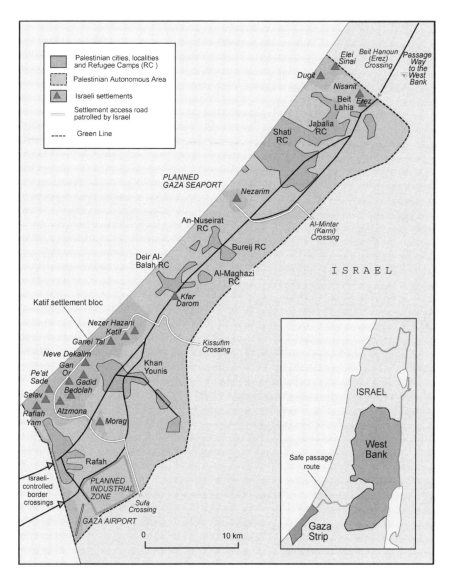

Map 4.3   The Gaza Strip   (Foundation for Middle East Peace)

as a result of the Israeli-Palestinian War, Israel has instituted a different three-pronged approach. Training consists of a brief yet difficult month-long training program followed by immediate deployment to either the occupied territories or the border with Lebanon. The training regimen, 40 percent of which has been altered, stresses the challenges soldiers will face during low-intensity conflict in an urban setting.

Forgoing the traditional 17-week course enables soldiers to acquire "on the job training," an experience at least one IDF official states cannot be replicated. The fluidity and rapidly changing tactics of the Israeli-Palestinian War renders many forms of lengthy training anachronistic by the time soldiers complete the various courses. Three field schools supplement the regimented and on the job training for IDF soldiers. Every month, each soldier spends four to five days in a field school being trained in the latest techniques tailored to their specific functions in the context of the most recent developments. After six months of deployment, soldiers train for yet another month and attend the field schools once more.

Israel makes good use of advanced military technology and of its access to arms transfers from the United States, and Israel had done more than procure high-technology equipment. While most Arab states focus on the "glitter factor" inherent in buying the most advanced weapons systems, Israel has given the proper weight to battle management, sustainability, and systems integration. Israel integrates technology into its force structure in ways that emphasize tactics, training, and all aspects of technology rather than relying on force strengths and weapons performance.

Trends in Manpower and Total Force Strength: Active vs. Reserve Forces

The recent trends in Israeli manpower and force structure are shown in Figure 4.2. These trends do not show dramatic changes, but they do reflect a significant downward shift in total manpower since 2000, in spite of the Israeli-Palestinian War, largely driven by cuts in reserve manpower. In contrast, cuts in active army manpower have been limited, and increases have taken place in the navy and the air force—in part driven by the added technological sophistication of these forces.

The shift in reserve manpower has been driven by a number of complex factors. One of the driving factors behind the development of Israel's military forces has been

Figure 4.2   Israeli Military: Manpower and Force Structure Trends: 1990–2006

	1990	2000	2005	2006
Manpower	645,000	697,500	~576,000	576,300
Active	141,000	173,500	~168,000	168,300
Conscript	110,000	107,500	107,500	105,000
Army	88,000	130,000	125,000	125,000
Navy	3,000	~6,500	~8,000	8,300
Air Force	19,000	20,000	35,000	35,000
Paramilitary	?	~6,050	~8,050	8,050
Reserve	504,000	425,000	408,000	408,000
Army	494,000	400,000	~380,000	380,000
Navy	1,000	5,000	3,500	3,500
Air Force	9,000	20,000	24,500	24,500

Source: Various editions of the International Institute for Strategic Studies (IISS) *Military Balance* and U.S., British, and Israeli experts.

the need to organize Israeli forces and military manpower in different ways from those of its Arab neighbors. As has been noted earlier, this is why comparisons of either total active manpower or total active and reserve manpower have only limited meaning in measuring comparative military effectiveness.

Israeli professional active military manpower is extremely expensive, and Israel faces major cost constraints in spite of the massive transfers of arms and technology it receives from the United States. Figure 4.3 shows the recent trends in Israeli arms transfers and is in many ways as important a summary indication of force trends as the force data in Figure 4.2 and the service-by-service figures that follow. While almost all of the U.S. supplied equipment shown in Figure 4.3 is provided in the form of grant aid, absorbing this equipment into Israel's force structure, supporting it throughout its life cycle, and adding major additional capabilities from Israel's military industries put a major strain on Israel's economy.

New Israeli Arms Agreements and Deliveries: 1993-2004 (in $US Current Millions)

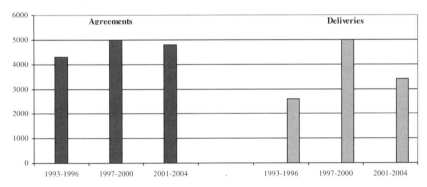

Israeli Arms Orders by Supplier Country: 1993-2004 (Arms Agreements in $US Current Millions)

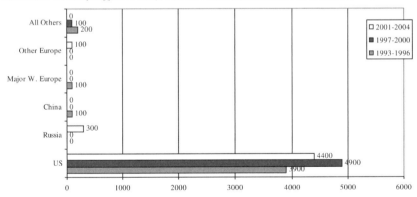

0 = less than $50 million or nil, and all data rounded to the nearest $100 million.

Source: Adapted by Anthony H. Cordesman, from Richard F. Grimmett, Conventional Arms Transfers to the Developing Nations, Congressional Research Service, various editions.

Figure 4.3   Recent Israeli Arms Sales

This helps explain why Israel cut its total active manpower from around 174,000 actives in its peacetime force structure in 2000 to 167,600 in 2006 in spite of the Israel-Palestinian War. This total, however, scarcely measures the number of true full-time professionals in Israeli forces. The number of total actives includes some 107,500 conscripts. Israeli male conscripts serve a total of 36 months (21 months for women and 48 months for officers), and a significant number are still in training or gathering combat experience at any given time.

At the same time, Israel has drawn on its reserves to deploy a significant number of reservists that are not included in the totals for its active manpower, and many of the personnel fighting in the Israeli-Palestinian War are reservists. Some of Israel's best troops consist of its younger reserves, and this gives Israel considerable strategic flexibility in dealing with asymmetric wars.

The problem with this approach is that calling up reservists for limited periods of active services is expensive and is disruptive to Israel's civil economy. The risk Israel takes in relying on reserves is also now largely limited to war with Syria. Israel's use of reserves still makes it dependent on timely mobilization for its war-fighting capability, and Israel requires 36–48 hours of strategic warning and reaction time to fully prepare its defenses in the Golan—its most vulnerable front. However, as a result of Syria's decline and the effective destruction of any Iraqi power projection capability following the Iraq War, the IDF has concluded that a major war with Syria is increasingly unlikely.

This has led Israel to try to find cheaper ways to deal with the realities of low-intensity and urban warfare. The IDF wants to reduce the number of expensive reservists it has to draw upon while growing the number of cheaper, regular troops to carry out tasks such as border patrol. Israel's reserve manpower pool has already been cut in recent years from 504,000 in 1990, to 425,000 in 2000, to 408,000 in 2006.

The IDF continues to examine different ways to man "high alert" forces. Some include larger numbers of career actives and fewer reserves. Others involve more use of attack helicopters, air support, and long-range firepower systems like rockets with advanced conventional warheads. The IDF places an increasing emphasis on improving combined arms and joint operations at every tactical level not only because of increased effectiveness, but as a way to reduce total manpower requirements.

Figure 4.3 shows Israel's heavy reliance on U.S. arms. Between 2001 and 2004, Israel imported $4.0 billion worth of new arms from the United States. It has been reported that due to Israel's financial crunch, the United States may allow Israel to defer payment for major arms purchases between 2009 and 2010. It plans to use most of its aid from the United States to buy U.S. weapons, according to the U.S. Defense Security Cooperation Agency. Israel argued that it will pay all the debt, but that it would need some time to do so. U.S. military grants and loans to Israel are the largest in the world. From 1949–2005, the U.S. military grants to Israel totaled $49.1 billion; from 1959–1984, U.S. military loans to Israel totaled $11.2 billion; and in 2004 alone the U.S. military development assistance reached

$2.68 billion. In 2006, the U.S. military grant to Israel will total $2.28 billion. Israel is required to use 75 percent of it to buy U.S. arms, but Israel can also use 25 percent of it for local military research. In addition, the United States is estimated to give Israel $78 million for its Arrow antimissile systems.[133]

The "Kela 2008 Plan"

Israel has begun to reshape its military forces in other ways. One effort that has been reported in the press is the "Kela 2008" plan. With the "eastern front" now gone, the IDF is discussing the possibility of combining the West Bank and the Gaza Strip under one command and whether a separate Southern Command is still needed against Egypt.

Other major aspects of the plan include transforming Merkava Mk 1 and 2 main battle tank (MBT) chassis or newly produced Merkava Mk 4 hulls into a new, heavily armored personnel carrier (APC) called the "Nemara" (Tigress). To improve their C^4I, Kela 2008 introduced the Tsayad Project, intended to fully integrate all ground platforms with broadband communications capabilities. The plan also calls for heavy investments into researching and procuring UAVs.

Currently Israel produces UAVs for countries such as India. Israel is India's sole provider of UAVs, and the contract signed in 2005 will ensure that continues. The contract between the two provides that Israel and India will begin to develop three new UAVs: the Rustam medium-altitude long-endurance UAV, the Pawan short-range UAV, and the Gagan tactical UAV. Needless to say, the development of the UAVs is beneficial to both countries.[134]

The military will outsource maintenance and administration functions in an effort to cut costs further. Initiatives that will surely raise concerns among soldiers and veterans are a move to cut wages up to 20 percent, the elimination of welfare programs for officers, and the increase in the minimum retirement age. Overall, the army will cut 10 percent of its regular forces and minimize the use of unskilled reservists who typically incur large operating expenses.[135]

In addition, a panel of industrialists, former generals, and security experts recommended further reductions on top of the Kela plan. The panelists want to decrease the number of combat helicopters by 20 percent, the number of tanks by an additional 10 percent, the older fighter planes by 5 percent, and the patrol boats by 15 percent. Reportedly, the resulting force numbers would be sufficient to face Israel's threats.[136]

Other reports indicate that Israeli concerns over funding and the threat of budget reduction had led the navy, the army, and the air force to fight fiercely over U.S. Foreign Military Financing allocations. The navy was once thought to have been assured a lion's share, but the other services have raised questions as to whether Israel would be best served by using those funds to purchase additional Arrow missile batteries, Apache AH-64Ds, or Stryker armored vehicles. It seemed likely that the navy would have used those funds to purchase additional missile corvettes, ostensibly to counter threats from Libya. However, Libya is perceived as somewhat less threatening and there has been a second successful test of the Arrow system, making it unclear which service will secure the funds.[137]

The effect these changes will have on the IDF's ability to confront the Palestinian militants is unclear. Some reports indicate that the IDF believes that Kela 2008 will streamline its forces, make them more effective, and cut unnecessary costs. However, some of the measures, such as the pay cuts and elimination of jobs, are likely to be highly unpopular and run the risk of fomenting discontent within the military. Such cuts in benefits may discourage Israelis from pursuing long-term military careers at a time when Israel leans increasingly heavily on the IDF despite reduced threats from Iraq and Syria.

Kushet (Rainbow) Plan

Other planning efforts are under way. Israel announced in February 2006 that it had launched its own Quadrennial Defense Review (QDR), or Kushet Plan, which would be completed in June or July 2006. The aim of this project is to guide Israel's defense spending and planning between 2007 and 2011.[138]

The Kushet Plan seeks to restructure the IDF based on threat assessment and the changing nature of warfare. This includes optimizing the IDF for low-intensity, urban, and asymmetric warfare without compromising Israel's conventional edge.[139]

The IDF Deputy Chief of General Staff, Major General Moshe Kaplinsky, stated the following in an interview with *Defense News:*[140]

> We [in Israel] need to achieve an appropriate balance between conventional high-intensity conflict [HIC]—which is no longer our principal threat, though it regrettably still exists—and all kinds of low intensity conflicts [LICs]...We've been trying to strike this balance while fighting over the past several years, but now we are emphasizing this as a bottom-up requirement for future plans.
>
> Our central direction is toward generic capabilities that can give us the flexibility we need for HIC and LIC, since we can't afford to put platforms and weapon systems in warehouses and save them for a war that might never come.

Kushet also focuses on strengthening Israel's capabilities against infiltrations and terrorist attacks including remotely monitored, sensor-fused, multilayered C^4I systems to control its borders with Lebanon, the Gaza Strip, and the West Bank. According to the IDF, this would improve Israel's monitoring and detection capabilities on its borders.[141]

It focuses on developing and deploying "multirole" and linked forces and limits the use of IDF troops. According to an IDF office, the new system reflects the view of the new Chief of General Staff, Major General Dan Halutz, which focuses on "replacing people with technology whenever possible, but he's equally intent on doing it in a methodical, very prudent, low-risk manner."[142]

This shift toward a "technocentric" force could include cutting active IDF manpower by 5,000 (10-percent cut) and substitute more advanced weapons and technology. The details of the actual plan, however, remain uncertain. Such numbers are not final and may change when the actual plan is presented to Israel's Knesset.

There are also other plans to restructure the IDF manpower, but it is unclear if those plans are part of Kushet. For example, it has been reported that the IDF is planning to reorganize its IDF command structure through merging commands, cutting back on manpower, and optimizing IDF ground capabilities. This process started on December 26, 2005, and was based on three principles:[143]

- Separate operating units from the staff units,
- Build up the IDF forces only from within the units, and
- Sever the General Staff from its role as the supreme commander of the IDF ground forces.

To accomplish this reorganization, the IDF plans to reorganize the ground forces in the following ways:

- Subordinate eight corps including the signals, ordnance, and personnel management corps to the ground forces by the end of 2006. The goal is to improve maneuver, auxiliary, and support capabilities.
- Some of the corps will be decommissioned.
- Combine artillery, intelligence, and field tactical intelligence corps into one, which the IDF hopes will be more effective.
- Create a "Special Forces school," which will offer joint training and weapons program.
- Create new divisions called "multiple corps tactical divisions."

ISRAELI LAND FORCES

The trends in Israeli land forces are shown in Figure 4.4 and reflect the same manpower trends discussed earlier. At of the end of 2005, Israel had an active army strength of 125,000 and had a well-trained and active reserve force of 380,000.[144]

The land forces were organized into three territorial and one home front command and into a combat structure of four corps. Its active forces had a nominal strength of two armored divisions, four infantry divisions, and three air-mobile brigades. Its reserves had a nominal strength of eight armored divisions, with a total of 15 armored brigades, four infantry brigades, and six artillery regiments. There were four infantry divisions with a total of 15 infantry brigades, four artillery regiments, and three mobile brigades. Each of these units had reserve elements. Another six of Israel's 11 armored "divisions" were reserve forces, as is one airmobile mechanized division. These reserve units had a total of 15 armored brigades, four infantry brigades, and at least four artillery regiments.

This makes the IDF a 14-division force, with some 8 divisions manned by reserves. However, the IDF may be moving toward a more flexible task force structure in which the independently controlled infantry brigades could be placed under the overall control of the armored divisions in order to enhance armored combat

Figure 4.4   Israeli Army Forces: Force Structure

	1990	2000	2005	2006
Manpower	645,000	697,500	~576,000	576,300
Active	141,000	173,500	~168,000	168,300
Reserve	494,000	400,000	~380,000	380,000
Combat Units	17+	~15	~18	~14
Armored Divisions	3	3	2	2
Mechanized Infantry Brigade	5	4	4	4
Infantry Division HQ	?	3	4	4
Reserve Armored Divisions	9	8	8	8
Nuclear capabilities	Yes	Yes	Yes	Yes
Warheads	100	100	200	200
Lance	?	0	0	0
Jericho I	?	?	?	Some
Jericho II	?	?	?	Some
Aircraft	0	0	0	Some
Main Battle Tank	3,794	3,800	3,090	3,657
Centurion	1,080	800	N/A	206
M-48A5	561	300	N/A	561
M-60	1,300	900	900	711
M-60A1	?	300	300	?
M-60A3	?	600	600	?
T-54	138	200	114	126
T-55	?	0	?	261
T-62	115	100	100	?
Merkava	600	1,100	1,790	1,681
Merkava I	?	?	?	407 (+441)
Merkava II	?	?	?	375
Merkava III	0	?	?	378
Merkava IV	0	0	?	80
Magach 7	0	400	186	111
Reconnaisance	~400	~400	~400	408
RAMTA RBY	BRDM-2	BRDM-2	Some	~400
M-2	?	?	?	?
M-3	?	?	?	?
Fuchs	0	~8	~8	~8 Tpz-1
APC	~10,380	~10,000	~12,940	10,419+
M-113A1/A2	5,900	5,500	7,700	6,131
Nagmashot	~80	~200	~400	?
BTR-50P	?	Inc. w/ Achzarit	?	?
M-2	4,400	4,000	4,300	180
M-3 half-track	?	?	? (Most in store)	3,386

Achzarit, Puma	0	~200	270	6
BTR 40/BTR-152	0	0	0	40
Nakpadon	0	0	?	Some
Towed Artillery	579	420	370	456
105 mm	70	70	70	70
M-101	70	70	70	70
122 mm	100	100	5	5
D-30	100	100	5	5
130 mm	109	100	15	100
M-46	109	100	15	100
155 mm	300	150	280	281
Soltam M-68/-71	300	50	50	50
M-839P/-845P	?	50	80	81
M-114A1	0	50	50	50
Soltam M-46	0	?	100	100
Self-Propelled Artillery	781	1,010	960	620
105 mm	0	34	N/A	N/A
M-7	0	34	N/A	N/A
155 mm	~605	700	852	548
L-33	?	150	148	148
M-50	75	120	0	50
M-109A1/A2	530	530	704	350
175 mm	140	140	72	36
M-107	140	140	72	36
203 mm	36	36	36	36
M-110	36	36	36	36
MRL	?	200+	212	224
122 mm	?	50	58	58
BM-21	?	50	58	58
160 mm	?	50	50	50
LAR-160	?	50	50	50
227 mm	0	48	48	60
MLRS	0	48	48	60
240 mm	?	30	36	36
BM-24	?	30	36	36
290 mm	?	20+	20	20
MAR-290	?	20+	20	20
Mortars	~230	~7,740	1,890	4,132
52 mm	0	0	0	2,000
60 mm	0	~5,000	0	?
81 mm	?	1,600	1,360	1,358
120 mm	~230	900	400	652
160 mm	?	240	130	122
M-43 (in reserve)	0	0	?	104

M-66 Soltam	0	0	?	18
Suface-to-Surface Missile	12+	~20+	~107	107
Lance	12	20	7	7
Jericho 1 (SRBM)/2 (IRBM)	?	Some	~100	~100
Antitank Guided Weapon	?	~1,325	~1,225+	1,225+
TOW [inc. Ramta (M-113) SP]	?	300	300	300
Dragon	?	1,000	900	900
AT-3 Sagger	?	?	Some	Some
Mapats	?	25	25	25
Gill/Spike	0	?	Some	Some
Rocket Launcher	?	?	?	Some
82 mm	?	?	?	Some
B-300	?	?	?	Some
Recoilless Rifle	250+	250	250	?
84 mm	?	0	0	?
Carl Gustav	?	0	0	?
106 mm	250	250	250	250
M-40A1	0	250	250	250
Air Defense Guns	~900	~1,010	?	815
20 mm	850	850	?	455
TCM-20	?	?	?	?
M-48 chaparral	?	?	?	?
M-163 Vulcan	30	35	?	?
M-167 Vulcan	?	?	?	?
M-1939	?	?	?	?
Stinger	?	?	?	0
23 mm	?	160	?	210
ZU-23	?	100	?	150
ZSU-23-4 SP	50	60	?	60
37 mm	?	?	?	?
M-39	?	?	?	?
40 mm	?	?	?	150
L-70	?	?	?	150
Surface-to-Air Missiles	?	1,298	1,250	1,250
Redeye	?	1,000	1,000	1,000
Stinger	0	250	250	250
Chaparral	0	48	0	0
Surveillance	0	?	?	?
EL/M-2140 (veh)	0	?	Some	Some
AN/TPQ-37 Firefinder (arty)	0	?	Some	Some
AN/PPS-15 (arty)	0	?	Some	Some

~ = Estimated amount; * = combat capable; + = more than the number given but not specified how much more; some = unspecified amount; ? = unspecified amount, if any.

Source: Various editions of the IISS *Military Balance,* the *Jane's Sentinel* series, and U.S., British, and Israeli experts.

under fire-saturated battlefield scenarios. The resulting units could operate independently in a number of scenarios.

The IDF's major combat equipment included 3,657 MBTs. It had an inventory of some 10,000 APCs: 670 armored infantry fighting vehicles (AIFVs), 3,386 obsolete half-tracks, 620 self-propelled artillery weapons, 456 towed weapons, 212 multiple rocket launchers, some 4,100 mortars, over 1,200 modern antitank guided weapons-launchers, some 250 recoilless rifles, and under 1,300 light surface-to-air missiles (many obsolete). The land forces are reported to operate Israel's nuclear-armed Jericho missiles.

Land Force Transformation

Israel has long led the region in creating and adopting new military tactics and technology and in adapting many elements of what the United States calls the "revolution in military affairs" and "netcentric" warfare to its own needs. By 2007, Israel hopes to begin the process of a service-wide transformation into a fully integrated combat ready multimission force under the Land Forces Command dubbed the Tzayad or "Hunter" Army Modernization Program. The Hunter Program is the IDF's attempt at integrating different services under one command to gain better control of situations and be more focused in operations.

The concept assumes Land Forces Command will have more expertise to find solutions in-house and shorten the time between planning and execution because everything will be subordinate to one command center. This transformation includes transferring the Signals Corps and the Ordnance Corps and the Technology and Logistics Branch directly under the auspices of the Land Force Command. The test brigade for this new combat unit is planned to include battalions of armor, infantry, engineering, artillery, and support forces all fighting together. In addition the brigade would be able to operate manned and unmanned air force aircraft and other intelligence assets.

Land Forces Command plans to establish a Special Operations Force that will combine military commando units with antiterror units that are currently managed by the General Staff. It is estimated within the military that the price tag for the Hunter Program will be around $900 million over the next decade in procurement and development. It is hoped that this program will lead the IDF into a fully digitized, integrated network structure.[145]

Command and Control Changes

Elbit, the IDF's prime contractor for the national command, control, communications, computers, intelligence, surveillance, and reconnoissance (C[4]ISR) effort, is seeking to develop an integrated strategic system for consumers and providers of national security. This system, dubbed "Big Brother" since the code name is secret, is planned to link imaging sensors, electronic signals, and communications systems from ground, sea, air, and space all on one secure command and control network.

The system will be designed to search for information and then through artificial intelligence decipher what is relevant and pass it on to the appropriate people. This system will be designed to process fragments, shards, and unstructured data in a relatively short time into a coherent, processed, and structured package in a format that can be used effectively.[146]

Israel has also moved closer to achieving the highly digitized, multioperational forces it has been working to achieve. Israel has a new C^4I system in addition to the Hunter Program. A test of this new C^4I system, dubbed Tirat Ha'agam (Castle on the Lake), was conducted during the disengagement from the Gaza Strip in August 2005.

Tirat Ha'agam has been developed since 2003 under the supervision of the IDF's C^4I Directorate and the Digital Army Program at an estimated cost of $22 million. It is intended to provide the senior command and decision makers with real-time high-resolution knowledge about the situations on the ground. Tirat Ha'agam cuts down on the time it takes forces on the ground to relay information to senior decision makers and the time it then takes for the decision to be handed down to the forces on the ground. It can provide maps, aerial images, units' weaponry, and ammunition supply and presents a "target bank" that the decision makers and the ground forces can both see and refer to without the need for physical briefings by lower lever commanders. Tirat Ha'agam incorporates within it another technology called Modern Mirror that collects and distributes real-time pictures from up to 24 different sources of the different IDF intelligence, reconnaissance, and surveillance sensors.[147]

The current version of the C^4I system—Beta 2—has been distributed to senior military officials and also to the senior directors of the Mossad, Israel's foreign intelligence agency, and Israel Security Agency, responsible for internal security. The next version of the system will be developed and manufactured in 2006 by Ness Technologies and will be supplied to all IDF commanders down to the division commander level. Access to the system's different usages will be given according to the user's level.

Israel's communications systems have also been improved. On September 19, 2005, Tadiran Communications (TadCom) was selected to provide broadband communications capabilities in a contract estimated at $15 million for 30 months. TadCom will "develop and provide a system that delivers long-range, high-capacity broadband data, video and voice telecommunications. The system will be based on wireless broadband technology, to be supplied by British Airspan Networks." Elbit Systems, which owns TadCom, is the primary contractor for the Digital Army Program and is assisting the IDF in connecting all three fighting platforms into one network with a unified communication infrastructure based on broadband communications for the ground, air, and naval units.[148]

Another innovation is a doctrine of low signature/no-signature warfare. This means the IDF is working toward a situation whereby there will be few troops/no troops in the field, yet the targets will be destroyed and the operations will be performed. One of the key elements is a remote controlled weapons station that can be mounted on many different vehicles such as jeeps, light armored vehicles, unmanned ground vehicles, and even on the Merkava tank.

For example, before the pullout from the Gaza Strip, Israeli forces within the territories began using a new weapon that put the soldiers less in danger, but provided similar capability as before. The new Israeli weapon was a rifle and video camera mounted on a segmented pole about six meters high attached to an armored vehicle. With this new weapon IDF forces can inspect an area that is actually beyond their vision from the ground, without endangering themselves because they can stay in the vehicle and not be subject to retaliatory fire.[149]

The three main Israeli military contractors, Rafael, Elbit Systems, and Israel Military Industries, are competing for the contract that will produce the weapon system first for Israeli use and then for international export. So far only a few dozen of the Katlanit (Lethal) by Rafael have been procured by the IDF and international customers, while the other two contractors are still developing various models.

According to Rafael marketing data the Katlanit can be operated by one soldier and is built to fire three different sizes of ammunition (NATO-standard 7.62 mm, 12.7 mm, and 40 mm) from several different platforms (land or sea).[150] The cost and force-wide impacts of the Israel-Palestinian War have had a major impact on Israel's military development. Israel does not face recapitalization problems that approach those of Jordan or Syria, but it does have problems. It cannot afford to convert its armor to a coherent force of first-line systems that had the mix the IDF would like of both the most advanced tanks and the most advanced infantry fighting vehicles.

Main Battle Tanks

The shifts in the balance, and reductions in the Syrian threat, have helped Israel maintain its "edge" by continuing to emphasize force quality over force quantity. Figure 4.4 shows a steady downward trend in main battle tank numbers, but it also shows a steady rise in tank quality. Israel's 1,680 Merkavas are designed for the specific tactical conditions Israel faces. They are more advanced than any tank in Arab hands, except for Egypt's 750 M1A1s, and can defeat most antitank weapons in Arab forces.

This is particularly true of the Merkava IV, Merkava III Baz, and Merkava III, which have excellent protection and some of the best fire control and sighting systems available. The Merkava IV has become operational and is much more powerful than the previous versions without an increase in weight. It also has much better day and night vision systems, better internal control of firepower, and a new and improved version of ballistic protection enhanced for urban warfare. The Ministry of Defense recently decided to forgo the development of the Merkava V, citing the success and cost effectiveness of the Merkava IV.[151]

Merkava program manager Brigadier General Amir Nir said the Merkava IV is being transformed into a true multipurpose combat vehicle for low-intensity conflict. A remote-controlled turret, underbelly protection, added armor, and new rubberized tracks are just part of the new modifications being added to the Merkava IV.

In addition the Merkava will be able to fire 50-mm machine guns and 40-mm grenade launchers safely from inside the hull. Elbit's remote control system has been tested and certified for Merkava use and will be available to the IDF not just for the Merkava but for other platforms as well. Elbit is a lightweight system that has capabilities of firing 7.62-mm rounds from platforms such as armored personnel carriers, tactical vehicles, and unmanned ground vehicles and a larger caliber model for 25-mm to 30-mm rounds.[152]

Money has been an issue. The cost of the existing Merkavas has raised questions about the viability of continuing the 34-year-old program. It has been reported that some elements within the Israeli Ministry of Defense are suggesting that the Merkava line be abandoned in favor of the U.S. M1A2 main battle tank. Viewed as widely successful, the M1A2 would also be paid for by U.S. Foreign Military Financing aid, making it an even more attractive option.

Others suggest that Israel should seek to be included in the U.S. Future Combat Systems (FCS) program which aims to develop a future armored force that is far lighter, easier to transport, and that integrates manned and unmanned vehicles while maintaining survivability and lethality. Critics argue, however, that, while they would be willing to participate in some aspects of the program, the FCS program is proving to be highly unstable and subject to increasing delays and uncertainty over exactly what vehicles it will create. They also argue that the U.S. Army's stress on weight and transportability does little to solve Israel's needs. They maintain that the Merkava line is sufficient and call for an increase in the program's budget.[153] A recent proposal to sell the Merkava tank production line, either to a private Israeli defense firm or to another owned by the government, has further clouded the tank's future. Proponents believe that the sale would increase efficiency and drastically cut the line's costs.[154]

Israel's 600 M-60A3s are not up to the standard of the Merkava, but have an edge in fire control and sights, and a marginal advantage in protection, over Syria's 1,500 export versions of the T-72 and the T-72M—the only relatively modern tank in Syrian forces. Israel's 300 M-60/M-60A1s have been upgraded to the point where they may well have a similar advantage. They may not have such an advantage over Egypt's nearly 1,000 M-60A3s and 400 M-60A-1s, or Jordan's 288 M-60A1/A3s or 288 Al Husseins (Challenger 1s)—which also have improved armor and other upgrades. Egypt also had some 1,400 M-60s, which have significant capabilities relative to Israel's first-line tanks.

Israel has upgraded at least 180–190 of its M-48s and M-60s to the MAGACH 6 and 7 modifications, with improved passive and reactive armor, power, guns, and fire control. It may upgrade the rest to a further improved version in the MAGACH series, and it has also developed a Sabra upgrade of the M-60, with improvements in fire control, protection, and mobility.

Israel's other tanks are much less advanced than its Merkavas and M-60s. They include Ti-67s (somewhat improved T-54/T-55s) and 100 T-62s. This means that some 114 of Israel's tanks are of low to medium quality, although many of these tanks have been upgraded to the point where they are considerably better than the original version.

One option Israel is considering is an "Iron First" system that would use a search and track radar to detect an incoming round or missile and fire an interception round or missile to deflect it, rather than relying on active or passive armor.

Other Armor

Figure 4.4 shows that Israel is not only continuing to rely on heavy tanks, but on modified tanks and heavily armored APCs. This reflects the changing dynamic of the war in several ways. They give Israel added freedom of maneuver and survivability against forces with main battle tanks and other antitank guided weapons. At the same time, Israel—like the United States in Iraq—has found that such vehicles can do a good job of protecting against ambushes by irregular forces with antitank weapons like remote piloted vehicles and provide better protection against roadside bombs —discouraging such attacks and reducing their numbers in the process. This mission requirement also explains why Israel is developing UAV and unmanned vehicle weapons capabilities that are supposed to see "over the hill" and reduce the need to expose men in any type of vehicles.

Israel has, however, had to choose between funding improved tanks and funding improvements of other armored fighting vehicles. As a result, it has a relatively limited number of modern AIFVs to supplement its tanks. The exact numbers of such weapons are uncertain, but they include some 400 light wheeled Ramtas and RBYs, BRDM-2 amphibious scout cars, and eight Fuchs. Israel's APCs include converted Centurions called Nagmaschons (400?), 270 heavy Achzarit APC conversions of the T-54 designed to accompany the Merkava, Puma combat engineer APCs, and Nakpadons.

Israel has upgraded large numbers of its fleet of some 5,000–6,000 M-113 to something approaching AIFVs. It is also examining ways to make significant improvements in its armor, perhaps using new "4th generation" light hybrid armor. Urban fighting in the Gaza Strip area in 2004 showed that the M-113 was too vulnerable for some missions, and the IDF is examining an up-armoring package called L-VAS.

The IDF is considering more intensive programs to create heavy armored engineering and support equipment and an AIFV or APC with many of the features of the Merkava Mark 4. It has recently begun to modernize its light armor and took delivery on 100 Ze'ev or "Wolf" armored wheeled vehicles in July 2005. It is evaluating heavier wheeled armored vehicles like the Stryker and Wildcat.

Its main weakness in other armored weapons systems is that it is still dependent on a stockpile of several thousand (some reports go as high as 4,300) half-tracks for support vehicles and reserves—although most are in storage or will be replaced in storage shortly. Israel is also paying close attention to the U.S. experience in Iraq and is considering armoring some of its HUMVEEs and logistic vehicles.

Israel is seeking to supplement this force, and possibly to replace the M113s, through its development and procurement of the "Nemara" APC as well as through the purchase of 100 Dingos.[155]

Antitank Weapons

Israel scarcely relies on armor and tanks to the exclusion of other weapons, a mistake it made before the October 1973 War. Its forces now have a wide range of advanced antitank guided weapons including 300 TOW 2A/B, many mounted on armored vehicles, 900 Dragon man-portable weapons, somewhat modified AT-3 Saggers, and an unknown number of Israel-developed weapons including 25 Mapats, Gill, Spike, and Dandy.

The Dandy can be fired from either a helicopter or a ground-based vehicle.[156] The Spike, available in medium range, long range, and extended range, has received a significant upgrade. This upgrade is named Spike C^4I; the upgrade included a global positioning system (GPS) receiver, computer, and data link as well as a handheld laser range finder and a laptop command unit and radio system. The C^4I decreases the chance of friendly fire incidents while providing a network capability to Spike units in the field.[157]

The IDF has large numbers of rocket launchers and some 250 106-mm recoilless rifles.

Up-Armoring Lighter Vehicles and Support Forces

Small Arms Detection Systems (SADS) are being integrated into 20–25 armor-protected Humvees so as to meet Israel's new operational requirements since the pullout from the Gaza Strip in August 2005. The SADS will provide each vehicle with real-time detection and location identification of small arms fire.

The System will provide audio and visual alarms to the crew and will be able to traverse the direction with an accuracy of 2° to 3°. SADS can be used when the vehicle is stationary or mobile with only a slight decrease in accuracy. The System has three main elements: an acoustic antenna with four microphones, a miniaturized processing unit, and the user interface on which the information is posted. The interface can define information from 360°, and information from events can be stored to be reviewed at a later date.

The Humvees will also be equipped with a battle management system, a navigational system, and an overhead weapon station, armed with a 7.62-mm or 12.7-mm machine gun or a 40-mm grenade launcher.[158]

The IDF has increasingly had to concentrate many of its recent efforts on internal security and counterinsurgency/counterterrorism missions, as well as to try to restructure its support and logistic elements to allow more rapid support of maneuver operations at the brigade or task force level, instead of supporting combat arms in "force to force" combat. As part of this effort, Israel is considering reequipping such forces with a mix of specialized armored and tracked support vehicles like the

Achsarit, the Puma, and the Nakpadon to provide better mobility and some degree of nuclear biological chemical (NBC) protection.

Artillery Forces

Israel has a modern artillery force of some 620 self-propelled weapons and more than 220 multiple rocket launchers—including 60 U.S. MLRSs. Its self-propelled weapons include 148 L-33 and 350 M-109A1/A2 weapons, 36 M-107 175-mm weapons, and 36 M-110 203-mm weapons. It has upgraded its 175-mm M-107 weapons into a version called the Romach and has upgraded many of its 155-mm M-109 weapons into a version called the Doher, which has improved mobility, NBC protection, and fire control and accuracy. The L-33 Soltam is an aging Israeli system placed on a Sherman M4A3e8 tank chassis. Its operational status was unclear. Some sources indicate that 200 were built and the system was in reserve. Israel also has 456 towed weapons, including 70 105-mm, 5 122-mm, 100 130-mm, and 280 155-mm weapons.

Israel's multiple rocket launcher strength includes 58 BM-21 122-mm, 50 LAR-160 160-mm, 48 MRLS 227-mm, 36 BM-24 240-mm, and 20 LAR-90 290–350-mm weapons. These weapons often have had substantial modifications and upgrades, and the LAR has both three 160-mm and one 290–350-mm versions. The 160-mm version has a range of 12–45 kilometers, and the 350-mm version from 30–100 kilometers, varying in range from 12–30 kilometers. Israel also has some 1,358 81-mm, 652 120-mm, and 122 160-mm mortars, many mounted on armored vehicles with the M-46 mostly in reserve.

Additionally, the IDF has absorbed 33 AFB-142F-1 and seven AGM-142 Have Nap Popeye Standoff Attack Missiles.[159] Israeli weapons manufacturers developed a deep-strike, precision-guided missile dubbed LORA, or Long-Range Artillery. The LORA, with a range of approximately 200 kilometers, is similar to the SS-26s employed by the Russians or the Army Tactical Advanced Conventional Munition System utilized by the Americans. The operational status of the missile remains uncertain, however, as the developers accidentally broadcast a failed LORA missile test in 2003.[160] LORA did succeed in four out of the past five live-fire weapons tests since that time. One of the tests was ground based, while the rest were sea launched. In March 2005, LORA flew more than 200 kilometers with a precision radius of less than 5 meters. LORA is expected to reach distances of up to 300 kilometers.

In 2004, Israel incorporated the Ramam Trajectory Corrected System into the army's battle of strength-increasing long-range accuracy. The Ramam is similar to the U.S. Army–Lockheed Martin Multiple Launch Rocket System (MLRS). In addition to the Ramam, Israel is developing another missile that will resemble the MLRS, the Extended Range Artillery (Extra) for land- or sea-based launches. Extra is designed to carry a 125-kilogram warhead and is guided by an inertial navigation system and GPS satellite signals.[161] Israel has over 100 active variants of the Jericho long-range ballistic missile, plus seven Lance surface-to-surface missile fire units in storage.

Israel wants to acquire much larger stocks of advanced and specialized ammunition, upgrade to weapons like an upgunned version of the M-109 and Soltam Slammer self-propelled 155-mm howitzers, and increase its number of MLRS and other advanced multiple rocket launchers.

It may, however, have to concentrate its resources on upgrading its targeting sensors like radars and UAVs and battlefield management systems.

The Ministry of Defense has ordered additional special surveillance coverage to be provided by Searcher UAVs that have been in service since 1992.[162] It is not clear, however, that the Searcher will satisfy the IDF's needs. The Israeli Army would like to acquire a number of Skylark mini UAVs for Special Operations purposes, but has yet to place a specific order.[163]

The IDF is also improving its communications and battle management in ways that improve its artillery capabilities. It has acquired the PNR-500 personal radio network system that allows units to communicate in a manner similar to a conference call, enhancing coordination and information transfer.[164] It has examined plans to develop a fleet of aircraft that would mimic the abilities of U.S. aircraft equipped with the Joint Surveillance Target Attack Radar System, or JSTARS. This would greatly enhance both long-range targeting and battle management.[165] The Israel Air Force is acquiring three signals intelligence collection (SIGINT) aircraft that can be used for land as well as air targeting.[166]

Asymmetric Warfare Capabilities

The IDF has acquired vast experience in counterterrorism and Special Operations, and virtually all of the intelligence elements it developed for conventional warfighting capabilities now have considerable capability for counterterrorism and counterinsurgency missions. The Directorate of Military Intelligence and Field Intelligence Corps are trained and organized for such missions. Even specialized IDF electronic intelligence and surveillance units like those in the Hei Modi'in HaSadeh (Intelligence Corps) and Aman (Israeli Military Intelligence Service) have steadily broadened their functions.

There are no reliable reports on IDF combat capabilities in such missions. A wide range of units have, however, been named in public sources. These include the following:[167]

- Sayeret Matkal (General Staff Deep Reconnaissance Unit), a rapid reaction commando force for "unconventional" action.
- Sayeret Duvdenvan, a deep cover unit that normally acts as Palestinians.
- Sayeret Haruv, IDF Central Command reconnaissance unit.
- Shaldeg or Unit 5101, long-range patrol and targeting in hostile territory.
- 1 Egoz, a special unit dealing with the threat from Hezbollah.
- Unit 5707, a unit operating behind the lines for targeting and damage assessment.
- Mista'arvin: undercover operatives speaking and acting as Arabs.

- Sayeret Golani (Special Forces Reconnaissance Platoon), commando unit in the Golani brigade, specializing in airborne operations and demolition.
- Givati Brigade, amphibious infantry.
- Sayeret Shimson, similar unit in the Givati brigade.
- Sayert Nahal, a reconnaissance unit in the Naval Infantry Brigade.
- Sayeret Tzanhanim (Paratroop Brigade Sayeret), mechanized paratroop force that can mobilize to full division.

Both IDF training and other aspects of its force development are increasingly tailored to asymmetric warfare, and this has included integrating Israel's security barrier into its concept of operations. This includes playing a role in designing security roads and access routes in the West Bank and greater Jerusalem area, and in sensor design.

The IDF has deployed a "Solid Mirror" integrated system along the expanding security barrier system and on the border of the Gaza Strip. Solid Mirror detects and identifies threats, tracks their progress, and has the ability to warn or set off an alarm. The system utilizes a variety of sensors and automated constructs to perform its mission. It has been deployed along the 120-kilometer border with Lebanon since 1999.[168]

Other Aspects of Land Force Development

Like most Western forces, the IDF is increasingly emphasizing joint operations in its training and doctrine and may develop fully mobile and airmobile infantry units that match or exceed the maneuver capability of its armored forces. It is pursuing netcentric approaches to warfare that reduce the "borders" between the services through a common intelligence, targeting, and force allocation system.[169]

Israel also is one of the few armies in the Middle East with anything approaching the advanced training facilities that the U.S. Army has at Fort Irwin or that the U.S. Marine Corps has at Twentynine Palms. Egypt and Jordan are the only two Arab powers acquiring somewhat similar capabilities. The Israeli army has a computer corps called Mamram. It has a training center at Mabat in the Negev Desert, which uses a modern computerized training range, an advanced command and control simulator, an area-weapons effect system, and over 1,000 MILES II instrumented player outfits for infantry, antitank weapons, and armored vehicles. There are other MILES systems for infantry and Special Forces training, and some form of equipment was used to simulate helicopter and fixed-wing aircraft in joint training. The facility is scarcely as advanced as its U.S. counterparts, but has well over $50-million worth of equipment.

Some reports indicate that Israel's Project Anog is seeking to apply existing technologies to create an integrated battle suite system in an effort to boost each individual soldier's effectiveness. It was reported that the system will sport interconnected weaponry, headgear, and body systems, providing soldiers with GPS receivers, laser range finders, wireless communicators, and a combined reflex sight and laser-aiming light. Field trials could begin as early as 2006 with full prototypes available by 2010 at a reported cost of less than $10 million.[170]

ISRAELI AIR FORCES

The trends in the size and the structure of the Israeli Air Force are shown in Figure 4.5. As of the end of 2005, the IAF had a nominal strength of 35,000. These included 20,000 conscripts, largely assigned to land-based air defense forces. It had some 400 active combat aircraft, plus 250 in storage, and some 95 armed helicopters.[171]

The IAF had 15 fighter and fighter attack squadrons with a total of 375 aircraft authorized. These included 36 F-15A/Bs, 28 F-15 C/Ds, 25 F-15Is, 110 F-16A/Bs, 126 F-16C/Ds, and 12 F-16Is that are now in the process of delivery and conversion at the rate of 2 per month for a total of 102 (which are expected to be delivered in 2008). It also has one attack squadron of 39 A4Ns, 2 Phalcon AEW aircraft, 23 EW and electronic intelligence aircraft, 95 attack helicopters (16 AH-1Es, 39 AH-1Ss, and 40 AH-64As), and 6 antisubmarine warfare helicopters. It has 5 KC130H tankers, around 63 major transport aircraft, and some scout and 89 transport helicopters. It also has more than 22 UAVs in a wide range, and a large inventory of advanced air-to-air and precision-guided air-to-surface weapons—including both Israeli- and U.S.–made weapons.

The IAF has recently absorbed 20–24 F-15Is, 50 surplus USAF F-16s, additional AH-64s, 10 Black Hawk helicopters, advanced new UAVs, and ongoing Israeli upgrades to existing aircraft like the F-15, F-16, and Phantom 2000. In April 2005, the first three Apache Longbows from Boeing arrived in Israel after nearly a decade of considerations regarding the necessity of an advanced attack helicopter squadron. All the aircraft are supposed to be delivered by 2007, and it will take at least two years to get the squadron fully operational.[172] The Israelis will leave their purchase of AH-64D Apache Longbow attack helicopters at 18 and not utilize their option of purchasing 6 more Apaches in addition to the original 18 in the contract.[173]

Additionally, the IAF is buying 102 F-16I fighters. Its older F-15Is will be fitted with Mk84 Joint Direct Attack Munitions (JDAMS) by late 2005.[174] The F-16-I is an upgrade version of the F-16D Block 50, which Israel feels has many of the capabilities of the USAF F-15E. It has Israeli developed advanced electronic warfare equipment, a special mission computer, add sensors, special secure communications gear, and two conformal wing tanks that free wing racks to carry added weapons, minimize drag, and can offer an unrefueled strike range close to 600 miles.

Israel has purchased four G550s, with an option for two more, to provide an airborne early-warning capability.[175] However, they will not be fully operational until 2007.

Figure 4.5   Israeli Air Force: Force Structure

	1990	2000	2005	2006
Manpower	65,000	93,000	?	59,500
Air Force	28,000	37,000	35,000	35,000
Conscript	19,000	20,000	?	?
Mobilized	37,000	57,000	?	?
Reserve	?	?	?	24,500
Total Combat Aircraft	651	592	494	402
Armed helicopters	77	133	95	?
Combat aircraft	574	459	399	?
FGA/Fighter (squad)	16/405	12/385	13/365	15/376
F-4E (+13 in storage)	112	20	Large #'s	Some
F-4E-2000	0	50	Large #'s	?
F-15	53	73	89	89
F-15A	35	38	29	29
F-15B	2	8	7	7
F-15C	11	16	17	17
F-15D	5	11	11	11
F-15I	0	25	25	25
F-16	145	237	238	248
F-16A	62	92	90	90
F-16B	8	17	20	20
F-16C	51	79	52	52
F-16D	24	49	75	74
F-16I Sufa (102 being delivered at the rate of 2/month)	0	0	1	12
Kfir C2/C7 (+95 in storage)	95	Stored	Large #'s	Some
A-4N Skyhawk	0	0	Large #'s	39
FGA	4/135	1/25	?	?
A-4H/N (+14 in store)	121	25	?	?
RECCE	14	10*	?	5
RF-4E (combat capable) (+10 in storage)	14	10*	?	0
RC-12D	0	0	?	5
Airborne Early Warning	4	6	2	2
E-2C	4	0	0	0
Boeing 707 with Phalcon system	0	6	2	2
Electronic Warfare	23	37	32	23
Boeing 707 (ELINT/ECM)	6	3	3	3
C-130H	0	?	2	2
EV-1E (ECM)	2	?	0	0
IAI-201 (ELINT)	4	0	0	0
IAI-200	0	3	0	0

IAI-202 Arava	0	0	6	6
RC-21D (ELINT)	6	6	5	5
RU-21A	3	?	0	0
Do-28	0	15	8	0
King Air	9	0	4	0
King Air 2000	0	10	0	0
Beech 200CT Super King Air	0	0	0	4
Gulfstream G-550	0	0	1 of 4	3
Maritime Reconnaissance	5	3	3	3
IAI-1124 Seascan	5	3	3	3
Tanker Aircraft	7	3	5	10
Boeing 707	5	0	0	5
KC-130H	2	3	5	5
Transport Aircraft	60	39	21	63+
C-130H	24	22	5	7
Boeing 707	3	5	5	2
IAI-201	10	0	0	0
IAI-1124	3	0	0	0
C-47	20	12	11	11
Liaison	77	32	32	?
Islander	4	2	2	2
Cessna U-206	41	20	22	22
Cessna U-172	2	0	0	0
Cessna U-180	2	0	0	0
Do-27	6	0	0	0
Do-28	10	0	0	8+
Queen Air 80	12	10	8	12
Helicopters	225	295	281	~278
Attack	77	129	95	95+
AH-1G/S	42	0	?	?
AH-1E	0	0	16	16
AH-1F	0	36	39	39
Hughes 500MD	35	30	0	0
AU-1G	0	21	0	0
AH-64A	0	42	40	40
AH-64D	0	0	0	Some
Apache (first of 18)	0	0	0	1
SAR	2	0	0	17
HH-65A	2	0	0	16
Transport	159	160	186	89
Heavy	35	38	41	41
CH-53	35	38	41	41
CH-53A	2	0	0	0

CH-53D	33	38	41	41
Medium	26	25	48	48
SA-321	9	0	0	0
UH-1D	17	0	0	0
UH-60	0	10	0	0
UH-60A	0	0	10	10
UH-60L Black Hawk	0	0	14	14
S-70A Black Hawk	0	15	24	24
Light	98	97	97	77
Bell 212	58	54	54	34
Bell 206A	40	43	43	43
Training Aircraft	169	128	86	110
Cessna 152	6	0	0	0
CM-170 Tzukit	80	77	43	0
CM-170 Magister (being replaced by A-4N)	?	0	0	43
F-4E	16	0	0	0
Kfir TC 2/7	5	0	0	0
Super Cub	35	28	0	20
TA-4H* (combat capable)	20	9	10	10
TA-4J* (combat capable)	7	10	16	16
Queen Air 80	0	4	4	4
Grob 120	0	0	17	17
Missile	?	?	?	?
Air-to-Surface	?	?	?	?
AGM-45 Shrike	?	?	Some	Some
AGM-62A Walleye	?	?	0	Some
AGM-62B Walleye	0	0	Some	?
AGM-65 Maverick	?	?	Some	Some
AGM-78D Standard	?	?	Some	Some
AGM-114 Hellfire	0	?	Some	Some
TOW	0	?	?	?
Popeye I+II	0	?	Some	Some
Luz	?	0	0	0
Gabriel III	?	0	0	0
GBU-31 JDAM undergoing IAF op/integration test	0	Yes	Some	Some
Air-to-Air	?	?	?	?
AIM-7 Sparrow	?	?	Some	Some
AIM-9 Sidewinder	?	?	Some	Some
AIM-120B AMRAAM	0	?	Some	Some
R-530	?	?	0	0
Shafrir	?	?	Some	Some

Python III	?	?	Some	Some
Python IV	0	?	Some	Some
UAV	0	?	?	22+
Scout, Pioneer, Searcher, Firebee, Samson, Delilah, Hunter Silver Arrow	0	?	?	22+

Source: Various editions of the IISS *Military Balance,* the *Jane's Sentinel* series, and U.S., British, and Israeli experts.

Modern Air Operations Are Joint Operations

What the force totals in Figure 4.5 cannot show is that Israel is the only Middle Eastern air force that combines all of the elements of modern air power into an efficient and integrated whole—although Egypt continues to make significant progress. Israel has long stressed joint warfare and combines its skills in land maneuver warfare with one of the most effective air forces in the world. The IAF is one of the most modern air forces in the world. It has systematically improved its conventional attack—or "soft strike"—capability. It now has many of the advantages U.S. air power enjoyed during the Gulf War, plus a wide range of subsystems and weapons tailored to deal with threats like Syria and the special conditions in its theater of operations.

The IAF has advanced combat, electronic warfare, intelligence and targeting, and battle management aircraft. These are supported by a host of advanced and special purpose weapons systems, combat electronics, unmanned airborne vehicles, night and all weather combat systems, and command and control facilities.

Israel not only has the technical resources to steadily modernize and improve the capability of its electronic warfare and reconnaissance aircraft, it also has the command, control, communications, computers, intelligence/battle management (C^4I/BM), training, night warfare, electronic warfare, support, sustainability, and other specialized qualitative capabilities necessary to exploit the revolution in military affairs. Over the next three years Israel plans on spending almost $5 billion on C^4ISR.

Although the air force still gets the bulk of the spending, increasing amounts are going to the navy and the ground forces so as to integrate all three branches into a functioning command and control network. C^4ISR capabilities will also decrease operation and maintenance costs because systems will be more automated and less manpower will be needed. For example, between 2002 and 2004 operational costs went down by 60 percent because money was invested in both land and aircraft technologies.[176] Its superior technology was fully supported by superior tactics and training, and this gave it all of the qualitative advantages over Syria that were discussed earlier.

Israel is one of the few countries capable of creating advanced chaff, electronic warfare, and electronic supporting measures and its own guided air weapons. According to some reports, the IAF is also pursuing the development of multispectral sensor systems to be fitted on UAVs, planes, and helicopters. Replacing forward-looking infrared systems with synthetic aperture radar or millimeter wave radio systems would drastically reduce the effects of poor weather conditions on reconnaissance and targeting. However, development and deployment may be 10 to 20 years away.[177]

The IAF benefits from Israel's intelligence satellites and their reconnaissance and targeting capability. These capabilities may improve significantly in the future. Two of Israel's biggest defense firms have joined together to create a new entity tentatively named MicroSat Ltd., which will develop and produce multimission satellites weighing between 10 and 120 kilograms. Although MicroSat is a commercial space program, national security and defense capabilities will also gain from the development of these satellites. These small satellites will be capable of operating as a unit for various intelligence gathering, targeting, and command-and-control missions, as well as housing a variety of "plug-and-play" payloads. Although the project may take 10–20 years to be realized, producers are hopeful that microsatellites will be as useful and as needed as laptops and handheld computers.[178]

Like its other services, the Israeli Air Force is organized for asymmetric warfare and counterterrorism. It has developed special intelligence and targeting techniques for killing targets it designates as terrorists and attacking their facilities. It has improved its IS&R systems to cover urban areas and suspect terrorist facilities and has developed specialized units like the Sayeret Shaldag (Kingfisher), a unit tied to the Army command which is also known as Unit 5101.[179] It has a variety of helicopters, aircraft, and UAVs for counterterrorism and air assault missions. Other elements include Unit 669.

Air Defense and Air-to-Air Combat Capability

While the Israeli air defense system is scarcely leakproof—a fact it demonstrated some years ago when a defecting Syrian pilot flew undetected deep into Israeli air space—a fully alert Israeli air defense is capable of coordinating its sensors, fighters, and land-based defenses with a level of effectiveness that no other Middle Eastern air force can approach.[180] Israel has a better overall mix of systems, better-trained personnel, and a far better ability to integrate all its assets with its own technology and software than any other Middle Eastern air force.

The Israeli Air Force has an unequalled record in air-to-air combat. It destroyed many of its opponent's aircraft on the ground in the 1967 war and then scored 72 air-to-air kills over the rest. It destroyed 113 Egyptian and Syrian aircraft in air-to-air combat during the war of attrition and killed 452 Egyptian, Syrian, Iraqi, and Jordanian aircraft during the October War in 1973.

It killed at least 23 Syrian aircraft between 1973 and 1982 and killed 71 fixed-wing aircraft during the fighting in 1982. It shot down three Syrian fighters between 1982 and 1992. While it has lost 247 aircraft in combat since the beginning of the 1948 war, only 18 have been lost in air-to-air combat. In contrast, Arab forces have lost at least 1,428 fixed-wing and rotary-wing aircraft in combat and 817 have been lost in air-to-air combat.

Air Offense and Air-to-Ground Combat Capability

Israel's advantages in strategic and long-range offensive operations are even greater. The IAF is the only air force in the Middle East that is seriously organized for strategic attacks on its neighbors. Other Middle Eastern air forces may have long-range strike aircraft, effective munitions, and even a limited refueling capacity. They were, however, essentially amateurs in using their assets to inflict strategic damage on an enemy nation or in conducting effective long-range strategic strikes.

Israel has shown it has the ability to strike deep into the Arab world and has greatly improved its long-range strike capability since its attacks on Osirak in 1981 and on Tunisia in 1985. It has the F-15I and greatly improved refueling capability, targeting capability, standoff precision munitions, and electronic warfare capability. Israel could probably surgically strike a limited number of key targets in virtually any Arab country within 1,500 nautical miles of Israel and could sustain operations against western Iraq. It would, however, probably be forced to use nuclear weapons to achieve significant strategic impact on more than a few Iraqi facilities, or if it had to simultaneously engage Syrian and Iraqi forces.

The IAF has also adapted its offensive tactics to gain an advantage over terrorists within urban areas. These tactics have included precision strikes against hostile leaders, such as targeting Ahmed Yassin, the spiritual leader of Hamas, in March 2004 in the Gaza Strip. When the IAF fully coordinates with the Shin Bet security service, Military Intelligence, and regional command authorities, it can assume a large part of the counterterror operations that would otherwise be assumed by forces on the ground at a much higher risk.

The IAF works not only in active air operations, but also uses UAVs for situations that require waiting and watching a possible target. The goal, according to one senior Israeli official, is to have the capability to strike an emerging target within 50 seconds or less, although the times when targets do emerge are fleeting, action is achieved by shortening the sensor-to-shooter loop.[181]

The IAF has long benefits from access to the most advanced U.S. air-to-ground, as well as air-to-air, munitions and has developed or modified many munitions on its own. According to some reports, Israel has been in talks with the United States to obtain $319-million worth of air-launched bombs, including 500 "bunker busters," possibly to use on Iran's alleged underground nuclear facilities.[182] Among the bombs Israel might get from the deal are 500 one-ton bunker busters, 2,500 regular one-ton bombs, 1,000 half-ton bombs, and 500 quarter-ton bombs.[183]

In addition the United States and Israel have discussed undertaking a joint project, the F-35 Joint Strike Fighter (JSF). The JSF is slated to replace the F-16 that has been Israel's primary assault aircraft for the past 25 years. Lockheed Martin and numerous other countries are developing the plane, yet for the time being Israel is being left out of the activities. The United States suspended Israel's involvement following an Israel-China arms deal that ended with Israel reneging on the deal with China and the former Defense Ministry Director General Amos Yaron resigning.[184]

Security relations between Israel and the United States became strained when the United States discovered that Israel was selling U.S. Patriot antimissile technology to China throughout the 1990s. Relations were intensified when the United States learned that Israel was providing China with Harpies, an unmanned aerial vehicle with a bomb that homes in on radar, in 2001 and conducted maintenance on the drones in 2003 and 2004. After learning that China now possessed the drones and that Israel was going to provide maintenance and upgrades for them, the United States drastically reduced weapons and technology transfers to Israel. The United States felt that the agreement between Israel and the United States, that each would be committed to global security, was damaged and only when Israel reneged on the deal, as was already stated, did the Pentagon agree to resume security and technological relations with Israel in August 2005.[185]

Following the disagreements between Israel and the United States regarding Israel's military sales to China, the United States also asked Israel to halt a military deal with Venezuela. (Hugo Chavez has been a vocal critic of the Bush administration and has been a partner with Cuban leader Fidel Castro in opposing U.S. policies.) The deal with Venezuela that was brought to a halt included upgrading the F-16 fighter jets for the Venezuelan Air Force, but since the jets are constructed from an American-made platform, Israel Aircraft Industries (IAI), which would have done the upgrading, needs the Pentagon's permission to work on the jets. It is not clear at the time of this writing whether the deal between Israel and Venezuela has been delayed or whether it is going to be canceled completely.[186]

Some IAF experts have called for Israel to advance in the direction of the Unmanned Combat Aerial Vehicle (UCAV) following the suspension of Israel's involvement in the JSF program. The costs of training pilots, the operational limitations of manned vs. unmanned aircraft, and the price a nation pays when a pilot is downed or taken hostage have all become part of the Israeli debate on UCAVs. There has also been research on manned vs. unmanned aircraft capabilities for the IAF by the Fisher Brothers Institute for Air and Space Studies. There is not, however, any current move toward building a UCAV fleet in the near future. Eitan Ben-Eliahu, former Israel Air Force commander and a key participant of the Fisher study about the JSF program and UCVAs, has stated that "[w]e need to solve all the problems with the Americans and that next-generation fighter our new center of gravity."[187]

IAF Readiness and Training Standards

Israeli pilot and aircrew selection and training standards are the highest in the Middle East and some of the highest in the world. In addition, Israel has developed a reserve system that requires exceptional performance from its air force reservists. There are no reserve squadrons in the IAF, and all squadrons can operate without mobilization. However, about one-third of the aircrew in each squadron are reservists. Reserve aircrews train 55–60 days a year and fly operational missions with the squadron to which they are assigned. In the event of a call-up, the reserve aircrews and operations support personnel report first and then support personnel for sustained operations. About 60 percent of the IAF reserves are in air and ground defense units.

In contrast, other Middle Eastern forces are weakened by their failure to enforce rigorous selection procedures for assignments other than combat pilot and by their failure to create a highly professional class of noncommissioned officers that were paid, trained, and given the status necessary to maintain fully effective combat operations. In most cases, these problems are compounded by poor overall manpower policies and promotion for political and personal loyalty. Other Middle Eastern air forces also tend to be weakened by a failure to see command and control, intelligence and targeting, high-intensity combat operations, and sustainability as being equal in importance to weapons numbers and quality. While Egypt, Iraq, and Saudi Arabia have moved toward the idea of force-wide excellence in supporting an overall concept of operations, they still have a long way to go before approaching Israel's level of capability.

Current Superiority and Future Challenges

Several Arab forces now have combat elements with moderate to high capabilities. Two Arab air forces—Egypt and Saudi Arabia—have relatively good training standards, modern combat aircraft, and advanced battle management systems like the E-3A and the E-2C. The IAF faces growing problems over the cost of advanced new aircraft, munitions, sensors, and battle management systems. Modernization will continue to present financial challenges. The IAF would like to buy up to 42 more AH-64 Apache or AH-64D Longbow attack helicopters, including at least one more squadron equipped with Longbow long-range, all-weather, fire-and-forget, antiarmor missiles.

More generally, the IAF faces two evolving challenges that could erode its present almost decisive superiority. One is the risk that a nation like Syria will acquire large numbers of truly modern surface-to-air missiles like the S-300 or S-400 and the necessary command-and-control system and sensors. The other is proliferation that has become an increasing threat from Iran over the past year. Long-range missiles and weapons of mass destruction pose a risk to all of Israel's conventional forces, but they pose a particular challenge to Israel's air forces because they (a) provide the ability to strike directly at Israel's densely packed main operating bases and (b) bypass its air combat capabilities. Israel's very strengths drive its opponents toward asymmetric warfare and to use proliferation as a way to exploit its remaining areas of vulnerability.

ISRAELI LAND-BASED AIR DEFENSES

The IAF operates Israel's land-based air defense units, and the trends in these forces are shown in Figure 4.6.[188] These are organized into six brigades covering five geographic regions (central, northwestern, southeastern, southwestern, and

Figure 4.6   Israeli Air Defense Force: Force Structure

	1990	2000	2005	2006
Manpower	?	?	18,000	18,000
Active	?	?	3,000	3,000
Reserve	?	?	15,000	15,000
SAM Batteries	15	17	17	66+
MIM-23 Hawk/Improved Hawk	15	17	17	Some
MIM-104 Patriot	0	0	0	Some
Patriot	0	3	0	?
Arrow battalions	0	0	2	?
Arrow II (launchers)	0	0	9	18
M-163 Chaparral (each with 4 FIM-92A Stinger MANPAD SAM)	0	8	0	35
M-163 Vulcan SP 20 mm (each with 4 FIM-92A Stinger MANPAD SAM)	0	0	0	35
M-163 Machbet Vulcan SP 20 mm (each with 4 FIM-92A Stinger MANPAD SAM)	0	0	0	35
PAC-2 battalions	0	0	3	48
Launchers	0	0	9	?
Forces Abroad	0	?	Occasional	Up to 1
Turkey (detachment of AF F-16) located at Akinci	0	?	Occasional	Up to 1
Paramilitary	~6,000+	~6,050	~8,050	~8,050
Border Police	6,000	6,000	~8,000	~8,000
BTR-152 APC	?	1,600	Some Walid	Some Walid
Coast Guard	?	~50	~50	~50
US PBR	3	1	0	0
PC	0	0	0	3
PCR (U.S.)	0	0	1	1
Other patrol craft	3	3	3	0
Foreign Forces	?	141	153	?
UN, UNTSO (observers)	?	141	153	?

Source: Various editions of the IISS *Military Balance,* the *Jane's Sentinel* series, and U.S., British, and Israeli experts.

northeastern), plus a training unit. Its air defense weapons are deployed into battalions organized by weapons type.

Israeli forces include Israel's Patriot/I Hawk battalions (136, 138, and 139 Battalions) that have one Patriot battery and three IHawk batteries each. Israel has 17 batteries of MIM-23 Improved Hawk surface-to-air missiles, and 3 batteries of upgraded Patriot missiles with improved antitactical ballistic missile capabilities. The Patriot batteries have three multiple launcher fire units each.

The Patriot has improved strikingly since the Gulf War and now has a nominal footprint with some five times the previous area coverage. The MIM-104, or PAC-2, has a speed of Mach 5, rather than Mach 3. Its maximum altitude is 24 kilometers, its minimum range is 3 kilometers, and its maximum range is 160 kilometers.

The PAC-3 is a further improvement over the PAC-2/GEM system in area coverage, lethality, and missile intercept capability. It has a new interceptor missile using a hit-to-kill warhead instead of an exploding warhead. The PAC-3 missile is also smaller. The launcher canister is approximately the same size as a PAC-2 canister, but contains four missiles and tubes instead of a single round.[189] It uses inertial/active millimeter-wave radar terminal homing.

Israel had deployed two Arrow batteries at Palmachim and Ein Shemer.[190] The first Arrow Weapon System (AWS) battery was deployed in the center of the country and became operational on March 12, 2000, at the Palmachim base (some reports suggest that the first battery was in the southern Negev Desert at the Dimona nuclear facility). The second battery was placed at Ein Shemer east of Hadera and was operational "for training purposes" as of mid-2002. The main warning and battle manage sensors are tied to the Green Pine radar system.[191]

The original Arrow 2, Green Pine radar, and battle management system have been steadily upgraded. Arrow 5s are now nearing deployment, or being deployed, and an Arrow 6 is in development. The nominal range of the system has evidently been increased from 300 to 500 kilometers and may be increasingly to 700 kilometers. These developments are discussed in the following section on Israeli weapons of mass destruction.

C⁴I/BM and Sensor Systems

The Israeli system is believed to make use of the Hughes technology developed for the U.S. Air Force (USAF), including many elements of the USAF 407L tactical command-and-control system and Hughes 4118 digital computers. The system had main control centers in the Negev and near Tel Aviv.

Israel had a mix of different radars, including at least two AN/TPS-43 three-dimensional radars with three AN/MPQ-53 radar sets and three AN/MSQ-104 engagement control stations bought in 1998. This system was tailored to Israel's local threats and had sufficient technology to meet these threats in combat. Israel also had the ability to coordinate its air defenses from the air, had superior electronic warfare and systems integration capability, and had a clear strategy for suppressing enemy land-based air defenses and the ability to execute it.

Israel is also steadily improving its missile warning and ballistic missile defense radars. These developments are discussed in the following section on Israeli weapons of mass destruction.

Short-Range Air Defense Systems

The Israeli Army also had eight short-range Chaparral missile fire units and units with large numbers of Stinger, Grail, Redeye man-portable missiles, and Vulcan antiaircraft guns. It had over 250 Stingers, 1,000 obsolescent Redeye man-portable surface-to-air missiles, and 45 Chaparral crew-served missile launchers. It also had some 455 20-mm antiaircraft (AA) guns—including TCM-20s and M-167 Vulcans. It had M-163 Vulcan/M-48 Chaparral gun-missile systems, 150 ZU-23 23, 60 ZSU-23-4 23-mm AA guns, some M-39 37-mm and 150 L-70 40-mm AA guns. The IAF had eight Stinger batteries and eight Chaparral batteries. These assets gave Israel fewer land-based air defense forces and mobility than some of its neighbors, but Israel relied primarily upon its air force for such defense.

Two Israeli defense firms had jointly produced a new surface-to-air missile platform dubbed the "SPYDER." The all-weather day/night system is truck mounted along with a surveillance radar and a command-and-control unit. The SPYDER was designed to target precision-guided munitions, helicopters, UAVs, and aircraft up to 15 kilometers away and up to 9,000 meters in the air.[192] The IDF had not, however, announced any plans to acquire SPYDER units.

Additionally, the IDF, in conjunction with the U.S. Army, is developing a Mobile Tactical High Energy Laser that will target UAVs, some types of cruise missiles, artillery shells, and short-range rockets. A similar system, albeit much larger and in prototype form only, had already been produced in the United States. The Ministry of Defense envisions deploying it by 2007.[193]

Readiness and Effectiveness

Israel remains the only Middle Eastern state with the resources, technology, organizational skills, war-planning capability, and leadership to provide a fully integrated approach to combining land-based air defense and air warfare. Jordan had the technical understanding, but lacked the equipment and resources.

Egypt combines some modern capabilities, but still has significant numbers of obsolete forces and a lack of overall systems integration and military coherence. Syria relies on aging Soviet systems, the most modern of which date back to the early 1980s. Its air defense deployments and battle management systems are poorly executed in detail and lack effective systems integration, electronic warfare capability, and modern C^4I/BM capabilities.

ISRAELI NAVAL FORCES

Israel's naval forces have 6,000 actives and 3,500 reserves. Conscripts serve three years. In 2006, the Israeli Navy had 3 submarines, 3 Sa'ar 5-class corvettes, 12 missile patrol craft, 32 inshore patrol craft, and 2 amphibious ships. It had a small commando force of around 300 men and had 5 AS 565SA Sea Panther antisubmarine warfare helicopters. Its forces are based at Haifa, Ashdod, and Eilat. The trends in these forces are shown in Figure 4.7.[194]

Surface Fleet Developments

Israel had three Sa'ar 5 (Eilat or Sa'ar V)-class missile corvettes delivered in the mid-1990s. A fourth has been delayed, The Sa'ar 5s are 1,227-ton ships, each of

Figure 4.7   Israeli Navy: Force Structure

	1990	2000	2005	2006
Manpower	19,000	~18,000	~19,500	11,500–23,000
Navy	9,000	~6,500	~8,000	6,000
Conscripts	3,000	2,500	2,500	2,500
Reservists	?	?	?	3,500
Mobilized forces	10,000	11,500	11,500	11,500
Patrol and Coastal Combatants	61	53	54	51
Commando	300	~300	~300	~300
Number of bases	3	3	4	4
Submarines	0	2	3	3
Gal (UK Vickers) SSC with Mk 37 HWT Harpoon USGW	3	3	0	0
SSK Dolphin (Sub-Harpoon USGW, 4×650-mm ASTT, 6×533-mm ASTT)	0	1	3	3
Corvettes	0	3	3	3
Eilat (Sa'ar 5) FSG (8 Harpoon SSM, 8 Gabriel II SSM, 2 Barak VLS SAM (2×32 mls), 1×76-mm gun, 6×324-mm ASTT, 1 SA-366G hel)	0	3	3	0
Eilat (Sa'ar 5) (either 1 AS-565SA Panther ASW hel or 1 AS-366G Dauphin II SAR hel)	0	0	0	3
Missile Craft	26	14	12	12
Aliya	2	2	2	2
(4 Harpoon, 4 Gabriel SSM, 1 AB-206 Kiowa hel)	2	0	0	0
(4 Harpoon SSM, 4 Gabriel SSM, SA-366G Dauphin hel)	0	2	2	2
Hetz (Sa'ar 4.5)	0	6	8	8
(8 Harpoons SSM, 6 Gabriel SSM, 6 Barak VLS SAM, 1×76-mm gun)	0	6	8	8
Romach	2	0	0	0
(8 Harpoon, 8 Gabriel)	2	0	0	0
Reshef	8	4	2	2
(2–4 Harpoon, 4–6 Gabriel)	8	0	0	0
(8 Harpoons SSM, 6 Gabriel SSM, 1×76-mm gun)	0	4	2	2
Mivtach/ Sa'ar	10	2	0	0
(2 Harpoon, 3–5 Gabriel)	10	0	0	0

(2–4 Harpoons SSM, 3–5 Gabriel SSM)	0	2	0	0
Shimrit (U.S. Flagstaff 2) PMH	3	0	0	0
(4 Harpoon, 2 Gabriel)	3	0	0	0
Dvora (under 100 tons)	1	0	0	0
Patrol, inshore	35	36	39	32
Super-Dvora PFI (under 100 tons)	4	13	13	13
Dabur PFI (under 100 tons)	31	17	18	18
Nashal PCI	0	3	3	3
Alligator	0	0	1	1
Type 1012 Bobcat catamaran PCC	0	3	3	3
Katler (SpecOps support craft)	0	0	0	1
Amphibious	9	2	2	2
LCT Ashdod	6	1	1	1
LCM U.S. type	3	1	1	1
Support and miscellaneous	2	0	0	0
Patrol Craft Depot Ship	1	0	0	0
Transport	1	0	0	0
Patrol Craft	0	0	0	0
U.S. Halter Marine PCI	0	0	0	0
Naval aviation	0	0	5	5
Helicopters (ASW, AS-565SA Panther)	0	0	5	5

Source: Various editions of the IISS *Military Balance,* the *Jane's Sentinel* series, and U.S., British, and Israeli experts.

which have two quad launchers for Harpoon missiles with a range of up to 130 kilometers, one 76-mm gun, a Dauphin SA-366G helicopter, a Phalanx close-in defense system, and six torpedo launchers. These ships have the mission of protecting Israel's shipping lanes.

The Sa'ar 5s have modern electronic support and countermeasure systems, and advanced software for target tracking and identification. These facilities included a sophisticated command information center sheltered deep within the ship that can act as task group command centers, as well as fight an individual ship. The sea and air tracking and battle management system are also advanced for a ship of this class.[195]

The ships also have extensive countermeasures and some stealth features and may be upgraded to use the Barak missile if suitable funds become available. The ships give Israel additional "blue-water capability" and are superior to any similar missile ships in service with Israel's Arab neighbors.

There have, however, been cost constraints in arming them. Some reports indicate that Israel planned to equip them with eight IAI MBT Gabriel 5 antiship missiles with radar and optical homing and ranges of up to 36 kilometers, but there have been top weight problems. Other plans called for giving each ship two 32-cell launchers for Barak air defense missiles. There have been cost problems in procuring this system, and some reports indicate that cost problems have limited the complement of Harpoon missiles.

Israel has sought funds for up to five more ships through U.S. aid, but it is unclear whether it will have sufficient funds to do so. Nevertheless, the Ministry of Defense continues to pursue funds for and development of sea-based vessels capable of interdicting air, surface, and submarine-fired missiles.[196]

Israel had 12 additional missile craft—including 6 to 8 operational Sa'ar 4.5 (Hetz)-class ships with 8 Harpoons and 6 Gabriels each. It had 2 Sa'ar 4.5 (Aliya)-class ships with 6 Harpoons and 6 Gabriels. Some reports indicate that 2 Sa'ar 4 (Reshef) class missile patrol boats were still being upgraded. All Sa'ar 2s and 3s have been retired.[197]

The Sa'ar 4.5s have been extensively modernized under the Nirit (4.5)-class upgrade program which incorporated a "modernization by cannibalization" approach, scrapping much of the material from the Sa'ar 4s while outfitting the vessels with new hulls, low-radar-signature masts, new fire-control detectors, and updated sensors. At least one ship has four eight-cell launchers for Barak point-defense missiles. The ships are also specially equipped to support Special Operations forces.

The Israeli Navy is seeking to purchase two or three multimission combat ships, dubbed the Sa'ar 5 plus program.[198] The vessels would extend the navy's sensor capability and possibly could serve as the platform for a sea-based missile defense system.[199]

Smaller Surface Ships

As is discussed shortly, Israel is changing its current force of smaller surface ships to improve its capability to defend the Gaza Strip and the rest of Israel against terrorism. Israel now has 13 Mark I/II Super Dorva-class fast attack craft (36 to 46 knots) with 20-mm guns and sometimes with short-range Hellfire missiles. These ships were built in the late 1980s and early 1990s. They can be equipped with depth charges or multiple rocket launchers. Two are based at Eilat on the Red Sea. The rest are in Haifa.

By early 2006, the Israeli Navy had also deployed two of eight new Wasp versions of the Defender-class boat (four 25-foot and four 31-foot). This is a $2.5 million program to provide seaborne counterterrorism protection for Israel's ports at Haifa, Ashdod, and Eilat. It has also signed a $45-million contract to buy four Super Dvoras and three Shaldag Mark IIIs to supplement the initial order it placed for six Super Dvoras and two Shaldags in January 2002.[200]

Four of the initial Super Dvora Mark IIIs were operational by early 2006, and all six should be operational by the summer of 2006. The next four will have a water-jet drive system to allow much more rapid maneuver in shallow water. They are 27.4 meters long and displace 58 to 72 tons, depending on the mission load. They have maximum speeds close to 50 knots. The Super Dvoras and Shaldags will have stabilized 25-mm bow guns and two machine guns on each side.

Israel once had 15 Dabur-class light patrol ships of 32-ton displacement. These are land transportable, but are too slow for their original purpose of antiterrorist operations (13 knots). They are being sold off and retired, but two are based at Eilat on the Red Sea. There were three small Bobcat (coast guard)-class patrol boats.

At this point in time, Israel has only light-patrol capability in the Red Sea—reflecting its peace with Egypt and Jordan.

Submarine Forces

Israel has replaced its three Gal-class submarines with three modern Dolphin-class submarines, which were commissioned in 1999 and 2000. Israeli Navy plans originally called for Israel to maintain five submarines, but such a force was not affordable.

The Dolphins give Israel considerably greater strategic depth in operating in Mediterranean waters. They can be operated at ranges of up to 8,000 miles and have an endurance of up to 30 days. They have modern sonars, torpedoes, and facilities for the launch of Harpoon antiship missiles. The Israeli-held version of Harpoon has GPS guidance for the land-attack role. There are "wet and dry" compartments for underwater swimmers and personnel craft for Special Operations.

The Dolphins are the most advanced submarines in the Middle East. They weigh 1,700 tons and are twice the size of the Gal-class subs. In addition, Israel is to receive the German Seahake active wire guided heavyweight torpedoes with a range of 13 kilometers. These may now be in service, and Israel also has NT 37E torpedoes.

The navy still seems to be considering the acquisition of two more Dolphins, and some reports indicate it might do so rather than buy two additional missile corvettes due to the concern that the corvettes would be vulnerable to terrorist attacks while in narrow waters like the Suez Canal.

Some within the navy have also stressed the importance of submarines over the corvettes in order to preserve a nuclear second-strike capability in the event of an attack.[201] There are reports that Israel can use its submarines to provide a secure and relatively invulnerable launch platform for nuclear-armed missiles. These initially would be a nuclear-armed version of a system like the Harpoon, with a nominal range of 70 miles or 130 kilometers. They could be followed by a new long-range cruise missile.

Israel is also believed to be working to develop a variety of conventionally armed longer-range missiles for both its submarines and surface forces. These include a loitering missile with a nominal range of 200 kilometers and a 220-kilogram warhead, with an endurance of up to one hour and an integrated radar and imaging seeker. Other systems include a large missile with a 570-kilogram warhead, terminal guidance, and a range exceeding 200 kilometers. Such systems could be openly or covertly equipped with nuclear warheads as well.[202]

Amphibious Forces

Israel has a Naval Infantry Brigade and a variety of Special Forces and intelligence units that can be inserted by sea. The Israeli Navy had one Ashdod-class LCT (400 tons, 730 tons fully loaded), and one U.S.–type LCM in 2006.

The Israeli Navy has considered the purchase of either a 13,000-ton amphibious ship that could carry troops, tanks, aerial vehicles, and helicopters as far as 2,000 miles away (the Multimission Combined Arms Platform) or a 3,000-ton Sa'ar 5 II Advanced Surface Warship.[203] However, due to budgetary concerns, the navy has shelved such procurement plans until at least 2008.[204]

Naval Aviation

The IAF's six Phalcons can provide maritime surveillance, as well as airborne early warning, and the IAF had 19 Bell 212 helicopters for coastal surveillance tasks.

Israel had four Sea Panther and one Dauphin SA 366G helicopters for its Sa'ar 5s, and Sea Scan UAVs for maritime surveillance and targeting.

The Navy's Role in Asymmetric Warfare

The navy's counterterrorist forces include Shayetet Shlosh-Esrai—13 Commando Yami—Kommando Yani. This is a 300-man commando unit based at Atlit. It is trained for at-sea, search and rescue, and counterterrorism operations. There is also LOTAR Eilat, a reserve counterterrorism unit based in Eilat, which works with 13 Commando. All of Israel's submarines are combat swimmer capable, and a number of its fast attack ships and boats are fitted for insertions and extractions and can rapidly deploy and recover Special Forces assault craft.[205]

The navy has shown its value in asymmetric warfare. In 2002, the Israeli Navy seized control of the *Karine A,* a ship headed for the shores of the Gaza Strip. When the cargo was uncovered the navy discovered 50 tons of weapons including 122-mm and 107-mm Katyusha rockets, mortar shells, rifles, mines, and a variety of antitank missiles and mines. The range of the 122-mm Katyushas, about 20 km, would have enabled the Palestinians in the Gaza Strip to threaten towns such as Ashkelon or other coastal cities, and the Palestinians in the West Bank to threaten Ben Gurion National Airport and several major cities.[206]

This may be critical in the future. The withdrawal from the Gaza Strip has opened up the prospect of significant new efforts at infiltration by sea, and the security barrier has created another incentive for infiltration from Lebanon or the Mediterranean.

Israel has reacted by creating new Snapir or Diving and Sea Warfare Units, mixing swimmers and frogmen with better port entry defense, and efforts to board and inspect suspect vessels.

The navy has built the first stage of a two-stage anti-infiltration barrier off of the southern end of the Gaza Strip that will extend from 150 meters to nearly a kilometer into the Mediterranean and be some 3–10 meters deep. The second phase will be a floating security barrier system 10 meters deep anchored to the bottom. These nets are supposed to be able to halt a boat traveling at speeds up to 50 knots. There already is a somewhat similar, but less-developed barrier, off Israel's coast near its border with Lebanon.[207]

These barriers include a variety of fixed optical, night-vision, and radar sensors mounted on high points on land like smokestacks and netted together by a common C4I/BM system. Israeli patrol boats have proven to be effective in land as well as coastal surveillance missions, particularly in the Gaza Strip. Patrol boats can use precision 25-mm guns against land targets that are slaved to these land sensors. Israeli vessels are also sometimes able to use their radars and sensors to target various aspects of Palestinian operations on land near the shore as well as use Doppler radars to detect infiltrators in small boats even in serious sea states. The navy is considering using UAVs as well to replace its aging Westwind Seascan manned aircraft, which date back to 1978.[208]

Israel has greatly improved port security, both in ports and nearby waters—where ships sometimes drop explosives and arms for later recovery. Containers have been used to smuggle in suicide bombers, and scuba divers have been dropped off to act as infiltrators.[209]

Naval Readiness and Mission Capability

Sea power is not likely to be a major factor in any near-term Arab-Israeli conflict —particularly one between Israel and Syria. Israel has massive naval superiority over Syria and Lebanon. It also can probably use joint naval-air operations win superiority over Egypt except in Egyptian waters.[210] It should be noted, however, that Israel has sharply limited its naval presence in the Red Sea and has had to make trade-offs that have reduced its naval capabilities.

Nevertheless, Israel is the only navy in the Middle East supported by an industrial base that had advanced electronic warfare design and modification capabilities and with the ability to manufacture and design its own sensors and antiship missiles. These developments should allow Israel to maintain a decisive edge over Syria in the Mediterranean and a more limited advantage in tactics, training, and technology over the Egyptian Navy—although the Egyptian Navy was receiving significant modernization.

Resources, however, remain a problem. The navy had to cut its procurement of new Sa'ar corvettes from eight to three and may have problems in funding all three Dolphin-class submarines. It also had to cut back substantially on its Barak ship defense missile—although these were armed with Harpoon and Gabriel ship-to-ship missiles. The practical issue is whether this matters given the strategic partnership between the United States and Israel and U.S. dominance of the sea. It simply is not clear that any of Israel's naval trade-offs erode its edge in any probable contingency.

ISRAEL'S COUNTERTERRORISM AND INTERNAL SECURITY FORCES

The open literature on Israel's military forces, like that on most Middle Eastern states, does not provide a clear or accurate picture of Israel's capabilities for asymmetric warfare. The role of police, intelligence, covert action, and security forces is just beginning to be seen as a critical part of the real-world military balance. Furthermore, only limited data are available on the expansion of such forces, and major changes in their role and structure, that have occurred in virtually every Middle East country over the last half-decade.[211]

The previous analysis has shown, however, that Israel has a wide mix of forces with exceptional experience and skill in counterinsurgency and counterterrorism efforts. These include civilian elements like the Mossad Merkazi Le Modin Uletafkidm (Central Institute for Intelligence and Special Missions), which is responsible for intelligence collection and operations and counterterrorism outside Israel. The Israel Security Agency (also called the General Security Service or Shinbet) is Israel's main internal security and counterespionage service.[212]

There are mixed civil-military units like the MALMAB (an acronym for Security Authority of the Israeli Ministry of Defense), which is responsible for the security of Israeli defense industries and a variety of intelligence activities, including industrial espionage. There also are a number of special units that are not public and special branch elements of the police.

The Israeli National Police (INP) have an intelligence and internal security mission. Once again, reliable data are not available, but unclassified sources have named elements like the Latam (works with Israel Security Agency), MATILAN (Intelligence Observation Interception and Mobile Warfare Unit) with a special mission to protect Jerusalem, and the YAMAM (Police Counterterrorist and Hostage Rescue Unit), which is a hostage rescue unit with over 100 men and units working in the Gaza Stirp, the West Bank, and Jerusalem. YAMAM is a self-sufficient unit within the INP with it its own dog units, snipers, bomb disposal and demolition teams, and specialist communications and intelligence personnel. There are teams within the YAMAM that are trained in scaling buildings and entering buildings undetected in counterterrorist operations.[213]

In addition, the INP includes some 8,000 personnel in the Mishmar Havgul-MAGAV (Border police or Green Police).[214] The MAGAV is trained in flexibility and rapid response to border incidents, public disorder, and regular police missions. The Border Police have at their disposal 1,600 BTR-152 APCs as well as other armored vehicles including Sufa jeeps that have been converted to operational armored plated vehicles. Specialized equipment includes night-vision equipment and grenade launchers, the weapons include Galil, Mini-Galil, M-16 assault rifles, Uzi, mini-Uzi submachine gun, and 9-mm IMI "Jericho" 941F DA semiautomatic pistols.[215]

YAMAS (Mista'aravim) is a specialist unit within Magav that conducts covert operations against terrorists and hard-line armed elements mainly in the West Bank and in Judea and Samaria. About 12 percent of the total Magav force is from ethnic minorities—Druze, Bedouin, Christian, Muslim, and Circassian—a fact that facilitates undercover operations in Arab-speaking areas.[216]

Other units subordinate to INP include the following:[217]

- Unit 33 (Gideonim)—elite intelligence oriented undercover unit,
- YAGAL—a paramilitary countersmuggling unit for the Lebanese border, and
- YAMAG—tactical countercrime and counterterror rapid deployment unit.

While Israel is no more immune to jurisdictional issues and interagency rivalries than any other country, its civilian services are used to working jointly with the IDF. While Israel's services are scarcely immune to turf fights and tensions in dealing with the military, there is far more "jointness" than in virtually all other Middle Eastern states. They are also linked by one of the most advanced computer and communications systems in the world, and one that uses data mining, advanced algorithms, and other data integration techniques to tie together open source material, human intelligence (HUMINT), and technical collection from platforms like UAVs to support both covert intelligence and military operations.

This "fusion" capability can provide real-time targeting to both police and military operations, and its graphics and data readouts have been steadily improved to support direct operational use. So has the automation of data routing to ensure the proper use gets immediate warning. This has been a major factor in allowing forces like the Shin Bet to intercept suicide bombers. While the details remain classified, it is scarcely coincidental that the same firm, Elbit Systems, is responsible for both Israel's new Intelligence Knowledge Management (IKM) and Digital Army Program.[218]

One thing is clear. Israel has very extensive counterterrorism and internal security forces that have been actively engaged in asymmetric warfare since Israel's founding. Since the late 1960s, Israel has faced an ongoing threat from violent Palestinian organizations like the Islamic Resistance Movement (Hamas), Al-Aqsa Martyrs' Brigades, Hezbollah, Islamic Jihad, and the Popular Front for the Liberation of Palestine; from foreign groups like Hezbollah, and potentially from Islamist extremist groups like Al Qa'ida. The nature and the capabilities of these forces are described in the following chapters on Lebanese, Palestinian, and Syrian forces. Most are individually weak, but they cumulatively confront Israel with a serious threat. Hamas also has emerged as the strongest single force in Palestinian politics in the Gaza Strip and the West Bank as a result of the January 25, 2006, parliamentary elections.

As has been noted earlier, this threat is changing as a result of Israel's unilateral withdrawals from the Gaza Strip and the West Bank and its creation of security barriers to separate Israelis and Palestinians. Quite aside from their political and diplomatic impacts, these policies require Israel to increasingly shift its security focus to defense of the barriers and lines of separation and maintain security within Israel and the territory Israel occupies on the Israel-held side of the barrier.

There have also been increasing problems with Israeli Arabs. Large numbers have been arrested or detained since October 2000. Israel has also reported that 14 Arab civilians were shot and killed by Israel policemen between October 2000 and January 2006, and another 5 were killed by Israel Defense Forces soldiers. These totals do not include 12 Israeli Arabs killed during the uprising that began in September 2000.[219]

The IDF is free of the need to occupy parts of the Gaza Strip and protect its settlers, but must now work with Egypt to secure the Egyptian-Gaza border. It must find ways to strike at hostile forces and points of attack in the Gaza Strip, with reoccupation as a desperate last resort. It must also redefine its security position around Jerusalem and throughout the West Bank, effectively creating a perimeter defense around the settlements Israel intends to retain and creating a de facto "border" with security barriers, rather than relying on broad freedom of action, security roads, and scattered settlements. At the same time, it must preserve its deterrent and warfighting capabilities to deal with any infiltration or threat across the Lebanese, Syrian, and Jordanian borders—more and more against the threat posed by nonstate actors working in concert with the Palestinians.

It is simply too soon to predict how serious the resulting pressure will be on the IDF. Much of the burden may fall on Israeli intelligence, counterterrorist, and security forces. This burden may also prove to be little more than a variation of threats that Israel has long had to deal with. There is no guarantee that any combination of the Palestinians, Israeli Arabs, and outside movements and states will pose a highly effective threat or develop ways to attack Israel that the IDF and the Israeli security services cannot counter. What does seem almost certain, however, is that they will try.

Israeli Capabilities

Israel has long maintained an extensive mix of security and intelligence services to deal with such threats. Some are civilian and some are elements within the military. Many have extensive experience in counterterrorism and counterinsurgency operations, including covert operations and target assassinations.

The structure of Israeli intelligence and covert operations capabilities is a separate study in itself and one where there is often more speculation than fact. What is clear is that Israel is still often able to target hostile leaders and attackers within the Gaza Strip and the West Bank and that Israel retains a network of Palestinian informers and agents who can act as Palestinians. There are some indicators that Palestinians aid Israel by giving Israel data that targets rival movements and leaders. Israel has developed a wide range of intelligence and surveillance systems like specialized UAVs, SIGINT, and communications intelligence to supplement its extensive HUMINT systems.

Israel has also done much more than create physical barriers or separation between Israeli and Palestinian areas. Its security barriers and procedures make extensive use of sensors and have defense in depth with coverage of Palestinian areas in the barrier area and security coverage on the Israeli side. The nature and control of such systems is classified, and journalistic reporting is uncertain. It also seems almost certain that Israeli defenses will change strikingly once the security barriers and systems are fully in place. Nevertheless, until a real peace settlement is achieved, the barrier areas, like Israel's borders, will remain the scene of an ongoing and constantly evolving asymmetric duel among Israeli forces and security services, the Palestinians, and outside forces hostile to Israel.

Israeli Terrorist Groups

Israel has its own terrorists as well as Palestinian threats. While most of the extreme settler groups have as yet used only very limited amounts of violence, some on the West Bank have become increasingly threatening. The U.S. State Department has also designated one Israeli group, Kahane Chai or Kach, as a terrorist organization and describes it as follows:[220]

> "Kahane Lives"), founded by Meir Kahane's son Binyamin following his father's 1990 assassination in the United States, were declared to be terrorist organizations in 1994 by the Israeli Cabinet under its 1948 Terrorism Law. This followed the groups' statements in support of Dr. Baruch Goldstein's attack in February 1994 on the al-Ibrahimi Mosque (Goldstein was affiliated with Kach) and their verbal attacks on the Israeli Government. Palestinian gunmen killed Binyamin Kahane and his wife in a drive-by shooting in December 2000 in the West Bank.
>
> . . . Kach's stated goal is to restore the biblical state of Israel. Kach, founded by radical Israeli-American rabbi Meir Kahane, and its offshoot Kahane Chai, (translation:
>
> . . . The group has organized protests against the Israeli Government. Kach has harassed and threatened Arabs, Palestinians, and Israeli Government officials, and has vowed revenge for the death of Binyamin Kahane and his wife. Kach is suspected of involvement in a number of low-level attacks since the start of the al-Aqsa Intifada in 2000. Known Kach sympathizers are becoming more vocal and active against the planned Israeli withdrawal from the Gaza Strip in mid-2005.
>
> . . . (Operates in) Israel and West Bank settlements, particularly Qiryat Arba' in Hebron.
>
> . . . . Receives support from sympathizers in the United States and Europe.

There have also been settler groups and other Israelis that have threatened and intimidated Palestinians, destroyed their business and olive groves, and committed acts of violence and sometimes killings that cannot be confirmed as large-scale terrorism but seem to be a growing problem. For example, the U.S. State Department human rights report issued in 2005 states that "[i]n December (2004), Israel convicted and sentenced an Israeli man for membership in the New Jewish Underground," a terrorist organization that aimed to carry out attacks on Arab civilians. On September 29, a group of five Israeli settlers attacked and seriously wounded two U.S. citizens, members of an NGO, who were escorting Palestinian children to school near Hebron. As of the end of 2004, the Israeli police had not arrested those responsible.

Internal Security vs. Human Rights and Political Impacts

The political dimension and impact of internal security has become a critical part of the military balance throughout the region. Asymmetric wars inevitably challenge human rights and make them an extension of war by other means. The ability to use and manipulate human fights organizations is a weapon, as is the effort to conceal abuses or practices that stretch legitimate security measures to the limit. Every nation in the Middle East faces such a struggle, regardless of the type of regime and the massive differences in the nature of the internal and external threats. Israel is no exception.

No matter how well Israel organizes and uses such forces, they are a source of major friction with the Palestinians and present major problems in terms of human rights and foreign perceptions of Israel. Few issues are the subject of so much controversy, but the human rights country report issued by the U.S. State Department provides a relatively neutral view of both Israeli actions and those of the other countries shaping the Arab-Israeli balance. The State Department reports issued in 2005 and 2006 noted that Israeli paramilitary and security forces have extensive powers that they often abuse, both in dealing with Palestinian extremists and peaceful dissidents,[221]

Internal security is the responsibility of the Israel Security Agency (ISA or Shin Bet), which is under the authority of the Prime Minister. The National Police, which includes the Border Police and the Immigration Police, are under the Minister of Internal Security and the Minister of Interior respectively. The Israel Defense Forces (IDF) are under the authority of a civilian Minister of Defense. The IDF includes a significant portion of the adult population on active duty or reserve status. The Foreign Affairs and Defense Committee in the Knesset oversees the IDF and the ISA. Security forces were under effective government control. Some members of the security forces committed serious abuses.

The country's population is approximately 6.8 million, including 5.2 million Jews, 1.3 million Arabs, and some 290,000 other minorities. It has an advanced industrial, market economy with a relatively high standard of living. Twenty one percent of the population lived below the poverty line in 2003. Unemployment was approximately 11 percent, and was higher among the Arab population. Foreign workers, both legal and illegal, constituted about 7 percent of the labor force.

The Government generally respected the human rights of its citizens; however, there were problems in some areas. Some members of the security forces abused Palestinian detainees. Conditions in some detention and interrogation facilities remained poor. During the year, the Government detained on security grounds but without charge thousands of persons in Israel. (Most were from the occupied territories and their situation is covered in the annex.) The Government did little to reduce institutional, legal, and societal discrimination against the country's Arab citizens. The Government did not recognize marriages performed by non-Orthodox rabbis, compelling many citizens to travel abroad to marry. The Government interfered with individual privacy in some instances.

. . . The law prohibits arbitrary arrest and detention, and the Government generally observed these prohibitions. (Palestinian security detainees fell under the jurisdiction of military law even if they were detained in Israel (see annex). When arrested, the accused is considered innocent until proven guilty, has the right to habeas corpus, to remain silent, to be represented by an attorney, to contact his family without delay, and to a fair trial. A bail system exists and decisions denying bail are subject to appeal. A citizen may be held without charge for 24 hours before he must be brought before a judge (48 hours for administrative detainees). If the detainee is suspected of committing a "security offense," the police and the courts can delay notification of counsel for up to 31 days. The Government may withhold evidence from defense lawyers on security grounds. In March, the Public Defender's Office charged that the police sometimes failed to apprise detainees of their rights under law and did not always provide detainees with legal counsel when required. The Public Defender's Office estimated that, as a result, approximately 500 persons were deprived of their rights to due process.

. . . Foreign nationals detained for suspected violations of immigration law are afforded an immigration hearing within 4 days of detention, but do not have the right to legal representation. According to the local advocacy organization Hotline for Migrant Workers, appropriate interpreters were not always present at the hearings. Hotline received complaints from Israeli attorneys of being denied access to their foreign clients. According to Hotline, foreign detainees were rarely released pending judicial determination of their status. If the country of origin of the detainee had no representation in the country, detention could last for months, pending receipt of travel documents. During the year, there were credible allegations that the police knowingly detained and deported legal foreign workers to meet deportation quotas.

. . . Pursuant to the 1979 Emergency Powers Law, the Ministry of Defense may order persons detained without charge or trial for up to 6 months in administrative detention, renewable indefinitely subject to district court review. Such detainees have the right to legal representation, but the court may rely on confidential information to which the defendant and his or her lawyer are not privy. Administrative detainees have the right to appeal their cases to the Supreme Court.

. . . The Judicial Branch is organized into three levels: Magistrate Courts; six District Courts; and the Supreme or High Court. District Courts prosecute felonies, and Magistrate Courts prosecute misdemeanors. There are military, religious, labor relations, and administrative courts, with the High Court of Justice as the ultimate judicial authority. The High Court is both a court of first instance and an appellate court (when it sits as the Supreme Court). All courts in the judicial system, including the High Court of Justice, thus have appellate courts of jurisdiction. Religious courts, representing the main recognized religious groups, have jurisdiction over matters of personal status for their adherents (see Section 2.c.).

The law provides for the right to a fair trial, and an independent judiciary generally enforced this right. The country's criminal justice system is adversarial, and professional judges rather than juries decide cases.

. . . Nonsecurity trials are public except in cases in which the interests of the parties are determined to be best served by privacy. Security or military trials are open to independent observers upon request and at the discretion of the court, but they are not open to the general public. The law provides for the right to a hearing with legal representation, and authorities generally observed this right in practice. In cases of serious felonies—subject to penalties of 10 years or more—indigent defendants receive mandatory legal representation. Indigent defendants facing lesser sentences are provided with representation on a discretionary basis. Counsel represented approximately 70 percent of defendants.

. . . The 1970 regulations governing military trials are the same as evidentiary rules in criminal cases. Convictions may not be based solely on confessions; however, according to PCATI, in practice, some security prisoners have been sentenced on the basis of the coerced confessions made by both themselves and others. Counsel may assist the accused, and a judge may assign counsel to those defendants when the judge deems it necessary. Indigent detainees are not provided with free legal representation for military trials. Charges are made available to the defendant and the public in Hebrew, and the court can order that they be translated into Arabic if necessary. Sentencing procedures in military courts were consistent with those in criminal courts. Defendants in military trials have the right to appeal through the Military High Court. Defendants in military trials also can petition the civilian High Court of Justice (sitting as a court of first instance) in cases in which they believe there are procedural or evidentiary irregularities.

Israel occupied the West Bank, Gaza Strip, Golan Heights, and East Jerusalem during the 1967 War. Pursuant to the May 1994 Gaza-Jericho Agreement and the September 1995 Interim Agreement, Israel transferred most responsibilities for civil government in the Gaza Strip and parts of the West Bank to the newly created Palestinian Authority (PA). The 1995 Interim Agreement divided the territories into three types of areas denoting different levels of Palestinian Authority and Israeli occupation control. Since Palestinian extremist groups resumed the use of violence in 2000, Israeli forces have resumed control of a number of the PA areas, citing the PA's failure to abide by its security responsibilities.

Israel exercised occupation authority through the Israeli Ministry of Defense's Office of Coordination and Liaison (MATAK).

...Violence associated with the Intifada has claimed the lives of 3,517 Palestinians, according to the Palestine Red Crescent Society (PRCS), 1,051 Israelis, according to the Israeli Ministry of Foreign Affairs website, and 52 foreign nationals, according to B'tselem, an Israeli human rights organization that monitors the occupied territories. During the year, over 800 Palestinians were killed during Israeli military operations in the occupied territories, a total of 76 Israeli civilians and 4 foreigners were killed in terrorist attacks in both Israel and the occupied territories, and 41 members of the Israeli Defense Forces were killed in clashes with Palestinian militants.

Israeli security forces in the West Bank and Gaza Strip consisted of the Israeli Defense Forces (IDF), the Israel Security Agency (Shin Bet), the Israeli National Police (INP), and the Border Police, an operational arm of the Israel National Police that is under IDF command when operating in the occupied territories. Israeli military courts tried Palestinians accused of security offenses. Israeli security forces were under effective government control. Members of the Israeli security forces committed numerous, serious abuses.

....There were reports that Israeli security forces used excessive force, abused and tortured detainees. Conditions in permanent prisons met international standards, but temporary facilities were austere and overcrowded. Many Israeli security personnel were prosecuted for committing abuses, but international and Israeli human rights groups complained of lack of disciplinary action in a large number of cases.

The Israeli Government continued construction of a security barrier along parts of the Green Line (the 1949 Armistice line) and in the West Bank. The PA alleged that the routing of the barrier resulted in the taking of land, isolating residents from hospitals, schools, social services, and agricultural property. Israel asserts that it has sought to build the barrier on public lands where possible, and where private land was used, provided opportunities for compensation. Palestinians filed a number of cases with the Israeli

Supreme Court challenging the routing of the barrier. In June, the Court ruled that a section of the barrier must be rerouted; determining that the injury caused by the routing of the barrier did not stand in proper proportion to the security benefits; various portions of the barrier route were rerouted. On July 9, the International Court of Justice issued an advisory opinion, concluding that "The construction of the wall built by Israel, the occupying Power, in the Occupied Palestinian Territory, including in and around East Jerusalem...and its associated regime, are contrary to international law."

...Israeli law, as interpreted by a 1999 High Court of Justice decision, prohibited torture and several interrogation techniques, such as violent shaking, holding and tying of prisoner in painful positions, shackling, sleep deprivation, covering the prisoner's head with a sack, playing loud music, and prolonged exposure to extreme temperatures, but allowed "moderate physical pressure" against detainees considered to possess information about an imminent attack. However, CATI and the Physicians for Human Rights in Israel (PHR) reported that techniques prohibited by the law were used against Palestinian detainees during interrogation and that security forces often beat Palestinians during arrest and transport. Israeli law prohibits the admission of forced confessions, but most convictions in security cases were based on confessions made before legal representation was available to defendants.

...Under applicable occupation orders, Israeli security personnel may arrest without warrant or hold for questioning a person suspected of having committed or to be likely to commit a security related offense. Israeli Military Order 1507 permits the Israeli army to detain persons for 10 days, during which detainees are barred from seeing a lawyer or appearing before court. Administrative detention orders could be issued for up to 6-month periods and could be renewed indefinitely by judges. No detainee has ever successfully appealed a detention order. Israeli military Order 1369 provides for a 7 year prison term for anyone who does not respond to a special summons in security cases. Suspects are entitled to an attorney, but this can be deferred during the interrogation phase, which sometimes lasts up to 90 days. Israeli authorities stated that they attempted to post notification of arrests within 48 hours, but senior officers may delay notification for up to 12 days. Additionally, a military commander may appeal to a judge to extend this period in security cases for an unlimited period, and many families reported serious problems in learning of the status and whereabouts of prisoners. Evidence used at hearings for administrative detentions in security cases was often unavailable to the detainee or his attorneys due to security classification.

...The Israeli Government maintained that it held no political prisoners, but Palestinians claimed that administrative detainees were political prisoners. At year's end, Israel held approximately 8,300 Palestinian security prisoners (up from 5,900 in 2003), of which at least 960 were in administrative detention.

...Israeli law provides for an independent judiciary, and the Government generally respected this in practice. Palestinians accused of security offenses usually were tried in military courts. Security offenses are comprehensively defined and may include charges as varied as rock throwing or membership in outlawed terrorist organizations, such as Hamas or the PFLP. Military prosecutors brought charges. Serious charges were tried before three-judge panels; lesser offenses were tried before one judge. The Israeli military courts rarely acquitted Palestinians of security offenses, but sentences in some cases were reduced on appeal.

Israeli military trials followed evidentiary rules that were the same as those in regular criminal cases. Convictions may not be based solely on confessions, although, in practice, some security prisoners were convicted on the basis of alleged coerced confessions of themselves and others. The prosecution must justify closing the proceedings to the public in security cases. The accused is entitled to counsel, and a judge may assign counsel. Charges are made available to the defendant and the public in Hebrew, and the court may order that the charges be translated into Arabic, if necessary. Defendants had the right to appeal through the Military High Court or to the Civilian High Court of Justice in certain instances. The court may hear secret evidence in security cases that is not available to the defendant or his attorney. However, a conviction may not be based solely on such evidence.

Trials sometimes were delayed for very extended periods, because Israeli security force witnesses did not appear, the defendant was not brought to court, files were lost, or attorneys were delayed by travel restrictions (see Section 2.d.). Palestinian legal advocates alleged that these delays were designed to pressure defendants to settle their cases.

. . . .According to the PA Ministry of Health, the Palestine Red Crescent Society, and B'tselem, at least 800 Palestinians were killed during the course of Israeli military and police operations during (2004). The PA Ministry of Health estimated that approximately half of those killed were noncombatants. B'tselem reported a figure of 452 innocent Palestinians killed this year. The IDF stated that the majority of Palestinians killed were armed fighters or persons engaged in planning or carrying out violence against Israeli civilian and military targets. According to the PRCS, IDF operations resulted in injuries to approximately 4,000 Palestinians.

. . .The IDF (has) conducted numerous military incursions into Palestinian population centers, in response to Palestinian mortar and antitank fire. These actions often resulted in civilian casualties. Israeli forces fired tank shells, heavy machine-gun rounds, and rockets from aircraft at targets in residential and business neighborhoods where Palestinian gunfire was believed to have originated. Palestinians often used civilian homes to fire upon Israeli forces and booby-trapped civilian homes and apartment buildings. In response to these actions, the IDF usually raided, and often leveled, these buildings.

ISRAELI WEAPONS OF MASS DESTRUCTION

Israel's nuclear capabilities, and efforts to develop weapons of mass destruction are some of its most controversial force developments. Although there have been many unclassified reports on such developments, only a few have had high credibility and these have consisted largely of reports on its missile forces. Many of the estimates of Israel's nuclear weapons trace back to rough estimates made a decade ago. No official data have emerged on Israel's strategic doctrine, targeting plans, or systems for planning and executing nuclear strikes.

Figure 4.8 provides an estimate of Israel's capabilities. It should be stressed again that all of the estimates of this kind provided in this analysis are highly uncertain and are heavily dependent on unclassified sources and the views of outside experts. It is equally important to note that little is known about Israeli doctrine and plans for using such weapons, although a great deal of speculation has been made over how Israel might act in a war or crisis.

Figure 4.8   Israel's Search for Weapons of Mass Destruction

Delivery Systems

- Israel has done technical work on a TERCOM-type smart warhead. It has examined cruise missile guidance developments using GPS navigation systems. This system may be linked to a submarine launch option.

- As part of its first long-range missile force, Israel deployed up to 50 "Jericho I" (YA-1) missiles in shelters on mobile launchers with up to a 400-mile range with a 2,200-pound payload, and with possible nuclear warhead storage nearby. These missiles were near copies of the two-stage, solid-fueled, French MD-620 missile. Some reports claim the first 14 were built in France. (Some reports give the range as 500 kilometers.)

- There are convincing indications that Israel has deployed nuclear-armed missiles on mobile launchers. Most outside sources call the first of these missiles the Jericho I, but Israel has never publicly named its long-range missile systems.
  - Israel is thought to have conventional, chemical and nuclear warheads for the Jericho I.
  - The current deployment of the Jericho I force is unclear. Some sources say it has been phased out for the Jericho II missile.[222]

- Israel has since gone far beyond the Jericho I in developing long-range missile systems. It has developed and deployed the "Jericho II" (YA-2).
  - The Jericho II began development in the mid-1970s and had its first tests in 1986.[223] Israel carried out a launch in mid-1986 over the Mediterranean that reached a range of 288 miles (460 kilometers). It seems to have been tested in May 1987. A flight across the Mediterranean reached a range of some 510 miles (820 kilometers), landing south of Crete.[224] Another test occurred on September 14, 1989.
  - Israel launched a missile across the Mediterranean that landed about 250 miles north of Benghazi, Libya. The missile flew over 800 miles, and U.S. experts felt it had a maximum range of up to 900–940 miles (1,450 kilometers)—which would allow the Jericho II to cover virtually all of the Arab world and even the southern USSR.[225]
  - The most recent version of the missile seems to be a two-stage, solid-fueled missile with a range of up to 900 miles (1,500 kilometers) with a 2,200-pound payload.
  - Commercial satellite imaging indicates the Jericho II missile may be 14 meters long and 1.5 meters wide. Its deployment configuration hints that it may have radar area guidance similar to the terminal guidance in the Pershing II and probably has deployed these systems.
  - Some Jericho IIs may have been brought to readiness for firing during the Gulf War.
  - Israel began work on an updated version of the Jericho II no later than 1995 in an effort to stretch its range to 2,000 kilometers. At least part of this work may have begun earlier in cooperation with South Africa.

- Israel is also seeking technology to improve its accuracy, particularly with gyroscopes for the inertial guidance system and associated systems software.

- Israel is actively examining ways to lower the vulnerability of its ballistic missiles and nuclear weapons. These include improved hardening, dispersal, use of air-launched weapons, and possible seabasing.

- There are also reports that Israel is developing a Jericho III missile, based on a booster it developed with South Africa in the 1980s.
  - The tests of a longer-range missile seem to have begun in the mid-1980s.[226] A major test of such a booster seems to have taken place on September 14, 1989, and resulted in extensive reporting on such cooperation in the press during October 25 and 26, 1989.
  - It is possible that both the booster and any Israeli-South African cooperation may have focused on satellite launches.[227] Since 1994, however, there have been numerous reports among experts that Israel is seeking a missile with a range of at least 4,800 kilometers, and which could fully cover Iran and any other probable threat.
  - *Jane's* estimates that the missile has a range of up to 5,000 kilometers and a 1,000-kilogram warhead. This estimate is based largely on a declassified DIA estimate of the launch capability of the Shavit booster that Israel tested on September 19, 1988.[228]
- Reports of how Israel deploys its missiles differ.
- Initial reports indicated that 30–50 Jericho I missiles were deployed on mobile launchers in shelters in the cases southwest of Tel Aviv. A source claimed in 1985 that Israel had 50 missiles deployed on mobile erector launchers in the Golan, on launchers on flat cars that could be wheeled out of sheltered cases in the Negev. (This latter report may confuse the rail transporter used to move missiles from a production facility near Be'er Yaakov to a base at Kefar Zeharya, about 15 kilometers south of Be'er Yaakov.)
- More recent reports indicate that Jericho II missiles are located in 50 underground bunkers carved into the limestone hills near a base near Kefar Zeharya. The number that are on alert, command and control and targeting arrangements, and the method of giving them nuclear warheads has never been convincingly reported.[229]
- *Jane's Intelligence Review* published satellite photos of what it said was a Jericho II missile base at Zachariah (God remembers with a vengeance) several miles southeast of Tel Aviv in September 1997.[230] According to this report, the transport-erector-launcher (TEL) for the Jericho II measures about 16 meters long by 4 meters wide and 3 meters high. The actual missile is about 14 meters long and 1.5 meters wide. The TEL is supported by three support vehicles, including a guidance and power vehicle. The other two vehicles include a communications vehicle and a firing control vehicle. This configuration is somewhat similar to that used in the U.S. Pershing II IRBM system, although there are few physical similarities.
- The photos in the article show numerous bunkers near the TEL and launch pad, and the article estimates a force of 50 missiles on the site. It also concludes that the lightly armored TEL would be vulnerable to a first strike, but that the missiles are held in limestone caves behind heavy blast-resistant doors. It estimates that a nuclear-armed M-9 or Scud C could destroy the launch capability of the site.[231]
- The same article refers to nuclear weapons bunkers at the Tel Nof airbase, a few kilometers to the northwest. The author concludes that the large number of bunkers indicates that Israel may have substantially more nuclear bombers than is normally estimated—perhaps up to 400 weapons with a total yield of 50 megatons.[232]
  - 76 F-15, 232 F-16, 20 F-4E, and 50 Phantom 2000 fighter-bombers capable of long-range refueling and of carrying nuclear and chemical bombs.

- Israel bought some Lance missile launchers and 160 Lance missiles, with a 130-kilometer range, from the United States in the 1970s. The United States removed them from active duty during 1991–1994. The status of the Israeli missiles is unknown.
  - IISS reports that Israel currently has some 20 Lance launchers in storage.
  - The Lance has a range of 130 kilometers with a 450-kilogram payload.
  - Reports indicate that Israel has developed conventional cluster munitions for use with the Lance rocket.
- Reports of a May 2000 test launch seem to indicate that Israel has a cruise missile with 1,500 kilometers that can be launched from its new Dolphin-class, German-built submarines.[233]
  - It is believed that such a cruise missile, an extended-range, turbofan powered variant of the Popeye cruise missile, called the Popeye Turbo, can carry a nuclear warhead.
- There are reports of the development of a long-range, nuclear-armed version of Popeye with GPS guidance and of studies of possible cruise missile designs that could be both surface-ship and submarine based.
  - Variant of the Popeye air-to-surface missile believed to have nuclear warhead.
  - The MAR-290 rocket with a 30-kilometer range is believed to be deployed.
  - MAR-350 surface-to-surface missile with a range of 56 miles and a 735-pound payload believed to have completed development or to be in early deployment.
  - Israel seeking supercomputers for Technion Institute (designing ballistic missile RVs), Hebrew University (may be engaged in hydrogen bomb research), and Israeli Military Industries (maker of Jericho II and Shavit booster).
  - Israel current review of its military doctrine seems to include a review of its missile basing options, and the study of possible hardening and dispersal systems. There are also reports that Israel will solve its survivability problems by deploying some form of nuclear-armed missile on its new submarines.

Chemical Weapons

- Reports of mustard and nerve gas production facility established in 1982 in the restricted area in the Sinai near Dimona seem incorrect. May have additional facilities. May have capacity to produce other gases. Probable stocks of bombs, rockets, and artillery.
- Extensive laboratory research into gas warfare and defense.
- An El Al 747-200 cargo plane crashed in southern Amsterdam on October 4, 1992, killing 43 people in the apartment complex it hit. This led to extensive examination of the crash, and the plane was found to be carrying 50 gallons on dimethyl methylphosphonate, a chemical used to make Sarin nerve gas. The chemical had been purchased from Solkatronic Chemicals in the United States and was being shipped to the Israel Institute for Biological Research. It was part of an order of 480-pounds worth of the chemical. Two of the three other chemicals used in making Sarin were shipped on the same flight. Israel at first denied this and then claimed it was being imported only to test gas masks.[234]

- Israel may have the contingency capability to produce at least two types of chemical weapons and has certainly studied biological weapons as well as chemical ones. According to one interview with an Israeli source of unknown reliability, Israel has mustard gas, persistent and nonpersistent nerve gas, and may have at least one additional agent.
- Development of defensive systems includes Shalon Chemical Industries protection gear, Elbit Computer gas detectors, and Bezal R&D aircrew protection system.
- Extensive field exercises in chemical defense.
- Gas masks stockpiled and distributed to population with other civil defense instructions during first and second Gulf Wars.
- Warhead delivery capability for bombs, rockets, and missiles, but none now believed to be equipped with chemical agents.
- An unconfirmed October 4, 1998, report in the *Sunday Times* of London quotes military sources as stating that Israeli F-16s have been able to carry out attacks using chemical and biological weapons produced at the Nes Ziona facility.[235]

Biological Weapons

- Extensive research into weapons and defense.
- Ready to quickly produce biological weapons, but no reports of active production effort.
- According to some reports, Israel revitalized its chemical warfare facilities south of Dimona in the mid-1980s, after Syria deployed chemical weapons and Iraq began to use these weapons in the Iran-Iraq War.
- Israel has at least one major research facility with sufficient security and capacity to produce both chemical and biological weapons.[236] There are extensive reports that Israel has a biological weapons research facility at the Israel Institute for Biological Research at Nes Tona, about 12 miles south of Tel Aviv, and that this same facility also has worked on the development and testing of nerve gas. This facility has created enough public concern in Israel so that the mayor of Nes Tona has asked that it be moved away from populated areas. The facility is reported to have stockpiled anthrax and to have provided toxins to Israeli intelligence for use in covert operations and assassinations like the attempt on a Hamas leader in Jordan in 1997.[237]
  - The Israel Institute for Biological Research is located in a 14-acre compound. It has high walls and exceptional security and is believed to have a staff of around 300, including 120 scientists. A former deputy head, Marcus Kingberg, served 16 years in prison for spying for the FSU.
- U.S. experts privately state that Israel is one of the nations included in U.S. lists of nations with biological and chemical weapons. They believe that Israel has at least some stocks of weaponized nerve gas, although they may be stored in forms that require binary agents to be loaded into binary weapons.
- They believe that Israel has fully developed bombs and warheads capable of effectively disseminating dry, storable biological agents in micropowder form and has agents considerably more advanced than anthrax. Opinion differs over whether such weapons are actively loaded and deployed. Unconfirmed reports by the British *Sunday Times* claimed

that IAF F-16s are equipped for strikes using both these weapons and chemical weapons.[238]

Nuclear Weapons

- Director of CIA indicated in May 1989 that Israel may be seeking to construct a thermonuclear weapon.
- Has two significant reactor projects: the 5-megawatt HEU light-water IRR-1 reactor at Nahal Soreq; and the 40–150-megawatt heavy water, IRR-2 natural uranium reactor used for the production of fissile material at Dimona. Only the IRR-1 is under IAEA safeguards.
- Dimona has conducted experiments in pilot scale laser and centrifuge enrichment, purifies UO_2, converts UF_6, and fabricates fuel for weapons purpose.
- Uranium phosphate mining in Negev, near Beersheba, and yellowcake is produced at two plants in the Haifa area and one in southern Israel.
- Pilot-scale heavy water plant operating at Rehovot.
- *Jane's Intelligence Review* published an article in September 1997 which refers to nuclear weapons bunkers at the Jericho 2 missile base at Zachariah (God remembers with a vengeance) several miles southeast of Tel Aviv and at Tel Nof airbase, a few kilometers to the northwest. The author concludes that the large number of bunkers indicates that Israel may have substantially more nuclear bombs than is normally estimated—perhaps up to 400 weapons with a total yield of 50 megatons.[239]
- Estimates of numbers and types of weapons differ sharply.
  - Stockpile of at least 60–80 plutonium weapons.
  - May have well over 100 nuclear weapons assemblies, with some weapons with yields over 100 kilotons.
  - U.S. experts believe Israel has highly advanced implosion weapons. Known to have produced Lithium-6, allowing production of both tritium and lithium deuteride at Dimona. Facility no longer believed to be operating.
  - Some weapons may be ER variants or have variable yields.
  - Stockpile of up to 200–300 weapons is possible.
  - There exists a possibility that Israel may have developed thermonuclear warheads.
- Major weapons facilities include production of weapons grade Plutonium at Dimona, nuclear weapons design facility at Nahal Soreq (south of Tel Aviv), missile test facility at Palmikim, nuclear armed missile storage facility at Kefar Zekharya, nuclear weapons assembly facility at Yodefat, and tactical nuclear weapons storage facility at Eilabun in eastern Galilee.

Missile Defenses

- Patriot missiles with future PAC-3 upgrade to reflect lessons of the Gulf War.

- Arrow 2 two-stage ATBM with slant intercept ranges at altitudes of 8–10 and 50-kilometer speeds of up to Mach 9, plus possible development of the Rafal AB-10 close in defense missile with ranges of 10–20 kilometers and speeds of up to Mach 4.5. Taas rocket motor, Rafael warhead, and Tadiran BM/C4I system and "Music" phased array radar.
- Israel plans to deploy three batteries of the Arrow to cover Israel, each with four launchers, to protect up to 85 percent of its population. The first battery was deployed in early 2000, with an official announcement declaring the system operational on March 12, 2000.
- The Arrow program has three phases:
  - Phase I: Validate Defense Concept and Demonstrate Pre-prototype Missile
    - Fixed price contract: $158 million.
    - The United States pays 80 percent, Israel pays 20 percent.
    - Completed in December 1982.
  - Phase II: Demonstrate Lethality, develop and demonstrate tactical interceptor and launcher.
    - Fixed price contract: $330 million.
    - The United States pays 72 percent, Israel pays 28 percent.
    - Began in July 1991.
    - Successfully completed.
  - Phase III: Develop and integrate tactical system, conduct weapon system tests, and develop and implement interoperability.
    - Program cost estimated at: $616 million.
    - The United States pays 48 percent, Israel pays 52 percent.
    - Began in March 1996.
    - System integration in progress.
  - The Arrow will be deployed in batteries as a wide area defense system with intercepts normally at reentry or exoatmospheric altitudes. Capable of multitarget tracking and multiple intercepts.
- Israel has designed the Nautilus laser system for rocket defense in a joint project with the United States. It has developed into the Theater High Energy Laser (THEL). The project has recently been expanded to include interception of not only short-range rockets and artillery, but also medium-range Scuds and longer-range missiles such as Iran's Shahab series.
- Israel is also examining the possibility of boost-phase defenses. The Rafael Moab UAV forms part of the Israeli Boost-phase Intercept System. This is intended to engage TBMs soon after launch, using weapons fired from a UAV. Moab would launch an improved Rafael Python 4 air-to-air missile. Range is stated as 80–100 kilometers depending on altitude of release.

Advanced Intelligence Systems

- Israeli space program to date:

Satellite	Launch Date	Status	Function
Ofeq 1	9/19/1988	Decayed 1/14/1989	Experimental
Ofeq 2	4/3/1990	Decayed 7/9/1990	Communications experiments
Ofeq 3	4/5/1995	Decayed 10/24/2000	Reconnaissance/experimental?
Ofeq 4 (Eros A)	1/22/1998	Launch failed during second-stage burn	Reconnaissance/commercial imaging?
Eros A1	12/5/2000	In orbit	Reconnaissance/commercial imaging?
Ofeq 5	5/28/2002	In orbit	Reconnaissance

- The Shavit launched Israel's satellite payload on September 19, 1989. It used a three-stage booster system capable of launching a 4,000-pound payload over 1,200 miles or a 2,000-pound payload over 1,800 miles. It is doubtful that it had a payload capable of intelligence missions and seems to have been launched, in part, to offset the psychological impact of Iraq's missile launches.
  - It is believed that the vehicle was launched for experimentation in generation of solar power and transmission reception from space; verification of system's ability to withstand vacuum and weightless conditions; data collection on space environment conditions and Earth's magnetic field.
- Ofeq 2 launched in April 3, 1990—one day after Saddam Hussein threatened to destroy Israel with chemical weapons if it should attack Baghdad.
  - This vehicle used the Ofeq 1 test-bed. Little open-source information exists on this vehicle although it is believed to be a test-bed for communications experiments.
- Israel launched first intelligence satellite on April 5, 1995, covering Syria, Iran, and Iraq in orbit every 90 minutes. The Ofeq 3 satellite is a 495-pound system launched using the Shavit 1 launch rocket and is believed to carry an imagery system. Its orbit passes over or near Damascus, Tehran, and Baghdad.
  - The Shavit 1 differs from the Shavit only in the use of a somewhat different first stage. This change has not significantly affected vehicle performance. The Ofeq 3 and all subsequent launches have used the Shavit 1.
  - Reports conflict regarding whether this was an experimental platform or Israel's first surveillance satellite. Although it is thought to carry visible and ultraviolet wavelength imaging technology, the resolution is thought to be on the order of feet. The relatively low resolution, combined with its orbit, suggests to some observers that the satellite was capable of producing imagery of limited military usefulness.
- On January 22, 1998, the Ofeq 4/Eros A satellite was launched. Due to a failure in the second-stage the satellite never made orbit. Reports conflict about whether this was a launch of a military reconnaissance satellite or was intended for producing commercial satellite imagery.
- The Eros A1 satellite was launched on December 5, 2000, on a Russian Start-1 rocket from Svobodny launch site. This satellite produces commercially available satellite images.

At a basic level, multispectral images with resolutions of 1.8 meters can be obtained. Currently, image processing techniques can yield resolutions of 1 meter. This is expected to improve to 0.6–0.7-meter resolutions in the next year or two. Some reports indicate that the Israeli government is a primary consumer of EROS imagery.

- The successor craft, the Eros B, will have a baseline ability to produce images with a panchromatic resolution of 0.87 meters and 3.5 meters for multispectral images. Launch on board a Russian vehicle is expected in early 2004.

- On May 28, 2002, the Ofeq 5 reconnaissance satellite was launched successfully.

- Development of the Ofeq 6 reconnaissance satellite has started for a 2007 launch.

  - Some sources claim a maximum resolution of 70 centimeters and geostationary reconnaissance capability.

- Agreement signed with the United States in April 1996 to provide Israel with missile early warning, launch point, vector, and point of impact data.

- Israeli Aircraft Industries, the manufacturer of the Shavit series SLV, is developing the additional launchers to place satellites in polar orbits:

  - LK-A—For 350–kilogram-class satellites in 240×600-kilometer elliptical polar orbits

  - LK-1—For 350–kilogram-class satellites in 700-kilometer circular polar orbits.

  - LK-2—For 800–kilogram-class satellites in 700-kilometer circular polar orbits.

  - It is likely that these SLVs designed to place satellites in polar orbits could not be launched from Israel and would require an overseas launching site, such as the American site at Wallops Island.

IRAN AS A WILD CARD

Many of the details of Israeli capabilities had limited importance as long as Israel did not face a regional threat with nuclear weapons and could rely on a nuclear monopoly as an undeclared deterrent. Israel now faces the possibility, however, that it may lose its present nuclear monopoly to Iran. Estimates differ sharply as to how soon Iran might get such a weapon if it continues to proliferate, although most put this time frame well after 2010.

Experts also differ over how serious a threat Iran would really be to Israel. Some experts feel that Iranian rhetoric calling for the destruction of Israel is more a smoke-screen and an excuse for creating an Iran nuclear monopoly in the Gulf than a sign of any serious willingness or desire to engage Israel. Others have said the opposite.

Moreover, even if Iran's nuclear ambitions are mainly centered on the U.S. presence in the Gulf and other Muslim and Arab states, this may not deter Israel from preventive or preemptive action in dealing with what it views an existential threat. Former Prime Minister Rabin made it all too clear long before the present tensions with Iran that one or two nuclear ground bursts centered on Tel Aviv and Haifa could virtually destroy Israel as a state.

Israeli officials like Prime Minister Olmert have stated that Israel cannot tolerate a nuclear-armed Iran. Such views are scarcely new. A number of Israeli officers, officials, and experts have said that Israel must not permit the Iranians to acquire nuclear capabilities, regardless of Tehran's motivations. Ephraim Inbar, the President of the Jaffee Center for Strategic Studies, said in 2004, "For self-defense, we must act in a pre-emptive mode."[240]

General Moshe Ya'alon, the Israeli Chief of Staff, was quoted as saying in August 2004 that Iran must not be permitted to acquire nuclear weapons. He added that Israel must not rely on the rest of the world to stop Iran from going nuclear because he said a nuclear Iran would change the Middle East where "Moderate States would become more extreme."[241] General Ya'alon also indicated that Israel might conduct such attacks without using its aircraft, triggering a wide range of speculation about Israeli and U.S. covert operatives and Special Forces conducting such strikes.

Israel bought 500 bunker busters from the United States in February 2005. Experts speculated whether the purchase was a power projection move or whether Israel was, in fact, planning to use these conventional bombs against Iranian nuclear sites. These speculations were further exacerbated with the Israeli Chief of Staff, Lieutenant General Dan Halutz, was asked how far Israel would go to stop Iran's nuclear program; he said, "2,000 kilometers."[242]

Israeli military officials were quoted in press reports in January 2006 as saying that the IDF got the order to get ready for a military strike against Iranian nuclear sites by March 2006.[243] It is unclear what type of military strikes Israel may choose, if it decides to respond preemptively. Some have argued that Israel may declare its nuclear weapons and establish a mutually assured destruction: deterrence. While the impact of an Israeli declaration remains uncertain, it is likely to have little impact on Israel's strategic posture in the region, since most states factor Israel's nuclear weapons into their strategic thinking.

Some Israeli experts have argued, however, that Israel does not have viable military options. They argue it does not have U.S. targeting capability and simply cannot generate and sustain the necessary number of attack sorties. Some argue that Israel might do little more than drive Iranian activity further underground, provoke even more Iranian activity, make it impossible for diplomatic and UN pressure to work, and make Israel into a real rather than a proxy or secondary target.

Brigadier General Shlomo Brom warned that Israel's capabilities may not be enough to inflict enough damage on Iran's nuclear program:[244]

> any Israeli attack on an Iranian nuclear target would be a very complex operation in which a relatively large number of attack aircraft and support aircraft (interceptors, ECM aircraft, refuelers, and rescue aircraft) would participate. The conclusion is that Israel could attack only a few Iranian targets and not as part of a sustainable operation over time, but as a one time surprise operation.
>
> Even if Israel had the attack capabilities needed for the destruction of the all elements of the Iranian nuclear program, it is doubtful whether Israel has the kind of intelligence needed to be certain that all the necessary elements of the program were traced and destroyed fully. Israel has good photographic coverage of Iran with the Ofeq series of reconnaissance satellites, but being so distant from Iran, one can assume that other kinds of intelligence coverage are rather partial and weak.

Covert action demands different kinds of operational capabilities and intelligence. There is no indication that Israel has capabilities of covert operations in Iran. The recent information about the development of the Iranian program indicated that it reached a status of being independent of external assistance. Moreover, the assistance Iran got was mostly from Pakistan, another place which is not a traditional area of operations for the Israeli secret services, like Europe or South America. It seems that there is no real potential for covert Israeli operations against the Iranian Nuclear program.

Israel would face operational problems in attacking. Israel does not have conventional ballistic missiles or land-/sea-based cruise missiles with the range or accuracy to carry out such a mission from Israel. The shortest flight routes would be around 1,500–1,700 kilometers through Jordan and Iraq, 1,900–2,100 kilometers through Saudi Arabia, and 2,600–2,800 kilometers in a loop through Turkey.[245]

Israel has configured its F-15s and F-16s for long-range strikes and has refueling capability. It is doubtful, however, that it has enough refueling capability to do more than send a strike force that would have to defend itself without a significant fighter escort or support from electronic warfare aircraft. Even then, forward area refueling would probably be required, and backup refueling and recovery would be an issue.

Israeli air or missile strikes would probably be detected relatively quickly by the radars in the countries involved, and very low-altitude penetration profiles would lead to serious range-payload problems. The countries overflown would be confronted with the need to either react or have limited credibility in claiming surprise. An overflight of Iraq would be seen in the region as having to have had a U.S. "green light." Iran would almost certainly see Jordanian, Turkish, and/or Saudi tolerance of such an IAF strike as a hostile act. It might well claim a U.S. green light in any case in an effort to mobilize hostile Arab and Muslim (and possibly world) reactions.

Israeli strike aircraft would probably need close to maximum payloads to achieve the necessary level of damage against most targets suspected of WMD activity, although any given structure could be destroyed with one to three weapons. (This would include the main Buhsehr reactor enclosure, but its real-world potential value to an Iranian nuclear program is limited compared to more dispersed and/or hardened targets).

The IAF's mix of standoff precision-guided missiles—such as Harpoon or Popeye —might not have the required lethality with conventional warheads. (Wildly differing reports exist about the range of the Popeye, which is deployed in the United States as the Have Nap missile. The base system has a range of around 60–70 kilometers. Popeye II has a range of 150 kilometers. Reports have been made about improved "turbo" versions with ranges of 200–350 kilometers.)[246] There have even been reports of air- or submarine-launched versions with ranges of 1,500 kilometers. (One report notes that "Israel is reported to possess a 200kg nuclear warhead, containing 6kg of plutonium, that could be mounted on cruise missiles."[247]

Israel's purchase of 500 BLU-109 Have Void "bunker busters" has given it 2,000-pound weapons that are far less effective against deeply buried targets than the much larger U.S. weapons described earlier. The standard version is a "dumb bomb" with a maximum penetration capability of 4 to 6 feet of reinforced concrete. An aircraft must overfly the target and launch the weapon with great precision to achieve serious penetration capability.[248]

It is possible to fit the weapon with precision guidance and convert it to a guided glide bomb and the United States may have sold such a version or Israel may have modified them. The Joint Direct Attack Munition (JDAM) GBU-31 can be fitted to the bomb to give it a nominal range of 15 kilometers with a Circular Error Probable (CEP) of 13 meters in the GPS-aided INS modes of operation and 30 meters in the INS-only modes of operation.[249] Open source reporting, however, does not provide any data on such capabilities. It is possible, however, that Israel purchased the BLU-116 Advanced Unitary Penetrator (AUP), GBU-24 C/B (USAF), or GBU-24 D/B (Navy) which has about three times the penetration capability of the BLU-109.[250]

Iran has at least 20 suspect facilities and over 100 potential aim points. Multiple strikes on the dispersed buildings and entries in a number of facilities would still be necessary to ensure adequate damage without restrikes. Restrikes would require repeated penetration into Arab airspace and do not seem feasible planning criteria for Israeli commanders to use.

Yet, these are problems to be solved, not insuperable barriers. Israel has the capabilities to carry out at last one set of air strikes, and senior U.S. officials have warned about this capability. Vice President Richard Cheney suggested on January 20, 2005, that, "[g]iven the fact that Iran has a stated policy that their objective is the destruction of Israel, the Israelis might well decide to act first, and let the rest of the world worry about cleaning up the diplomatic mess afterwards."[251]

POSSIBLE IRANIAN RESPONSE

Iran has considerable capability to retaliate and has threatened retaliation if attacked by Israel. Iranian Foreign Minister Manouchehr Mottaki has been quoted as saying that an attack by Israel or the United States would have "severe consequence," and threatened that Iran would retaliate "by all means" at its disposal. Mottaki added: "Iran does not think that the Zionist regime is in a condition to engage in such a dangerous venture and they know how severe the possible Iranian response will be to its possible audacity...Suffice to say that the Zionist regime, if they attack, will regret it."[252]

Iran has several options to respond to an Israeli attack:

- Multiple launches of Shahab-3 including the possibility of chemical, biological, or radiological (CBR) warheads against Tel Aviv, Israeli military and civilian centers, and Israeli suspected nuclear weapons sites.

- Escalate the conflict using proxy groups such Hezbollah or Hamas to attack Israel proper with suicide bombings, covert CBR attacks, and missile attacks from southern Lebanon and Syria.

- Covert attacks against Israeli interests by its intelligence and Islamic Revolutionary Guards Corps assets. This could include low-level bombings against Israeli embassies, Jewish centers, and other Israeli assets outside and inside Israel.

An Israeli strike against Iranian nuclear facilities might also strengthen the Iranian regime's stance to move toward nuclear capabilities and drive many neighboring states to support Iran's bid for nuclear weapons. The United States will be seen as having given the green light for such Israeli strikes, which could lead to further escalation of the Iraqi insurgency, increase the threat of asymmetric attacks against American interests and allies in the region, or, even worse, be used as a justification cry for attacks against the U.S. homeland with CBR weapons by proxy groups or through an alliance with groups such as Al Qa'ida.

On the other hand, Israeli officials have expressed the concern that if Iran is allowed to acquire nuclear weapons, and the means to deliver them, this will lead to further proliferation in the region. They feel Iran's actions would lead to a race to acquire such capabilities around the Middle East and greatly increase the threat of CBRN attacks against Israel and the entire region.[253] They feel that waiting also has its penalties.

SHIFTS IN ISRAELI STRATEGIC NUCLEAR FORCES

If Israel does not preempt, it will almost certainly take steps to both ensure that it has a survivable strike capability and can retaliate immediately with nuclear strikes against all of Iran's cities. Experts have speculated for several years that this will lead Israel to create a submarine-based nuclear missile force and longer-range missiles for air strikes. Israel is also known to have tested much larger boosters than it is presently believed to arm with nuclear warheads, and these might be used to carry several Multiple Reentry Vehicle or Multiple Independent Reentry Vehicle warheads each.[254]

One key uncertainty is the nature of Israel's efforts to arm its submarines and aircraft with what is sometimes called the turbo version of the Popeye. A report by Global Security notes reports that Israel may be developing a Popeye Turbo missile similar to the submarine-launched cruise carried on the Dolphin-class submarines. Press reports appeared claiming Israel had tested a submarine-launched cruise missile (SLCM) with a range of 1,500 kilometers in May 2000. It is possible that Israel could develop a variant of the Popeye Turbo with a range of 1,500 kilometers by lengthening the fuel tank associated with a 300–350-kilometer variant reported by U.S. intelligence.

Israel's submarines are outfitted with six 533-mm torpedo tubes suitable for the 21-inch torpedoes that are normally used on most submarines, but may have 650-mm tubes. If they have two to four larger 25.5-inch diameter torpedo tubes, these could be used to launch a long-range nuclear-capable (SLCM).[255]

The problem for both Israel and Iran is that Israel's vulnerability virtually forces it into a countervalue strike against Iran's population, and any other state then at war with Israel, the moment even one nuclear armed missile hits Israeli soil. Israel cannot win by riding out an attack and has no reason for delay and restraint. There would also be questions about missile accuracy and lethality against small military targets and the need to send the message that no stage could afford to risk trying to exploit Israel's weakness after an Iranian attack.

SHIFTS IN ISRAELI MISSILE DEFENSES

As for missile defenses, Israel did declare that the improved Block 3 version of its Arrow ballistic missile defense system became active in April 2006, and further improvements in software are expected by 2007. It has improved its Green Pine and other radar warning and sensor systems and created a new battle management system, nicknamed the "Cube." It is working on Block 4 versions of both the Arrow and Green Pine to be deployed by 2009 capable of handling significantly greater numbers of missile tracks at the same time and intercepting incoming missiles with a higher closing velocity and at ranges of more than 700 kilometers. It is believed to be developing more advanced counter-countermeasures and the ability to detect decoy warheads.[256]

It should be noted, however, that the Israel missile defense test program has been very limited in terms of operational data and that Israel must rely to a very high degree on engineering models and estimates. While Iran has conducted some ten tests of the Shahab series since 1997, and conducted a 2,000-kilometer test in May 2006, it too might be using missiles whose accuracy and reliability would not be fully established with nuclear warheads that were largely untested. There is at least some possibility of an exchange in which the blind tried to use unproven systems to kill the blind.

ISRAEL'S CONTINUING STRATEGIC CHALLENGES

The problems Israel would face in a new conventional war with Egypt, Jordan, and/or Syria are described in later chapters. At this point, Israel has such a decisive edge in conventional forces, backed by a monopoly of nuclear weapons, that such wars seem very unlikely. If they do occur, the issue is much more likely to be the cost to Israel of winning and not the risk of defeat. Maintaining Israel's edge is an ongoing strategic challenge, but one that seems well within Israel's capabilities.

It is asymmetric warfare and wars of attrition that currently put the main burden on Israel, and Chapters 7 through 9 each outline a different mix of threats from Hezbollah in Lebanon, from Palestinian militants, and from Syria. At this point in time, the one certainty is that a war of attrition already exists between Israel and the Palestinians whether it is called a "peace process" or a "war process." This conflict could escalate to something far more serious.

Iranian proliferation is also becoming a major issue. Israel faces a potential existential threat for the first time since 1973, and it faces hard choices about how to respond to the Iranian challenge.

As a result, Israel faces continuing strategic challenges in spite of its conventional military superiority and nuclear forces:

- The IDF must make hard trade-offs between technology and force size, mass intakes of conscripts for "nation building" and real war-fighting needs, and high-quality, long call-up reserves, and large reserve forces. In the process, it must make equally hard trade-offs among capabilities for conventional warfare, asymmetric warfare, and counterproliferation.
- Israel must maintain relations with the United States that will sustain high levels of military aid and low-cost transfer of advanced U.S. military technology.
- Israel must fight at least a low-level ongoing asymmetric war with the Palestinians and deal with the constant threat of extremist and terrorist attacks. These partly offset its advantages in conventional force strength, force it to constantly devote major resources to offensive missions, and are a major threat to any new peace process.
- Israel faces a growing threat that the Gaza Strip and the West Bank could come under the control of hard-line and Islamist movements like Hamas and the PIJ and/or a radicalized Palestinian Authority. The victory of Hamas in the January 25, 2006, elections has greatly increased this risk.
- Israel must redefine its security position to secure the Gaza Strip from the outside, working with Egypt in defending the Egyptian-Gaza border and providing security for the coast and air space as well as the Gaza Strip's borders with Israel.
- Israel must create a new defensive concept around its security barriers on the West Bank and in dealing with Jerusalem, which mixes perimeter security with defense in depth against the risk of longer-range weapons like rockets, UAVS, mortars, etc. If it withdraws from many of its outlying settlements, it must adjust its entire security position—including the deployment of IDF forces, use of security roads, and coverage of the Jordanian and part of the Syrian border to maintain deterrent and war-fighting capabilities while allowing some form of Palestinian state or entity to function as well as possible.
- With or without peace, the IDF must design its forces and strategy around the prospect of continued unilateral withdrawals and security barriers and infiltration into Israel from the Gaza Strip and the West Bank. Efforts to use Israeli Arabs and create identities that will allow penetration into Israel are certain to increase. Separation is an easy strategy to call for. It is much more difficult for a military force to implement and secure.
- Israel must plan for peace with the Palestinians as well. A sovereign Palestinian state or entity would also change the strategic geography of Israel at virtually every level, and a failed peace could mean massive problems in terms of terrorism and urban, asymmetric, and occupation warfare.
- Israel must work with Egypt and the Palestinians to secure the Egyptian border with the Gaza Strip, a mission that has also been greatly complicated by the victory of Hamas in the January 25, 2006, parliamentary elections.
- Israel must simultaneously plan to deter Syria, to fight Syria, and to make peace with Syria, with or without peace with Lebanon. It must also prepare for low-level war, large-scale conventional combat, and warfare involving chemical and biological weapons. Under worst cases, this could involve outside Arab intervention.

- The IDF must plan for the risk of an extended low-intensity war on its border with Lebanon and for Iran's more hard-line position calling for Israel to be wiped from the face of the map. Israel not only faces a threat from Hezbollah, but the threat of growing Iranian and Syrian aid to Hamas and the PIJ.

- Israel is increasingly the target of Islamist extremist groups like Al Qa'ida, which have long opposed Israel's existence, but increasingly attempt to exploit Israeli-Arab tensions to gain popular support in the Arab world.

- Israel must decide how to both strengthen its alliance with the United States and best secure peace with Egypt, Jordan, and other powers in the region. So far, this has meant closer strategic cooperation with the United States and Turkey, but the IDF must also be prepared to rethink the way in which it would assist Jordan in the event of Iraqi or Syrian pressure or attack, and the possibility of extending missile defense over Jordan and Palestinian territory.

- The IDF must look beyond defense against its neighbors, most of whom now have peace treaties with Israel, to a broader range of threats like Iran which will acquire very long-range strike capabilities and which can support proxies in asymmetric warfare.

- Israel and the world must deal with the emerging threat of Iran producing nuclear weapons. If Israel has to do it alone, according to one minister, it will, but it would be more influential if the international community were to contain the situation.[257]

- Finding the right mix of nuclear and retaliatory survivability is becoming a growing problem, as is reliance on an undeclared nuclear deterrent. Israel continued to use its limited resources to build more nuclear warheads, but its shelters are not hardened silos and do not protect its existing warheads and Jericho medium-range missiles from a preemptive surprise nuclear attack.

- Any Israeli move to place a number of nuclear missiles in submarines is likely to be challenged by other Middle Eastern countries that may respond by acquiring attack subs, helicopters, and planes with antisubmarine warfare capabilities and more sensitive detection devices. Iran had acquired three older submarines and while they may not be able to challenge the Israeli subs, it may signify a new proliferation arena. Saudi Arabia had expressed interest in purchasing submarines and is seeking ten NH-90 helicopters with antisubmarine warfare capabilities for their Alriyadh-class frigates.

- Counterproliferation involves both offense and defense. In 1981, the IAF was able to destroy an Iraqi nuclear reactor before it could start to produce material or waste that could be used for atomic weapons. Now Iran has been successful in using Chinese and Russian support to develop a nuclear program that is spread out and not susceptible to long-range attack. This requires a shift to missile defense, but it also requires a broader counterproliferation strategy and possibly a new approach to deterrence and retaliation—making nuclear deterrence more overt and mixing it with credible long-range precision conventional strikes.

Most of these challenges are less severe than those Israel's forces have faced in the past, but they are anything but easy to deal with. Israel must maintain massive conventional forces for a country its size in order to deter any risk of conventional attack and ensure that no future Egyptian, Jordanian, or Syrian regime will take the risk of attacking Israel.

Israel must plan both its defensive capabilities and nuclear retaliatory and strike capabilities to deal with the potential emergence of a new, existential threat from Iranian nuclear weapons. This threat is likely to take years to materialize, if it does become real, but would represent a fundamental change in the regional balance.

More generally, Israel will be locked into at least a low-level war of attrition as long as it does not have a full peace with the Palestinians, and even if a peace could be reached, it will have significant extremist and terrorist opposition. Israel's efforts to respond with security barriers, separation, and unilateralism may change the rules of the Israel-Palestinian conflict and may provide some degree of added security. They also, however, will almost inevitably provoke the Palestinian side to acquire longer-range weapons to seek to carry out attacks inside the barrier and strike at Israeli and Jewish targets outside the region.

Israel also faces threats from Islamic extremist movements like Al Qa'ida, hostile outside movements like Hezbollah, and anti-Israeli states like Iran and Syria. It faces the risk of steadily improving linkages between such groups and the Palestinians and increased outside aid to Palestinian extremist groups. Finally, the Israel-Palestinian conflict threatens Israel's peace with Egypt and Jordan, the support of other Arab states for a more general peace, and the stability of Jordan.

The Military Forces of Egypt

Egypt is the leading military power of the Arab world, and one of its most populous nations. Egypt had a population of over 78 million in 2006. Unlike most states in the region, its population had few ethnic differences. It was roughly 99 percent of Eastern Hamitic stock (Egyptians, Bedouins, and Berbers). Only about 1 percent consisted of other groups: Greek, Nubian, Armenian, and other European (primarily Italian and French). It did, however, have sectarian divisions that had long led to religious clashes between Muslims and Christians. While some 94 percent of Egypt's population was Sunni Muslim, the remaining 4 percent was Coptic Christian and other religious minorities.[1]

Egypt is an African as well as an Arab-Israeli power, and its control of the Suez Canal and coastlines on the Mediterranean and the Red Sea give it an import naval role as well. Its strategic position is illustrated by the nature of its borders: the Gaza Strip, 11 kilometers; Israel, 266 kilometers; Libya, 1,115 kilometers; and Sudan, 1,273 kilometers. It has a total area of over 1 million square kilometers, and some 2,450 kilometers of coastline.

Egypt has been at peace with Israel since 1979 and has scrupulously honored the terms of this peace. Nevertheless, it had never been able to plan on a secure peace because of ongoing conflicts between Israel and the Palestinians and the risks illustrated by Israel's past conflicts with Lebanon. Egypt had also planned for the risk of a military confrontation with the Sudan over the control of the Nile, to provide security for the transit of shipping through the Suez Canal and the Red Sea, and for potential conflicts with Libya—although the risk of these latter conflicts has diminished steadily in recent years.

At least for the near term, Egypt's major problems will be to maintain internal security against the threat posed by violent Islamist extremist groups and to deal with the challenge of securing its border with the Gaza Strip in the face of an ongoing low-level asymmetric war between Israeli and hostile Palestinian groups. Maintaining its peace with Israel will remain a major strategic problem as well as a major objective. At the same time, it will face the reality of serious internal instability in the Sudan and the long-term strategic issue of how the other nations in the Nile riverine system seek to use its water.

FORCE SIZE VS. FORCE QUALITY

Egypt faces major challenges in creating a more modern and effective force structure. Its historical threat from Israel, the political and bureaucratic momentum behind maintaining a large force posture for status purposes, and the fact that Egypt's armed forces play a major role in its government, have all led Egypt to preserve larger forces than it needs. It has preserved many force elements with little effectiveness and has spent far more on military and internal security forces than it can really afford.

In the process, it has used U.S. grant assistance for military purposes that would be far better spent on economic development and reform. Such spending also limits Egypt's ability to deal with a serious Islamic extremist and terrorist threat, caused in part by deteriorating economic conditions and living standards for much of the population.

The end result is that Egypt has formidable military forces by regional standards. Egypt has sought to retain much of the force levels it developed for the October War in 1973, in spite of its long peace with Israel. In early 2006, it had an active strength of 468,500 men—although between 190,000 and 220,000 were conscripts serving 12–36 months, who often lacked adequate training. It had more than 3,800 tanks, some over 5,700 other armored vehicles in inventory, over 4,300 artillery weapons, some 570 combat aircraft, massive land-based air defenses, and a navy with 4 submarines, 11 major surface combatants, and 63 smaller surface combat ships.[2]

The recent manpower trends in Egyptian forces are shown in Figure 5.1. Many of the shifts shown in Figure 5.1 are more from changes in the method of reporting than in actual force strength. It is striking, however, that Egypt has never had a real "peace dividend" in terms of force size. Its army was much smaller before its peace with Israel. Once it had carried out a limited demobilization after the October War, its army had 275,000 actives—only about 60 percent of its recent strength—although it had some 500,000 reserves. Its air force had roughly the same number of actives, and its land-based air defense forces were somewhat smaller—some 70,000 actives vs. 80,000 at present. Its navy had 17,500 men vs. 18,500–20,000 in recent years. Egypt also remains a force focused more on conventional war fighting than internal security. It had some 120,000 men in its paramilitary forces vs. over 300,000 in recent years. It had roughly the same amount of armor and fewer combat aircraft (500).

Figure 5.2 shows the recent trends in Egypt's arms imports. Like Israel, most of the transfers from the United States come in the form of grant aid and provide major advances in military technology at limited cost to Egypt. Egypt has far less capable military industries than Israel, however, and spends its own funds on imports to

Figure 5.1 Egyptian Military: Force Structure

	1990	2000	2005	2006
Manpower	704,000	704,000	890,000	947,500
Active	448,000	450,000	450,000	468,500
Army	320,000	320,000	320,000	340,000
Navy	18,000	~20,000	20,000	18,500
Air Force	30,000	30,000	30,000	30,000
Air Defense Command	80,000	80,000	80,000	80,000
Paramilitary	~74,000	230,000	~330,000	330,000
Reserve	604,000	254,000	410,000	479,000
Army	500,000	150,000	300,000	375,000
Navy	14,000	14,000	20,000	14,000
Air Force	20,000	20,000	20,000	20,000
Air Defense	70,000	70,000	70,000	70,000

Source: Various editions of the International Institute for Strategic Studies (IISS) *Military Balance* and U.S., British, and other experts.

sustain its aging and obsolete Soviet-bloc equipment, on relatively low-capability systems from China, and European arms whose quality is often imparted by support and interoperability problems.

Even so, Figures 5.3–5.6 show that Egypt's greatest military strength lies in its pool of advanced modern equipment. Egypt has benefited from some two decades of large amounts of U.S. grant aid and is the only Arab state bordering Israel that has been able to compete in arms imports during the 1990s. Egypt has had massive supplies of U.S. and other Western arms and had a substantial backlog of new orders. Egypt is extremely dependent on U.S. aid, and this dependence could present problems if U.S. aid declines in the future or if Egypt should ever back away from the peace process. Egypt would face an immediate cutoff of U.S. aid and resupply if it should come under extremist Islamist rule, and this would present major near-term problems in Egypt's effort to support U.S.–supplied systems as well as probably lead to an immediate internal economic crisis. This may explain why Figures 5.3–5.6 show that Egypt has retained large amounts of worn and obsolete Soviet-bloc equipment and small amounts of European systems that sometimes present more interoperability problems than they are worth.

Egypt has, however, tended to retain force strength at the expense of force quality, often limiting its ability to make effective use of its modern weapons. Its active forces are so large, and conscript dependent, that they have serious manpower quality, readiness, and sustainability problems. Egypt has maintained massive 479,000-man reserve forces (375,000 army, 20,000 air force, 70,000 air defenses, and 14,000 navy) that have been allowed to collapse into near decay since the 1973 war. Its reserves still have nominal assignments to fill in badly undermanned regular units, but most reservists received little or no training. Those reserves that do train usually do not receive meaningful training above the company to battalion level, with many training on obsolete equipment that is different from the equipment in the active units to which they are assigned.

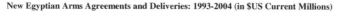

New Egyptian Arms Agreements and Deliveries: 1993-2004 (in $US Current Millions)

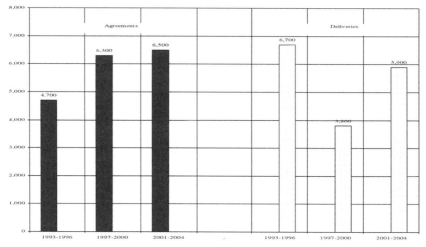

Egyptian Arms Orders by Supplier Country: 1997-2004 (Arms Agreements in $US Current Millions)

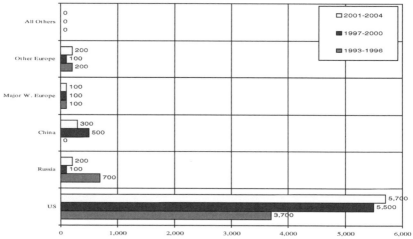

0 = less than $50 million or nil, and all data rounded to the nearest $100 million.
Source: Adapted by Anthony H. Cordesman, from Richard F. Grimmett, Conventional Arms Transfers to the Developing Nations, Congressional Research Service, various editions.

Figure 5.2   Recent Egyptian Arms Transfers

EGYPTIAN LAND FORCES

The Egyptian Army had a strength of 340,000 actives in early 2006, including between 190,000 and 220,000 conscripts, plus a reserve pool of up to 375,000 men. Egypt's command structure was organized into five military zones: the Central Zone (Cairo), the Eastern Zone (Ismailiya), the Western Zone (Meksa Matrun), the Southern Zone (Aswan), and the Northern Zone (Alexandria).[3]

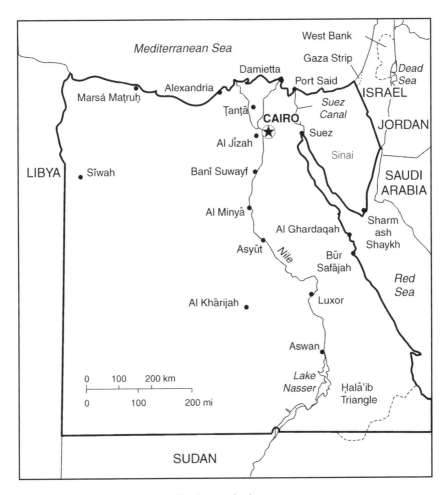

Map 5.1   Egypt   (Cartography by Bookcomp, Inc.)

Each military zone had a nominal strength of one armored division with one mechanized and two armored brigades, except for the Central Zone. The mechanized divisions were concentrated in the Eastern Zone, but some were in the other zones. Each mechanized division had one armored and two mechanized brigades. The Republican Guard was under the command of the Central Zone, but took its orders directly from the President. The air mobile and paratroop units also seemed to be under presidential command. The army's main bases were in Cairo, Alexandria, El Arish, Ismailiya, Luxor, Matruh, Port Said, Sharm el-Sheik, Taba, and Suez.

In spite of the fact that Egypt had strictly adhered to the terms of its peace with Israel since the Camp David Accords, the Eastern Zone and defense of Suez and the Sinai were still its major military priorities. Its two field armies (the 2nd Field Army and 3rd Field Army) were placed under the Eastern Zone Command. Egypt's forces, however, were not trained and organized for rapid maneuver or supply and sustainment into the Sinai. Their structure had become increasingly static with time, centered around their peacetime casernes. In effect, Egypt had adopted some of the defensive posture of a garrison army.

Force Structure and Major Deployments

The trends in Egypt's land forces are shown in Figure 5.3. Egypt's combat strength has continued to emphasize heavy forces, although it has built up a significant strength of airborne, Special Forces, and commando units. It has four armored divisions, each with a nominal organization of two armored, one mechanized, and one artillery brigade. It has eight mechanized infantry divisions, each with a nominal strength of one armored, one artillery, and two mechanized brigades. It also has one Republican Guard armored brigade, four independent armored brigades, one airmobile brigade, four independent mechanized brigades, two independent infantry brigades, one Special Forces group, and five to seven commando groups.

Its Special Forces units and elite units, and several of its armored and mechanized units, were well equipped and well trained. However, a substantial part of the Egyptian army's order of battle was composed of relatively low-grade and poorly equipped units, many of which would require substantial fill-in with reservists—almost all of which would require several months of training to be effective. Major combat support forces included 15 independent artillery brigades, one FROG surface-to-surface rocket brigade, and one Scud-B surface-to-surface missile brigade.

The recent trends in Egyptian combat unit strength reflect an increase in mechanized and elite commando units, although some of the changes shown are more the product of a lack of consistent reporting than actual force changes. Egypt has fully modern equipment for 30–40 percent of its land forces. However, roughly 30 percent of its equipment inventory is worn and obsolete or obsolescent Soviet-bloc equipment. This equipment has been partly reconditioned in recent years, but several decades of attempts to modernize fire control and computers, up-armor, up-gun, and improve drive trains have had limited effectiveness.

Main Battle Tanks and Other Armor

The equipment holdings of the Egyptian army are also shown in detail in Figure 5.3. Egypt had large holdings of modern land force equipment and Figure 5.3 shows that it continues to modernize. In 2006, the Army had 755 M-1A1 tanks, plus 300 M-60A1s and 1,200 M-60A3s. This was a total of 2,255 relatively modern tanks out of a total of 3,855, or 58.5 percent. These forces compare with 2,392 modern tanks for Israel, out of overall holdings of 3,657 tanks (65 percent). A decade and a half earlier, Egypt only had 785 M-60A3s out of a total of 2,425 tanks.

Egypt's first-line 755 M-1A1s compare with 1,681 Merkavas—less than half of the Israeli total. However, Egypt is scheduled to produce additional M-1A1s by June

Figure 5.3   Egyptian Army: Force Structure

	1990	2000	2005	2006
Manpower	704,000	704,000	890,000	947,500
Active	448,000	450,000	450,000	468,500
Reserve	500,000	150,000	300,000	375,000
Combat Units—Army	48	44	48	37
Republican Guard Armed Brigade	1	1	1	1
Armored Divisions	4	4	4	4
Mechanized Brigade	3	4	4	4
Mechanized Infantry Brigade	6	0	8	8
Air Mobility Brigade	2	1	1	1
Infantry Brigade	4	2	2	2
Special Forces Group	0	?	1	1
Commando Group HQ	?	?	?	1
Strength	?	?	?	300
Commando Group	7	6	5	5–7
Counterterrorist Unit	0	0	?	1
Heavy Mortar Brigade	2	0	0	0
Paramilitary Brigade	1	1	1	1
Artillery Brigade	14	15	15	15
Surface-to-Surface Missile Brigade	2	2	2	2
FROG-7 Brigade	1	1	1	1
Scud-B	1	1	1	1
MBT	2,425	3,855	3,755	3,855
M-1-A1	0	555	650	755
M-60	785	1,700	1,400	1,500
M-60A1	0	400	400	300
M-60A3	785	1,300	1,000	1,200
T-62	600	500	550	500 (in store)
T-54/-55	1,040	840	895	80 (in store)
Ramses II (modified T-54/55)	0	260	260	260
RECCE	300	312	412	412
BRDM	300	300	300	300
BRDM-2	300	300	300	300
Commando Scout	0	112	112	112
AIFV	470	770	690	520
BMP	470	460	470	220
BMP-1	220	220	220	220
BMP-600P	250	260	250	?
YPR-765	0	310	220	300
APC	~2,925	4,280	4,300	4,750
APC (T)	1,000	?	?	2,100
M-113	0	0	?	2,100
M-113A2 (inc. variants)	1,000	2,320	1,900	2,100

APC (W)	1,075	?	?	2,650
BMR-600P	0	0	?	250
BTR-50/OT-62 (most in store)	1,075	1,075	500	500
BTR-60	0	0	250	250
YPR-765	0	70	?	?
Fahad-30/TH 390	?	?	1,000	1,000
Fahd	200	165	1,000	1,000
Walid	650	650	650	650
Artillery	~1,120+	1,222	1,460	1,435
TOWED	1,120	971	971	946
120 mm	620	515	551	526
D-30	220	156	?	190
D-30M	0	0	156	190
M-1931/37	0	0	36	336
M-30	0	0	?	36
M-1938	400	359	359	300
122 mm	48	36	0	0
M-31/37	48	36	0	0
130 mm	440	420	420	420
M-46	440	420	420	420
152 mm	12	0	0	0
M-1937	12	0	0	0
SP	~140+	251	489	489
122 mm	Some	76	124	124
SP 122	?	76	124	124
D-30	Some	0	0	0
155 mm	140	175	365	365
M-109	0	0	365	365
M-109A2	140	175	196	164
M-109A2/A3 (surplus U.S. stock delivered Nov. 2005)	0	0	169	201
MRL	~300++	156+	~356+	498
80 mm	~300	0	0	0
VAP-80-12	~300	0	0	0
122 mm	Some	156	356	356
BM-11	?	96	96	96
BM-21	?	60	60	60
SAKR	?	?	200	200
Sakr-10	0	?	?	50
Sakr-18	?	?	?	50
Sakr-36	0	?	?	100
130 mm	Some	0	0	36
Kooryong	0	0	0	36
M-51/Praga V3S	Some	0	0	0

132 mm	Some	0	0	0
BM-13-16	Some	0	0	0
140 mm	Some	0	0	32
BM-14	Some	0	0	32
227 mm	0	0	Some	26
MLRS	0	0	Some	26
240 mm	Some	0	0	48
BM-24	Some	0	0	48 (in store)
MOR	~624	2,400	2,370	2,415
81 mm	0	0	0	50
M-125A2	0	0	0	50
82 mm	~50	540	540	500
SP	~50	?	~50	?
120 mm	450	1,800	1,800	1,835
M-43	450	0	0	0
M-38	0	1,800	0	0
M-106A2	0	0	0	35
M-1943	0	0	1,800	1,800
160 mm	100	60	30	30
M-43	100	0	0	0
M-160	0	60	30	30
240 mm	24	0	0	0
M-1953	24	0	0	0
ATGW	?	2,350	4,600	2,672
MSL	~3,340+	?	4,600	2,152
AT-1 Snapper	1,000	0	0	0
AT-2 Swatter	?	0	0	0
AT-3 Sagger (including BRDM-2)	1,400	1,400	1,200	1,200
Milan	220	220	200	200
Swingfire	200	200	?	?
TOW	520	530	3,200	752
M-901	52	52	50	52
YPR-765 SP	?	210	210	?
TOW-2	?	0	?	700
RCL 107 mm	Some	0	0	520
B-11	Some	?	0	520
UAV	0	?	Some	Some
R4E-50 Skyeye	0	?	Some	Some
AD	~1,200+	~3,220	~2,770+	~2,800+
SAM	~1,200+	?	2,096+	2,096+
SP	0	530	96	96
FIM-92A Avenger	0	0	50	50
M-54 Chaparral	Some	26	26	26
SA-9 Gaskin	Some	20	20	20

MANPAD	0	0	2,000+	2,000+
FIM-92A Stinger	0	0	?	Some
Ayn al-Saqr/SA-7 Grail	1,200	2,100	2,000	2,000
GUNS	~1,105+	1,074	~674+	705+
14.5-mm, TOWED, ZPU	Some	200	200	300
ZPU-4	Some	200	200	300
23 mm	615	434	434	365
SP	155	154	154	165
Sinai-23	45	36	36	45
ZSU-23-4	110	118	118	120
TOWED	460	280	280	200
ZU-23-2	460	280	280	200
37 mm	150	200	?	?
M-1939	150	200	?	?
57 mm	340	240	40+	40+
SP	40	40	40	40
ZSU-57-2	40	40	40	40
TOWED	300	200	Some	Some
S-60	300	200	Some	Some
RADAR, LAND	0	?	Some	Some
AN/TPQ-36 Firefinder	0	?	Some (new)	Some
AN/TPQ-37 Firefinder	0	?	Some	Some
MSL, TACTICAL	21	0	~21+	51+
SSM	12	0	12+	42+
FROG-7	12	0	12	9
Sakr-80	0	0	0	24
(trials)	0	0	Some	Some
SCUD	9	?	9	9
Scud-B	9	?	9	9

Notes: ~ = Estimated amount; * = combat ready; + = more than the number given but not specified how much more; Some = unspecified amount; ? = unspecified amount, if any

Source: Various editions of the IISS *Military Balance*, the *Jane's Sentinel* series, and Egyptian, U.S., British, and other experts.

2008.[4] Egypt had bought M88A2 Hercules heavy recovery vehicle kits from the United States.[5] The lack of Egyptian battlefield recovery and repair capability has been a major weakness in the past. Egypt has had to largely abandon damaged vehicles or breakdowns, while Israel has rapidly returned them into service.

The Egyptian army has, however, weakened its ability to use its tanks and other modern weapons effectively, however, by overextending its force structure. It tried to support far too large a land force structure at the cost of relying on low-quality conscripts, poor training for most of its forces, and increasingly underpaid officers and other ranks.

In spite of a decade of ongoing modernization, about 35–40 percent of Egypt's total inventory of major land combat weapons still consisted of obsolete and badly worn Soviet-bloc systems supplied in the late 1960s, and none of its Soviet-bloc inventory was supplied after 1974. For example, the rest of its tanks consisted of obsolete to obsolescent Soviet-bloc models, with some conversions and upgrades of dubious value. These included 1,155 T-54/T-55s most of which are in storage, only 260 of which had had any real upgrading into the Ramses version, and 550 T-62s, 500 of which are in store. The most Egypt could do to modernize the rest of these tanks was to obtain British aid in upgrading its ammunition.

Armored warfare training is best at the battalion and brigade levels, although some of Egypt's U.S.–equipped divisions train realistically and do well by regional standards. Unit training for units with Soviet-bloc equipment ranges from poor to moderate and is largely poor. Training in rapid armored maneuver and sustained operations is mixed and often of uncertain quality. Some units do well; others do not show the ability to carry out more than set-piece exercises.

Other Armored Forces

Egypt has lagged in modernizing its armored fighting vehicles and armored personnel carriers (APCs). It has over 400 armored reconnaissance vehicles, but they were largely obsolescent BRDM-2s, plus 112 more modern Commando Scout light-wheeled armored reconnaissance vehicles. It has over 500 armored infantry fighting vehicles (AIFVs), but 220 were worn BMP-1s, many in storage. The rest were reconditioned YPR-465 upgrades of the M-113. Its other holdings consisted of 250 Spanish lightly armored, wheeled BMR-600Ps.

There are different estimates of some of these holdings. The International Institute for Strategic Studies (IISS) estimates that only 300 YPR-765s of Egypt's holdings of 520 AIFVs were relatively advanced types, although *Jane's* reports that some 611 were delivered, including 304 with 25-mm cannons, 6 command post vehicles with 25-mm cannons, 210 PRAT-TOW vehicles with a twin TOW antitank guided missile launcher, 79 other command post vehicles with 12.7-mm machine guns, and 12 other communications and command post variants.

Egypt had 300 worn and aging BRDM-2s, and its 4,750 APCs included some 2,400 relatively low-quality systems: 650 Walids, 1,000 Fahds, 500 worn and aging BTR-50/OT-62s (most in storage), and 250 aging BRT-60s. Many of the Soviet-bloc systems had limited capability or were in storage. Egypt may upgrade around 350 BTR-50s with the help of Belarus.[6] They also, however, included some 2,100 variants of M-113A3. Some of Egypt's M-113s have been upgunned and may have add-on armor. The Egyptian Armed Forces are trying to procure 100 up-armored armament carrier 4×4 high-mobility multipurpose wheeled vehicles.[7]

Antitank Weapons

Egypt had 752 advanced U.S.–made TOW antitank guided weapons (including the TOW-2A that had a significant capability against reactive armor), 50 mounted on M-901 armored vehicles and 210 on YPR-765s. Egypt was seeking TOW-2B missiles.

Egypt also had 200 relatively effective Milan man-portable weapons. However, Egypt also had 1,200 aging, second-generation AT-3 Saggers and 200 Swingfires.

Training with its U.S.–supplied weapons is adequate, but live firings are limited and some exercises lack realism. Training in using the AT-3 and the Swingfire is limited and unrealistic.

Artillery

Egypt had significant artillery strength, with over 4,300 major artillery weapons and over 2,400 mortars. It had around 490 self-propelled weapons. These included 365 modern self-propelled M-109A2 155-mm howitzers, and 201 M-109A2/A3s delivered in 2005. They also included 124 122-mm self-propelled systems using a mix of Soviet-supplied and U.S.–supplied chassis.

Egypt had some 1,000 towed tube artillery weapons, including 551 Former Soviet Union (FSU)–supplied 122-mm and 420 FSU-supplied 130-mm weapons. Its roughly 356 multiple rocket launchers included 96 BM-l1 60 BM-21 and, 200 Saqr 10/18/36 122-mm weapons. It had some 26 227-mm MLRS weapons, and 2,850 rockets, entering service and in delivery.

Unlike some Arab states, Egypt has made a major effort to improve and modernize its artillery targeting and fire-control systems and had procured AN/TPQ-37 counterbattery radars, unmanned aerial vehicles (UAVs), and RASIT artillery support vehicles to support its artillery in maneuver warfare. The best Egyptian units are very good by regional standards, although more static and mass-fire oriented than comparable Western forces.

Other Egyptian artillery units are of very mixed quality. The rest of Egypt's self-propelled artillery consists of 76 aging FSU-supplied 122-mm self-propelled weapons, 971 towed weapons, and 156 operational multiple rocket launchers, only a limited number of which have been modernized.

Egypt has never fully trained and organized the forces using its older weapons into a modern war-fighting force, and most of its artillery forces still lack modern support vehicles, C^4I, battle management and fire control, and target acquisition and counterbattery radars and sensors. Many of its forces are not trained or equipped for effective beyond-visual-range (BVR) targeting, counterbattery fire, and rapid shifts of fire.

Air Defense Forces

Egypt has large numbers of short-range air defense weapons, which included over 1,000 antiaircraft guns. Most were obsolete weapons suitable only for suppressive fire, but as many as 230 are ZSU-23-4 radar-guided, self-propelled systems. These are vulnerable to electronic countermeasures, but still have considerable capability.

Egypt had over 2,000 man-portable surface-to-air missiles in 2006, largely Egyptian made or upgraded versions of the SA-7 but also including some Stingers. It had 20 SA-9s, 26 M-54 Chaparrals, and 50 Avengers. Live firings and realistic exercises were limited.

Readiness and Modernization

In spite of its obvious successes in many aspects of force modernization, the Egyptian Army is still heavily dependent on aging and obsolescent Soviet-supplied systems, many of which are inoperable or incapable of sustained combat. The Egyptian Army could probably be much more effective if it concentrated its manpower and training resources on a much smaller and better-equipped force. It could also use the resulting savings in military spending either to improve its readiness and sustainability or for economic development.

Egypt has honored its peace treaty and is currently postured largely as a defensive force. It has not taken the steps necessary to improve its ability to rapidly deploy and then sustain its heavy forces for war with Israel. In spite of ongoing improvements, it has emphasized modernizing its weapons holdings over support, logistic, and sustainment capabilities—although some Egyptian combat engineering units are reporting to be quite good. It has not modernized its infrastructure near the Suez Canal in ways that aid it in efficiently mobilizing and assembling a massive armored force that can rapidly thrust across the Sinai and then sustain itself in intense combat. It is much better postured to defend in depth than to attack in a massive war of offensive maneuver.

The Egyptian Army has also cooperated with Israel and the Palestinian Authority in strengthening a key aspect of the peace process. When Israel pulled out of the Gaza Strip in August 2005, the Egyptian Army took over the responsibility for the security of the Philadelphi Road, which runs along the border of the Gaza Strip and Egypt. U.S. Secretary of State Condoleezza Rice negotiated with Israel, Egypt, and the Palestinians to allow a border crossing at Rafah to be opened on the condition that EU observers would man the crossing and Egypt would secure it. This move to normalize life within the Gaza Strip has helped to strengthen relations between Israel, the Palestinians, and Egypt.

EGYPTIAN AIR FORCES

Egypt has long given high priority to modernizing its air force, a priority that is no surprise, given the fact that President Hosni Mubarak is an ex-commander of the air force. In the 1967 October War it was still a Soviet-style air force that relied more on mass, ground-controlled intercepts, and ground-based surface-to-air missiles than a modern concept of air operations. It has limited capability for joint operations and effective ground support and focused on maximizing initial aircraft numbers at the expense of sustainability and effective sorties generation capability.[8]

It has since developed the only air force in the Arab "ring states" with large numbers of modern fighters capable of advanced strike/attack missions and BVR/lookdown shoot-down air-to-air combat. It also is the only Arab force with adequate airborne warning and command and control assets and relatively modern electronic intelligence (ELINT), communications intelligence, electronic warfare (EW), and targeting/damage assessment aircraft and UAVs. Jordan can afford only a limited number of relatively low-performance versions of such "force enablers," Lebanon cannot afford any, and Syria risks becoming a museum for air warfare.

The evolving strength of the Egyptian Air Force (EAF) is shown in Figure 5.4 and shows a steady emphasis on acquiring modern U.S.–made systems. The EAF had 30,000 actives in early 2006, including 10,000 conscripts, and a reserve pool of 20,000 men. Egypt had 26 F-16As, 113 F-16Cs, and 15 Mirage 2000Cs in 2005. This was 154 advanced aircraft out of a total of 572 combat aircraft (27 percent). Egypt's holdings compared with 64 F-15A-Ds, 25 F-15Is, and 248 F-16A-Ds for Israel. Israel had a total of 337 advanced combat aircraft out of a total of 402, or 83 percent. Egypt's 139 first-line F-16s compared with 337 first-line Israeli F-15s and F-16s (41 percent).

Combat Air Strength

Egypt's total forces included 131 attack fighters, 334 fighter-attack aircraft, and 20 reconnaissance fighters. Its forces have 7 attack squadrons, equipped with 2/42 Alphajets, 2/44 obsolete PRC-made J-6s, 29 aging F-4Es, and 16 aging Mirage 5E2s. Its fighter-attack units included 2/26 F-16As, 7/113 F-16Cs, 1/15 Mirage 2000Cs, 2/53 aging Mirage 5D/Es, 6/74 obsolete MiG-21s, and 3/53 obsolescent J-7s. It had two reconnaissance squadrons, equipped with 6 aging Mirage 5SDRs and 14 obsolete MiG 21-Rs. It also had 12 F-16B, 6 F-16D, 3 Mirage 2000B, 15 MiG-21U, 6 JJ-6, and 35 L-59E armed aircraft in its training units.

Egypt had 110 armed helicopters. It had 36 AH-64 Apache attack helicopters and had 6/74 SA-342Ks (44 with HOT and 30 with 20-mm guns). It also had 5 SA-342L, 5 Sea King 47, and 10 SH-2G antisubmarine warfare helicopters, many serving with the Navy.

Force "Enablers" and Transport Aircraft

Egypt is one of the few Arab air forces with Airborne Early Warning aircraft and some modern electronic warfare, intelligence, and reconnaissance aircraft—including 4 E-2Cs, 2 C-130H ELINT, 1–4 Beech 1900 ELINT, and 4 Commando 2E ECM helicopters. It had 4 Beech 1900C surveillance aircraft.

Egypt makes growing use of UAVs, including 20 R-E-50 Skyeyes and 29 Teledyne-Ryan 324 Scarabs. The EAF absorbed the first of a planned six E-2C Hawkeye 2000 aircraft. The fleet will eventually replace Egypt's older E-2Cs.[9] Egypt has moderate performance in using these assets, but cannot match Israel in electronic warfare systems, advanced intelligence collection and emission analysis, and in air combat control and targeting/damage assessment capability.

The EAF had large transport assets. It had some 60 fixed-wing transport aircraft, including 22 C-130Hs. It had 127 transport helicopters, including 19 CH-47C/D heavy transports, 40 Mi-8s, 28 Commandos, and 2 S-70 medium helicopters

Figure 5.4   Egyptian Air Force: Force Structure

	1990	2000	2005	2006
Manpower	30,000	30,000	30,000+	50,000
Air Force	30,000	30,000	30,000	20,000
Conscript	10,000	10,000	10,000	10,000
Reservist	?	?	?	20,000
Total Combat Aircraft	589	712	692	572
Fighter (squad)	16/272	21/337	22/327	21/334
Mirage	70	71	68	68
5DE	54	53	53	53
M-2000C	16	18	15	15
F-16	67	139	139	139
F-16A Fighting Falcon	33	25	26	26
F-16C Fighting Falcon	34	114	113	113
MiG-21 Fishbed	83	74	67	74
J-7 (MiG-21) Fishbed C	52	53	53	53
FGA	10/170	7/133	7/131	7/131
F-4E Phantom II	33	28	29	29
J-6 (MiG-19S) Farmer	76	44	44	44
*Alpha Jet**	15	41	42	42
Mirage	16	20	16	16
MiG-17	30	0	0	0
ASW/Helicopter		24	20	20
*SH-2G Super Seasprite**		10	10	10
*Sea King MK47**		5	5	5
*SA-342L Gazelle**		9	5	5
Tactical, Helicopter, training	101	158	141	127
CH-47C Chinook	15	15	3	3
CH-47D Chinook (medium)	0	14	16	16
Commando (VIP)	24	25	25	28
S-70 Black Hawk (VIP, Light)	0	2	2	2
UH-60A Black Hawk	0	2	2	2
UH-60L Black Hawk	0	2	2	5
Mi-4	12	12	0	0
Mi-6 Hook	6	0	10	12
Mi-8 Hip	27	66	62	40
AS-61	0	3	2	2
UH-12E	17	17	17	17
RECCE	1/20	2/20	2/20	2/20
*MiG-21R Fishbed H**	14	14	14	14
Mirage 5SDR (Mirage 5R)*	6	6	6	6
MR	1	2	2	Some
Beech 1900C	1	2	2	4
Electronic Warfare	10	10	7	Some

Beech 1900 (ELINT)	4	4	1	1
C-130H Hercules (ELINT)	2	2	2	2
Commando 2E (ECM)	4	4	4	4
Airborne Early Warning	5	5	4	4
E-2C	5	5	4	4
Transportation	30	32	41	41
B-707-366C	0	0	3	3
B-737-100	0	0	1	1
Beech 200 Super King Air	0	1	1	1
C-130H Hercules	19	19	22	22
DHC-5D Buffalo	5	5	5	5
Falcon 20	0	3	3	3
Gulfstream III	0	3	3	3
Gulfstream IV	0	1	3	3
An-12	5	0	0	0
C-123B	1	0	0	0
Attack Helicopters	4/72	4/105	6/101	6/110
AH-64A Apache	0	69	36	36
SA-342K Gazelle (,)	72	69	69	74
With HOT	42	44	44	44
With 20 mm	30	25	25	30
Training	176	275	404	411
F-16B Fighting Falcon*	7	10	12	12
F-16D Fighting Falcon*	6	29	6	6
FT-6	0	0	6	0
DHC-5 Buffalo	4	4	4	4
Alpha Jet	29	0	70	70
EMB-312 Tucano	40	54	34	34
Gomhouria	36	36	39	36
Grob 115EG	0	0	74	74
K-8 (being delivered to replace L-29)	0	0	80	80
L-29 Delphin	20	40	?	26
L-39 Albatros	0	48	10	10
L-59E Albatros*	0	30	35	35
M-2000B Mirage*	3	3	3	3
Mirage 5SDD	5	5	0	0
JJ-6 (MiG-19UTI) Farmer	16	16	16*	6
PZL-104	10	0	0	0
MiG-21U Mongol A*	0	Some	15	15
UAV	0	29	49	Some
R4E-50 Skyeye	0	0	20	20
Teledyne-Ryan 324 Scarab	0	29	29	29
MSL, Tactical	?	?	Some	500+
ASM	0	0	?	245+

AGM-119 Penguin	0	0	?	Some
AGM-65	0	Some	?	245
AGM-65A Maverick	0	0	0	80
AGM-65D Maverick	Some	0	0	123
AGM-65F Maverick	0	0	0	12
AGM-65G Maverick	0	0	0	30
AGM-84 Harpoon	0	0	Some	Some
AM-39 Exocet	0	Some	Some	Some
ARM, Armat	0	Some	Some	Some
AS-1 Kennel	Some	0	0	0
AS-5 Kelt	Some	0	0	0
AS-12 Kegler	0	Some	Some	Some
AS-30	Some	Some	Some	Some
AS-30L	Some	Some	Some	Some
AAM, AA-2 Atoll	Some	Some	Some	Some
AIM-7	Some	Some	Some	Some
AIM-7E Sparrow	0	Some	Some	Some
AIM-7F Sparrow	Some	Some	Some	Some
AIM-7M Sparrow	0	Some	Some	Some
AIM-9	Some	Some	Some	Some
AIM-9F Sidewinder	0	Some	Some	Some
AIM-9L Sidewinder	Some	Some	Some	Some
AIM-9P Sidewinder	Some	Some	Some	Some
R-550 Magic	Some	Some	Some	Some
R530	Some	Some	Some	Some

Source: Various editions of the IISS *Military Balance,* U.S., British, and other experts.

coupled with 12 Mi-6, 17 UH-12E, 2 UH-60A, 5 UH-60L, and 2 AS-61 light helicopters. The readiness and operational status of its older helicopters was, however, uncertain.

Ongoing Force Improvements

Egypt has significant force improvements under way. It is currently scheduled to receive a total of 220 F-16C/Ds and to upgrade its AH-64s to Longbow. Egypt already has large numbers of modern U.S. air-to-surface, antiradiation, and air-to-air precision-guided weapons. It is taking delivery on the advanced medium-range air-to-air missile and had the technology to make fuel-air-explosive weapons, although it is not clear it has done so. Egypt is seeking an additional 414 AIM-9M-1/2 Sidewinder missiles and 459 Hellfire II missiles.[10]

The Egyptian Air Force also plans to upgrade 35 of the AH-64As with the Modular Mission Support System that will enable Egypt to integrate the attack operations of its modern fixed-wing jets with that of its rotary-wing Apaches.[11] The air force will be equipping several of its F-16s with reconnaissance pods as part of its ongoing Theater Airborne Reconnaissance Systems program. To be completed by 2007, the program will include the construction of two ground stations as well as extensive training and repair programs.[12]

Readiness and Mission Capabilities

The Egyptian Air Force is still developing modern joint warfare capabilities and needs to improve both its training and command-and-control systems, but can already do a far better job of supporting its land and naval forces than most Arab air forces. Some Egyptian squadrons have excellent readiness and proficiency. However, the Egyptian Air Force sets higher training and readiness standards for its more modern aircraft than for the rest of its forces and does still tend to emphasize modern combat aircraft numbers over sustained and sortie generation capability.

More generally, the Egyptian Air Force cannot compete with the Israeli Air Force in overall battle management, the exploitation of modern sensors and targeting systems, electronic warfare, beyond-visual-range warfare, and in using precision strike and attack munitions. It also focuses more on numbers than sustainability and had limited ability to sustain high sortie rates. Air combat and joint warfare training still need improvement, as does the ability to manage large numbers of aircraft in air combat and attack missions. The air force badly needs to speed up its decision-making cycle.

The EAF has slowly phased out its older aircraft, but still has nearly 190 obsolete aircraft (33 percent). It wastes significant resources on ineffective systems like its J-6s, J-7s, and MiG-21s. The EAF has not done well in keeping its Mirage 5s at a high degree of combat readiness. Egypt still has aging Alpha Jets and well-worn F-4Es. The operational readiness of many of its 74 SA-342K armed helicopters is limited.

EGYPTIAN LAND-BASED AIR DEFENSES

Egypt learned the value of land-based air defenses the hard way. It lost a large portion of its air force in 1967 because it lacked both combat air patrol and long-range sensors, and land-based defenses that could defend its airspace against surprise or preemptive attack. It steadily improved and expanded its land-based air defenses as a result of the Canal War of 1970, however, and made them a key part of its strategy in defending the forces that attacked across the Suez Canal in 1973. As a result, Egypt developed one of the largest and most effective air defense forces in the Middle East.[13]

This Russian-supplied force became steadily more obsolescent after Egypt broke with Russia in 1974. Egypt has been able to get some upgrades and modernization, as well as additional missiles and spare parts, from the FSU and Eastern Europe, but has not fully upgraded its Russian-supplied systems. Most Russian-supplied surface-to-air missiles and radar sensors are now obsolete when faced by a modern air force with advanced electronic warfare and jamming capability and antiradiation missiles (ARMs).

The Egyptian Air Defense Force does, however, have a significant number of Improved Hawks (IHawks). Israel probably has substantial electronic warfare capability to defeat such systems and to attack them with Unmanned Combat Aerial Vehicle and ARMs, but the IHawk is more survivable than Soviet-supplied systems. Egypt is also buying modern Patriot missiles and improved U.S. radars and command-and-control systems.

Egyptian Force Structure

Egypt has a separate Air Defense Command with nearly 80,000 personnel. In 2006, its forces were organized into four divisions with regional brigades and a countrywide total of 100 air defense battalions. As Figure 5.5 shows, Egypt now has large holdings of U.S.–supplied systems, but relies largely on older Soviet-bloc systems.

These forces include large numbers of worn obsolete Soviet-bloc systems that had only limited upgrading. These assets included 40 SA-2 battalions with 282 launchers, 53 SA-3 battalions with more than 212 launchers, and 14 SA-6 battalions with more than 56 launchers. Egyptian SA-2 and SA-3 forces had particularly low readiness and operational sustainability and only a limited capability to resist modern jamming and other air defense suppression techniques. The SA-6 units were marginally better and more mobile, but all three types of surface-to-air missiles were vulnerable to modern antiradiation missiles.

Egypt also had substantial holdings of more modern and more effective Western-supplied systems. They include 12 batteries of Improved Hawks with 78 launchers. Egypt is also developing an integrated command-and-control system, with U.S. assistance, as part of Program 776. This system is not highly advanced by U.S. standards, but it will allow Egypt to (a) integrate airborne and land-based air defenses into a common air defense system, (b) create a single command, control, communication, computers, intelligence/battle management (C^4I/BM) network, and (c) manage a defense against air attacks that bring a moderate number of sorties together at the same time and near the same area.

Modernization and Upgrades

Egypt had long been trying to upgrade its older air defense systems and will improve its surface-to-air missile capabilities in the near future. Egypt first considered trying to update some of its systems with modern Russian-made S-300 or S-400 surface-to-air missiles. In 1997, Egypt was reported to have submitted a proposal to Russia whereby it would purchase the S-300 in a package containing 224 missiles and nearly 100 mobile launchers and radar systems at a cost of at least $700 per missile. The S-300 is not only an effective surface-to-air missile, but also a competent antitactical ballistic missile system and defense against cruise missiles. Egypt lacked the funds to complete this contract, however, and could not use U.S. aid funds for such a purpose. It limited its purchase from Russia to a $125-million

Figure 5.5 Egyptian Air Defense Command: Force Structure

	1990	2000	2005	2006
Manpower	80,000	80,000	80,000+	150,000
Air Defense Command	80,000	80,000	80,000	30,000
Conscript	50,000	50,000	50,000	50,000
Reserve	?	?	?	70,000
AD Systems	~18+	~18+	~72+	108+
Amount each with RIM-7F Sea Sparrow SAM	18	18	72+	72+
Quad SAM, Skyguard towed SAM	0	0	0	36+
Sinai-23 short range (Dassault 6SD-20S radar)	Some	Some	Some	0
SAM	858+	~452	~900	702+
SA-3	240	212	50	212+
Pechora (SA-3A) Goa/SA-3 Goa SAM	0	212	50	212+
SP	0	92	130	130+
Crotale	~50	36	24	24+
M-48 Chaparral	0	0	50	50+
SA-6 Gainful	6	56	56	56+
TOWED	0	?	~360	360+
SA-9	Some	0	0	0
MIM-23	0	?	78	78+
I-HAWK MIM-23B	108	78	78	78+
SA-2 Guideline	~400	282	282	282+
Skyguard	0	0	?	Some
GUNS	~2,500	~2,000	~2,000	1,566+
20 mm	Some	?	?	0
23 mm	Some	?	266	266+
Sinai-23 (SPAAG) each with Ayn al Saqr MANPAD SAM	?	?	36	36+
Dassault 6SD-20S	?	?	0	?
ZSU-23-4	?	?	230	230
57 mm, TOWED	Some	?	600	600
S-60	?	?	600	600
85 mm, TOWED	Some	?	400	400
M01939 KS-12	?	?	400	400
100 mm, TOWED	Some	?	300	300
KS-19	?	?	300	300

Source: Various editions of the IISS *Military Balance,* U.S., British, and other experts.

contract to upgrade 50 of Egypt's SA-3a missile launchers and their associated units by 2003.

As a result, Egypt turned to the United States. In March 1999, the United States agreed to sell Egypt $3.2-billion worth of new American weapons, including 24 F-16C/D Block 40 fighter jets, 200 M-1A1 tanks. and 32 Patriot missiles. The sale gave Egypt its first battery of Patriot-3 missiles at a cost of $1.3 billion. The battery consisted of eight firing units, each containing four missiles. At the same time, the United States announced that it would provide Egypt with the same warning data on the launch of any hostile ballistic missile that it provided to Israel. Egypt will almost certainly acquire several more batteries over time, acquiring far better air, cruise, and tactical ballistic missile defenses than it had.

Egypt is also upgrading its AN/TPS50(V)2 air defense radars to the (V)3 standard. This will provide new software and hardware, including new signal processing centers. It will also give Egypt considerably more ballistic missile attack warning and tracking capability, and advanced long-range, three-dimensional air-surveillance capabilities. The radars are linked to 12 operations centers in Egypt, which will be able to pass intercept data to both airborne and ground-based air defenses and anti-ballistic missile warning data to Egypt's IHawks and Patriots.

Short-Range Air Defenses

The Egyptian ground forces have large numbers of antiaircraft (AA) weapons. The army's surface-to-air missile assets include some 2,000 obsolete SA-7s and slightly better performing Egyptian-made variants of the SA-7 called the Ayn-as-Saqr. The army also had 12 batteries of short-range Chaparrals with 26 M-54 self-propelled Chaparral fire units, 14 batteries of short-range Crotales with more than 24 launchers, and additional SA-9 fire units.

The Egyptian Army's holdings of air defense guns included 300 4.5-mm ZPU-4, 120 23-mm ZU-23-2-4, an estimated 200 37-mm M-1939, and an estimated 200 57-mm S-60 towed-unguided guns. They also include 118 ZSU-23-4 and 36 Sinai radar-guided self-propelled guns. The SA-9s, Chaparrals, ZSU-23-4s, and Sinais provided the Egyptian Army with maneuverable air defenses that can accompany Egyptian armored forces.

In addition, Egypt's Air Defense Command had some 2,000 Soviet-bloc-supplied unguided-towed AA guns ranging from 20 to 100 mm, and a number of light air defense systems. These include more than 72 Amoun (Skyguard/RIM-7F Sparrow) systems with 36 twin guns and 36 quad launchers, a number of ZSU-23-4s, and Sinai-23 systems that are composed of Dassault 6SD-20S radars, 23-mm guns, and short-range Ayn-as-Saqr missiles. These weapons provide low-altitude defense of military installations and critical facilities and can often be surprisingly effective in degrading attack sorties or destroying attack aircraft that attempt to fly through a "curtain" of massed antiaircraft fire.

Readiness and Mission Capability

Egypt's mix of surface-to-air missiles is still effective against its Arab and African neighbors, but has serious limitations in dealing with an attack by the Israel Air Force (IAF). Israel would have to use a much larger and more sophisticated mode of attack than it used against Syria in 1982, but Egypt's land-based air defenses are vulnerable to Israeli suppression and countermeasures.

Readiness is a problem. Egypt's land-based air defense force became an elite force during the buildup to the Canal War in 1970 and was a key component of Egyptian operations in the 1967 October War. It did serious damage to the IAF until Egyptian land forces moved outside the cover of layered Egyptian air defenses and Egypt's forward-deployed units could be attacked by Israeli land forces advanced across the Suez. Its status and readiness has slowly declined, however, and training and operational capabilities are mixed. Significant numbers of units with Soviet-bloc equipment have limited capability.

Egypt cannot rapidly project large mobile land-based surface-to-air missile forces into the Sinai and would then have to operate individual fire units outside the full sensor and C^4I/BM capabilities of its current central air defense command-and-control system. It would have to support its advancing land forces with individual surface-to-air missile units that would become progressively more vulnerable to the IAF as they moved across the Sinai. Unless Egypt had months in which to build up its forces near Israel's border, they would become progressively more vulnerable to air attack in terms of both Israel's ability to rapidly suppress Egyptian air defenses and target and attack Egyptian land units.

EGYPTIAN NAVAL FORCES

Egypt has played a significant naval role in the Red Sea and in guarding the approaches to Egyptian ports and the Suez Canal, In 2006, Egypt had a 20,000-man navy, including a 2,000-man coast guard. More than half of this force (12,000 men), however, consisted of conscripts with limited experience and training. Its headquarters was in Alexandria, and its forces were based primarily at Port Said, Mersa Matruh, Safaqa, Port Tewfiq, and Hurghada.[14]

The Egyptian Navy has had a lower force modernization priority than the other services and has tended to emphasize force quantity over force quality, trying to retain its strength levels even at the cost of obsolescence and limited readiness. As a result, Egypt's naval forces are numerically much larger than those of Israel—4 submarines and 11 principal surface combatants vs. 3 submarines and 12 principal surface combatants for Israel.[15]

While Figure 5.6 shows that the Egyptian Navy continues to maintain impressive combat strength by regional standards, some of this strength has been maintained at the cost of holding on to aging and low-capability ships and limited overall effectiveness. The Egyptian Navy is, however, improving as it continues to modernize.[16]

Submarine Forces

Egypt's submarine forces have successfully attacked Israeli surface forces in past wars and have been an effective way of dealing with Israel's air supremacy. Submarine forces are, however, very difficult to maintain and require extensive technical support

Figure 5.6   Egyptian Navy: Force Structure

	1990	2000	2005	2006
Manpower	18,000	~20,000	20,000	32,500
Navy	18,000	~12,000	20,000	~8,500
Coast Guard	?	~2,000	~2,000	2,000
Conscript	10,000	~10,000	~12,000	10,000
Reservists	?	?	?	14,000
Fleet HQ—Mediterranean and Red Sea	2	?	2	2
Naval Organization	?	?	?	5
Submarine Brigade	?	?	1	1
Destroyer Brigade	?	?	1	1
Patrol Brigade	?	?	?	1
Fast Attack Brigade	?	?	?	1
Special Ops Brigade	?	?	?	1
HQ	2	2	2	2
Alexandria	1	1	1	1
Port Tewfig, Red Sea, Hurghada	1	1	1	0
Safaqa	0	0	0	1
Submarines, Tactical	10	4	4	4
SSK	10	4	4	0
Romeo (USSR, 4Ch Type-033 with 533-mm TT)	10	0	0	0
Romeo (PRC, sub-Harpoon and 533-mm TT)	0	4	4	4
Romeo (Each with 1+ single 533-mm TT with UGM-84C Harpoon tactical USGW)	0	0	0	4
Principal Surface Combatants	6	11	11	11
Destroyer	1	1	1	1
DD	0	3	1	1
El Fateh training (UK "Z")	1	1	1	1
Frigates	5	10	10	10
Abu Qir (each with 2 triple ASTT, Sting Ray LWT, 2 Mk 141 Harpoons quad, 1 RGM-84C Harpoon tactical SSM, 1 2 tube Bofors 375 mm, 1 76-mm gun)	0	0	0	2
El Suez (2×3 ASTT, 1×2 ASW RL, plus 2×4 Harpoon SSM)	2	2	2	0
Damyet (each with 1 Mk 16 Mk 112 octuple with 8 RGM-84C Harpoon tactical SSM, tactical ASROC, 2 twin 324-mm TT, 1 127-mm gun)	0	2	2	2
Mubarak (each with 1 Mk 13 GMLS with 36 SM-1 MR SAM, 4 RGM-84 Harpoon tactical SSM, 1 76-mm gun)	0	3	4	4
Najim al-Zaffir (each with 2 twin each with 1 HY-2 Silkworm tactical SSM, 2 RBU 1200)	2	2	2	2
Tariq (UK Black Swan, with 6 102-mm gun)	1	1	0	0

Patrol and Coastal Combatants	43	39	44	48
PFC	18	15	19	18
Hainan (PRC, each with 2 triple 324-mm TT, 4×1 RL)	8	4	6	4
Hainan in reserve (PRC, each with 2 triple 324-mm TT, 4×1 RL)	0	4	0	4
Shanghai II (PRC)	4	5	4	4
Shershen (each with 1+SA-N-5 Grail SAM, 1 12 tube BM-24 MRL)	6	0	0	4
Shershen (FSU, each with 4 single 533-mm TT, 1 8 tube BM-21 MRL)	0	6	6	2
Polnochny LSM	0	0	3	0
PFM	25	24	25	30
5 October (each with 1 Ootomat tactical SSM)	0	0	0	6
6 October (each with 2 Ootomat SSM)	6	4	6	0
Hegu (Komar type, PRC, each with 2 single, each with 1 SY-1 tactical SSM)	6	6	6	6
Komar (FSU, each with 2 single, each with 1 SY-1 tactical SSM)	0	4	3	3
Osa I (FSU, each with 4 single, each with 1 SS-N-2A Styx tactical SSM) (one may not be operational)	7	5	4	4
Ramadan (each with 4 single, each with 1 Ootomat tactical SSM)	6	5	6	6
Tiger	0	0	0	5
Mine warfare, mine countermeasures	9	14	12	15
SRN-6 hovercraft	3	N/A	N/A	N/A
MSI El Fayoun (Soviet T-301)	2	N/A	N/A	N/A
MSC Aswan (FSU Yurka)	4	5	4	4
MSO Assiout (FSU T-43 class)	0	6	6	6
MHC Dat Assawari	0	0	0	3
MHI Safaga Swiftships	0	3	2	2
Amphibious	3	3	3	12
LS, LSM	3	3	3	3
Polnochny B (FSU, capacity 180 troops, 6 MBT)	0	0	0	3
Polnochny LSM (capacity 100 troops, 5 tanks)	3	3	3	0
Craft, LCU	0	9	9	9
Vydra (capacity either 100 troops or 3 AMX-30 MBT)	0	9	9	9
Logistics and Support	7	20	20	20
AOT (Small)	0	7	7	7
AT	0	6	6	6
Tugs	4	0	0	0
Spt (diving)	1	1	1	6
Training	2	5	5	5

Tariq	?	1	1	1
Coastal Defense—Army troops, Navy control	~30+	?	?	Some
MSL, tactical	30	Some	?	Some
SSM	30	Some	?	Some
SSC-2b Samlet	?	0	?	Some
Ootomat	?	Some		
LNCHR	0	0	?	3
3 twin each with 1 Mk 2 Ootomat SSM	0	0	?	3
Gun	?	Some	Some	Some
100 mm	0	0	Some	Some
130 mm SM-4-1	?	Some	Some	Some
152 mm	0	0	Some	Some
Naval Aviation	17	24	31	31
Aircraft, TPT, Beech 1900	0	0	2	2
Beech 1900C	0	0	2	2
Helicopters (armed operated by the Air Force)	17	24	24	27
ATK	12	9	12	12
SA-342 Gazelle	12	9	12	12
ASW	5	15	15	15
SH-2G Super Seasprite (each with Mk 46 LWT)	0	10	10	10
Sea King MK47	5	5	5	5
UAV	0	0	2	2
Camcopter 5.1	0	0	2	2

Source: Various editions of the IISS *Military Balance,* U.S., British, and other experts.

and high readiness standards. The Egyptian Navy has serious problems in meeting these criteria.

Egypt's current major combat ships include four ex-Chinese, Romeo-class Type 033 submarines. These are badly aging designs, but they were modernized in the mid-1990s to use Western periscopes, trailing global positioning systems, passive sonars, and fire-control systems and fire modern wire-guided torpedoes and Harpoon missiles (130-kilometer maximum range). They have since been further updated with more modern periscopes and other modifications. One of the submarines (849) has not, however, been operational since its modernization. All are based at Alexandria. The navy stores its decommissioned Russian submarines there as well, but none are believed to be combat capable.

Egypt has examined buying two former Royal Dutch-Navy Zwaardvis-class submarines, which could be specially refitted for Egypt. Egypt hoped at one point to use its U.S. Foreign Military Financing grants to purchase these subs and to buy two new-build RDM-designed Moray 1400 submarines or German Type-209s. These deliveries would significantly increase the capabilities of the Egyptian Navy, but there was little evidence that the United States will agree to the use of funds for foreign ships and the RDM-designed ships are not yet under contract.

Egypt also has some small, two-man Italian-made submarines for underwater Special Operations missions.

Major Surface Forces

Egypt's surface fleet is a mix of aging and more modern ships. It has two low- to medium-quality 1,425-ton Jianghu 1-class Chinese frigates dating back to the early 1980s, which have never been upgraded and refitted as the Egyptian Navy once planned. Each is equipped with four HY-2 antiship missiles (with a maximum range of 80 kilometers) and four 57-mm guns. These ships are both active in the Red Sea. Plans to modernize these ships with better battle management and other electronics, and with helicopters, have not been funded. However, no other regional navy in the Red Sea area, except Saudi Arabia, deploys more modern major combat vessels and the Saudi Red Sea fleet has low training and activity levels.

Egypt has two 3,011-ton Damyat (ex–U.S. FF-1051 Knox)-class guided missile frigates. While they date back to the 1970s, they were recommissioned in 1995. Each had eight Harpoon missiles, antisubmarine rocket (ASROC) launchers, Phalanx close-in air/missile defenses, and a 127-mm gun. They had two twin torpedo tubes, relatively modern combat data systems, electronic countermeasures, search and surface radars, and fire-control systems. Each can carry one Kaman Seasprite SH-2G helicopter, and their electronic warfare suites have had further updating. However, they have had persistent boiler problems and limited operational capability. Their ASROC system is dated, and they lack long-range air defenses.

Egypt has two more capable El Suez (Spanish Descubierta-class) frigates. These ships date back to the early 1970s, but each was modernized in the early 1980s and mid-1990s. These are 1,479-ton ships equipped with eight Harpoon antiship missiles (maximum range 70 nautical miles, 130 kilometers) in two quadruple launchers, an octuple Albatros antiair missile launcher, a 76-mm gun, two triple torpedo tubes, and antisubmarine mortars. Their combat data systems, air search, and fire-control radars were updated in 1995–1996. They can be modified to carry up to eight Otomats. Both ships continued to be well maintained and modernized and are operational.

In 1996, the Egyptian Navy began to acquire four Oliver Hazard Perry–class frigates in a $600-million deal with the United States. These frigates are 2,750-ton vessels that were originally commissioned in the early 1980s. They have been put in service as the Mubarak class and are armed with four Harpoon antiship missiles, 76-mm guns, Standard SM-1 surface-to-air missiles, Vulcan, and six torpedo tubes with Mk 46 antisubmarine torpedoes. All of these ships have been upgraded and had relatively modern radars, sonars, fire control, combat data management, and electronic warfare capability. Each could carry two Kaman Seasprite SH-2G helicopters. All have been operational since 1999, and one operates regularly in the Red Sea area.

The Egyptian Navy still has an obsolete British frigate of the Black Swan class dating back to 1949. It is evidently in restricted training status. If it is operational, it can be used only as a support ship or tender.

The navy received an additional four Phalanx systems in 2005.[17] It also received an additional 62 Harpoon missiles.[18]

Missiles and Other Patrol Craft

The Egyptian Navy has some 30 missile patrol craft, 12 of which are relatively capable ships armed with the Harpoon and Ootomat antiship missiles. The more capable ships include six British-made 307-ton Ramadan-class ships, each with 76-mm guns and four Ootomat I antiship missiles. These date back to the 1980s and lack air defense. They had their EW and combat data systems updates in the 1990s and again in the early 2000s. They have not been modified to have modern eight missile launcher fire units.

There seemed to be five operational 82-ton October-class craft with one Ootomat I missile and 30-mm guns. (One may be sidelined.) They have aging hulls similar to the Russian Komar class, but were refitted in Britain in the early 1980s. These are small vessels with limited capability.

Egypt had six 68-ton Hegu-class (the Chinese version of the FSU Komar-class) vessels with SY-1 missiles dating back to the late 1970s/early 1980s. They were refitted with improved electronic support measures in 1996. Two seem to be sidelined on what may be a permanent basis.

Egypt still has four obsolete Osa I-class vessels with four SS-N-2A Styx missiles and had three Komar-class vessels with SS-N-2A missiles in reserve. Two of the Osa-class vessels had been taken out of service, but four Osa-class boats were still operational.

Israel is believed to have significant countermeasure capabilities against the missiles and electronics on these vessels and superior sensors and antiship missiles. Israel also has probable air supremacy and significant air-to-ship attack capabilities.

Egypt has 16 other operational patrol ships (4 Shanghai class, 6 Shershen class, and 8 Hainan class, with 4 of the 8 Hainan in reserve). Some are armed with 122-mm multiple rocket launchers, torpedoes, or 57-mm guns. They could also be used to lay mines. These had some value in the patrol mission and the fire-support mission in secure waters.

Mine Warfare Capability

Egypt had 15 operational mine vessels, including 3 relatively modern Swiftship coastal mine hunters and 2 Swiftship route survey vessels. The minehunters have had problems with their minehunting equipment and their effectiveness is uncertain. The rest of its mine vessels could lay mines, but its 4 ex-Soviet Yurka and 6 T-43-class mine vessels are obsolete, had little modern mine detection and mine sweeping capability, and uncertain operational status. Plans to modernize their capabilities had never been implemented.

In the past, the Egyptian Navy has faced a mine threat in the Red Sea. A Libyan ship was used to scatter mines, and as was the case in the Iran-Iraq and Gulf Wars, this threat can inhibit commercial traffic through an area like the Red Sea. Egypt could probably deal with low-level covert and scattered terrorist mining, but would have serious problems in dealing with a serious mine warfare threat in the Red Sea.

Amphibious Forces

The Egyptian Navy had three Polnochny-class amphibious vessels (180 troops and 6 tanks capacity each) and nine Vydra-class landing ships (100 troops or 3 tanks capacity each). It had some 20 support ships, including diving and support ships. All were in active service. It had eight specialized Seafox ships for deliveries of underwater demolition teams. Two do not seem to be operational.

Egypt could also draw on significant numbers of ferries to move forces toward the Gulf or reinforce Jordan.

Coastal Defense Forces

The army operates three land-based, truck-mounted batteries of Ootomat antiship missiles with Plessey targeting radars, and two brigades of 100-mm, 130-mm, and 152-mm SM-4-1 coastal defense guns. These defenses are located near major ports and the approaches to the Suez Canal and are under Egyptian Navy command.

Such forces have become something of an anachronism in an era of long-range antiship and air-to-ground missiles, but might be useful against some forms of terrorist attack.

Naval Aviation

The EAF had four operational E-2C Hawkeyes in 2006, with search and warning radars and electronic support and countermeasures that it could use to support naval as well as air-land operations. It also had four (some sources indicate two) Beech 1900C surveillance aircraft with surveillance and multimode radars and electronic support measures that it could use in the maritime patrol role. The Egyptian Air Force is equipping a limited number of F-16s to carry Harpoon antiship missiles.

Egypt has acquired 15 antisubmarine warfare helicopters. It had 10 SH-2(G)E Seasprite helicopters equipped for antisubmarine warfare, which carried dipping sonars and two torpedoes or depth charges. These Seasprites were designed to be ship based and had search radars, electronic support measures, and EW suites.

The EAF had nine operational SA-342L helicopters (out of a total of 11) armed with AS-12 air-to-surface/ship guided missiles, and five Westland Mark 47 Sea Kings equipped for both the antiship and antisubmarine warfare roles.

Readiness and Mission Capability

The Egyptian Navy is improving, but has not yet received the funding necessary to fully modernize its ships or to carry out the levels of advanced joint warfare training it needs. It had difficulties in maintaining ships from so many different countries, and many of its ships and boats are worn and obsolete and have little operational effectiveness. At the same time, it has many capable vessels and does not face a meaningful peer threat except from Israeli forces in the Mediterranean. It has a good capability to defend Egypt's coast, the approaches to the Suez Canal, and Egypt's interests in the Red Sea.

Egypt could not defeat Israel at sea, particularly given Israel's probable air supremacy. It may have the capability to pose a limited to moderate threat to Israel, but it would face major problems. It does not have the training, electronic warfare, or navy-air force joint operations capabilities to challenge Israel's best Sa'ar-class vessels in joint operations, except in Egyptian waters, where Egyptian ships might have air cover and protection from its submarines. Most importantly, Egypt's navy would not have the air cover and air defense capability necessary to protect itself from the Israeli Air Force.

The Egyptian Navy is, however, the dominant regional naval power in the Red Sea. It had moderate capabilities to defend the approaches to the Suez Canal. Egypt can play an important role in dealing with the less sophisticated naval and air forces of potentially hostile Red Sea countries and in securing the Egyptian coastline and approaches to the Suez Canal. The better-crewed and funded Egyptian ships have drawn considerable praise from their U.S. counterparts during joint exercises.

EGYPTIAN PARAMILITARY, SECURITY, AND INTELLIGENCE FORCES

Egypt has faced serious internal threats from a range of violent Islamist extremist groups. It has also long enforced tight state control over internal security and all political activity. Figure 5.7 shows that Egypt has extensive paramilitary and security forces, but it does not include substantial additional intelligence and secret police units.[19]

Egypt has developed a wide range of paramilitary forces, including the National Guards, Central Security Force, Border Guards, Internal Security Forces, General Intelligence Service, and Department for Combating Religious Activity. The National Guard, Central Security Force, and Border Guards are all under the command of the Ministry of Interior. Egyptian military intelligence had a separate, and large, internal security force to preserve the loyalty of the armed forces.

Key Egyptian Security, Intelligence, and Paramilitary Forces

The Ministry of Interior is responsible for most internal security, counterterrorism, and paramilitary activity and is formally responsible for some intelligence activity, although much is not formally part of the Egyptian government and reports directly to the President and the Minister of Defense.

The National Guard is under the Ministry of the Interior and has some 60,000 personnel. It plays a role in counterterrorism, but is not a particularly

Figure 5.7   Egyptian Paramilitary and Security Forces: Force Structure

	1990	2000	2005	2006
Manpower		230,000	~330,000	~330,000
Active	?	230,000	~330,000	~330,000
Central Security Forces *(inc. conscripts)*	300,000	150,000	250,000	325,000
APC	?	110	110	100+
APC (W)	0	?	?	100
Walid	0	?	?	Some
National Guard	60,000	60,000	60,000	60,000
Light weapons only	?	Yes	Yes	Yes
Paramilitary cadre status	?	8	8	8
APC (W) Walid	Some	?	?	250
Border Guard Forces	?	20,000	20,000	12,000
Light weapons only	?	Yes	Yes	Yes
Border guard regiment	?	19	19	18
Coastal Guard (inc. in Naval entry)	~2,000	~2,000	~2,000	2,000
Patrol and coastal combatants	?	?	?	99+
Patrol, inshore	20	40	40	?
Misc. Boats/craft	Some	60+	60+	60+
PB Bertram	0	?	?	7
PCI	14	34	34	26
Nisr (sid)	5	5	5	5
Swiftship	9	9	9	9
Timsah less than 100 tons	0	20	20	12
PFI	6	6	6	6
Crestitalia	6	6	6	6
Deployment	?	?	?	176
Burundi (observers)	?	?	?	2
UN, ONUB	?	?	?	2
Democratic Republic of Congo (observers)	?	?	?	15
UN, MONUC	?	?	?	8
Georgia (observers)	?	?	?	4
UN, UNOMIG	?	?	?	4
Iraq (advisors)	Some	0	0	0
Kuwait (advisors)	Some	0	0	0
Liberia	?	?	?	8
UN, UNMIL (observers)	?	?	?	8
Oman (advisors)	Some	?	?	?
Saudi Arabia (advisors)	Some	0	0	0
Serbia and Montenegro	?	?	?	21
UN, UNMIK (civilian police)	?	?	?	21
Sierra Leone	?	?	?	5
UN, UNAMSIL (observers)	?	?	?	5
Somalia (advisors)	Some	?	?	?

Sudan	?	?	?	100
UN, UNMIS	Some	?	?	100
Air element	?	?	?	1
Transportation platoon	?	?	?	1
Engineer detachment	?	?	?	1
Minesweeping detachment	?	?	?	1
Observers	?	?	?	2
Western Sahara	?	?	?	21
UN, MINURSO (observers)	?	?	?	21
Zaire (advisors)	Some	0	0	0
Foreign Forces	~2,600	~1,896	~1,685	1,722
Peacekeeping (MFO - Sinai)	~2,600	~1,896	~1,685	1,722
Australia	0	?	?	25
Canada	?	?	?	29
Colombia (infantry battalion)	?	?	?	358
Fiji (infantry battalion)	?	?	?	338
France Air Force (DHC-6 Twin Otter transportation aircraft)	?	?	?	15
Hungary (MP)	0	?	?	41
Italy	?	?	?	76
New Zealand	?	?	?	26
Norway	?	?	?	4
United States (infantry battalion, support battalion)	?	?	?	750
Uruguay	?	?	?	60

* Included in the army total.
** Includes 108 fighters in the Air Defense Command.
Source: Various editions of the IISS *Military Balance,* U.S., British, and other experts.

effective force and tends to get the manpower the army does not want or need. Its training and effectiveness have improved in recent years, however, and it has become an important element of Egypt's efforts to suppress violent Islamic extremists. It is dispersed throughout the country and had automatic weapons, armored cars, and some 250 Walid armored personnel carriers.

The Central Security Force is also under the Ministry of Interior and plays a role in fighting Islamic extremists. It is a large force with some 325,000 men, but training, equipment, readiness, and morale are poor. It was this force that mutinied near the pyramids in 1986. It has remained relatively poorly trained, paid, and equipped and is given lower-grade conscripts while the army got the better educated intake.[20]

The Border Guards included some 12,000 men in 18 regiments with only light weapons.[21]

The General Directorate for State Security Investigations (Mubahath Al-Dawla), the Internal Security Forces, and General Intelligence Service (GIS or Mukhabarat Al-Aama) are all more professional services that play a major role in dealing with

Islamic extremists, other militant opposition groups, and foreign agents. These services report to both ministers and the President. The GIS has played a particularly important role in dealing with Islamist extremist elements.

The Department for Combating Religious Activity is under the command of an army general and had focused on the most extreme religious groups. These included the Islamic Jihad, Jamaat Islamiya (Islamic Group), and Vanguards of Conquest. The Muslim Brotherhood was the subject of considerable government concern, but was more a political party than an extremist movement.

Egypt has a strong mix of additional intelligence, security, and counterterrorism forces. As is the case with most such forces, the details of their strength and capability are not well described in the open literature. It is clear, however, that Egyptian internal security forces and intelligence operations are largely and often highly effective.

The U.S. State Department office dealing with counterterrorism reports that the Egyptian and U.S. governments have maintained close cooperation on a broad range of counterterrorism and law enforcement issues and regularly exchange information on a variety of terrorism, security, and law enforcement matters.

The U.S. State Department report on terrorism issued in 2005 reported that a high-level Egyptian judicial delegation visited the United States in June 2005 and met with representatives of the U.S. Departments of Justice, State, and the FBI to discuss cooperation in the areas of counterterrorism, law enforcement, and the mutual legal assistance treaty. Egypt trains some of its personnel in the United States. For example, in September 2005, 20 generals from Egyptian security services attended a crisis management seminar in Washington, D.C., funded by the Department of State's Antiterrorism Assistance Program.

The U.S. State Department also reports that Egypt has tightened its assets-freezing regime in keeping with relevant UN Security Council Resolutions. Egypt passed strong antimoney laundering legislation in 2002 and established a financial intelligence unit in 2003. Egypt maintained its strengthened airport security measures and security for the Suez Canal and continued to institute more stringent port security measures.

Major Internal Security Threats

Egypt faces several serious terrorist threats, although it sometimes labels legitimate political opposition groups as terrorists. There are also questions about some political groups and whether they have terrorist cells or operations. This includes the main opposition party, the Muslim Brotherhood.

One particularly violent internal threat is the Gama'a al-Islamiyya (IG), or Islamic Group, al-Gama'at. The U.S. State Department identifies the IG as a terrorist group, and its 2005 report on terrorism described it as follows:[22]

> The IG, Egypt's largest militant group, has been active since the late 1970s, and is a loosely organized network. It has an external wing with supporters in several countries. The group's issuance of a cease-fire in 1997 led to a split into two factions: one, led by

Mustafa Hamza, supported the cease-fire; the other, led by Rifa'i Taha Musa, called for a return to armed operations. The IG issued another ceasefire in March 1999, but its spiritual leader, Shaykh Umar Abd al-Rahman, sentenced to life in prison in January 1996 for his involvement in the 1993 World Trade Center bombing and incarcerated in the United States, rescinded his support for the cease-fire in June 2000. IG has not conducted an attack inside Egypt since the Luxor attack in 1997, which killed 58 tourists and four Egyptians and wounded dozens more. In February 1998, a senior member signed Usama Bin Ladin's fatwa calling for attacks against the United States.

In early 2001, Taha Musa published a book in which he attempted to justify terrorist attacks that would cause mass casualties. Taha Musa disappeared several months thereafter, and there is no information as to his current whereabouts. In March 2002, members of the group's historic leadership in Egypt declared use of violence misguided and renounced its future use, prompting denunciations by much of the leadership abroad. The Egyptian Government continues to release IG members from prison, including approximately 900 in 2003; likewise, most of the 700 persons released in 2004 at the end of the Muslim holy month of Ramadan were IG members.

For IG members still dedicated to violent jihad, their primary goal is to overthrow the Egyptian Government and replace it with an Islamic state. Disaffected IG members, such as those inspired by Taha Musa or Abd al-Rahman, may be interested in carrying out attacks against US interests.

...The IG conducted armed attacks against Egyptian security and other Government officials, Coptic Christians, and Egyptian opponents of Islamic extremism before the cease-fire. After the 1997 cease-fire, the faction led by Taha Musa launched attacks on tourists in Egypt, most notably the attack in November 1997 at Luxor. IG also claimed responsibility for the attempt in June 1995 to assassinate Egyptian President Hosni Mubarak in Addis Ababa, Ethiopia.

...At its peak IG probably commanded several thousand hard-core members and a like number of sympathizers. The 1999 cease-fire, security crackdowns following the attack in Luxor in 1997 and, more recently, security efforts following September 11 probably have resulted in a substantial decrease in the group's numbers.

...(The IG) Operates mainly in the al-Minya, Asyut, Qina, and Sohaj Governorates of southern Egypt. Also appears to have support in Cairo, Alexandria, and other urban locations, particularly among unemployed graduates and students. Has a worldwide presence, including in the United Kingdom, Afghanistan, Yemen, and various locations in Europe.

...There is some evidence that Usama bin Ladin and Afghan militant groups support the organization. IG also may obtain some funding through various Islamic nongovernmental organizations (NGOs).

The other major extremist threat comes from the Al-Jihad (AJ), which is also known as the aJihad Group, Egyptian Islamic Jihad, or EIJ. The State Department describes this group as follows:[23]

This Egyptian Islamic extremist group merged with Usama Bin Ladin's al-Qa'ida organization in 2001. Usama Bin Ladin's deputy, Ayman al-Zawahiri, was the former head of AJ. Active since the 1970s, AJ's primary goal has been the overthrow of the Egyptian Government and the establishment of an Islamic state. The group's primary targets, historically, have been high-level Egyptian Government officials as well as US and Israeli interests in Egypt and abroad. Regular Egyptian crackdowns on extremists, including on AJ, have greatly reduced AJ capabilities in Egypt.

. . . The original AJ was responsible for the 1981 assassination of Egyptian President Anwar Sadat. It claimed responsibility for the attempted assassinations of Interior Minister Hassan al-Alfi in August 1993 and Prime Minister Atef Sedky in November 1993. AJ has not conducted an attack inside Egypt since 1993 and has never successfully targeted foreign tourists there. The group was responsible for the Egyptian Embassy bombing in Islamabad in 1995 and a disrupted plot against the US Embassy in Albania in 1998. . . . (It) probably has several hundred hard-core members inside and outside of Egypt.

. . . Historically AJ operated in the Cairo area. Most AJ members today are outside Egypt in countries such as Afghanistan, Pakistan, Lebanon, the United Kingdom, and Yemen. AJ activities have been centered outside Egypt for several years under the auspices of al-Qa'ida.

. . . Since 1998 AJ received most of its funding from al-Qa'ida, and these close ties culminated in the eventual merger of the groups. Some funding may come from various Islamic non-governmental organizations, cover businesses, and criminal acts.

Egypt has limited the activities of the various terrorist groups it faces, but has continued to be subject to terrorist attacks. On October 7, 2004, for example, terrorists attacked tourist targets in Taba and Nuweiba on the Sinai Peninsula in three separate but coordinated actions. Thirty-four people were killed, including Egyptians, Israelis, Italians, a Russian, and an American-Israeli dual national, and over 140 were injured.

On October 25, 2004, the Minister of Interior announced that the government had identified nine individuals responsible for the attack. According to the Egyptian Government, the group's ringleader was a Palestinian resident in North Sinai. The government reported that the Palestinian and an accomplice were killed in the course of the attack in Taba and that five others had been taken into custody. Two remain at large. The government has stated that the nine perpetrators were not part of a wider conspiracy and did not receive assistance from international terrorist organizations. Some experts feel this statement disguises ongoing support for extremist activity both from organizations like the IG and AJ and Al Qa'ida.

In March 2005, an emergency court convicted 26 persons accused of trying to reconstitute the Islamic Liberation Party (Hizb al-Tahrir al-Islami), which was banned in Egypt in 1974 for its efforts to overthrow the Egyptian Government. The court sentenced 12 of the defendants (including three U.K. citizens) to prison. In April, Ahmad Hussein Agiza, an Islamist militant returned to Egypt by Sweden in 2001, was sentenced by a military court to 25 years in prison for membership in a banned organization, although his sentence was subsequently commuted to 15 years.

The U.S. State Department report on terrorism, issued on April 28, 2006, noted the following:[24]

On April 7, a lone suicide bomber killed three foreigners, including an American, at the Khan el-Khalili market; several other Americans were seriously injured in this incident.

On July 23, three bombs exploded in Sharm el-Sheikh, at the tip of the Sinai Peninsula, killing 67, including one American. Hundreds of Egyptians and a number of foreign tourists were also injured as a result of the blasts. One vehicle penetrated security positions along the driveway of a hotel and detonated in the lobby area. Another vehicle-borne improvised explosive device (VBIED) exploded on a street in the old section of Sharm el-Sheikh. A third bomb was concealed in a bag that exploded in a pedestrian area frequented by tourists. There was no evidence these attacks were directed at Americans, but they were widely regarded as targeting the Egyptian tourism industry.

On August 15, near the Rafah border crossing into the Gaza Strip, a small improvised explosive device (IED) detonated near a Multinational Force and Observers vehicle, causing minor injuries to its occupants. This incident was preceded by the discovery of a one-ton cache of explosives in El Arish, on the Mediterranean coast of the Sinai. Separately, on August 13, an intercity bus was shot at on a road crossing the Sinai.

. . . two related but unsuccessful attempts to target tourists near the Citadel and the Egyptian Museum that were thwarted by Egyptian authorities. Only the perpetrators of the incidents were killed in the failed attempts; the government described both as the remaining members of the terrorist cell responsible for the April 7 bombing.

Between August and late November, the Egyptian Government conducted an intensive security operation in Jebel Helal, a remote region in northeast Sinai, in pursuit of fugitives from a Salafist-Bedouin group suspected of links to the terrorist incidents cited above and to other crimes. During the course of this operation, several Egyptian security personnel, including two high-ranking police officers, were killed. In separate skirmishes, several of the fugitives were shot and killed, including Salim Khadr Al-Shanoub and Khalid Musa'id, whom the government identified as key planners of the July Sharm el-Sheikh attacks and three 2004 attacks in Taba involving tourism interests. The Egyptian Government maintained that all of the terrorist incidents that occurred in 2004-05 were conducted by small domestic groups.

During his campaign for the September 7 presidential elections, President Mubarak called for new "anti-terrorism" legislation to replace the decades-old Emergency Law, emphasizing that constitutional and legislative reforms were needed to eliminate terrorism. In explaining his proposal, Mubarak said, "the time has come to create a decisive mechanism to fight terrorism." While defending the use of the Emergency Law, President Mubarak said Egypt should follow the example of other countries that recently passed comprehensive laws to combat terrorism. The Egyptian judicial system does not allow plea bargaining, and historically terrorists have been prosecuted to the full extent of the law. Terrorism defendants may be tried in military tribunals or emergency courts.

New attacks took place at resorts in Dahab, the Sinai, on April 24, 2006. Triple suicide bombing attacks killed 24 people, and it was clear that the attackers had links to Islamist groups outside Egypt. These attacks had patterns very similar to those conducted elsewhere by Al Qa'ida, and attacked secular resorts that had been called "jihad zones." They were later tied to Egyptians who had had Palestinian training in the Gaza Strip, although Hamas condemned the attacks and denied involvement. Egypt has tended to downplay both such links to outside groups and the scale of the continuing struggle between its internal security forces and Islamist extremist and terrorist groups.[25]

Internal Security vs. Human Rights and Political Impacts

As is the case with Israel, and with the other states that make up the Arab-Israeli balance, no discussion of Egypt's efforts to deal with terrorism and internal security can ignore the fact that some Egyptian efforts violate human rights and do as much or more to provoke opposition, extremism, and terrorism as they do to fight them. There are a number of statements by human rights and opposition groups that exaggerate such problems.

Egypt did, however, put serious pressure on legitimate opposition groups during the 2005 presidential elections and has imprisoned legitimate political leaders and human rights activists. While it has legitimate threats, the human rights country report issued by the U.S. State Department in 2005 notes that Egypt's paramilitary and security forces have extensive powers which they often abuse, both in dealing with extremists and peaceful dissidents and members of the opposition:[26]

> The Emergency Law allows detention of an individual without charge for up to 30 days, after which a detainee may demand a court hearing to challenge the legality of the detention order, and may resubmit his motion for a hearing at 1-month intervals thereafter. There is no limit to the detention period if a judge continues to uphold the detention order or if the detainee fails to exercise his right to a hearing. Incommunicado detention is authorized for prolonged periods by internal prison regulations. Human rights groups and the U.N. Committee Against Torture both expressed concern over the application of measures of solitary confinement
>
> ...In addition to the Emergency Law, the Penal Code also gives the State broad detention powers. Under the Penal Code, prosecutors must bring charges within 48 hours following detention or release the suspect. However, they may detain a suspect for a maximum of 6 months pending investigation. Arrests under the Penal Code occurred openly and with warrants issued by a district prosecutor or judge. There is a functioning system of bail for persons detained under the Penal Code. The Penal Code contains several provisions to combat extremist violence, which broadly define terrorism to include the acts of "spreading panic" and "obstructing the work of authorities."
>
> Hundreds, perhaps thousands, of persons have been detained administratively in recent years under the Emergency Law on suspicion of terrorist or political activity. Several thousand others have been convicted and were serving sentences on similar charges (see Section 1.e.). In a July 2003 interview published in Al-Ahram Weekly, HRAAP (formerly HRCAP) estimated that the total number of persons held in administrative detention was approximately 15,000. HRAAP further estimated that about 7,000 additional persons have been released over the past 3 years. According to HRAAP, approximately 300 detainees, including convicts with remaining sentences and those who had been held under emergency administrative detention, were released during the year. In addition to these individuals, a much larger number of regular convicts were released during the year, as [a] result of having completed their sentences.
>
> ...In May 2003, the Government formally abolished State Security Courts. The courts had been criticized for restricting the rights of defendants, particularly the right to appeal. A number of cases referred to the State Security Courts were transferred to regular criminal courts. However, skeptical observers of the legal system argued that as long

as the Government retained and used Emergency Courts, the abolition of State Security Courts did not constitute a fundamental improvement.

In 1992, following a rise in extremist violence, the Government began using military tribunals to adjudicate cases involving persons accused of terrorist activity or membership in terrorist groups. In 1993, the Supreme Constitutional Court ruled that the President may invoke the Emergency Law to refer any crime to a military court. The 1993 ruling in effect removed hundreds of civilian defendants from the normal process of trial by a civilian judge. The Government defended the use of military courts as necessary to try terrorism cases, maintaining that trials in the civilian courts were protracted and that civilian judges and their families were vulnerable to terrorist threats. One case involving civilian defendant Ahmed Hussain Agiza was referred to a military court during the year.

Military verdicts were subject to a review by other military judges and confirmation by the President, who in practice usually delegated the review function to a senior military officer. Defense attorneys claimed that they were not given sufficient time to prepare and that military judges tended to rush cases involving a large number of defendants. Judges had guidelines for sentencing, defendants had the right to counsel, and statements of the charges against defendants were made public. Observers needed government permission to attend. Diplomats attended some military trials during the year. Human rights activists have attended, but only when acting as lawyers for one of the defendants.

. . . The Emergency Courts share jurisdiction with military courts over crimes affecting national security. The President can appoint civilian judges to these courts upon the recommendation of the Minister of Justice or military judges upon recommendation of the Minister of Defense. Sentences are subject to confirmation by the President. There is no right to appeal. The President may alter or annul a decision of an Emergency Court, including a decision to release a defendant.

Egypt has, however, grown more repressive in recent years as the Mubarak regime ages and may be moving toward a close. It has arrested legitimate political opposition leaders, blamed the Muslim Brotherhood for actions that the U.S. government does not believe it was guilty of, and called peaceful demonstrations by other opposition groups the actions of the Muslim Brotherhood. The human rights report that the State Department issued on March 6, 2006, summarized these problems as follows:[27]

The country has both local and national law enforcement agencies, all of which fall under the Ministry of Interior. Local police operate in large cities and governorates. The ministry controls the State Security Investigations Service (SSIS), which conducts investigations, and the Central Security Force (CSF), which maintains public order. SSIS and CSF officers are responsible for law enforcement at the national level and for providing security for infrastructure and key officials, both domestic and foreign. Single-mission law enforcement agencies, such as the Tourist and Antiquities Police and the Anti-Narcotics General Administration, also work at the national level. As a whole, the security forces operated under a central chain of command and were considered generally effective in their efforts to combat crime and terrorism and preserve and maintain public order. However, a culture of impunity militated against systematic prosecution of security personnel who committed human rights abuses.

There were continued instances of torture by police, and human rights monitors believed the use of torture by police was widespread. Although some police were prosecuted, human rights monitors believed most incidents of torture went unpunished. Security forces continued to mistreat and torture prisoners, arbitrarily arrest and detain persons, hold detainees in prolonged pretrial detention, and engage in mass arrests.

There was widespread petty corruption in the police force, especially below senior levels...In addition to acceptance of bribes or simple theft, there were instances of accompanying assault and even murder....security forces killed a number of opposition voters and protesters during the parliamentary elections. The death toll was at least 11; although several of the deaths resulted from violence between supporters of competing candidates, the majority of the killings in the parliamentary elections resulted from the security forces' use of rubber bullets and live ammunition.

...During October protests by Muslim demonstrators against a theatrical production staged by members of the Mar Guirguis Church in Alexandria, security forces reportedly killed three Muslim demonstrators who were threatening the church.

In November and December, during the second and third rounds of the parliamentary elections, security forces in the Nile Delta region used lethal force against multiple groups of opposition voters. At least 11 persons were killed during election-related violence. According to EOHR, those killed included Mohamed Khalil Ibrahim (Alexandria); Gomaa Saad al-Zeftawy (Kafr Al-Sheikh); Islam Ahmed Shihata (Al-Daqahlia governorate); Magdy Hassan Ali al-Bahrawy (Al-Daqahlia); Tamer Mahmoud Abdu al-Qamash (Al-Daqahlia); Al-Saeed al-Deghidy (Damietta); Ihab Saleh Ezz al-Deen (Damietta); Shaaban Abdu Abu Rabaa (Damietta); Mostafa Abdel Salam (Al-Sharqia governorate); Mohamed Karam al-Taher Eliwa (Al-Sharqia); and Mohamed Ahmed Mahdy Gazar (Al-Sharqia). According to EOHR, the violence also left at least 500 persons injured.

EOHR asserted that responsibility for the elections related clashes could be attributed to supporters of the ruling party, as well as independents and MB supporters. EOHR also noted, however, that most of the fatalities occurred on December 7 after security forces closed at least 496 polling stations, which led to clashes between security forces who were enforcing the closure of the voting stations and opposition voters who were prevented from voting.

...there were numerous, credible reports that security forces tortured and mistreated prisoners and detainees. Domestic and international human rights groups reported that the State Security Investigations Service (SSIS), police, and other government entities continued to employ torture to extract information or force confessions. Reports of torture and mistreatment at police stations remained frequent. In prominent cases, defendants alleged that police tortured them during questioning (see sections 1.e. and 2.c.). Although the government investigated torture complaints in some criminal cases and punished some offending police officers, punishments generally have not conformed to the seriousness of the offense. The government has not prosecuted any SSIS officers for torture since 1986, according to a senior Ministry of Interior official during a February meeting with HRW. There was no indication during the remainder of the year that the government prosecuted or otherwise penalized State Security officials for human rights abuses.

Principal methods of torture reportedly employed by the police and the SSIS included stripping and blindfolding victims; suspending victims from a ceiling or doorframe with feet just touching the floor; beating victims with fists, whips, metal rods, or other objects; using electrical shocks; and dousing victims with cold water. Victims frequently reported being subjected to threats and forced to sign blank papers for use against themselves or their families should they in the future complain about the torture. Some victims, including male and female detainees and children, reported sexual assaults or threats of rape against themselves or family members. While the law requires security authorities to keep written records of detentions, human rights groups reported that the lack of such records often effectively blocked investigations.

The Emergency Law—applied almost continuously since 1967 under the state of emergency—and most recently renewed in 2003 through May 2006—authorizes incommunicado detention for prolonged periods. Detentions under this law frequently were accompanied by allegations of torture. The government responded to terrorist attacks in April and July with a crackdown authorized by the Emergency Law; authorities conducted mass arrests of scores or hundreds of persons acquainted with the suspects and reportedly tortured some of them in custody (see section 1.d.).

In May 2004, the government's Central Audit Agency directed the Ministry of Interior to require any security or police officers found responsible for torture to be financially liable for any judgments levied against the ministry. According to the Human Rights Association for the Assistance of Prisoners (HRAAP), punitive damages awarded by the courts during the year to victims of torture mounted to approximately $35,500 (LE 204,500).

The government continued efforts during the year to hold some security personnel accountable for torturing prisoners in their custody; however, the government has not investigated any SSIS officials for torture in the last two decades.

Egypt's internal security problems continue to be exacerbated by poor distribution of income in a grindingly poor population, a steady decline in government services, and problems in its security forces. State employment is no longer a right, much of the educational system has broken, and health care has sharply deteriorated.

Egypt had 6 percent growth in GNP in purchasing power parity (ppp) terms in 2005 and tripled its rate of foreign investment. The practical problem is that little of this new wealth has trickled down to the ordinary Egyptian, and the marginal middle and professional classes have come under increasing economic pressure. Egypt has a population of nearly 79 million, and a median age of 24. While its population growth rate has dropped, nearly a third of its population is 14 years of age or younger. Its GDP was $339 billion in ppp terms in 2005, and $93 billion in market terms. Its per capita income is $4,400 in ppp terms, but most Egyptians live on the equivalent of well under $1,000 a year. Unemployment is well over 10 percent and is particularly severe for young men and women. Some 803,000 males and 763,000 females reach the age where they need employment each year, and many cannot find productive jobs for several years, if at all.[28]

EGYPTIAN WEAPONS OF MASS DESTRUCTION

Little is known about Egypt's current holdings of missiles and weapons of mass destruction or how serious its efforts to maintain some kind of technical and production base now are. It seems likely that it has limited any nuclear and biological weapons efforts to research, rather than active development and production. It may, however, have some chemical weapons and probably retains some capability to produce them or to rapidly convert civil facilities for this purpose. Egypt has pursued the development of more advanced surface-to-surface missiles, but largely in the form of updating its existing Scud systems.

Figure 5.8 summarizes recent reporting on Egyptian capabilities. It should be stressed, however, that such reporting is often speculative and is highly uncertain. Egypt has publicly stressed President Mubarak's call for a "weapons of mass destruction free zone" in the Middle East and has seemed to be willing to reluctantly live with an Israeli nuclear monopoly. The wild card, however, may be Iran's acquisition of long-range missiles and nuclear weapons. President Mubarak has already warned of the threat of Iranian ties to other Shi'ite or non-Sunni regimes in Iraq, Lebanon, and Syria and is virtually certain to see Iran proliferation as both further destabilizing and a threat to Egypt's status and prestige.

Figure 5.8   Egypt's Search for Weapons of Mass Destruction

Delivery Systems

- Began three major design programs based on the V-2 missile in the 1950s, with help from German scientists. Test two missiles by 1965: A 350-kilometer range al-Zafir and a 600-kilometer range Al Kahir. A 1,500-kilometer range Ar-Ra'id was designed but never tested. These missiles were liquid-fueled aging designs and development ceased around 1967.

- Cooperated with Iraq in paying for development and production of "Badr 2000" missile with a 750–1,000-kilometer range. This missile is reported to be a version of the Argentine Condor II or Vector missile. Ranges were reported from 820–980 kilometers, with the possible use of an FAE warhead.

  - Egyptian officers were arrested for trying to smuggle carbon materials for a missile out of the United States in June 1988.

  - Covert U.S. efforts seem to have blocked this development effort.

  - The Condor program seems to have terminated in 1989–1990.

- Has Scud B TELs and missiles with approximately 100 missiles with 300-kilometer range.

- Reports have developed plans to produce an improved version of the Scud B, and possibly Scud C, with North Korean cooperation.

  - North Korean transfers include equipment for building Scud body, special gyroscope measuring equipment, and pulse-code modulation equipment for missile assembly and testing.

  - Unconfirmed reports in June 1996 that Egypt has made major missile purchase from North Korea and will soon be able to assemble such missiles in Egypt. Seven shipments from North Korea reported in March and April.

  - Other unconfirmed reports that Egypt had another liquid-fueled missile under development known as "Project T" with an estimated range of 450 kilometers. It is believed to be an extended-range Scud designed with North Korean assistance. These unconfirmed reports indicate Egypt may have as many as 90 Project T missiles.

- Media reports that U.S. satellites detected shipments of Scud C missile parts to Egypt in February–May 1996—including rocket motors and guidance devices—do not seem correct. The Scud C has a range of roughly 480 kilometers.
- The CIA reported in June 1997 that Egypt had acquired Scud B parts from Russia and North Korea during 1996.
- The CIA reported in January 1999 that Egypt continues its effort to develop and produce the Scud B and Scud C and to develop the two-stage Vector short-range ballistic missiles (SRBMs). Cairo also is interested in developing a medium-range ballistic missile (MRBM). During the first half of 1998, Egypt continued to obtain ballistic missile components and associated equipment from North Korea. This activity is part of a long-running program of ballistic missile cooperation between these two countries.
- The United States suspects Egypt is developing a liquid-fueled missile called the Vector with an estimated range of 600–1,200 kilometers.
- FROG 7 rocket launch units with a 40-kilometer range.
- Cooperation with Iraq and North Korea in developing the Saqr 80 missile. This rocket is 6.5 meters long, 210 mm in diameter, and weighs 660 kilograms. It has a maximum range of 50 miles (80 kilometers) and a 440-pound (200-kilogram) warhead. Longer-range versions may be available.
- AS-15, SS-N-2, and CSS-N-1 cruise missiles.
- 28 F-4E fighter ground attack aircraft.
- 20 Mirage 5E2 fighter ground attack.
- 53 Mirage 2000EM fighters.
- 33 F-16A/B and 174 F-16C/D fighters.
- Multiple rocket launcher weapons.
- Tube artillery.
- The Center for Nonproliferation Studies at the Monterey Institute of International Studies has compiled a chronology of North Korean assistance to Egypt through 2003:[29]

Date	Item(s)	Remarks
1987	Technical assistance for Scud-B production plant	
1989	Scud-B parts, improved missile components, such as guidance systems	Information from retired Israeli Brigadier General Aharon Levran.
Early 1990s	Scud-C missile production technology	North Korea reportedly helps Egypt set up Scud-C production facility outside of Cairo.
1996 March–April	Seven shiploads of equipment and materials for producing Scud-C missiles	Could have included steel sheets for Scuds and support equipment, rocket engines, and guidance systems. Possible assistance for producing Scud-C TELs.

1997	Several shipments of equipment for Scud-C production	
1999 July	Specialty steel	Probably maraging steel; shipped by Chinese firm in Hong Kong
1999–2001	50 to 300 missile experts	
2000	No Dong missiles and TELs	Unconfirmed; North Korean firm Ch'ongchon'gang reportedly delivers 50 No Dong missiles and seven TELs to Syria. Missiles possibly procured on behalf of Iraq, Egypt, and Libya for $600 million.
2001	24 to 50 No Dong engines	Unconfirmed; some reports claim that delivery occurred in the first half of 2001, but others claim engines have yet to be delivered. Egypt insists that missile cooperation with North Korea ended in 1996.

Chemical Weapons

- Produced and used mustard gas in Yemeni civil war in 1960s, but agents may have been stocks British abandoned in Egypt after World War II. Effort was tightly controlled by Nasser and was unknown to many Egyptian military serving in Yemen.
- Completed research and designs for production of nerve and cyanide gas before 1973.
- Former Egyptian Minister of War, General Abdel Ranny Gamassay stated in 1975, that "if Israel should decide to use a nuclear weapon in the battlefield, we shall use the weapons of mass destruction that are at our disposal."
- Seems to have several production facilities for mustard and nerve gas. May have limited stocks of bombs, rockets, and shells. Unconfirmed reports suggest that Egypt had developed VX nerve gas.
- Unconfirmed reports of recent efforts to acquire feedstocks for nerve gas. Some efforts to obtain feedstocks from Canada. May now be building feedstock plants in Egypt.
- Industrial infrastructure present for rapid production of cyanide gas.
- Egypt is thought to have an offensive chemical warfare capability, but the extent of this capability is unknown.

Biological Weapons

- Research and technical base.
- Unconfirmed Israeli sources allege that Egypt has pursued research into anthrax, plague, botulinum toxin, and Rift Valley fever virus for military purposes, but no other open-source data confirms these allegations.

- Egypt is thought to have a significant microbiological capability, but no substantiated, open-source evidence exists that suggests Egypt has pursued biological weapons.
- No evidence of major organized research activity.

Nuclear Weapons

- Research and technical base.
- Egypt currently operates two research reactors, both of which are under IAEA safeguards.
  - A 2 MW Soviet-built reactor 40 kilometers from Cairo which started operation in 1961.
  - A 22 MW Argentine reactor at the Ishas facility, 60 kilometers from Cairo, started operation in 1997. The Argentine reactor is thought to be capable of producing enough plutonium for one weapon each year.[30]
- Numerous discussions over the years with the United States, China, and other nations for large-scale power generation facilities. No current agreements for construction of power reactors.
- No evidence of major organized research activity for development of a usable weapon.
- President Mubarak did say in October 1998 that Egypt could acquire nuclear weapons to match Israel's capability if this proves necessary,[31] "If the time comes when we need nuclear weapons, we will not hesitate. I say 'if' we have to because this is the last thing we think about. We do not think of joining the nuclear club." This speech was more an effort to push Israel toward disarmament talks, however, than any kind of threat.
- Mubarak also said that Israel "enhances its military expenditure and develops its missile systems that are used for military purposes. It knows very well that this will not benefit it or spare it from harm. Its efforts to use the help of foreign countries will plunge the region ban into a new arms race which serves nobody's interests." Egypt has supported the indefinite extension of the NNPT, has long been officially committed to creating a nuclear weapons–free zone in the Middle East, and had advocated an agreement that would ban all weapons of mass destruction from the region.

EGYPT'S CONTINUING STRATEGIC CHALLENGES

Egypt faces different strategic challenges than it did at the time it was at war with Israel. It has scarcely eliminated the internal threat it faces from Islamist extremism and terrorism, and from movements both inside and outside Egypt. Its economic growth has increased the disparity in income between Egypt's rich, its small middle class, and its poor. The government has pursued economic reform that has opened up Egypt's markets, but virtually all government services, including health and education have deteriorated for more than a decade. Unemployment and housing are major problems. This is a recipe that tends to breed violence and extremism, and it has been exacerbated by political repression and suppression of legitimate dissent. Egypt needs more than broad economic growth and strong and effective security forces. Stability requires political, economic, and social reform.

The Sinai Contingency

Internal security challenges, however, are only part of the story. In spite of Egypt's firm commitment to peace, it cannot ignore the risk of some unexpected political crisis or strategic shift that could again make Israel a threat. It must maintain a suitable deterrent and defense capability to deal with the risk of some unlikely breakdown in its peace with Israel, although it has nothing to gain from a new war in the Sinai, and other challenges now dominate Egypt's security interests.

Egypt also cannot distance itself from the Israeli-Palestinian war of attrition that has gone on ever since September 2000. Egypt's strategic challenge in dealing with Israel is to advance the peace process and avoid war. It has nothing to gain from a new war with Israel and much to lose. Even if a new, radical Islamic government should come to power in Egypt, or Egypt should be driven to attack by some breakdown in the peace process or new Arab-Israeli crisis, any buildup in its capabilities for such an attack would give Israel ample strategic warning. Furthermore, Egypt could prepare for such an attack and execute it only by violating an international treaty, thereby risking the almost certain loss of U.S. aid.

As a result, the one war that can now challenge Egypt's present military capabilities is still another war with Israel. Its outcome would be shaped as much by the outcome of the air war as the land war, and it is almost impossible to see how Egypt could achieve surprise in building up a massive additional force in the Sinai and not have Israel react.

If one does ignore Israel's probable victory in the air war, an Egyptian attack across the Suez Canal would require a massive repositioning and reorganization of Egyptian forces, without an Israeli response. Egypt would have to carry out these redeployments without anything approaching the required major support and staging facilities in the Sinai.

It would then face the problem of dealing with the geography of the Sinai. The Suez Canal, the Mediterranean Sea, the Gulfs of Suez and Aqaba, and the border with Israel define the Sinai. The distances are about 190 kilometers from the Suez Canal to the Israeli border, about 145 kilometers along the Suez Canal and the Great Bitter Lakes, and about 370 kilometers from the coast of the Mediterranean down to the southern most tip of the Sinai. The terrain is very barren and rugged.

Movement through the Sinai is limited in ways that increase the difficulty in moving forces and sustaining them, and increase their vulnerability to air attack. There are only a limited number of roads through the Sinai. The main roads go along the northern coast and through two passes, the Giddi in the north and Mitla in the south. The two passes are about 20 kilometers apart. The Mitla Pass is about 32 kilometers long and the Giddi Pass is about 29 kilometers long.

The Mitla Pass is more open and has a relatively wide slope. The Giddi Pass has rough terrain and narrows down to as little as 100 meters. South of these passes, the terrain becomes very rugged and large-scale armored movement becomes very difficult. The north coast road is vulnerable to air and land attacks. The ocean blocks northern movement and extensive southern movement is highly restricted by "seas of sand." Further, Egypt's border with Israel is far from most Israeli population centers, and the Negev Desert gives Israel strategic depth.

The paved and graded roads in the north central Sinai are channeled through the Giddi and Mitla passes, and bypassing them is difficult. This makes them the preferable route for large mechanized forces, and such movements involve hundreds of armored vehicles and nearly 600 support vehicles for each heavy division. Combat and service support units must also accompany combat units to sustain them in combat and provide artillery support, and most Egyptian support vehicles are wheeled rather than tracked. This further limits the areas in which they can move and makes the passes more important. Further, unless Egypt moves its heavy land-based air defenses forward to create the kind of defensive belt it had near the Suez in 1970–1973, its forces would be exposed to the IAF—which would be far more effective against armor than in any previous Arab-Israeli conflict.

Once Egypt moved into the Sinai, it would also be exposed to an Israeli attack in far more depth than a Syrian force advancing into the Golan. The Sinai is an exposed killing ground where land forces are exposed and/or must move through narrow predictable routes. The IAF is now organized and equipped to use a combination of electronic intelligence aircraft, jammers, stand-off munitions, land-based strike systems, UAVs, and other countermeasures to suppress Egyptian air defenses. If the Golan has become a high-technology killing ground, it is even truer of the Sinai and the Negev.

Egypt *might* be more successful in advancing under the defensive envelope of its surface-to-air missiles than in 1973. More probably, it would find that the Israeli Air Force could use a combination of electronic warfare, antiradiation missiles, UAVs, and precision strike systems to strip away such land-based air defenses before Egyptian troops could come close to the Israeli border. Similarly, the Egyptian Air Force is not strong and effective enough to provide survivable air cover. The end result would probably be to turn the Sinai into a killing ground for the Israeli Air Force, which would be supported by Israel's long-range artillery and multiple rocket launchers. These attacks would seriously degrade the cohesion of any Egyptian advance and delay or potentially halt it. This part of the fighting would be expensive to both sides, but Israel would almost certainly win.

If the armored forces of both nations did close in on the Sinai, the resulting massive armored engagement between Israel and Egypt would be a tragic, bloody mess. Egyptian armored and artillery forces are now good enough so that the resulting attrition would be high for both sides. Egypt, however, would almost certainly take far greater losses than Israel. Egypt still needs to make major improvements in its manpower quality, emphasize joint warfare and combined arms, change many of its training methods above the brigade and squadron levels, and allocate funds to buy the high-technology equipment necessary to support more advanced training methods.

Yet, Egypt's land forces remain vulnerable to a combination of Israeli air and artillery attacks and armored maneuver. They would be relatively exposed and have to operate in an environment where Israel's superior sensors, UAVs, and battle management capabilities would give it the equivalent of information dominance. Israel's superior targeting and battlement systems would probably allow it to out-range and out-kill Egyptian artillery, and its Merkavas would certainly outrange all Egyptian armor except the M-1A1. Even then, superior Israeli training, battle man-agement, and situational awareness might give the Israel Defense Forces (IDFs) a decisive edge in range and kill capability. It would be an exceedingly unpleasant war for both sides, but it is not a war that Egypt can now win.

Egypt would also be strategically vulnerable. It has far better air defenses than Syria, but Israel could probably win enough air superiority in several days to launch the same kind of strategic strikes using conventional weapons that have been described in the case of Syria. In this case, geography is both one of Egypt's strengths and weaknesses. Egypt has a larger total area than any other country of territory in the ring states. This means that Egypt is forced to defend a large amount of airspace. At the same time, Egypt's economy, infrastructure, and population centers are heav-ily concentrated in the Cairo area and lower Egypt, and in areas well within the range of Israel strikes.

While an Israeli attack on Egypt seems even more improbable than an Egyptian attack on Israel, such a contingency illustrates why Egypt's deterrent and defensive strength in facing Israel is important both in terms of Egyptian perceptions and those of moderate and friendly Arab states. It demonstrates that Egypt's support of the peace process does not mean that it had to accept strategic inferiority or the kind of "edge" that gives Israel offensive freedom of action as distinguished from defensive security and that Arab strategic alliances with the United States can involve parity in technology transfer. Egypt's military modernization also gives it a decisive edge over regional rivals like Libya and the Sudan and makes it a major potential player in any coalition involving Arab forces in the Gulf.

Israel would face significant problems if it did attack Egypt through the Sinai. Egypt has developed much of the combat capability it needs to defend against an Is-raeli attack through the Sinai. As long as the Sinai remains largely demilitarized, Isra-el might be able to move rapidly into the area, just as Egypt could move north. At some point, however, Israel would have to engage dug-in Egyptian armor and infan-try in large numbers, as well as fight a massive battle for air superiority.

This means Israel would probably require a one-front war and considerable free-dom of action to be able to concentrate enough armor to advance through the Sinai without taking major losses. Unless Israel was free to react quickly and decisively, any battle could become a two-way race for the passes or have to be fought farther north and close to Israel. The situation would also become progressively more difficult for Israel as the IDF advanced toward the Suez. An Israel fighting on more than one front—or with a large portion of its forces tied down on other fronts—would then face an Egyptian army organized to fight a defense in depth and which could be a formidable opponent.

Egypt might lose the Sinai—as it did in 1973—but the cost would probably be far higher to Israel than in the October War. Israel might be able to retake the Suez Canal, but it would involve significant military risks. It would also confront Israel with then having to either hold the area at immense political, economic, and military cost or repeat its past withdrawal.

Moreover, Israel and Egypt confront a common strategic problem. A conflict would lead to almost immediate U.S. political and possibly military intervention. Any tactical or theater victory would confront Egypt with the reality that no defeat of the IDF in the Sinai is going to lead to total victory or the occupation of a nuclear-armed Israel, and it would confront Israel with the reality that a return to the edge of Suez does not amount to a total victory over Egypt. Although many previous conflicts were not prevented by knowledge that war would be pointless, it is especially hard in this case to see any form of such a war as anything other than a mutually self-defeating strategic disaster for both Egypt and Israel.

The New Security Mission in the Gaza Strip

The irony in this situation is that in spite of such "worst-case" risks, Egypt's peace mission in the Sinai is at least as much of a strategic challenge as is the war mission. Egypt has also a new paramilitary mission in seeking to secure the border between the Gaza Strip and Egypt. Egypt has long worked with Israel to crack down on smuggling through the Sinai to the Gaza Strip. Egypt has destroyed more than 40 tunnel openings since 2003 and long ago cleared sensitive portions of the border area spanning the tunneling area. Egypt has actively engaged Palestinian leaders on the question of reorganizing the Palestinian Authority's security services to better police the border area.[32] Egypt also organized an Israeli-Palestinian summit at Sharm al-Shaykh and the Palestinian Authority–Hamas cease-fire in spring 2005 and has begun to train Palestinian security forces.

On September 1, 2005, Egypt went further. It signed an agreement with Israel called the Agreed Arrangements Regarding the Deployment of a Designated Force of Border Guards along the Border in the Rafah Area (the Agreed Arrangements). The agreement allowed Israel to evacuate the Philadelphia corridor, an eight-mile (13-kilometer) military zone along the Gaza-Egypt border, by deploying Egyptian border patrol forces to the Egyptian side of the border in order to prevent smuggling into the Gaza Strip.

Work by Michael Herzog and Brooke Neuman of the Washington Institute summarizes the key features of the agreement as follows:[33]

> The Agreed Arrangements stipulate that they are wholly subject to the provisions of the 1979 Israel-Egypt Peace Treaty and do not constitute an amendment, revision, or modification of it. Article IV of the new document describes its purpose as "additional mission-oriented security measures...in order to augment the security arrangements contained in the Security Annex (of the Peace Treaty)." ...The new agreement specifies that the newly permitted Egyptian forces are to deal exclusively with the acts or threats of smuggling, infiltration, or terrorism. The agreement explicitly stipulates that the new force should serve no military purpose.

An Egyptian border guard force (BGF) replaces the Egyptian police force previously deployed in the area, which was not adequate for the task of halting smuggling.

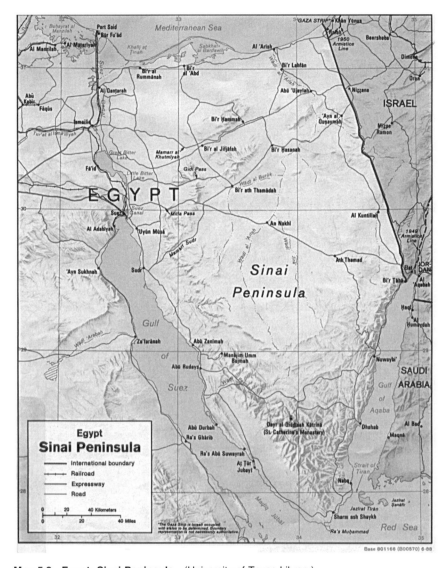

Map 5.2   Egypt: Sinai Peninsula   (University of Texas Library)

It must include only border patrol personnel, a requirement that implicitly excludes military personnel. The BGF can have a maximum of 750 personnel, divided between headquarters and four companies. An additional several dozen auxiliary aerial and naval personnel can support the mission of the BGF. Its weapons are light and include some 500 assault rifles, 67 light machine guns, and 27 light antipersonnel launchers. Some ground radars are permitted. No heavy armored vehicles can be deployed, and vehicles are limited to 31 police-style vehicles as well as 44 logistical and auxiliary vehicles. Heavy armored vehicles are prohibited. Facilities can include a fixed number of sentry posts, watchtowers, and logistics facilities. No fortifications, intelligence facilities, or arms deports are permitted.[34]

Egypt can use a maximum of six unarmed police-mode Gazelle and two unarmed MI or Westland police-mode helicopters, bearing consistent markers of the BGF. Their operations must be coordinated with the IDF in advance. Egyptian naval forces can also patrol the area south of the Gaza Strip more extensively, while Israel will patrol the coast off the Gaza Strip. The infrastructure and equipment of the naval force include four coastal patrol ships. As Herzog and Neuman note, the agreement is an extension of the arms control provisions in previous peace agreements. It limits the weapons each naval force can use, and Israel and Egypt must jointly enforce civilian-no-sail and military-no-training zones one mile (1.6 kilometers) on either side of the sea border.

New liaison arrangements are made to improve coordination and intelligence sharing on a 24 hour a day basis. The existing U.S.–headed Multinational Force and Observers is to provide independent monitoring of the implementation of the Agreed Arrangements and carry out weekly ground and aerial inspections and report any deviations from the Agreed Arrangements to Israel and to Egypt.

As might have been expected, when Israel withdrew, the Palestinians immediately tested the new arrangements and thousands of people crossed the borders in both directions without permission. At least some Hamas and PIJ activists crossed into the Gaza Strip then and have done so since, and some arms and other equipment smuggling may have taken place. Since that time, some further incidents have taken place, but Egypt has improved the operations of the BGF. It may not be able to fully secure the corridor and the key Rafah crossing, but seems committed to making a serious effort and treating it as a key part of its efforts to secure an Israeli-Palestinian peace agreement.

Egypt's Other Strategic Challenges

Egypt faces other strategic challenges because it is a major regional power and may be called upon to project military and peacekeeping forces far beyond its own borders. Virtually all of its African neighbors have some degree of political instability. It is a target of Islamist extremists and has to deal with hostile terrorist organizations in Egypt:

- Egypt needs to further rationalize its force posture and emphasize force quality over force quantity. It retains too many aging Soviet-bloc and European systems, which have limited military value and complicate its interoperability, training, maintenance, and sustainability problems.
- As part of this force rationalization and restructuring, Egypt needs to place less emphasis on equipment numbers and major weapons modernization and more emphasis on sustainability and overall war-fighting effectiveness.

- Human factors remain a major challenge. Egypt needs to improve the quality of its personnel management and career development. It needs to improve its educational efforts and the realism of its training—particularly for large-scale force employment and joint warfare.

- Egypt must modernize its internal security forces and make them more effective in targeting and destroying actual terrorists and violent movements while making them less repressive in dealing with legitimate political opponents and human rights issues.

- Egypt needs to continue to fight its internal Islamist extremist threats, as well as external movement like Al Qa'ida. It must find ways to strengthen its cooperation in counterterrorism in dealing with its neighbors and allies outside the region.

- Peace with Israel is both a key strategic priority and an ongoing challenge. Egypt plays a critical role in mediating between Israel and the Palestinians and must find ways to expand its training and security cooperation with the Palestinians as a counterbalance to antipeace elements and extremists in the Palestinian movement. At the same time, it is a key voice in persuading Israel to compromise with the Palestinians, take their needs into consideration, and move toward recognition of a Palestinian state.

- Egypt must work with Israel and the Palestinians to secure the Egyptian border with the Gaza Strip, a mission that has been greatly complicated by the victory of Hamas in the January 25, 2006, parliamentary elections.

- Egypt does and should continue to play a stabilizing role in the Red Sea Area and Africa. This includes security cooperation.

- Proliferation remains a major problem. Egypt continues to pursue weapons of mass destruction or a nuclear-free zone, but must now deal with the prospects of Iranian proliferation and Egypt's status in the region. The prospect of a new nuclear arms race between Israel and Iran is not one that involves Egypt directly, but it is also one Egypt cannot ignore. Such an exchange would inevitably have a massive strategic impact on Egypt, and even in peacetime, could push Egypt back toward a more active effort to proliferate to maintain its status and prestige in the region and guard against wild card contingencies.

- Egypt must define the role it seeks to play in stabilizing the Sudan. So far, this has been ambiguous. Stability on Egypt's southern border, however, is important and Egypt must either find a way to bring added stability or devote more effort to protecting its borders against infiltration and possible spillovers of Sudanese conflicts.

- Egypt must decide whether to play a more active role as a major power in the region; Egypt has sat on the sidelines during several recent conflicts including Iraq and Afghanistan.

- Egypt must find the right balance between sizing its military forces and expenditure and the priority it must give to economic and social development. Egypt requires more than effective police and counterterrorism forces. Economic, social, and political reforms are important to ensuring internal stability. Modernization and reform remain the key long-term weapons in effective counterterrorism.

- Egypt must consider the broader struggle outside its borders to define Islam and its political role. As a major regional power, it cannot ignore the threat Neo-Salafi Sunni Islamist extremists pose to all moderate and secular regimes and to cooperation and progress in the Arab world.

It is clear, however, that Egypt's central strategic focus must be on internal security and not on external threats. It must address the causes of internal instability in Egypt, liberalize its political system, and broaden the popular base of its economic development. Barring some radical new development in the region, this seems likely to be the case indefinitely into the future.

Egypt also needs to consider whether it is spending too much on too large a military force structure. It would take a new war outside the Arab-Israeli conflict, or an explosive deterioration in the struggle between Israel and the Palestinians, to change Egypt's position on the peace process. Its African neighbors, while troublesome and unstable, are not a threat. As a result, Egypt may have to make some hard choices about reducing a conventional force posture that is too large and too expensive for its current needs and shifting resources to internal security and to the kind of economic development that may do more to improve such security than additional paramilitary and internal security forces.

The Military Forces of Jordan

Jordan has spent much of its modern history caught up in the pressures of various Arab-Israeli conflicts while facing pressures from nations like Iraq and Saudi Arabia to its east. Jordan still suffers from its division during the 1967 War, when it lost the territory it had occupied in Jerusalem and the West Bank. Jordan is now a relatively small country with an area of 92,300 square kilometers. It has borders with Israel (238 kilometers), Iraq (181 kilometers), Saudi Arabia (744 kilometers), Syria (375 kilometers), and the West Bank (97 kilometers). It has a 26-kilometer-long coastline on the Gulf of Aqaba.

While it avoided subsequent conflicts, the Canal War, the 1973 October War, and the Israeli invasion of Lebanon in 1982 all created problems for Jordan. They put new pressures on Jordan's problems in dealing with Palestinian refugees and in integrating Palestinian citizens into the nation. The fact that Jordan sympathized with Saddam Hussein after Iraq's invasion of Kuwait in 1990 did more serious damage. Jordanians, like Palestinians, were pushed out of many of the Gulf countries, Jordan lost much of its foreign aid, energy assistance, and the United States ceased to provide military assistance.

The situation has improved in several important respects. Jordan's peace agreement with Israel in 1994 put an end to any near-term risk of involvement in another conflict with Israel and defined Jordan's western border. Like Egypt, Jordan has consistently met the terms of its peace agreements with Israel, and this has greatly reduced the risk of any clash or conflict that could lead to a major conventional war or clash.

A combination of the Jordanian peace agreement with Israel and the fact that Jordan distanced itself from Saddam Hussein's regime also improved relations with the United States and nations like Saudi Arabia. U.S. aid resumed and helped Jordan's military and economic development. Jordan's security also benefited from a shift away from the support of Saddam Hussein and improvements with its relations with other Arab states. The end of Saddam Hussein's regime in Iraq in 2003 then removed the only serious potential military threat to its eastern border, although Syrian-Jordanian relations have never been smooth and some form of a clash between the two countries remains a possibility.

Jordan's security does, however, remain fragile. Jordan still has to plan to deter Israeli military incursions. At the same time, Jordan must secure its borders with Israel and the West Bank and face new problems because of a flood of Iraqi exiles into Jordan and the threat posed to Jordan by the insurgency in Iraq.

Jordan faces a growing threat from Islamist extremist groups and has been the subject of attacks by elements of Al Qa'ida based in Iraq. It fears the potential division of Iraq among Arab Sunnis, Arab Shi'ites, and Arab Kurds. King Abdullah of Jordan has expressed his fear of the potential role that Iran might play in creating a "Shi'ite crescent" out of Iran, Iraq, Syria, and Lebanon—creating potential new pressures on Jordan from the north and the west.

Jordan's support of the United States in the invasion of Iraq has been highly unpopular with Jordan's people. At the same time, Jordan faces growing internal instability because of the hostility its population feels toward Israel and toward the United States for being Israel's ally. No precise breakout of how many Jordanians are "Palestinian" is available, and many Transjordanians and Palestinians have intermarried, but some experts feel that Jordan has a Palestinian majority. Jordan must also deal with a large population of Iraqis in Amman. Some experts feel Jordan now has more than 1-million Iraqi exiles and that Amman alone has nearly 400,000 Iraqis working and living there since the mid-1990s.

The end result is that the most immediate security threats to Jordan are internal instability and terrorism. Jordan still faces constant problems with Palestinian infiltration, often by elements hostile to its regime. At the same time, it faces a growing threat from Iraq and its border with Iraq is relatively easy for jihadists to cross. Jordan has been able to block a number of major terrorist strikes, but some attacks have been successful.

On August 19, 2005, three rockets were launched from a building in Aqaba aimed at the USS *Ashland* and at the Israeli city of Eilat. Both organizations claiming responsibility for the attack were Al-Qa'ida organizations, one of which was Abu Musab al-Zarqawi's Al-Qa'ida in Mesopotamia who said they sent their people from Iraq.[1] Another such attack came in early November when three Iraqis strapped with explosives blew themselves up in three different hotels around Amman killing 57 people and wounding more than 100. Al Qa'ida in Iraq claimed responsibility for this terrorist act as well, threatening that attacks against Jordan will continue.[2]

At the same time, Jordan cannot ignore the constant pressure that the Israeli-Palestinian conflict puts on Jordan's internal stability and the risk that some sudden escalation of the conflict could force Jordan to become involved on the Palestinian side or lead to an active domestic Palestinian threat to the regime. Political risks currently seem to be much more serious than military ones, but the risk of some kind of military clash over Israel's future treatment of the Palestinians cannot be ignored.

TRENDS IN JORDANIAN FORCE DEVELOPMENT

The recent trends in the size of Jordanian forces are shown in Figure 6.1. There have been no significant increases in recent years, and Jordan has concentrated on force quality rather than force quantity. In fact, Jordan has long maintained some of the best-trained and most professional military forces in the Middle East and maintained a force structure of 100,500 actives and some 35,000 reserves.

Jordan has continued to modernize its forces and has taken on peacekeeping as a major new mission. It is seeking to modernize its Intelligence, Surveillance, and Reconnaissance (IS&R) capabilities and to adopt some of the "digital" and "netcentric" approaches to warfare used by the United States and Israel. It has concentrated on counterterrorist and Special Forces in recent years, developing better intelligence cooperation with other nations in this mission, and improving its border defenses. Jordan's Special Forces and counterterrorism forces are seen as some of the most effective forces in the developing world.

It was in the process of a major strategic review in 2006, but it had developed the following priorities for each of its military services:[3]

- *Land forces:* Strengthen weapons, personal equipment, armed helicopters, and air transport. Develop faster and more efficient response for counterterrorism and humanitarian missions. Modernize artillery, air defenses, and antiarmored weapons. Strengthen IS&R capabilities with better sensors, alarms, and monitoring equipment. Improve information technology and night-vision equipment.

- *Air forces:* Dispose of outdated aircraft. Improve logistics and maintenance systems. Create
  a search and rescue unit and obtain more attack helicopters. Reinforce air defense systems. Modernize the command-and-control system to support joint warfare for the entire military.

- *Naval forces:* Complete and equip new naval base on Gulf of Aqaba. Add special wing to Special Operations Training Center for naval, coastal, and port security training. Build a complete naval training center.

Figure 6.1 Jordanian Military: Force Structure

	1990	2000	2005	2006
Manpower	124,250	149,000	145,500	145,500
Active	85,250	~104,000	~100,500	100,500
Army	74,000	90,000	85,000	85,000
Navy	250	~480	~500	500
Air Force	11,000	13,500	15,000	15,000
Paramilitary	4,000	~10,000	~10,000	10,000
Reserve	35,000	35,000	35,000	35,000
Army	30,000	30,000	30,000	30,000
Joint	N/A	N/A	N/A	5,000

Source: Various editions of the International Institute for Strategic Studies (IISS) *Military Balance,* U.S., British, and other experts.

At the same time, Jordan has faced massive problems in financing its military modernization. This recapitalization crisis in Jordanian forces is shown in the steady decline in the value of Jordan arms imports reflected in Figures 6.2 and 6.3. Figure 6.2 shows the precipitous decline in the value of Jordanian arms imports that began long before the Gulf War, and which essentially marked the end of Jordan's effort to compete with Egyptian and Israeli force modernization. Figure 6.3 shows

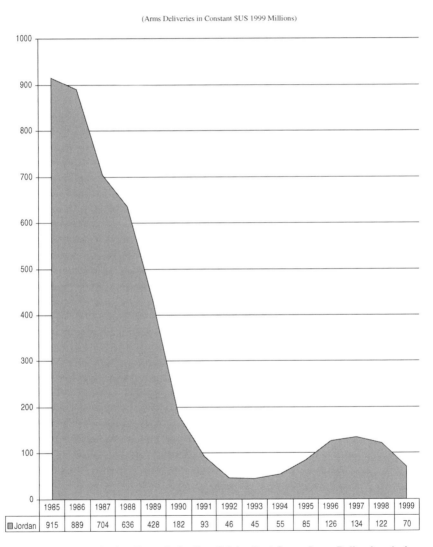

(Arms Deliveries in Constant $US 1999 Millions)

	1985	1986	1987	1988	1989	1990	1991	1992	1993	1994	1995	1996	1997	1998	1999
Jordan	915	889	704	636	428	182	93	46	45	55	85	126	134	122	70

Figure 6.2 The Jordanian Recapitalization Crisis: Part One—Arms Deliveries during 1985–1999

New Jordanian Arms Agreements and Deliveries by Country: 1993-2004 (in $US Current Millions)

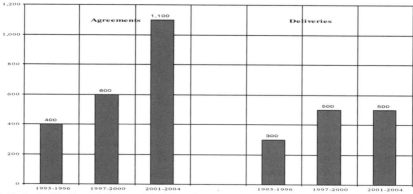

0 = Data less than $50 million or nil. All data rounded to the nearest $100 million.

New Jordanian Arms Orders by Supplier Country: 1993-2004 (Arms Agreements in $US Current Millions)

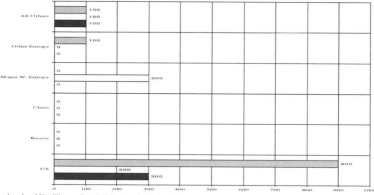

0 = less than $50 million or nil, and all data rounded to the nearest $100 million.

Source: Adapted by Anthony H. Cordesman, from Richard F. Grimmett, Conventional Arms Transfers to the Developing Nations, Congressional Research Service, various editions.

Figure 6.3   The Jordanian Recapitalization Crisis: Part Two

that Jordan's situation has improved since its peace treaty with Israel and that Jordan has been able to get significant numbers of arms from the United States, but that these imports still fall far below Egyptian and Israeli levels.

Jordan has dealt with this situation as effectively as its resources permit. It has focused on buying the key weapons systems that do the most to improve its capabilities and has developed a steadily improving domestic capability to modify and upgrade its weapons. It has also developed steadily better light forces, including some of the best-trained and most combat effective Special Forces in the region. These steps, however, have still not enabled Jordan to keep up with the rate of military modernization in Israel and in Egypt.

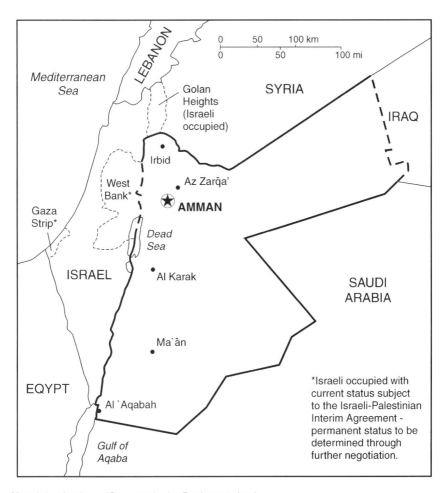

Map 6.1   Jordan   (Cartography by Bookcomp, Inc.)

JORDANIAN MANPOWER

Jordan has a large manpower pool to draw upon with only limited sectarian and ethnic differences. It had a population of over 5.9 million in mid-2006. Some 1.6 million males were available for military service, and 1.3 million were fit for service. Nearly 61,000 males reached the military age of 17 in 2006.[4]

The CIA estimates that its population was 98 percent Arab. Its only significant minorities were Circassian (1 percent) and Armenian (1 percent). In terms of religion, Jordan was about 92 percent Sunni Muslim, 6 percent Christian (majority Greek Orthodox, but some Greek and Roman Catholics, Syrian Orthodox, Coptic Orthodox, Armenian Orthodox, and Protestant denominations), and 2 percent other (several small Shi'a Muslim and Druze populations).

The fact Jordan has so many Palestinians that may not be loyal to the regime presents problems in drawing fully on its manpower resources, however, and Jordan cannot afford to significantly increase its combat unit numbers with reserves. It has had to cut back on reserve training to the point where its reserves have limited effectiveness, and it has recently frozen its intake of conscripts for its active forces to reduce the cost of its forces. This freeze effectively ensured that Jordan's active and reserve forces would not grow with its population, and Jordan may have to make additional cuts in both its active and reserve strength.[5]

JORDANIAN ARMY

The Jordanian Army is regarded as one of the best trained and organized military forces in the Middle East, although it has long faced serious resource limitations on its ability to modernize its equipment and military technology. It had a total of some 85,000 actives and 30,000 reserves in 2006. In spite of funding problems, it had highly effective armored, mechanized, artillery, and Special Forces units.

The Jordanian Army Command Structure

The trends in the Jordanian Army are summarized in Figure 6.4. In 2006, the army was organized into four commands, with a strategic reserve and Special Operations Command.

- The North Command had two mechanized, one infantry, one artillery, and one aid defense brigade, and it defended Jordan's border with Syria. Its structure and deployment reflected the fact that Syria had threatened to invade Jordan in the past, and Jordan was still forced to plan for a conflict with an Arab neighbor.

- Two of Jordan's other commands were designed to act as a deterrent and defense against an Israeli incursion, as well as provide for internal security. The Central Command had one mechanized, one light infantry, one artillery, and one air defense brigade. The Southern Command had one armored and one infantry command.

- The Eastern Command does not seem to have been reorganized since the fall of Saddam Hussein's regime, but may be in the future. It had two mechanized, one artillery, and one air defense brigade.

- Jordan's Strategic Reserve is a heavy, highly mobile force composed of the Royal Armored Division, with three armored, one artillery, and one air defense brigade.

- The Special Operations Command had two Special Force brigades, a Ranger unit, and a counterterrorism battalion.

Jordan has reorganized its land force deployments to improve coverage of the Iraqi and Syrian borders and provide a lighter border force to cover its border with Israel to emphasize border security over defense against Israel. This new border force is highly mobile, has improved surveillance technology, and could be supported by an

Figure 6.4   Jordanian Army: Force Structure

	1990	2000	2005	2006
Manpower	104,000	120,000	115,000	115,500
Active	74,000	90,000	85,000	85,000
Reserve	30,000	30,000	30,000	30,000
Combat Units—Army	~8	17	24	24
Infantry Brigade	2	3	1	1
Lt. Infantry Brigade	N/A	N/A	1	1
Artillery Brigade	N/A	4	4	4
Artillery Battalion	16	N/A	N/A	N/A
Air Defense Brigade	2	2	3	3
Mechanized Brigade	3	3	5	5
Armored Brigade	N/A	N/A	1	1
RECCE Battalion	N/A	1	N/A	N/A
Reserve	1	N/A	5	5
Armored Royal Division	1 (not res)	1 (not res)	1	1
Artillery Brigade	N/A	N/A	1	1
Air Defense Brigade	N/A	N/A	1	1
Armored Brigade	N/A	N/A	3	3
Special Operation	4	4	4	4
Ranger Battalion	N/A	N/A	1	1
Counterterrorism Army Battalion	N/A	N/A	1	1
Special Forces Brigade	1	2	2	2
Airborne	3	2	N/A	N/A
MBT	1,131	1,204	1,120	1,120
CRI Challenger 1 (Al Hussein)	N/A	N/A	390	390
FV4030/2 Khalid	360	270	274	274
M-60	218	354	288	288
M-60A1/M-60A3	218	354	288	288
Tariq Centurion	293	280	90 (stored)	90 (stored)
M-47/M-48A5	260	300	78 (stored)	78 (stored)
Scorpion	19	19	19	19
RECCE	144	N/A	N/A	N/A
Ferret	144	N/A	N/A	N/A
AIFV	N/A	~35	226+	226+
BMP-2	N/A	~35	~26	26+
FSV 90	N/A	N/A	~200	200
MK III-20 Ratel-20	N/A	N/A	~200	200
APC		1,400	~1,350	1,350
APC (T)	1,269+	1,400	1,300	1,300
FV 103 Spartan	0	0	~100	~100
M-113A1/M-113A2	1,235	1,400	1,200	1,200
APC (W)	34+	0	50	50
BTR-94 (BTR-80)	0	0	50	50

Saracen	34	In paramilitary	In paramilitary	In paramilitary
EE-11 Urutu	Some	In paramilitary	In paramilitary	In paramilitary
Artillery	~247+	1,321	1,233	1,233
TOWED	95	115	94	94
105 mm	36	50	54	54
M-101	36	N/A	N/A	N/A
M-102	0	50	36	36
MOBAT (being delivered in 2005)	0	0	18	18
155 mm	55	40	36	36
M-1/M-59	17	10	18	18
M-114	38	30	18	18
203 mm	4	25	4	4
M-115	4 (stored)	25 (stored)	4	4
SP	152	406	399	399
105 mm	0	30	35	35
M-52	0	30	35	35
155 mm	128	240	282	282
M-109	108	220	253	253
M-109A1/M-109A2	108	220	253	253
M-44	20	20	29	29
203 mm	24	136	82	82
M-110A2	24	136	82	82
MOR	Some	800	740	740
81 mm	Some	450	450	450
107 mm	Some	50	60	60
M-30	Some	50	60	60
120 mm	Some	300	230	230
Brandt	Some	300	230	230
AT	970	5,440	~5,470	~5,470
MSL	640	640	670	670
Javelin	N/A	N/A	30	30
M47 Dragon	310	310	310	310
TOW	330	330	330	330
TOW msl/TOW-2A	330	330	330	330
RL	Some	Some	4,800+	4,800+
73 mm	0	0	Some	Some
RPG-26	0	0	Some	Some
94 mm	N/A	2,500	2,500	2,500
LAW-80	N/A	2,500	2,500	2,500
112 mm	Some	2,300	2,300	2,300
APILAS	Some	2,300	2,300	2,300

RCL	330	330	N/A	N/A
106 mm	330	330	N/A	N/A
M-40A1	?	330	N/A	N/A
AD	560+	1,258	~1,387	~1,387
SAM	80+	890+	992+	992+
SP	40	100	152	152
SA-13 Gopher	20	50	92	92
SA-8 Gecko	20	50	60	60
MANPAD	Some	790+	840+	840+
FIM-43 Redeye	Some	250	250	250
SA-14 Gremlin	Some	300	300	300
SA-16 Gimlet	N/A	240	240	240
SA-18 Grouse (Igla)	0	0	Some	Some
SA-7	Some	Some	50	50
SA-7B2 Grail	Some	Some	50	50
GUNS	408	368	395	395
20 mm	100	100	139	139
M-163	100	100	139	139
23 mm	44	52	40	40
ZU-23-4	44	52	40	40
40 mm	264	216	216	216
M-42	264	216	216	216
Radar	N/A	Some	Some	Some
AN/TPQ-36 Firefinder	N/A	Some	Some	Some
AN-TPQ-37 Firefinder	N/A	Some	Some	Some

~ = Estimated amount; * = combat capable; + = more than the number given but not specified how much
more; Some = unspecified amount; ? = unspecified amount, if any; N/A = not available; { } = serviceability in doubt.
Source: Various editions of the IISS *Military Balance,* U.S., British, and other experts.

electrified border security barrier system and systems of thermal TV cameras. These efforts are designed to provide protection from infiltration and smuggling from Iraq and Syria as well as to counter terrorist threats. Talks have also been under way between Israel and Jordan on cooperative border surveillance.

The changes in this command structure since the late 1980s also reflect Jordan's conversion to a lighter force structure emphasizing smaller combat formations and fewer tank battalions. Its army has become more professional, cheaper, more mobile, and better able to deal with internal security problems and the defense of Jordan's borders against threats like smuggling and infiltration across the Jordanian border. As part of this conversion, Jordan has put more emphasis on Special Forces, on lighter equipment like the AB3 Black Iris light-utility vehicle, and on remotely piloted helicopters for border surveillance.

Jordan's Special Operations Command is one of the most effective in the Middle East and North African area. It has been extensively reorganized since 1992 and had extensive special equipment, including advanced intelligence, communications, night-vision devices, and special purpose vehicles. It also includes the Royal Guard Brigade, elements of the police, and an air wing with AH-1F attack helicopters and UH-1H utility helicopters. It has taken over responsibility for operating its attack helicopters from the air force, one of the few commands in the region strong enough to do so.[6]

The Special Operations Command was under the Command of King Abdullah II before he became king, and it has received strong support from the Jordanian government. It played a critical role in securing the Iraqi border in the years before the Iraq War, where almost nightly clashes took place with Iraqi smugglers, and now plays a major role in blocking infiltration across the Syrian border. It conducts joint training with the British 5th Airborne Brigade and Parachute Regiment.

Jordan also has 10,000 men in its Public Security Directorate, which is under the command of the Ministry of the Interior and includes the police and Desert Patrol. The Desert Patrol had about 2,500 men and 25 EE-11 and 30 aging Saracen armored infantry and scout vehicles. The People's Army is a broad pool of reserves with some military training and which would assume part of the internal security mission in time of war. It had a large pool of mobilizable manpower, but little equipment and recent training. Its current strength is estimated at 35,000.

Jordanian Main Battle Tanks

The Jordanian Army has developed one of the most effective equipment mixes in the Middle East, in spite of its resource limitations, and it has been able to retain significant defensive and war-fighting capabilities in spite of its economic problems.

Jordan is one of the few countries that has succeeded in upgrading and modifying much of its land force combat equipment. It has developed a very efficient defense industrial and research and development base for a small nation, and one capable of cost-effective modifications of its armor and some aspects of its aircraft. Its King Abdullah II Design and Development Bureau (KADDB) has worked well in creating upgrade programs for its Challenger and M-60 tanks, and developing variants of equipment for its Special Forces and light armored vehicles.[7]

Jordan's main battle tank strength has stayed consistent at 1,200. In 2006, its first-line tanks consisted of 390 Challenger Is (Al Hussein), and 288 upgraded M-60A1/A3 conversions, supported by 274 much less capable Khalid (Chieftain) tanks. Jordan had 78 additional M-47/M-48s and 90 Centurions (Tariq).[8] Some of these older tanks had been heavily modernized, but most were not operational or were in storage.

Figure 6.4 shows that the transfer of the British Challengers or Al Husseins made a major improvement in Jordan's forces. Jordan's Al Husseins' capabilities are being improved by the addition of a 120-mm mechanical load assist system that will give the tanks a 120-mm smoothbore gun capability.[9] In addition, Jordan is studying a "Hybrid Turret" upgrade to the Al Hussein that would give the tank a greater degree of system commonality with Jordan's other tanks.[10]

Some 100 of Jordan's M60's will be upgraded with the Integrated Fire-Control System, or IFCS. The IFCS will boost the tanks' target acquisition and surveillance abilities during mobile conflicts, improve long-range fire, and enable them to engage multiple targets more rapidly.[11] The Jordanian military recently placed an order for 100 Turkish tracked FNSS ACVs to be delivered over the next three years.[12]

Jordanian Other Armored Vehicles

Jordan's other armor is less effective, although it has recently acquired some 200 Ratel FSV 90s and 100 FV103 Spartans. The Ratel 90 is a 6X6 armored wheeled fire-support vehicle. It is normally equipped with a turret-mounted 90-mm gun, a coaxial MG-4 (the South African–made version of the MAG), another MG-4 (C), and yet another MG-4 pintle mounted on the rear deck. The Spartan is a derivative of the CVR(T) (Combat Vehicle Reconnaissance tracked) which is usually specially configured for particular support and combat missions.

Most of its 245 armored infantry fighting vehicles consist of 19 aging Scorpions, 26 BMP-2s, and 200 Ratel 20s. Jordan has converted some of its roughly 1,200 M-113s from APCs (armored personnel carriers) to AIFVs (armored infantry fighting vehicles), but some of the rest of its M-113s are not fully operable. Jordan also has 50 BTR-94 APCs, for a total of 1,250.

Jordan has developed its own prototype of an AIFV called the Temsah (Crocodile) which would convert a Tariq tank chassis in ways somewhat similar to the Israeli conversions of main battle tanks. It would give Jordan one of the few AIFVs with the passive armor and other protection necessary to accompany its tanks into maneuver warfare and deal with well armed infantry and insurgent threats.

The Jordanian Public Security Directorate ordered 60 AB2 Al-Jawad armored troop carriers in 2002, but it seems that these vehicles have not yet been delivered.[13]

Jordanian Antitank Weapons

Jordan is relatively well armed with antitank guided weapons: 330 TOW (tube-launched optically tracked wire-guided missile) and TOW-2As, 20 on M-901 AFVs, with 310 Dragons, and 30 Javelins. It had large numbers of light antitank weapons, including RPG-26s, 2,500 LAW-80, and 2,300 APILAS.

Jordanian Artillery

As Figure 6.4 shows, Jordan has steadily modernized its artillery force and has relatively large amounts of self-propelled artillery for a force its size, although some of its inventory is now aging or obsolescent. In 2006, its total holdings included 35 M-52 105-mm and 29 M-44 155-mm weapons which are older systems, and 82 M-110A2 203-mm weapons, which offer long ranges and significant lethality but are also older weapons. The core of its strength included 253 M-109A1/A2 conversions and 82 M-110A2 203-mm weapons.

Jordan also had 94 towed artillery weapons: 36 M-102 105-mm, 18 MOBAT [(MOB ArTillery) delivered in 2005] 105-mm, 18 M-114 155-mm, 18 M-59/M-1 155-mm, and 4 M-115 203-mm guns.

The Jordanian army has begun replacing its existing M102 105-mm field pieces with 18 truck-mounted MOBAT 105-mm howitzers throughout 2005.[14] These guns will be fitted with the newly ordered Laser Inertial Automatic Pointing System that will allow operators to aim them faster and more accurately.[15]

Jordan cannot, however, afford to fully support its artillery with advanced target acquisition, fire and battle management, and counterbattery capabilities. It must rely on presiting most towed weapons and using them defensively to get the maximum effect against any serious conventional threat, although it does train its forces in maneuver and in rapidly targeting individual weapons and switching fires.

The data on lighter weapons holdings is more uncertain. According to the IISS, Jordan had 450 81-mm mortars (130 on AFVs), 60 107-mm mortars, and 230 120-mm mortars.

Jordanian Antiaircraft

Jordan had some 400 AA (antiaircraft) guns—including 139 M-163 20-mm, 40 ZSU-23-4 radar-guided 23-mm, and 216 M-42 40-mm guns. It had 60 self-propelled SA-8s, plus 92 SA-13s, 50 SA-7B2s, 300 SA-14s, 240 SA-16s, and 250 obsolete Red Eye man-portable surface-to-air missile launchers. Jordan also has some radar capabilities including some AN/TPQ-36/37 Firefinders.[16]

These weapons were capable of protecting ground troops only at short ranges and against aircraft flying at low altitudes. The Jordanian Army would be highly vulnerable to Israeli missile and guided bomb attacks if the Israel Air Force (IAF) suppressed its air force and longer-range surface-to-air missile forces. The Jordanian Army would be particularly vulnerable while its armored units were maneuvering or have not yet dispersed and dug into defensive positions. As Iraq was shown during the First Gulf War, however, even dispersed and dug-in major weapons systems are now highly vulnerable to precision air attack.

Jordanian Army Readiness and Effectiveness

Jordanian Army training and readiness is generally good to very good by regional standards. Jordan carries out meaningful maneuver exercises, organizes and trains for effective sustainability, and practices combined arms warfare more realistically than most of its neighbors. Jordan also has an effective defense industry for a nation its size, capable of modernizing many of its weapons and repairing combat damage.

Jordan would have little offensive capability against Israel, but is strong enough to be a major deterrent to any Israeli incursion. While its forces are far smaller than those of Syria, they again are strong enough to deter Syrian action, and the Jordanian Army no longer faces a meaningful threat from Israel. The Jordanian Army is particularly well organized for asymmetric warfare and internal security missions. The

King's emphasis on Special Forces has created one of the most respected Special Operations capabilities in any Middle Eastern force, and Jordanian units regularly practice a variety of realistic operations, including the use of helicopter assaults and mobility.

JORDANIAN AIR FORCE

Jordan's 15,000-man air force had 100 operational combat aircraft in 2006, and 140 attack helicopters. Air force training and readiness are good, and air and air-to-ground combat training is more demanding and realistic than that of most regional powers. As Figure 6.5 shows, however, Jordan has been slow to modernize and has faced major funding constraints in buying and operating first-line combat aircraft. It has not been able to afford airborne warning and control aircraft, advanced targeting systems, or advanced electronic intelligence and other intelligence aircraft. The Royal Jordanian Air Force (RJAF) has the skill levels to operate such systems, but cannot afford them.[17]

Fixed-Wing Air Units

Most of Jordan's aircraft are comparable in quality to those held by Syria, but not comparable to those held by Israel. Jordan's F-16A/Bs are its only modern fighter, but they do not have the advanced avionics performance capability of Israel's F-16C/Ds or F-15s.[18]

In 2006, the RJAF had seven fighter attack/reconnaissance squadrons with 3/54 F-5E/Fs and 1/15 F-1EJ. It had one fighter squadron with 1/15 Mirage F-1 CJ/BJ and was building up to a total of two fighter squadrons with 32 operational F-16A/Bs. Jordan first took delivery of 16 F-16s as part of the Peace Falcon One program and lost one in a training accident. It received 17 more in Peace Falcon Two and signed a letter of intent in November 2005 to buy three more F-16Bs for training purposes.

The RJAF has ordered 17 upgrade kits to boost the service life of its F-16s and has contracted with Turkey to install them.[19] It also is acquiring Link 16 secure communications and more advanced C4I capabilities for its F-16s and other aircraft.

Its Mirage F-1 aircraft could not hope to engage modern IAF fighters with a high rate of success. It is seeking to sell some F-1Cs, but has replaced the F-1D trainer it lost in an accident.

Jordan's F-5Es are aging. Although they may be upgraded as a result of an agreement with Singapore, the F-5E is nearing the end of its useful life, and even upgrade versions have limited mission capability. As a result, Jordan may sell some of its F-5s as its new F-16s come fully into service. There are also reports that it is examining the purchase of 20 used Belgian and Dutch F-16s to allow a more comprehensive modernization of its F-5s and some of its Mirages.[20]

Jordan lacks any form of Airborne Early Warning (AEW) aircraft and Jordan's ground-based air battle management capabilities have severe technical limitations. Jordan is, however, examining the possible purchase of UAVs. It also is looking at

Figure 6.5   Jordanian Air Force: Force Structure

	1990	2000	2005	2006
Manpower	11,000	13,500	15,000	15,000
Air Force	11,000	13,500	15,000	15,000
Air Defense	?	3,400	3,400	3,400
Total Aircraft*	135	109	121	100
Fighter	6/93	6/91	6/101	7/85
F-5	59	50	55	54
F-5E Tiger II	52	50	55	54
F-5F Tiger II	7	?	?	?
F-16	0	16	16	16
F-16A Fighting Falcon	0	12	12	28
F-16B Fighting Falcon	0	4	4	4
F-1	34	25	30	15
Mirage F-1BJ	2	?	?	?
Mirage F-1CJ	15	?	15	N/A
Mirage F-1E	17	?	15	15
Operational Conversion Unit	18	N/A	N/A	N/A
F-5A	14	N/A	N/A	N/A
F-5B	4	N/A	N/A	N/A
MP, surveillance	N/A	N/A	2	2
RU-38A Twin Condor	N/A	N/A	2	2
Transport	13	26	14	14
A-340	0	N/A	1	1
A-340-211	0	N/A	1	1
C-130	6	8	4	4
C-130B	2	3	0	0
C-130H Hercules	4	5	4	4
CASA 212	3	4	2	2
CASA 212A Aviocar	3	4	2	2
CL-604 Challenger	0	N/A	2	2
CN-235	0	N/A	2	2
Gulfstream III	2	2	N/A	N/A
Gulfstream IV	0	N/A	2	2
L-1011 Tristar	0	Some	1	1
Boeing 727	2	0	0	0
Utility	0	N/A	2	2
TB-20 Trinidad	0	N/A	2	2
Training	52	51	28	43
Bulldog 103	18	16	15	15
CASA C-101 Aviojet	16	15	13	13
*F-1BJ (F-1B)**	N/A	2	N/A	15
PA-28-161	N/A	12	N/A	N/A
PA-34-200	N/A	6	N/A	N/A

Piper	18	N/A	0	0
Warrior-II	12	N/A	0	0
Seneca-II	6	N/A	0	0
Helicopter	63+	65	91	111
Attack	24	16	20	40+
AH-1F Cobra	N/A	N/A	20	40+
AH-1S	24	16	N/A	N/A
Support	29	12	15	15
AS-332M Super Puma	12	9	12	12
S-70A Black Hawk	3	3	3	3
S-76	14	N/A	N/A	N/A
Utility	10+	37	56	56
BO-105	Some	3	3	3
EC-635	2	N/A	9	9
HUGHES 500D	8	8	8	8
UH-1H Iroquois	N/A	18	36	36
UH-60 Black Hawk	N/A	8	N/A	N/A
AD	126	80	~80+	1,120+
SAM	N/A	N/A	3 battalions	Some
PAC-2	N/A	N/A	3 battalions	Some
TOWED	126	80	80	1,120
I-HAWK MIM-23B	126	80	80	1,120
MSL Tactical	Some	Some	Some	Some
ASM	N/A	Some	Some	Some
AGM-65D	N/A	Some	Some	Some
TOW	Some	N/A	Some	Some
AAM	N/A	Some	Some	Some
AIM-7 Sparrow	N/A	N/A	Some	Some
AIM-9 Sidewinder	Some	Some	Some	Some
R-550 Magic	Some	Some	Some	Some
R530	N/A	Some	Some	Some

Source: Various editions of the IISS *Military Balance,* U.S., British, and other experts.

possible replacements for its CASA 101 trainers, such as the Super Tucano, BC-21, or PC-9.

Rotary-Wing Air Units

Jordan does have more than 40 AH-1F attack helicopters, some with TOW antiarmor missiles. These are effective systems, and Jordanian proficiency in using them is good. Jordanian doctrine, tactics, and exercises are modern—unlike those of most regional powers. Joint warfare and Special Operations exercises set high standards, and Jordan has 3 S-70 Black Hawk helicopters and 12 AS-332 Super Pumas to provide support.

These helicopter forces could provide significant support to the Jordanian Army in both maneuver warfare and Special Operations missions, but would face major problems in flying evasive attack profiles along most of the border with Israel because they would be highly vulnerable to Israeli air power.

Jordan is currently studying long-term replacements for its UH-1s, AB-212s, and Super Pumas. It decided to buy additional EC 636s in January 2006 and has eight more S-70 Black Hawks coming into service by the end of 2006. Some will be specially equipped for Special Forces missions.

JORDANIAN LAND-BASED AIR DEFENSES

Jordan has modernized some aspects of its ground-based air defense C^4I/BM system with U.S. aid, but has lacked the funds to compete with Israel in systems integration, sensor and sensor integration capability, digital data links, and electronic warfare capabilities. It now has two air defense systems with limited interoperability: its air force and Improved Hawk forces use a U.S. system supplied by Westinghouse, and its land forces use a Russian system.[21]

In 2006, Jordan had two air defense battalions divided into 14 batteries each with 80 Improved Hawk launchers, organized into two brigades with a total of 24 launchers. Jordan's Improved Hawk forces, however, have important limitations. They are not mobile, they have blind spots in their low-altitude coverage, and Israel can target them. The Improved Hawks have been upgraded to Phase 3 Pip (product improvement program) status, but may still be vulnerable to Israeli and even Syrian electronic countermeasures.

According to *Jane's*, the Jordan military maintains three PAC-2 Patriot missile batteries around Amman and Irbid.[22] As has been discussed earlier, the Patriot is a highly advanced surface-to-air missile system with advanced radars and high resistance to electronic countermeasures. It has a limited missile defense capability against Scud-type systems with a limited area or "footprint" of defensive coverage.

Jordan is steadily improving other aspects of its C4I systems and has signed a contract with Northrup Grumman for a major upgrade of its current capabilities.

JORDANIAN NAVAL FORCES

The trends in Jordan's Navy are shown in Figure 6.6. Jordan's small naval forces report to the Director of Operations at the headquarters of the general staff and consist of a 500-man force with several coastal patrol boats. In 2006, these included three 124-ton Al Hussein class, and four small 8-ton Faysal class (Bertram) patrol boats. Most patrol boats were based at Aqaba, but some can deploy to the Dead Sea.[23]

Jordan's three 30-meter, Al Hussein-class boats were built by Vosper in the late 1980s and early 1990s. They are well maintained, are in active service, and have twin 30-mm guns, radars, and chaff launchers.

The four 8-ton Faysal-class boats only had machine guns. Jordan also had three Rotork class for patrolling the Dead Sea. These craft are normally kept on shore. They are light 9-ton craft, capable of carrying 30 troops each.[24]

Figure 6.6   Jordanian Navy: Force Structure

	1990	2000	2005	2006
Manpower	250	~480	~500	~500
Navy	250	~480	~500	~500
Facilities	1	1	1	1
Aqaba	1	1	1	1
Patrol and Coastal Combatants	Some	13	20	20
PB	N/A	3	7	7
Al Hashim	N/A	3	3	3
Bertram	0	N/A	4	4
PCC (less than 100 tons)	N/A	N/A	10	10
PFI	N/A	3	3	3
Al Hussein (less than 100 tons)	N/A	3	3	3
Other armored boats	N/A	4	N/A	N/A

Source: Various editions of the IISS *Military Balance,* U.S., British, and other experts.

In addition, Jordan has four 17-foot launches and four 14-foot rocket propelled grenade boats used by its frogman units.[25]

JORDANIAN PARAMILITARY, SECURITY, AND INTELLIGENCE FORCES

Like all of its neighbors, Jordan maintains a large mix of paramilitary, security, and intelligence forces. The unclassified portion of these forces is shown in Figure 6.7. It should be noted that some of these numbers are uncertain and that other sources show the manning of the Public Security Directorate—which includes some police and the Desert Patrol—as only 3,000.

Jordan's Special Forces, including its Special Forces Brigade (which includes the 71st and 101st Counterterrorist Battalions, the 81st and 91st Paratroop Battalions, and a psyops unit) also play a major role in internal security and counterterrorism. The Jordanian Special Operations Command coordinates the Royal Jordanian Special Forces (RJSF), Police Public Security, or Police Security Force Brigade, Royal Guard, an airlift unit, and special intelligence elements.[26]

These Jordan security services—and particularly the General Intelligence Directorate (GID or Dairat al Mukhabarat)—are generally felt to be some of the most effective in the Middle East, although they have not been able to prevent all "Al Qa'ida in the Two Rivers" attacks or some operations by Palestinian terrorist groups.[27]

While Jordan could not prevent incidents like the hotel bombings in 2005, it has halted many other attacks since the late 1990s. For example, Jordanian border officials intercepted and killed armed individuals attempting to infiltrate northern Israel from Jordan in July 2004. Jordanian border officials intercepted suspects involved in a Abu Mus'ab al-Zarqawi plot in April 2004 to use truck bombs against Jordanian

Figure 6.7 Jordanian Paramilitary and Security Forces: Force Structure

	1990	2000	2005	2006
Manpower	19,000+	~30,000	~45,000	~45,000
Active	4,000	~10,000	~10,000	10,000
Public Security Directorate	4,000	~10,000	~10,000	~10,000
Civil Militia "People's Army" (reservist)	15,000+	~20,000	~35,000	~35,000
Equipment By Type	N/A	55+	55+	55+
Tank, light	N/A	Some	Some	Some
Scorpion	N/A	Some	Some	Some
APC (W)	N/A	55	55	55+
EE-11 Urutu	N/A	25	25	25+
FV603 Saracen	N/A	30	30	30
Deployment	N/A	12	1,246	2,331
Burundi, UN	N/A	N/A	N/A	62
ONUB, observers	N/A	N/A	N/A	5
Cote D'Ivoire, UN	0	0	8	210
UNOCI, observers	0	0	4	7
Croatia, UN	N/A	1	N/A	N/A
UNMOP, observer	N/A	1	N/A	N/A
Democratic Republic of Congo, UN	0	0	30	20
MONUC, observers	0	0	23	6
East Timor, UN	0	0	2	1
UNOTIL, observer	0	0	2	1
Ethiopia/Eritria, UN	0	0	966	962
UNMEE Observers	0	0	7	7
Haiti, UN	0	0	N/A	755
MINUSTAH	0	0	N/A	755
Georgia, UN	N/A	6	8	9
UNOMIG observers	N/A	6	8	9
Liberia, UN	0	0	N/A	124
UNMIL observers	0	0	N/A	7
Serbia and Montenegro	0	0	100	101
NATO, KFOR I	0	0	99	99
UN, UNMIK	0	0	1	2
Sierra Leone, UN	0	0	132	84
UNAMSIL observers	0	0	10	4
Sudan, UN	0	0	N/A	3
UNMIS observers	0	0	N/A	3
Tajikistan, UN	N/A	5	N/A	N/A
UNMOT, observers	N/A	5	N/A	N/A

Source: Various editions of the IISS *Military Balance,* U.S., British, and other experts.

Government targets and the U.S. Embassy in Amman as they tried to enter Jordan from Syria. They also stopped a terrorist driving a vehicle loaded with large amounts of explosives as he tried to cross the Iraqi-Jordanian border in November 2004.

Major Terrorist and Extremist Threats

The movement led by Abu Mus'ab al-Zarqawi has maintained a serious threat in Jordan as well as in Iraq, and Jordan has continued to purse Zarqawi and his supporters. Abu Mus'ab al- Zarqawi's group, Tanzim Qa'idat al-Jihad fi Bilad al-Rafidayn (QJBR) is based in Iraq, but Zarqawi is a Jordanian, and he attacked the Jordanian monarchy and the regime long before he shifted operations to Iraq. The U.S. State Department describes his movement as follows:[28]

Tanzim Qa'idat al-Jihad fi Bilad al-Rafidayn (QJBR) is also known as the Al-Zarqawi Network, Al-Qa'ida in Iraq, Al-Qa'ida of Jihad Organization in the Land of The Two Rivers, and Jama'at al-Tawhid wa'al-Jihad

...Zarqawi's group has been active in the Levant since its involvement in the failed Millennium plot directed against US, Western, and Jordanian targets in Jordan in late 1999. The group assassinated USAID official Laurence Foley in 2002, but the Jordanian Government has successfully disrupted further plots against US and Western interests in Jordan, including a major arrest of Zarqawi associates in 2004 planning to attack Jordanian security targets.

...The Jordanian Palestinian Abu Mus'ab al-Zarqawi (Ahmad Fadhil Nazzal al-Khalaylah, a.k.a. Abu Ahmad, Abu Azraq) established cells in Iraq soon after the commencement of Operation Iraqi Freedom (OIF), formalizing his group in April 2004 to bring together jihadists and other insurgents in Iraq fighting against US and Coalition forces. Zarqawi initially called his group "Unity and Jihad" (Jama'at al-Tawhid wa'al-Jihad, or JTJ).

...In August 2003, Zarqawi's group carried out a major international terrorist attack in Iraq when it bombed the Jordanian Embassy in Baghdad, followed 12 days later by a suicide vehicle-borne improvised explosive device (VBIED) attack against the UN Headquarters in Baghdad, killing 23, including the Secretary-General's Special Representative for Iraq, Sergio Vieira de Mello....Zarqawi's group fulfilled a pledge to target Shi'a; its March attacks on Shi'a celebrating the religious holiday of Ashura, killing over 180, was its most lethal attack to date. The group also killed key Iraqi political figures in 2004, most notably the head of Iraq's Governing Council.

...Zarqawi and his group helped finance, recruit, transport, and train Sunni Islamic extremists for the Iraqi resistance. The group adopted its current name after its October 2004 merger with Usama Bin Ladin's al-Qa'ida. The immediate goal of QJBR is to expel the Coalition—through a campaign of bombings, kidnappings, assassinations, and intimidation—and establish an Islamic state in Iraq. QJBR's longer-term goal is to proliferate jihad from Iraq into "Greater Syria," that is, Syria, Lebanon, Israel, and Jordan.

....QJBR's numerical strength is unknown, though the group has attracted new recruits to replace key leaders and other members killed or captured by Coalition forces. Zarqawi's increased stature from his formal relationship with al-Qa'ida could attract additional recruits to QJBR.

...QJBR's operations are predominately Iraq-based, but the group maintains an extensive logistical network throughout the Middle East, North Africa, and Europe.

...QJBR probably receives funds from donors in the Middle East and Europe, local sympathizers in Iraq, and a variety of businesses and criminal activities. In many cases, QJBR's donors are probably motivated by support for jihad rather than affiliation with any specific terrorist group.

Jordanian Counterterrorism

According to the U.S. State Department, Jordan's State Security court has maintained a heavy caseload in dealing with Zarqawi-affiliated suspects. It has sentenced eight men to death, including Zarqawi and five others in absentia, for the murder of USAID official Laurence Foley in Amman outside his home on October 28, 2002. The list of other convictions in 2004 provides a similar picture of how serious the Zarqawi movement is. Three Jordanians—including one of Zarqawi's nephews —were found guilty of plotting attacks against U.S. and Israeli tourists in May. Ahmad al-Riyati and eight men being tried in absentia (including Zarqawi and reputed Ansar al-Islam leader Mullah Krekar) were sentenced to prison in June. Bilal al-Hiyari, a Zarqawi fundraiser, was sentenced to six months in jail in October. Some 14 other Zarqawi supporters were indicted in 2004. The State Security Court has also, however, indicted other Jordanians for plotting to attack foreign diplomats and attacks against U.S. and Israeli targets. Operations against Jordanian Palestinians remain a major priority.

Jordan has not, however, been able to insulate itself from attack by Al Qa'ida. The U.S. State Department annual report summarized Jordanian counterterrorism activity in 2005 as follows:[29]

The Jordanian Government aggressively pursued the network of fugitive Jordanian terrorist Abu Musab al-Zarqawi, believed responsible for attacks in Jordan and Iraq, including the November 9 bombing of three hotels in Amman that killed 63 people and the August 19 rocket attack in Aqaba that also impacted Eilat, Israel. Jordan publicly condemned terrorist acts throughout the world, introduced heightened security measures, and began drafting new counterterrorism legislation. Jordanian security forces disrupted numerous terrorist plots during the year, including several that targeted U.S. interests. Jordan's State Security Court, which oversees terrorism-related cases, processed a heavy caseload, many of which involved suspects affiliated with Zarqawi.

The November 9 hotel bombings, the country's worst-ever terrorist attacks, left many Jordanians shocked. The targeting of a wedding reception, in particular, eroded support for Zarqawi and al-Qa'ida within Jordan. Surveys taken in the weeks after the bombings showed that approximately 80 percent of those polled had negative opinions of al-Qa'ida; 90 percent believed al-Qa'ida was a terrorist organization; and approximately 65 percent changed their views as a result of the bombings. The televised confession of would-be suicide bomber Sajida al-Rishawi further reduced support for Zarqawi and Islamic extremists in general.

In mid-November, in response to the hotel bombings, members of the royal family, including Queen Rania and Princess Basma, led a series of street protests, vigils, and marches against terrorism; approximately 200,000 people participated in the largest of these events. The government promoted religious tolerance, interfaith dialogue, and shared values between civilizations with a number of initiatives, including the July International Islamic Conference in Amman, and the ensuing "Amman Message" of tolerance and moderation in Islam. In December, Jordan called on the Organization of the Islamic Conference to dedicate itself to combating extremism.

After the November bombings, Jordanian Public Security Department commanders met with representatives of hotels, banks, restaurants, and tourist sites to discuss implementing security measures to prevent future attacks. Many hotels, shopping malls, and other major institutions installed metal detectors and electronic surveillance systems. In response to King Abdullah's call for a strategy to preempt terrorist plots, 23 Jordanian academics created an NGO called The Scientific Society to Combat Terrorism.

Border security remained a top concern of Jordanian officials. Since the Aqaba rocket attack in August, Jordan has enforced strict security measures at the Karama-Trebil border crossing, including thorough manual searches of all vehicles and persons attempting to enter the country. In addition, Jordanian authorities issued a zero tolerance policy toward fuel smuggling. Notably, Jordan and Iraq signed a security agreement to establish a committee to exchange information on terrorists, organized crime, and border infiltration.

The State Security Court (SSC) moved forward several high-profile al-Qa'ida-related terrorism cases. Legal action against 13 men accused of plotting a chemical bomb attack in Amman in April 2004 continued as reputed cell leader Zamia Jays threatened court officials and admitted meeting with Abu Musab al-Zarqawi in preparation for the attack. In November, prosecutors demanded the death penalty for the plotters. Four of the accused, including Zarqawi, are being tried in absentia. Separately, Zarqawi was sentenced to death by the SSC in 2004 for the 2002 murder of U.S. diplomat Laurence Foley. He is also being tried in absentia for a December 2004 attack at the Karama-Trebil border crossing. In November, the SSC charged Muammar Jaghbir with plotting subversive acts for the 2003 attack against the Jordanian Embassy in Baghdad that killed 17.

Jaghbir was arrested in Iraq in 2004 by U.S. forces and handed over to authorities in Jordan, where he is standing trial for the assassination of Laurence Foley. In September, the SSC sentenced 12 Islamist militants to prison terms ranging from one and one-half to three years (falling well short of the maximum penalties of death or 15 years of hard labor) for plotting terrorist attacks against the U.S. and Israeli embassies. During their sentencing, the defendants praised the September 11 al-Qa'ida attacks and claimed that the verdict would not dissuade them from pursuing the path of extremism.

The SCC heard several non-al-Qa'ida-related terrorism cases. The highly contentious trial of more than 100 Jordanians charged with involvement in the 2002 Ma'an riots, which left six dead, began in early 2005. Ninety-five of the defendants are being tried in absentia. The main defendant in the case, Abu Sayyaf, retracted his earlier confession, claiming he was tortured and forced to confess. In January, the SSC sentenced two men to two and one-half year prison terms for plotting attacks against foreign diplomats in Amman. In October, the SSC sentenced five Jordanians to prison terms ranging from one to five years of hard labor for plotting attacks in Israel and against tourists in Jordan. Another three men were sentenced to five years' imprisonment for plotting attacks on liquor stores and tourists in Aqaba. In November, the SSC said it would re-examine guilty verdicts issued against seven militants convicted of a bungled conspiracy to use poison gas against American and Israeli tourists during Jordan's millennium celebrations in December 1999. An appeals court had ordered a retrial on the grounds that the plotters may be covered under a general amnesty issued by King Abdullah.

In November, the Jordanian Government proposed counterterrorism legislation that would authorize penalties for anyone who condones or supports acts of terrorism. The proposed bill, still in the drafting stage, would also allow authorities to hold terror suspects indefinitely.

Jordan has since had to deal with other problems like Al Qa'ida organized riots in its prisons, and almost certainly faces a steadily rising mix of threats for at least the next few years.[30] Islamist extremist terrorist movements like Al Qa'ida see Jordan as both an ally of the United States and the new Iraqi government and as a target in itself. They see Jordan's modern regime as an enemy of their concept of Islam and as having given up the struggle against Israel. These problems are compounded by the presence of as many as 1 million Iraqi refugees, some of which are Islamists or supporters of Saddam Hussein, and by the sectarian struggles in Iraq between Sunnis and Shi'ites that threaten to drag Jordan in on the Sunni side.

At the same time, the Israeli-Palestinian war of attrition puts constant stress on the very fabric of Jordanian society. It makes it harder for the regime to support and enforce its peace settlement with Israel, and it creates new incentives for Palestinians to try to infiltrate across Jordan's border with Israel and the West Bank. Coupled to similar problems in securing the border with Iraq, and less publicized "end runs" across the Saudi and Syrian borders, Jordan faces a major border security problem. It also faces growing problems in ensuring that arms are not moved into Jordan through its ports.

Security vs. Reform

Unlike the security forces of many other Arab states, Jordanian forces generally are less repressive and tightly focus their operations on actual terrorist or potentially violent opposition groups. Nevertheless, they present many of the same problems as all the paramilitary and security forces in the region. Their operations do affect legitimate opposition movements and can be harsh enough to breed opposition as well as counter it.

The human rights report that the U.S. State Department issued in February 2005 summarized the role—and limitations—of Jordanian paramilitary and security forces as follows:[31]

> The Public Security Directorate (PSD) controlled general police functions. The PSD, the General Intelligence Directorate (GID), and the military shared responsibility for maintaining internal security, and had authority to monitor security threats. The PSD reports to the Interior Minister and the independent GID reports directly to the King. The civilian authorities maintained effective control of the security forces. Members of the security forces committed a number of serious human rights abuses.
>
> ...police forces fall under the leadership of the Director of the PSD, who in turn answers to the Minister of Interior. The Director has access to the King when the

seriousness or urgency of a matter demands it. A total of 13 different offices form the basic structure of the PSD. Two of these offices include Preventative Security and the Office of Complaints and Human Rights. Each of the 12 provinces has a police department that also falls under the authority of the PSD Director. Security and Policing activities were effective.

...The Preventative Security Office enforces strict rules regarding officer performance. Incidents of poor officer performance ultimately are reported to the PSD Director's Office. (Corruption within the PSD has not been an issue of significant debate, and there are mechanisms in place to investigate police abuses. Preventative Security actively investigates security issues, including police corruption. Following the initial investigation, Preventative Security forwards the findings to the Legal Affairs Office for further investigation and possible prosecution in Police Court. Citizens may file a complaint about police abuse or corruption to the Office of Complaints and Human Rights (see Section 4). The head of this office reports directly to the PSD Director. New officers in training receive special instruction on how to avoid corruption.

...In cases involving state security, the security forces arbitrarily arrested and detained citizens. The authorities frequently held defendants in lengthy pretrial detention, did not provide defendants with the written charges against them, and did not allow defendants to meet with their lawyers until shortly before trial. Defendants before the State Security Court usually met with their attorneys only 1 or 2 days before their trial. The Criminal Code prohibits pretrial detentions for certain categories of misdemeanors.

...The State Security Court consists of a panel of three judges, two military officers and one civilian. More than a dozen cases were tried or are ongoing in the State Security Court during the year. Most sessions are open to the public, though some are limited to the press. Defendants tried in the State Security Court often were held in pretrial detention without access to lawyers, although they were permitted regular visits by representatives of the ICRC. State Security Court judges inquired into allegations that defendants were tortured and allowed the testimony of physicians regarding such allegations (see Section 1.c.). The Court of Cassation ruled that the State Security Court may not issue a death sentence on the basis of a confession obtained as a result of torture. Defendants in the State Security Court have the right to appeal their sentences to the Court of Cassation, which is authorized to review issues of both fact and law, although defendants convicted of misdemeanors in the State Security Court have no right of appeal. Appeals are automatic for cases involving the death penalty.

...Although the Government respected human rights in some areas, its overall record continued to reflect many problems. Reported continuing abuses included police abuse and mistreatment of detainees, allegations of torture, arbitrary arrest and detention, lack of transparent investigations and of accountability within the security services resulting in a climate of impunity, denial of due process of law stemming from the expanded authority of the State Security Court and interference in the judicial process, infringements on citizens' privacy rights, harassment of members of opposition political parties, and significant restrictions on freedom of speech, press, assembly, and association.

...the police and security forces sometimes abused detainees during detention and interrogation, and allegedly also used torture. Allegations of torture were difficult to verify because the police and security officials frequently denied detainees timely access to lawyers. The most frequently reported methods of torture included beating, sleep deprivation, extended solitary confinement, and physical suspension. Defendants in high-profile cases before the State Security Court claimed to have been subjected to physical and psychological abuse while in detention. Government officials denied allegations of torture and abuse.

Defendants in at least six cases before the Security Court during the year alleged that they were tortured while in custody. For example, affiliates of fugitive Jordanian Abu Musab al-Zarqawi, convicted in April of killing USAID official Laurence Foley in 2002, claimed their confessions were derived under duress. Zarqawi's nephew Omar al-Khalayleh, who was sentenced in May with two others for plotting against U.S. and Israeli tourists, also claimed torture. Other Zarqawi accomplices in custody for activities made similar accusations in their trials during the year, including Ansar al-Islam member Ahmad al-Riyati (sentenced in June), fundraiser Bilal al-Hiyari (sentenced in October), and Miqdad al-Dabbas, whose trial was ongoing at years end.

...Human rights activists reported a number of cases of beatings and other abuses of individuals in police custody during the year. These included accusations surrounding a disturbance at the Juweideh Correctional and Rehabilitation Center and allegations by security detainees. Human rights activists also claimed that detainees are often held incommunicado for up to 2 months after arrest.

The State Department report of March 8, 2006, was virtually identical.[32]

JORDAN'S CONTINUING STRATEGIC CHALLENGES

Like Egypt, Jordan's strategic challenges have changed from planning for war with Israel to deterring such a war, dealing with internal security challenges, and securing its borders. At the same time, Jordan still does face the risk of being dragged into some form of military confrontation with Israel.

Jordanian Support of Palestinian Forces in the West Bank, Jerusalem, and Israel

Any form of war with Israel would be a worst-case contingency for Jordan, but there are three forms that such a conflict could take: support of Palestinian forces, a unilateral attack on the West Bank, and joint action with Syria in an "Eastern Front."

The first type of conflict—which would involve the least risk for Jordan—would be a low-level conflict in which Jordan actively and covertly supported Palestinian attacks on Israel, but did not overtly use its military forces. Jordan has not acted as a sanctuary for hostile Palestinian elements since 1970 and has put serious new limits on Hamas operations in Jordan in 1998 and 1999. Nevertheless, the war of attrition between Israel and the Palestinians might create political conditions that virtually force Jordan to take the Palestinian side. Jordan might then be willing to provide bases, training facilities, and arms to Palestinian extremists on the West Bank. Such Jordanian support for a low-intensity war in the West Bank might significantly complicate Israel's internal security problems.

Jordan could escalate its involvement in such a conflict by sending in cadres of lightly armed Special Forces from the Jordanian Army under civilian cover. Such Jordanian covert forces would be easier for Israel to identify than native Palestinians, but would have far more training than the Palestinians. They could make a significant contribution to any Palestinian military effort that involved urban warfare, or terrorism that required high levels of discipline and technical expertise. Cadres of trained advisors and troops have played a significant role in previous guerrilla and low-level wars—often under conditions where they preserved "plausible deniability." Such a use of Jordanian forces would allow Jordan to exploit its strengths—a highly trained and well-disciplined army—with less risk than other uses of Jordanian forces.

At the same time, Israel has established a secure perimeter along the border with Jordan in the past, and the terrain favors such a security perimeter as long as a Palestinian entity does not exist on the West Bank that cannot be cut off from Jordan. Israel can also retaliate with the kind of air and artillery strikes it has used against Hezbollah in Lebanon and retaliate economically by sealing off the border between Jordan and Israel. Anything but very low-level covert Jordanian support of a Palestinian conflict would be detected by Israel in a matter of hours or days and would also present major problems in terms of U.S. reactions and those of other states. Jordan would risk serious problems in terms of access to foreign investment, trade, loans, and aid.

The IDF might take time to reestablish a firm control over movements from Jordan into the West Bank and might be unable to deal with any covert Jordanian presence on the West Bank. Even so, such a contingency is something of a contradiction in terms. Israel is only likely to give up its ability to secure the border after it secures and tests a "warm peace" with both Jordan and its Palestinians. Further, Jordan's current regime is unlikely to cooperate with any Palestinian entity that falls under Islamist extremist or other radical control because such an entity would be as much of a threat to Jordan as it would to Israel.

As a result, low-level Jordanian support of Palestinian military efforts does not seem likely to have a significant effect on the Palestinian-Israeli military balance. If anything, it would be more likely to prolong a conflict the Palestinians could not win with or without Jordanian support and risk dragging Jordan into conflict with Israel and a confrontation with the United States.

Jordanian "Rescue" of Palestinians in the West Bank

The second contingency would be a crisis-driven Jordanian intervention in the West Bank. Such a contingency is extremely unlikely under current conditions. It would either require Israel to abandon the peace process so catastrophically that Jordan would feel compelled to go to the aid of the Palestinians or a massive change in the character of Jordan's government. Even then, Jordan would be willing to take risks of this kind only if Islamic extremists dominated it or if extreme Israeli provocation threatened Jordan's existence. This would effectively require a contingency like a forced Israeli expulsion of the Palestinians living in the West Bank. Such events are conceivable, but they presently strain the limits of political credibility.

If such a battle did occur, Jordan would almost certainly lose decisively during the first day or days of combat. Jordan's forces are well trained and disciplined, with some of the best officers, noncommissioned officers, and career troops in the developing world. They have significant defensive capability against limited to mid-intensity Israeli attacks that attempt to move across the Jordan and up the East Bank. Jordanian forces have performed well in exercises with U.S. troops, such as the desert warfare exercises the United States and Jordan have conducted since August 1995. In fact, Israel might find it as painful and futile to attack deep into Jordan, and particularly into the area above the East Bank of the Jordan River, as Jordan would find it to attack Israel.[33]

The previous analysis has shown, however, that air power, technology, and land force quality and strength ratios do decisively favor Israel. Jordan could attack across the Jordan only by moving virtually its entire land forces down to the East Bank. This would provide clear strategic warning and allow Israel to use its air force extensively with only limited resistance by the Jordanian air force and ground-based air defenses. Jordanian land forces would then have to fight their way across Jordan, and up the West Bank, in the face of overwhelming Israeli superiority in the air, a high level of Israeli superiority on the ground, and Israeli ability to exploit a wide range of defense barriers.

Jordan does not have the kind of forces that could survive a move down to the Jordan River through narrow and predictable routes, cross a relatively open river plain averaging about 30 kilometers wide with a water barrier in the middle, and fight through Israeli forward defenses and then up in the heights on the West Bank. Only a few roads go down the 900 meters from the heights above the East Bank and the 400–600 meters up from the Jordan River. Israel can also couple its advantage in modern unmanned aerial vehicles, reconnaissance and strike aircraft, and AEW to extraordinarily short flight times from Israel to land targets moving through the West Bank. Flight times vary from 2 to 5 minutes once an aircraft is airborne, and Israel has demonstrated excellent capabilities to surge high sortie rates and manage large numbers of sorties.

Jordanian Cooperation with Syria

Jordan is strategically isolated from Egypt both in terms of land warfare and in any ability to manage an effective air war. Jordan's political differences and tensions with Syria now preclude any meaningful military cooperation, but if a crisis or war changed this situation, Jordan's chances of military success are marginally better—but only marginally better.

Syria has become a largely defensive force of limited quality, and the Jordanian Army would be highly vulnerable. Jordan would be exposed to far more devastating IAF attack capabilities than in previous wars, and the only area where the Jordanian Army could hope to take advantage of rough terrain to partially shield itself is in the

Map 6.2   The Jordan River Valley and Heights   (Foundation for Middle East Peace)

far northwestern part of Jordan at the junction of the Yarmuk and Jordan rivers, just south of Lake Tiberius.

The Jordanian heights of Umm Qays also overlook Lake Tiberius and the Galilee and would allow Jordan to use its artillery against targets in Israel. This, however, is an area where there are no easy routes up and down the heights, and where Israel has excellent surveillance capabilities. The Yarmuk River is also a significant terrain barrier with only a few crossing points, and any attack through Irbid that involved armored or mechanized forces would be highly vulnerable to air power, systems like the Multiple Launch Rocket System, and attack helicopters.

The Jordan River Valley becomes progressively harder to fight across at any point about 10 kilometers south of the junction between the Yarmuk and Jordan rivers. It opens up into a plain 5 to 40 kilometers wide. Israel is geographically vulnerable through the Beit Shean or Jezreel Valley, but forces attacking in this direction also become vulnerable to Israeli air and armor. Furthermore, it would take Jordan days to mass a sustainable force to launch such an attack and at least six hours to cross the terrain and river barrier.

The distances involved are short by the standards of most wars, but they are still long enough for Israel to employ air power with great effect. It is roughly 40 kilometers from Irbid to Beisan/Beit Shean, 85 kilometers from Jerash to Irbid, 55 kilometers from Salt to Amman, 55 kilometers from Amman to Jericho via the King Hussein Bridge and 45 kilometers by the King Abdullah Bridge. The southern route along the Dead Sea is 100 kilometers from Amman and the route to Eilat through Aqaba and Maan is 130 kilometers.

Jordan's Current Security Challenges

These factors help explain why Jordan's real-world strategic challenges are to deter any military incursion from a neighboring state and to maintain internal security in the face of the threat of terrorism and the potential backlash from the Israeli-Palestinian war of attrition. Jordan has created good capabilities to deal with these missions, but it does face the following strategic challenges:

- Maintaining its peace with Israel in the face of the ongoing war of attrition between Israel and the Palestinians on the West Bank and the Gaza Strip.
- Preventing Palestinian military or terrorist activities from being planned and supported in Jordan, and infiltration across Jordan's borders with Israel and the West Bank.
- Deterring any form of Syrian action in Jordan from military threats and incursions to hostile actions by Syrian intelligence agencies and proxies.
- Securing Jordan's port at Aqaba and the Jordanian coast of the Gulf of Aqaba.
- Securing the Iraqi border. Helping Iraq develop effective military, security, and police forces while dealing with the threat of terrorist infiltration from Iraq, and ensuring Iraqis in Jordan do not support the insurgency in Iraq or become a further source of Iraqi instability. Also preparing for the risk that Iraq could divide between Arab Sunnis and Arab Shi'ites or become the scene of a more intense civil war.
- Preparing for the possibility of a nuclear Iran.
- Finding ways to ensure continued control over the large Palestinian and Iraqi populations inside the country. The conflicts in Iraq and Palestine could lead these communities to become a source of instability inside Jordan.
- Maintaining internal security in the face of serious internal threats from internal and external extremists and terrorist threats from movements like Al Qa'ida.
- Planning for the risk that Jordanian territory or airspace could be involved in any exchange between Iran and Israel, and that if Iran develops nuclear armed missile, Jordan might have to deal with an inaccurate missile or fallout.

Like its neighbors, Jordan must balance its security efforts with the need to deal with major demographic problems and an expanding workforce, the need for economic developing and job creation, and the need for political liberalization. These are not easy trade-offs to make and the problems caused by the near breakdown of the Israeli-Palestinian peace process and the aftermath of the Iraq War have made Jordan's problems significantly worse.

These problems are further compounded by shifts in Palestinian politics toward Hamas, instability in Syria, and the broader threat of Islamist extremist terrorist movements like Al Qa'ida. The same is true of the deteriorating security situation in Iraq, the growing split between Sunnis and Shi'ites in the region, and Iran's growing assertiveness in both the Gulf region and Syria and Lebanon. King Abdullah may exaggerate in warning about the threat of a "Shi'ite crescent," but it is clear that Jordan sees developments in the east as posing growing problems, if not yet a serious threat.

So far Jordan has done well in shaping its forces to meet such challenges, but its security situation has deteriorated for reasons beyond its control. Jordan faces serious and continuing challenges to its security and stability indefinitely into the future.

The Military Forces of Lebanon

Lebanon is more played against in the current Arab-Israeli balance than a player. It is a small country caught in the middle between Israel and Syria. It has a total area of some 10,400 square kilometers, a 375-kilometer border with Syria, a 79-kilometer border with Israel, and a 225-kilometer coastline on the Mediterranean.

Lebanon has never been a meaningful military power, but it has been caught up in several Arab-Israeli conflicts. It has long experienced sectarian violence, and sometimes serious intrasect violence, particularly among the leading families of its once dominant Maronites. Its population in 2006 was approaching 4 million. It was 95 percent Arab (4 percent Armenian and 1 percent other), but Lebanon officially recognized some 17 religious sects and had deep sectarian divisions. The CIA estimated that its main religious groups were Muslim, 59.7 percent (Shi'ite, Sunni, Druze, Isma'ilite, Alawite, or Nusayri); Christian, 39 percent (Maronite Catholic, Greek Orthodox, Melkite Catholic, Armenian Orthodox, Syrian Catholic, Armenian Catholic, Syrian Orthodox, Roman Catholic, Chaldean, Assyrian, Copt, or Protestant); and other, 1.3 percent.[1]

Lebanon is still recovering from a long period of religious civil war between these factions that began in the 1970s and from the Israeli and Syrian occupations that resulted from Israel's invasion of Lebanon in 1982. It suffered from repeated Syrian interventions in Lebanon's civil war before 1982, and Syria effectively dominated Lebanon once its troops and intelligence services moved into Lebanon as part of the Taif Accords peace settlement in 1990.

It is still far from clear whether Lebanon will remain united and avoid future civil conflicts. There are still serious tensions between virtually all factions and Lebanon's Shi'ites have become more assertive in recent years. The Taif Accords did, however, create a political system that gave Muslims and other non-Maronite groups a larger role in the political system that more accurately reflected their share of the population while ensuring that all major sectarian groups would have some representation at the top of the government by requiring that given posts be held by a representative of given groups.

There have been several elections since the end of the civil war in 1990, and a major drop in civil violence. Many sectarian militias have been weakened, partially disarmed, or disbanded, although every major group retains arms and some militia capability. However, key Shi'ite militias like Amal and Hezbollah have never been disarmed. Syrian forces have officially left Lebanon, but Syria and the Syrian security services still play a major political role in Lebanon. Both Syria and Iran continue to arm and support Hezbollah and use it as a proxy, and both use Lebanon to funnel arms and money to anti-Israeli Palestinian factions.

Lebanon's "unity" is still more a shell than a reality. Its leadership and politics remain divided along sectarian lines. The Prime Minister and the Deputy Prime Minister are appointed by the President in consultation with the National Assembly. However, the President must be a Maronite Christian, the Prime Minister must be a Sunni Muslim, and the Speaker of the Legislature must be a Shi'ite Muslim.

The Lebanese Armed Forces (LAF) have gradually been rebuilt as a unified or "national force" (although troops retain strong sectarian loyalties), and Syria allowed the LAF to exert central government authority over the northern two-thirds of the country by 2005. Hezbollah still exerts a major degree of control over southern Lebanon Beka Valley, although the LAF is present in the area.

These problems are compounded by tensions between Israel and Hezbollah. Israel left southern Lebanon in 2000, after years of low-intensity civil conflict with Shi'ite militias like Hezbollah and Amal. While Israel viewed this withdrawal as a strategic choice and part of its effort to create a peace process with Syria and the other Arab states, it had failed to secure the area, and Hezbollah was largely credited in Lebanon and much of the Arab world with "defeating" the Israel Defense Forces (IDF) in asymmetric warfare. Hezbollah forces remain in the Israel-Lebanese border area, and Hezbollah has shown it retains the ability to strike across the border at Israel and inflict damage to Israeli forces at the border.

THE SYRIAN FACTOR

Lebanon has faced far more serious problems in recent years with Syria, however, than it has with Israel. The Arab League effort to settle the civil war through the Taif Accords led to the deployment of some 30,000 Syrian troops. These forces suppressed Lebanese resistance, particularly from Maronite-led forces. They then remained in Lebanon, with some 16,000 Syrian troops based mainly east of Beirut and in the Beka Valley.

Syrian political pressure, the presence of Syrian forces, and the permeating presence of Syrian intelligence then allowed Syria to continue to dominate Lebanon. Syria justified this by arranging a Lebanese government request for its forces to stay, claiming that the Lebanese government failed to implement all of the constitutional reforms in the Taif Accords.

Israel's withdrawal from southern Lebanon in May 2000 did, however, encourage some Lebanese factions to demand that Syria withdraw its forces. They slowly gained significant foreign support, and the UN Security Council passed UNSCR 1559— which stated that Syria should withdraw from Lebanon and end its interference in Lebanese affairs—in early October 2004. This resolution passed largely because of the support provided by the United States, France, and then Lebanese Prime Minister Rafik Hariri.

Hariri was killed in a car bomb in Beirut in February 2005, along with 20 other people. It soon became apparent that the Syrian government had played a major role in this assassination, and almost certainly with the knowledge and consent of Syrian President Bashar al-Assad. The UN investigated and issued a Report of the International Investigation Commission, established pursuant to Security Council Resolution 1595 (2005).[2] The Report found evidence that pointed conclusively to the involvement of both Syrian and Lebanese officials in Hariri's death.[3]

Syria attempted to limit its reaction to a partial withdrawal, but failed. Largely as result of the political turmoil following the investigation of its role in Hariri's assassination, Syria withdrew the remainder of its forces from Lebanon in April 2005 after 29 years of occupation.[4]

In May–June 2005 Lebanon held its first legislative elections free of the Syrian presence since the end of the civil war in 1990. These elections, however, were scarcely free of major sectarian divisions and did not unite the country. Hezbollah remains a major independent force, with Iranian and Syrian support, and the risk of new civil clashes remains all too real. President Emile Lahud remained in office, although it was Syrian pressure to extend his term to six years that was the key to Hariri's clash with Asad and Hariri's assassination. A more independent Prime Minister, Fuad Siniora, took office on June 30, 2005, but the elections for a new national assembly in May and June 2005 produced an assembly divided in terms of both sect and ties to Syria.[5]

Elements of Syrian intelligence stayed in Lebanon despite Syrian declarations otherwise, and Syria continued to finance and put pressure on Lebanese political factions. The UN investigation, however, continued to put Syria in a problematic situation in both the international community and within the Arab world. These pressures are compounded by the fact the Uunted States is militarily active in Iraq and views Syria as playing a hostile and uncooperative role in Iraqi politics and in supporting the Iraqi insurgency.[6]

LEBANESE SECURITY AFTER SYRIAN WITHDRAWAL

The Lebanese government has authorized deployment of a small joint force of army commandos and military police to join its internal security personnel already in the south since the Israeli pullout from southern Lebanon in May 2000. Lebanon has been subjected to criticism from the UN concerning its inaction in disbanding Syrian- and Iranian-backed Hezbollah since the Israeli pullout. Lebanon has replied that it has chosen to act against the militant groups through dialogue and not more violence.[7]

The Lebanese government has tried to assert more control over its other borders since the Syrian withdrawal from Lebanon. In late October 2005, Lebanese commandos blocked smuggling routes along the Syrian border, established guard posts, and deployed tanks along the border with Syria. In addition, the Lebanese set up positions close to Palestinian militant bases to keep a closer watch on their activities.

The pullout of Syrian forces has also put more pressure on the Lebanese to disband the militias, including the Palestinian militias within the refugee camps. The Lebanese government, at the urging of the UN, said it would disband the militias through national dialogue and not through confrontation. The United Nations Interim Force In Lebanon has said that it would cut the number of its forces down by half, the second reduction in size since the Israeli pullout in May 2000.

Reducing the number of UN peacekeepers in southern Lebanon could bring about a situation in which the Lebanese Army will have either to deploy more forces to the south or see the region come further under Hezbollah control and see an increased risk of clashes with Israel. The government, however, has shown great caution in attempting to actively control southern Lebanon and bring Hezbollah under its control. The Lebanese government must still evaluate every use of military force in the context of Lebanon's history of civil war and the risk of dividing its military forces if they are used for any mission that major factions do not perceive as being in Lebanon's national interest.

Furthermore, as a UN report issued in October 2005 recounts, Hezbollah is still receiving arms from Iran. Not only are Hezbollah and Palestinian organizations receiving weapons and materials from Iran, the equipment is still being transported through Syria with no apparent Syrian objection.[8] There are concerns that this continued support by Iran and implicit support from Syria will destabilize the situation in Lebanon. The Syrian pullout could destabilize Lebanon and possibly bring about a clash between Israel and Lebanon and/or even involve the United States in a direct way.[9]

THE TRENDS IN LEBANESE FORCES

Lebanese forces are lightly armed, poorly organized for maneuver warfare and lack both a meaningful air force and modern land-based air defense assets. The recent trends in Lebanese forces are shown in Figure 7.1 and then are explained by military service in Figures 7.3–7.6. Lebanon's recent arms imports are summarized in Figure 7.2. Lebanon's military forces remain small and totaled some 72,100 actives in 2006, including some 22,600 conscripts. It was unclear, however, that all this strength was actually present. It is also clear from Figure 7.2 that Lebanese forces have lacked the resources to make many major moves toward modernization and recapitalization in recent years.

Lebanese forces have moved toward a higher degree of unity, and many Lebanese officers are deeply committed to avoiding any further civil conflict, Syrian

Figure 7.1   Lebanese Military: Force Structure

	1990	2000	2005	2006
Manpower	70,000?	80,900	85,100	85,100
Active	~30,300	67,900	72,100	72,100
Conscript	0	27,400	22,600	N/A
Army	21,000	65,000	70,000	70,000
Navy	500	1,200	1,100	1,100
Air Force	800	1,700	1,000	1,000
Paramilitary	8,000	~13,000	~13,000	~13,000

Source: Various editions of the International Institute for Strategic Studies (IISS) *Military Balance*, U.S., British, and other experts.

interference in Lebanese affairs, or clashes with Israel that could affect the country's recovery and development. Nevertheless, the Lebanese command structure reflects the nation's serious religious divisions. The President is the commander of the army and is Maronite Christian, the Deputy Commander is a Muslim (Shi'ite), and the Army Council has Druze and Sunni members.

THE LEBANESE ARMY

The army had an authorized strength of about 70,000 men in 2006. Its order of battle had 11 mechanized infantry brigades, a Presidential Guard Brigade, a commando/Ranger Regiment, five Special Forces regiments, an air assault regiment, and two artillery regiments. The trends in the Lebanese Army are shown in Figure 7.3.[10]

The army is the only element of Lebanon's military forces with any serious potential war-fighting capability against a well-organized military force. There was strong public and Lebanese Army support for the Syrian withdrawal. Since the first parliamentary election after the Syrian withdrawal the Lebanese Army has begun to be more active: it surrounded Palestinian bases in the Beka Valley, detained, and deported Palestinian infiltrators.[11] It has played a steadily more important internal security role since the final battles of the civil war in October 1990. It has deployed south from Beirut and occupied Lebanese territory as far south as Sidon and Tyre, north to Tripoli, and in the Shuf Mountains.

While Hezbollah remains a major problem, and Amal has not been disarmed, most militias have been contained to their local territory, and most are largely disarmed. Some militias have been integrated into the army, and most have turned over or sold their heavy weapons. Although some members of the army's command structure may still have covert links to Syria, it is doubtful they would take any overt action in support of Syria or at Syrian direction. As a result, Hezbollah is the only armed force within Lebanon that might deploy in support of Syria if it came under intense pressure to do so.[12]

Lebanese New Arms Agreements and Deliveries: 1993-2004 (in $US Current Millions)

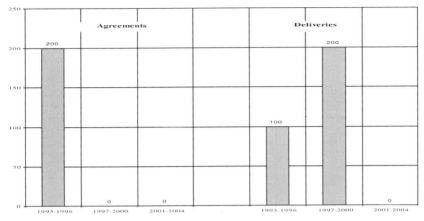

Lebanese Arms Orders by Supplier Country: 1993-2004 (Arms Agreements in $US Current Millions)

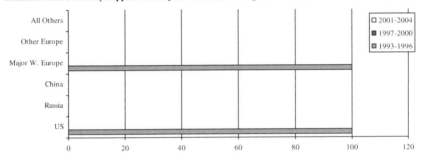

0 = less than $50 million or nil, and all data rounded to the nearest $100 million.
Source: Adapted by Anthony H. Cordesman, from Richard F. Grimmett, Conventional Arms Transfers to the Developing Nations, Congressional Research Service, various editions.

Figure 7.2   Recent Lebanese Arms Sales

Major Combat Equipment

The Lebanese Army has a relatively large pool of major combat equipment for a force its size, although much is of low to moderate capability and consists of worn transfers from other countries. Since the end of Lebanon's civil war in 1990, the army has benefited from its relationship with the U.S. military. The United States either donated or sold at minimal prices 16 Huey helicopters and earmarked another 16 for future delivery, comprising the entirety of Lebanon's air force. The United States furnished a large portion of Lebanon's ground transportation, including 850 armored personnel carriers, 3,000 trucks and jeeps, and 60 ambulances. The Pentagon also provided much equipment, labeled as "excess defense articles," which had included small weapons, spare parts, grenade launchers, night-vision goggles, and communications equipment.

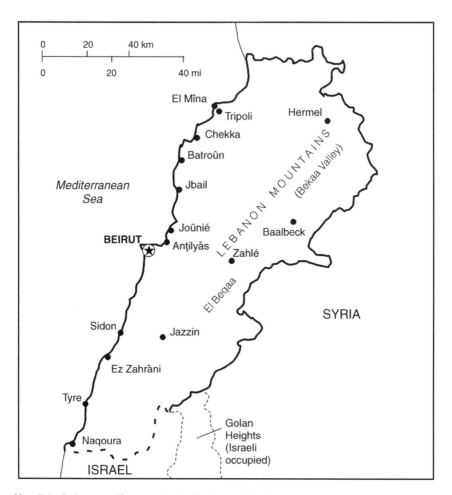

Map 7.1 Lebanon (Cartography by Bookcomp, Inc.)

Much of the army's inventory is worn or obsolete, however, and is useful largely for internal security purposes. The Lebanese Army is far too lightly equipped, and its equipment is too old or limited in capability to engage either Israeli or Syrian forces.

In 2006, its holdings included 310 tanks—with an estimated 110 M-48A1 and M-48A5 tanks and 200T-54 and T-55 tanks. The army had phased out its Ferret and Staghound light-armored reconnaissance vehicles. It did, however, have 125 other armored fighting vehicles: some AMX-13 light tanks and an unspecified number of Saladins. It had some 1,275 APCs (armored personnel carriers), including the operational portion of an inventory of 1,164 M-113s, 81 VAB-VCIs, 81 AMX-VCI, and 12 M-3/VTTs. This was a relatively high level of mechanization for such

Figure 7.3   Lebanese Army: Force Structure

	1990	2000	2005	2006
Manpower	704,000	80,900	85,100	85,100
Active	~30,300	67,900	72,100	72,100
Reserve	?	?	?	?
Combat Units—Army	10	23	28	28
Regional command	N/A	N/A	5	5
Mechanized Infantry Brigade	?	11	11	11
Marine Commando Regiment	?	1	1	1
Special Forces Regiment	1	5	5	5
Commando/Ranger Regiment	1	1	1	1
Air Assault Regiment	?	1	1	1
Artillery Regiment	?	2	2	2
Presidential Guard Brigade	?	1	1	1
Mountain Infantry Coy	?	1	?	?
Military Police	0	?	1	1
MBT	105	304	310	310
T-54/-55	N/A	212	200	200
M-48	105	92	110	110
M-48A1	?	?	?	?
M-48A5	?	?	?	?
RECCE	70	67	85	60
AML	?	67	60	60
Ferret	5	0	0	0
Saladin	65	?	25	N/A
APC	320	1,281	1,338	1,275
APC (T)	300	1,164	1,164	1,164
M-113A1/A2	300	1,164	1,164	1,164
APC (W)	20	117	174	174
VAB-VTT	20	0	0	0
M-3/VTT	0	37	12	12
VAB-VCI	N/A	80	81	81
AMX-VCI	0	N/A	81	81
Artillery	579	486	541	541
TOWED	~69+	151	147	147
105 mm	15	13	13	13
M-101	15	13	13	13
M-101A1	15	13	13	13
122 mm	18+	62	56	56
D-30	Some	?	24	24
M-102	18	0	0	0
M-30 M-1938	Some	?	32	32
130 mm	?	11	16	16
M-46	?	11	16	16

155 mm	36+	65	62	62
M-114A1	Some	18	15	15
M-198	Some	35	32	32
Model-50	36	12	15	15
MRL	N/A	23	25	25
122 mm	N/A	23	25	25
BM-21	N/A	23	25	25
MOR	25+	312	369	369
81 mm	Some	93	158	158
82 mm	0	111	111	111
120 mm	25	108	100	100
Brandt	?	?	100	100
AT	~20+	~20+	~120+	~130+
MSL	?	~20+	70	70
ENTAC	?	Some	30	30
Milan	?	Some	16	16
TOW	20	20	24	24
RCL	Some	Some	50	60
106 mm	Some	Some	50	60
M-40	Some	Some	50	60
RL	Some	Some	Some	Some
73 mm	0	0	N/A	Some
RPG-7 Knout	0	0	N/A	Some
85 mm	Some	Some	Some	N/A
RPG-7	Some	Some	Some	N/A
89 mm	Some	Some	Some	Some
M-65	Some	Some	Some	Some
AD	15+	~10+	~50+	~50+
SAM-*MANPAD*	N/A	N/A	20	20
SA-7	N/A	N/A	20	20
SA-7A Grail	N/A	N/A	?	?
SA-7B Grail	N/A	N/A	?	?
GUNS	15	10	~10+	10+
20 mm	?	?	Some	Some
23 mm	?	?	Some	Some
TOWED	?	?	Some	Some
ZU-23-2	?	?	Some	Some
40 mm	15	10	10	10
SP	15	10	10	10
M-42A1	15	10	10	10

~ = Estimated amount; * = combat capable; + = more than the number given but not specified how much more; Some = unspecified amount; ? = unspecified amount, if any; N/A = not available; {} = serviceability in doubt.

Source: Various editions of the IISS *Military Balance,* U.S., British, and other experts.

a small force, but significant numbers had limited or no operational readiness and/or sustainability in combat.

The Lebanese Army had 147 towed artillery weapons—many of which are operational: 13 105-mm M-101A1s, 32 M-1938, and 24 D-30 122-mm weapons, 16 130-mm M-46s, and 15 Model 50, 15 M-114A1, and 32 M-198 155-mm weapons. It also had 25 BM-21 rocket launchers and over 370 81-mm, 82-mm, and 120-mm mortars.

Antitank holdings were limited for a force that might have to engage Syrian on Israeli armor. The army had 24 BGM-71A TOWs, 16 Milan and 30 ENTAC antitank guided missiles, plus large numbers of light antitank weapons—including 60 M-40A1 106-mm recoilless rifles.

Lebanon has only token land-based air defenses. In 2006, the army had 20 SA-7A/B fire units, and some 20-mm and 23-mm antiaircraft guns, plus 10 M-42A1 40-mm guns.

Training and Readiness

The Lebanese Army does seem, however, to be shifting its force structure to put more emphasis on mortar and light antitank weapons. This may be driven by the problems it has in maintaining heavy weapons, but may also be affected by plans to slowly take Hezbollah's place as the armed force in southern Lebanon. Lighter weapons and disperse infantry forces are useful in both border security and in defending against incursions by the Israeli forces across the border. They are able to inflict damage, but not enough so that a massive retaliation from Israel would be in order.

More broadly, the Lebanese Army underwent a massive reorganization in 1997, integrating Muslim and Christian brigades in an attempt to end factional rivalries and bias. Units became subject to rotation to prevent any regional bias from forming and commanders within units are rotated regularly to ensure that religious prejudice does not create informal hierarchies. Although these changes cannot compensate for Lebanon's weaknesses in materiel or its client relationship with Syria, many hope they will insulate the military from the religious tensions that plague the country.

In spite of these improvements, the army is still emerging from the chaos of civil war. Lebanon may have some excellent individual officers and some good combat elements, but there are still ethnic and sectarian divisions within its forces. Its "brigades" and "regiments" are often undermanned. Conscripts train only for one year. Career soldiers still tend to be politicized, are generally low in quality, and receive limited training for anything other than defensive infantry combat. The Lebanese Army's seemingly impressive equipment pool is worn, often obsolescent, and much of it is inoperative.

The army is seeking to recreate itself as an independent national force and many Lebanese officers are struggling hard to maintain the army's independence. The fact the army was under heavy Syrian influence is no longer such a hurdle, but even the best leaders cannot quickly overcome the military's heritage of incompetence, corruption, and ethnic divisions. It will be years before the Lebanese Army can emerge as an independent fighting force that could engage Israeli or Syrian forces in anything other than well-positioned defensive combat.

THE LEBANESE AIR FORCE

Lebanon has no real air force or navy. The trends in its small air force are shown in Figure 7.4 In 2006, the Lebanese Air Force had 1,000 men on paper, but its real strength was much lower. It had only six worn, obsolete, low-capability Hunter light attack and five Fouga fixed-wing aircraft, all in storage.

Figure 7.4   Lebanese Air Force: Force Structure

	1990	2000	2005	2006
Manpower	800	1,700	1,000	1,000
Air Force	800	1,700	1,000	1,000
Total Aircraft	51	19	51	54
FGA	12	?	11	6
Hawker Hunter	6	?	6	6
F-70	5	0	0	0
T-66	1	0	0	0
Fouga	0	?	5	?
MK9 in store	0	?	N/A	Yes
Training	8	3{}	3	8
Bulldog	5	3+	3	3
(Bulldog in store)	?	?	N/A	127
CM-170 Magister (in store)	3	0	N/A	5
Helicopter	31	16	37	40
Attack	4	?	2	2
SA-342 Gazelle	4	?	2	2
Support	9	?	2	3
SA-330 Puma	9	?	2	3
Utility	16	?	33	35
Bell 212	7	?	5	5
R-44 (utility/training)	0	?	N/A	2
SA-313	2	?	0	0
SA-316 Alouette III	7	?	3	3
SA-318 Alouette II	0	?	1	1
UH-1	0	16	24	24
UH-1H Iroquois	0	16	24	24
Transport	2	0	0	0
Dove	1	0	0	0
Turbo-Commander 690A	1	0	0	0

Source: Various editions of the IISS *Military Balance,* U.S., British, and other experts.

It also had two SA-342 attack helicopters armed with obsolete short-range AS-11 and AS-12 missiles. It had no significant surface-to-air missile defenses. The only significant assets of the Lebanese Air Force are its transport helicopters, which consist of about 24 UH-1Hs, 1 SA-318, 5 Bell-212s, and 3 SA-330s. A substantial number of these helicopters need major overhauls or are only semioperational.

LEBANESE NAVAL FORCES

Lebanon has some 1,100 men assigned to its navy, including 100 marines. The trends in its small naval forces are shown in Figure 7.5. All of its ships are based in Beirut and Jounieh. In 2006, it had seven coastal patrol craft, including five British-made, 38-ton, Attacker-class inshore patrol craft with radars and twin 23-mm guns. These are aging 38-ton vessels dating back to the early 1980s. Their maximum speed is 21 knots and is slow for antiterrorist and infiltration missions.[13]

It had two British-made, 31-ton, Tracker-class inshore patrol craft with radars and either twin 23-mm guns or 12.7-mm machine guns. They have a simple I-Band surface search radar. Their 20-knot maximum speed again is slow for antiterrorist and infiltration missions.

The United States transferred 27 M-boot river patrol boats to the navy in 1994. These are small six-ton vessels used for inshore coastal patrol. They have 5.56-mm machine guns and a relatively slow 22-knot maximum speed. Some 10–12 are operational. The rest are sidelined.

Figure 7.5   Lebanese Navy: Force Structure

	1990	2000	2005	2006
Manpower	500	1,200	1,100	1,100
Navy	500	1,200	1,100	1,100
Facilities	1	2	2	2
Jounieh	1	1	1	1
Beirut	0	1	1	1
Patrol and Coastal Combatants	4	7	7	32
Misc. boats/craft	N/A	27	25	25
Armed boats	N/A	27	25	25
PCI	4	7	7	7
Tarablous	1	0	0	0
Byblos	3	0	0	0
Attacker (UK, under 100 tons)	0	5	5	5
Tracker (UK, under 100 tons)	0	2	2	2
Amphibious	2	2	2	2
LCT	2	0	0	0
LS, LST	0	2	2	2
Sour (capacity 96 troops)	0	2	2	2

Source: Various editions of the IISS *Military Balance,* U.S., British, and other experts.

The navy also had two 670-ton Sour-class (French Edic-class) landing craft built in the mid-1980s. They can carry about 96 troops each, 11 trucks, or 8 APCs. They were damaged in 1990, but have been repaired and are fully operational. They are used by Lebanon's marines.

The navy had other small-armed boats in its inventory, including 13 6-ton inshore patrol craft and two more Tracker-class boats in the Customs service for a total of 25 armored boats/crafts. It is not clear how many are operational.

The Lebanese Navy had a coastal patrol capability, and some troop lift capability, but no war-fighting capability against Israel or any neighboring state. It can perform a surveillance role, inspect cargo ships, and intercept small infiltrating forces along a limited part of Lebanon's coastline.[14]

LEBANESE PARAMILITARY FORCES AND HEZBOLLAH

The trends in Lebanon's paramilitary forces are shown in Figure 7.6. In 2006, they included a large 13,000-man internal security force that was part of the Ministry of the Interior, and which included the regional and Beirut Gendarmerie and Judicial Police. It was armed with automatic weapons and had 60 Chaimite APCs. There was a small customs force, equipped with seven light patrol boats.[15]

The effectiveness of these forces, Lebanese intelligence, and the Lebanese military has been severely hampered by the ethnic and religious divisions in Lebanon and by the role Syria played while its forces occupied the country. Many Lebanese Shi'ites see local movements like Hezbollah as a guarantee to their security, and even many non-Shi'ites see it as the force that defeated Israel and forced it to end its occupation of southern Lebanon. Other movements have remained in Lebanon because of Syrian pressure or because the Lebanese government was not willing to confront them. At the same time, the Lebanese security and intelligence forces have been heavily penetrated by Syrians and many other Lebanese have good reason to distrust them.[16]

The U.S. State Department summarized Lebanon's overall efforts to deal with extremist and terrorist groups as follows in its report on terrorism in April 2005:[17]

> The Lebanese Government recognized as legitimate resistance groups organizations that target Israel and permitted them to maintain offices in Beirut. Lebanon also exempts what it terms "legal resistance" groups, including Lebanese Hezbollah, from money laundering and terrorism financing laws. Lebanese leaders, including President Emile Lahud, reject assessments of Lebanese Hezbollah's global terror activities, though the group's leadership has openly admitted to providing material support for terror attacks inside Israel, the West Bank, and Gaza. Hezbollah, which holds 12 seats in the Lebanese parliament, is generally seen as a part of Lebanese society and politics. The Lebanese Government has failed to comply with numerous UN resolutions to extend sole and effective authority over all Lebanese territory. The Lebanese security forces remain unable or unwilling to enter Palestinian refugee camps, the operational nodes of terrorist groups such as Asbat al-Ansar and other Palestinian terror groups, and to deploy forces into areas dominated by Lebanese Hezbollah, including the Beka'a Valley, southern Beirut, and the south of the country up to the UN-demarcated Blue Line.

Figure 7.6   Lebanese Paramilitary and Security Forces: Force Structure

	1990	2000	2005	2006
Manpower	8,000	~13,000	~13,000	~13,000
Active	8,000	~13,000	~13,000	~13,000
Internal Security Force	8,000	~13,000	~13,000	~13,000
Force By Role	N/A	3	3	3
Police (Judicial) Unit	N/A	1	1	1
Regional Coy	N/A	1	1	1
Paramilitary (Beirut Gendarmerie) Coy	N/A	1	1	1
Equipment By Type	30	30	60	60
APC (W)	30	30	60	60
V-200 Chaimite	30	30	60	60
Customs	2	7	7	7
Patrol and Coastal Combatants	?	?	?	7
PCI	2	7	7	7
Aztec (less than 100 tons)	N/A	5	5	5
Tracker (less than 100 tons)	2	2	2	2
Foreign Forces	37,500	26,646	17,994	17,995
Fiji (UNIFIL)	Some	Inf bn	?	?
Finland	Some	?	0	0
France (Army and 1 logistic battalion) (UNIFIL)	Some	Spt unit	Spt unit	204
Ghana (UNIFIL)	Some	Inf bn	Inf bn	652
India (UNIFIL)	Some	Inf bn	Inf bn	648
Iran (Revolutionary Guard)	2,000	~150	~150	N/A
Ireland (UNIFIL)	Some	Inf bn	Spt unit	5
Italy (UNIFIL)	Some	Spt unit	Spt unit	53
Nepal	Some	?	0	0
Norway	Some	0	0	0
Poland (UNIFIL)	0	Spt unit	Inf bn	236
Sweden	Some	0	0	0
Ukraine (UNIFIL)	0	?	Inf bn	197
Syria (until the pullout in 2005)	30,000	22,000	16,000	N/A

Note: Lebanese combat aircraft shown in parentheses are in storage or are for sale.
Source: Various editions of the IISS *Military Balance,* U.S., British, and other experts.

Its updated report of April 2006, which was issued after the Syrian withdrawal from Lebanon, summarized Lebanese activity in more detail,

In April, Syrian military forces and overt intelligence agents departed Lebanon after 29 years of occupation. Terrorist activities were still carried out in Lebanon, however. Is-raeli positions in the Blue Line village of Ghajjar in the Israeli-occupied Golan region were attacked on November 21, probably by Hizballah. Al-Qa'ida in Iraq claimed responsibility for a rocket attack on Israel from Lebanese territory on December 27, but some analysts suspected "rejectionist" Palestinian groups or Hizballah as the perpe-trator and, thus far, a clear determination of culpability has not been possible.

Throughout the year, Hizballah continued to claim the right to conduct hostile operations along the Blue Line on the premise of a legitimate "resistance" to the occupation of Lebanese territory.

Since October 2004, when a protracted campaign of domestic political violence began, there have been 15 bombings and assassination attempts that resulted in more than 30 deaths, including that of former Prime Minister Rafiq Hariri. More than 230 people have been injured. The attacks have targeted Lebanese journalists and politicians critical of Syrian interference in Lebanon, including Telecom Minister Hamadeh, MP Gebran Tueni, journalist May Chidiac, Defense Minister Elias Murr, and journalist Samir Kassir. These attacks remain unsolved, but the UN International Independent Investigation Commission (UNIIIC) is investigating the Hariri assassination and the Lebanese Government, assisted by the UNIIIC, is investigating the other acts of political violence.

Since July, when the government of Prime Minister Fouad Siniora took office, Lebanon has taken small but important steps against several terrorist groups, specifically the PFLP-GC and Fatah al-Intifada. Under Prime Minister Siniora, the Lebanese Armed Forces (LAF) surrounded several Palestinian terrorist militia bases and restricted access to them. Similarly, since late 2005, the Lebanese Armed Forces strengthened border control posts and increased patrols along the Lebanese-Syrian border to prevent the flow of weaponry to terrorist groups.

Even with the advances Lebanon has made against terrorism, considerable work remains. The most significant terrorist group in Lebanon is Hizballah, because of its power and influence in Lebanon's Shi'a community, which makes up about one-third of Lebanon's population. The Lebanese Government still recognizes Hizballah as a "legitimate resistance group." Hizballah maintains offices in Beirut and elsewhere in the country and has elected deputies in Lebanon's Parliament and a minister in Prime Minister Siniora's Council of Ministers (Cabinet). Hizballah also operates a comprehensive system of health and education services in several regions of the country. Although Syria withdrew its military forces in April, it continued to maintain a covert intelligence presence in Lebanon. In addition, Syria continued to offer support for, and facilitated arms smuggling to, Hizballah and Palestinian terrorist groups. Given that the Government of Lebanon does not exercise authoritative control over areas in the Hizballah-dominated south and inside the Palestinian-controlled refugee camps, terrorists can operate relatively freely in both locations

The Lebanese and Syrian governments have not fully complied with UNSCR 1559, which calls for respect for the sovereignty and political independence of Lebanon, the end of foreign interference in Lebanon, and the disarming and disbanding of all Lebanese and non-Lebanese militias, including Hizballah. The Government of Lebanon, however, has indicated it will abide by its international obligations, including UNSCR 1559's call to disarm all militias. The Lebanese Government and its political leaders maintain that implementation of Hizballah's disarmament should be accomplished through "national dialogue" rather than force. This position complicates the process of implementing UNSCR 1559, because under Lebanon's "consensus" political system, all the country's sectarian communities, including the powerful Shi'a community, have to agree on a course of action on matters of national security.

A number of Lebanese leaders, including pro-Syrian President Emile Lahoud, reject categorizing Hizballah's activities as terrorist, even though the group's leaders openly admitted to providing support for terrorist attacks inside Israel, the West Bank, and Gaza. Hizballah, which holds 14 seats in Parliament as well as a seat on the Council of Ministers, is widely considered a legitimate participant in Lebanese society and politics. Some government officials and members of Parliament attended the annual militaristic Hizballah parade in southern Beirut on October 28, known locally as "Jerusalem Day."

Lebanese authorities maintain that their provision of amnesty to Lebanese individuals involved in acts of violence during the civil war prevents Beirut from prosecuting many cases of concern to the United States. These cases include the 1985 hijacking of TWA flight 847, during which a U.S. Navy diver was murdered, and the abduction, torture, and murder of U.S. hostages in Lebanon from 1984 to 1991. U.S. courts brought indictments against Lebanese Hizballah operatives responsible for a number of those crimes.

Despite evidence to the contrary, the Lebanese Government has insisted that Imad Mugniyah, wanted in connection with the TWA 847 hijacking and other terrorist acts, and placed on the FBI's list of most-wanted terrorists in 2001, is no longer in Lebanon. Mohammad Ali Hamadi, who spent 18 years in a German prison for his role in the TWA hijacking, was released in December and is now believed to be in Lebanon. The United States continued its efforts to bring him to trial before a U.S. court and has formally requested his return. The Lebanese Government's legal system failed to hold a hearing on a government prosecutor's appeal in the case of Tawfic Muhammad Farroukh, who, despite the evidence, was found not guilty of murder for his role in the killing of U.S. Ambassador Francis Meloy and two others in 1976.

The Lebanese Government took judicial action on two terrorist incidents that occurred in 2004: an attempted bombing of the Italian Embassy, and an attempt to bring a bomb onto the U.S. Embassy grounds. Two Lebanese citizens, Mehdi Hajj Hasan and Abed Karim Mreish, were tried and convicted for the U.S. Embassy incident; they are serving sentences of five and two years at hard labor, respectively. Other members of the terrorist cell involved in these actions were freed as part of an amnesty law passed in June, but a judicial investigation is still taking place.

On terrorism finance, Lebanon's Special Investigation Commission (SIC), an independent legal entity with judicial status that is empowered to investigate suspicious financial transactions, investigated 165 cases involving allegations of money laundering and terrorist financing activities. Lebanon assumed a leadership role in the Middle East and North Africa Financial Action Task Force.

The Lebanese government decided in February 2006 to avoid a political crisis with Hezbollah by designating it a "resistance" force against Israel, rather than a militia, and allowing it to keep its arms. Lebanon's problems with irregular and terrorist forces, however, go beyond the problem of Hezbollah. The Lebanese government has been willing to take action against various Sunni neo-Salafi and other Sunni extremist groups, including those similar in ideology to Al Qa'ida. However, Lebanon has been the location of a number of Palestinian groups that the United States designates as terrorist organizations. These include the Palestinian Islamic Jihad, the Popular Front for the Liberation of Palestine-General Command, the Abu Nidal Organization, and elements of Hamas. This could prove to be more important in the future, now that Hamas has emerged as the dominant political force in the Gaza Strip and the West Bank.

Nonstate Forces: Hezbollah

Virtually every ethnic and religious faction in Lebanon still has some form of militia and conceals arms in spite of the supposed disarming of most such movements. The main threat to Lebanese internal stability, however, now consists of two Shi'ite militias: Amal and Hezbollah.

Syria and the Lebanese Army have allowed both to retain significant numbers of weapons, but Hezbollah (also Hezballah, Party of God, Islamic Jihad, and Islamic Jihad for the Liberation of Palestine) is clearly the most important independent paramilitary element in Lebanon. The U.S. State Department describes Hezbollah as follows:[18]

...Formed in 1982 in response to the Israeli invasion of Lebanon, this Lebanon-based radical Shia group takes its ideological inspiration from the Iranian revolution and the teachings of the late Ayatollah Khomeini. The Majlis al-Shura, or Consultative Council, is the group's highest governing body and is led by Secretary General Hasan Nasrallah. Hezbollah is dedicated to liberating Jerusalem and eliminating Israel, and has formally advocated ultimate establishment of Islamic rule in Lebanon. Nonetheless, Hezbollah has actively participated in Lebanon's political system since 1992. Hezbollah is closely allied with, and often directed by, Iran but has the capability and willingness to act independently. Though Hezbollah does not share the Syrian regime's secular orientation, the group has been a strong ally in helping Syria advance its political objectives in the region.

...Known or suspected to have been involved in numerous anti-US and anti-Israeli terrorist attacks, including the suicide truck bombings of the US Embassy and US Marine barracks in Beirut in 1983 and the US Embassy annex in Beirut in 1984. Three members of Hezbollah, 'Imad Mughniyah, Hasan Izz-al-Din, and Ali Atwa, are on the FBI's list of 22 Most Wanted Terrorists for the 1985 hijacking of TWA Flight 847 during which a US Navy diver was murdered. Elements of the group were responsible for the kidnapping and detention of Americans and other Westerners in Lebanon in the 1980s. Hezbollah also attacked the Israeli Embassy in Argentina in 1992 and the Israeli cultural center in Buenos Aires in 1994. In 2000, Hezbollah operatives captured three Israeli soldiers in the Shab'a Farms and kidnapped an Israeli noncombatant.

...Hezbollah also provides guidance and financial and operational support for Palestinian extremist groups engaged in terrorist operations in Israel and the occupied territories. In 2004, Hezbollah launched an unmanned aerial vehicle (UAV) that left Lebanese airspace and flew over the Israeli town of Nahariya before crashing into Lebanese territorial waters. Ten days prior to the event, the Hezbollah Secretary General said Hezbollah would come up with new measures to counter Israeli Air Force violations of Lebanese airspace. Hezbollah also continued launching small scale attacks across the Israeli border, resulting in the deaths of several Israeli soldiers.

...In March 2004, Hezbollah and HAMAS signed an agreement to increase joint efforts to perpetrate attacks against Israel. In late 2004, Hezbollah's al-Manar television station, based in Beirut with an estimated ten million viewers worldwide, was prohibited from broadcasting in France. Al-Manar was placed on the Terrorist Exclusion List (TEL) in the United States, which led to its removal from the program offerings of its main cable service provider, and made it more difficult for al-Manar associates and affiliates to operate in the United States.

...In 2005 Hizballah's status quo changed due both to the withdrawal of Syrian troops from Lebanese territory and Hizballah's broadened role in Lebanese politics following the Lebanese legislative elections that spring. Hizballah has actively participated in Lebanon's political system since 1992. The party now claims 14 elected officials in the 128-seat Lebanese National Assembly and is represented in the Cabinet for the first time, by the Minister of Water and Electricity. Hizballah maintains a military presence in southern Lebanon, a presence it justifies by claiming to act in defense of Lebanon against acts of Israeli aggression, such as regular Israeli overflights of Lebanese airspace. Hizballah alleges that Israel has not withdrawn completely from Lebanese territory because, in Hizballah's view, the Sheba'a Farms area belongs to Lebanon. Hizballah and Israel clashed twice in this disputed part of the Golan Heights in 2005.

...Several thousand supporters and a few hundred terrorist operatives....Operates in the southern suburbs of Beirut, the Beka'a Valley, and southern Lebanon. Has established cells in Europe, Africa, South America, North America, and Asia....Receives financial, training, weapons, explosives, political, diplomatic, and organizational aid from Iran, and diplomatic, political, and logistical support from Syria. Hezbollah also receives funding from charitable donations and business interests.

Hezbollah's role has evolved over time. When Hezbollah was established in 1982, its primary goal was to force Israel to withdraw from southern Lebanon. When it achieved this goal in May 2000, its focus began to broaden, although it still challenged Israel over disputed territories like the Shebaa Farms region in the foothills of Mount Hermon. Since September 2000, following Ariel Sharon's visit to the Muslim holy sites in Jerusalem and the subsequent Palestinian uprising, Hezbollah became more outspoken in its support for the Palestinian cause. It has repeatedly said that it sought Israel's withdrawal from all territory it considers occupied and as rightfully belonging to Arabs. In the wake of the February 2005 assassination of former Lebanese Prime Minister Rafik Hariri and the subsequent pullout by Syria, many believe that Hezbollah will seek to expand its influence and role in Lebanese politics.

Hezbollah engages in both political and military activity, and its structure is hierarchical, disciplined, and secretive. Its central decision-making body is the seven-member Majlis Shura al-Qarar ("Decision-making Consultative Council"), which is presided over by Sheik Seyyed Hassan Nasrallah. Though he is clearly recognized as Hezbollah's leader, Nasrallah shares power with the other members of the council. Their decisions are generally reached by consensus or a vote. There are also a number of other bodies and committees below the Consultative Council, including the Politburo, which provides advice to the Council, and the General Convention, which implements Council orders and plans day-to-day operations in Lebanon.[19]

Other elements influence Hezbollah decision making. High-ranking resistance fighters are influential, due in part to their privileged status in the General Convention and the fact that their former commanders are often elected to the Consultative Council. In addition, the security and intelligence agencies play an important role in the group, particularly Amn al-Hizb (the "Party's Security"), which is believed to protect Hezbollah leaders, preserve discipline, and monitor all levels of Hezbollah's hierarchy, including the Consultative Council. Moreover, Iran and Syria, due to their financial and political support, also significantly impact Hezbollah decisions.[20]

Hezbollah reacted strongly to the outbreak of the Israeli-Palestinian War in September 2000. An official statement from the group referred to Sharon's visit as "a deliberate desecration of Muslim holy places in Jerusalem, a criminal act and an insolent provocation of the feelings and dignities of the Arab and Muslim people." The group further described Sharon's visit as a crime and "a declaration of war on Muslim sacred places in Jerusalem."[21]

In October 2000, Al Manar broadcast speeches by Sheik Nasrallah that were clearly designed to incite Palestinian hostility. One such speech included a call to stab Israelis to death: "If you don't have bullets, who among you doesn't have knives? Hide the knife, and when he comes close to the enemy let him stab him. Let the stab be fatal."[22] In another instance, Sheik Nasrallah appeared on the independent al-Jazeera and addressed the Palestinians as "holy war comrades-in-arms," and he proposed a strategy of gradually escalating the uprising from stones to daggers to firearms and other means of military combat.[23] He also reportedly encouraged Palestinians to fight Israelis using suicide operations.

Hezbollah has since offered continued political support and guidance to Palestinian fighters. In October 2000, Nasrallah stated that Hezbollah was concerned with all Israeli prisoners, "whether Lebanese, Palestinian or Arab."[24] He also exhorted Arab leaders to protect the Palestinian struggle "by providing support and assistance to Palestinians fighting Israeli troops."[25] Then in January 2001, he pledged to Palestinian families that he would work to secure the release of their loved ones from Israeli jails.[26] Later that year in August, he told his fighters to prepare to join the Intifada (although they have yet to participate actively in the uprising).[27] Finally, in April 2002, Nasrallah made public overtures to the Israeli government to bargain for the lives of Palestinian fighters threatened by IDF forces. However, a framework for an Israeli-Hezbollah prisoner release agreement was not reached until late 2003 and no exchanges took place until early 2004.[28]

Hezbollah is also suspected of providing significant material assistance to Palestinian militants, probably with Iranian and Syrian encouragement and support and the tolerance of the Lebanese government. There have been a number of reports since October 2000 that Hezbollah has smuggled arms to Fatah and the Palestinian security services, as well as to Hamas and the Islamic Jihad.[29] In February 2002, following the Israeli seizure of a shipment of arms on board the freighter *Karine-A* in the Red Sea, Yasser Arafat accused Hezbollah of attempting to ship the arms to the Palestinian Authority illegally. Within a matter of days, he retracted his comments and instead blamed the Israeli government, which he accused of framing the Palestinians and Hezbollah.[30] Just over a year later, on May 22, 2003, the Israeli Navy captured a fishing vessel off the coast of Haifa carrying weapons and evidence of plans for terrorist attacks. Israeli authorities suspected the items were being smuggled by Hezbollah, but there was no conclusive evidence that they were bound for Palestinian territory.[31]

In addition to suspected arms smuggling, there is evidence that Hezbollah actively trains Palestinian fighters. On April 21, 2002, Hezbollah official Mohammed Raab acknowledged that Hezbollah provides Palestinians with military intelligence and suggestions for stockpiling supplies, trench building, and destroying tanks.[32] In addition, a December 2003–January 2004 investigation by the Israel Security Agency uncovered a Hezbollah-financed and guided terrorist infrastructure within the State of Israel. On February 8, 2004, two Arab Israeli citizens, brothers Jassan and Sirhan Atmallah, were indicted in Israel's Northern District Military Court for attempting to establish "a terrorist infrastructure among Israeli Arabs that would be financed by Hezbollah and under its military guidance," and for "preparing a list of candidates for military training, types of war material that [they] would need, etc."[33] The Shin Bet claimed that Hezbollah provided the individuals with "military training...and ...large sums of money to prepare terrorist attacks."[34]

On July 20, 2004, Hezbollah leader Sheik Seyyed Hassan Nasrallah publicly acknowledged that Hezbollah provided covert assistance to Palestinian militants for the first time. At the funeral of Ghaleb Awwali, a senior Hezbollah official killed by an allegedly Israeli-planted car bomb in Beirut on July 19, Nasrallah said that Awwali was "among the team that dedicated their lives in the last few years to help their brothers in occupied Palestine." He added that "we [Hezbollah] do not want to hide this truth. We want to declare it and boast about it."[35] According to a senior Israeli intelligence official, ten Hezbollah "controllers" in Beirut manage 44 cells of Palestinian militants throughout the West Bank and the Gaza Strip.[36]

Moreover, although Hezbollah has traditionally restricted its support of Palestinian militants to Islamic-based groups such as Hamas and Islamic Jihad, evidence suggests that it has also provided assistance to secular resistance groups as well. For instance, leaders of the Al-Aqsa Martyrs' Brigades in Nablus claimed in July 2004 that they "speak to their Hezbollah handlers by telephone almost daily."[37] Specifically, they stated that Hezbollah "was transferring $50,000 every two or three months to [their] operatives in Nablus," and that "one cell in the nearby Balata refugee camp received $1,000 a month [from Hezbollah] for ammunition and cell phone calling cards, plus $10,000 to $15,000 to help plan specific attacks." And a Brigades' leader, who identified himself as Abu Mujahed, suggested that "we are receiving funding from Hezbollah because we have no other option."[38]

Hezbollah has also engaged in a number of low-intensity attacks on Israeli military outposts and civilian settlements since the Israeli withdrawal from Lebanon in May 2000.[39] There is an ongoing possibility that Hezbollah could further expand its use of armed violence to create a "Northern Front" that might significantly influence the Israeli-Palestinian conflict

If such a Northern Front were to emerge, it might start in the Shebaa Farms region. The conflict over the area dates to the French and British Mandates' post–World War I division of territory, which placed the Shebaa Farms in Syria. Following World War II, United Nations cartographers accepted this position. The Israeli seizure of the Golan Heights from Syria during the 1967 Six Day War included the seizure of the Shebaa Farms as well. When Israel withdrew from Lebanese territory in May 2000, Israeli forces remained in Shebaa, considering the land part of annexed Syrian territory. However, Hezbollah and the Lebanese and Syrian governments claim that Shebaa belongs to Lebanon, arguing that the Syrian government gave the territory to Lebanon in 1951. Thus, in Hezbollah's view, Israel has not yet completed its withdrawal from Lebanon. This makes the Shebaa Farms a major point of contention.[40]

On October 7, 2000, Hezbollah seized three IDF soldiers—Staff Sergeant Binyamin Abraham, Staff Sergeant Adi Avitan, and Staff Sergeant Omar Sawaid—in the Shebaa Farms region and kidnapped Israeli reservist Elhanen Tennenbaum, suspected by Hezbollah of being a Mossad agent, a few days later. The three soldiers were seized by Hezbollah forces that allegedly were disguised as UN soldiers, using a mock UN vehicle. Sheik Nasrallah clearly stated the reason for the October 2000 kidnappings. "We took Israelis prisoner in order to trade them—there is no other solution," he said in a public statement on the day the soldiers were kidnapped.[41]

These kidnappings threatened to expand the Israeli-Arab conflict beyond Israel's northern borders within weeks of the outbreak of open hostilities in the Palestinian territories. It prompted Israeli Prime Minister Ehud Barak to issue an ultimatum to the Palestinians on October 7, 2000, and to demand Hezbollah to halt its assaults on Israeli military outposts and civilian settlements. Barak warned, "We shall direct the IDF and the security forces to use all means at their disposal to halt the violence."[42]

This ultimatum did not halt Hezbollah activity, but within a few months the group did begin to negotiate with the Israeli government for an exchange of prisoners. In December 2000, Israel offered to exchange the bodies of slain south Lebanese guerrillas for information concerning the missing Israelis. Hezbollah insisted on a trade of prisoners for the Israelis, with no other concessions. On April 6, 2001, Israeli Defense Minister Binyamin Ben-Eliezer stated that he would consider the release of the Lebanese guerrilla Mustafa Dirani if it led to the release of the Israeli prisoners.[43] A month later, he said he was willing to pay "any price" for information concerning the hostages' whereabouts.[44] In late October 2001, the Israeli government publicly stated that it believed the three soldiers were dead, though negotiations for the release of their bodies continued.[45] In July 2003, Hezbollah representatives insisted they still held the Israeli prisoners and pledged to capture more if Israel did not negotiate a prisoner exchange with them.[46]

On November 9, 2003, a German-brokered deal was reached for Hezbollah to turn over Elhanen Tennenbaum and the bodies of the three IDF soldiers (who by that time had been confirmed dead) in return for the release of 430 Hezbollah, Lebanese Shi'ite, Jordanian, and Palestinian security prisoners and administrative detainees and the reinternment of the remains of 60 Lebanese decedents and members of Hezbollah from the IDF's Cemetery of the Fallen Enemy to Lebanon. The exchange took place on January 29, 2004.[47] The agreement was widely criticized by many Israeli political leaders and defense analysts who warned that because the exchange was so unbalanced, it would "simply serve to encourage yet more kidnapping of Israeli citizens, particularly military personnel, as a means of putting pressure on the Israel authorities."[48] Nevertheless, as of mid-June 2004 the four seizures of October 2000 are the only reported Hezbollah kidnappings since the start of the war. Yet Nasrallah has stated on at least two occasions that the group would consider doing so again to secure the release of Lebanese and Palestinian prisoners still being held in Israel.[49]

On April 14, 2001, another incident that killed an IDF soldier in the Shebaa Farms area demonstrated how quickly the Israeli-Palestinian War could escalate and broaden to a regional conflict. Israel responded to Hezbollah's attack by firing at least 40 tank and artillery shells into suspected Hezbollah hideouts in the Lebanese hills near Israel's northern border. The Israeli Air Force (IAF) then dispatched planes that struck targets in southern Lebanon. It was the first time that fighter jets attacked Lebanon since Ariel Sharon assumed office.[50]

This incident too provoked an international reaction. The day after the attack, UN Secretary-General Kofi Annan's representative in southern Lebanon, Staffan de Mistura, characterized the incident as "very regretful" and as having occurred "in a way and place that represent a clear violation of Resolution 425 and the Blue Line as far as the UN is concerned passes there."[51] The Bush administration accused Hezbollah of causing a new wave of violence in the region.[52] The Lebanese newspaper *Al-Mustaqbal* was also critical, questioning the timing of the operation.[53]

In November 2004 and April 2005, Hezbollah successfully flew a UAV, the Mirsad, over Israeli communities in the northwestern portion of the country, allegedly in response to frequent flights of Israeli aircraft over Lebanon. Hezbollah was able to pilot the UAV safely back to Lebanese territory in the second incident, sparking fears that the organization may try to arm UAVs for future attacks.

Hezbollah has been the cause of a number of other incidents in the Israel-Lebanon border area and occasional IDF reprisals against Syria and Lebanon. On June 8, 2004, the IDF claimed that 14 infiltration attempts and 105 antiaircraft attacks, 42 antitank missile attacks, 5 Katyusha rocket attacks, 7 shooting attacks, and 10 explosive device attacks had been made against Israeli targets since the Israeli pullout from southern Lebanon in May 2000. In total, the IDF reported that 11 IDF soldiers and 6 Israeli civilians were killed and 53 soldiers and 14 civilians were wounded in these attacks.[54] In March 2004, Hezbollah and Hamas signed an agreement in which they stated that the two organizations would work together more closely to bring about a greater number of attacks against Israel.

Long before the Israeli-Palestinian War began, Israeli officials claimed that Iran financed and armed Hezbollah and that the Syrian and Lebanese governments claimed responsibility for Hezbollah attacks, accusing the former of supplying the group and permitting it to operate from Lebanese territory, while charging the latter with refusing to deploy Lebanese troops along its border with Israel, and thus giving Hezbollah free reign in the southern part of Lebanon. It also threatened to attack interests of both countries.

On April 16, 2001, Israeli warplanes attacked Syrian radar sites in Lebanon's central mountain region, Dar al Baidar. The attacks killed one Syrian soldier and wounded four others. These were the first strikes against Syrian military installations in five years. The previous attack was in 1996, when Israeli gunships hit Syrian Army positions near the Beirut airport during a bombing campaign against Lebanon.

The Israeli attack against Syrian positions led to more criticism of Israel by Arab and Islamic leaders, as well as fears of an escalation of the Israeli-Palestinian violence into a possible regional conflict. The Syrians and Hezbollah, while refraining from immediate retaliatory measures, vowed to respond in due course. Hezbollah's deputy leader, Sheik Naim Kassem, pledged vengeance against Israel at an "appropriate time and manner...contrary to Israeli expectations," while Syrian foreign minister Farouk al-Sharaa pledged that Israel would "pay a heavy price...at the convenient and appropriate time."[55]

Neither Syria nor Lebanon retaliated for the Israeli attacks, at least in an overt manner. On July 1, 2001, Israeli jets again attacked a Syrian radar position, this time in Sarin Tahta in eastern Lebanon, injuring three Syrian soldiers and one Lebanese. The assault was in retaliation for a Hezbollah attack in Shebaa Farms two days earlier.[56] On October 22, 2001, Israeli aircraft fired on a Lebanese border position, in response to a Hezbollah attack that same day.[57]

Hezbollah activity did decrease between October 2001 and July 2003. Indeed, there were only seven major reported altercations between Israel and Hezbollah during that time. It seems likely that Syrian President Bashar al-Asad applied pressure on Hezbollah to reduce its number of attacks, in particular when such attacks were perceived to increase the likelihood of a military confrontation against Syria and/or Lebanon. Syria may want tension and clashes to maintain the pressure on Israel, but it is doubtful that Syria perceives an escalation from a low-intensity Israeli-Palestinian intrastate conflict to an interstate war against a militarily and economically superior Israel to be in its interest.

Tensions between Hezbollah and Israel flared again in August 2003. On August 2, Hezbollah leader Ali Hussein Saleh was killed in a car bomb in Beirut. Hezbollah blamed Israel for the assault, saying that, "All information available...proves beyond a doubt complete Israeli responsibility for this heinous crime."[58] Hezbollah retaliated against Israel on August 8, when militants fired rockets, antitank missiles, mortar shells, and light weapons at Israeli military positions in the Shebaa Farm region. Israeli warplanes and artillery quickly responded with attacks on suspected Hezbollah positions in Shebaa Farms and southern Lebanon.[59] Hezbollah shelled Israeli positions again two days later. Israel destroyed the cannon that launched the shells, but took no other action against the group.

Hezbollah is far more than a Lebanese resistance movement, but Hezbollah maintains a large militia and sizable arsenal that, if used in conjunction with coordinated Palestinian attacks, could pose a serious threat to Israel and the resumption of peace. By most accounts, Hezbollah reportedly has between 2,000 and 5,000 "conventional" fighters based in Lebanon that have received Special Operations training from Iranian, Syrian, and mercenary military instructors.[60] It also allegedly fields 500 to 1,000 operatives that have received special training and are capable of carrying out various types of terrorist attacks. Such operatives are stationed throughout the world. Furthermore, Israeli and Western military sources believe the group has between 8,000 and 10,000 Katyusha rockets, with an estimated range of 12 miles.[61]

Israeli intelligence believes Hezbollah possesses wire-guided TOW missiles, artillery, and 57-mm antiaircraft guns.[62] Some Israeli officials have warned that Iran is providing the group with 240-mm Fajr-3 missiles, with a 25-mile range, and 333-mm Fajr-5 missiles, with a possible 45-mile range.[63] There also are reports that Syria is providing rockets to the group. And on October 25, the Lebanese newspaper *Al-Mustakbal* reported that Sheik Nasrallah had recently vowed that, "in the current situation, the resistance [code name for Hezbollah] must be stronger than in the past, and if there is a possibility to acquire stronger weapons, we should acquire them because the national interest requires it."[64]

In April 2005, Israeli President Moshe Katsav alleged that Syria had transferred an unspecified quantity of additional antiaircraft missiles to Hezbollah that same month. Katsav expressed his concern with Russian President Vladimir Putin during a visit to Israel when it became apparent that Russia would sell Syria a number of short-range antiaircraft missiles.[65]

Hezbollah launched a new wave of Kaytusha rocket firings on Israel in May 2006, after IAF aircraft struck at PIJ targets in Lebanon. These strikes were targeted in part at IDF targets and showed considerable accuracy, indicating Hezbollah was becoming better at long-range strikes. The IDF replied with air, attack helicopter, and artillery fire. The fact that Iran is believed to have supplied Hezbollah with some 10,000–13,000 long-range rockets—some with ranges of 70 to over 100 kilometers—is a subject of considerable concern to the IDF, as is the fact that some Kaytusha-like rockets have been fired by Palestinian forces. The IDF is examining ways to intercept such rockets through laser or high-energy beam weapons and antimissile missiles, as well as air and ground operations against Hezbollah forces.

Although Hezbollah has yet to play a major direct role in the Israeli-Palestinian War, the group is capable of playing a considerably larger role in the conflict in the future. At least publicly, Hezbollah members perceive the Palestinians' situation as an extension of their own. And while Hezbollah's independence is constrained, it still has more flexibility to fight against Israel in ways that states such as Syria, Lebanon, and Iran do not have.

Estimates differ regarding Hezbollah's current force strength, but Figure 7.7 provides a rough estimate of its current military capabilities. Hezbollah had already defeated the South Lebanese Army and was the force that drove Israel out of Lebanon. It would have far more difficulty in attacking across the Israeli border or infiltrating into the country, but it does have rockets and other weapons that it can fire into Israel and had shown it can conduct small border raids and shown it could kidnap Israeli soldiers in the Shebaa Farms area as in October 2000. In late November 2005 IAF flew north to Beirut and dropped pamphlets denouncing Hezbollah and explaining that Hezbollah was "causing enormous harm to Lebanon." This came after two days of intense fighting on the border between the IDF and Hezbollah fighters.[66]

Hezbollah has had significant Iranian and Syrian support in the past and is helping to train anti-Israeli Palestinian groups. Hezbollah forces now have modified AT-3 Sagger antitank missiles reworked to carry tandem warheads designed by an Iranian engineer, thousands of Katushya rockets that have been upgraded to 30-km range, and Al-Fajr 3 surface-to-surface and Al-Fajr 5 that can deliver a 200-kg payload up to a 75-km range, and an Iranian Mohajer UAV that they have used for surveillance over the north of Israel.[67]

Hezbollah's UAVs have flown over northern Israel at least twice: once in November 2004 and again in May 2005. This brought about an increase in the level and intensity of Israeli surveillance flights over southern Lebanon.[68] One of the UAV sorties reached the coastal town of Nahariya and the other Hezbollah claims reached Akko. Israel disputes this claim asserting that the second UAV flight reached just south of Nahariya before turning back. The Israeli Air Force did not initially detect either of the two UAV flights, explaining that the air defenses do not pick up on such small, low-flying, slow-moving objects. Should the UAV missions continue to be undetected for the first few minutes of their flight over Israel, it is feared in Israel that Hezbollah will use the UAVs to carry chemical agents, biological agents, or even small bombs.[69]

Hezbollah has also succeeded in forcing the Lebanese government to allow it to keep its arms in spite of all the political turmoil in 2005 and the expulsion of Syrian forces. When Prime Minister Fuad Siniora threatens to raise the issue of disarming Hezbollah by calling for a full examination of all the activities that led to Hariri's assassination, Hassan Nasrallah removed Hezbollah's five ministers from the Lebanese cabinet and made it clear that Lebanese political stability was at stake. As a result, in early February 2006, the Lebanese government designated Hezbollah as a "resistance movement" to Israel, allowing it to operate as a paramilitary force and keep its arms.[70]

Figure 7.7   Developments in Hezbollah Military Forces in Lebanon in 2004–2006

- Roughly 2,500–3,500 men, heavily dependent on part-time and irregular forces. Many are now highly experienced, often well-educated forces.

- Composed of a core of around 300 guerrillas. Has deliberately cut its force over the past years to prevent infiltration and leaks.

- Hezbollah fighters are old by comparison to Israeli fighters. Any age up to 35, usually married, often university students or professional men.

- Still seems to have Iranian Revolutionary Guards as advisors. Heavily supplied and financed by Iran, but Syrian personnel seem to be involved in training and in coordinating with Iran. Iranian and Syrian coordination of support for military supply and possibly operations of Hezbollah seems to occur at the general officer, deputy minister level.

- Conflicting intelligence reports estimate Iranian aid to Hezbollah to involve tens of millions of dollars a year.

- Equipped with APCs, artillery, multiple rocket launchers, mortars, antitank guided missiles (including AT-3 Sagger, AT-4 Spigot ATGMs, and captured TOWs), recoilless rifles, SA-7s, antiaircraft guns.

- Guerrilla mortar strikes have improved in both accuracy and range, indicating better range-finding systems, low signature weapons, and the use of mortar boosters that enable consistent hits for 2 to 3 miles.

- Supply of rockets is estimated to have risen to 1,000. These include Iranian produced 240-mm rockets with a range of 40 kilometers, according to Israeli intelligence reports. Most of the rockets are 120-mm and 127-mm variants with a maximum range of 22 kilometers. Types include the Katyusha, Fajr 3/5, and Zelzal-2.

- Has great expertise in using improvised explosive devices like the improved radio detonated roadside bombs that proved effective against the Israelis. Some are disguised as large rocks. These rock-like explosives are reportedly produced in Iran.

Source: Various editions of the IISS *Military Balance,* U.S., British, Lebanese, and other experts.

Nonstate Forces: Asbat al-Ansar

While Lebanon does not extend official tolerance to Islamist extremist terrorist groups, significant numbers of fighters have joined such groups in the fighting in Iraq, and Tripoli is increasingly becoming a center of Sunni Neo-Salafi extremist activity. There is also at least one such group operating in Lebanon with ties to Al Qa'ida.[71] This movement is Asbat al-Ansar, or the League of the Followers or Partisans' League. U.S. State Department reporting on terrorism describes it as a Lebanon-based Sunni extremist group, composed primarily of Palestinians with links to Usama Bin Ladin's Al Qa'ida organization and other Sunni extremist groups. It provides the following details:[72]

> The group follows an extremist interpretation of Islam that justifies violence against civilian targets to achieve political ends. Some of the group's goals include overthrowing the Lebanese Government and thwarting perceived anti-Islamic and pro-Western influences in the country.
>
> ...Asbat al-Ansar has carried out multiple terrorist attacks in Lebanon since it first emerged in the early 1990s. The group assassinated Lebanese religious leaders and bombed nightclubs, theaters, and liquor stores in the mid-1990s. The group raised its operational profile in 2000 with two attacks against Lebanese and international targets. It was involved in clashes in northern Lebanon in December 1999 and carried out a rocket-propelled grenade attack on the Russian Embassy in Beirut in January 2000. Asbat al-Ansar's leader, Abu Muhjin, remains at large despite being sentenced to death in absentia for the 1994 murder of a Muslim cleric.
>
> Suspected Asbat al-Ansar elements were responsible for an attempt in April 2003 to use a car bomb against a McDonald's in a Beirut suburb. By October, Lebanese security forces arrested Ibn al-Shahid, who is believed to be associated with Asbat al-Ansar, and charged him with masterminding the bombing of three fast food restaurants in 2002 and the attempted attack on a McDonald's in 2003. Asbat forces were involved in other violence in Lebanon in 2003, including clashes with members of Yassir Arafat's Fatah movement in the 'Ayn al-Hilwah refugee camp and a rocket attack in June on the Future TV building in Beirut.

In 2004...operatives with links to the group were believed to be involved in a planned terrorist operation targeting the Italian Embassy, the Ukrainian Consulate General, and Lebanese Government offices. The plot, which reportedly also involved other Lebanese Sunni extremists, was thwarted by Italian, Lebanese, and Syrian security agencies.

...Asbat al-Ansar remained vocal in its condemnation of the United States' presence in Iraq...the group urged Iraqi insurgents to kill US and other hostages to avenge the death of HAMAS leaders Abdul Aziz Rantisi and Sheikh Ahmed Yassin. In October, Mahir al-Sa'di, a member of Asbat al-Ansar, was sentenced in absentia to life imprisonment for plotting to assassinate former US Ambassador to Lebanon David Satterfield in 2000. Until his death in March 2003, al-Sa'di worked in cooperation with Abu Muhammad al-Masri, the head of al-Qa'ida at the 'Ayn al-Hilwah refugee camp, where fighting has occurred between Asbat al-Ansar and Fatah elements.

...The group commands about 300 fighters in Lebanon.

...The group's primary base of operations is the 'Ayn al-Hilwah Palestinian refugee camp near Sidon in southern Lebanon.

...Probably receives money through international Sunni extremist networks and possibly Usama Bin Ladin's al-Qa'ida network.

The Role of the Lebanese Security Forces

As is typical of internal security and paramilitary forces in the region, Lebanon's internal security forces have serious problems that go far beyond their sectarian differences and penetration by Syrian intelligence. The human rights report by the U.S. State Department issued in February 2005 summarized the role—and limitations—of Lebanese paramilitary and security forces as follows:[73]

The security forces consist of the Lebanese Armed Forces (LAF) under the Ministry of Defense, which may arrest and detain suspects on national security grounds; the Internal Security Forces (ISF) under the Ministry of the Interior, which enforce laws, conduct searches and arrests, and refer cases to the judiciary; and the State Security Apparatus, which reports to the Prime Minister and the Surete Generale (SG) under the Ministry of the Interior, both of which collect information on groups deemed a possible threat to state security. These security forces committed numerous, serious human rights abuses, sometimes acting independently, and other times on instruction of senior government officials.

...Members of the security forces used excessive force and tortured and abused some detainees. Prison conditions remained poor. The Government also arbitrarily arrested and detained persons who were critical of government policies. Lengthy pretrial detention and long delays in trials remained problems. The courts were subject to political pressure, seriously hampering judicial independence.

...The Government acknowledged that violent abuse usually occurred during preliminary investigations conducted at police stations or military installations, in which suspects were interrogated without an attorney. Such abuse occurred despite laws that prevented judges from accepting any confession extracted under duress.

Methods of torture reportedly included beatings and suspension by arms tied behind the back. Some former Southern Lebanese Army (SLA) detainees reported that they were abused or tortured. Amnesty International (AI) and other human rights organizations reported that some detainees were beaten, handcuffed, blindfolded, and forced to lie face down on the ground.

. . .Abuses also occurred in areas outside the Government's control, including in Palestinian refugee camps. During the year, there were reports that members of the various groups that controlled specific camps detained their Palestinian rivals. Rival groups, such as Fatah and Asbat al-Nur, regularly clashed over territorial control in the various camps, sometimes leading to exchanges of gunfire and the detention of rival members.

. . .The law requires the ISF to obtain warrants before making arrests; however, the Government used arbitrary arrest and detention. Military intelligence personnel made arrests without warrants in cases involving military personnel and those involving espionage, treason, weapons possession, and draft evasion. The 2004 report by the Parliamentary Commission for Human Rights estimated that of the approximately 5,000 persons being held in prison, one third had not been convicted of any crime.

. . .Defendants have the right to legal counsel, but there was no state-funded public defender's office. The bar association operated an office for those who could not afford a lawyer, and the court panel on many occasions asked the bar association to appoint lawyers for defendants.

Security forces continued the practice of arbitrary arrest and detention. On several occasions during the year, security forces detained and arrested citizens on grounds of national security. Protestors were also arbitrarily detained and arrested

. . .The Military Court has jurisdiction over cases involving the military as well as those involving civilians in espionage, treason, weapons possession, and draft evasion cases. Civilians may be tried for security issues, and military personnel may be tried for civil issues. The Military Court has two tribunals—the permanent tribunal and the cassation tribunal—the latter hears appeals from the former. A civilian judge chairs the higher court. Defendants on trial under the military tribunal have the same procedural rights as defendants in ordinary courts.

. . .The Government and Syrian intelligence services used informer networks and monitored telephones to gather information on their perceived adversaries. The Army Intelligence Service monitored the movements and activities of members of opposition groups. The Government conceded that security services monitored telephone calls but claimed that monitoring occurred only with prior authorization from competent judicial authorities.

. . .Syrian and Palestinian security forces operated independently of Lebanese security forces and also committed numerous, serious human rights abuses. There were credible reports that Lebanese security forces personnel detained individuals on the instruction of Syrian intelligence agencies.

. . .Syrian military and Lebanese and Palestinian militias, particularly Hezbollah, retained significant influence over much of the country. Approximately 15,000 Syrian troops were stationed in locations throughout the country, excluding the area bordering on Israel in the south of the country. In September, Syria claimed to have carried-out a redeployment of its troops in the country, withdrawing approximately 3,000; however, the actual number is believed to be less than 1,000.

. . .An undetermined number of Syrian military intelligence personnel in the country continued to conduct their activities independently. In 2000, following the Israeli Defense Forces (IDF) withdrawal from the south, the Government deployed more than 1,000 police and soldiers to the former Israeli security zone. However, the Government has not attempted to disarm Hezbollah, a terrorist organization operating in the region, nor have the country's armed forces taken sole and effective control over the entire area. Palestinian groups, including armed factions, operated autonomously in refugee camps throughout the country.

This report did not change significantly in the update that the State Department issued on March 8, 2006.[74]

LEBANON'S CONTINUING STRATEGIC CHALLENGES

Lebanon's major security challenge has long been national unity, and this challenge is likely to remain its key security problem indefinitely into the future. Lebanese forces can only be as effective as Lebanese political unity and the ability of its various sects to compromise and live in peace. If its political system fails, there are no lasting military solutions, and Lebanese attempts at warlordism have done far more to provoke further division and outside intervention than provide even authoritarian security.

At the same time, Lebanon needs to develop forces that can secure its borders and act as a deterrent to any further Syrian and Israeli incursions. It needs forces that can bring Hezbollah and Palestinian paramilitary and terrorist elements under control and fully disarm them, and that can ensure that Iran, Israel, and Syria cannot use Lebanon as a proxy in their conflicts and struggles. Once again, this requires national unity from a nation that has been the victim of a self-inflicted sectarian wound for more than half a century.

Lebanon also faces the following more detailed strategic challenges:

- Continuing to train and organize truly integrated and national military, paramilitary, and security forces.
- Removing officers and elements penetrated by Syrian intelligence and subject to Syrian influence.
- Establishing full military and security control over both the Syrian and Israeli border areas.
- Disarming Hezbollah and Amal, seizing the hidden military assets of other militias.
- Preventing Palestinian military or terrorist activities from being planned and supported in Lebanon and preventing infiltration across Lebanon's borders with Israel.
- Organizing and modernizing its military forces to deter Israeli and Syrian military incursions, including air and naval forces capable of deterring incursions into Lebanese airspace and waters.
- Reducing the risk that Jordanian territory or airspace could be involved in any exchange between Iran and Israel, and that if Iran develops nuclear armed missile, Jordan might have to deal with an inaccurate missile or fallout.

Lebanon cannot prepare for large-scale conventional war, or even play a significant military role on the periphery of a broader Arab-Israeli conflict. It can, however, become involved in such a war if Iran, Syria, and or Hezbollah involve the Hezbollah in a serious proxy war with Israel or a missile attack on northern Israel.

If Lebanon is to be a player, rather than simply played, it must develop adequate capabilities to deal with internal security threats and to deter a limited expansion of a conflict between its neighbors into Lebanese territory, waters, or airspace. The key to such success is bringing Hezbollah under central government control, disarming Hezbollah and the concealed weapons stashes in other militias, and putting Lebanese central government forces truly in control. It must also be to fully expel the remaining Syrian and Iranian intelligence and security presence in the country and stop the expansion of Sunni Islamist extremist activity before it becomes yet another threat.

It cannot be stressed too firmly, however, that Lebanese military success is totally dependent on political unity and compromise. Whether or not nature abhors a vacuum, the Middle East abhors a political vacuum. Disunity and internal political conflict not only risk tearing Lebanon apart from the inside, they are an open invitation to some form of outside action—as Iran, Israel, and Syria have already shown.

The Military Forces of Palestine

The current Israeli-Palestinian war of attrition is only the latest form of what is now the oldest conflict in the Middle East, and one of the oldest conflicts in the modern world. It began well before World War II and has been a steady war of attrition ever since 1947. While state actors dominated the struggle from 1948 to 1967, Jordan's expulsion from Jerusalem and the West Bank made a fundamental shift in the nature of the struggle that took on organized form in the late 1960s, was officially recognized by the Arab League, and then was given further recognition when Jordan declared it would no longer seek to recover Jerusalem and the West Bank.

From 1970 to the Oslo Accords, virtually every Palestinian faction, including the Palestine Liberation Organization (PLO) and Yasser Arafat's dominant Fatah faction, not only declared itself at war with Israel but also denied Israel's right to exist. The rise of Palestinian activism and the Palestinian struggle with Israel was a key factor leading to the clash between Palestinian forces and Jordan that drove Palestinian leaders into Lebanon in 1970. The Palestinian presence in Jerusalem was the official reason for Israel's invasion of Lebanon in 1982. While some initially felt the expulsion of Arafat and Palestinian forces from Lebanon marked an end to the Israeli-Palestinian struggle, the various Palestinian factions found new host countries, and internal riots in the West Bank that began in 1988 led to a popular uprising or Intifada that became an asymmetric war of attrition so exhausting that it pushed both sides into signing the peace agreement that became the Oslo Accords.

The present size and character of the Gaza Strip, West Bank, Israel, and Jordan are shown in Figure 8.1. The numbers in Figure 8.1 illustrate just how the different character of the nations and peoples involved really is, and it shows the disparities in living standards that help exacerbate the Israeli-Palestinian conflict. They reflect the major demographic pressures on the Palestinians in both the Gaza Strip and the West Bank. Figure 8.2 shows how such demographic pressures will grow sharply with time. This population growth already challenges Palestinian ability to create a

Figure 8.1   CIA Profile of the Gaza Strip and West Bank—Part One

Category	The Gaza Strip	West Bank	Israel	Jordan
Total Area (sq. km)	360	5,860	20,770	92,300
Land Area (sq. km)	360	5,640	20,330	91,971
Land Borders (km)	62	404	1,017	1,635
Egypt	11	–	266	–
The Gaza Strip	–	–	51	–
Iraq	–	–	–	181
Israel	51	307	–	238
Jordan	–	97	238	–
Lebanon	–	–	79	–
Saudi Arabia	–	–	–	744
Syria	–	–	76	375
West Bank	–	–	307	97
Coastline (km)	40	0	273	26
Land Use (Percent)				
Arable	26.32	NEGL	17.02	2.87
Permanent Crops	39.47	0	4.17	1.52
Meadows & Pastures	0	32	7	9
Forest & Woodland	11	1	6	1
Other	34.21	100	78.81	95.61
Irrigated (sq. km)	120	–	1,990	750
Population	1,376,289	2,385,615	6,276,883	5,759,732
(% 0–14 years)	48.5	43.4	26.5	34.5
(% 15–64 years)	48.8	52.2	63.7	61.7
(% 65+ years)	2.6	3.4	9.8	3.8
Growth Rate (%)	3.77	3.13	1.48	2.56
Birth Rate (per 1,000)	40.03	32.37	18.21	21.74
Fertility Rate (Per Woman)	5.91	4.77	2.54	2.71
Net Migration Rate (per 1,000)	1.54	2.88	–	6.42
Death Rate (per 1,000)	3.87	3.99	6.18	2.63
Infant Mortality (per 1,000)	22.93	21.24	7.03	17.35
Life Expectancy (yrs.)	71.8	73.08	79.32	78.24
Ethnic Divisions				
Arab	99.4	83	19.9	98
Armenian	–	–	–	1
Circassian	–	–	–	1
Jew	(0.0)	17	80.1	–
Religion				
Christian	0.7	8	2.1	6.0
Jew	0.0	17	80.1	–
Muslim	99.3	75	15.9	92.0
Other	–	–	5.5	2.0

Figure 8.2   CIA Profile of the Gaza Strip and the West Bank—Part Two[1]

Category	The Gaza Strip	West Bank	Israel	Jordan
Literacy	–	–	95.4	86.6
Labor Force	278,000	614,000	2,420,000	1,460,000
Construction (%)	–	–	8	–
Agriculture (%)	11.9	9.0	2.6	5.0
Industry (%)	18.0	28.0	20.2	12.5
Commerce (%)	–	–	12.8	82.5
Other Services (%)	70.1	63	26.8	–
Public Services (%)	–	–	31.2	–
GDP (PPE in $billion)	0.768	1.8	139.2	27.7
Real Growth Rate (%)	4.5	6.2	4.3	5.5
GDP Per Capita ($US)	600	1,100	22,200	4,800
Inflation Rate (%)	3.0	3.3	1.3	–
Unemployment Rate (%)	31.0—	19.9	8.9	15.0–30.0
Population Below Poverty Line (%)	81.0	46.0	21.0	30.0
Budget ($B)				
Revenues	(0.964------------0.964)		43.8	3.68
Expenditures	(1.34--------------1.34)		58.0	4.69
Trade ($M)				
Exports	(270------------270)		40,100	4,226
Imports	(1,952------------1,952)		43,200	8,681
External Debt ($M)	(0------------------0)		44,600	8,459
Economic Aid ($M)	(2,000------------2,000)		662	500
Transportation				
Railroads (km)	0	0	647	505
Roads (km)	–	4,500	17,237	7,364
Paved (km)	–	2,700	17,237	7,364
Airports	2	3	51	17
Runways 1,500M+	–	1	13	6
Runways 3,000M+	1	0	2	7
Telephones	(301,600--------301,600)		3,006,000	622,000
Cellular	(480,000--------480,000)-		6,334,000	1,325,300
Internet Users	(145,000---------145,000)		2,000,000	
Televisions	–	–	1,690,000	500,000
Stations	2	–	17	20
Radios	–	–	–	1,660,000
AM Stations	0	1	23	6
FM Stations	0	20	15	5
Short-wave	–	–	2	1

Source: Adapted from CIA, *World Factbook, 2006,* various country sections.

viable state under the best of conditions and helps explain why Israel's efforts at separation are seen very differently from the Palestinian side than they are from the Israeli side.

THE OSLO ACCORDS AND THE NEW ISRAELI-PALESTINIAN WAR

It was not until the Oslo Accords led to the Israel-PLO Declaration of Principles on Interim Self-Government Arrangements (the DOP), that was signed in Washington, D.C., on September 13, 1993, that efforts at creating an Israeli-Palestinian peace process acquired real meaning. The PLO gave up a formal state of war with Israel to become a "protostate" as the dominant part of a new Palestinian Authority (PA). Even then, however, significant numbers of Palestinian organizations rejected the new peace process, and the PLO was reluctant at best to act on the portion of the Accords that called for it to reject the portions of its charter that called for Israel's destruction.

The resulting peace process did make progress. A transfer of powers and responsibilities for the Gaza Strip and Jericho occurred as the result of the Israel-PLO Cairo Agreement on the Gaza Strip and the Jericho Area of May 4, 1994. This transfer was expanded to cover additional territory on the West Bank as a result of the Israel-PLO Interim Agreement of September 28, 1995; the Israel-PLO Protocol Concerning Redeployment in Hebron, the Israel-PLO agreement of January 15, 1997; the Wye River Memorandum of October 29, 1998; and the Sharm el-Sheikh Agreement of September 4, 1999.

Yasser Arafat's Fatah was the ruling party within the PA at this time and remained so until the elections of January 2006. It had members that were Christian, Muslim (Sunni mainly), and secularist and saw the new peace in relatively pragmatic terms. However, although it was formally willing to accept Israel's right to exist and to exchange land for peace, it never proved able to agree with Israel on three main issues: the status of Jerusalem, Palestinians' right of return, and the issue of Palestinian sovereignty and independence.[2]

As a result, the DOP agreement did not put an end to the Israeli-Palestinian conflict. A number of secular factions remained antipeace and anti-PLO. New, radical Islamist groups like Hamas and the Palestinian Islamic Jihad actively carried on the struggle against Israel. Israel continued to expand its settlements and the Palestinians continued to carry out acts of violence and terrorism. The "peace process" was always a "war process" as well, and the creation of Palestinian security forces in the Gaza Strip and the West Bank was as much a potential future threat as an ongoing effort to bring security to both the Palestinians and Israel.

Both sides sought peace and both made critical mistakes. Both in their own way worsened the plight of the Palestinian people and helped create the conditions for a more intense and open form of asymmetric struggle. Whether Israeli rigidity and settlements or the corruption and incompetence of the Palestinian Authority cause the Palestinians more suffering is moot. Both were deeply to blame.

Both sides failed fundamentally in delaying serious negotiations for a permanent peace, although for very different political reasons. The DOP has provided that Israel would retain responsibility during the transitional period for external and internal security and for public order of settlements and Israeli citizens, but called for direct negotiations to determine the permanent status of the Gaza Strip and the West Bank. These negotiations began in September 1999, and even a major effort by President Bill Clinton at Camp David could not move them forward rapidly enough to avert new major clashes.

A new and far more violent Intifada broke out in September 2000. In spite of various peace efforts—most notably by the Quartet (the United States, European Union, United Nations, and Russia) in June 2003 to create a "road map" for a final settlement, the most that could be accomplished was a faltering series of cease-fires. The proposed date for a permanent status agreement had to be postponed indefinitely.

Major clashes took place, and the new Palestinian security forces became involved along with radical Palestinian opponents of Israel like Hamas. The Palestinian Authority came under siege and in many ways ceased to function—consuming large amounts of aid money but failing to provide anything approaching effective governance or even an honest accounting of its actions and expenditures. Meanwhile, Israeli settlements continued, and Israel moved to create security barriers that would separate Israel, "greater Jerusalem," and the territory it wished to keep on the West Bank from the Palestinians in both the Gaza Strip and the West Bank.[3]

THE DEATH OF ARAFAT AND THE VICTORY OF HAMAS: REDEFINING PALESTINIAN POLITICS AND THE ARAB-ISRAELI MILITARY BALANCE

The death of Yasser Arafat in November 2004 triggered new hopes that the peace process might be revived, and a respected propeace leader, Mahmoud Abbas, was elected President of the Palestinian Authority in January 2005. Israel and the PA reached new agreements on security issues, in an effort to move the peace process forward, as part of the Sharm el-Sheikh Commitments, in February 2005.

Israel and the PA remained at odds over how the peace process could be moved forward, however, and new talks and cease-fire efforts had little practical effect. Worse yet, the Palestinian Authority remained corrupt and incompetent and lost popular support. Abbas had little to offer the Palestinians by way of peace incentives and could neither effectively unify and rebuild the Palestinian security forces nor offer honest and effective governance, economic hope, or security.

Israel continued to increase the size of the settlements in the West Bank and the Gaza Strip, created more barriers and walls, did little to show a peace would offer real hope of a successful Palestinian state, and focused more on unilateral separation than peace. In September 2005, Israel withdrew all Israeli settlers and military forces from the Gaza Strip and vacated and destroyed its military facilities. It did not, however, give up control over the Gaza Strip's waters, airspace, and access to the Gaza Strip.

Israel did sign an agreement with the PA to authorize the reopening of the Rafah border crossing in Israel in November 2005. The agreement stipulated Egyptian and Palestinian control of the Rafah border with monitoring by the EU. It soon became clear, however, that Israel would take strong action against the Palestinians if there were evidence of arms smuggling or that they permitted Palestinians that Israel regarded as terrorists to enter the Gaza Strip.

Moreover, many Palestinians saw the Israeli withdrawal as more of result of the continuing violence and attacks launched by Hamas and the Palestinian Islamic Jihad (PIJ) than as a result of progress toward a meaningful peace. As was the case when Israel withdrew from Lebanon, many Arabs saw the withdrawal more as an Israeli defeat than an Israeli strategic choice. Palestinian anger was further fueled by the ongoing expansion of Israeli settlements, the steady deterioration of social and economic conditions, and Abbas's ongoing failure to improve Palestinian governance.

HAMAS COMES TO POWER

The end result was a stunning shift in the Palestinian leadership growing out of the elections for the Palestinian national assembly on January 25, 2006. The PA's failures, corruption, and internal divisions left it far more politically vulnerable than either preelection polls or political experts had predicted. Although Fatah and its supporters gained more votes, splits in their list of candidates and attempts to rig the electoral system in their favor backfired. Hamas and its supporters emerged as the dominant political party in both the Gaza Strip and the West Bank in spite of Israeli threats, prior efforts by Abbas to gerrymander a Fatah/PLO victory, and U.S. efforts to support propeace Palestinian candidates. Hamas had already won several local elections, but this time it won 76 out of 132 seats in the legislature vs. only 43 for Fatah, which had dominated Palestinian politics since the 1960s.[4]

A largely secular and propeace Palestinian government was suddenly and unexpectedly replaced by a radical Islamist group whose charter and ideology called for Israel's destruction. Some Hamas leaders in the Gaza Strip and the West Bank did indicate that they would consider a mutual cease-fire. However, Hamas's formal leader, Khaled Meshal, based in Damascus, made it emphatically clear that Hamas would not abandon its struggle with Israel and would transform its armed wing into a national Palestinian army.[5]

President Abbas continued in office, but initially took the position that Hamas should be given office and would find it could not govern. He felt it would either have to turn to the PA or be forced to agree to Israel's right to exist and to negotiate with Israel. Israel and many outside powers refused to deal with Hamas and shut off aid to the Palestinian government when Hamas continued to refuse to recognize Israel's right to exist or support the effort to revive the peace process.

As least through mid-2006, however, Hamas not only showed that it could take power in spite of such opposition, Abbas became steadily weaker. Hamas appointed its own leaders for Palestinian security forces and created new Hamas forces. The PA security forces and civil service—some 150,000 men and women—went unpaid or got a small fraction of their pay. The regular PA security forces reacted by becoming more violent and corrupt, while the Hamas forces began to play an open role as part of the Palestinian forces and showed they were strong enough to clash with various elements of the PA forces.

The end result was to convince many Israelis that the Palestinians could not become a negotiating partner for years to come, if ever, and that Israel was right in creating security barriers, moving toward more formal separation, and declaring new unilateral boundaries—steps that could only further exacerbate Palestinian anger and the Israeli-Palestinian war of attrition.

History provides equal warnings that there is no way to predict how much given movements like Hamas and the PIJ will or will not moderate over time, or whether they will become more extreme and violent. There is no doubt, however, that Hamas's victory is a further catalyst in a fundamental change in the Arab-Israeli military balance. At the same time, it has interacted with the rise of Neo-Salafi Islamist terrorism and efforts to dominate the Islamic world. Like the interaction among Hezbollah, Syria, and Iran; the shifts in the Israeli-Palestinian conflict have become regional as well as internal. The Palestinians have also been driven primarily by local tensions and dynamics. They have never been anyone's proxies; they use as much as they are used.

THE CHANGING STRUCTURE OF PALESTINIAN AUTHORITY FORCES

The nature and the structure of Palestinian Authority forces have changed as often as the cycles in the peace process and the war process. For the last half a decade, they have been driven by the Israeli-Palestinian conflict that began in September 2000.[6] Palestinian forces have been caught in the dilemma of having to support the shell of a peace while increasingly being involved in a grim asymmetric war that has mixed popular resistance to Israel with the most brutal forms of terrorism, while producing equal violence from Israel. The pauses and cease-fires in this conflict did not prevent PA forces from being gutted during periods of fighting or many members of these forces from coming to feel that any form of violence against Israel was better than waiting for peace negotiations that would never happen.

Palestinian Authority Forces during the Peace Process

In order to understand how Palestinian Authority forces developed before Hamas won the 2006 election, it is necessary to understand both that Chairman Arafat never allowed the Palestinian security forces to be unified and effective before the new round of fighting began in September 2000, and that Israel had largely shattered the forces that were created by the end of 2002.

Arafat's "divide and rule" shaped the history of the Palestinian Authority security forces until Arafat's death. The PA security forces first acquired formal status in May 1994, when Israel and the PA signed the Cairo Agreement on the Gaza Strip and the Jericho Area. This agreement officially created the General Security Service

(GSS), which included most of the PA police and intelligence organizations. In the process, the GSS came to coordinate ten different security and intelligence services.

A study by the Washington Institute for Near East Policy summarized their respective duties before the outbreak of the Israeli-Palestinian War as follows:[7]

- National Security Force (Quwat al-Amn al-Watani): Conducted most security missions along Area A borders and inside cities;
- Civil Police (al-Shurta Madaniyya): Main PA law-enforcement agency; also conducted riot control and counterterrorist operations;
- Preventive Security Force (al-Amn al-Wiqa'i): Largest PA intelligence organization; plain-clothes; involved in counter-terrorist and anti-opposition actions, and surveillance in Israel;
- General Intelligence (Mukhabbarat al-Amma): Official PA intelligence body; involved in intelligence gathering, counterespionage, and maintaining relations with foreign intelligence services;
- Military Intelligence (Istkhabbarat al-Askariyya): Not recognized in the Oslo Accords; dealt primarily with antiopposition activities; investigated other intelligence and security agencies;
- Military Police (MP): Also unrecognized by Oslo; dealt with riot control, protected important people and facilities, oversaw prisons, and maintained "order and discipline" among the other security agencies;
- Coast Guard (Shurta Bahariyya): Located in the Gaza Strip; protected the PA's territorial waters;
- Aerial Police (Shurta al-Jawiya): Not recognized by the peace agreements; maintained the PA's helicopters;
- Civil Defense (al-Difa'a al-Madani): Fire department and rescue services; and
- County Guard (al-Amn al-Mahafza): Unrecognized by the peace accords; provided security for county governors and settled local disagreements.

The formal structure of the PA forces, however, disguised that fact that all essentially revolved around Arafat. Moreover, Arafat established two additional security organizations outside the GSS, which reported only to him. The Special Security Force, Al-Amn al-Khass, existed ostensibly to gather information on opposition groups in other countries, although some analysts speculate that it might have actually existed to monitor the other Palestinian security services. The Presidential Security Service (al-Amn al-Ri'asa), also known as Force 17, consisted largely of Special-Forces operatives from the supposedly defunct PLO special security organization. It retained its mission of protecting Arafat and other PA leaders and gathering intelligence about domestic opposition. Many of these organizations were restructured over the course of the war.

Experts believe these services had grown roughly from 35,000 to 50,000 PA security, intelligence, and law enforcement operatives by 1998, and were well over 45,000 by 2000.[8] Even when the war began in September 2000, however, the PA security forces had only token strength as conventional military forces. They were also caught between the need to act as a counterbalance to the IDF and the need to establish control over movements like Hamas and the PIJ.

The Impact of the Israeli-Palestinian War

The IDF began to attack PA security forces early in the Israeli-Palestinian War. By early 2001, the Israeli Defense Force (IDF) had begun to attack PA security operatives and facilities in retaliation for Palestinian violence against Israelis. In response to a Hamas sponsored suicide bombing on March 28 near Qalqilyah in the West Bank, the IDF bombarded the bases and training camps of Force 17, Arafat's personal security force. Then in April, the IDF responded to Hamas mortar attacks by attacking PA police installations in the Gaza Strip on three different occasions. The IDF retribution served the purposes of not only the Israeli government, but of Hamas and its allies as well. Israeli attacks on the PA security infrastructure meant that Hamas faced a weaker opponent in its struggle to capture Palestinian public support.

The IDF steadily increased the intensity of these attacks during 2001 and early 2002, and matching increases took place in the form of increased attacks by militant Palestinians and sometimes elements of the PA forces. These IDF attacks steadily weakened the capabilities of the PA security forces, as the following chronology demonstrates:[9]

- February 13, 2001—Israeli gunships kill a member of Force 17, Arafat's personal security force. Israel claims the man, Colonel Masoud Ayad, was a leader of Hezbollah.
- March 21, 2001—The Israeli Army shells a Force 17 training base, killing one Palestinian officer.
- March 28, 2001—In a Hamas suicide bombing two Israeli teenagers are killed near the Palestinian city of Qalqilya. In response, Israeli helicopter gunships bombard bases and training camps of Yasser Arafat's personal security forces. One member of the Force and two other Palestinians are killed.
- April 6, 2001—Israeli helicopters fire rockets at Palestinian police installations north of Gaza City. At least four rockets are fired, damaging a two-story headquarters building and two other structures. Israel attacks after three Hamas mortar shells fired from the Gaza Strip landed near Netiv Haasara, an Israeli village next to the Gaza Strip.
- April 10, 2001—Hamas continues to fire mortar rounds at Israeli targets in the Gaza Strip and inside Israel. The shellings do not result in any casualties. Israel responds by firing antitank missiles at Palestinian police posts in the Gaza Strip. The attack on one target, a Palestinian naval post, kills a lieutenant and wounds seven police officers; the second strike, on a police headquarters in a refugee camp, wounds ten. In contrast to recent nighttime raids, these are daylight attacks without warning on occupied buildings.
- April 21, 2001—Israeli tanks roll into the Palestinian-controlled town of Rafah and level a border police post before pulling out. There are no reported injuries.
- May 13, 2001—Israeli helicopter gunships bombard Palestinian security targets across the Gaza Strip and naval boats strike at least eight Palestinian armored personnel carriers with rockets.

- May 14, 2001—Israeli troops shoot and kill five Palestinian officers stationed at a roadblock in Beitunya, in the West Bank. The IDF says that the post served as a base for firing on Israeli bypass roads. Arafat describes the operation as a "dirty [and] immoral" killing of officers doing mundane, postmidnight guard duty while they were preparing a snack.

- May 20, 2001—IDF tanks fire three shells at the home of Col. Jibril Rajoub, director of Palestinian security forces in the West Bank. Palestinians accuse Israel of trying to assassinate him, while the IDF denies aiming its attack personally at Mr. Rajoub, saying its troops had come under fire and responded by shelling "the precise source of the fire, which was definitely from the courtyard of Jibril Rajoub's house."

- August 9, 2001—Israel takes hold of and closes the East Jerusalem office of the PA. In Ramallah, F-16s flatten a Palestinian police station. Israel is retaliating in response to the bombing in Jerusalem.

- August 14, 2001—Israeli tanks enter the West Bank city of Jenin, leveling the city's police station.

- August 26, 2001—Israeli F-16s and F-17s destroy security installations in the West Bank and the Gaza Strip.

- October 3, 2001—Israel responds by demolishing seven Palestinian police posts in the Gaza Strip—nearby the Jewish settlement two gunmen had attacked the night before.

- December 13, 2001—Israeli helicopter gunships shoot at Palestinian buildings in the West Bank and the Gaza Strip. A Palestinian police station in Ramallah is among the targets.

- February 11–13, 2002—In response to Hamas rocket attacks, Israel bombs PA security compounds in Gaza City. Searching for the manufacturing and launching sites of the rockets, the IDF initiates a military incursion into the Gaza Strip.

- February 15, 2002—Palestinian mines blow up an Israeli tank. Three crew members are killed in the explosion. This is the first time that one of Israel's highly sophisticated tanks is destroyed. Over the Jabalya refugee camp in the Gaza Strip, Israeli jets attack a PA police compound.

- February 20, 2002—Israel initiates an attack on buildings belonging to the PA. Arafat's headquarters in Ramallah and the PA compound in Gaza City are attacked. Sixteen Palestinians are killed.

- June 25, 2002—Israeli troops seize control of Hebron. Israeli forces surround the governor's compound, arrest the leader of Palestinian intelligence, and exchange fire with PA forces. Four Palestinian policemen are killed.

- December 4, 2002—Israeli helicopters fire several missiles at a room in the Palestinian Authority Preventive Security headquarters compound in Gaza City where Mustafa Sabah, a bomb maker responsible for destroying three Israeli battle tanks and killing seven soldiers, is employed as a guard. Sabah dies in the assault and five others are wounded.

By April 2002, the Associated Press reported that the IDF had destroyed most of the 150 PA security facilities, leaving agents to "roam the streets, stay at home, or work from tents."[10] According to PA Chief of Preventative Security Colonel Rashid Abu Shbak, by June 2003 three-quarters of PA national security officers were being held in Israeli detention camps and nine out of ten of the security services offices had been destroyed.[11] According to Dr. Gal Luft, by July 23, 2003, IDF operations had destroyed all the PA's aerial capabilities and left them with only minimal communications and land-based transportation equipment. The end result was that they had "no effective mechanism to coordinate military operations."[12]

The Uncertain Size of Current Palestinian Authority Security Forces

This fighting has made it almost impossible to estimate the present size of various Palestinian forces. A rough estimate of the size and structure of Palestinian forces shortly before Hamas came to power is shown in Figure 8.3.

Figure 8.3   Military and Paramilitary Strength of Key Palestinian Factions and Hezbollah at the Start of the Israel-Palestine War

Palestinian Authority

- 29,000 Security and paramilitary pro-PLO forces enforcing security in the Gaza Strip and Jericho, including:
- Public Security (14,000)—6,000 in the Gaza Strip and 8,000 in the West Bank
- Civil police (10,000)—4,000 in the Gaza Strip and 6,000 in the West Bank
- Preventive Security (3,000)—1,200 in the Gaza Strip and 1,800 in the West Bank
- General Intelligence (1,000),
- Presidential Security (500),
- Military Intelligence (500), and
- Additional forces in Coastal Police, Air Force, Customs and Excise Police Force, University Security Service, and Civil Defense.
- Equipment includes 45 APCs, 1 Lockheed Jetstar, 2 Mi-8s, 2 Mi-17s, and roughly 40,000 small arms. These include automatic weapons and light machine guns. Israeli claims they include heavy automatic weapons, rocket launchers, antitank rocket launchers and guided weapons, and man-portable antiair missiles.
- The PA wants 12,000 more security forces after further withdrawals. Israel had proposed some 2,000.

Pro PLO

- Palestinian National Liberation Army (PNLA)/Al Fatah—5,000–8,000 active and semiactive reserves that make up main pro-Arafat force, based in Algeria, Egypt, Iraq, Lebanon, Libya, Jordan, Sudan, Syria, and Yemen under the tight control of the host government.
- Palestine Liberation Front (PLF)—Abu Abbas Faction—200 men led by Al-Abbas, based in Syria.

- Arab Liberation Front—500 men led by Abdel al Rahim Ahmad, based in Lebanon and Iraq.
- Democratic Front for the Liberation of Palestine (DFLP)—400–600 men led by Naif Hawatmeh, which claims eight battalions, and is based in Syria, Lebanon, and elsewhere.
- Popular Front for the Liberation of Palestine (PFLP)—800–1,000 men led by Ahmed Sadaat, based in Syria, Lebanon, the West Bank, and the Gaza Strip.
- Palestine Popular Struggle Front—200 men led by Samir Ghawsha and Bahjat Abu Gharbiyah, based in Syria.

Anti-PLO

- Palestinian Islamic Jihad (PIJ)—500 men in various factions, led by Assad Bayud al-Tamimi, Fathi Shakaki, Ibrahim Odeh, Ahmad Muhana, and others, based in the West Bank and the Gaza Strip.
- Hamas—military wing of about 300 men, based in the West Bank and the Gaza Strip.
- As-Saiqa—600–1,000 men in pro-Syrian force under Issam al-Qadi, based in Syria.
- Fatah Revolutionary Council/Abu Nidal Organization (ANO)—300 men led by Abu Nidal (Sabri al-Bana), based in Lebanon, Syria, and Iraq.
- Popular Front for the Liberation of Palestine–General Command (PFLP–GC)—500 men led by Ahmad Jibril, based in Syria, Lebanon, elsewhere.
- Popular Front for the Liberation of Palestine–Special Command—50–100 men led by Abu Muhammad (Salim Abu Salem) based in Lebanon, Syria, and Iraq.
- Palestine Liberation Army—2,000 men, based in Syria.
- Fatah Intifada—400–1,000 men led by Said Musa Muragha (Abu Musa), based in Syria and Lebanon.

Hezbollah (Party of God)

- About 300–500 actives with 2,000 men in support, Shi'ite fundamentalist, APCs, artillery, MRLs (107 and 122 mm), rocket launchers, recoilless launchers, AA guns, SA-7 SAMs, antitank missiles (AT-3 Saggers, AT-4 Spigots).

Source: Adapted from U.S. Department of State, *Patterns of Global Terrorism,* various editions; and IISS, *The Military Balance,* various editions.

According to the International Institute for Strategic Studies (IISS) *Military Balance,* there were some 56,000 Palestinian Authority security forces in late 2005.[13] The Jaffee Center estimates that the size of the Palestinian security forces increased from 36,000 in 2000 to 45,000 in 2002. The Center estimated that in 2002, the Palestinian Authority had the following force strength: Public Security or National Security Force, 14,000; Coastal Police, 1,000; Aerial Police, 50; Civil Police, 10,000; Preventive Security Force, 5,000; General Intelligence, 3,000; and Presidential Security Force, 3,000. There were additional men in the Military Intelligence and Civil Defense forces.[14]

According to the Jaffee Center the PA security forces numbers totaled some 45,000 in 2005, including both the Gaza Strip and the West Bank.[15] These forces were being reformed. Yasser Arafat's death in Paris on November 11, 2004, had removed a political leader that had constantly played one element of the Palestinian security forces off against another, allowed widespread corruption and abuses, tolerated violence against Israel whenever this was a useful political weapon, and blocked U.S. and other aid efforts from creating effective Palestinian forces.

There was a desperate need to act. Meaningful peace negotiations could not take place without meaningful Palestinian forces, However, a half-decade of war had shattered the PA forces, and many existed largely on paper or could do little more than claim a paycheck. Many Palestinians saw the PA forces as repressive and corrupt, as did many younger members of the forces—which had been increasingly radicalized by the fighting and the lack of meaningful leadership at any level from mid-level officers to the President.

The new leadership that replaced Arafat understood many of these problems. Following Arafat's death, Prime Minister Ahmed Qurei and PLO Chairman, and the PA's new President Mahmoud Abbas attempted to bring some degree of unity to Palestinian forces and to bring about a cease-fire between the different militant organizations and the Israeli forces.[16] They had significant U.S. support in these efforts, but they largely failed. Palestinian Authority political leaders and heads of the security forces were too divided to allow decisive reforms in the PA forces.

On March 1, 2005, for example, Abbas publicly announced the Palestinian Authority's decision and readiness to restructure its security forces and to create a unified command structure at an international meeting in London.[17] Unity was a key issue because Arafat had created 14 separate units that Arafat said he intended to unify into three distinct divisions but never made serious efforts to reform.[18]

The security situation in the West Bank and the Gaza Strip had also deteriorated to the point by March 24, 2005, where members of the Palestinian Parliament openly urged the PA to immediately institute much stronger security reforms.[19] Shortly after hearing the findings of the Parliamentary Human Rights Committee, Palestinian MPs passed a resolution that criticized the heads of security for the "lack of attentiveness in taking action to stop the situation from deteriorating." They also urged recently appointed Interior Minister Nasr Yussuf to "unveil his promised plans to rectify the lawlessness and reform the security services as soon as possible."[20]

Events made the need for such reform all too clear a week later. On March 31, Palestinian militants in the West Bank town of Ramallah opened fire on Abbas's compound in response to the President's recent efforts to establish control in the area. This forced security officials to compromise with the militants. They allowed the reinstatement of many of the militants, who were former security officers, to their old units—with demotion of one rank.[21]

Abbas's plan to "integrate the fighters [militants] into official Palestinian security agencies...with the ultimate aim...of creating 'one law, one authority, one weapon'" remained at the core of his efforts before the January 25, 2006, elections.[22] While the general Palestinian population largely supported the plan, the Israeli government opposed it, since the "integration proposal" would effectively allow individuals whom Israel considered to be "terrorists" to maintain arms under Palestinian law.[23] Abbas, however, strongly disagreed with the Israeli government stance and was convinced that it would be far more effective to "co-opt" militants as opposed to going after them militarily.[24]

Palestinians militants, such as members of Al-Aqsa, also opposed the integration plan, which many perceived as a means of undermining their long-standing political struggle.[25] Nevertheless, Abbas moved forward. In further efforts to improve security, Abbas fired West Bank Security Chief Ismail Jaber and the local security chief in Ramallah, Younis al-Aas (two days after the incident at Abbas's compound in Ramallah).

Abbas announced that he would enforce a new law that required security personnel to retire at the mandatory age of 60—meaning many hundreds, and even thousands, of security officers (predominantly from Arafat's era) would be forced to retire in efforts to jump-start the much needed reform.[26] By May 2005, efforts were already under way to retire 1,076 officers, and an additional 1,000 were scheduled to retire in a second phase.[27] Abbas also requested that MPs impose a law that allowed commanders to serve in the same position only for a term of four years. However, the proposal has yet to be voted on by the Parliament at the time of this writing. It was also opposed by most senior security officials.

Abbas continued with such reform efforts through the January 25, 2006, election. In fact, he planned to use a Fatah victory to disarm the militias and make further security reforms. In practice, however, the election not only halted most reform activity, it raised serious questions as to whether Abbas and the PA could maintain control of Palestinian forces and whether their future mission would be to try to bring order and peace or support a renewed Israeli-Palestinian war of attrition.

PALESTINIAN SECURITY FORCES AND INTERNAL SECURITY IN THE GAZA STRIP AND THE WEST BANK

Abbas had good reasons to seek reform. The failings, the repressiveness, and the corruption of the Palestinian security forces have had a major impact on Palestinian politics since they were first created and were a significant factor in Hamas's January 2006 election victory. As is the case with all of the countries and entities that form the Arab-Israeli balance, the Palestinian security services have performed both a security function and acted as an instrument of repression.[28]

There are various reports that either exaggerate or understate these abuses. However, the human rights report the U.S. State Department issued in February 2005 provides an objective summary of the role of both Palestinian and Israeli security forces in the Gaza Strip and the West Bank during the period before Hamas won the 2006 election:[29]

> The Palestinian security forces included the National Security Forces (NSF), the Preventive Security Organization (PSO), the General Intelligence Service, or Mukhabarat, the

Presidential Security Force, and the Coastal Police. Other quasi-military security organizations, such as the Military Intelligence Organization, also exercised de facto law enforcement powers. Palestinian police were normally responsible for security and law enforcement for Palestinians and other non Israelis in PA-controlled areas of the West Bank and Gaza Strip. Palestinian security forces were under the authority of the PA. Members of the PA security forces committed numerous, serious abuses.

Israeli security forces in the West Bank and Gaza Strip consisted of the Israeli Defense Forces (IDF), the Israel Security Agency (Shin Bet), the Israeli National Police (INP), and the Border Police, an operational arm of the Israel National Police that is under IDF command when operating in the occupied territories. Israeli military courts tried Palestinians accused of security offenses. Israeli security forces were under effective government control. Members of the Israeli security forces committed numerous, serious abuses.

The PA's overall human rights record remained poor, and it continued to commit numerous, serious abuses. There were credible reports that PA officers engaged in torture, prisoner abuse, and arbitrary and prolonged detention. Conditions for prisoners were poor. PA security forces infringed privacy and freedom of speech and press. The PA did not take available measures to prevent attacks by terrorist groups either within the occupied territories or within Israel. Impunity was a serious problem. Domestic abuse of women persisted. Societal discrimination against women and persons with disabilities and child labor remained problems.

There were reports that Israeli security forces used excessive force, abused and tortured detainees. Conditions in permanent prisons met international standards, but temporary facilities were austere and overcrowded. Many Israeli security personnel were prosecuted for committing abuses, but international and Israeli human rights groups complained of lack of disciplinary action in a large number of cases.

The Israeli Government continued construction of a security barrier along parts of the Green Line (the 1949 Armistice line) and in the West Bank. The PA alleged that the routing of the barrier resulted in the taking of land, isolating residents from hospitals, schools, social services, and agricultural property. Israel asserts that it has sought to build the barrier on public lands where possible, and where private land was used, provided opportunities for compensation. Palestinians filed a number of cases with the Israeli Supreme Court challenging the routing of the barrier. In June, the Court ruled that a section of the barrier must be rerouted; determining that the injury caused by the routing of the barrier did not stand in proper proportion to the security benefits; various portions of the barrier route were rerouted. On July 9, the International Court of Justice issued an advisory opinion, concluding that "The construction of the wall built by Israel, the occupying Power, in the Occupied Palestinian Territory, including in and around East Jerusalem...and its associated regime, are contrary to international law."

...Palestinian members of Fatah, HAMAS, and PFLP attacked and killed civilians in Israel, Israeli settlers, foreign nationals, and soldiers. They used weapons designed to inflict casualties on noncombatants, such as suicide bombs, and fired area weapons such as rockets and mortars at their targets without regard for noncombatants. In addition, they often fired at Israeli security forces from civilian population areas, increasing the risk that Israeli return fire would harm noncombatants. The PA did not take sufficient steps to prevent terrorist attacks, enforce a ban on militant groups, or prevent such groups from seeking shelter in civilian areas. By year's end, some PA officials made statements questioning the utility of violence. During the presidential campaign, PA presidential candidate Abbas called the armed Intifada counterproductive to Palestinian interests.

According to the PA Ministry of Health, the Palestine Red Crescent Society, and B'tselem, at least 800 Palestinians were killed during the course of Israeli military and police operations during the year. The PA Ministry of Health estimated that approximately half of those killed were noncombatants. B'tselem reported a figure of 452 innocent Palestinians killed this year. The IDF stated that the majority of Palestinians killed were armed fighters or persons engaged in planning or carrying out violence against Israeli civilian and military targets. According to the PRCS, IDF operations resulted in injuries to approximately 4,000 Palestinians.

The IDF conducted numerous military incursions into Palestinian population centers, in response to Palestinian mortar and antitank fire. These actions often resulted in civilian casualties. Israeli forces fired tank shells, heavy machine-gun rounds, and rockets from aircraft at targets in residential and business neighborhoods where Palestinian gunfire was believed to have originated. Palestinians often used civilian homes to fire upon Israeli forces and booby-trapped civilian homes and apartment buildings. In response to these actions, the IDF usually raided, and often leveled, these buildings.

The State Department report issued in March 2006 was very similar. It indicated that little real progress had been made in reforming Palestinian forces and noted a wide range of abuses by both Palestinian and Israeli forces:[30]

Israeli security forces in the West Bank and Gaza consisted of the IDF, the Israel Security Agency (Shin Bet), the Israeli National Police (INP), and the Border Police, an operational arm of the INP that is under IDF command when operating in the occupied territories. Israeli military courts tried Palestinians accused of security offenses.

...Palestinian security forces were under the authority of the PA. Palestinian police were normally responsible for security and law enforcement for Palestinians and other non-Israelis in PA-controlled areas of the West Bank and Gaza. Palestinian security forces included the National Security Forces, the Preventive Security Organization (PSO), the General Intelligence Service, or Mukhabarat, the Presidential Security Force, and the Coastal Police. Other quasi-military security organizations, such as the Military Intelligence Organization, exercised the equivalent of law enforcement powers. The General Intelligence Law, signed into effect in October, placed the Mukhabarat under PA President Abbas's authority.

In April Abbas placed operational control of the security services under the interior minister. While the order was given to consolidate the security forces under the interior minister, this was not done in practice, and there were ongoing problems in the delineation of responsibilities, with no clear chain of command. In practice the Mukhabarat and the PSO maintained independent commands and reported directly to the president. On September 25, Abbas restructured the Palestinian National Security Council, incorporating competing security interests. The PA lacked full control over security forces. On December 20, armed members of Fatah-affiliated Al-Aqsa Brigades briefly seized Bethlehem's municipal building, reportedly demanding employment.

The PA generally did not maintain effective control over its security forces, and there were reports that members of the PA security forces committed numerous, serious abuses, including torture. The Israeli government maintained effective control of its security forces; however, there were reports that Israeli security forces used excessive force and abused and tortured detainees.

...Regarding the PA, there were reports of the following problems:

- torture
- arbitrary and prolonged detention
- poor prison conditions
- infringement of privacy and freedom of speech
- insufficient measures to prevent attacks by terrorist groups either within the occupied territories or within Israel
- numerous instances of violence against Israeli civilians, resulting in deaths and injuries in the West Bank, the Gaza Strip, and Israel
- corruption and lack of transparency
- domestic abuse of women
- societal discrimination against women and persons with disabilities and child labor

Regarding the Israeli occupying forces, there were reports of the following:

- damage to civilians in the conduct of military operations
- numerous, serious abuses of civilians and detainees
- failure to take disciplinary action in cases of abuse
- improper application of security internment procedures
- use of temporary detention facilities that were austere and overcrowded
- limited cooperation with nongovernmental organizations (NGOs)

...Palestinian members of Hamas, Fatah-affiliated militant groups, and Palestinian Islamic Jihad attacked and killed Israeli civilians, foreign nationals, and soldiers, both in Israel and in the occupied territories. They used weapons in such a manner as to inflict casualties on noncombatants, such as suicide bombs, rockets, and mortars. In addition they often fired at Israeli security forces from civilian population areas, increasing the risk that Israeli return fire would harm noncombatants.

The PA took some steps to prevent terrorist attacks and banned the display of weapons in public, but these steps did not prevent or deter numerous attacks. Armed members of various groups ignored PA directives; PA security has not consistently prevented them from displaying weapons in public. During the presidential campaign, Fatah presidential candidate Abbas publicly called the armed Intifada counterproductive to Palestinian interests.

...In March the PA and Palestinian factions agreed to uphold a tahdiyah, or period of calm, whereby armed Palestinian groups would refrain from attacks on Israeli targets; however, during the year militant factions broke this agreement killing and injuring Israelis.

There was a widespread public perception of PA corruption, notably within the security forces. Many social and political elements called for reform. The PA security forces made little progress in rationalizing the security forces payroll and rooting out corruption in the services. On September 18, Abbas appointed a new attorney general to focus on corruption. Local NGOs praised the appointment and hoped he would effectively address PA corruption. At year's end the attorney general had announced investigations into several corruption cases. PA members and the general Palestinian public widely criticized the growing lawlessness inside the West Bank and Gaza and the failure by PA security forces to provide security.

...The law requires official PA institutions to "facilitate" acquisition of requested documents or information to any Palestinian; however, the law does not require any PA agency to provide such information. Many Palestinians cited the law when seeking to acquire information; however, there were no PA court cases. NGOs sought to make it mandatory to provide information to Palestinians; however, there was no action during the year.

...Torture by PA security forces reportedly was widespread. Documentation of abuses by PA security forces was very limited, due partly to hesitancy by alleged victims to make public claims of torture or abuse against PA authorities. Palestinian security officers have no formal guidelines regarding legal interrogation conduct; most convictions were based largely on confessions.

PA prison conditions were poor. Facilities were dilapidated and neglected; most were destroyed during the Intifada, and prisoners were kept informally incarcerated. There were separate facilities to hold juvenile prisoners. Prison facilities were poorly protected and subject to intrusions by outsiders. The PA generally permitted the ICRC access to detainees and allowed regular inspections of prison conditions; however, the PA denied access to some detainees for 14 days following their arrests. The PA permitted monitoring of its prisons, but human rights groups, humanitarian organizations, and lawyers reported difficulties gaining access to specific detainees. Human rights organizations stated their ability to visit PA prisons and detention centers varied depending on which organization ran the facility. Human rights monitors said prison authorities did not consistently permit access to PA detention facilities, and they rarely could see inmates being interrogated.

PA security forces detained persons without informing judicial authorities and often ignored laws protecting detainee rights and court decisions calling for release of alleged security criminals. At year's end Palestinian sources estimated the PA imprisoned approximately 239 suspected of collaboration with Israel. Alleged collaborators often were held without evidence and denied access to lawyers, their families, or doctors.

Similarly, the State Department reports on terrorism continued to describe PA efforts to reform the PA forces as ineffective, and PA forces as having failed to make serious efforts to put an end to attacks on Israel:[31]

Though the PA Security Forces (PASF) made some improvements in their command and control mechanisms, and contributed to the security of Israel's withdrawal from the Gaza Strip and four settlements in the northern West Bank in August, the PA failed to take resolute action against terrorist groups based in the West Bank and Gaza. President Abbas' public condemnation of terrorist acts was not matched by decisive security operations following attacks against Israelis.

The U.S. Security Coordinator worked with the PASF to encourage comprehensive security sector reform and to enable the PASF to confront militant groups. The PASF, however, did not take serious action against known terrorist groups such as HAMAS, PIJ, PFLP, or AAMB. On two occasions immediately following the Israeli withdrawal from Gaza, PASF units were involved in military confrontations with HAMAS militants, resulting in clashes that exposed the PASF's lack of sufficient military equipment and organization to confront militant groups operating in areas under PA control.

organization to confront militant groups operating in areas under PA control. In September, the U.S. Consulate General signed a Letter of Agreement with the PA to provide a limited amount of non-lethal assistance to the PASF. The PA took some actions to curtail terrorist violence through its political activities. In February, the PA—supported by the Government of Egypt—brokered a deal between HAMAS, PIJ, and AAMB for a period of "calm" to allow Israel to withdraw from Gaza and four settlements in the northern West Bank.

Although terrorist activity against Israel was reduced during this period, attacks continued. PIJ and PRC were particularly active. Palestinian terrorist groups continued to operate from Palestinian areas controlled by the PA and the Israeli military. The PASF did not take decisive actions to end the use of Palestinian territory for attacks on Israeli civilians. Terrorist groups, such as PIJ and HAMAS, received support from foreign terrorist organizations and foreign governments, including Syria and Iran, and operated extensively in areas of the West Bank and Gaza under both PA and Israeli military control.

The PA did not make any sustained effort to dismantle terrorist infrastructure in territory under its control. There was periodic low-level cooperation between the PA and Government of Israel security services. The PA worked with the Israeli Government in preparation for the Israeli disengagement from Gaza and areas of the northern West Bank. PASF occasionally provided information to the Israeli Government regarding planned terrorist operations and handed over explosives and other materials located by PA forces.

The PA failed to take action, however, in several instances when the Government of Israel provided intelligence on the location and activities of wanted terrorists. In many cases, the individuals were briefly arrested and subsequently released. The PA's lack of action in this area was an obstacle to broader security cooperation. In the West Bank, the PASF was hindered by restrictions on movement imposed by the IDF.

PASF officials frequently raised concerns about operational difficulties imposed by the Government of Israel. While operational issues may have limited the effectiveness of the PASF, a lack of political will from the senior Palestinian leadership was the primary cause of the PA's failure to arrest and prosecute terrorists. In an effort to crack down on terrorists, following the December 5 bombing of a shopping center in Netanya, the PASF arrested nearly 70 militants and activists, most of them affiliated with PIJ.

Efforts to arrest and prosecute terrorists were impeded by a disorganized legal system, the Palestinian public's opposition to action, lack of political will, a weak security apparatus, and inadequate prison infrastructure. Deficiencies in training, equipment, and leadership of the PASF in Gaza were a significant obstacle to PASF actions there. PA courts were inefficient and failed to ensure fair and expeditious trials

...Although progress was slow in creating a Financial Follow-Up Unit (FFU) under the Palestinian Monetary Authority (PMA), the PMA expressed its commitment to build capacity to track and deter financial transactions used to fund terrorist activity. Despite the lack of coordination between the PMA and other ministries, a new Prosecutor General was named. The FFU also continued to lack the legal framework in which to act. The PA does not have an Anti-Money Laundering/Countering Financing of Terrorism (AML/CFT) law.

It is important to note that the State Department report also states that Israeli security forces were reported to have killed 190 Palestinians in 2005, and wounded some 900, plus carried out some 30 targeted killings. It also reports a wide range of legal and human rights abuses by IDF forces. Cease-fires or no cease-fires, PA forces effectively operated in a war zone—although one that was asymmetric rather than conventional. Nevertheless, these State Department reports show the internal divisions in the Palestinian security forces, factionalism and corruption, and the impact of nearly half a decade of Israeli attacks had all combined to make the PA security forces as much a part of the problem as part of the solution.

So far, however, the main real-world shifts since the death of Arafat have been the creation of an overt Hamas security force, the inability to pay much of the PA security force, and significant clashes between PA and Hamas forces and supporters. The only tangible improvement that has been put in place is the creation of a new Counterterrorist Unit made up of the best and most loyal elements of the Presidential Special Guard, which is one of the few elements of PA forces with good special mission training and which is trained by the Jordanian Unit 14, a counterterrorist force with training facilities near Amman. The total manning of the Special Presidential Guards has been increased from around 100 to 900 since May 2005. They have training camps near Jericho and Bethlehem in the West Bank, but are lightly equipped and do not have secure communications.

PALESTINIAN MILITANT ORGANIZATIONS AND THEIR MILITARY IMPACT

The Israeli-Palestinian balance has been shaped by a wide range of additional forces. Palestinian militant movements—some independent and some affiliated with Fatah and the Palestinian Authority—have opposed peace and shaped most Palestinian violence ever since Israel seized the West Bank, the Gaza Strip, and the rest of Jerusalem in 1967.[32]

Like the PA forces, such militant elements have been in constant flux. They have also acquired a steadily more militant Islamist character since September 1990. A rough estimate of the size of the various Palestinian and Lebanese forces that currently pose a threat to Israel is shown in Figure 8.4. The major active militant groups in the Gaza Strip and West Bank with paramilitary elements include the Fatah Tanzim, the Islamic Resistance Movement (Hamas), Palestinian Islamic Jihad (PIJ), the Al-Aqsa Martyrs Brigade (Fatah's militant wing), and the Popular Front for the Liberation of Palestine (PFLP).

The U.S. State Department summarized the activities of such groups as follows in its 2005 country report on terrorism:[33]

> The Palestinian Authority's efforts to thwart terrorist operations were minimal...The PA security services remained fragmented and ineffective, hobbled by corruption, infighting, and poor leadership. Following the November 11 death of PA Chairman Arafat, Prime Minister Ahmed Qurei and then PLO Chairman Mahmoud Abbas engaged in an effort to convince militant Palestinian groups to agree to a cease-fire. Cease-fire talks

Figure 8.4 Current Palestinian and Lebanese Forces

Origin	Organization and Aims (Remarks)	Established	Estimated Strength	Status	Operates
Lebanon	**Asbat al-Ansar** Advocates Salafism, opposed to any peace with Israel	1990s	300	Active	Lebanon
Lebanon	**Hezbollah (Party of God) • Islamic Jihad-Revolutionary Justice Organization • Organization of the Oppressed on Earth ▲** Iran-style Islamic republic in Lebanon; all non-Islamic influences removed from area (Shi'ite; formed to resist Israeli occupation of south Lebanon with political representation in Lebanon Assembly).	1982	2,000+	Active	Bekaa Valley, Beirut, south Lebanon, Shebaa Farms
Palestinian Autonomous Areas of Gaza and Jericho	**Al-Aqsa Martyrs' Brigade ▲** Associated, though not officially backed, by Arafat Military offshoot of Fatah	2000	Not known	Active	Palestinian Autonomous Areas of Gaza and Jericho, Israel
Palestinian Autonomous Areas of Gaza and Jericho	**Al Saika** Military wing of Palestinian faction of Syrian Ba'ath Party (Nominally part of PLO)	1968	300	Active	Palestinian Autonomous Areas of Gaza and Jericho, Israel
Palestinian Autonomous Areas of Gaza and Jericho	**Arab Liberation Front** Achieve national goals of Palestinian Authority (Faction of PLO formed by leadership of Iraq Ba'ath party)	1969	500	Dormant	Palestinian Autonomous Areas of Gaza and Jericho, Israel

Organization	Year	Size	Status	Location
Democratic Front for the Liberation of Palestine (DFLP) Achieve Palestinian national goals through revolution (Marxist-Leninist; splintered from PFLP)	1969	100+	Active	Palestinian Autonomous Areas of Gaza and Jericho, Israel
Fatah Tanzim Armed militia link to Fatah	1995	1,000+	Active	Palestinian Autonomous Areas of Gaza and Jericho, Israel
Harakat al-Muqawama al-Islamiyya (Hamas) Islamic Resistance Front Establish an Islamic Palestinian state in place of Israel	1987	Not known	Active	Palestinian Autonomous Areas of Gaza and Jericho, Israel
Izz al-Din al-Qassam Brigades (IDQ) ▲ Replace Israel with Islamic state in Palestinian Areas [Armed wing of Harakat al-Muqawama al-Islamiyya (Hamas); separate from overt organization]	1991	500	Active	Palestinian Autonomous Areas of Gaza and Jericho, Israel
Palestine Islamic Jihad (PIJ) ▲ Destroy Israel with holy war and establish Islamic state in Palestinian areas (One of the more extreme groups from the Palestinian areas.)	1970s	Estimated 500	Active	Palestinian Autonomous Areas of Gaza and Jericho, Israel

Location	Group	Year	Strength	Status	Location
Palestinian Autonomous Areas of Gaza and Jericho	**Palestine Liberation Front (PLF)** ▲ Armed struggle against Israel (Splintered from PFLP)	1977	300–400	Dormant	Palestinian Autonomous Areas of Gaza and Jericho, Israel
Palestinian Autonomous Areas of Gaza and Jericho	**Popular Front for the Liberation of Palestine (PFLP)** Armed struggle against Israel (Marxist-Leninist)	1967	1,000	Active	Palestinian Autonomous Areas of Gaza and Jericho, Israel
Palestinian Autonomous Areas of Gaza and Jericho	**Popular Front for the Liberation of Palestine—General Command (PFLP-GC)** ▲ Armed struggle against Israel (Marxist-Leninist; Split from PFLP to focus on fighting rather than politics)	1968	500	Dormant	Palestinian Autonomous Areas of Gaza and Jericho, Israel

Notes: ▲ = Group known to carry out suicide attacks; dormant = inactive for the past 12 months.
Source: Various editions of the IISS *Military Balance*, U.S., British, and other experts.

were inconclusive by the end of 2004. Palestinian officials, including Mahmoud Abbas, and some Palestinian intellectuals have called for an end to armed attacks against Israelis.

. . . Palestinian terrorist groups conducted a large number of attacks in Israel, the West Bank, and Gaza Strip in 2004. Hamas, Palestinian Islamic Jihad (PIJ), the al-Aqsa Martyrs Brigade, and the Popular Front for the Liberation of Palestine (PFLP)—all US-designated Foreign Terrorist Organizations—were responsible for most of the attacks, which included suicide bombings, shootings, and mortar and rocket firings against civilian and military targets. Terrorist attacks in 2004 killed almost 100 people (mostly Israelis, as well as a number of foreigners, including one US citizen), a decrease from the almost 200 people killed in 2003.

The October 15, 2003, attack on a US diplomatic convoy in Gaza that killed three Americans is the most lethal attack ever directly targeting US interests in Israel, the West Bank, or Gaza. The Popular Resistance Committees (PRC), a loose association of Palestinians with ties to various Palestinian militant organizations such as Hamas, PIJ, and Fatah, claimed responsibility, although that claim was later rescinded. Official investigations continued and resulted in the arrests of four suspects. A Palestinian civil court ordered the four suspects freed on March 14, citing a lack of evidence. Palestinian Authority (PA) Chairman Arafat rescinded the order and kept the suspects in custody until Palestinian gunmen attacked the Gaza prison and released the four suspects on April 24. Since the April 24 incident, the PA has failed to re-arrest the four suspects or to identify and bring to justice the perpetrators of the October 2003 attack.

Palestinian terrorist groups in Israel, the West Bank, and Gaza continue to focus their attention on the Palestinians' historical conflict with Israel, attacking Israel and Israeli interests within Israel and the Palestinian territories, rather than engaging in operations worldwide. Israel employed a variety of military operations in its counterterrorism efforts. Israeli forces launched frequent raids throughout the West Bank and Gaza, conducted targeted killings of suspected Palestinian terrorists, destroyed homes—including those of families of suicide bombers—imposed strict and widespread closures and curfews in Palestinian areas, and continued construction of an extensive security barrier in the West Bank.

. . . Israeli counterterrorism measures appear to have reduced the lethality of attacks; continuing attacks and credible threats of attacks, however, show that the terrorist groups remained potent. Israel also took action in February to block what it labeled terrorist funding in two Palestinian banks. The Israeli Defense Forces (IDF) and Shin Bet raided the West Bank offices of the Arab Bank and the Cairo-Amman Bank, seizing almost $9 million in cash from 310 accounts. Israeli law does not allow seizure of funds via correspondent accounts in Israel, and the Israeli Government claimed that the PA had failed to act on earlier intelligence. PA officials asserted that the funds belonged to reputable clients, with no connection to terrorism. The funds remain seized by order of an Israeli court.

Hamas was particularly active in 2004, carrying out attacks that included shootings, suicide bombings, and standoff mortar and rocket attacks against civilian and military targets, many of them joint operations with other militant organizations. Hamas was responsible for the deadliest attack of the year in Israel—the August 31 double suicide bombing of two buses in Beersheva that killed 16 people and wounded 100. Hamas was also responsible for an increase in Qassam rocket attacks. A rocket attack on Sderot on June 28 was the first fatal attack against Israelis using Qassam rockets. Two Israelis died in the attack. In September, two Israeli children were killed in Sderot from another Qassam rocket attack. In response to the continued Qassam rocket fire, the IDF launched a three-week operation on September 28, in which 130 Palestinians (among them 68 Hamas and Palestine Islamic Jihad militants) and five Israelis died, according to press reports.

. . . The Popular Front for the Liberation of Palestine (PFLP) was active in 2004. The group was responsible for the November 1 suicide bombing at the Carmel Market in Tel Aviv, which killed three people and wounded 30. Palestinian Islamic Jihad conducted numerous attacks on Israeli settlements and checkpoints, including the April 3 attacks on the Avnei Hafetz and Enav settlements in the West Bank that killed one Israeli and seriously wounded a child.

. . . Fatah's militant wing, the al-Aqsa Martyrs Brigade, conducted numerous shooting attacks and suicide bombings in 2004. It was responsible for two suicide bus bombings in Jerusalem during January and February. The attacks killed 21 people and wounded over 110. Al-Aqsa also claimed responsibility along with Hamas for the March 14 suicide attack in the port of Ashdod. The double suicide attack killed ten people and wounded at least 15. The group also claimed responsibility for a suicide bomber attack that killed two people and wounded 17 at a checkpoint near Jerusalem on August 11. On May 2, Palestinian gunmen belonging to the al-Aqsa Martyrs Brigade and PIJ shot and killed an Israeli settler and her four daughters in the Gaza Strip. The group also claimed responsibility for a suicide bomber attack that killed two people and wounded 17 at a checkpoint near Jerusalem on August 11. Lebanese Hezbollah remained a serious threat to the security of the region, continuing its call for the destruction of Israel and using Lebanese territory as a staging ground for terrorist operations. Lebanese Hezbollah was also involved in providing material support to Palestinian terrorist groups to augment their capacity and lethality in conducting attacks against Israel.

The Palestinian Authority did make new attempts later in 2005 to limit such attacks, but its efforts were not satisfactory or successful according to the United States and Israel.[34] Hamas also agreed, however, to a cease-fire before the January 2006 elections on the grounds that it was preparing for the elections and did restrain its members from violent acts against Israeli targets.[35] As a result, the State Department report issued in 2006 described some limited improvements in the situation:

Between August 15 and 22, Israel withdrew approximately 8,000 settlers from the Gaza Strip and four northern West Bank settlements, as well as the Israeli Defense Forces (IDF) units protecting them, thus implementing Prime Minister Sharon's disengagement plan. Responsibility for Gaza was turned over to the Palestinian Authority (PA). Following the Israeli disengagement, Egypt deployed 750 border guards along the Egyptian-Gaza border. Egypt also dispatched security advisers to Gaza to advise the Palestinian Authority Security Forces (PASF) on their new security role along the border.

. . . . Palestinian terrorist groups conducted a significant number of attacks in Israel, the West Bank, and the Gaza Strip even after a "period of calm" was agreed in February. All of these groups used a variety of terrorist tactics, including suicide bombs, rocket attacks, pipe bombs, mortar attacks, roadside bombings and ambushes, and shooting at Israeli homes and military and civilian vehicles. The number of victims killed in Israel in terrorist attacks was less than 50, down from the almost 100 individuals killed in 2004.

...Israeli security forces successfully thwarted other planned attacks. Palestinian Islamic Jihad (PIJ), the Fatah-linked al-Aqsa Martyrs Brigade (AAMB), HAMAS, and the Popular Resistance Committees (PRC) were responsible for most of these attacks. Within Gaza, Palestinian militants engaged in occasional bloody skirmishes with PA police and security service officials, and periodically shot at polling stations, electoral offices, and PA security complexes. According to claims by HAMAS, AAMB, and the PRC, a number of terrorist attacks were perpetrated by one or more organizations acting together, including the January 13 truck bombing of the Qarni cargo crossing terminal on the Israeli-Gaza border, which killed six Israeli civilians and wounded another five. Palestinian Islamic Jihad claimed credit for several terrorist attacks that occurred in Israel, including:

- The February 25 suicide bombing of a Tel Aviv nightclub.
- The July 12 suicide bombing near a mall in Netanya.
- The October 26 suicide bombing at the market in Hadera.
- The December 5 suicide bombing at the mall in Netanya.

HAMAS activity dropped significantly in 2005, in part because of its adherence to the ceasefire, but also because much of its leadership in the West Bank was arrested or killed. HAMAS claimed credit for the pre-ceasefire January 18 suicide bombing in Gaza that killed an Israeli security officer and injured eight other soldiers and security agents. Individuals linked to HAMAS were involved in the September 21 kidnapping and murder in the West Bank of an Israeli resident of Jerusalem. Fattah's militant wing, the al-Aqsa Martyrs Brigade, claimed credit for the following terrorist attacks, after agreeing to the ceasefire:

- The October 16 drive-by shooting attack at Gush Etzion south of Jerusalem, and a shooting attack the same day in the West Bank in which an Israeli teenager was wounded.
- Qassam rocket launches from the Gaza Strip into the western Negev desert that destroyed property and injured Israeli civilians and soldiers.

The Popular Resistance Committees (PRC) carried out a significant number of terrorist attacks from the Rafah area on the Gaza-Egyptian border, notably rocket attacks against Israel. The PRC was also responsible for armed attacks against construction teams and IDF forces in Gaza during the disengagement process. The Popular Front for the Liberation of Palestine (PFLP) made no claims to perpetrating any terror attacks, though it continued to coordinate with other foreign terrorist organizations to carry out attacks.

Lebanese Hizballah continued to provide support to Palestinian terrorist groups to augment their capacity for conducting attacks against Israel. Hizballah also continued to call for the destruction of Israel and used Lebanese territory as a staging ground for terrorist operations. On November 21, Hizballah fighters launched a rocket barrage against border communities and IDF outposts.

Acting on threat information that Hizballah intended to kidnap Israelis, the IDF stopped the incursion, killing four Hizballah fighters. Israeli Government sources reported an upsurge in the PIJ's purchase and resale of goods. Israeli security forces and customs authorities seized containers at the port of Ashdod that contained thousands of dollars worth of merchandise suspected of having been purchased by the PIJ for resale. IDF and civil administration forces also shut down two illegal "Daawa" charity organizations in the West Bank to prevent their possible use as conduits for terror finance.

...After Israel's withdrawal from Gaza, IDF sources reported an increase in the number of explosive devices planted along the fence separating Gaza from Israel. In response to these terrorist attacks, Israel deployed forces along the perimeter of Gaza to prevent rocket and mortar attacks, delayed the expected transfer of West Bank towns to PA control, postponed planned meetings with Palestinian negotiators, and used aircraft to set off sonic booms over Gaza.

In response to continuing mortar and rocket attacks against Israel, the IDF also fired rockets and artillery against sites in Gaza used for mortar and Qassam rocket attacks. In response to continuing threat information, Israeli security forces launched frequent arrest and detention raids throughout the West Bank and Gaza, conducted targeted killings of suspected Palestinian terrorists, imposed strict and widespread closures and curfews in Palestinian areas, conducted airborne rocket attacks on buildings affiliated with designated Foreign Terrorist Organizations (FTOs) in Gaza, and continued the construction of an extensive separation barrier in the West Bank. Israel did not destroy the homes of any suicide bombers or their families.

The Differing Character of Palestinian Militant Groups

While Islamist Palestinian forces have increasingly dominated attacks on Israeli and IDF targets, there are a wide range of Palestinian militant organizations. Some key groups—like Hamas and the PIJ—have emerged as major rivals to the Palestinian Authority; other key groups—like Fatah Tanzim and the Al-Aqsa Martyrs Brigade—are closely tied to Fatah and the Palestinian Authority. Some of these movements are largely based outside the Gaza Strip and the West Bank, or are small and relatively ineffective. All, however, have had at least some impact on Palestinian politics, Palestinian security, and Palestinian relations with Israel.

Some organizations are more violent than others, a few are little more than political proxies for Syria, and some have not been active or effective for years. It is also misleading to label such groups as either "terrorists," "militants," or "freedom fighters." The difference not only is a matter of perspective, but also involves categories that can easily overlap. Most Palestinian militant groups do, however, attack Israeli and Palestinian civilians with the deliberate purpose of causing terror and using terror to get media attention.

As the following group-by-group descriptions show, different groups tend to use different tactics and methods of asymmetric warfare. Their weaponry, however, is changing. They now have some systems like mortars, a small amount of artillery, and Qassam rockets that they can fire across the security boundaries and barriers between the Gaza Strip and the West Bank and Israel and Israeli-occupied areas. They are learning how to make steadily more sophisticated bombs, short-range missiles, and suicide devices. They have long had smuggling tunnels and other ways of moving equipment across the Egyptian-Gaza border, and some smuggling of arms and equipment does move into the West Bank. At least some infiltration and smuggling penetrates across the Israel security barriers and comes in by sea. The rise of Hamas to power may make it significantly easier to move equipment into the Gaza Strip and lead to more tolerance of mortar and rocket firings and preparation of attacks.

Hamas or Harakat Al-Muqawwama Al-Islamia (Islamic Resistance Movement)

Hamas has become the leading Palestinian Islamist organization and is now the dominant Palestinian political party as well. Its name is an acronym for Harakat Al-Muqawwama Al-Islamia (Islamic Resistance Movement) and also means "zeal" or "courage and bravery." Hamas's foremost objective is a *jihad* (holy war) for the liberation of Palestine and the establishment of an Islamic Palestine "from the Mediterranean Sea to the Jordan River."[36] Hamas has stated that the transition to the stage of *jihad* "for the liberation of all of Palestine" is a personal religious duty incumbent upon every Muslim and rejects any political arrangement that would relinquish any part of Palestine.[37]

Hamas has always advocated violence in pursuit of its objectives, not only against Israeli armed forces, but against Israeli civilians as well. Its views also conflict with those Palestinian factions affiliated with Yasser Arafat and the PA, which advocate the creation of a secular Palestine through the resolution of negotiations with Israel.

Hamas has employed a variety of unconventional tactics, ranging from mass demonstrations and graffiti to roadside murders and suicide bombings. Its gradual escalation of violence has influenced the course of the Israeli-Palestinian War. According to the U.S. counterterrorism center knowledge database, Hamas carried out approximately 545 "incidents" between 1968 and February 2006, which caused 2,904 injuries and 595 deaths—where 84 percent of the attacks were against private property and civilians, 5 percent against transportation, and the rest against other targets.[38]

Hamas first became active during the early stages of the Intifada. It was formed in early 1987, out of the religious-social Al-Mujama' Al-Islami (Islamic Center) association in the Gaza Strip, by Sheikh Ahmad Yassin, which was considered the parent organization that represented the Muslim Brotherhood, which originated in Egypt in the 1920s. Sheikh Yassin was involved in the Muslim Brotherhood activities in Palestine throughout the 1960s. Many senior members of Al-Mujama' formed Hamas and used the existing infrastructure of Al-Majama' as a basis for semicovert activity once the Intifada began. Following the start of the "First Intifada" in December 1987, Hamas expanded its activity into the West Bank with at least some cells in Israel proper, becoming the dominant Islamic organization in the West Bank and the Gaza Strip. It also founded a political arm and issued its charter in 1988. As noted earlier, its charter argues that the movement's goal is the creation of an Islamic state in all the territories of historical Palestine.

Hamas has since evolved as a loosely structured organization, with some elements working clandestinely, while others worked openly through mosques and social service institutions to recruit members, raise money, organize activities, and distribute propaganda. Its strength was concentrated in the Gaza Strip and a few areas of the West Bank, where it engaged in political activity, such as running candidates in the West Bank Chamber of Commerce elections.

During the period before the present Israeli-Palestinian war of attrition, Hamas's operations in the Gaza Strip and the West Bank consisted of a combination of regional and functional organizations. It had several identical, parallel frameworks that operated in each region. One framework, called Dawa (literally "call" or "outreach"), engaged in recruitment, distribution of funds, and appointments. Another framework, called Amn ("security"), gathered information on suspected collaborators during the Intifada. This information was passed on to "shock committees," which interrogated and sometimes killed suspects. Amn became a key element in Hamas's rivalry with the Palestinian Authority and in intelligence-gathering operations.

Hamas had a well-organized fundraising apparatus in the Gaza Strip, the West Bank, and Jordan, as well as outside the region. According to the International Policy Institute for Counter-Terrorism (ICT), an Israeli institute in Herzilya, it also received considerable financial support from unofficial Saudi Arabian channels, the Iranian government, and other Gulf States. ICT estimates Hamas's total yearly budget in the tens of millions of dollars. Such ample funding is one of the principal reasons for Hamas's primacy among the militant Palestinian factions.[39]

During the period between the Oslo Accords and September 2000, the paramilitary elements of Hamas played a major role in violent fundamentalist subversion and radical terrorist operations against both Israelis and Arabs. Its shock troops (Al-Suad Al-Ramaya—the "throwing arm") were responsible for popular violence during the Intifada and continued to play a role in violent opposition to the peace process. Hamas also had two paramilitary organizations for more organized forms of violence. The first was the Palestinian Holy Fighters (Al-Majahidoun Al-Falestinioun)—a military apparatus that included the Izzedin al-Qassam Brigades. The second was the Security Section (Jehaz-Amn).

The Al-Majihadoun Al-Falestinioun was established by Sheik Ahmad Yassin in 1982. It procured arms and planned an armed struggle against both Palestinian rivals and Israel. This activity was uncovered in 1984, and Yassin was sentenced to 13 years in prison, but was released shortly afterward as part of the Jibril prisoner exchange in May 1985.

Yassin then resumed his effort to set up a military apparatus. He began by focusing on the struggle against "heretics" and collaborators in accordance with the view of the Muslim Brotherhood that jihad should come only after the purging of rivals from within. At the same time, he prepared a military infrastructure and stockpiled weapons for war against Israel. Shortly before the outbreak of the Intifada, operatives were recruited to execute the military jihad and regular terrorist attacks. The new military apparatus executed a large number of attacks of various kinds, including bombings and gunfire, mostly in the northern part of the Gaza District.

Hamas's spiritual leader Sheik Ahmad Yassin retained considerable personal popularity among Palestinians.[40] His ability to raise millions of dollars in funds for Hamas and his anti-Israel stance led some to fear that he would eventually rival Arafat for power over the PA, despite his frail health and physical disabilities.[41]

The PA was careful to keep Yassin under close observation and scrutiny during the peace process. Following the signing of the Wye Accords, hundreds of Hamas activists were detained and Yassin was placed under house arrest in November 1998. This spurred an angry response from Hamas's members and other Palestinians, who vowed violent retaliation against Arafat and the Palestinian Authority.[42] Although Yassin was released in late December 1998, relations between Hamas and the PA have remained strained.

The main function of Hamas's Security Section (Jehaz Amn), established in early 1983, was to conduct surveillance of suspected collaborators and other Palestinians who acted in a manner contrary to the principles of Islam, such as drug dealers and sellers of pornography. In early 1987, it began to set up hit squads, known as MAJD, an Arabic acronym for Majmu'at Jihad wa-Dawa ("Holy War and Sermonizing Group"). MAJD became the operational arm of the Security Section. Its purpose was to kill heretics and collaborators. Yassin instructed the leaders of these sections to kill anyone who admitted under interrogation to being a collaborator, and he reinforced this instruction with a religious ruling.

After the outbreak of the Intifada, Hamas began to organize military actions against Israeli targets as well. The MAJD units then became part of the Al-Majahadoun network. At the same time, the military apparatus of Hamas underwent several changes as a result of preventive measures and exposure by the Israeli forces following major terrorist attacks. The military apparatus formed the Izzedin al-Qassam Brigades, which were responsible for most of the serious attacks perpetrated by Hamas after January 1, 1992. These squads were formed out of dozens of proven personnel from the Gaza Strip who later also began to operate in the West Bank. Palestinians from the West Bank were recruited to carry out attacks inside the Green Line. Since the peace accords, these groups have been formed into cells that sometimes recruit young Palestinians and form smaller cells to carry out attacks and suicide bombings.

Hamas has long used its overt political operations to recruit members into the units that engaged in riots and popular violence. Those who distinguished themselves were then recruited into the military apparatus, which carried out attacks against Israelis and other Palestinians. There is no way to know exactly how many Arabs that Hamas killed in the years following the signing of the Oslo Declaration of Principles in September 1993. The Israeli government estimates that Hamas killed 20 Israelis and one Jewish tourist from the beginning of the Intifada (December 9, 1987) until December 1992, and assassinated close to 100 Palestinians.

This violence caused a considerable backlash within the Palestinian community during the time when the peace process still seemed likely to be successful and led Hamas to limit its more violent actions. A combination of the Palestinian desire for peace and the loss of jobs and income as a result of Israeli economic retaliation led to a steady drop in Hamas's public support. Public opinion polls showed that support dropped from nearly 40 percent in 1993, to 18 percent in June 1995, and to 11 percent in October 1995. As a result, Hamas began to conduct talks with the

PA in the summer of 1995.[43] The outbreak of the Israeli-Palestinian War (the Second Intifada in September 2000), however, reversed this trend. By late May 2001, Palestinian support for Hamas, which was responsible for the majority of suicide attacks on Israelis, rose to 18.5 percent.[44]

Like Hezbollah in Lebanon, Hamas maintained a distinction between the overt and covert aspects of activities of its various divisions. This compartmentalizing was principally for the purposes of secrecy and security, which was further achieved by limiting internal communication to encoded messages. These measures resulted in an internal structure that remains unclear to outside analysts while debate continues among experts over the degree of overlap between Hamas's social and militant elements. It is clear that Hamas has strong civil elements that perform charitable roles and have little or no direct connection to violence. At the same time, it seems to have used its charity committees—and the ideological instruction, propaganda, and incitement it delivers in mosques and other institutions—as a recruiting base for violence and terrorism. Moreover, parts of its religious and social network almost certainly provide moral and financial support for its militant operatives.[45]

The escalation of the Israeli-Palestinian War can be attributed, in no small part, to the actions of Hamas. As early as October 2000, Hamas leaders called for an escalation of the violence. On November 14, Sheikh Yassin urged Palestinians to "transform the Intifada into an armed struggle against the Israeli conquest."[46] This statement preceded Hamas's first car bomb of the war by only eight days.

In October 2000, the PA released Hamas activists who had been imprisoned during the peace process, in order to placate Hamas and its growing number of supporters and increase pressure on Israel in order to gain greater concessions.[47] This had a significant impact on the fighting. Some of these militants later participated in orchestrated violence against Israel. Their release deepened Israeli suspicions that Arafat was at least a tacit supporter of terrorism and extremism.

Shortly after the activists' release, Hamas organized its first "day of rage" against Israel in the West Bank and the Gaza Strip. The "days of rage" appeared to increase Hamas support in the Gaza Strip. Thousands of supporters marched in protests, shouting militant slogans.[48] In addition to building unity among ordinary Palestinians, Hamas also encouraged solidarity among the other extremist factions. On October 7, the *Washington Post* noted that Hamas, the Revolutionary Communist Party, and even Fatah supporters were appearing at rallies together.[49]

In addition, there is evidence of cooperation between the PA and Hamas during the early weeks of the war. On October 12, Arab mobs overran a Palestinian police station in Ramallah, where two Israeli soldiers were detained, ostensibly for their own protection. The mobs seized them, beat them to death, and dragged their bodies through the streets. Israel responded with an attack on PA security facilities throughout the West Bank and the Gaza Strip. Shortly before the Israeli attack, the PA announced that at least 85 Hamas and PIJ militants had been released from jails. Some conflicting reports stated that it was intentional, because the PA was unable to guarantee their safety, and others stated that they escaped. Among those released were Mohammed Deif and Ibrahim Makadmeh, leaders of the Izzedin al-Qassam.[50]

Hamas's role in organizing demonstrations became official by the end of the month. On October 25, 2000, the *Washington Post* reported that Arafat had allocated seats on a decision-making committee called the High Committee Follow-Up Intifada Nationalist Islamic Organizations to Hamas, PIJ, and Fatah representatives.[51] A day later, Mahmoud Zahar confirmed this, stating that Hamas was designating times and places for street marches.[52] It is likely that this represented an attempt on Arafat's part to placate Hamas and its supporters. However, it also contributed to the spread of Hamas's brand of extremism from the Gaza Strip to the West Bank.

Hamas's tactics have changed over the course of the Israeli-Palestinian War. In the first weeks of the war, Hamas's activities consisted primarily of demonstrations and rallies, confined for the most part to the Gaza Strip. The largest of these initial rallies was in the Gaza refugee camp of Jebaliya on October 27, 2000. An estimated 10,000 Hamas supporters attended, reportedly led by masked men wearing white t-shirts reading "The martyrs of al-Qassam."[53]

Hamas became more active in November 2000, with the first of a series of car and roadside bombs. On November 22, a powerful car bomb detonated in the northern Israeli town of Hadera, killing one and wounding 20. Though Hamas did not directly claim responsibility, it distributed a leaflet reading, "If Israel tries to kill any of the Islamic or national Palestinian figures, militants or leaders, the gates of hill [sp] would be opened for Israel and the price would be so high."[54] Not surprisingly, Israel responded a day later, with a car bomb that killed Ibrahim Beni Ouda, a leader of the Izzedin al-Qassam Brigades, on furlough from prison.[55]

Israel created its policy of "targeted killings" of Palestinian militants in response to such extremist Palestinian violence. Although other groups like the PIJ and Al-Aqsa Martyrs have also been targeted regularly by Israel, Hamas has borne the brunt of its attacks. Of the 52 Israeli targeted killings of senior Palestinian militants between November 2000 and the June 2003 hudna (cease-fire), 50 percent were successfully directed at Hamas activists. After the cease-fire dissolved in late August 2003, Israel continued to have success in thinning the leadership ranks of Hamas through "targeted" killings—including most prominently the assassinations of Sheik Yassin on March 22, 2004, and Abdel Aziz Rantisi on April 17, 2004.[56]

Through early 2004, Hamas had typically responded to IDF assassinations of its members with deadly retaliatory attacks. As previously stated, Hamas had employed suicide bombings throughout the Oslo-Wye peace process. On March 4, 2001, Hamas unleashed its first suicide bomber since the start of the war in Netanya, where a member's self-detonation killed three Israelis and injured dozens of others. Hamas's use of suicide bombings has since become one of the defining characteristics of the war.

According to the Israel Ministry of Foreign Affairs, from the beginning of the war in September 2000 through March 22, 2004, Hamas perpetrated 452 attacks of various kinds, which in total killed 377 Israelis and wounded 2,076 civilians and IDF personnel—including 52 suicide attacks that produced 288 of the deaths and 1,646 of the injured.[57] Thus, while suicide bombings have remained Hamas's deadliest tactic, the group has employed other tactics as well. On April 17, 2001, the

Izzedin al-Qassam launched five mortar shells at the Israeli town of Sderot, near the Gaza Strip. The attack was allegedly in retaliation for recent targeted killings of Hamas leaders. The Sharon government believed the mortar assaults represented a serious and unexpected escalation. Sharon called the act a "major provocation" and seized Palestinian-controlled areas in the Gaza Strip for the first time during the conflict. The Israelis also rocketed PA security bases and divided the Gaza Strip into three parts, barring north-south traffic, a move that U.S. Secretary of State Colin Powell deemed "excessive and disproportionate."[58]

Despite Israel's strong response, Hamas launched five more mortars at the farming village of Nir Oz on April 19, 2001, and fired shells onto a Jewish neighborhood in Jerusalem three months later on July 17. The mortar attacks were carefully orchestrated moves, designed to force Israel to take measures that would further inflame Palestinians and encourage them to strike at the PA, thus weakening Hamas's major rivals for control over the Palestinian populace. Israel again targeted the PA due to Hamas's actions on May 18, after the Netanya shopping mall suicide bombing. Israeli F-16 warplanes, used for the first time since the onset of the war, attacked PA facilities throughout the West Bank and the Gaza Strip.[59]

Hamas's tactics changed again in early 2002. On January 24, Hamas spokesman Moussa Abu Marzook acknowledged that the group was developing a rocket (Qassam-3) with a range long enough to hit targets in the Jewish districts of Jerusalem from inside the West Bank. The Qassam-3 rockets were expected to have an eight-mile range, much longer than the 0.5-mile range of the Qassam-1 and the 1.8-mile range of the Qassam-2.[60] On February 16, Hamas militants fired a Qassam-2 model into an open field near Kfar Azza. Though no one was injured, it represented an ominous new addition to Hamas's repertoire. On May 9, 2003, six more crude rockets, though apparently not the Qassam-3, landed in the vicinity of Sedrot in the Negev Desert, wounding a 10-year-old girl.[61]

At the same time, Hamas was able to build up Palestinian public support through its support of Islamic charities and social services. The PA had to slowly reduce its social services over the course of the war, due to an ever-shrinking budget, a weakening infrastructure, corruption, and poor leadership. Hamas, however, proved able to increase some of its activities and maintain most others. On March 2, 2001, the Associated Press reported that Hamas was believed to support several Islamic charity organizations in the West Bank and the Gaza Strip, including the Islamic Charity Organization in Hebron, which distributes food packages to destitute Palestinian families in the West Bank. Islamic charities continue to fill a growing need due to rampant poverty and widespread unemployment. In addition, Hamas also operates health clinics and kindergartens.[62]

The end result was that the Palestinian Authority had to conduct an increasingly delicate balancing act between satisfying Israeli demands and placating Hamas. For example, while the PA released Hamas militants from jail on October 12, 2000, it began rearresting them just four days later. At the same time, Fatah has never accepted Hamas, and despite their mutual dislike of Israel, Hamas and the Fatah are very different groups. Fatah is secular, advocates a nominally democratic government in an independent Palestine, and for the most part, has been willing to negotiate with Israel to achieve its objectives. Hamas, however, is an Islamic fundamentalist movement. It supports the creation of an Islamic theocratic government in Palestine and is unwilling to accept any long-term agreements or treaties that recognize Israel as a state deserving of land in what it regards as Palestine.[63]

Hamas's popularity has varied according to Palestinian confidence in the peace process, and the level of Israeli violence against Palestinians. Public support for Hamas decreased dramatically during the Oslo-Wye period, but experienced a resurgence in popularity at the outbreak of the Israeli-Palestinian War, while the PA's support diminished. This was due in part to Hamas's charitable social services, but also to the fact that it rejected negotiations, while Arafat was seen as placating Israel. An opinion poll by the West Bank's Birzeit University showed that support for Hamas and other Islamic fundamentalist groups by Palestinians rose from 23 to 26 percent between October 2000 and February 2001, while Arafat's Fatah dropped from 33 to 26 percent (margin of error 3 percent).

On June 16, 2001, Palestinian political analyst Ghassan Khatib said that Hamas had become part of the political mainstream, with 17 to 19 percent of Palestinians "hav[ing] confidence" in the group, compared to 10 percent during the Oslo period.[64] A May 2002 poll indicated that Hamas's approval ratings had increased to 25 percent, drawing ever closer to Fatah's 32 percent. Sheikh Yassin was ranked as the third most popular Palestinian leader,[65] reinforcing some prewar fears that he might one day surpass Arafat in popularity. A Palestinian public-opinion poll conducted in early 2004 indicated that support for Hamas had increased to 30 percent of Palestinians in the West Bank and the Gaza Strip and thus "is increasingly seen as a rival to Yasser Arafat's mainstream Fatah movement."[66]

Animosity between Hamas and the PA grew during the course of the war, due in large part to Hamas's unwillingness to cooperate with the PA's efforts to secure a lasting cease-fire with Israel, ease the IDF's pressure on the PA, and move back toward negotiations. On June 2, 2001, the day after a Hamas/PIJ attack on a Tel Aviv discotheque, Arafat announced that he would encourage a cease-fire with the Palestinian militant groups. At least initially, Hamas seemed to agree to the cease-fire. However, later that same day, the group publicly renounced it. Sheikh Yassin said, "When we are talking about the so-called cease-fire, this means between two armies. We are not an army. We are people who defend themselves and work against the aggression."[67]

The negative impact of Hamas on the PA, the refusal of Hamas to cooperate with the cease-fire, and Arafat's continued arrests of Hamas personnel following the June 1 discotheque attack led to new tension between Arafat's Fatah and the PA forces, and Hamas and its supporters. On August 23, 2001, Fatah and Hamas activists engaged in a shootout at a funeral in the Gaza Strip, leaving three Palestinians dead.[68] On October 10, 2001, the PA police force, conscious of the negative effect a rally in favor of Osama bin Laden could have on world opinion, used clubs, guns, and tear gas to battle hundreds of pro–bin Laden protestors in Gaza City. Most of these protestors were supporters of Hamas. At least three Palestinians were killed and many more were wounded.

The irony of the situation was that the PA became more active against Hamas, while Israel became more active against Arafat's PA. Fearing repercussions from the murder of right-wing Israeli Tourism Minister Rahavem Zeevi by the PFLP in late October, Arafat chose to ban the armed wings of Hamas, the DFLP, the PFLP, and the PIJ. A high-ranking PA official said that the decision was made after it became obvious that the groups were giving Israel an excuse to destroy the PA.[69] Each time Hamas and other factions committed attacks on Israelis, the PA suffered. Following the rash of Hamas suicide bombings on December 1 and 2, 2001, Ariel Sharon declared the PA a "terror-supporting entity" and launched three missiles at a PA security installation in Arafat's West Bank compound. F-16s flattened the offices of the Preventive Security Services, though Hamas was not attacked.[70]

The PA responded by arresting more militants. Sheikh Yassin himself was placed under house arrest. In a series of demonstrations, Hamas marchers demanded that the PA stop arresting their leaders. Riots broke out in Gaza City, leading to clashes between PA/Fatah supporters and Hamas activists.[71] On December 13, Arafat ordered all Hamas and PIJ offices in the West Bank and the Gaza Strip to be shut down.[72] When PA agents attempted to arrest Abdelaziz Rantisi, PA and Hamas forces clashed once more, resulting in the deaths of six Palestinians. In order to "preserve Palestinian unity," Hamas announced a self-imposed cease-fire.[73] On January 9, 2002, two Hamas militants broke the cease-fire, when they killed four Israeli soldiers in a village near the Gaza Strip. Israeli Special Forces responded by killing four Hamas militants in Nablus. Hamas vowed "all-out war" against Israel on January 23, and Hamas supporters tried to storm PA jails in order to free Hamas militants. This led to even further clashes with PA security forces.[74]

Hamas sometimes joined Israel in trying to remove Arafat from power. In May 2002, Hamas leaders claimed that Arafat could no longer lead the resistance against Israel because he was not capable of defending himself against U.S. and Israeli pressure. On June 3, in an attempt to rein in Hamas, Arafat offered the group positions in a new Palestinian Cabinet. Hamas leaders promptly rejected the new Cabinet, saying it would not serve their goals.[75]

On June 18, 2002, at rush hour, a Hamas suicide bomber blew himself up aboard a bus in Jerusalem, killing 19 people and injuring 74. As a result, on June 19, Israel said it would reoccupy the West Bank. In a leaflet, Hamas said it would wage a "war on the buses."[76] Fearing Hamas's actions, Arafat placed Yassin under house arrest once more.[77] Hamas accused the PA of serving the interest of the Israeli occupation and bowing to "Zionist–U.S. pressures." Between August 12 and 15, Arafat again made overtures to Hamas and other militant organizations to participate in the PA government. It was an attempt to prevent more suicide bombings. Hamas refused and rejected a cease-fire.

The tension between the PA and Hamas reached a new boiling point on October 7, 2002. In the Nuseirat refugee camp in the Gaza Strip, a PA police colonel, Rajeh Abu Lehiya, was ambushed and killed by Hamas member Emad Akel, who was seeking vengeance for the death of his brother at the hands of PA riot police a year ago. Hamas sent in large numbers of militants to the camp to prevent PA police from taking action. Street fights broke out between Hamas militants and PA troops that lasted all day and resulted in the deaths of five Palestinians. Other Hamas members assisted in the killing and then protected Akel afterward. Abu Shanab said, "He practiced the justice that was lost by the Palestinian Authority."[78]

On February 7, 2003, Hamas discussed succeeding Arafat's government. Dr. Mahmoud al-Zahar said that Hamas was in position to take over from the PA, "politically, financially, [and] socially." Interestingly, he said that Hamas would take over by elections, not by force.[79] Though Hamas and the PA have continued to abide each other's presence, their shared animosity and differing objectives do not bode well for future Palestinian unity.

When Arafat reluctantly appointed Abbas as his Prime Minister on March 19, 2003, Hamas said it would not cooperate with him. Hamas also responded negatively to the unveiling of the United States "road map for peace" one month later on April 30. Hamas and other militant groups said they would not disarm, as required by the document, and would not honor a cease-fire. However, the Abbas government announced that it would use persuasion, not force, to disarm the militants.[80]

Public support for Hamas in the Gaza Strip seemed to diminish in response. On May 21, 2003, an estimated 600 Palestinians in the town of Beit Hanoun demonstrated against Hamas and other militant factions whom they felt caused Israeli incursions into their homes. On May 22, Abbas began conducting cease-fire talks with Hamas leaders. Eight days later, Sharon announced that he would ease Israeli restrictions on the West Bank and the Gaza Strip if Abbas would crack down on militia groups. In doing so, Sharon placed Hamas in a position where it had to accept a cease-fire or be directly responsible for further violence against the Palestinian people. Moreover, Israel was successful in assassinating senior Hamas militants at an average rate of one a month during the first six months of 2003.

These pressures led Hamas and the PIJ to agree to a three-month cease-fire on June 29. They declared, however, that their observance of the cease-fire was contingent upon Israel abiding by two conditions. First, Israel had to halt all aggression against Palestinians, including demolitions, village closures, sieges, assassinations, arrests, and deportations. Second, Israel was required to release all Palestinian and Arab detainees from prisons and return them to their homes. If Israel did not act in accordance with the conditions, then the cease-fire was officially over, and the militant groups would "hold the enemy responsible for the consequences."[81]

There are several reasons why Hamas agreed to the cease-fire. Rantisi said Hamas agreed to do it "to prevent internal conflict."[82] However, participation allowed Hamas not only to challenge the PA's role as the sole architect of Palestinian diplomacy, but also to craft a document that served its own purposes. The three-month cease-fire gave Hamas an opportunity to regroup and recuperate from the constant Israeli retaliation of recent months. Furthermore, it could allow Hamas to portray Israel as the belligerent in the future. Any Israeli act that could be construed as aggressive could lead to a renewal of hostilities, which Hamas could portray as Israel's responsibility.

In any case, the cease-fire was limited in scope. On July 13, the PA began a campaign to disarm the militant groups. Hamas and the PIJ responded in a joint declaration, stating they would not surrender their weapons and warned Israel that attempts to do so could jeopardize the delicate truce. In addition, Israel continued its policy of targeting militant leaders throughout the cease-fire. And then on August 19, a Hamas suicide bomber detonated a device aboard a crowded Jerusalem bus, killing 18 people and wounding more than 100. The attack was publicly alleged to be in response to the recent Israeli targeted killings; however, a videotaped statement by the suicide bomber indicated that the bombing was actually in response to an Israeli assassination that occurred in June—long before the cease-fire began. Israel responded to the bombing two days later with the assassination of senior Hamas political activist Abu Shanab. The renewed violence crippled the cease-fire, and Hamas announced shortly afterwards that it would no longer honor the agreement. Hamas blamed Israel for "the assassination of the cease-fire."[83]

Hamas did choose to participate in local municipal elections in the West Bank in December 2004 and in the Gaza Strip in January 2005. Candidates associated with Hamas but campaigning under different affiliations ran for office in 26 communities in the West Bank and won approximately 35 percent of 306 races. According to Ghazi Hamad, the Editor of Hamas's weekly newspaper, *Ara Salah,* "It was a very big percentage...No one expected Hamas to take that percentage."[84] Such results reflect a voting population that is "disenfranchised by their leaders, frustrated by years of corruption and worn down by conflict with Israel."[85] According to Birzeit University political scientist Ali Jerbawi, "People wanted change...They were tired of 10 years of negotiations [with Israel] that went nowhere....Hamas was the political opposition, and people identified with the opposition, if not with the Hamas ideology itself."[86]

Hamas also participated in the first-ever Gazan local elections at the end of January 2005—marking the first time Hamas openly campaigned for positions in Palestinian elections. The group obtained overwhelming support in the Gaza Strip where they secured 75 of the 118 council seats, while Abbas's Fatah and its allies won 39. Although the election was for less than half of the councils in the Gaza Strip, the results indicate the widespread support and clout Hamas has continued to maintain in the Gaza Strip. Hamas won further important victories in April and July 2005, when the second and third stages of local elections took place, and went on to win the legislative elections on January 2006.

Part of the reason for the success of Hamas is reflected in a broader-range public-opinion poll conducted by the United States Institute of Peace (USIP). Politics can be as local in the Gaza Strip and the West Bank as in the United States, and Palestinian relations with Israel and other countries were only part of the issues driving Palestinian perceptions. The survey—shown in Figure 8.5—found broad Palestinian willingness to compromise with Israel on a variety of issues, but it also found trends in Palestinian popular opinion regarding the operations of the Palestinian Authority,

Figure 8.5   Palestinian Public Opinion on the Palestinian Authority, Fatah, and Hamas

Palestinian Authority Governance and Legitimacy (in Percent)							
	1996	2000	2001	2002	2003	2004	2005
Support President	71	47	33	25	35	38	44
Adequate Quality of Democracy	43	21	21	16	19	23	35
Adequate Quality of Performance	64	44	40	32	37	23	41
Corruption a Major Problem	49	76	82	85	82	84	87

Support for Fatah vs. Islamists (in Percent)								
	1993	1996	2000	2001	2002	2003	2004	2005
Fatah	41	55	37	28	28	26	28	39*
Islamists	23	13	17	26	25	30	32	34*

*After Arafat's death.

Source: Adapted from Khalil Shikaki, "Willing to Compromise, Palestinian Public Opinion and the Peace Process," Washington, USIP, Report 158, January 2006.

and Fatah vs. Hamas, which do much to explain the results of the 2005 and 2006 elections.[87]

Hamas has enjoyed considerable foreign support, particularly from Iran and Syria. The ties between Hamas and Iran developed gradually. Initially, the Sunni Hamas ignored or rejected the Iranian revolution as Shi'ite—although a few leaders of Al-Majama' quoted leading Iranian revolutionaries—and focused almost exclusively on Sunni groups and issues. It also took a relatively ambiguous position on the 1991 Gulf War because of its dependence on rich Gulf donors, its rivalry with the PLO, and lack of support from the secular regime of Saddam Hussein.

Iran actively courted Hamas after the 1991 Gulf War, and meetings took place between a Hamas delegation and Iran's foreign minister in October 1992. While it is unclear just how much Iranian support Hamas obtained, Hamas did set up a small office in Iran, and its leaders visited there regularly. The leaders of Hamas also met regularly with the leaders of Hezbollah in Lebanon and Syria. It is also believed that Hamas kept contact with Iran through its Damascus office.

Iran seems to have provided Hamas with up to several million dollars a year from 1993 onward, and some Israeli estimates reach as high as $20 to $30 million. In early 1999, Palestinian police reported that Hamas might have already received $35 million to carry out sabotage operations against Israelis in the Gaza Strip.[88] However, it is doubtful that Iran was able to provide such large amounts of arms and military training and that the assistance and support it provided had costs this high. It is also doubtful that extensive cooperation between Hamas and Hezbollah existed in training or operations, although there certainly has been some coordination.[89]

Cooperation between Hamas and Hezbollah increased as the Israeli-Palestinian War continued. Iran has played a pivotal role in trying to unite Islamic forces in the struggle against the Jewish state. In late April 2001, "The International Conference on the Palestinian Intifada" was convened in Tehran and was attended by

Sheikh Hassan Nasrallah of Hezbollah, Khalid Meshal of Hamas, and the PIJ's Ramadan Shalah. At the conference, Meshal stressed the linkage of the brotherhood between the Palestinian and Lebanese resistance movements.

One of the first trips Hamas took, following its victory in the January 2006 election, was to Tehran. Khalid Meshal traveled to Iran on February 20. Meshal met with Ali Khameni, who emphasized Iran's support to the Palestinians, and attributed Hamas's win in the election to its resistance against the "Zionist regime." Iranian President Mahmoud Ahmadinejad also praised Hamas's resistance as the reason for its victory in the election and called on Hamas not to "give in" to Western financial and economic pressures.[90]

Hamas has also enjoyed considerable support from Syria, which included allowing Hamas to train and operate in Lebanon and providing it with logistical support and safe havens.[91] The present status of Hamas's relationship with Syria has become less clear, partly because of the Syrian reaction to pressure from the United States. On May 3, 2003, Syrian President Bashar al-Asad ordered the closures of the offices of Hamas, the PIJ, and other Palestinian militant groups in Syria. The move was in response to pressure from the U.S. State Department, which threatened economic or diplomatic penalties against Syria if the Asad government did not act.[92] However, it is not apparent that the closures ended Syria's role in Hamas activity. A Western diplomat, speaking on the condition of anonymity, told the *New York Times* on July 14 that, "While there has certainly been a diminution of activity, there is still evidence that operational activity is continuing of a terrorist nature...As long as some of these leaders have a cell phone and a laptop, they will be able to operate."[93]

As for the future, it is simply too soon to know whether Hamas will moderate to the point where any cease-fires or participation in a peace process can be more than a tactic. The charter of Hamas effectively rejects Israel's right to exist, and Senior Hamas leaders rejected any compromise before and after the January 2006 elections. However, some Hamas leaders have repeatedly said they are willing to offer a long-term truce to Israel, and other Hamas voices were at least somewhat more ambiguous following Hamas's electoral victory.

An analysis by Louisa Brooke of the British Broadcasting Corporation (BBC) notes the following:[94]

Abdul Aziz al Rantissi told the Israeli newspaper Haaretz (18.6.03) "No one can guarantee that Hamas will be able to bring about the land's liberation within 100 or 200 years. Without dramatic changes in the region, it will be impossible. We can't tell our people to continue in an unequal struggle. But we also can't tell them to give in." This led him (Rantissi) to a view that has hitherto been associated with those defined as the movement's "moderates": If Israel would withdraw from all the land it captured in 1967, dismantle all the settlements and enable an independent Palestinian state, "there will be an end to the struggle, in the form of a long-term truce."

This echoes comments Rantissi made to the BBC in 2002, when he said "the main aim of the intifada (uprising) is the liberation of the West Bank, Gaza and Jerusalem, and nothing more. We haven't the force to liberate all our land. It is forbidden in our religion to give up a part of our land, so we can't recognise Israel at all. But we can accept a truce with them, and we can live side by side and refer all the issues to the coming generations."

Mahmoud al-Zahar, the top Hamas official in Gaza, told CNN's "Late Edition with Wolf Blitzer" that a "long-term hudna or long-term truce" is possible. He would not commit to negotiating with Israel and would not say whether recognizing Israel's existence is a long-term possibility.[95]

Al-Zahar said if Israel "is ready to give us the national demand to withdraw from the occupied area [in] '67; to release our detainees; to stop their aggression; to make geographic link between Gaza Strip and West Bank, at that time, with assurance from other sides, we are going to accept to establish our independent state at that time, and give us one or two, 10, 15 years time in order to see what is the real intention of Israel after that ....We can accept to establish our independent state on the area occupied [in] '67."

Zahar did not say how long an independent state in the West Bank and Gaza would be acceptable. Key conditions could allow Palestinians to give a "long-term hudna or long-term truce," and "after that, let time heal," he said. But asked about Hamas' call for Israel's destruction, Zahar would not say whether that remains the goal. "We are not speaking about the future, we are speaking now," he said.

Zahar argued that Israel has no true intention of accepting a Palestinian state, despite international agreements including the Road Map for Middle East peace. Until Israel says what its final borders will be, Hamas will not say whether it will ever recognize Israel, Zahar said. "If Israel is ready to tell the people what is the official border, after that we are going to answer this question."

"Negotiation is not our aim. Negotiation is a method," Zahar said. Asked whether Hamas would renounce terrorism, Zahar argued the definition of terrorism is unfair. Israel is "killing people and children and removing our agricultural system—this is terrorism," he said. "When the Americans [are] attacking the Arabic and Islamic world whether in Afghanistan and Iraq and they are playing a dirty game in Lebanon, this is terrorism." He described Hamas as a "liberating movement."

Asked whether a Hamas-led government would cancel the security and civilian liaison offices and security coordination with the Israelis, Ismail Haniyah said: "Sir, there were agreements in history that were called the Sykes-Picot agreements. They divided the Arab and Islamic world into countries. However, we deal with these agreements as a status quo, but we do not approve of them. We do not approve of dividing the Arab and Islamic world. The same applies to the situation on the ground in the Palestinian territory, where an occupation is imposed. There is a reality imposed on the Palestinian people. We deal with this reality, but we do not recognize it. We deal with this reality, but we do not recognize its legitimacy. Rather, we employ the resistance, steadfastness and unity to expel the occupation, so that the Palestinian people would live freely and honourably."[96]

It is unclear whether Israel and its supporters can pressure Hamas to changes its ideology and political goals or find ways to undercut popular support for the Hamas government. The United States and the European Union decided to cut off financial support to the Palestinian Authority following the election of Hamas. Israel froze the transfer of all Palestinian Authority money—money that Israel collects in the form of taxes, tariffs, and savings that was agreed to during the Oslo Accord. Israel also halted payments of some $50 million a month.

The result has been to create major economic and fiscal problems for the PA, but it is unclear this has done anything to weaken Hamas. The PA has not been able to pay its workers their salary. Most of its funds have been frozen by Israel and the United States or mismanaged and wasted. The Palestinian territories also suffer from high-unemployment rates. Palestinians depend on trade with Israel and the ability to work in Israel proper (the UN estimates that 100,000 Palestinians of the 125,000 who used to work in Israel lost their jobs in 2001)[97] and travel between the Gaza Strip and the West Bank. The Israeli-Palestinian War added more hurdles and increased the unemployment rates.

Hamas's longer-term ability to manage these difficulties depends on outside support. Whether Israel and the United States relax their restrictions of financial support to the PA largely depends on Hamas's recognition of Israel's right to exist. The future of Hamas's position and the dynamics between its political and military activities remain uncertain. The Arab League support to the PA is unlikely to change.

Despite Israeli and U.S. objections, many countries have pledged to help the PA. The European commission agreed to pay $144 million to the PA, and the Arab League pledged to continue its support.[98] In addition, Saudi Arabia and other Gulf States will likely continue their support. Between 2002 and 2005, on average, Saudi aid to the Palestinian Authority was estimated to be about $500 to $550 million per year. Russia has also signaled that it would support Hamas. Following the victory of Hamas in the election, Russia announced that it planned to maintain its contacts with Hamas and expressed interest in continuing its support to the PA.

Special Middle East envoy James D. Wolfensohn has warned that cutting off aid and funds may backfire. In a letter to the United States, the UN, and the European Union on February 25, 2006, he argued that the PA might collapse in weeks unless the flow of financial and economic aid into the Palestinian areas resumed. Mr. Wolfensohn argued that the PA needed $60–$80 million by the first week of March 2006 to pay the salaries of 165,000 civil servants—*half of which are security forces*. He also argued that Israel should release Palestinian money and that it was holding an estimated $55 million from taxes and tariffs.[99] Wolfensohn warned the Quartet that the PA could face an estimated $260 million budget deficit if Israel did not release the money and if the United States demands its financial aid be returned.[100]

Senior IDF officers and security officials have since echoed Wolfensohn's warning and have added to warning that isolating the Gaza Strip in economic terms and limiting activity at the few remaining crossings into Israel and Egypt may also make things worse.[101] These concerns over the consequences of a PA collapse stem from the fact that most of the money that is needed goes to salaries of civil servants, of which half are security forces. A failure to pay may drive large parts of the PA forces to join militant groups and cripple any effort to make the PA internal security forces effective. In addition, the collapse could lead to civil strife and further divisions between Palestinian factions and eliminate the prospects for peace in the short-run.

Another key uncertainty is the longer-term Israel policy of targeted killing. As noted earlier, this policy has been under scrutiny by human rights groups, the

United States, and the United Nations due to its collateral damage. The election of Hamas adds another dimension: Israel would be targeting a member of the Palestinian government. This policy could further legitimize Hamas's stance in the eyes of the Palestinians and could enhance international pressure on Israel to abandon this policy.

Hamas may, however, face problems of its own. In addition to balancing it charter with the political realities of the peace process, it must balance its own factions. While there had not been evidence that internal fighting was taking place, Hamas faces several decisions that could change the nature of its organization. The President of the PA does have control over the security forces, but whether these forces can be aggressive at curbing Hamas's actions remain largely a political issue as much as it is an internal security problem. Abbas may not have the political clout to direct the security forces against Hamas's security apparatus. It is also unclear if the PA security forces—due to Israel's attacks and PA mismanagement—*can* stand up to Hamas and stop attacks.

In the past, Hamas has been more effective and disciplined at achieving security in the areas it controlled than the PA internal security forces have been. Hamas has also taken steps to create its own "official forces." On April 26, 2006, the new Hamas Minister of the Interior, Said Siyam, renamed his ministry the Ministry of the Interior and Internal Security and declared it was creating its own 3,000-man security branch. He put the new security branch under the command of Jamal Abu Samhadana, a long-stranding tribal enemy of Abbas and head of Hamas's Popular Resistance Committee—an organization that had conducted terrorist attacks on Palestinian, Israeli, and U.S. targets. Hamas declared that these new forces would exist in parallel with the PA forces and "support" them, but only report to the Minister of the Interior and Internal Security. These actions effectively bypassed Abbas's postelection efforts to consolidate control of Palestinian security forces—including firemen and police—under Rashid Abu Shabak, the former head of preventive security in the Gaza Strip.[102]

Hamas acted after a period of increasing political tension with Abbas and a significant number of clashes between Hamas and PA forces and elements of Fatah in both the Gaza Strip and the West Bank.[103] Hamas may also have made at least two assassination attempts on senior PA security officials and a bombing on May 19, 2006, in the General Intelligence Service (GIS) headquarters in the Gaza Strip that wounded Major General Tareq Abu Rajab—a senior figure in the GIS. Certainly, Abbas saw Hamas as enough of a threat to make major increases in his personal guard from 3,500 to 5,000 and give it new vehicles and weapons. He may also quietly have turned to Israel for support and more weapons.[104]

These developments raise growing questions about whether Hamas and Fatah will come to an open struggle for power using their respective forces. If not, there seems to be a growing possibility that Hamas will transform its "irregular" forces into some more formal militia or official paramilitary force, perhaps absorbing some of the more hard-line PA forces in the process.

Islamic Jihad

Palestinian Islamic Jihad has also employed unconventional tactics in the war against Israel. The PIJ, however, is more secretive than Hamas and does not play the high-profile charitable and social role in Palestinian society that Hamas does. It does not operate schools, hospitals, or health clinics, although it does give money to the families of militants killed in action.[105]

Hamas and Palestinian Islamic Jihad do share several similarities. Attacks by the PIJ, however, have been less intense. According to the Memorial Institute for the Prevention of Terrorism (MIPT) Terrorism Knowledge Database, between 1968 and February 2006, 130 incidents were linked to PIJ (compared to 545 with Hamas), which caused 997 injuries and 193 deaths.[106]

Islamic Jihad's objective, however, is the same as that of Hamas: to drive the State of Israel from historical Palestine. Both movements ultimately hope to construct an Islamic theocracy in Palestine, and both are committed to violence in order to achieve their objectives. Like Hamas, the Islamic Jihad's struggle is directed against both non-Muslims and Arab regimes that have "deviated" from Islam and which have attacked or suppressed the Muslim Brotherhood.[107] Throughout the Israeli-Palestinian War, the Islamic Jihad and Hamas have been allies and, on some occasions, collaborators in their conflicts with both Israel and the PA.

Islamic Jihad began as a radical, ideological offshoot of the Muslim Brotherhood, the original Sunni pan-Arab Islamist movement, and was formed in reaction to the Brotherhood's growing rejection of militancy. Unlike Hamas, however, Islamic Jihad is not simply a Palestinian group. Elements of the Islamic Jihad have appeared in almost all the Arab states and in some parts of the non-Arab Islamic world under various names. These groups have been influenced by the success of the revolution in Iran and by the growth of Islamic militancy in Lebanon and Egypt. According to Israeli sources, the Palestinian factions of the Islamic Jihad are part of the Islamic Jihad movements that appeared in the Sunni Arab world in the 1970s. These movements are characterized by a rejection of the Brotherhood's "truce" with most of the existing regimes in the Arab world. They perceive violence as a legitimate tool in changing the face of Arab societies and regimes.

The Palestinian factions of the Islamic Jihad (known collectively as the PIJ) do see the "Zionist Jewish entity" embodied in the State of Israel as their foremost enemy and primary target. They see "Palestine" as an integral and a fundamental part of the Arab and Muslim world where Muslims are "subjected" to foreign rule. The fact that Israel is perceived as foreign and non-Muslim allows the Islamic Jihad to use different methods of resistance than those adopted by similar groups operating against Muslim and Arab regimes. The PIJ calls for armed struggle against Israel through guerrilla groups composed of the revolutionary vanguard. These groups carry out terrorist attacks aimed at weakening Israel and "its desire to continue its occupation." These attacks lay the groundwork for the moment when an Islamic army will be able to destroy Israel in a military confrontation.

The PIJ movement has always been divided into factions. The element that has become dominant since the signing of the Declaration of Principles between Israel and the PLO was originally named "Shekaki/Ouda," after its co-founders Dr. Fathi Shekaki and Abed el-Aziz Ouda. Ouda also served as the organization's spiritual leader. Shekaki and Ouda were both from the Gaza Strip, and they founded their faction based on their exposure to similar political groups in Egyptian universities. They coordinated various groups in the Gaza Strip when they returned from their studies and may have had some responsibility for a grenade attack on an Israeli army induction ceremony at the Western Wall in October 1986 that killed one person and wounded 69.

Both Shekaki and Ouda were deported from the Gaza Strip to Lebanon in 1988. They then reorganized their faction to establish a military unit to carry out attacks against Israeli targets, alongside the existing political unit. This unit seems to have played a role in an assault on an Israeli tourist bus in Egypt in February 1990 that killed nine Israelis and two Egyptians and wounded 19. There is also evidence that they were responsible for killing two people and wounding eight in a knifing attack in Tel Aviv in March 1993. Around the time of the signing of the Declaration of Principles between Israel and the PLO in September 1993, Shekaki used his close ideological and political ties with Iran to gradually push aside Ouda. He soon became recognized as the sole head of the group. He renamed the Syrian-based organization the Shekaki Faction and remained in Damascus serving as its undisputed leader until alleged Mossad agents assassinated him in Sliema, Malta, on October 26, 1995.[108]

The PIJ made no secret of its commitment to violence after the Oslo Peace Accords or about its ties to Iran.[109] It distributed antipeace propaganda, material, and tapes and used the mosques as centers for antipeace activity. It also established a newspaper called *Al-Istiqlal,* which appears in the area under the jurisdiction of the PA and is edited by Ala Siftawi. Shekaki often boasted of his ties with Iran—which, he said, were strengthened following his first visit to Tehran in December 1988. Unlike Hamas, his faction had close ties to Hezbollah from the start.[110] Shekaki praised the Islamic Republic and its political and spiritual support of the Palestinian people's efforts to continue the jihad and to achieve independence. In 1994, however, he claimed that the PIJ did not receive Iranian military aid and did not have a base in Iran, yet he claimed that Iranian support for his organization and Hamas amounted to $20 million a year.[111]

The PIJ intensified the tone of its anti-Israeli statements after the murder of PIJ activist Hani Abed in the Gaza Strip on February 11, 1994. Shekaki said, "The continuation of the jihad against the Zionist occupation is our primary concern and the center of our lives."

The PIJ was less successful between late 1995 and the outbreak of war in September 2000, but it scarcely abandoned violence. Similar to Hamas, the PIJ also changed the character of its operations, focusing heavily on suicide bombers. Whereas Hamas began its campaign against Israel with organized demonstrations and car bombs, and later escalated to suicide bombings, an emphasis on the use of suicide bombings characterized the PIJ's operations from the beginning of the war.

Roughly one month after the war began, on October 26, 2000, the PIJ claimed responsibility for a suicide bombing in the Kisufim settlement in the Gaza Strip that injured one Israeli soldier. The bombing marked the fifth anniversary of the death of Shekaki and was the first suicide bombing of the war. PIJ leader Ramadan Abdallah Shallah, a former professor from the University of South Florida, suggested that the bombing was "a new opening for suicide action" and would "be the beginning for more operations against Israeli soldiers."[112]

On November 2, 2000, the PIJ demonstrated what was to become its secondary tactic of the war. A car bomb exploded in a Jerusalem marketplace killing, *inter alia,* the daughter of National Religious Party leader Rabbi Yitzhak Levy and wounding ten Israelis. Between November 2, 2000, and early October 2001, the PIJ claimed responsibility for at least five additional car-bomb attacks in which two Israelis were killed and at least 110 were injured.[113] These attacks included a car bomb that exploded in Jerusalem's Talpiot area (the city's "industrial" zone where there are many nightclubs and dance bars) on March 27, 2000, a car bomb that exploded at the central bus station of Hadera on May 25, one that exploded outside of a Netanya school on May 30, and one that exploded in a residential area of Jerusalem on October 1, but caused no serious injuries.

In addition to suicide attacks and car bombs, the PIJ carried out other forms of attack. On May 27, a bomb exploded in central Jerusalem, containing several mortar shells, some of which were propelled hundreds of meters from the site of the explosion. The Israeli police conducted extensive searches for the shells and found six mortars intact in a 300-meter radius. The Israeli police expressed grave concern, emphasizing the likelihood that such an attack could only have been possible had mortars been smuggled into the West Bank and the Gaza Strip from areas outside of Israel.[114]

The PIJ reportedly has had little difficulty finding recruits for suicide bombings.[115] By 2003, a number of recruits had allegedly defected from Hamas and the Al-Aqsa Martyrs Brigade. On January 6, 2003, Knight Ridder reported that the new recruits could number from several dozens to several hundreds. According to Israeli officials, the increase in membership began after the Megiddo Junction attack on June 5, 2002, and resulted from the fact that the PIJ will not make long-term peace with Israel, but is less strict than Hamas. Another attraction was that the PIJ reportedly paid $5,000 (U.S.) to the surviving family members of suicide bombers, which on average was $2,000 more than Hamas typically paid during 2002.[116]

Despite Islamic religious constraints, PIJ suicide bombers have come to involve women. On May 19, 2003, a 19-year-old woman, Hiba Daraghmeh, detonated a bomb at a shopping mall in the northern Israeli town of Afula. Three people died and dozens more were wounded. This was the PIJ's first use of a female suicide bomber, which was particularly surprising due to the group's radical beliefs. After the attack, the PIJ distributed newsletters to universities throughout the West Bank and the Gaza Strip, praising its female fighters.[117] One PIJ trainer reportedly said, "Our women are no longer the type of women who cry or weep. We have

martyrdom women now."[118] The PIJ adopted the tactic because of its element of surprise, and its use marked a clear distinction from Hamas, which has long opposed the
use of female suicide bombers.

The success of the PIJ's suicide attacks is another example of the impact of asymmetric warfare on the conventional balance of military forces. A quarter of a century
of military and paramilitary training and terrorist training camps have had a limited
impact on Israel. Untrained youths, however, had a major impact during the first
Intifada. Since that time, the PIJ and Hamas have found that using Islamic organizations to locate idealistic "true believers," giving them a short indoctrination for preparation, and then sending them out on suicide missions gives the Palestinian Authority and Israel far less warning than using trained personnel and produces far more
casualties and has a greater political impact. Like Hamas, its loose, decentralized,
and compartmentalized organization lacks the transparency of the hierarchical structures of military and paramilitary groups and thus makes it more difficult for Israeli
antiterror units and the Palestinian security services to detect and penetrate those
cells.[119]

The PIJ has had a largely adversarial relationship with the PA. As mentioned previously, in the first few months of the war, Yasser Arafat attempted to placate the militant factions and encourage anti-Israeli demonstrations by releasing Hamas and PIJ
militants from PA jails.[120] In October 2000, PIJ activists were granted representation
in the PA High Committee Follow-Up Intifada Nationalist Islamic Organizations,
which planned rallies in the West Bank and the Gaza Strip.[121]

The Tel Aviv discotheque bombing on June 1, 2001, marked the first time that the
PIJ not only had a dramatic impact on the war, but also on the PA. As a result of the
deaths, injuries, and sheer terror of the incident, Arafat announced that he would
attempt to enforce a cease-fire among the militant factions. While he had previously
ignored Sharon's calls for a truce, the PA now began to arrest PIJ and Hamas supporters. On June 23, PA security forces arrested Sheikh Abdullah Shami, the PIJ's
spiritual leader. PIJ supporters formed a human wall around Shami's house, delaying
the arrest.[122]

On November 4, 2001, the PA arrested PIJ militant Mahmoud Tawalbi in Jenin.
The arrest set off protests by 3,000 Palestinians, who fired guns, threw grenades, and
burned cars. The PA was forced to fight against its own people, who were encouraged
by Hamas.[123] Throughout November and December 2001, the PA arrested Hamas
and PIJ militants, and the two sides clashed on several occasions.

The PIJ's relationship with Arafat's government worsened in 2002. This was
caused in part by Israeli retaliation against the PA for PIJ actions. For example, on
June 5, following the Megiddo Junction suicide bombing, Israeli troops stormed
Arafat's Ramallah compound and destroyed PA buildings.[124] Four days later, PA
security personnel again arrested al Shami, allegedly for criticizing Arafat in Palestinian newspapers.[125]

The PIJ has expressed the desire to replace the Arafat regime. On January 24–28,
2003, PIJ representatives met with delegates from 11 other Palestinian factions in
Cairo to discuss intergroup cooperation and a possible cease-fire. They were unable

to agree on the cease-fire but did agree to form a coalition, which could ultimately take over the Palestinian Authority.[126]

On March 11, 2003, the PIJ dismissed the notion of a Palestinian Authority prime minister, saying it could never accept a post created under pressure from the United States and Israel.[127] Following the introduction of the U.S.–drafted road map for peace on April 29, the PIJ also rejected cease-fire efforts. However, surprisingly, on June 19, PIJ and Hamas leaders met with Abbas to discuss a halt in the violence.

On June 25, senior PIJ militant Mohammed al-Hindi reported that Hamas had asked the PIJ to issue "a joint declaration which is based on a comprehensive three-month cease-fire."[128] On June 29, both Hamas and the PIJ agreed to the temporary cease-fire, though both parties refused to surrender their weapons to the Abbas government on July 13.

Publicly, the PIJ stated that it agreed to the cease-fire because of Hamas's requests.[129] However, at least three other factors seem to have influenced the group. First, a number of countries had become actively hostile to militant extremism and terrorist activity in the preceding months. This was reflected in both the U.S.–led Coalition's removal of the Saddam Hussein regime from power in Iraq and increasing U.S. pressure on countries known to support terrorism, such as Syria. Second, antimilitant protests broke out in the Palestinian village of Beit Hanoun in the Gaza Strip in May, following repeated Israeli incursions. The villagers blamed Hamas and the PIJ for the Israeli operation. This indicated a possible decline in the PIJ's public support. Finally, both the PIJ and Hamas likely required a three-month period to recuperate from recent Israeli retaliation.

The PIJ initially adhered to the cease-fire agreement despite the Israeli assassination of the PIJ militant Muhammed Sider in Hebron on August 14. However, the PIJ followed Hamas's lead and withdrew from the truce on August 22, following the Israeli targeted killing of the Hamas senior activist Abu Shanab a day earlier.

The PIJ has benefited from continued foreign support. Iran is often perceived as its key foreign sponsor. Indeed, on April 24, 2001, representatives from Hamas, Hezbollah, and the PIJ met in Tehran in a gesture of solidarity. According to the Associated Press, they issued a joint message to Israel: Expect combat, not dialogue.[130] On July 18, 2002, the American Jewish Committee released a new report, stating that the PIJ was responsible for "Islamicizing" Palestinians and establishing a deadly relationship between Palestinians and Iran.[131]

Syria has also been a major supporter. When the PIJ joined in the protests of a Jordanian crackdown against Hamas in September 1999, it did so out of its office in Damascus and in cooperation with the Popular Front for the Liberation of Palestine (PFLP), the Popular Front for the Liberation of Palestine-General Command (PFLP-GC), and Fatah Intifada.[132]

On May 3, 2003, Syrian President Bashar Asad ordered the closures of Hamas, PIJ, PFLP-General Command, and other militant factions' offices in Damascus. However, Western diplomats believe that the groups are still using Syria as a base for planning future terrorist activity.

The PIJ has a small membership base and support network compared to Hamas, but has nonetheless succeeded in executing many suicide attacks against Israelis, even inside Israel. The PIJ's main areas of support are in the West Bank cities of Hebron and Jenin. It is believed that the group is trying to develop weapons capabilities similar to the Qassam rockets used in the Gaza Strip.[133]

Fatah Tanzim ("Organization")

Fatah Tanzim ("Organization") is the youthful paramilitary wing of Fatah. Unlike Hamas or the PIJ, Tanzim is largely secular. In 1995, Fatah created the Tanzim to counter the growing strength of the anti-PA factions on the streets, especially from Islamist groups that saw Fatah as corrupt. It was created in part from the remnants of Fatah militias from the Intifada known as the "Fatah Hawks."[134] Though the Tanzim supported Yasser Arafat and the PA, it has taken a "no-compromise position" on the peace process and supports a unilateral declaration of Palestinian statehood.[135] It has participated in demonstrations as well as armed violence against Israelis throughout the war.

Many of its senior leaders participated in the Intifada in 1987. Fatah leaders have largely attempted to exclude Tanzim members from Fatah's higher offices. Indeed, only Tanzim leader Marwan Barghouti also holds a high office in Fatah.[136]

Tanzim cells, which are active in most Palestinian neighborhoods, reportedly take their orders from Tanzim's commanders—not from Fatah or the Palestinian Authority. The Israeli Ministry of Foreign Affairs insists that Arafat has active links with the Tanzim leadership, though responsibility for their actions cannot be traced to him. The Israeli newspaper *Yediot Aharonot* has reported that the Tanzim is financed directly by the PA, though this has not been reported elsewhere.[137] Tanzim's strongest concentration is within the Palestinian universities, particularly in Bethlehem's Birzeit and An-Najah universities.[138]

It is unknown exactly how many Tanzim members there were at the time the war began in September 2000. A 2001 United Press International report stated that the group had "3,500 militants but no tangible military assets."[139] However, in October 2000, the Israeli Ministry of Foreign Affairs alleged that "[t]he Tanzim has tens of thousands of weapons of all kinds—from pistols to machine guns."[140] While in 2001, Gal Luft alleged in the *Middle East Quarterly* that Tanzim possessed roughly 30,000 weapons.[141] The ICT further stated that the group had stockpiled German MP-5 submachine guns, as well as assault rifles and antitank missiles.[142]

If Fatah served as the "brains" of the initial uprising in late 2000, then the Tanzim served as the "fists." The Tanzim took the leading role in organizing the first wave of hostilities against Israel in the Israeli-Palestinian War. Tanzim forces were initially led by Marwan Barghouti, who was also the leader of Fatah in the West Bank. The highly charismatic and popular Barghouti called upon ordinary Palestinians to rise up against Israel in protests and riots. Barghouti also attempted to coordinate early efforts between the various armed factions until the violence escalated beyond his control.

The Tanzim repeatedly organized days of rage, in which gun battles broke out between IDF soldiers and Tanzim militiamen. One Israeli official remarked that a pattern emerged in the Tanzim-organized street violence by October 2000: stone throwing during the day and "a full-fledged shooting war" at night.[143] Tanzim militants targeted both Israeli soldiers and settlements. Some reports suggested that Tanzim militiamen were interspersed with PA security personnel and the two organizations cooperated on attacks against Israelis.[144]

Since the beginning of the war, the Tanzim employed two main tactics in its attacks against Israel—shootings and car/roadside bombings. From September 27, 2000, to January 1, 2004, the ICT counted 54 separate shooting incidents in which Tanzim militants attempted to injure or kill Israeli soldiers or settlers.[145] The group has also conducted bombings of Israeli cars and buses, though much less frequently. Unlike other militant groups, most of the Tanzim's attacks have generally occurred within the borders of the West Bank and the Gaza Strip. The group has also notably rejected the use of suicide bombings, which has become characteristic of movements such as the Al-Aqsa Martyrs' Brigades, Hamas, and the Palestinian Islamic Jihad.

The Tanzim has become more violent during the course of the conflict. On April 15, 2002, Israeli forces arrested Tanzim leader Barghouti in Ramallah. In August, nearly four months later, he was formally charged with multiple counts of murder against Israeli civilians. The indictment accused him of heading Tanzim operations, as well as those of the West Bank Al-Aqsa Martyrs' Brigades. Nevertheless, even in jail, Barghouti continued to play a significant role in the Israeli-Palestinian War by helping to negotiate the cease-fire between the various Palestinian militant factions, including the Tanzim, in June 2003. However, in May 2004 Barghouti was convicted in an Israeli court for the murder of five Israeli civilians and being involved in four terrorist attacks. On June 6, 2004, the court sentenced Barghouti to five consecutive life sentences plus 40 additional years in prison (20 for attempted murder and 20 for membership in a terrorist organization).[146]

Tanzim has a membership that is made up of mostly adult Palestinian males between the ages of 25–30 within the Palestinian autonomous areas, "graduates of the Intifada," most of who are either university students or recent graduates. Its membership is supposedly in the tens of thousands with some of the Tanzim's leadership serving in the Palestinian security services as field commanders under Jibril Rajoub.[147]

Al-Aqsa Martyrs' Brigades

The Al-Aqsa Martyrs' Brigades first appeared in September 2000, shortly after the Palestinian uprising began. It has since become one of the most active and violent militias in the Israeli-Palestinian War. The group is closely aligned with Fatah. Similar to Fatah, it is both secular and nationalist. Al-Aqsa activist Maslama Thabet attempted to define the relationship: "The truth is, we are Fatah itself, but we don't operate under the name Fatah. We are the armed wing of the organization. We receive our instructions from Fatah. Our commander is Yasser Arafat himself."[148]

Like the Tanzim, the Al-Aqsa Martyrs' Brigades rejects concessions to Israel. It supports an unconditional Israeli withdrawal from the Occupied Territories, as well as a right of return for Palestinians to their former homes in Israel. The Brigades believes that the use of violence, including terrorist activity, is a legitimate tactic for achieving its objectives. As an armed militia independent of the PA, the group serves largely the same role as the Tanzim, allowing Arafat and his allies to strike adversaries without being directly implicated. Based on this mandate, the Brigades has carried out attacks against Palestinians as well as Israelis, with the targets ranging from those who opposed Arafat's rule, such as moderate journalists and politicians, to those suspected of collaborating with Israeli authorities.

Little is known about the Brigades' leadership and organizational structure. The group is composed of a network of cells in the main cities of the West Bank and the Gaza Strip. These cells include military units, which are responsible for carrying out anti-Israeli terrorist attacks, and security units, which are in charge of both planning these attacks and safeguarding the group's internal security. The Brigades' main strongholds are in the West Bank cities of Nablus and Ramallah and the refugee camps in the surrounding areas.[149] Its total strength in manpower and material is unknown. Israeli officials believe that Fatah and Tanzim member Marwan Barghouti originally provided leadership, before his arrest and later conviction. They also believe that the group's current executive high commander, Taufik Tirawi, has taken refuge in Arafat's Ramallah compound.

More is known about the Brigades' finances. The Israeli government has provided evidence that the PA provides financial support for the Brigades, paying members' salaries and providing weapons. On April 2, 2002, Israel released an invoice that was seized in Arafat's office during Israel's Operation Defensive Shield. The Al-Aqsa Martyrs had sent the invoice to General Fouad Shoubaki, the PA's chief financial officer for military operations. The invoice requested reimbursement for electrical and chemical components of explosives. It also asked for additional funds to construct bombs and to finance propaganda posters.[150]

In early June 2004 the Al-Aqsa Martyrs' Brigades began threatening to break away from Fatah over accusations that Yasser Arafat and other top Fatah leaders had halted financial aid to the militia's members. This led a senior Fatah official in Ramallah to inadvertently confirm that Brigades members had been receiving monthly salaries from the Palestinian Authority. The *Jerusalem Post* quoted the official as saying, "We [(the PA) no longer]...have enough money to pay them. Besides, we are under heavy pressure from the international community to cut off our links with the group."[151] On June 12, in response to the Brigades' potential mutiny, Arafat invited its members to be incorporated into various branches of the PA security forces. The group, however, rejected Arafat's offer. According to Nayef Abu Sharkh, one of the Brigades' West Bank leaders, they "feel disgusted and disgraced at belonging to a movement that is led by corrupt officials. We feel this way because we have been abandoned and neglected by the Fatah leadership."[152]

Then on June 15, the Fatah Central Council decided to form a special committee of senior Fatah officials and cabinet officials to study the Al-Aqsa Martyrs' Brigades' demands for renewed financing and, in doing so, for the first time formally acknowl-edged the Palestinian Authority's responsibility for the militia.[153] In early July 2004, the Brigades presented senior Palestinian officials with a ten-page formal proposal "outlining its demands and recommendations for participation in the govern-ment."[154] Specifically, the document called for "the expulsion and prosecution of government officials involved in corruption, a wholesale purge of relatives and cro-nies of senior officials from government payrolls and a halt to the practice of govern-ment officials monopolizing sectors of the Palestinian economy to 'line their private pockets.'"[155]

Although the Al-Aqsa Martyrs' Brigades' manifesto was widely circulated among senior Palestinian officials, the Palestinian Authority did not provide the group with an official response. Evidence indicates that Arafat chose to ignore the group's con-cerns and refuse its demands. On July 16, 2004, militants from the Popular Resist-ance Committees—including gunmen affiliated with the Al-Aqsa Martyrs' Brigades —temporarily kidnapped the Palestinian Authority's senior security chief in the Gaza Strip, Ghazi Jabali, in the attempt to draw attention to their allegations that he had stolen $22 million in public funds. In response, Arafat fired Jabali and appointed his cousin, Moussa Arafat, to take his place. The Al-Aqsa Martyrs' Brigades perceived the move as a clear indication that Arafat remained reluctant to "surrender some of his powers and reform a government system riddled with corruption."[156] Frustrated by Arafat's failures to address their concerns, Al-Aqsa gunmen in Rafah began shoot-ing at uniformed Palestinian security forces soon after the announcement regarding Moussa Arafat's appointment.

Through early August 2004, Brigades members continued to play a prominent role in the uprising against Palestinian Authority corruption in the Gaza Strip. In addition to leading anticorruption demonstrations and making numerous public statements calling for governmental reform, members' actions included exchanging gunfire with PA security personnel, conducting raids on PA security force offices, and preventing PA representatives from speaking at public engagements.

It is difficult to predict how the relationship between Fatah and the Brigades will evolve following Arafat's death. Nevertheless, it is likely that any lasting split will neg-atively affect the peace process since the PA would lose control over the Brigades' ter-rorist activities and as Abu Sharkh has stated, the Brigades "will not abide by any [cease-fire] agreement if they do not negotiate with us face to face."[157]

The Brigades' combat tactics were similar to the Tanzim's throughout 2001. The group participated in shootings against Israeli soldiers and settlers, primarily within the West Bank and the Gaza Strip. However, in January 2002, the Brigades began what became a long series of suicide bombings. On January 27, the Martyrs' employed the first female suicide bomber in the war. The young woman blew herself up on a busy shopping street, Jaffa Road, in Jerusalem.

The Brigades grew increasingly more effective and violent in 2002. On August 17, the *Washington Post* reported that in the course of the previous year the Brigades had established the largest number of militant cells among the known extremist groups in the West Bank and had accepted responsibility for more than twice as many suicide bombings as Hamas. The Palestinian psychiatrist and civil rights activist Eyad Sarraj said, "[Al-Aqsa was] thrown into the competition of suicide bombing in Israel because they want the support of the public and they felt the public support swinging towards Hamas, so they had to do the same thing."[158]

This did not prevent some of the Brigades' leaders from playing a role in trying to establish a cease-fire. On June 9, 2003, Mahmoud Abbas (with the help of Marwan Barghouti) concluded a cease-fire arrangement between Hamas, the PIJ, and the militias aligned with Fatah, including the Martyrs' Brigades. The Brigades initially condemned the cease-fire, though it eventually agreed to a six-month truce (which was ultimately cut short as described earlier).[159]

It became apparent in the weeks following the Brigades' signing of the cease-fire, however, that the militia was loosely organized and lacked the authoritative, centralized leadership necessary to ensure its members adhered to the cease-fire. For instance, the leader of the Brigades' faction in Nablus stated that his specific group had not agreed to the cease-fire and was still planning attacks against Israelis. The Brigades' branches in Jenin and Qalqilyah also publicly announced opposition to the truce.[160] Hence, attacks by Brigades members continued throughout the cease-fire. In fact, Brigades operatives in Nablus murdered a Bulgarian worker that they believed was Israeli less than 24 hours after the cease-fire was signed.[161]

After the cease-fire was terminated in late August, the Al-Aqsa Martyrs' Brigades remained one of the most active Palestinian militant groups. According to the International Policy Institute for Counter-Terrorism's Casualties Database, the Brigades was responsible for at least nine more terrorist attacks against Israeli military personnel and civilian settlers throughout the rest of 2003. These included three suicide bombings and six shootings that killed a total of nine Israelis and seriously injured another seven.[162]

In 2004, the Al-Aqsa Martyrs' Brigades continued to be one of the most active Palestinian factions conducting terrorist attacks against Israeli targets. From January–May 2004, the Brigades claimed sole responsibility for two suicide bombings and nine shootings that in total killed 18 people and wounded 83.[163] In addition, some of the most prominent Brigades' operations in early 2004 were carried out in collaboration with other Palestinian militant groups not aligned with the Palestinian Authority. These four joint attacks—three suicide bombings, a suicide car bomb and small arms assault on the Erez crossing and a roadside shooting ambush—killed 33 people and wounded an additional 85 people.

As of early January 2005, the Al-Aqsa Martyrs' Brigades had not unilaterally conducted a suicide bombing since April 17 and only three smaller-scale strikes, shootings on July 6 and on August 13 and a bus stop bombing on July 11, since April 25. The Israeli government claims the reduction in Brigades attacks against Israeli targets is due to increased border security brought on by the construction of the security barrier system and Israeli counterterrorism efforts, mainly their targeted assassination policy. For example, between late February and late June 2004, the IDF killed most of the Al-Aqsa Martyrs' Brigades' leaders in Nablus.

On February 29, IDF soldiers fatally shot wanted Brigades member Muhammad Oweiss in a "capture or kill" raid on the Balata refugee camp in Nablus. Later that day, at Oweiss's funeral the IDF assassinated another wanted Nablus Brigades member, Rihad Abu Shallah. In another capture or kill operation on May 2, the IDF killed the group's senior military commanders in Nablus, Nadir Abu-Layl and Hashim Abu Hamdan, along with two other Brigades members.[164] On June 14, Khalil Marshud, the head of the Al-Aqsa Martyrs' Brigades in Nablus, was killed in a targeted IAF helicopter gunship strike.[165] And on June 6, during a capture or kill raid on the Old City of Nablus, IDF soldiers killed Naef Abu Sharh, the military leader of the Al-Aqsa Martyrs' Brigades in the city.[166]

Although Israeli efforts have had a significant impact on Brigades activities, Brigades' members such as Hani Uwaidah, the Al-Aqsa Commander in Tulkarm, have offered a different explanation. In mid-June he told the *Jerusalem Post* that the fact that "the PA stopped paying his salary a few months ago....was the main reason why he and his friends had halted their attacks against Israel."[167] Since mid-June 2004 Members of the Al-Aqsa Martyrs' Brigades have also played a leading role in acting out against corruption in the Palestinian Authority.

Thus, whether or not the downward trend in the Brigades' operational capabilities can primarily be attributed to Israeli counterterrorism activities or internal Fatah-Brigades tensions—and whether it will continue to decline—remains to be determined.

It is equally important, however, to note that Fatah as an organization has been weakened since the death of Yasser Arafat. Tanzim and the Al-Aqsa Martyrs' Brigades legitimacy and support were largely due to their association with the PLO and Fatah. The election of Hamas in Palestine, the perceived corruption and incompetence of Fatah leaders, and the overall radicalization of the Palestinian population may drive the support of these two organizations even further. Their influence on Palestinian internal security and their impact on the overall intensity in the Palestinian-Israeli conflict remain highly uncertain.

These dynamics may also drive more secular nationalist resistance groups such as Tanzim or even Fatah itself to drift toward religious extremism. The vacuum created by the violence and Israeli actions contributed, at least in part, to Hamas's success and to Abas's failure to unite Palestinian factions. These developments can also fragment Fatah even further across ideological lines, increase Palestinian-on-Palestinian violence, and strengthen the hands of more independent groups such as Hamas and the PIJ.

Smaller Militant Groups

The United States provides the following declassified intelligence data on the size and activities of the smaller Palestinian militant groups in its annual country reports on terrorism:[168]

Abu Nidal Organization (ANO) a.k.a. Fatah Revolutionary Council, Arab Revolutionary Brigades, Black September, Revolutionary Organization of Socialist Muslims

The ANO international terrorist organization was founded by Sabri al-Banna (a.k.a. Abu Nidal) after splitting from the PLO in 1974. The group's previous known structure consisted of various functional committees, including political, military, and financial. In November 2002 Abu Nidal died in Baghdad; the new leadership of the organization remains unclear.

...The ANO has carried out terrorist attacks in 20 countries, killing or injuring almost 900 persons. Targets include the United States, the United Kingdom, France, Israel, moderate Palestinians, the PLO, and various Arab countries. Major attacks included the Rome and Vienna airports in 1985, the Neve Shalom synagogue in Istanbul, the hijacking of Pan Am Flight 73 in Karachi in 1986, and the City of Poros day-excursion ship attack in Greece in 1988. The ANO is suspected of assassinating PLO deputy chief Abu Iyad and PLO security chief Abu Hul in Tunis in 1991. The ANO assassinated a Jordanian diplomat in Lebanon in 1994 and has been linked to the killing of the PLO representative there. The group has not staged a major attack against Western targets since the late 1980s.

...Strength: Few hundred plus limited overseas support structure.

...Al-Banna relocated to Iraq in December 1998 where the group maintained a presence until Operation Iraqi Freedom, but its current status in country is unknown. Known members have an operational presence in Lebanon, including in several Palestinian refugee camps. Authorities shut down the ANO's operations in Libya and Egypt in 1999. The group has demonstrated the ability to operate over a wide area, including the Middle East, Asia, and Europe. However, financial problems and internal disorganization have greatly reduced the group's activities and its ability to maintain cohesive terrorist capability....The ANO received considerable support, including safe haven, training, logistical assistance, and financial aid from Iraq, Libya, and Syria (until 1987), in addition to close support for selected operations.

Palestine Liberation Front (PLF) a.k.a. PLF-Abu Abbas Faction

The Palestine Liberation Front (PLF) broke away from the PFLP-GC in the late 1970s and later split again into pro-PLO, pro-Syrian, and pro-Libyan factions. The pro-PLO faction was led by Muhammad Abbas (a.k.a. Abu Abbas) and was based in Baghdad prior to Operation Iraqi Freedom.

...Abbas' group was responsible for the attack in 1985 on the Italian cruise ship Achille Lauro and the murder of US citizen Leon Klinghoffer. Abu Abbas died of natural causes in April 2004 while in US custody in Iraq. Current leadership and membership of the relatively small PLF appears to be based in Lebanon and the Palestinian territories. The PLF has become more active since the start of the al-Aqsa Intifada and several PLF members have been arrested by Israeli authorities for planning attacks in Israel and the West Bank.

...Strength: Unknown.

...Based in Iraq since 1990, has a presence in Lebanon and the West Bank.

...Received support mainly from Iraq; has received support from Libya in the past.

Popular Front for the Liberation of Palestine (PFLP)

. . .Formerly a part of the PLO, the Marxist-Leninist PFLP was founded by George Habash when it broke away from the Arab Nationalist Movement in 1967. The PFLP does not view the Palestinian struggle as religious, seeing it instead as a broader revolution against Western imperialism. The group earned a reputation for spectacular international attacks, including airline hijackings that have killed at least 20 US citizens.

. . .The PFLP committed numerous international terrorist attacks during the 1970s. Since 1978, the group has conducted attacks against Israeli or moderate Arab targets, including killing a settler and her son in December 1996. The PFLP has stepped up its operational activity since the start of the current Intifada, highlighted by at least two suicide bombings since 2003, multiple joint operations with other Palestinian terrorist groups, and assassination of the Israeli Tourism Minster in 2001 to avenge Israel's killing of the PFLP Secretary General earlier that year.

. . .Strength: Unknown.

. . .Location/Area of Operation: Syria, Lebanon, Israel, the West Bank, and the Gaza Strip.

. . .Receives safe haven and some logistical assistance from Syria.

Popular Front for the Liberation of Palestine–General Command (PFLP-GC)

The PFLP-GC split from the PFLP in 1968, claiming it wanted to focus more on fighting and less on politics. Originally it was violently opposed to the Arafat-led PLO. The group is led by Ahmad Jabril, a former captain in the Syrian Army, whose son Jihad was killed by a car bomb in May 2002. The PFLP-GC is closely tied to both Syria and Iran.

. . .Carried out dozens of attacks in Europe and the Middle East during the 1970s and 1980s. Known for cross-border terrorist attacks into Israel using unusual means, such as hot-air balloons and motorized hang gliders. Primary focus is now on guerrilla operations in southern Lebanon and small-scale attacks in Israel, the West Bank, and the Gaza Strip.

. . .Strength: Several hundred.

. . .Headquartered in Damascus with bases in Lebanon.

. . .Receives logistical and military support from Syria and financial support from Iran.

PALESTINIAN APPROACHES TO ASYMMETRIC WARFARE

The Palestinians have had far fewer opportunities than the Israelis to use new weapons and tactics. They have been tightly contained and pushed into a defense mode. As the previous discussion of Palestinian militant groups has shown, however, they have made some shifts in both their tactics and their equipment.

Suicide Bombings

The primary Palestinian counter to Israel's conventional strength has been suicide bombings: the same tactic hard-line Palestinian militants used to undermine the peace process before the Israeli-Palestinian war began. There have, however, been some changes. Five weeks after Sharon's visit to the Temple Mount in September 2000 and the ensuing riots in the compound in Jerusalem's Old City, an additional element was introduced into the Israeli-Palestinian War in the form of car bombings and suicide bombings. On November 2, 2000, a car-bomb explosion, near Jerusalem's popular downtown Mahane Yehuda market, marked the beginning of a new wave of fatal bombings.

By early June 2001, extremist Palestinian groups carried out at least nine suicide and ten car-bombing attacks and had left several explosive devices on roadsides. Their attacks killed 51 Israelis and injured at least 630, not to mention the psychological damage of countless witnesses.[169] While Hamas and the Palestinian Islamic Jihad claimed responsibility for the majority of these attacks, the Popular Front for the Liberation of Palestine (PFLP) claimed responsibility for a car-bomb attack in the center of Jerusalem on May 27, 2001. In addition, there were several car and suicide bombings for which responsibility has never been clarified due to that fact that either no group claimed responsibility, or for which several groups claimed responsibility.[170]

The extent to which the Palestinian Authority encouraged, turned a blind eye to, or attempted to prevent suicide bombers from perpetrating attacks has been the subject of constant dispute since the start of the conflict. What has been verified, however, was that in the first days of the Israeli-Palestinian War, the PA leadership released a substantial number of prisoners known to have planned, or have been involved in, attacks including suicide bombings, against Israeli targets prior to the start of the war including suicide bombings.

According to Israeli sources, the released prisoners—dozens of Hamas and PIJ activists—included Muhammad Deif, one of the men responsible for several bombings in Israel; Adnan al-Ghul, a top bomb-making expert responsible for several suicide bombings that swept Israel in February to March 1996, killing 59 Israelis; and Mahmud Abu-Hannud, another wanted man whose whereabouts remained unknown. Israeli officials immediately charged that this mass release created an atmosphere for future bombings.[171]

There are a number of possible explanations for this release. The most widely speculated has been that the PA released the prisoners for internal reasons—in order to unify Palestinians of various political streams in light of an anticipated long-term confrontation with Israel. Another explanation has been that it was done in order to increase the pressure on the Israeli public and leadership.

In any case, it is still unclear whether any bombings can be classified as an "official" Palestinian tactic. Much depends on the actual degree of coordination between the Palestinian leadership on the one hand and the organizers and perpetrators of the attacks on the other hand. It is most often nearly impossible to determine the PA's role in such attacks since they are, for obvious reasons, reluctant to claim responsibility—at least to the international community.

Some analysts note that the number of suicide attacks declined after early June 2001, when international pressure on Yasser Arafat intensified following a suicide bombing in a Tel Aviv discotheque that killed 21 Israelis. At the time, Arafat called for an immediate cease-fire. Still others point to statements by Hamas and other organizations following that suicide bombing which made it clear that such groups opposed the Palestinian Authority and stated that they would not adhere to a cease-fire and would continue with their attacks. Such analysts argue that these statements prove that Hamas and other groups not associated with the PA were defying Arafat's orders and thereby concluded that those organizations are not receiving orders from the PA, or might otherwise have grown more independent in the course of the Israeli-Palestinian War.

What has been clear during both the peace process, and throughout the fighting that has followed, is that antipeace groups can successfully use suicide bombings for their own political and military purposes. Such bombings have given small Palestinian factions the ability to block or shatter cease-fires and peace efforts regardless of their size and political support.

The willingness of suicide bombers to die—and the willingness of those who sponsor, organize, and equip such bombers to sacrifice them—makes it extremely difficult to deter or defend against suicide attacks. At the same time, suicide bombings often succeed in causing physical destruction and even greater and more extensive psychological damage to their targets.

The IDF has tried a number of different solutions to suicide bombings, from closures to increased patrolling of border areas, and from large-scale retribution and assassinations to a policy of restraint. None has yet been fully successful, although a combination of such tactics and new barrier defenses has seemed to offer at least temporary reductions in the number and the effectiveness of such bombings.

Mortars and Rockets

Although the IDF has been able to keep the Palestinians from obtaining conventional artillery, it has not been able to prevent them from employing other, less accurate forms of long-range attack systems. The Palestinians introduced two new elements into the Israeli-Palestinian crisis in early 2001—mortar and rocket attacks.

Initially, Palestinians mortar fire concentrated on IDF outposts and Jewish settlements in the Gaza Strip, but they eventually began reaching targets in Israel proper as well. On January 3, 2001, six mortar shells were fired at an IDF base near the disputed Shebaa Farms region on the Israel-Lebanon border. At the time, the IDF did not rule out that a faction supported by the PA was responsible for the attack, since the tactic was considered atypical of Hezbollah.[172]

On January 30, 2001, Palestinian elements in the Gaza Strip fired mortars for the first time. A mortar landed on the roof of a house in a neighborhood close the Netzarim junction. The IDF established that standard 82-mm Soviet mortars and improvised 60-mm mortars were being used. They labeled such attacks a "new trend" in Palestinian warfare and "a clear escalation" in tactics. The 82-mm mortars were believed to have been smuggled into the Gaza Strip from Egypt through underground tunnels near Rafah, or perhaps underwater by sea. The 60-mm mortars appeared to be manufactured in the Gaza Strip, possibly with the help of Hezbollah.

On June 21, 2001, a 120-mm mortar round with a range of 4–5 kilometers—the largest type used since the beginning of the Israeli-Palestinian War—was fired on the Karni industrial zone. The mortar was also thought to have been made in the Gaza Strip.

The IDF attributed the introduction of mortar capability in large part to Massoud Ayyad, a lieutenant colonel in Arafat's Force 17 security force. Israelis suspected him of leading a Gaza-based cell of Hezbollah and assassinated him in the Gaza Strip on February 13, 2002.[173] While Palestinian mortar attacks have not caused extensive injuries or harm to infrastructure to date, they have acted as psychological weapons and have the potential to escalate a crisis. On April 17, 2001, for example, the IDF responded to Palestinian mortar fire targeted at Sderot—a town near the Gaza Strip and only a few miles away from a farm owned by Prime Minister Sharon—by mounting a 24-hour invasion of Palestinian-ruled areas in the Gaza Strip, destroying houses and military posts, and uprooting trees. This was the first time that mortars landed on a town in Israel proper.

In an interview with the *Los Angeles Times* on April 10, 2001, a Palestinian leader of a unit that carried out mortar attacks against Israeli targets described the rationale of Palestinian mortar attacks. Using his nom de guerre, Abu Jamal, the interviewee said, "it's true that it is not a very accurate weapon, but we don't actually care that it's not 100% accurate. Whether or not it hits the target, we want to create confusion and terror. We want the Israelis to think that their army cannot protect them."[174]

Mortars have been used in more direct attacks. For example, in central Jerusalem on May 27, 2001, 52-mm mortar shells shot from a vehicle landed unexploded on a porch of a house and in a public park hundreds of yards away. While mortar shells had been used before in bombs, up until this point, such attacks had all taken place in or near the Gaza Strip. The mortars used in the May 27 attack were thought to have originated in the West Bank. This was a grave concern for Israelis, for they had long feared that extremist Palestinian groups in the West Bank might one day obtain mortars. Because of the proximity of Israeli population centers to the West Bank, they can be used to inflict casualties and damages with considerably more precision than rockets launched from fire points in the Gaza Strip.

In another mortar attack on November 24, 2001, one IDF reservist was killed and two other IDF soldiers were wounded when Hamas militants fired mortar shells at the Gush Katif community of Kfar Darom in the Gaza Strip. This marked the first fatal mortar attack since the war began. It was not until one year later, on December 2, 2002, that another mortar was reportedly launched. This time one Palestinian was killed, and nine others were wounded, when members of Islamic Jihad launched two mortars at the Erez industrial zone in the Gaza Strip—clearly revealing the inaccuracies of such weapons.

Palestinian militants began constructing crude unguided rockets in workshops throughout the Gaza Strip in early 2001. The initial model was designed and produced by Hamas and dubbed the Qassam-1, after Hamas's military wing, the Ezzedine al-Qassam Brigades. The 79-cm-long, 60-mm-caliber Qassam-1 had a 4.5-kilogram warhead and a maximum range of 1.5–2 kilometers. The first

Qassam-1 was fired on July 10, 2001, destroying an IDF bulldozer in the Gaza Strip. In October and November 2001, multiple Qassam-1 rockets were fired at the Israeli settlement of Gush Katif, IDF outposts around the Erez border crossing, and the town of Sderot in Israel, although none of these launchings caused any serious injuries or damage.[175]

By early 2002, Hamas had developed and began production on an upgraded version of the Qassam rocket. The 180-cm-long and 120-mm-diameter Qassam-2 is capable of carrying 5–9 kilograms of explosive payload and has an average range of 8–9 kilometers. The first Qassam-2 rockets were launched at Kibbutz Saad and Moshav Shuva on February 10, 2002. The relatively unsophisticated design of all Qassam rocket variants has made them fairly easy to produce using generally available components and makeshift facilities.[176]

Although Hamas has been the principal manufacturer of Qassam rockets, both Hamas and Fatah's Al-Aqsa Martyrs' Brigades members have carried out Qassam rocket attacks. Israeli security officials allege that the Al-Aqsa Martyrs' Brigades has consistently supported Hamas's efforts with the tacit approval of the Palestinian Authority.[177] In addition, by the summer of 2003 the Palestinian militant group Islamic Jihad had developed and began launching its own type of rocket, called the Al-Quds, although these have been less effective than the Qassam series.[178]

As of late 2004, all rocket attacks have occurred in or originated from the Gaza Strip, although evidence indicates that Palestinian militants have been trying to extend the capabilities to manufacture Qassam rockets to the West Bank for some time. For instance, a truck carrying eight Qassam-II rockets was stopped at an IDF roadblock southeast of Nablus on February 6, 2002, and two rocket assembly workshops were uncovered by the IDF in the Balata refugee camp outside of Nablus later that month.[179] During an August 7, 2003, raid on the West Bank town of Jericho, IDF forces arrested 18 Palestinian security personnel who allegedly were setting up Qassam factories there.[180]

In total, over 350 rockets were launched at Israeli targets in and around the Gaza Strip from mid-2001 to late 2004. Because of their simplistic design and haphazard construction, however, the rockets have produced few casualties and little collateral damage. In fact, as of late 2004, only two rocket attacks have resulted in fatalities —June 29 and September 29, 2004, Qassam-2 rocket attacks on Sderot each killed two Israeli civilians.[181] Despite the minimal physical impact that launching rockets has produced, as in the case with mortar fire, Palestinian militants have continued to utilize this tactic due to the effect it has on the Israeli psyche.

Political Warfare and Weapons of Mass Media

Palestinian tactics responded to the outbreak of the Israeli-Palestinian War as much by political means as by military means. Arafat sought to rebuild his image in the eyes of the Arab world and international community, maintain his influence over the Palestinian people, and survive Israeli military assaults. He fought back with both political statements and attempts to reform the Palestinian Authority.[182] On

December 16, 2001, in a speech broadcast on Palestinian television, Arafat called for "a complete cessation of any operation or actions, especially suicide attacks" which provides Israel with a pretext for "military aggression."[183] In this speech, Arafat repeatedly affirmed that the Palestinian Authority had always condemned suicide-bombing attacks.

This address marked the first time during the Israeli-Palestinian War that Arafat pleaded so broadly and visibly for an end to the violence against Israel.[184] However, it was scarcely an altruistic appeal. Arafat was responding to the IDF effort to isolate him—by making a public speech that sought to place him "above the fray" and remove himself as far as possible from accusations of being associated with terrorist networks. Arafat also acted due to increased pressure from the international community. In a meeting in Brussels on December 10, the EU's foreign ministers told Arafat that he must "arrest and prosecute all 'suspects' and appeal, in Arabic" for an end to the Palestinians' armed struggle.[185] If Arafat wanted to maintain some degree of European support, he had to comply.

Arafat also showed he could still do much to curb the daily fighting, ambushes, roadside booby traps, and suicide attacks against Israel.[186] Between the beginning of the Israeli-Palestinian War and December 21, 2001, Arafat detained at least 185 Hamas and Palestinian Islamic Jihad members—although only five were estimated to be among the top 36 on U.S. envoy General Zinni's "most-wanted" list, and the other 180 were low-level Hamas and PIJ members. Most of the 180 low-level militants were placed under "loose 'house arrest.'"[187] Then on December 12, 2001, Arafat shut down Hamas and PIJ offices.

Arafat, however, continued to mix politics with warfare. Only two days later, he withdrew the order. Moreover, he failed to confiscate the illegal weapons found in the hands of popular resistance committees and Fatah-associated groups. There is also no evidence of a serious attempt to dismantle activities such as mortar-manufacturing factories and the smuggling infrastructure established across the Egypt-Gaza border.[188]

This mix of political statements, arrests, and asymmetric warfare is typical of Arafat's tactics in negotiating without abandoning armed struggle up to the time of his death. Arafat also responded to Israeli and international pressure on a number of occasions by making token or limited arrests; while many militants on the Israel and U.S. most-wanted list were able to escape Arafat's law enforcement. It is likely that some were not arrested because Arafat's forces were unable to operate effectively, in part due to the damage they had suffered from Israeli forces. In most cases, however, it seems more likely that Arafat responded to Israeli pressure by offering a slight "crackdown" on terrorism—enough to help bolster his international credibility and maintain his support at home among the Palestinian people.

More broadly, the Palestinian advantage in exploiting political warfare has had a powerful impact in international relations and the world media, but it also had limits. Palestinian suicide bombings, for example, have a major detrimental effect on the Palestinian image. For example, the series of Palestinian suicide bombings that culminated in an explosion in front of a Tel Aviv discotheque that killed 21 Israelis on

June 1, 2001, drastically shifted the balance of world opinion in favor of Israel.[189] The Palestinians can exploit their "underdog" status when they are under attack by Israel, but become terrorists when they go on the offensive.

PALESTINIAN STRATEGIC CHALLENGES

The Palestinians must make hard choices about their future. A political struggle between the more secular elements of Fatah and its supporters, and Islamist groups like Hamas and the PIJ, is already a major fact of life in the Gaza Strip and the West Bank. This could expand into a major clash between rival Palestinian paramilitary forces as well.

More generally, Palestinians will have to decide on whether they should try to create a new and more effective peace process or pursue their ongoing asymmetric war of attrition with Israel. These are not necessarily contradictory goals. Since the Oslo Accords, the Palestinians have consistently tried both options at the same time, just as Israel has pursed both peace and settlements.

The contradictions and tensions in Palestinian and Israeli politics do, however, make any mix of Palestinian efforts based on attacks on Israel extremely costly and have already triggered Israeli efforts to create security barriers through the West Bank and Jerusalem, and unilateral "boundaries" that expand Israeli control over the greater Jerusalem area and West Bank. The Israeli cutoff of financial support to the Palestinian government, crackdowns on any activity at the Gaza Strip crossings, tightening of security measures on the West Bank, and new attacks on Hamas and PIJ activists and officials all illustrate that the Palestinians may be able to keep up an asymmetric war indefinitely, but that the cost is likely to continue to be far higher to the Palestinians than Israel.

More generally, the Palestinians face the following strategic challenges:

- Creating a new political balance, new structure of government, and a new balance of control over Palestinian security forces as a result of Hamas's victory in the January 25, 2006, elections;
- Dealing with the hostile reaction to that victory from Israel and the United States.
- Deciding whether Hamas is willing to evolve into a political party that can advocate a meaningful peace process and some kind of accommodation with Israel.
- Determining whether the new government can create unified and effective Palestinian security forces and the role they should play.
- Finding out what new balance of financing and aid can be achieved to support the Palestinian Authority and its security forces as a result of Hamas's victory and Israeli and U.S. threats to reduce or eliminate aid and financing.
- Developing new political, aid, and security arrangements with other Arab states. These include security arrangements with Egypt, and security relations with Iran, Hezbollah, and Syria.

- Dealing with the political, economic, and military impact of Israel's steadily improving security barriers.
- Finding sources of advice, funding, and arms for its security forces.
- Determining the extent to which militias and forces outside the Palestinian Authority security forces should now be integrated with the Palestinian Authority security forces.

There is no way to make a mid- or long-term estimate of how well the Palestinians will deal with these security challenges, but the short-term prognosis is clear. Whatever happens, relations between the Palestinians and Israel will now be more troubled than before. Similarly, creating effective Palestinian security forces will be more difficult, regardless of the focus of their mission.

There seems to be little prospect that the PA security forces can be rebuilt to support the search for peace when the elected government at most accepts a cease-fire, there is no money, President Abbas has limited authority, outside advisors can do little more than try to keep hope alive, and Israel has effectively rejected the present Palestinian government as a peace partner. Financial pressure is far more likely to both weaken and corrupt the PA forces developed under Arafat and favor the Hamas forces by comparison.

If the Palestinians choose to focus on asymmetric war, they face the near certainty of having to find ways to fight across Israel's growing security barriers and dealing with steadily escalating Israeli controls and attacks on Palestinian territory, leaders, and forces. The Palestinians may be able to respond with rockets and smuggled or homemade artillery and long-range weapons. They may be able to take advantage of the fact that many parts of the present security barriers are little more than chain-link fences with 1970s vintage sensors, if any. The Gaza Strip already is enclosed in far more advanced barriers, however, and Israel can expand its security barriers, sanctions, and attacks far more easily and at less cost than the Palestinians can escalate.

The Military Forces of Syria

In the past half century, Syria has gone from a major intellectual, cultural, and power center in the Arab world to the status of a local irritant. Over the last two decades, Syria has entered in a strange strategic limbo. It maintains far larger conventional forces than it can hope to make effective or modernize. At the same time, its consistent failures to modernize and reform its economy have made it fall further and further behind the pace of global economic modernization and steadily reduced its ability to fund effective and modern forces.

The forces that achieved surprise against Israel and major initial advances in the Golan in 1973, and that resisted the Israeli advance in 1982, have steadily decayed in capability. It is difficult to know just how much. Syrian forces never engaged in meaningful combat in the Gulf War in 1991, and never met meaningful resistance in Lebanon. It is clear that their equipment is now often obsolete, that many of the units deployed to Lebanon became corrupt and exploited their position, and that much of the Syrian force structure is now a garrison force with little realistic experience and training. At the same time, some elements do carry out realistic training, and there are armored/mechanized, Special Forces and attack helicopter units that still maintain significant proficiency.

The end result is that Syria has steadily less real-world offensive and defensive capability against Israel, but it continues to act as if it has the resources and the access to cheap and free Soviet-bloc arms that it had in the 1970s and early 1980s. It rejected a unique opportunity to regain the Golan in negotiating with former Israeli Prime Minister Barak even though its forces had already decayed to a purely defensive posture of uncertain effectiveness.

Syria is, however, a relatively large country by regional standards, and its strategic geography makes it a major factor in the regional balance. It has an area of 185,180 square kilometers (including 1,295 square kilometers of Israeli-occupied territory). It has borders with Israel (76 kilometers), Iraq (605 kilometers), Jordan

(375 kilometers), Lebanon (375 kilometers), and Turkey (822 kilometers). It has a 193-kilometer-long coastline on the Mediterranean.[1]

Syria also can play a spoiler role in spite of its military weakness. It retains enough influence in Lebanon to use Hezbollah as a proxy in its struggle with Israel, and it acts as a conduit for Iranian shipments of arms to both Hezbollah and Palestinian groups opposed to Israel. It continues to play a destabilizing role in Lebanese politics, and it has played a significant role in the insurgency in Iraq—allowing Iraqi insurgent groups to operate in Syria and acting as a transit point for infiltrating volunteers and arms into Iraq. Syria's Alawite-controlled regime is also increasingly seen by leaders like President Mubarak and King Abdullah as a potential member of a "Shi'-ite" crescent involving Iran, Iraq, Lebanon, and Syria.

The question is whether its present regime can survive indefinitely by juggling local alliances and maintaining the equivalent of a police state. Basher Asad has shown little more economic pragmatism to date than his father and has done little to arrest the relative decline in Syria's economic position and make serious increases in its per capita income and government services. Income distribution remains poor, Syria's Ba'ath Party has little popular political credibility, and Syria seems to have increasing problems with Islamist internal resistance in spite of the repressive nature of its regime.

Syria's demographics also do not favor Alawite dominance. Its population was slightly over 18.5 million in 2006. Some 74 percent of the population was Sunni Arab, and 16 percent was Alawite, Druze, and other Muslim sects. Another 10 percent was various sects of Christian, and there were small Jewish communities in Damascus, Al Qamishli, and Allepo. Ethnically, the population was 90.3 percent Arab and 9.7 percent Kurds, Armenians, and other.[2]

LEBANON AND SYRIA'S PROXY WAR WITH ISRAEL

Although Syria has had quiet borders with Israel for the past 32 years, it has used Lebanon as an arena for a low-level proxy war against Israel, and it hosted various Palestinian antipeace and terrorist movements. At the same time, Syria exploited its occupation of Lebanon in virtually every form possible. This included actions like military-organized car theft rings and official sanctioned trafficking in narcotics.

Beginning with the first Syrian military occupation of Lebanon in 1976, Lebanon became a major global provider of hashish and, later on, opium. The U.S. House of Representatives Subcommission on Crime and Criminal Justice reported in 1992 that many Syrian officers and troops were benefiting directly from the Lebanese drug-trafficking trade. Although Syria and Lebanon have since made explicit publicized efforts to appear as though they were cracking down on the drug trade, in 2001 the CNN Beirut bureau chief who had uncovered evidence that this was actually not the case was made to surrender his film footage.

Syria used this drug trade and Lebanese banks to launder money it was counterfeiting. $100 bills circulating were at such high quality that even the U.S. Federal Reserve Bank's scanners could not identify the money as counterfeit. The laundered money was then used by terrorist organizations that Syria supports.[3] Syrian support for terrorism is a cause of much concern for Israel as well as the United States and the United Nations.

Syria provides logistical and financial assistance to Hezbollah, Hamas, Islamic Jihad, and other groups. Although the Syrian government denies assistance and safe-guarding of terrorists, the denial stems more from the unwillingness to recognize the organizations as terrorist organizations and not from any Syrian denial of such ties or that it provides a sanctuary for Palestinian militants and other sources of instability in the region like some of the men who killed Rafik Hariri in Beirut.[4]

This effort has had distinctly mixed results. Syrian (and Iranian) support for Hez-bollah and Amal did help to push Israel out of southern Lebanon. Since that time, however, Syria's support of Hezbollah and Palestinian militants has been more as an irritant to Israel than a meaningful effort to achieve a useful strategic objective. Moreover, Syria has now been forced out of Lebanon, a country that may have been a strategic liability for Israel, but was a key source of revenue for Syria.

As for proliferation, Syria has developed some elements of a force capable of strik-ing Israel with long-range missiles and chemical weapons. This force cannot be dis-regarded as a threat or deterrent, but it is so much less lethal than Israel's nuclear forces that if it was used, it might trigger massive Israeli retaliation without having the capability to do truly serious damage to Israel. It is the kind of proliferation that invites preemption if it is not used, and disaster if it is.

SYRIA'S BROADER REGIONAL PROBLEMS

Syria has also failed to set meaningful strategic goals for dealing with Turkey, Iraq, and the United States. It attempted to exploit Turkey's problems with its Kurds by giving aid and sanctuary to Turkish Kurdish separatists, with the end result that Tur-key threatened military action and Syria was forced to accede to virtually every Turk-ish demand.

Syria has supported a range of Sunni insurgent factions in Iraq since the fall of Saddam Hussein, but again more as an irritant to the United States than to achieve any clear objective for Syria.[5] Syria at most can succeed in creating prolonged tur-moil in Iraq. These Syrian actions may weaken Iraq and the United States, but seem more likely to provoke them than produce any benefits for Syria. While Syria has sporadically taken a more active approach to border control in the southwest where the Syrian border meets Iraq, it has also clearly tolerated infiltrations from Syria into Iraq on other occasions, and Iraqi leaders have repeatedly condemned it for provid-ing sanctuary to Iraqi insurgents.[6] Syrian actions might make more sense if Syria believed it could benefit from the insurgency, but it is more likely to divide Iraq and polarize Iraqi Arab Sunnis and Shi'ites in ways that could come back to haunt Syria's ruling Alawite minority.

Syria's alleged involvement in the death of Rafik Hariri has also marginalized Syria and distanced it from its regional neighbors. Egypt, Jordan, and Saudi Arabia saw the attack against Hariri as a turning point in their relationship with Syria. Despite sharp disagreements among Arab nations in the past, there has been an informal under-standing that assassinating rival leaders was unacceptable.

Egyptian and Saudi leaders urged Bashar al-Asad to withdraw Syrian troops from Lebanon and pressured him to cooperate with the UN investigation. This enhanced the pressure against Syria and concerned many Syrian leaders. In the past, Egypt, Jordan, and Saudi Arabia have also played a moderating role between the United States and Syria. They may be more reluctant to try to halt U.S. pressure on Syria in the future, not only because of the assassination of Rafik Hariri but because of Syria's role in supporting the insurgency in Iraq.

THE TRENDS IN SYRIAN FORCES

The trends in Syrian forces are shown in Figure 9.1. More detail by service is shown in Figures 9.4–9.7. They reflect the fact that Syria still treats Israel as an enemy power, but had to abandon its search for conventional parity. As a result, it had to minimize the risk of a future military clash with Israel and make shifts in its strategy and procurement effort that has included a new focus on "asymmetric warfare." These shifts are as follows:[7]

- Emphasize the procurement of long-range ballistic missiles and weapons of mass destruction (WMD) as a relatively low cost offset to Israel's conventional superiority while giving Syria a limited counterweight to Israel's nuclear strike capability. There are allegations that Syria is working with Iran to achieve chemical warfare capabilities although there has been no mention of nuclear capability acquisitions.[8]

Figure 9.1   Syrian Forces: Force Structure

	1990	2000	2005	2006
Manpower	704,000	~820,000	758,800	769,600
Active	404,000	~316,000	296,800	307,600
Conscript	130,000	?	?	?
Army	300,000	~215,000	200,000	200,000
Navy	4,000	~6,000	7,600	7,600
Air Force	40,000	40,000	35,000	40,000
Air Defense Command	~60,000	~55,000	~54,200	~60,000
Paramilitary	24,300	~108,000	~108,000	~108,000
Reserve	400,000	396,000	354,000	354,000
Army	392,000	300,000	280,000	280,000
Navy	8,000	4,000	4,000	4,000
Air Force	N/A	92,000	70,000	70,000

~ = Estimated amount; * = combat capable; + = more than the number given but not specified how much more; Some = unspecified amount; ? = unspecified amount, if any; N/A = not available; {} = serviceability in doubt.

Source: Various editions of the International Institute for Strategic Studies (IISS) *Military Balance,* U.S., British, and other experts.

- Give priority to elite commando and Special Forces units that can be used to defend key approaches to Syria and spearhead infiltrations and attacks. Many of these forces are equipped with modern antitank guided weapons and other modern crew and man-portable weapons that allow them to disperse without relying on armored weapons and other systems Israel can target more easily. They are supported by attack helicopters. There has been no real change in the number of attack helicopters since 2000.[9] Air defense (AD) and antitank (AT) missile capabilities have increased continuously since 2000.[10]

- Maintain a large tank force both as a deterrent to any Israeli attempt to penetrate Syria and to maintain a constant threat to the Golan, even if Syria had no hope of achieving overall parity.

- Use Hezbollah and Amal as proxies to attack Israel [there is no Symbionese Liberation Army (SLA) anymore; it was disbanded after the Israeli pullout when the SLA leadership and others fled to Israel], the Golan Heights, and the Shebaa Farms area. Following the October 5, 2003, bombing of a suspected Islamic Jihad training camp near Damascus by Israel, it was speculated that the Golan Heights in particular could become a new battleground. However, critics of such a view argue that it would be very difficult for Syria to establish a credible resistance movement among the Syrians in the Golan Heights, mostly the Druze, since they have faced little repression. Some Druze serve in the Israel Defense Forces (IDF). They contend that attacks on the Shebaa area by Hezbollah are much more likely.

The trends in Figure 9.1 reflect serious uncertainties and inconsistencies in unclassified sources, but they seem to reflect a reduction in Syrian force sizes, except the paramilitary forces that have stayed constant throughout since 2000. Although missile capabilities (antitank and air defense) have increased since 2000, there is little evidence to show that the increase has led to a qualitative improvement in Syrian forces. Syria has rather tended to emphasize mass and procure more of the same.

The Syrian Modernization and Recapitalization Crisis

As the data in Figures 9.2 and 9.3 show, Syria has faced massive problems in recapitalizing its forces and in modernization, which have grown worse in recent years rather than better. Its weapons systems and military equipment continue to age since there has been little procurement, even for the few areas Syria has modernized in the past like AD and AT missiles. There also has been a cut in foreign forces operating within Syria, with a remaining 150 Russian Army forces at the final IISS count.[11]

For over two decades, Syria has had to cope with the recapitalization crisis reflected in Figure 9.2 and/or the failure to acquire modern arms and military technology shown in Figure 9.3. Syria had attempted to remedy some of its growing modernization problems by procuring upgrades and technology from Russia and the West, but Syria had not done well in obtaining such help.

Its only major conventional force improvements during the mid- and late-1990s were some Ukrainian modifications for part of the T-55 tank fleet and AT-14 Kornet antitank guided missiles (ATGMs). Some reports indicate that the Syrian Armed

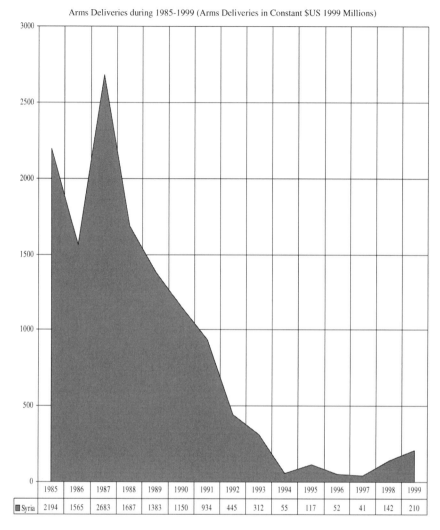

Arms Deliveries during 1985-1999 (Arms Deliveries in Constant $US 1999 Millions)

	1985	1986	1987	1988	1989	1990	1991	1992	1993	1994	1995	1996	1997	1998	1999
■ Syria	2194	1565	2683	1687	1383	1150	934	445	312	55	117	52	41	142	210

Source: Adapted by Anthony H. Cordesman from US State Department, World Military Expenditures and Arms Transfers, various editions.

Figure 9.2   The Syrian Recapitalization Crisis: Part One

Forces did acquire an additional 1,500 Kornets, as well as upgrade packages for up to a brigade of T-72 tanks. The upgrade will boost the T-72's armor while adding an attachment that would enable the tank to fire ATGMs.[12] Yet it is important to note that Syria tried four previous times to upgrade the T-72s with little success, and past attempts to incorporate elements of the current upgrade package were met with great difficulty.

As Figures 9.2 and 9.3 show, Syria, however, has not yet succeeded in negotiating major new arms agreements with Russia and other suppliers. Western companies

Syrian New Arms Agreements and Deliveries: 1993-2004 (in $US Current Millions)

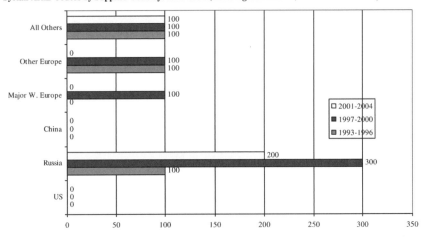

0 = less than $50 million or nil, and all data rounded to the nearest $100 million.

Figure 9.3   The Syrian Recapitalization Crisis: Part Two

want firm cash guarantees and are reluctant to sell to Syria. China and North Korea cannot supply the quality of conventional arms Syria needs, and any purchase of equipment that does not come from Russia will create interoperability problems that will compound Syrian weaknesses in sustainability and combined arms.

Bulgaria, for example, could supply Syria with much of the Soviet-era replacement parts that it needs, as an illegal sale by a Bulgarian firm of 50 sets of gear boxes and engines for T-55s in 2001 illustrates, but the country had expressed its desire to join NATO. NATO clearly does not support the export of arms to Syria, and Bulgaria had launched an investigation into the sale of Soviet armored personnel carrier (APC) parts to Syria in 2003, culminating in at least six arrests. Bulgaria hopes to rid itself of the perception that it will sell arms to almost any group interested to support its flagging defense industry and thus is unlikely to continue or strengthen ties with Syria.[13]

The Russian Connection?

Russia is Syria's most logical source of new conventional arms, and there were reports during the early 1990s that indicated that Syria would be able to spend some $1.4 billion on military modernization between 1992 and 1994. Syria found, however, that post-Communist Russia did not make concessionary arms sales that approached the level of gifts or show the past tolerance for unpaid loans. This was a major stumbling block throughout the 1990s. Syria had plied up a massive debt over the years. It owed Russia roughly $7.0–11.0 billion for past arms purchases and a total of $20 billion for both its military and civil debt. Russia was well aware that there was little prospect that it would ever be paid and this had a chilling impact on Syria's ability to obtain arms.[14]

Russia and Syria have claimed to resolve the issue on several occasions. Syria signed a new cooperation agreement with Russia in April 1994 for "defensive weapons and spare parts." Syria held extensive new arms purchasing talks with Russia in 1997 and 1998. In February 1999, Syria announced plans to spend as much as $2 billion on a range of Russian armaments, including more antitank systems—which seem to have included deliveries of more AT-14 Kornets.[15]

Syria and Russia held talks in May 1999 to discuss expanding military cooperation and, in particular, to arrange the sale of Russian advanced weapons systems to Syria.[16] According to some reports, Russia now seemed willing to put repayments of its debt on hold.[17] A five-year, $2-billion contract was under discussion.[18] According to one report, Syria apparently requested Su-27 fighters and the S-300 air defense system, but was offered the cheaper MiG-29 fighters and Tor-M1 air defense systems.[19]

Syria and Russia held new high-level talks on military cooperation in September 1999. These talks seem to have again involved a $2–2.5 billion deal over five years and the possible purchase of the S-300 surface-to-air missile (SAM) defense system, the Sukhoi Su-27 multirole fighter, MiG-29SMT fighters, T-80 tanks, and more antitank weapons. Once again, however, the contractual status of such agreements, the weapons involved, and delivery schedules remained unclear.[20]

It is not clear how Hafez Asad's death, and Basher's succession, will ultimately affect this situation. Even if reports of major new Russian arms sales in 2004 and 2005 should eventually prove true, any foreseeable new agreements will still leave Syria with far fewer funds than it needs to recapitalize its current force structure and compete with Israel in modernization.

There may, however, have been real progress on the military debt issue. In a meeting between Asad and Russian Finance Minister Alexei Kudrin, Russia agreed to write off 73 percent of Syria's $13.4-billion debt, thus reducing the Syrian foreign debt to less than 10 percent of its gross domestic product and allowing it to allot more funding to weapon acquisitions.[21] In talks between the Syrians and the Russians in January 2005, the two countries were reported to have reached six cooperation agreements, one of them focusing on military issues.[22]

This may make it easier for Syria to finance some of the equipment it needs to modernize its forces such as its older land force equipment, surface-to-air missiles, and aircraft in the near- to mid-term. There have been such reports in the past, however, that led to token or no actual arms imports. Moreover, even if Syria could order all of the arms it wants, it would still take at least three to five years to fully absorb all of the new technology it needs, integrate it into effective combat systems, and retrain its forces—assuming it recognizes the need to do so.

The Israeli Problem

Syria must also deal with the risk that Russia may be seeking to develop a closer relationship with Israel. Israeli Prime Minister Sharon stated that Russia had decided not to sell the SA-18 Grouse surface-to-air missile systems to Syria over Israeli concerns that the weapons might fall into the hands of Hezbollah.[23] Sharon indicated that Israel and Russia intend on sharing intelligence in their respective fights against "terrorism."

If Israel and Russia continue to strengthen their ties, Syria could face additional weapons procurement problems, as Israel is likely to pressure Russia on other arms sales. Israel's relations with Russia may not be progressing as previously thought since in late November 2005 Russia and Iran signed a contract whereby Russia would supply Iran with antiaircraft missile systems to be delivered over the next two years, Tor-M1.[24] Although Russia claims there is no need for Israel to worry, this sale may put a strain on the Russia-Israel relations in the coming months.

Another point of tension between the Russians and Israelis is over Russian intentions to sell Syria new Iskandar missiles, which would give Syria the ability to hit anywhere inside Israel save the southernmost areas,[25] as well as the Igla man-portable air-defense systems. Putin has agreed to sell only the vehicle-mounted 9K38 Igla (SA-18) low-altitude surface-to-air missiles to Syria, but has not specified the number of missiles to be sold. Israel's concern about the transfer of weapons to Hezbollah or Palestinian insurgent groups continues since the vehicle-mounted missiles can be dismantled and transferred to the individual militia groups.[26]

The Igla and possibly the Iskandar sale were part of discussions to sell not only the missiles, but also dozens of AT-14 Kornet-E, AT-13 Metis, and possibly in addition the Almaz S-300PMU medium-range low- to high-altitude SAM system.[27] Syria has also been in advanced negotiations with Russia for the procurement of new United Arab Emirates' development-funded Pantsir S1 short-range surface-to-air missile systems and is said to have spent more than $400 million on several dozen systems. Earlier in 2005, it was reported that Syria was interested in acquiring Iskander-E short-range ballistic missiles that have a range of 280 kilometers. The Iskander-E is the exported version of the Kolomna-designed 9M72 short-range ballistic missile currently in use in the Russian military.[28]

Continuing to Go "Hollow"

Barring massive outside aid, Syrian forces are almost certain to continue to go "hollow" for the foreseeable future, although moderate deliveries of advanced modern aircraft, tanks, and surface-to-air missile systems like the S-300 could still help correct key Syrian weaknesses. It is interesting to note that Syria has not yet invested or explored acquisitions for an integrated air defense system.[29]

Syria's limitations will be further compounded by its problems in absorbing new equipment. These include endemic corruption. They also include a politicized and compartmented command structure, inadequate military pay, poor manpower management, poor technical training, and poor overall training—particularly in realistic combat exercises and aggressor training. Syrian forces have inadequate combat and service support, equipment for night and poor weather warfare, long-range sensors and targeting systems, and mobile rapidly maneuverable logistics, recording, and combat repair capability. While individual Syrian officers have shown an understanding of many of these problems, Syria had never taken effective action to deal with them.

SYRIAN LAND FORCES

Syria's military forces have never lacked courage, and they performed with considerable skill in the October 1973 War with Israel. Elements of the Syrian Army fought equally well during Israel's 1982 invasion of Israel, particularly some Special Forces, commando, and attack helicopter units. The Syrian Army has, however, suffered badly from a lack of proper modernization, from poor overall command direction, from corruption, and from the debilitating impact of occupying Lebanon and acting as a static defensive force in the Golan.[30]

The primary mission of the Syrian Army remains defensive and to counter Israeli attacks. In 2006, Syria organized its ground forces into two corps that reported to the Land Forces General Staff and Commander of the Land Force. The chain of command then passes up to the Chief of the General Staff and Deputy Defense Minister, Minister of Defense (Deputy Commander in Chief of the Armed Forces), and Supreme Commander of the Armed Forces.

This chain of command has become steadily unstable in recent years. Veteran security chiefs are being systematically removed from office. In April 2004 a presidential decree changed the retirement age for generals to 62, for lieutenant generals to 60, for major generals to 58, and so on. Note the trend as follows since 2004:[31]

- October 2004—Army Deputy Commander in Chief Lieutenant General Farouq l'ssa was dismissed,
- January 2004—Army Deputy Commander in Chief Lieutenant Tawfiq Jaloul was dismissed,

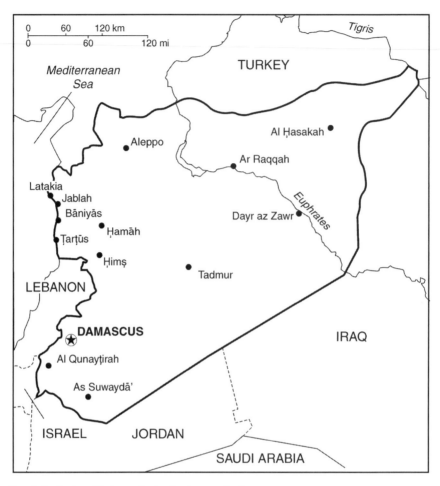

Map 9.1   Syria   (Cartography by Bookcomp, Inc.)

- January 2004—Deputies in the Defense Ministry Lieutenant General Ahmad Abd al-Bani and Lieutenant General Ibrahim Al-Safi were dismissed,
- January 2002 to January 2005—Command of the First Corps was replaced three times,
- June 2002 to January 2005—Second Corps commander was replaced three times, and
- June 2002 to January 2004—Third Corps commander was replaced twice.

Syrian Force Strengths and Deployments

The Syrian 1st Corps was headquartered near Damascus in 2006, and it commanded forces in southeastern Syria, opposing Israel. The 2nd Corps was headquartered near Zabadani, near the Lebanese border, and covers units in Lebanon, but this is changing now that Syria has officially extracted its forces out of Lebanon. The 1st Corps had two armored and three mechanized divisions. The 2nd Corps had three armored and two mechanized divisions. The command relationships Syrian Army forces would have in contingencies involving Jordan, Turkey, and Iraq are unclear.

The trends in the Syria Army are shown in Figure 9.4. In 2006, it had a total of 200,000 active men and was organized into seven armored divisions, including the 1st, 3rd, 9th, 11th, and 569th. Syrian armored divisions vary in size. Most have three armored brigades, two mechanized brigades, and one artillery regiment. A typical division had around 8,000 men. A typical armored brigade had 93 main battle tanks, and 30 other armored fighting vehicles like the BMP. The Syrian Army had three mechanized divisions. They normally had about 11,000 men, but also varied in structure. They have one to two armored brigades, two to three mechanized brigades, and one artillery regiment. A typical mechanized brigade had 40 main battle tanks and 90 other armored fighting vehicles like the BMP.

Syria also had one Republican Guard division, with three armored brigades, one mechanized brigade, and one artillery regiment that reports directly to the Commander of the Land Forces, plus a Special Forces division with three Special Forces regiments and ten independent Special Forces regiments.

Syria's other independent formations included four independent infantry brigades, two independent artillery brigades, and two independent air tanker brigades. Its active smaller formations include one border guard brigade, three infantry brigades, one antitank brigade, one independent tank regiment, eight Special Forces regiments, three surface-to-surface missile brigades with an additional coastal defense brigade, and two artillery brigades.[32]

On paper, Syria had one low-grade reserve armored unit with about half the effective strength of its active divisions, plus 31 infantry, three artillery reserve regiments, and four armored brigades. Most of these Syrian reserve units are poorly equipped and trained. Those Syrian reserves that do train usually do not receive meaningful training above the company to battalion level, and many train using obsolete equipment that is different from the equipment in the active units to which they are assigned. The Syrian call-up system is relatively effective, but the Syrian Army is not organized to make use of it. Virtually all of the Syrian reserves called up in the 1982 war had to be sent home because the Syrian Army lacked the capability to absorb and support them.

Syrian Main Battle Tanks

Although Syria now had a total of some 4,600 tanks, at least 1,200 of these tanks were in static positions or in storage. Roughly half were relatively low-grade T-54s and T-55s, and only 1,600 were relatively modern T-72s.

Even the T-72s, however, lacked the advanced thermal sights, fire-control systems, and armor to engage the Israeli Merkavas and M-60s on anything like a 1:1 basis. The T-72 also performed surprisingly poorly in Iraqi hands during the Gulf War. Its armor did not prove to be as effective against modern Western antitank rounds

Figure 9.4   Syrian Army: Force Structure

	1990	2000	2005	2006
Manpower				
Active	300,000	~215,000	200,000	200,000
Reserves	392,000	300,000	280,000	280,000
Combat Units—Army	19	22	26	26
Corps HQ	2	3	3	3
Armored Division	5	7	7	7
Mechanized Division	3	3	3	3
Infantry Brigade	2	4	4	4
Special Forces Division	1	1	1	1
Artillery Brigade	2	N/A	2	2
Air Tanker Brigade	N/A	1	2	2
SSM Brigade	4	4	5	5
Border Guard Brigade	N/A	1	1	1
Republican Guard Division	N/A	1	1	1
Reserves	9	30	38	38
Division HQ	N/A	N/A	1	1
Armored Brigade	N/A	N/A	4	4
Infantry Regiment	9	30	31	31
Artillery Regiment	N/A	Some	3	3
MBT	4,050	4,650	4,600	4,600
T-55	2,100	2,150	2,000	2,000
T-55MBT/T-55MV	2,100	2,150	2,000	Some stored
T-62	1,000	1,000	1,000	1,000
T-62K/T-62M	1,000	1,000	1,000	Some stored
T-72	950	1,500	1,600	1,600
T-72MBT/T-72M	950	1,200	1,600	1,600
Stored	1,100	Some	N/A	Some
RECCE	500	935	800	800
BRDM-2	500	850	800	800
BRDM-2 Rkh	0	85	N/A	N/A
AIFV	2,350	~2,350+	2,200	2,200
BMP	2,350	~2,350+	2,200	2,200
BMP-1	2,350	2,250	2,100	2,100
BMP-2	0	100	100	100
BMP-3	0	Some	?	?
APC	1,450	1,500	~1,600	1,600+
APC (W)	1,450+	1,500	~1,600	1,600+
BTR-50	?	?	?	?
BTR-60	?	?	?	?
BTR-70	?	?	?	?
BTR-152	?	?	?	?

OT-64	Some	0	0	0
Artillery	~2,150	1,930	2,060	1,960
TOWED	~2,000	~1,480	1,630	1,530
122 mm	600	700	850	850
D-30	500	450	600	600
M-1931/37	100 (stored)	100 (stored)	100 (stored)	100 (stored)
M-1938	Some	150	150	150
ISU-122	Some	0	0	0
130 mm	650	700	600	600
M-46	650	700	600	600
155 mm	Some	70	70	70
D-20	0	20	20	20
M-1937	Some	50	50	50
152 mm	Some	0	0	0
M-1943	Some	0	0	0
180 mm	Some	10	10	?
S23	Some	10	10	?
SP	150	450	430	430
122 mm	108	400	380	380
2S1 Carnation	72	400	380	380
T-34/D-30	36	?	?	?
152 mm	42	50	50	50
ISU-152	?	0	0	0
2S3	42	50	50	50
MRL	~250+	480	480	480
107 mm	0	200	200	200
Type-63	0	200	200	200
122 mm	250	280	280	280
BM-21	250	280	280	280
220 mm	Some	0	0	0
BM-27	Some	0	0	0
240 mm	Some	0	0	0
BM-24	Some	0	0	0
MOR	Some	~908	710	710
82 mm	Some	200	200	200
120 mm	Some	600	400	400
M-1943	Some	600	400	400
160 mm	Some	100	100	100
M-160	Some	100	100	100
240 mm	Some	~8	10	10
M-240	Some	~8	10	10
AT	1,300+	3,390	~4,190	~4,190+
MSL	1,300+	3,390	4,190	4,190+

AT-3 Sagger	1,300	3,000	3,000	3,000
AT-4 Spigot	Some	150	150	150
AT-5 Spandrel	N/A	40	40	40
AT-7 Saxhorn	N/A	N/A	Some	Some
AT-10	N/A	Some	800	800
AT-14 Kornet	N/A	Some	Some	Some
Milan	Some	200	200	200
RL	0	N/A	Some	Some
73 mm	0	N/A	Some	Some
RPG-7 Knout	0	N/A	Some	Some
105 mm	0	N/A	Some	Some
RPG-29	0	N/A	Some	Some
AD	1,700+	6,115	6,285	6,385
SAM	Some	~4,055	4,235+	4,335+
SP	N/A	55	235	235
SA-8 Gecko	N/A	N/A	160	160
SA-9 Gaskin	Some	20	20	20
SA-11 Gadfly	N/A	N/A	20	20
SA-13 Gopher	Some	35	35	35
MANPAD	Some	4,000	~4,000+	4,100+
SA-7 Grail	Some	4,000	4,000	4,000
SA-14 Gremlin	N/A	N/A	N/A	100
SA-18 Grouse	N/A	N/A	Some	Some
GUNS	1,700	2,060	2,050	2,050
23 mm	Some	1,050	1,050	1,050
TOWED	Some	650	650	650
ZSU-23-4	Some	650	650	650
SP	Some	400	400	400
ZU-23-2	Some	400	400	400
37 mm	Some	300	300	300
TOWED	Some	300	300	300
M-1939	Some	300	300	300
57 mm	Some	675	675	675
TOWED	Some	675	675	675
S-60	Some	675	675	675
100 mm	Some	25	25	25
TOWED	Some	25	25	25
KS-19	Some	25	25	25
MSL, Tactical	~54	72+	72+	72+
SSM	36+	72+	72+	72+
Frog-7	18	18	18	18
SS-21 Scarab (Tochka)	18+	18+	18+	18+
SS-C-1B Sepal	Some	4	4	4

SS-C-3 Styx	Some	6	6	6
SCUD	18	26	26	26
SCUD-B	18	?	?	?
SCUD-C	N/A	?	?	?
SCUD-D	N/A	?	?	?

Source: Various editions of the IISS *Military Balance,* U.S., British, and other experts.

as was previously expected, and its sensors and fire-control systems proved inadequate for night and poor visibility combat and could not keep up with Western thermal sights in range and target acquisition capability.

Syrian Other Armored Vehicles

Syria had some 4,600 armored vehicles, of which approximately 2,200 are BMPs. These armored fighting vehicles could supplement and support Syria's tanks in combined arms combat and increase its potential ability to overwhelm immobilized Israeli forces with sheer mass. Only about 100 of these BMPs were the more modern BMP-2s, plus a limited number of BMP-3s.

Even the BMP-2 had relatively light armor and retained many of the ergonomic problems in fighting from the vehicle and using its guns and antitank guided missile launchers as with the BMP-1. The BMP had only moderate ability to escort tanks in a combat environment where the opponent had modern sensors and antitank guided weapons.

Nearly half of Syria's other armor consisted of low-grade BRDM-2 and BTR-50, 60, 70, and 152 reconnaissance vehicles and APCs.

Syrian Antitank Weapons

Syrian has some relatively modern antitank guided weapons like the Milan, AT-10, and AT-14. Much of its inventory, however, consists of older antitank guided weapons that require constant training for their crews to be effective. Such live-fire training is generally lacking.

Syria's more modern third-generation antitank guided missile launchers consist of 200 Milans, 40 AT-5s, 800 AT-10s, and an unknown number of AT-14s. This is about 20 to 25 percent of its total holdings of some 4,190 antitank guided missile launchers.

Syria also has large numbers of RPGs and other antitank rockets, some recoilless rifles, and some obsolete antitank guns.

These holdings can defeat most of Israel's other armored fighting vehicles, and the more modern weapons may have some effectiveness even against Israel's more modern Merkavas. Syrian forces would, however, have serious problems in using such weapons in the face of combined operations of Merkava tanks, suppressive artillery force, and attack helicopter and other air operations.

Syrian Artillery

Syria can mass large numbers of towed artillery weapons and multiple rocket launchers. Syria maintained an inventory of 150 122-mm M-1938, 600 122-mm D-30, 100 122-mm M-1931 (mostly in storage), 600 130-mm M-46, 20 152-mm D-20, 50 152-mm M-1937, and 10 180-mm S23 towed weapons. These are difficult to maneuver at anything like the rate required for modern armored warfare or to meeting Israel's ability to combined air and armored operations. They can, however, deliver large amounts of long-range firepower from static positions and are more difficult to target once they are dug in and revetted.

Syria deploys some 200 107-mm Type-63 and 280 122-mm BM-21 rocket launchers. These weapons are best suited for mass fires from relatively static positions against area targets.

Such weapons could have a major impact in an area like the Golan where ranges are relatively short and where Syria normally deploys much of its artillery. At the same time, massed artillery fire has only limited lethality against well dug-in defenses and armor, and Syria lacks the sensors and battle management systems to concentrate its artillery fire with great precision and to rapidly switch fires. Syria would also have problems in maneuvering its artillery.

Only about 28 percent of Syria's artillery consists of self-propelled weapons. These weapons include 380 122-mm 2S1 and 50 152-mm 2S3s. So far, Syria has shown only limited ability to use such weapons in rapid maneuvers, to target them effectively, and to manage rapid shifts of fire with some degree of precision. Counterbattery radars, unmanned aerial vehicles (UAVs) and other targeting systems, and battle management vehicles and advanced fire-control systems, seem to be in limited supply even for Syria's self-propelled artillery.

Syrian Army Air Defenses

The Syrian Army had roughly 4,000 man-portable light surface-to-air missiles, including SA-7s. It had a number of vehicle-mounted, infrared systems that included 20 SA-9s and 35 SA-13s. Syria's 160 radar-guided SA-8 fire units are assigned to its air force as part of its Air Defense Command. These systems have low-individual lethality, but help keep attacking aircraft at standoff distances, can degrade the attack profile of aircraft they are fired at, and have some cumulative kill probability.

The Syrian Army had over 2,000 antiaircraft guns, including some 650 radar-guided 23-mm ZSU-23-4s. It also had 650 23-mm ZU-23, 300 M-1939 37-mm, 675 57-mm S-60, and 25 100-mm KS-19 unguided towed guns. These antiaircraft guns have limited lethality even at low altitudes, except for the ZSU-23-4. They can, however, be used effectively in "curtain fire" to force attacking aircraft and helicopters to attack at high altitudes or at standoff ranges.

Syrian Army Training and Readiness

The Syrian Army retains some elite elements with reasonable training and proficiency. The bulk of the army, however, is now a relatively static garrison force with limited real-world maneuver, combined arms, and joint warfare training. It is largely defensive in character, lacks leadership, and has suffered from serious corruption as a result of nepotism, political favoritism, and the impact of deployment in Lebanon. It lacks modern tactics, still restricts the initiative of its junior officers, and has not developed an effective noncommissioned officer corps or adequate numbers of technical specialists.

Maintaining large numbers of weapons has priority over maintenance, sustainability, and recover and repair capability, although combat engineer and some other combat support forces seem adequate. Overall logistic and service support capabilities are suited largely for static defensive warfare.

Syria does have good physical defenses of its positions on the Golan. Syria has spent decades improving its terrain barriers and creating antitank barriers and ditches. Many of its units in the area between Damascus and the Golan have considerable readiness and effectiveness. However, Syria has not come close to Israel in developing the kind of capabilities for joint and combined operations, and rapid maneuver.

SYRIAN AIR AND AIR DEFENSE FORCES

The Syrian Air Force and Air Defense Command have more severe qualitative problems than Syrian land forces. Again, courage is not an issue. Syrian Air Force pilots continued to fly what were little more than suicide missions after President Asad demanded that they be committed to combat in 1982 even after it was obvious they could not survive against a far superior Israel Air Force (IAF).

Syria lacks significant numbers of modern aircraft, however, and the modern airborne and other command-and-control and sensor systems needed for today's forms of warfare. It is in many ways more a military museum dedicated to obsolete Soviet-bloc forms of air combat than a modern air force.

Syrian Combat Air Strength

The trends in the Syrian Air Force (SAF) are shown in Figure 9.5. Although Syria possessed 632 combat aircraft and a force of 40,000 men, the 20 Su-24s were its only relatively modern attack fighters and these are export versions of the aircraft, largely limited to the technology available in the late 1970s and early 1980s. while they have had limited upgrades, they lack the avionics and precision all-weather strike capabilities of first-line Israeli attack aircraft.

Similarly, Syria's 80 MiG-29s and 8 Su-27s are its only modern fighters with reasonably capable beyond-visual-range and look-down, shoot-down capabilities. These too are export aircraft with largely late 1970s/early 1980s avionics. Syria has

Figure 9.5 Syrian Air Force: Force Structure

	1990	2000	2005	2006
Manpower	40,000	132,00	105,000	110,000
Air Force	40,000	40,000	35,000	40,000
Reserve	N/A	92,000	70,000	70,000
Total Aircraft	609	661	591	632
Fighter	17/311	17/310	16/289	18/390
MiG-21	172	170	102	200
MiG-21H fishbed/MiG-21J Fishbed	?	?	?	160
Combat capable	?	?	?	40
MiG-23	80	90	107	N/A
MiG-25	30	30	30	110
MiG-25 Foxbat	?	?	?	30
MiG-25 Flogger	?	?	?	80
MiG-25U	5	0	0	0
MiG-29	24	20	42	80
MiG-29A Fulcrum A	?	20	42	80
SU-27	0	N/A	8	N/A
FGA	9/148	9/154	9/130	8/136
Su-7	15	0	0	0
Su-17	0	90	50	56
Su-17M	0	90	50	56
Su-22 (Su-17M-2) Fitter D	0	90	50	50
Combat capable	0	?	?	6
Su-20	35	0	0	0
Su-24	0	20	20	20
Su-24 Fencer	0	20	20	20
MiG-17	38	0	0	0
MiG-23B	60	44	60	60
MiG-23BN Flogger H	60	44	60	60
RECCE	6	14	46	8
*MiG-21H/J**	0	8	40	N/A
*MiG-25R Foxbat**	6	6	6	8
Transport	27	29	21	22
An-12	6	0	0	0
An-24 Coke	4	4	N/A	1
An-26 Curl	4	5	4	6
Falcon 20	2	2	2	2
Falcon 900	0	1	1	1
Il-76 Candid	4	4	4	4
PA-31 Navajo	0	N/A	N/A	2
Yu-134	0	6	4	N/A
Yak-40 Codling	7	7	6	6
Training	220	177	81	139

L-29	70	N/A	N/A	N/A
L-39 Albatros*	90	80	23	70
MBB-223 Flamingo (basic)	20	20	35	35
MFI-17 Mushshak	N/A	6	6	6
MiG-17	10	N/A	N/A	N/A
MiG-21U Mongol A*	20	20	20	20
MiG-23UM*	N/A	6	6	6
MiG-25U Foxbat 2*	N/A	5	2	?
MiG-29UB*	N/A	N/A	6	N/A
Su-7U	10	N/A	N/A	N/A
Du-22*	N/A	N/A	6	N/A
Yak-11	Some	N/A	0	0
Helicopter	245	182	174	191
Attack	110	72	36	71
Mi-24	25	N/A	N/A	N/A
Mi-25	35	49	36	36
Mi-25 Hind D	?	49	36	36
SA-342	50	23	Some	35
SA-342L Gazelle	?	23	?	35
Transport	20	N/A	N/A	N/A
Mi-4	10	N/A	N/A	N/A
Mi-6	10	N/A	N/A	N/A
Support	115	110	138	120
Mi-8	60	100	138	100
Mi-17 (Mi-8MT) Hip H/Mi-8 Hip	45	100	138	100
PZL Mi-2 Hoplite	10	10	N/A	20
MSL tactical,	0	Some	Some	Some
ASM	Some	Some	Some	Some
AS-2 Swatter	Some	Some	0	0
AS-7 Kerry	0	Some	Some	Some
AS-10 Karen	0	0	Some	N/A
AS-11 Kilter	0	0	Some	N/A
AS-12	Some	Some	Some	N/A
AS-14 Kedge	0	0	Some	N/A
HOT	Some	Some	Some	Some
AAM	Some	Some	Some	Some
AA-2 Atoll	Some	Some	Some	Some
AA-6 Acrid	Some	Some	Some	Some
AA-7 Apex	Some	Some	Some	Some
AA-8 Aphid	Some	Some	Some	Some
AA-10 Alamo	0	Some	Some	Some

Source: Various editions of the IISS *Military Balance*, U.S., British, and other experts.

so far shown little ability to use such aircraft effectively in training and simulated combat or to generate high sortie rates.

The SAF's other aircraft include 50 Su-22s, around 100 MiG-23 and 60 MiG-23 BNs, 200 MiG-21s, and 110 MiG-25s with 80 MiG-25 Floggers. The exact number in service was unclear.

The bulk of Syria's air defense fighters have poor look-down, shoot-down capabilities and beyond visual range combat capability and still operate largely using obsolete and electronically vulnerable ground-controlled intercept techniques.

Syria does have some UAVs and reconnaissance aircraft, but their sensors were limited and are vulnerable to countermeasures. Some aspects of SAF electronic warfare, electronic support measures, and communications have been modernized in recent years, but the SAF lags far behind Israel and significantly behind Egypt.

Syria had no airborne early warning and electronic intelligence and warfare aircraft that approach Israel's capabilities.

Syrian Rotary-Wing Combat Strength

Syria had some 36 Mi-25s and 35 SA-342ls in service, with up to another 35 in storage. These forces have declined in readiness and sustainability since 1982. They are still largely mission capable, but Syria has been slow to modernize its attack helicopter tactics.

While Syria's attack helicopter tactics were successful in the 1982 war, they were successful largely because the IDF did not expect them and was often trying to rush its advances without adequate coordination. The IDF had now greatly improved its counterattack helicopter training and tactics, arms its helicopters to attack other helicopters, and its antiaircraft systems and light air defense weaponry.

SYRIAN LAND-BASED AIR DEFENSES

As Figure 9.6 shows, Syria has a large separate Air Defense Command with nearly 60,000 personnel. In 2006, its forces were organized into 25 regional brigades and a countrywide total of 150 air defense batteries.

There were two major air defense commands, a North Zone and a South Zone. The defenses were concentrated to protect the south, but Syria had recently redeployed some forces to strengthen the North Zone and defenses against Turkey and Iraq. Some forces were deployed to cover Lebanon.[33]

Syrian Air Defense Weapons

Syrian forces included large numbers of worn obsolete Soviet-bloc systems which have only had limited upgrading. These assets included 11 SA-2 and SA-3 brigades with 60 batteries and some 468 launchers. They included 11 brigades with 27 batteries that were armed with 195 SA-6 launchers and some air defense guns. In addition, there were two regiments that had two battalions with two batteries each, and which were armed with 44 SA-5 and an unspecified number of SA-8 surface-to-air missile launchers. The SA-5s seemed to be deployed near Dumayr, about 40 kilometers east of Damascus, and at Shansur near Homs.

The SA-2 and SA-3 were effectively obsolete. They were hard to move, large enough to be easy to target, and were vulnerable to Israeli, Jordanian, and Egyptian countermeasures. The SA-5 was an obsolescent long-range system whose primary value was to force large, fixed-wing aircraft like Israel's E-2Cs to stand off outside their range. The SA-6 was Syria's only moderately effective long-range system. The SA-8 was a mobile medium-range system that was effective, but limited in capability.

Shorter-Range Syrian Air Defenses

Syria's 160 radar-guided SA-8 fire units are assigned to its air force as part of its Air Defense Command. These systems have low-individual lethality, but help keep attacking aircraft at standoff distances, can degrade the attack profile of aircraft they are fired at, and have some cumulative kill probability.

Syria is keenly aware, however, that Iraqi short-range air defenses proved relatively ineffective in the Gulf War and Iraq Wars and that Israel was now equipped with standoff air-to-ground missiles, high-speed antiradiation missiles, UAVs that can target mobile and concealed systems, and extensive countermeasures.

Syrian Air Defense Training and Readiness

Syria has learned a great deal from the air defense duel Iraqi air defense forces conducted with U.S. and British forces between the end of the Gulf War and the Coalition's invasion in 2003. Some crews and subsystems are well manned and have a high degree of readiness. However, Syria has not modernized its C^4I/BM system to anything approaching a high-capability automated system, and most of its systems required active radar to operate with any lethality. This again makes it forces vulnerable to Israeli antiradiation missiles, target location and identification systems, and electronic warfare capabilities.

While such land-based air defenses can scarcely be disregarded and are certain to both force Israel to conduct a massive air defense suppression campaign and fly attack missions that avoid or minimize exposure to surviving defenses, Syrian air defenses did not have the quality necessary to match their quantity.

Syria's Need for Air Defense Modernization

Syria has badly needed a new type of missile system, and a modernized sensor and command-and-control system to support it, for more than a decade. This is the only way it can develop the range of air defense capabilities it requires. Its SA-2s, SA-3s, SA-6s, SA-5s, and SA-8s are simply vulnerable to active and passive countermeasures.

If Syria is to create the land-based elements of an air defense system capable of dealing with the retaliatory capabilities of the Israeli Air Force, it needs a modern, heavy surface-to-air missile system that is part of an integrated air defense system. Such a system will not be easy for Syria to obtain. No European or Asian power can currently sell Syria either an advanced ground-based air defense system or an advanced heavy surface-to-air missile system. The United States and Russia are the only current suppliers of such systems, and the only surface-to-air missiles that can meet Syria's needs are the Patriot, S-300 series, and S-400.

In practice, Russia has long been Syria's only potential source of the required land-based air defense technology. This explains why Syria has sought to buy the S-300 or S-400 heavy surface-to-air missile/antitactical ballistic missile systems and a next generation warning, command, and control system from Russia for more than ten years.[34]

The SA-10 (also named the Fakel 5300PMU or Grumble) had a range of 90 kilometers or 50 nautical miles. It had a highly sophisticated warning radar, tracking radar, terminal guidance system, and warhead and had good electronic warfare capabilities. The SA-10 is a far more advanced and capable system than the SA-2, SA-3, SA-5, or SA-6.[35]

As is the case with other aspects of Syrian modernization, success has depended on Russian willingness to make such sales in the face of Syria's debt and credit problems. Russia has the capability to provide Syria with the SA-300 or S-400 quickly and in large numbers, as well as to support it with a greatly improved early warning sensor system, and an advanced command-and-control system for both its fighters and land-based air defenses.

Figure 9.6   Syrian Air Defense Command: Force Structure

	1990	2000	2005	2006
Manpower	~60,000	~55,000	~54,200	~60,000
Active	~60,000	~55,000	~54,200	~60,000
AD	640	4,788	4,828	4,707
SAM	392	480	560	148
SA-3 Goa	?/392	?/480	?/560	148
SP	200	200	220	195
SA-6 Gainful	200	200	220	195
TOWED	392	480	560	320
SA-2 Guideline	?/392	?/480	?/560	320
STATIC	48	48	48	44
SA-5 Gammon	48	48	48	44
MANPAD	N/A	4,000	4,000	4,000
SA-7	N/A	?	?	4,000
SA-7A Grail/SA-7B Grail	N/A	?	?	4,000
SA-8	60	N/A	N/A	N/A

Source: Various editions of the IISS *Military Balance,* U.S., British, and other experts.

There have been many reports that Syria has reached an accommodation with Russia, and it seems likely that at some point such reports will prove to be true. Such a Russian-supplied system would, however, still have important limits. Russia had not fully completed integration of the S-300 or S-400 into its own air defenses. It also had significant limitations on its air defense computer technology and relies heavily on redundant sensors and different, overlapping surface-to-air missiles to compensate for a lack of overall system efficiency. A combination of advanced Russian missiles and an advanced sensor and battle management system would still be vulnerable to active and passive attack.

It would take Syria at least three to five years to deploy and integrate such a system fully, once Russia agreed to the sale. Its effectiveness would also depend on Russia's ability to both provide suitable technical training and to adapt a Russian system to the specific topographical and operating conditions of Syria. A Russian system cannot simply be transferred to Syria as an equipment package. It would take a major effort in terms of software, radar deployment, and technology—and considerable adaptation of Russian tactics and sighting concepts—to make such a system fully combat effective. As a result, full-scale modernization of the Syrian land-based air defense system has not occurred thus far and will probably lag well beyond 2010.[36]

SYRIAN NAVAL FORCES

Syria has a small 7,600-man navy, manned largely by conscripts with 18 months of service. It is based in Latakia, Tartous, and Minet el-Baida. Junior naval officers receive training at the Jableh Naval Academy. Senior officers receive training as part of the normal program of the general staff's center at Quabon. Petty officer and enlisted training is conducted at Minet el Baida, Lattakia, and on ship. Syria has some 4,000 naval reserves, but they have little training and war-fighting capability.[37]

The trends in Syrian Naval Forces are shown in Figure 9.7. The navy had 25 surface ships in 2006. It also had three nonoperational Romeo-class submarines transferred by the Soviet Navy in 1985 moored at Tartous.[38] These submarines are out of commission, have no combat capability, and now are little more than potential deathtraps.

Syrian Surface Forces

Syria's only significant surface ships include two obsolete Petya III class frigates. These obsolete 950-ton ships were transferred to Syria by Russia in the mid-1970s. They are equipped with torpedo tubes and rocket launchers, but have no modern air defense capability or antiship missiles. They remain in commission, but they have never been modernized or refitted. Their radars and electronic suites are obsolete and have low capability. Their seagoing status is unclear, they are very poorly maintained, and one may no longer be functional. They are based at Tartous.

The Syrian Navy has two obsolescent Osa I and eight Osa II missile patrol boats dating back to the 1970s. Each is equipped with four SS-N-2 Styx antiship missiles.

Figure 9.7   Syrian Navy: Force Structure

	1990	2000	2005	2006
Manpower	12,000	~10,000	11,600	11,600
Navy	4,000	~6,000	7,600	7,600
Reserve	8,000	4,000	4,000	4,000
Facilities	3	3	3	3
Latakia	1	1	1	1
Tartous	1	1	1	1
Minet el-Baida	1	1	1	1
Submarines	3	3	N/A	N/A
SSK Romeo (nonoperative)	3	3	N/A	N/A
Frigates	2	2	2	2
FF2	2	2	2	2
FSU Petya III	0	0	2	2
Sov Petya II	2	2	0	0
Patrol and Coastal Combatants	18	20	20	20
PFI	6	8	8	8
Zhuk (less than 100 tons)	6	8	8	8
Hamelin (less than 100 tons)	0	2	0	0
PFM	12	10	12	12
Osa I/II	12	10	12	12
Mine warfare	9	5	5	5
MSC	1	1	1	1
Sonya	1	1	1	1
MSI	4	3	3	3
Yevgenya	4	3	3	3
MSO	1	1	1	1
T-43 (FSU)	1	1	1	1
Amphibious	3	3	3	3
Polnochny B	3	3	3	3
Logistics and support	N/A	4	4	4
AGOR	N/A	1	1	1
Support	N/A	1	1	1
Division	N/A	1	1	1
Training	N/A	1	1	1
Naval Aviation	17	48	41	50
Helicopters	5	24	16	25
Attack	5	24	16	25
Anti-Submarine Warfare	0	24	25	25
KA-27	0	4	5	5
Ka-28 (Ka-27PL) Helix A	0	4	5	5
Mi-14	12	20	20	20
Haze	12	20	20	20

Source: Various editions of the IISS *Military Balance*, U.S., British, and other experts.

The Osa Is are not operational. The Osa IIs were transferred to Syria in the late 1970s and early 1980s. Some of the Osa IIs have only limited operational capability, while others are on the edge of being sidelined or may already lack operational capability. These boats have never been modernized or refitted. Syria did, however, partially modernize two of its Osas in the mid-1980s.[39] They are based at Latakia.

Syria had eight light Soviet Zhuk-class patrol boats that the FSU transferred to Syria in the 1980s. These are light 39-ton coastal patrol boasts with little firepower and combat capability. They are capable of 30-knot speeds, however, and do have I-band surface search radars. All are based at Tartous. They are suitable for their undemanding patrol missions, but some are no longer operational.

Syria had five operational FSU-supplied mine warfare craft, including one Natya-class, one T-43, one Sonya, and three Yevgenya-class ships. Only some of these mine craft are operational in the mine warfare mission (although all the operational vessels could release mines.) The three 50-ton Yevgenya-class ships are coastal minesweepers that are relatively modern. Syria has had trouble in operating these ships, however, and has had to cut its force of this class from five to three.

The 804-ton Natya-class vessel had its guns' minesweeping gear removed. It retains its 2X4 SA-N-5 antiaircraft missiles. It is painted white and is now a training and patrol ship. The 450-ton Sonya is a relatively capable wooden hulled ship transferred in the mid-1980s, with adequate equipment and electronics, but may not be operational. The T-43 is a 1950s vintage, iron-hulled ship that has negligible mine warfare capability and does not seem to be operational.

Syrian Amphibious Capability

Syria had three Polnochny-class landing ships with a lift capacity of 100–180 troops, 350 tons of cargo, or five tanks. All are based at Tartous and are active.

Syrian Naval Aviation

The navy has a small naval aviation branch with 25 armed helicopters. These include 20 operational Mi-14P Hazes and five Kamov Ka-28 Helixes, and they were manned with air force operators. The Mi-14s have dipping sonar, radar, and magnetic anomaly detector (MAD), could use sonobuoys, and could launch torpedoes, depth bombs, or mines. The Ka-28s are relatively modern and have dipping sonar, radar, and MAD. They could use sonobuoys, and could launch torpedoes, depth bombs, or mines.

Syrian Coastal Defense Forces

The coastal defense force was placed under naval command in 1984. It had two infantry brigades for coastal surveillance and defense, two artillery brigades with 18 130-mm M-46 coastal guns and around six KS-19 antiaircraft guns. Its main armament consists of 8–12 batteries of aging SSC-1B Sepal and SS-N-2 Styx anti-ship missiles.[40]

Syrian Naval Readiness and Training

The Syrian Navy has negligible ocean going or "blue-water" war-fighting capability. Its primary mission is the defense of Syria's ports at Lattakia and Tartous, coastal surveillance and defense, and peacetime patrol missions. Its major bases are at Banias, Mina el Beida, Lattakia, and Tartous, with small marine detachments at Banias, Lattakia, and Tartous. There were scuba and undersea defense technology units at Mina el Beida. Most surface forces were based at Lattakia and Tartous, and the submarines at Tartous.[41]

Overall readiness, training, and funding levels are low. The Syrian Navy rarely practices meaningful exercises, has almost no joint warfare training, and has little war-fighting capability against either Israel or Turkey.[42] It is largely a coastal surveillance and patrol force.

SYRIAN PARAMILITARY, SECURITY, AND INTELLIGENCE FORCES

Like Egypt, Syria has a large mix of paramilitary forces. These forces are shown in Figure 9.8. These forces have little or no military value, but do serve as effective

Figure 9.8   Syrian Paramilitary and Security Forces: Force Structure

	1990	2000	2005	2006
Manpower	19,800	~108,000	~108,000	~108,000
Gendarmerie	8,000	8,000	8,000	8,000
Workers' Militia (People's Army)	N/A	~100,000	~100,000	~100,000
Desert Guard	1,800	N/A	N/A	N/A
Republican Guard	10,000	N/A	N/A	N/A
Forces Abroad	30,000	23,179	17,179	N/A
Lebanon	30,000	22,000	16,000	N/A
Mechanized Division HQ	1	1	1	N/A
Element armored	1	1	1	N/A
Mechanized Infantry Brigade	2	4	4	N/A
Element of Special Forces	8	10	10	N/A
Artillery Regiment	0	2	2	N/A
Foreign Forces	37,500	1,179	1,179	150
Russian Army	3,000	~150	~150	150
UNDOF	1,400	1,029	1,029	N/A
Austria (UNDOF)	?	428	364	N/A
Canada (UNDOF)	?	183	186	N/A
Finland (UNDOF)	?	0	0	0
Japan (UNDOF)	0	30	30	N/A
Norway (UNDOF)	0	N/A	1	N/A
Poland (UNDOF)	?	353	356	N/A
Slovakia (UNDOF)	0	35	92	N/A

Source: Various editions of the IISS *Military Balance*, U.S., British, and other experts.

instruments of state control, and they helped Syria secure its occupation of Lebanon before Syrian forces had to withdraw in 2005.[43]

Syrian security and intelligence forces have been willing to take major risks in the past, and they have supported terrorist and militia forces in covert attacks against Israel and against the United States and its allies in Lebanon after they deployed to that country in 1982. They have covertly supported a number of the Sunni insurgent elements in Iraq since 2003 and have joined Iran in supporting Hezbollah. They played a major role in the assassination of Prime Minister Harriri in 2005.

Syrian security forces are notorious for their repressiveness, although their operations are generally focused on actual opponents of the regime. Ordinary Syrians are well aware of the security forces, but rarely see them in operation. The services do, however, often conduct operations against citizens with Kurdish ethnicity or suspected ties to the Muslim Brotherhood and other Islamic organizations. The U.S. State Department report on terrorism issued in April 2005 summarizes their conduct as follows:[44]

> The Syrian Government in 2004 continued to provide political and material support to both Lebanese Hezbollah and Palestinian terrorist groups. Hamas, Palestinian Islamic Jihad (PIJ), the Popular Front for the Liberation of Palestine (PFLP) and the Popular Front for the Liberation of Palestine-General Command (PFLP-GC), among others, continue to operate from Syria, although they have lowered their public profiles since May 2003, when Damascus announced that the groups had voluntarily closed their offices. Many of these Palestinian groups, in statements originating from both inside and outside of Syria, claimed responsibility for anti-Israeli terrorist attacks in 2004. The Syrian Government insists that these Damascus based offices undertake only political and informational activities. Syria also continued to permit Iran to use Damascus as a transshipment point for resupplying Lebanese Hezbollah in Lebanon.
>
> Syrian officials have publicly condemned international terrorism, but make a distinction between terrorism and what they consider to be the legitimate armed resistance of Palestinians in the occupied territories and of Lebanese Hezbollah. The Syrian Government has not been implicated directly in an act of terrorism since 1986, although Israeli officials accused Syria of being indirectly involved in the August 31, 2004, Beersheva bus bombings that left 16 dead. Damascus has cooperated with the United States and other foreign governments against al-Qa'ida and other terrorist organizations and individuals; it also has discouraged signs of public support for al-Qa'ida, including in the media and at mosques.
>
> In September 2004, Syria hosted border security discussions with the Iraqis and took a number of measures to improve the physical security of the border and establish security cooperation mechanisms. Although these and other efforts by the Syrian Government have been partly successful, more must be done in order to prevent the use of Syrian territory by those individuals and groups supporting the insurgency in Iraq.

The updated U.S. State Department report issued in April 2006 was little different, highlighting Syria's spoiler role in the region and growing problems with its own internal security:[45]

> The Syrian Government insists that the Damascus-based groups undertake only political and informational activities. However, in statements originating from outside Syria,

many Palestinian groups claimed responsibility for anti-Israeli terrorist acts. Syria's public support for the groups varied, depending on its national interests and international pressure. In 2003, these groups lowered their public profile after Damascus announced that they had voluntarily closed their offices in Syria. In September, however, Syrian President Bashar al-Asad held a highly publicized meeting with rejectionist leaders, and a month later the rejectionist leaders participated in a meeting in Damascus with the Speaker of the Iranian Parliament, Gholam Ali Haddad Adel. Syria continued to permit Iran to use Damascus as a transshipment point to resupply Hizballah in Lebanon.

. . . preliminary findings of a UN investigation into the February assassination of former Lebanese Prime Minister Rafik Hariri have indicated a strong likelihood of official Syrian involvement.

In the past, Damascus cooperated with the United States and other foreign governments against al-Qa'ida and other terrorist organizations and individuals. In May, however, the Syrian Government ended intelligence cooperation, citing continued U.S. public complaints about the inadequate level of Syria's assistance to end the flow of fighters and money to Iraq.

Syria made efforts to limit the movement of foreign fighters into Iraq. It upgraded physical security conditions on the border and announced that it has begun to give closer scrutiny to military-age Arab males entering Syria (visas are still not required for citizens of Arab countries). The government claimed that since 2003 it has repatriated more than 1,200 foreign extremists and arrested more than 4,000 Syrians trying to go to Iraq to fight.

In the last six months of 2005, Damascus highlighted clashes on Syrian territory with terrorist groups, particularly with the Jund a-Sham group associated with Abu Musab al-Zarqawi, in its government-controlled press information.

The human rights country report issued by the U.S. State Department in February 2005 provides additional data and a summary of how repressive Syria's forces can be:[46]

The powerful role of the security services, which extends beyond strictly security matters, is due to the state of emergency, which has been in place since 1963. The Government justifies ongoing martial law because of its state of war with Israel and past threats from terrorist groups. Syrian Military Intelligence and Air Force Intelligence are military agencies; the Ministry of Interior controls general security, state security, and political security. The branches of the security services operated independently of each other and outside the legal system. The Government maintained effective control of the security forces, and members of the security forces committed numerous, serious human rights abuses.

. . . There are four major branches of security: Political Security Directorate (PSD); Syrian Military Intelligence (SMI); General Intelligence Directorate (GID); and Air Force Security (AFS), all of which devote some of their overlapping resources to monitoring internal dissent and individual citizens. Only PSD, supervised by the Ministry of Interior, is under civilian control. The four branches operate independently and generally outside of the control of the legal system.

. . . The Government prevented any organized political opposition, and there have been few antigovernment manifestations. Continuing serious abuses included the use of torture in detention, which at times resulted in death; poor prison conditions;

arbitrary arrest and detention; prolonged detention without trial; fundamentally unfair trials in the security courts; and infringement on privacy rights. The Government significantly restricted freedom of speech and of the press. The Government also severely restricted freedom of assembly and association. The Government did not officially allow independent domestic human rights groups to exist. The Government placed some limits on freedom of religion and freedom of movement. Violence and societal discrimination against women were problems. The Government's discrimination against the stateless Kurdish minority resulted in a series of riots in March centered in the Hassakeh province which spread to other parts of the country during which more than 30 persons were reportedly killed by security forces and more than 1000 arrested. The Government also restricted worker rights.

...The Ministry of Interior controlled the police forces, which consist of four separate divisions: emergency police; local neighborhood police; riot police; and traffic police. The emergency division responds to 911 calls and operates through roving patrols. The local neighborhood police are responsible for general security in the neighborhood they patrol and respond to non-emergency situations. The Government uses the riot police to break up demonstrations and marches.

During the year, the security forces again conducted mass arrests of suspected Islamists: 25 in Hama; 18 in Hayaleen; 19 in Qatana; and an unknown number in Damascus and Aleppo. In March, the Supreme State Security Court (SSSC) sentenced 33 persons to 2 years in prison who had been arrested in Aleppo in August 2003 and accused of belonging to the Muslim Brotherhood. The suspects remained in detention at year's end.

In April, military security arrested the human rights activist Aktham Naiissa, head of the Committee for the Defense of Democracy, Freedom, and Human Rights (CDF), for his involvement in a protest in front of the Parliament in March and for communiqués issued by the CDF critical of the Government's treatment of the Kurdish minority (see Section 2.b.). Naiissa was held at Saidnaya prison without access to his lawyer and was tried by the SSSC; he was released on bail in August. His trial has been postponed twice, and it is now scheduled for April 4, 2005.

Throughout the year, the security services also conducted mass arrests of Kurds in Hassakeh province, Aleppo, Damascus, and other areas. Human rights organizations and Kurdish groups reported that 1,000–2,000 Kurds were detained in the aftermath of the March riots. Most were freed after a few months detention; however, 200–300 Kurds remain in custody and are awaiting trial at the SSSC and military courts

...Media sources reported that in April, security forces increasingly staged nighttime raids on Kurdish homes in Hassakeh province and arbitrarily arrested male members of households. Press reports also stated that on April 8, following a dispute between Kurdish children and Arab students at a school in Qamishli, security forces took four school children, ages 12 and 13, from the school during the day and transferred them to a prison in Hassakeh. At year's end, the children were reportedly still detained.

...The Government, through its security services, also threatened families or friends of detainees to ensure their silence, to force them to disavow publicly their relatives, or to force detainees into compliance. For example, the family of a human rights activist received numerous calls from security service personnel alleging misconduct and inappropriate social behavior by the activist. These calls continued during the year and became increasingly threatening.

The number of remaining political detainees was unknown. AI's 2003 report stated that 800 political detainees were held in Saidnaya prison and that hundreds of others were held in other prisons. There also were Jordanian, Lebanese, and Palestinian political detainees. Estimates of detainees were difficult to confirm because the branches of the security services, which maintain their own prison facilities, hold a large number of prisoners. These prisoners are frequently held for extended periods of time without trial and without information given to their families. Estimates were also difficult to confirm because the Government did not verify publicly the number of detentions without charge, the release of detainees or amnestied prisoners, or whether detainees subsequently were sentenced to prison...

The Constitution provides for an independent judiciary; however, the Supreme State Security Court (SSSC), in dealing with cases of alleged national security violations, was not independent of executive branch control. Political connections and bribery sometimes influenced verdicts in regular courts.

The SSSC tried political and national security cases and operated under the provisions of the Emergency Law. The SSSC did not observe the constitutional provisions safeguarding defendants' rights. The Emergency Law and the Penal Code are so broad and vague, and the Government's powers so sweeping, that many persons have been convicted and many remain in prison for the mere expression of political opposition to the Government. In April 2001, the U.N. Commission on Human Rights stated that the procedures of the SSSC are incompatible with the provisions of the International Covenant on Civil and Political Rights, to which the country is a party.

Charges against defendants before the SSSC were vague. Defendants appeared to be tried for exercising normal political rights, such as free speech. For example, the Emergency Law authorizes the prosecution of anyone "opposing the goals of the revolution," "shaking the confidence of the masses in the aims of the revolution," or attempting to "change the economic or social structure of the State." The Government stated that the SSSC tries only persons who have sought to use violence against the State, but the majority of defendants who appeared before the SSSC this year were prosecuted for exercising their political rights.

Under SSSC procedures, defendants were not present during the preliminary or investigative phase of the trial, during which the prosecutor presents evidence. Trials usually were closed to the public. Lawyers were not ensured access to their clients before the trial and were excluded from the court during their client's initial interrogation by the prosecutor. Lawyers submitted written defense pleas rather than making oral presentations.

During the year, there was one case in which a lawyer representing defendants in a national security case had his license to practice law suspended. The Government's case was based on confessions, and the defendants were not allowed to argue that their confessions were coerced.

On July 11, the SSSC acquitted for lack of evidence a Syrian-Canadian citizen arrested in 2002 when he returned home to Syria to visit his family. The individual was charged with belonging to a religious group and was reportedly tortured while in detention (see Section 1.c.).

Defendants did not have the right to appeal verdicts, but the Minister of Interior, who may ratify, nullify, or alter them, reviews sentences. The President also may intervene in the review process.

Accurate information regarding the number of cases heard by the SSSC was difficult to obtain, although hundreds of cases were believed to pass through the court annually. Many cases reportedly involved charges relating to membership in various banned political groups, including religious parties such as the Muslim Brotherhood, the Islamic Liberation Party, the Party of Communist Action, Syrian Kurdish Parties and the pro-Iraqi wing of the Ba'ath Party. Sentences as long as 15 years have been imposed in the past. Human rights NGOs were not permitted to visit the SSSC; however, local lawyers affiliated with local NGOs acted as defense counsel in some cases (see Section 4).

...Military courts have the authority to try civilians as well as military personnel. A military prosecutor decides the venue for a civilian defendant. There have been reports that the Government operated military field courts in locations outside established courtrooms. Such courts reportedly observed fewer of the formal procedures of regular military courts.

...Corruption continued to be a serious problem throughout the police forces and security services. International and regional human rights groups continue to consider the police forces corrupt.

The report issued in 2006 was very similar, although it highlighted Syria's role in assassinating Lebanese Prime Minister Rafik Hariri, its use of torture, and provided a long chronology of Syrian actions to suppress all political dissent.[47]

On October 19 and December 12, Chief Investigator for the UN International Independent Investigation Commission (UNIIIC) Detlev Mehlis presented two interim reports on the February 14 assassination of former Lebanese prime minister Rafiq al-Hariri to UN Secretary-General Kofi Annan. Hariri and 22 other individuals killed in a blast in central Beirut. The October report concluded that evidence pointed toward the involvement of Syrian authorities in the assassination of al-Hariri. The report also made it clear that Syrian officials, while purporting to cooperate, deliberately misled investigators. In response to the UN report, citizens rallied in front of the Central Bank in Damascus on October 24, protesting its findings (see section 2.b), and in smaller demonstrations throughout November and early December. The December report stated that the ongoing investigation reinforced the conclusions of the October report and requested a six-month extension, noting Syrian authorities' "reluctance and procrastination" and citing its attempt to "hinder the investigation internally and procedurally." The UN Security Council passed Security Resolution 1644 on December 15, extending the UNIIIC's mandate.

...Former prisoners, detainees, and reputable local human rights groups, reported that torture methods included electrical shocks; pulling out fingernails; burning genitalia; forcing objects into the rectum; beating, sometimes while the victim was suspended from the ceiling; alternately dousing victims with freezing water and beating them in extremely cold rooms; hyperextending the spine; bending the detainees into the frame of a wheel and whipping exposed body parts; and using a backward-bending chair to asphyxiate the victim or fracture the victim's spine. Torture was most likely to occur while detainees were held at one of the many detention centers operated by the various security services throughout the country, particularly while authorities attempted to extract a confession or information.

The details of Syria's intelligence forces are not shown in Figure 9.8, but are equally notorious for their operations in Lebanon, and support of operations like assassinations and insurgent infiltration into Iraq (and previously Jordan.) This is particularly true of Syrian Air Force intelligence

Syrian military and civil intelligence cooperates with Iran in supporting Hezbollah. It has also long supported those Palestinian movements, including Hamas, that Syria believes it can use as leverage against Israel.

SYRIAN WEAPONS OF MASS DESTRUCTION

Syria has long sought missiles and weapons of mass destruction to match Israel's capabilities. In practice, however, it has never had the resources or technology base to compete with Israel or to develop a meaningful nuclear weapons effort.

Figure 9.9 summarizes current reporting on Syrian weapons of mass destruction. Like the previous figures dealing with Israeli and Egyptian weapons of mass destruction, the data are often speculative. It is clear, however, that Syria has pursued the updating of its surface-to-surface missiles in spite of all of its resource constraints and has given such forces high priority.

Figure 9.9 Syria's Search for Weapons of Mass Destruction

Delivery Systems

- Four SSM brigades: 1 with FROG, 1 with Scud Bs, 1 with Scud Cs, and 1 with SS-21s.

- Has 18 SS-21 launchers and at least 36 SS-21 missiles with 80–100-kilometer range. May be developing chemical warheads.

- According to the May 1998 estimate of the Center for Nonproliferation Studies at the Monterey Institute of International Studies, Syria possessed 200 SS-21 Scarab missiles.[48]

- Some experts believe some Syrian surface-to-surface missiles armed with chemical weapons began to be stored in concrete shelters in the mountains near Damascus and in the Palmyra region no later than 1986 and that plans have long existed to deploy them forward in an emergency since that date.

- Up to 12 Scud-B launchers and 200 Scud-B missiles with 310-kilometer range. Believed to have chemical warheads. Scud-B warhead weighs 985 kilograms. The inventory of Scud-B missiles is believed to be approximately 200.

- The Monterey Institute of International Studies' Center for Nonproliferation Studies reports that the Chinese provided technical assistance to upgrade Scud-B missiles in 1993.[49]

- New long-range North Korean Scud Cs deployed.

  - *Jane's* cites an American Department of Defense document published in 1992 alleging that Syria had purchased 150 Scud-C missiles.

  - Two brigades of 18 launchers each are said to be deployed in a horseshoe shaped valley. This estimate of 36 launchers is based on the fact there are 36 tunnels into the hillside. The launchers must be for the Scud C since the older Scud Bs would not be within range of most of Israel. Up to 50 missiles are stored in bunkers to the north as possible reloads. There is a maintenance building and barracks.

- Underground bunkers are thought to have sufficient storage for some 1,000 Scud-C missiles according to a fall 2002 article in the *Middle East Quarterly.*[50]
- Estimates indicate that Syria has 24–36 Scud launchers for a total of 260–300 missiles of all types. The normal ratio of launchers to missiles is 10:1, but Syria is focusing on both survivability and the capability to launch a large preemptive strike.
- The Scud Cs have ranges of up to 550–600 kilometers. They have a circular error probable (CEP) of 1,000–2,600 meters. Nerve gas warheads using VX with cluster bomblets seem to have begun production in early 1997. Syria is believed to have 50–80 Scud-C missiles.
- A training site exists about 6 kilometers south of Hama, with an underground facility where transporter-erector-launchers (TELs) and missiles are stored.
- *Jane's* reports that "[i]t was reported in early 1998 that Israeli intelligence experts had estimated that there were between 24 and 36 'Scud' launchers at most Syrian missile sites —far more launchers than previously estimated." Traditionally, armies deploying Scuds stock about ten missiles per launcher. The higher number of Syrian launchers suggests a ratio closer to two missiles per launcher—this would enable Syria to launch a large first-wave strike before launchers were destroyed.
- Syria can now build both the entire Scud B and Scud C. It has sheltered and/or underground missile production/assembly facilities at Aleppo, Hama, and near Damascus, which have been built with aid from Chinese, Iranian, and North Korean technicians. Possibly some Russian technical aid.
- Israeli defense officials have been reported as stating that Syria has been producing about 30 Scud-C missiles per year at an underground facility.[51]
- A missile test site exists 15 kilometers south of Homs where Syria has tested missile modifications and new chemical warheads. It has heavy perimeter defenses, a storage area and bunkers, heavily sheltered bunkers, and a missile storage area just west of the site. According to some reports, Syria has built two missile plants near Hama, about 110 miles north of Damascus; one is for solid fueled rockets and the other is for liquid fueled systems. North Korea may have provided the equipment for the liquid fuel plant, and Syria may now be able to produce the missile.
- Reports of Chinese deliveries of missiles but little hard evidence:
  - Reports of People's Republic of China's (PRC) deliveries of missile components by China Precision Machinery Company, maker of the M-11, in July 1996. The M-11 has a 186-mile (280-kilometer) range with a warhead of 1,100 pounds. Missile components may have included "contained sensitive guidance equipment."[52]
- All reports of Syrian purchases and production of Chinese M-9 missiles are unconfirmed and of uncertain value:
  - Some sources believe M-9 missile components, or M-9-like components, delivered to Syria. Missile is reported to have a CEP as low as 300 meters.
  - Some intelligence reports indicate that 24 M-9 launchers were sighted in late 1991.[53] Other reports suggest that the 1991 missile deliveries were subsequently cancelled due to U.S. pressure.
  - "Since 1989 there have been persistent rumors that Syria was trying to import the M-9 form [from] China. Up to the mid-1990s, Israeli sources believed that these attempts

ended in failure—Beijing reportedly backed out of the deal due to US pressure. The reports surfaced again in the late 1990s, with suggestions that the M-9 had been delivered from China—possibly in kit form, or partly assembled."

- *Jane's* reported in March 1999 that Syria had created a production facility to build both the M-11 (CSS-7/DF-11) and M-9 missiles with ranges of 280 and 600–800 kilometers, respectively. It reports that production of the booster stage of the M-11 began in 1996 and that missile production is expected to start "soon."

- An April 1993 report in *Jane's Intelligence Review* indicated that North Korea and Iran (with Chinese assistance) helped in the construction of underground production facilities for the Scud-C and M-9 missiles. At the time of the article (April 1993), production of the Scud C was believed to be 12–18 months off, while M-9 production was believed to be 2–3 years away.[54]

- Senior administration officials were quoted as stating that China had sold missile technology to Syria. By mid-1992, 30–90 tons of chemicals for solid propellant were sold to Syria.[55]

- Syria has also developed, with considerable North Korean assistance, a Syrian version of the Korean No Dong (sometimes referred to as the Scud D).

  - A number of sources reported the September 23, 2000, test flight of the Syrian No Dong.

  - Four tunnels for shelters for No Dong launchers have been excavated, as of late 2002.[56]

  - Syria expected to produce or have already started production at the rate of about 30 missiles per year.[57]

  - Israeli officials claimed that Syria was developing "multiple warhead clusters" in a bid to defeat Israel's Arrow missile defense system.[58]

- The Center for Nonproliferation Studies at the Monterey Institute of International Studies has compiled a chronology of North Korean assistance to Syria through 2000:[59]

Date	Item(s)	Remarks
1991 March	24 Scud Cs and 20 TELs	Syria pays approximately $250 million, and Libya reportedly helps finance transaction.
1991 April	60 Scud Cs and 12 TELs	First delivery after agreement for Syria to acquire 150 Scud Cs for an estimated $500 million.
1991 May	36 Scud Cs	Missiles transported by Yugoslavian freighter.
1991 summer	Unknown number of Scud Cs	Missiles delivered by North Korean ship *Mupo* and transferred to Syria via Cyprus.
1992	24 Scud-C missiles; missile-production and assembly equipment	Delivered by North Korean freighter *Tae Hung Ho* in March. Part of the shipment was airlifted to Syria via the Iranian port of Bandar Abbas, and the remaining cargo was transported directly to the Tartous. The manufacturing equipment reportedly destined for suspected missile factories in Hama and Aleppo.

1992	Approximately 50 Scud Cs	A North Korean ship carrying 100 Scud Cs departs for the Iranian port Bandar Abbas in October. Half of the delivery transported overland to Syria.
1993	Seven MAZ 543 chassis and unknown number of Scud Cs	In August, two Russian Condor aircraft transport the missiles and chassis from Sunan International Airport to Damascus. According to Israeli Foreign Minister Shimon Peres, North Korea offered to stop the delivery if Israel paid $500 million.
1994	Unknown number of Scud-C missiles and TELs	
1994	Unknown number of Scud-C cluster warheads	
1996	Missile expertise	Syrian missile technicians spend two weeks training in North Korea.
1999	10 tons of powdered aluminum	Originally from China, shipment delivered to the Centre des Etudes de Recherche Scientifique, the institute in charge of Syria's missile program.
2000	Scud-D missile	Unconfirmed; Syria conducted Scud-D flight test on September 23, 2000.
2000	No Dong missiles and TELs	Unconfirmed; North Korean firm Ch'ongchon'gang reportedly delivers 50 No Dong missiles and seven TELs to Syria. Missiles possibly procured on behalf of Iraq, Egypt, and Libya for $600 million.

- Sheltered or underground missile production/assembly facilities at Aleppo and Hamas have been built with aid from Chinese, Iranian, and North Korean technicians. Possibly some Russian technical aid.

- A missile test site exists 15 kilometers south of Homs where Syria has tested missile modifications and new chemical warheads. It has heavy perimeter defenses, a storage area and bunkers, heavily sheltered bunkers, and a missile storage area just west of the site.

  - Syria has shorter range systems:

  - Short-range M-1B missiles (up to a 60-mile range) seem to be in delivery from PRC.

  - SS-N-3, and SSC-1b cruise missiles.

- May be converting some long-range surface-to-air and naval cruise missiles to use chemical warheads.

- 20 Su-24 long-range strike fighters.

- 44 operational MiG-23BN Flogger F fighter ground attack aircraft.

- 20 Su-20 fighter ground-attack aircraft.

- 90 Su-22 fighter ground-attack aircraft.[60]

- 18 FROG-7 launchers and rockets.

- Negotiations for PRC-made M-9 missile (185–375-mile range).
- Multiple rocket launchers and tube artillery.
- Syria thought to be interested in purchasing Russia's Iskander-E (SS-X-26) ballistic missile when once it has finished development.[61]
- Syria has improved its targeting capability in recent years by making extensive direct and indirect use of commercial satellite imagery, much of which now offers 3-meter levels of resolution and comes with coordinate data with near GPS-like levels of accuracy. One-meter levels of resolution will become commercially available.
- The CIA estimated in January 1999 that Syria continued work on establishing a solid-propellant rocket motor development and production capability. Foreign equipment and assistance have been and will continue to be essential for this effort.

Chemical Weapons (CW)

- First acquired small amounts of chemical weapons from Egypt in 1973.
- Began production of nonpersistent nerve gas in 1984. May have had chemical warheads for missiles as early as 1985.
- Experts believe has stockpiled 500 to 1,000 metric tons of chemical agents. Holdings thought to include persistent (VX) and nonpersistent nerve agents (Sarin) as well as blister agents.
- Believed to have begun deploying VX in late 1996, early 1997.
  - CIA reported in June 1997 that Syria had acquired new chemical weapons technology from Russia and eastern Europe in 1996.
  - Unconfirmed reports of sheltered Scud missiles with unitary Sarin or Tabun nerve gas warheads, now being replaced by cluster warheads with VX bomblets, deployed in caves and shelters near Damascus.
  - Tested Scuds in manner indicating possible chemical warheads in 1996.
  - Seems to have cluster warheads and bombs.
  - May have VX and Sarin in modified Soviet ZAB-incendiary bombs and PTAB-500 cluster bombs. Reports stated that U.S. intelligence source had obtained information indicating a late October 1999 test of a live chemical bomb dropped by a Syrian MiG-23.[62]
- Acquired design for Soviet Scud warhead using VX in 1970s.
- Major nerve gas, and possible other chemical agent production facilities north of Damascus. Two to three plants.
  - One facility is located near Homs and is located next to a major petrochemical plant. It reportedly produces several hundred tons of nerve gas a year.
  - Reports show building new major plant at Safira, near Aleppo.
  - Reports that a facility co-located with the Center d'Etdues et de Recherche Scientifique (CERS) is developing a warhead with chemical bomblets for the Scud C.

- Many parts of the program are dispersed and compartmented. Missiles, rockets, bombs, and artillery shells are produced/modified and loaded in other facilities. Many may be modified to use VX bomblets.
- Wide range of delivery systems:
  - Extensive testing of chemical warheads for Scud Bs. May have tested chemical warheads for Scud Cs. Recent tests include a July 2001 test of a Scud B near Aleppo and a May 1998 test of a Scud C with a VX warhead near Damascus.
  - Shells, bombs, and nerve gas warheads for multiple rocket launchers.
  - FROG warheads may be under development.
  - Reports of SS-21 capability to deliver chemical weapons are not believed by U.S. or Israeli experts.
  - Israeli sources believe Syria has binary weapons and cluster bomb technology suitable for delivering chemical weapons.
- The CIA estimated in January 1999 that Syria continued to seek CW-related precursors from various sources during the reporting period. Damascus already has a stockpile of the nerve agent Sarin and may be trying to develop more toxic and persistent nerve agents. Syria remains dependent on foreign sources for key elements of its CW program, including precursor chemicals and key production equipment.
- The CIA stated that Chinese entities sought to supply Iran and Syria with CW-related chemicals during this reporting period.

Biological Weapons

- Signed, but not ratified the 1972 Biological and Toxin Weapons Convention. Extensive research effort.
- U.S. State Department, Bureau of Arms Control report in August 1996 indicated that "it is highly probable that Syria is developing an offensive biological capability."
- Extensive research effort. Reports of one underground facility and one near the coast.
- Probable production capability for anthrax and botulism, and possibly other agents.
- Israeli sources claim Syria weaponized botulinum and ricin toxins in early 1990s, and probably anthrax.
- Limited indications may be developing or testing biological variations on ZAB-incendiary bombs and PTAB-500 cluster bombs and Scud warheads.
- Major questions exist regarding Syria's strike capabilities. Older types of biological weapons using wet agents, and placed in older bomb and warhead designs with limited dissemination capability, can achieve only a small fraction of the potential effectiveness of biological weapons. Dry micropowders using advanced agents—such as the most lethal forms of anthrax—can have the effectiveness of small theater nuclear weapons. It is difficult to design adequate missile warheads to disseminate such agents, but this is not beyond Syrian capabilities—particularly since much of the technology needed to make effective cluster munitions and bomblets for VX gas can be adapted to the delivery of biological weapons.[63]

- The design of biological bombs and missile warheads with the lethality of small nuclear weapons may now be within Syrian capabilities, as is the design of UAV, helicopter, cruise missile, or aircraft-borne systems to deliver the agent slowly over a long line of flight and taking maximum advance of wind and weather conditions. U.S. and Soviet texts proved that this kind of "line source" delivery could achieve lethalities as high as 50–100 kiloton weapons by the late 1950s, and the technology is well within Syria's grasp. So is the use of proxy or covert delivery.

- According to CIA estimates, it is considered "highly probably [probable] that Syria also is developing an offensive BW capability."[64]

Nuclear Weapons

- Ongoing research effort.
- No evidence of major progress in development effort.
- Announced nuclear reactor purchase plans including 10 megawatt research reactor from Argentina. Discussions with Argentina were resumed in the mid-1990s, but plans to build a Syrian reactor were scrapped under U.S. pressure.
- Syria tried to obtain six power reactors (for a total of 6,000 megawatts of generating capacity) in 1980s from a number of countries, including the Soviet Union, Belgium, and Switzerland, but plans were never implemented.
- The Center for Nonproliferation Studies at the Monterey Institute of International Studies quotes a *Jane's Intelligence Review* article from 1993 claiming Syria attempted to purchase "large (thousand ton) quantities" of yellowcake from Namibia.[65]
- In December 1991 Syria purchased a 30-kilowatt neutron-source research reactor from China; the reactor is not suitable for weapons production. The Atomic Energy Commission of Syria received 980.4 grams of 90.2 percent enriched Uranium 235 as part of the deal.
- Russia and Syria have approved a draft of a plan for cooperation on civil nuclear power, which is expected to provide opportunities for Syria to expand its indigenous nuclear capabilities.[66] Reports surfaced in January 2003 indicating that Syria and Russia had reached an agreement on the construction of a $2-billion facility which would include a nuclear reactor. Although within several days, Russian Foreign Ministry officials had indicated that no reactor would be sold.[67]

Missile Defenses

- Seeking Russian S-300 or S-400 surface-to-air missile system with limited antitactical ballistic missile capability.

Syrian Progress in Weapons Development

Syria has chemical weapons, and most experts believe it has mustard agents and at least ordinary nerve gas. It may have persistent nerve gas as well. It is believed to have cluster warheads for delivering chemical weapons, and it probably has chemical bombs and rocket warheads as well. It may have chemical artillery shells.

There are reports that Syria imported hundreds of tons of hydrochloric acid and ethylene glycol-MEG from Iran. These chemical agents are precursors for the production of mustard blister agents and Sarin nerve gas. The precursors are going to be used and mounted on Scud-B/C warheads and/or on aerial bombs. Construction of the chemical facilities is due to start in late 2005 with construction estimated at taking one year. Thereafter production of precursors will start in Syria and the Syrian dependence on Iran for chemical agents will diminish if not disappear completely.[68]

There are also reports that Syria has recently benefited from sales and technology transfers by Iran. These reports indicate that Syria is undertaking "an innovative chemical warfare (CW) program in cooperation with Iran." Syria's CW program began in the mid-1970's and its facilities are known to have successfully produced VX and Sarin nerve agents as well as mustard blister agents, but not independently. The Scientific Studies and Research Center (CERS) runs the facilities in Dumayr, Khan Abou, Shamat, and Furklus.[69]

The same reports indicate that no contract has yet been signed, but that the draft agreements would lead Iranian scientists from the Iranian Defense Industries Organization to assist Syria in establishing the infrastructure and location of the new chemical facilities. It will also supply Syria with reactors, pipes, condensers, heat exchangers, and storage and feed tanks, as well as chemical detection equipment for airborne agents. Then Iran will assist in producing and piloting the first four or five CW facilities throughout Syria, producing precursors for VX and Sarin nerve agents and mustard blister agents.

Syria may be working on biological weapons. The nature of its progress, if any, is unclear.

As for delivery systems, some sources have reported that Syria has tried to upgrade its missile forces by buying the Russian SS-X-26 or Iskander E missile from Russia. The missile has a maximum range of 280–300 kilometers and could hit Israeli cites like Haifa, Jerusalem, and Tel Aviv. Unlike Syria's present missiles, the SS-X-26 is solid fueled and could improve Syria's ability to rapidly disperse its missiles and fire without delays for fueling or preparation. So far, however, Russia seems to have rejected such sales, as well as the sale of new surface-to-air missiles that might be converted for such use.[70]

The SS-X-26 is believed to be a replacement for both the Scud and the SS-23, which had to be abandoned as a result of the intermediate-range ballistic missile treaty. It is a mobile system mounted on a tracked TEL that can carry two missiles. Work by the Federation of American Scientists (FAS) indicates that it is a high-technology system that could have a cluster munition warhead, a fuel-air explosive enhanced-blast warhead, a tactical earth penetrator for bunker busting, and an electromagnetic pulse device for antiradar missions. It does, however, have a small 480-kilogram warhead, and the FAS indicates it would need advanced terminal precision guidance. It speculates that this could be provided by using an "active terminal sensor such as a millimeter wave radar, satellite terminal guidance using GLOSNASS, an improved inertial platform, or some combination of these approaches."[71]

The only major positive recent development in Syria capabilities is that Syria fired three Scud missiles in 2005 which all seem to have been tested in an "airburst" mode where the warheads might be using cluster munitions that could carry chemical or biological weapons. One was an older Scud B, with a range of about 300 kilometers, but two were the improved No Dong missiles sometimes called the Scud D, with a range of up to 700 kilometers. There are also some analysts who still feel Syria might have acquired Iraq's weapons of mass destruction when Saddam Hussein had them smuggled out of Iraq before the U.S.–led invasion. Such reporting is anecdotal and so far has little credibility.

Possible Syrian Strategy, Tactics, and Employment

Various experts have postulated that Syria could use its chemical and possibly biological weapons against Israel or any other neighbor in range as terror weapons, and they see them as at least a partial deterrent to Israeli strikes with weapons of mass destruction in anything other than an existential conflict.

Other experts have suggested that Syria might use chemical weapons against Israeli army forces as they mobilized to support a surprise attack on the Golan, on Israel's weapons of mass destruction, or in attacks on some other critical Israeli target or facility. There have also been suggestions that Syria might attempt covert attacks or use a terrorist or other proxy.

It is impossible to dismiss such possibilities, and there are no reliable unclassified sources on Syrian doctrine, plans, or intentions for using weapons of mass destruction. Syria does, however, face the fact that any such attack might be seen as the prelude to a Syrian attack on Israeli population centers and that a mass attack producing high lethality against Israel's mobilization centers would probably be viewed as being too unacceptable for Israel to ignore.

As little is known about Israeli plans and doctrine as Syrian. However, given Israel's past actions, the response might well be Israeli massive retaliation with a mix of air and missile strikes designed to destroy much of Syria's continuity of government, military facilities and capabilities, and economy and infrastructure. A major Syrian attack on Israeli civilian targets might well lead to Israeli retaliation against Syrian cities with nuclear weapons. If Israel sought to send a decisive signal as to the cost of strikes on Israel, these might be nuclear ground bursts designed to both cripple Syria and prevent its recovery.

It also seems likely that if Israel ever came to believe Syria was acquiring highly lethal biological weapons, or nuclear weapons, it would massively preempt and possibly without warning.

SYRIA'S CONTINUING STRATEGIC CHALLENGES

Syria faces several major strategic challenges: dealing with Israel, finding ways to profit from its "spoiler role" in regional security, and maintaining internal security for a regime that fails to modernize and develop the country.

Real-World Syrian Options on the Golan

In theory, Syria's strategic challenge is to create modern and effective enough military forces to be able to liberate Syrian territory on the Golan Heights and conduct a major offensive operation against Israel. In practice, however, Syria has no practical chance of ever acquiring such a capability without massive new transfers of weapons and technology, and it is extremely unlikely that Israel would allow such transfers to take place in a world where Russia no longer can intervene unilaterally against it.

Syria can maintain large enough forces to exploit Syrian defensive positions and act as a major deterrent to any Israeli attack on invasion. Its forces are not particularly effective, but sheer numbers or mass act as a deterrent, and Israel has little to gain from occupying more Syrian territory. They cannot, however, prevent Israel from launching devastating conventional air or missile attacks on any Syrian target, or using nuclear weapons.

Syria fought major wars over the Golan in 1967 and 1973. The October War, in particular, showed that the balance of forces that each side could bring to bear in the critical 24-hour periods before the attack began and after it commenced is a critical factor in assessing the Israeli-Syrian balance. Israel miscalculated the compromises it could make in reducing the size and readiness of its reserve forces between 1970 and 1973. As a result, Syria successfully launched a surprise attack with 1,400 tanks and 28,000 other weapons and vehicles against unprepared Israel forces on the Golan and thrust 15 kilometers into Israeli territory

Syria has since become a largely ineffective garrison force. At the same time, it has been over 20 years since the IDF faced the kind of challenge that forced it to fully mobilize under true wartime conditions and test its system *in extremis*—a "learning experience" that military history shows is inevitably more demanding than even the best peacetime exercises and training. Much has changed since 1973, and any new war would have a very different character.

Israel's main challenge in defending the Golan would be having sufficient mobility and killing capability over the entire battlefield to halt any sudden Syrian advance. To do this, Israel must be able to commit the IDF and the IAF in ways that react to initial warning indicators on a near "hair trigger" basis to prevent significant initial Syrian gains. Much of the Syrian Army is forward deployed and could rapidly mobilize and attack across the Golan with roughly five to six armored division equivalents. This attack could potentially be supported by a thrust through Jordan and/or Lebanon, although such a thrust is now politically unlikely.

Israel has greatly improved its defenses and fortifications on the Golan, and Syria cannot prevent Israel from retaliating with powerful air strike capabilities. Even so, the IDF can halt an all-out Syrian surprise attack with minimal casualties only if it has time to redeploy its active forces and mobilize its reserves. The IDF needs at least 24 hours of strategic warning that Syria is massing and ready for an attack to mobilize and man its forward defenses. Ideally, it needs 36 to 48 hours of reaction time to fully complete its plans.

This makes the success of any Syrian attack highly dependent upon whether Syria can attack with enough surprise or speed to prevent Israel from mobilizing before Syria creates new facts on the ground, such as seizing back the Golan or even penetrating into the Galilee and then using diplomatic pressure to reach a cease-fire. If Syria could attack before Israel fully mobilized and deployed, such an attack might make serious initial gains, and Syria might then be able to hold the territory it seized, dig in, and try to obtain a political settlement.

For all its defects, the Syrian Army has large forces near the Golan area, with an active strength of nearly 40,000 men. Although Syria would need sustained training and exercise activity to properly prepare its forces for a massive all-out attack, and some 48 to 72 hours of intensive mobilization and redeployment activity to properly support and sustain such an attack, it might still take the risk of attacking with the forces on hand and supporting them with follow-on echelons. Under these conditions, Syria could use its existing forces to attack with minimal warning and mass large amounts of artillery to support its armored advance.

According to some experts, the Syrian I Corps, which is headquartered in Damascus, has the 5th and 7th Mechanized Divisions in the Golan area, the 9th Armored Division in support, the 1st Armored Division northeast of Qatana, and the 569th Armored Division and a Republican Guards Division near Damascus. Three more armored divisions—the 11th, 17th, and 18th—are located in the general area between Homs and Hama.[72]

Some IDF experts also feel Syria could put simultaneous pressure on Israel by attacking across the Lebanese border with the 30,000 men it stations in the Beka'a, or using the men in Hezbollah.[73] Syria does have at least two high-quality heavy divisions and three Special Forces regiments that performed well in 1982 and could bring two other heavy divisions to bear in support. It could reinforce such units relatively rapidly, although the readiness and training of many of these Syrian reinforcements would be limited.

Virtually all heavy units in the Syrian Army now suffer from a sustained lack of spare parts and outside support, a result of Syria's lack of funds and the breakup of the Soviet Union. Syria would face other mobilization, deployment, and sustainability problems. The Israeli-Syrian disengagement agreement signed on May 31, 1974, limits the forces Israel and Syria can deploy in the Golan area. There is a 3–6-kilometer-wide disengagement zone where no forces are permitted, except for a UN disengagement observer force (UNDOF) of about 1,000 men assisted by some 80 military observers of the United Nations Truce Supervision Organization Observer Group Golan. This force has been in place since May 31, 1974, and has manning from Austria, Canada, Japan, Poland, and the Slovak Republic, and it has a budget of roughly $33.7 million a year.[74]

Israeli and Syrian forces are then separated by a 10-kilometer-wide force limitation zone where each side can deploy a maximum of 6,000 soldiers, 75 tanks, and 36 short-range howitzers (122-mm equivalent). There is a third 10-kilometer-wide force limitation zone where both sides are limited to 450 tanks and 162 artillery weapons with a range not exceeding 20 kilometers. Finally, each side is forbidden to deploy surface-to-air missiles closer than 25 kilometers from the disengagement zone.

The IDF completely reorganized its defenses on the Golan after 1973, and it has progressively improved these defenses ever since. Although the May 31, 1974, separation of forces agreement between Israel and Syria cost Israel about 600 square kilometers of territory on the Golan, particularly control over the dominant Bahta ridge line in the south and Rafid junction, Israel is also aided by the fact it no longer is forced to split its forces to defend against both Egypt and Syria.

The IDF has built up major strong points in the Golan, specially tailored heavy armored brigades designed to blunt any initial attack, and improved its mining and artillery capabilities in the Golan. It has significantly improved its ability to rapidly reinforce its forward-deployed forces and to provide artillery and rocket support. It has developed much stronger attack helicopter forces and fixed wing air attack capabilities that can attack Syrian armor with considerable precision and lethality even at night or in relatively poor weather. Israel has also improved its real- and near real-time long-range surveillance and battle management capabilities.

It is also unclear how much surprise Syria could achieve, even if it practiced substantial deception and attacked during a supposed training exercise. The IDF has deployed a wide range of all-weather sensors and can detect virtually any major Syrian movement in time to mobilize and react—although such indicators can never assure that the IDF makes the right assessment of Syrian moves, or whether its political leaders choose to react. Israeli coverage of Syria includes advanced airborne radar reconnaissance that extends north of Damascus from positions in Israeli airspace, coverage from advanced UAVs which include electronic intelligence (ELINT) as well as imagery systems, airborne ELINT coverage capable of characterizing and precisely locating any Syrian electronic emitter including radars, and land-based sensors in the Golan and on Mount Hermon.

In short, a "race for the Golan" would be an extremely high-risk strategy for the Syrian Army even if it could achieve a substantial degree of surprise, could ignore the fact that this time the IAF can intervene with excellent precision-strike capabilities and little fear of Syrian surface-to-air missiles, and Israel has a monopoly of nuclear weapons.

Israeli Options Against Syria

As for any Israeli attack in the other direction, the IDF now shows much less interest in meeting engagements between massed armored forces and preserving the option to drive forward into Syrian territory. Armored wars of maneuver that penetrate into Syria are still an option, but defense in depth offers higher attrition of Syrian forces with fewer Israeli casualties. Defense in depth also allows Israel to decide whether to counterattack, rather than rely on such attacks, and to vary its mix of armor, artillery, close air support, and air interdiction to strike deep into Syria while defending forward.

The IAF has learned from its mistakes and successes in the 1973 and 1982 wars, and from the Gulf War. It has steadily improved its coordination with the land forces in combined operations. It can do a much better job of coordinating the air-land battle in both tactical operations and at the strategic level. Its C^4I and battle management systems may lack all the sophisticated technology and techniques used by U.S. forces, but they are tailored to a unique area and set of missions and allow given assets to be used with great effectiveness. At least some Israeli planners have argued since 1973—reinforced by Israel's experience in 1982—that Israel must either fight very limited military actions or strategically decisive ones.

The approaches to the Golan force Syria to channel its armor in any major offensive and it has little ability to provide effective air defense or even prevent the IAF from making intensive air-to-ground strikes deep into the battlefield without waiting to win an air battle for air supremacy. Israel not only has advanced antitank weapons and attack helicopters, it can now use rockets and submunitions to kill advancing armor in large numbers at ranges well over 60–80 kilometers. Night and poor weather would no longer be Syria's friend. Israel has superior night-warfare capability and warning and intelligence assets that can function in virtually any weather. The confusion factor Syria would face in operating under such conditions would, on the other hand, slow Syrian movement and allow Israel to inflict more attrition during an advance.

The IAF does, however, face certain basic operational constraints in using such a defense. The IAF alone cannot destroy all of the land forces of a major enemy like Syria within a short period, although it might be decisive in cooperation with the IDF in an air-land offensive. It can contribute to the land battle, but Syria's forces near the Golan are too close to the border and too large for any combination of interdiction bombing and close air support to act as a substitute for effective defensive action by the IDF's land forces.

There also are limits to Israel's ability to exploit some of its technical capabilities at lower thresholds of conflict. If the IAF is to minimize IAF losses and inflict maximum damage on Syria, it must achieve a high degree of technological surprise in air defense suppression—either through preemption or deception. As Israel learned in 1982, it does not make sense to reveal its air defense suppression capabilities in limited attacks with limited objectives and give an enemy time to improve its own defense and develop countermeasures.

Israel can easily escalate to striking virtually any mix of Syrian targets outside the Golan. Any major Syrian success in an attack on the Golan would involve the risk of Israeli strategic retaliation using conventional forces. Israel currently has so large a qualitative "edge" in air, precision attack, and electronic warfare capabilities that it could probably win air superiority in a matter of hours and break through part of Syria's land-based air defenses in a day. Israel could then strike high-value targets in Syria with relative impunity in a conventional war—and Syria would be able to launch only limited numbers of air and missile attacks in retaliation.

Since 1973, the IDF has organized its targeting, battle management, and strike plans for both conventional and nuclear strategic strikes on key potential enemies.

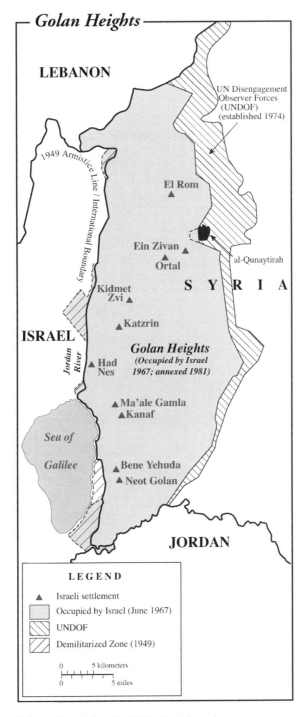

Map 9.2 The Golan (Foundation for Middle East Peace)

Israel gives high priority to destroying and suppressing the enemy's air- and land-based air defense capability during the initial stages of the battle. The potential scale of Israel's success in suppressing Syrian air defenses in a future battle over the Golan is indicated by the fact that during the 1982 war, Israel essentially broke the back of the Syrian surface-to-air missile network in the Beka'a Valley in one day, on June 9. Israel shot down over 80 Syrian fighters and lost only one A-4 in flying a total of over 1,000 combat sorties—including the sorties delivered against Syrian ground-based air defenses in the Beka'a. Israel also was able to devote an extraordinary percentage of its total sorties to the attack mission, although it should be noted that even in the 1973 war, some 75 percent of all IAF sorties were attack sorties.[75]

Israel has sufficient long-range precision munitions, land-based missile and rocket systems, and UAVs to then use conventional weapons to cripple the power, water, refining, key communications and command centers, and critical industrial facilities of either or both confrontation states before the United States or outside powers could intervene. If Israel was to launch such attacks on a surprise or preemptive basis, or do so before Syrian and/or Jordanian air forces were fully alert and dispersed, it would achieve nearly certain success. It would have a very high probability of success even against fully alert Syrian and Jordanian forces.

Such strategic attacks would, however, risk Syrian escalation to biological and chemical weapons. They might require a level of Israeli strategic commitment to achieving rapid strategic success that could force Israel to escalate to weapons of mass destruction if conventional IAF attacks failed. Further, they would involve sudden unilateral Israel military action under conditions where Israel must expect U.S. and outside pressure to limit such military action. On the one hand, the IAF would have to operate under political conditions that deter large-scale action. On the other hand, the IAF would have to operate under military conditions that could lead it toward sudden and massive escalation.

The existence of Israeli nuclear weapons might also succeed in deterring Syrian use of biological and chemical weapons in response to conventional strategic air attacks. Furthermore, Israel might have no other way to achieve a decisive victory over Syria. It is unclear that any land victory over Syria would be sufficient to force Syria to accept a peace or so weaken it that it could not recover as a threat in a few years.

The IDF continues to make further improvements to warning and the sensors and battle management capabilities necessary to fight intense "24-hour a day" battles in all-weather conditions.[76] Many of the sensors and other assets that improve Israel's warning and ability to characterize Syrian movements provide all-weather targeting capabilities that make it much more difficult for Syria to take advantage of weather and terrain masking. Israel also plans to steadily improve its air, missile, and rocket assets in ways that allow Israel to strike far deeper into the Golan battlefield, and even near Damascus. In contrast, Syria lacks matching intelligence, warning, battle management, and strike capabilities. It is half-blind compared to Israel.

The use of UAVs, other sensors, smart precision munitions, and more lethal area munitions increasingly allows the IDF to simultaneously engage a Syrian advance at virtually every point from the forward edge of the battle to the limits of its rear areas. Long before such attacks defeated Syria through attrition, they would seriously degrade or break up the coherence of its military advance. In a number of simulations, they would create movement problems that froze substantial Syrian forces of armor and vehicles in place in the open, allowing Israeli forces to destroy them in detail without directly engaging Syrian forces in a war of maneuver.

Syrian Risk Taking

Syria might do better in some theoretical contingency in which Israel faced a multifront war with Egypt. It has, however, lost any chance of a major direct reinforcement by another Arab power following the disintegration of Iraq's Air Force and heavy land forces in 2003. Syria might also find that it accomplished little more in engaging in such a war than leading Israel to attack its economy and infrastructure to force Syria to end a conflict. Syria is critically vulnerable to such an attack.

Nevertheless, Syria might still risk war—if it felt it could achieve strategic surprise and hold a significant amount of the Golan long enough for world opinion to bring a halt to fighting and use such "shock therapy" to achieve its goals in the peace process. Syria might be reluctant take such a risk without a superpower patron to support it diplomatically, but it might try to use the threat of escalation to chemical warfare as a substitute for outside diplomatic and military support.

Even though Syria cannot hope to penetrate much beyond the Golan, it might still launch such an attack in an effort to create new facts on the ground and at least shallow defenses and emergency fortifications. Syria might also attempt to use such an attack to alter the outcome of peace negotiations, to respond to a failure of the peace negotiations, or to try to exploit a peace agreement that disrupted or weakened the IDF presence on the Golan without placing compensating limitations on Syria.

Syria's conventional military weakness does not, however, preclude Syria from taking risks like using proxy groups such as Hezbollah. If Syria is pressured, it could unleash and equip militant groups in southern Lebanon and other Palestinian groups such as Hamas and PIJ. This asymmetric threat, even if it is low intensity, can distract the Israeli attention away from Syria's conventional military and WMD threat. Such a threat could include intensified mortar attacks from southern Lebanon against IDF and Israeli towns in northern Israel, spectacular suicide attacks in Israel proper against military and civilian targets, or equip proxy groups with chemical, biological, or radiological capabilities to be use asymmetrically against Israel.

Syria's Real-World Strategic Priorities

That said, prudent Syrian decision makers cannot ignore the fact that Syria has become a third-rate regional military power. Without a major outside patron, it cannot obtain the arms it needs to modernize its forces, and it is far from clear that its armed forces have the leadership, professionalism, and technical base to use such arms if they did become available. The failure of Syria's leadership to carry out economic modernization and reform has crippled Syria's ability to fund modern military forces and keep up with modern technology, as well as severely cut Syria's overall economic growth and development.

As a result, Syria's real-world strategic challenges are not war with Israel, or efforts to recover the Golan, but considerably more modest. Syria must do the following:

- Maintain the best defensive posture it can to deter Israel without provoking major Israeli retaliation.
- Find some way to better modernize its forces, particularly its major surface-to-air missile systems and C^4I/BM net and sensor systems.
- Seek to find the delicate balance between some modernization of its weapons of mass destruction and delivery systems to deter Israel and provoking Israel into preemption or massive escalation in the event of war.
- Seek to balance its domestic economy and social needs with its defense modernization expenditures.
- Decide what type of armed forces structure it wants to have. Syrian military forces continue to be largely equipped and organized to fight long wars with other Arab armies against Israel. They lack mobility and the capabilities to win decisive victories early in any war.
- Create a new relationship with Lebanon that is not based on occupation or continuing efforts at intervention.
- Reach some strategic decision about its role in seeking a meaningful peace process with Israel.
- Decide whether to try to exploit Hamas's victory or reach some different and more stable relationship with the Palestinians.
- Deter any form of Syrian action in Jordan from military threats and incursions to hostile actions by Syrian intelligence agencies and proxies.
- Secure the Iraqi border and decide whether continuing support to Iraqi insurgents serves Syria's strategic interest, particularly given the prospect the United States will withdraw most or all of its forces once Iraq seems secure and politically stable.
- Maintain internal security in the face of serious internal threats from Islamist extremists, elements of the Muslim Brotherhood, and external threats from movements like Al Qa'ida.
- Improve its fiscal and monetary situation. Its economy is still largely controlled by the central government, and its key sectors lack necessary foreign and domestic investment.
- Find a balance among its strategic relationship with Iran, the prospect of a peace settlement with Israel, and its relationship with other states. Syria is being isolated not from the West, but also from key Arab states following its alleged involvement in the Hariri assassination.
- Balance the funding of its internal security needs with its needs for a strategic and defense posture against Israel.

One key issue that affects all of these decisions is what Syria gains from playing a spoiler role in the region. Its support of Hezbollah and Palestinian factions has not given it any strategic traction in dealing with Israel or negotiating leverage in recovering the Golan. In fact, Syria may have created a situation where Israel has lost any real interest in negotiating a peace and giving up the Golan and feels it can gain more from keeping the Golan and containing Syria if its various adventures become too provocative. Hafaz Asad may well have lost the Golan for the second time, and "permanently," when he refused Ehud Barak's offer to trade it for peace.

Syria may well be able to ride out its role in assassinating Lebanese Prime Minister Rafik Hariri on February 14, 2005, and help keep Lebanon's pro-Syrian president, Emil Lahood, in office. It has, however, been forced to withdraw virtually all of its open military and security presence as a result of the disclosure made in the Detlev Mehlis report to the UN. (Syria withdrew its forces in two phases on September 1, 2005.) Syria can also scarcely hope to live down its role in the assassination even though the UN is unlikely to take serious action. Four senior Lebanese officers with close ties to Syria have been publicly implicated. Syria's Minister of Interior Ghazi Kanaan committed "suicide" because of his involvement. Basher Asad has been personally implicated, along with his brother Maher al-Asad (commander of the key security brigade stationed near Damascus), and General Asaf Shawkat, head of Syrian military intelligence.[77]

It seems unlikely that continuing to play the game in Lebanon can restore Syria's political and economic position in that country, and it may alienate more and more Lebanese over time.[78] Playing the Hezbollah card also has serious dangers, including allowing Iran to provoke Israel in ways that can create a powerful backlash against Syria.[79] Israel may well hold Syria accountable for permitting the Iranian transfer of 10,000s of long-range artillery rockets to Hezbollah.[80] If a massive rocket attack is made on northern Israel, Israel may use its air and missile power to conduct strikes on Syria's forces and economy. The same could be true at a lesser scale if Syria is too supportive of Palestinian groups.

The game Syria plays in Iraq may to some extent deter the United States from putting political and military pressure on Syria because of U.S. military involvement in Iraq. It also, however, may provoke the United States to strike at Syria or use force to seal off the Syrian border with Iraq. The more serious issue from Syria's perspective is that playing a spoiler role in Iraq is not going to bring back the Ba'ath or a secular power on Syria's border. It instead is strengthening Neo-Salafi Sunni extremist movements that ultimately are a threat to Syria's Alawite-controlled regime and secular status. Syria has alienated at least some Iraqi Shi'ite leaders in the process, and closer ties to Iran's Shi'ite extremists do little to improve Syria's strategic position or deter Israel and the United States. If anything, they provoke. The ability to string out a losing hand while others gather in the chips is not strategic success.

More broadly, Syria cannot rely on repression for internal security and stability. So far, Basher Asad has shown little serious interest in reform. The new hard-line cabinet he installed on February 11, 2006, changed 15 of 34 senior positions and promoted figures like Faruq al-Shar'a—a key player in shaping Syrian control of Lebanon—to Vice President. Syria's conservative (if incompetent) Minister of Defense, General Hasan Turkmani, kept his job, but another hard-liner—General Adb al-Majid—

was made Minister of the Interior. He has distinctions: He is a member of the Circassian minority and his whole "military career" has been based on roles in intelligence and internal security operations.[81]

Syria must balance its security efforts with the need to deal with major demographic problems and an expanding workforce, the need for economic development and job creation, and the need for political liberalization. At present, it is committed to maintaining far larger forces than it can hope to modernize or make effective, and this inevitably affects its economic growth and ability to maintain its internal stability.

The need for basic changes in both Syria's strategy and force posture is obvious, but has now been obvious for roughly a quarter of a century. The end result may be that the regime's external ambitions and actions may be exacerbating the internal tensions and security problems that should be the primary focus of its political decision makers. Syria's real strategic challenge is social modernization and economic growth—something its military and internal security forces cannot possibly accomplish.

An Uncertain Future

The Arab-Israeli balance does not dominate the Middle East as it did in much of the Cold War era. Israel's peace with Egypt and Jordan has changed the military face of the region, as has Syria's steady decay in military modernization and effectiveness. New threats in the Gulf Region have gained importance, and the challenge of violent Islamist extremism has mobilized the world in ways that the Arab-Israeli conflict never did.

At the same time, the Arab-Israeli conflict still has a powerful impact on Arab and Muslim perceptions throughout the world. It may now be largely an Israeli-Palestinian conflict, with a largely impotent Syria on the sidelines, but it still captures imaginations and perceptions in every part of the Middle East. It remains one of the key factors behind popular anger at the West and the United States and one of the causes that Islamic extremists can exploit both in attacking moderate regional governments and Western targets. Israel may see the struggle as a war against Palestinian extremists and terrorists, but most Arabs and Muslims see it as Israeli state terrorism arrayed against weak and largely defenseless Palestinians.

In this sense, the perceptual balance has become as important as the real-world military balance. For all the very real threat posed by weapons of mass destruction, it is weapons of mass media that shape the political struggle and much of Arab and Muslim anger. There is also little prospect of change. Hamas's legislative victory over Fatah is almost certain to extend and intensify the Israel-Palestinian war of attrition. Israel's search for separation and a unilateral solution is likely to have the same effect. There will be new images of terrorism and new images of Israeli forces creating barriers against the Palestinians by force. At least in the short run, there is little prospect that any combination of the Quartet, the Arab League, and propeace Israelis can make real progress.

The Israel-Palestinian war of attrition will also create new facts on the ground, and most of them will be negative. Palestinian efforts to attack Israeli targets behind

Israel's security barriers will intensity Israeli efforts at separation and creating the kind of barriers that severely hurt the Palestinians in developing their economy, day-to-day movement, and becoming a real state. Palestinian efforts to acquire longer-range weapons will put new pressure on Egypt and Jordan to secure their borders and create more problems for both countries in dealing with popular unrest and anger against Israel. Successful Palestinian attacks with either longer-range weapons or militants in Israel will lead to new Israeli reprisals and new security pressure on Israeli Arabs and Palestinians.

While major conventional wars have become less and less likely, there will be no new peace dividends. Egypt, Israeli, Jordan, and Syria will remain locked into a conventional arms race and a pattern of mutual deterrence. The economic burden of this arms race may be lower than in the past, but it is still significant and can be made stable only by large amounts of U.S. military aid. Ironically, the best form of arms control is not fewer weapons and less spending, but rather a massive flow of U.S. military aid that enables Israel to sustain its military edge while giving Egypt and Jordan a strong incentive to support the peace process, and their own deterrents against Israel. The end result is to steadily further weaken a Syria that simply cannot compete with Israel, without bringing peace or stability.

All of the countries in the region will be forced to continue to build up their internal security capabilities, although there is a major difference in the nature of the threat each nation faces. Jordan will face new internal problems because of the shifts in Palestinian politics in favor of Hamas, and the deterioration of the Israeli-Palestinian conflict. Egypt will have further problems with popular anger against Israel and the United States. Lebanon will face its own problems with Hamas and the fear of new clashes and sectarian divisions. At the same time, these same tensions will give new openings to outside movements like Al Qa'ida. There is no way to know just how much Palestinian militancy and Islamist extremist terrorism will interact. What is certain is that they will.

The pace of Egyptian-Israel-Syrian proliferation is unlikely to have a major impact in changing the Arab-Israeli military balance, either in terms of deterrence or war fighting. The "wild card" is rather Iran. It is far from clear how much Iran truly opposes Israel as distinguished from finding a convenient scapegoat to explain its own military buildup in asymmetric warfare capabilities and efforts to acquire nuclear weapons and long-range missiles. Iran has consistently supported Hezbollah and Palestinian militants in their attacks on Israel, however, and the real answer may be that Iran is both seeking to develop military deterrents and capabilities to deal with its Gulf neighbors and the United States *and* is acting as an enemy of Israel.

There seems little near-term change that relations between Iran and Israel will not further deteriorate or that Iran will not sustain its aid to Hezbollah and Palestinian militants. Iran can conduct such a proxy war at a relatively safe distance, build up support in the Arab and Sunni world, and serve its own ideological ends.

The key wild card remains the response Israel will make to a nuclear armed Iran. Israel has argued that Iran must not be permitted to acquire nuclear weapons, but has also argued that it is an international problem and not an Israeli problem. Many in Israel do, however, see a nuclear armed Iran as an existential threat to Israel, and some have called for military strikes to stop Iran from acquiring nuclear capabilities. When Israeli Chief of Staff Lieutenant General Dan Halutz was asked how far Israel would go to stop Iran's nuclear program, he said "2,000 kilometers."[1] Iran has said in response that an attack by Israel on Iranian nuclear facilities will be met with a "crushing response from the armed forces."[2] Much depends on the EU3 and the UN's ability to negotiate a viable agreement with Iran.

Syria is equally likely to play out its own low-level proxy war against Israel and support the insurgency in Iraq. Just what this really means for Syria is unclear. There are new signs in Syria of Sunni militancy against Syria's Alawite ruling elite. Since Syria is supporting elements with the same beliefs against Iraq and the United States, it is playing a game it may not be able to fully control.

The alternatives to these developments are obvious: an Israeli-Palestinian peace settlement; an Israeli-Syrian peace settlement; some form of weapons of mass destruction free zone in the region that includes Iran and Israel; an agreed upon build-down in conventional forces and arms transfers; support for an independent and unified Lebanon; and a new and far more intensive focus on political, social, and economic reform and modernization.

It is equally obvious, however, that none of these developments will take place quickly or effectively in the near term and that most efforts to achieve them will be able to do little more than lay potential groundwork for the future. A half-century of peace efforts, arms control efforts, and good intentions have had some major effects. The peace among Israel, Egypt, and Jordan is more than enough to justify such efforts. The grim fact, however, is that further progress depends far more on the nations in the region than outside efforts and good intentions, and such cooperation will be tenuous and uncertain at best. The Arab-Israeli military balance will continue to provide a kind of security, but it will also continue to be a self-inflicted wound.

The final wild card in the Arab-Israeli balance is Iraq. The insurgency in Iraq may be local, but the tensions over the U.S. presence in the region and the intensity of the insurgency reach beyond the border of Iraq. Many in the region, particularly Jordan, fear the spillover of the insurgency into neighboring states and/or the creation of a new "Shi'ite crescent" that extends to include Iran, Iraq, Lebanon, and Syria to counterbalance a "Sunni crescent" that includes Jordan, Egypt, Saudi Arabia, and the other southern Gulf States.

Given the nature and the source of threat, building effective internal security and military forces to deal with this asymmetric threat is only part of the picture. Economic, social, and political reforms in the Middle East are as important if not more important than equipping armies with the most advanced weapons. Most of the tensions outlined in this analysis are political in nature and until these issues are addressed internally and externally, the status quo will not change.

The security, political, economic, social, and demographic forces are evolving during a time when the strategic outlook in the region is changing in terms of the nature of threat from conventional armies (Saddam Hussein's Iraq) toward asymmetric war

(Al Qa'ida and other extremists organizations) and proliferation (Iran's WMD and missile capabilities).

These changes in both the internal dynamics in the Arab-Israeli ring states, and the overall strategic posture in the region, make any analysis of military forces highly unpredictable. As noted earlier, most of the forces in Egypt, Israel, Jordan, Lebanon, Palestine, and Syria have just started to adjust their forces to deal with this threat.

It is equally important to note that the Arab-Israeli countries have to make trade-offs between spending on conventional defense, internal security, and social services. Historically, social services have been the victims of defense spending, but as the threat of Islamist extremists increases and the "youth explosion" nears, countries are realizing that revitalizing their economies, reforming their employment systems, and reducing their commands of their economies is part of their defense and internal security planning to deal with the changing nature of threat.

Notes

CHAPTER 1

1. Steve Erlanger, "Abbas Declares Victory in Election; Exit Polls Give Him About 65% of Vote," *International Herald Tribune,* January 10, 2005, 1.

2. The text of the speech is available at http://www.jewishvirtuallibrary.org/jsource/Peace/sharon_1203.html.

3. Steve Erlanger, "Sharon Narrowly Wins Approval for New Government," *International Herald Tribune,* January 11, 2005, 4.

4. Greg Myre and Steven R. Weisman, "'Major Step Forward' Ends Bitter Dispute After Israeli Pullout," *International Herald Tribune,* November 16, 2005, 1.

CHAPTER 4

1. These data are extrapolated from the CIA, *World Factbook, 2006,* http://www.odci.gov/cia/publications/factbook/geos/is.html.

2. Barbara Opall-Rome and Riad Kawahji, "Rendering Asad Unviable," *Defense News,* October 20, 2003, 1.

3. *Jane's Defence Weekly,* "Israel, Turkey Sign Security Accord," January 21, 2004, http://jdw.janes.com (accessed January 27, 2004); and *Jane's Defence Weekly,* "Russia Halts Plans to Sell Igla to Syria," November 6, 2002, http://jdw.janes.com (accessed January 9, 2004).

4. Khaled Abu Toameh, "Life After Rantisi," *The Jerusalem Post,* April 23, 2004, 12.

5. Elliot Chodoff, "Taking the War on Terror to Syria," *National Post, National Edition,* September 28, 2004, A18.

6. Barbara Opall-Rome, "Tactical Successes, Strategic Failures," *Defense News,* December 22, 2003, 32.

7. Barbara Opall-Rome, "Israel Security Experts Seek Strategy," *Defense News,* December 22, 2003, 6.

8. Nina Gilbert, "Israeli Defense Forces: Significant Decline in 2004 Terror," *Jerusalem Post,* December 21, 2004 (accessed January 13, 2005).

9. Barbara Opall-Rome, "Tactical Successes, Strategic Failures," 34.

10. Barbara Opall-Rome, "In Israel, Air Power Takes on Ground Jobs," *DefenseNews.com,* February 28, 2005 (accessed May 5, 2005).

11. Alon Ben David, "Israel Bolsters Security Before Gaza Pull-Out," *Jane's Defence Weekly,* April 22, 2005 (accessed May 5, 2005).

12. Deborah Sontag, "Gun Lessons Are Suddenly All the Rage in Israel," *New York Times,* October 25, 2000.

13. *Washington Post,* November 30, 2000, A-32 and A-33.

14. "Report of the United Nations High Commissioner for Human Rights and Follow-Up to the World Conference on Human Rights," New York United Nations, E/CN.42001/114, November 29, 2000.

15. Ibid., 8 and 16.

16. Ibid., 15.

17. B'Teslem, "Through No Fault of Their Own: Punitive House Demolitions during the Al-Aqsa Intifada," November 2004, www.btselem.org.

18. "Report of the Special Rapporteur of the Commission on Human Rights, John Dugard, on the Situation of Human rights in the Palestinian territories Occupied by Israel since 1967," E/CN.4/2004/6/Add.1, February 27, 2004, in B'Teslem, "Through No Fault of Their Own: Punitive House Demolitions during the Al-Aqsa Intifada."

19. B'Teslem, "Through No Fault of Their Own: Punitive House Demolitions during the Al-Aqsa Intifada."

20. Ibid.

21. Ibid.

22. Israel Ministry of Foreign Affairs Spokesman, "Initial Israeli Response to Amnesty Report on Demolitions," Israel Ministry of Foreign Affairs, May 18, 2004, http://www.mfa.gov.il/MFA/Terrorism+Obstacle+to+Peace/Terror+Groups/Demolition+of+Palestinian+Structures+Used+for+Terrorism+-+Legal+Background+-+May+2004.htm.

23. "Israeli High Vourt Bans Demolition of 10 Palestinian House in Gaza," *Financial Times,* July 22, 2004.

24. AFP, "Israel Hold US Woman's Body," March 18, 2003.

25. Richard Boucher, Spokesman, U.S. State Department, "Daily Press Briefing," March 19, 2003.

26. Joshua Hammer, "The Death of Rachel Corrie," *Mother Jones,* September/October 2003.

27. Rachel Corrie, http://en.wikipedia.org/wiki/Rachel_Corrie (accessed December 6, 2004).

28. Adam Shapiro, "Under Siege with Arafat," *The Nation,* November 12, 2004.

29. Rema Hammami, "Interregnum: Palestine after Operation Defensive Shield," *Middle East Report,* No. 223, Summer 2002.

30. Nitsan Alon, "Operation Defensive Shield: The Israeli Actions in the West Bank," *Peacewatch,* April 10, 2002.

31. Ruth Wedgewood, "Law in the Fog of War: On Urban Battlefields, Principles Can Be Elusive," *Time,* May 13, 2002.

32. Hammami, "Interregnum: Palestine After Operation Defensive Shield."

33. Serge Schmemann, "13 Israeli Troops Killed in Ambush at Refugee Camp," *New York Times,* April 10, 2002.

34. "Israel Redefines Tactics: Doctrine Highlights Limited, Urban Combat," *Defense News,* June 10–16, 2002.

35. Wedgewood, "Law in the Fog of War."

36. Barbara Opall-Rome, "Objective: Re-Create the Fog of War," *Defense News,* June 24, 2002.

37. Ibid.

38. Ibid.

39. Heath Minister Ephraiam Sneh admitted Israel's role in killing a leader of Islamic Jihad in an interview on November 2, 1995, but retracted his remarks. Executive News Service, October 29, 1995, 1431; November 2, 1995, 0704.

40. International Policy Institute for Counter-Terrorism, "Casualties and Incidents Database," Herzliya, Israel, www.ict.org.il/ (accessed July 29, 2003).

41. Ibrahim Barzak, "Hamas Leader Yassin Killed in Airstrike, Prompting Threats of Revenge Against Israel, US," *Associated Press,* March 22, 2004.

42. John Ward Anderson and Molly Moore, "Israeli Strike Kills Another Hamas Chief: Gaza Leader, Two Others Slain in a Missile Attack," *Washington Post,* April 18, 2004, A1.

43. Paul Martin, "'Crisis' in Hamas as Leaders Killed," *Washington Times,* April 20, 2004.

44. Army Spokesperson quoted in William Orme, "Israeli Army Removes Angry Settlers Blocking Gaza Road," *New York Times,* December 5, 2000.

45. Deborah Camiel, "Israeli Copters Attack Palestinian Gunmen," *Washington Post,* December 5, 2000.

46. Joel Greenberg, "Tank Warfare on Jerusalem's Outskirts," *New York Times,* February 22, 2001, A8.

47. Tracy Wilkinson, "Israeli Armor Storms West Bank Town in Fierce Attack on Gunmen," *Los Angeles Times,* May 7, 2001, 3. See also "Seven Palestinians Killed; In Gilo, Four Israelis Hurt by Gunfire," *Ha'aretz,* May 15, 2001.

48. Barbara Opall-Rome, "Israel: Training Moves to Front," *Defense News,* February 9, 2004.

49. Reuters "Israelis Kill Palestinian in New 'Assassination'" December 14, 2000; Arieh O'Sullivan, "IDF Soldiers Killing of a Hamas Activist Spurs Charges of Assassination," *Jerusalem Post,* December 15, 2000; Deborah Sontag, "Israel Acknowledges Hunting Down Arab Militants," *New York Times,* December 21, 2000.

50. Deborah Sontag, "Killings of Palestinian Officers Push Tension to Boiling Point," *New York Times* (Internet Edition), May 15, 2001.

51. Daniel Williams, "Old Tactics Get New Life Under Sharon," *The Washington Post,* April 21, 2001.

52. Lee Hockstader, "Israel Plans Big Assault If Truce Talks Fail: Army and Government Back Aggressive Action," *The Washington Post,* March 25, 2002.

53. "IDF Spokesperson Denial of Harming Religious Sites and Structures in Beit Jala," *Israeli Defense Forces* (Internet Source), August 28, 2001.

54. Tal Muscal, "Shekel Rises Slightly on Beit Jala Withdrawal," *The Jerusalem Post,* August 31, 2001.

55. "Israeli Troops Take Positions in West Bank Town," CNN.com / WORLD, August 27, 2001, http://www.cnn.com/2001/WORLD/meast/08/27/mideast/index.html; "Capturing Posts in the Town of Beit Galla Following the Shooting in Gilo," *Israeli Defense Forces* (Internet Source), October 19, 2001.

56. "IDF Activity Last Night in the Cities of Ramallah, Nablus, and Jenin," *Israeli Defense Forces* (Internet Source), October 17, 2001.

57. Nitsan Alon, "Entering the Refugee Camps: The Israeli Counterterrorist Offensive in the West Bank and Gaza Strip," *Peacewatch*, March 22, 2002.

58. Hockstader, "Israel Plans Big Assault."

59. Alon, "Operation Defensive Shield."

60. Alon, "Entering the Refugee Camps."

61. Joel Brinkly, "Frantically Figuring Results of Military Force," *New York Times*, April 2, 2002.

62. Hockstader, "Israel Plans Big Assault."

63. Brinkly, "Frantically Figuring Results."

64. Keith Richburg, "Israeli Armor Enters Center of Bethlehem," *Washington Post*, April 2, 2002.

65. Hammami, "Interregnum: Palestine after Operation Defensive Shield."

66. Ibid.

67. "Showdown: After a Savage Spasm of Terror, Sharon and Arafat Face Off in a Cold Test of Wills," *Time*, December 12, 2001.

68. "Israel's War on Terror: Sharon Aims Israel's Guns at Arafat," *The Economist*, December 8, 2001.

69. Elaine Sciolino, "U.S. Questions If Arafat Can Lead the Palestinians," *New York Times*, December 5, 2001.

70. Dan Williams, "Arafat Calls for End to All Attacks: After His Address, a Skeptical Israel Says, 'Start Making Arrests,'" *International Herald Tribune*, December 17, 2001.

71. Lev Grinberg, "The Arrogance of Occupation," *Middle East Policy*, Vol. IX, No. 1, March 2002.

72. "Showdown: After a Savage Spasm of Terror, Sharon and Arafat Face Off in a Cold Test of Wills," *Time*.

73. Ibid.

74. John Kifner, "3 Are Left Dead By Suicide Blasts in Tel Aviv Street," *New York Times*, July 18, 2002.

75. "The Palestinians: Arafat's Choice," *The Economist*, December 15, 2001.

76. "Israel's War on Terror: Sharon Aims Israel's Guns at Arafat," *The Economist*, December 8, 2001.

77. "Israel and the Palestinians: Sharon's Strategy, If He Has One," *The Economist*, December 22, 2001.

78. "Israelis Attack Arafat's Compound and 7 Other Sites," *New York Times*, December 5, 2001; "Showdown: After a Savage Spasm of Terror, Sharon and Arafat Face Off in a Cold Test of Wills," *Time*.

79. "Breaking with Arafat," *The Economist*, December 13, 2001.

80. Barbara Opall-Rome, "Israel AF Wants Wider Role in Anti-Terror War," *Defense News*, January 5, 2004.

81. Barbara Opall-Rome, "In Israel, Air Power Takes on Ground Jobs," *Defense News*, February 28, 2005.

82. Ibid.

83. Ed Blanche, "IDF Uses Armed UAVs against Gaza Militants," *Jane's Missiles and Rockets*, December 1, 2004.

84. Matt Rees, "Untangling Jenin's Tale," *Time*, May 13, 2002.

85. *Jane's Defence Weekly,* October 11, 2000, 30.

86. Lee Hockstader and Daniel Williams, "Palestinian Leaders Adapt to Life Altered by Israeli Threats," *Washington Post,* December 8, 2001.

87. Edward Cody, "Israel Takes Another Tack," *Washington Post,* November 1, 2000.

88. Larry Kaplow, "Barak Vows to Increase Attacks; Palestinians Demand Revenge for Killings," *The Atlanta Journal and Constitution,* November 11, 2000, 3A.

89. "Chronology of Israel's Deadly Strikes Against Palestinian Militants," *Agence France Press,* May 6, 2001, http://in.news.yahoo.com/010505/6/u5bv.html/.

90. Molly Moore, "Israel's Lethal Weapon of Choice; As Assassinations of Militants Increase, Citizens' Uneasiness Grows," *The Washington Post,* June 29, 2003, A1.

91. Molly Moore, "Top Israeli Officer Says Tactics Are Backfiring," *The Washington Post,* October 31, 2003, section A1.

92. Barabara Opall-Rome, "Israel AF Wants Wider Role in Anti-Terror War," *Defense News,* January 5, 2004.

93. Gal Luft, "The Seizure of Gaza-Bound Arms: Military Implications," *Peacewatch,* January 8, 2002.

94. Barbara Opall-Rome, "Israel Reorganizes for Underground Warfare," *Defense News,* February 14, 2005.

95. Anne Barnard, "Pullout Plan Tears Rift in Israeli Society," *Boston Globe,* August 7, 2005.

96. Margot Dudkevitch, "Pullout Over in Less Than 12 Hours," *The Jerusalem Post,* September 13, 2005.

97. Sheldon Kirshner, "Israel Faces Uncertainty After Evacuation," *Canadian Business and Current Affairs,* 35, no. 35 (September 1, 2005): 11.

98. "Israel Army to Leave Gaza After 38 Years," *Agence France Presse,* September 11, 2005.

99. Deborah Sontag, "Israel Weighs Border Pal to Proclaim if Talks Fail," *New York Times,* October 22, 2000, A-8.

100. Ibid.

101. "A New Leader Makes New Distinctions," *Washington Post,* March 11, 2001, B1.

102. "Unilateral Separation Supported by 60 percent of Israeli Jews," *Ha'aretz,* June 5, 2001.

103. John Ward Anderson, "Israel Starts Building Fence Along West Bank; Palestinian Interim State is Rejected by Sharon," *The Washington Post,* June 17, 2002.

104. Daniel Williams, "For Al-Aqsa Brigades, a Change of Tactics; Israeli Offensive Leaves West Bank Cells Battered, More Likely to Pick Close Targets," *The Washington Post,* June 13, 2002.

105. Israel Ministry of Defense, "Israel's Security Fence," www.securityfence.mod.gov.il.

106. Ibid.

107. Laurie Copans, "Israeli Leader Discloses West Bank Speration Plan," *Associated Press,* February 7, 2006.

108. These details are taken from the map published in the *Washington Post,* May 30, 2006, A11. The details were confirmed in interviews with Israeli officials and officers.

109. Jerrold Kessel, "Opposing Views of West Bank Fence," *CNN,* July 3, 2003, www.cnn.com.

110. Israel Ministry of Defense, "Israel's Security Fence."

111. Ibid.

112. Alon Ben-David, "Israel Closes Intelligence Picture Gap," *Jane's Defence Weekly*, March 18, 2005, www.janes.com (accessed March 5, 2005).

113. Barbara Opall-Rome, "Roving Sensors, High-Powered, Ground-Mobile FLIRs Protect Israeli Borders Autonomously," *DefenseNews.com*, June 28, 2004 (accessed May 5, 2005).

114. Ibid.

115. David Hoffman, "Arab-Israeli Barrier Has Both Sides Divided," *The Washington Post*, July 2, 2002.

116. Ibid.

117. Jewish Virtual Library, "Israel's Security Fence," http://www.usisrael.org/jsource/Peace/fence.html, May 2004.

118. Ibid.

119. Tel Aviv University Peace Project poll, October 2003, http://spirit.tau.ac.il/socant/peace/peaceindex/2003/files/oct2003e.doc.

120. Jewish Virtual Library, "Israel's Security Fence."

121. Tel Aviv University Peace Project poll.

122. John Ward Anderson, "Israel's Fence Mixes Security and Politics; As Scope Grows, So Does Hostility," *The Washington Post*, September 23, 2003.

123. Ibid.

124. Ibid.

125. JPost.com Staff, "Mufti: Muslims Helping Build Fence-Traitors," *Jerusalem Post*, June 11, 2004.

126. Anderson, "Israel's Fence Mixes Security and Politics."

127. Ibid.

128. Daniel Seidemann, "Erecting a Barrier to Peace," *Washington Post*, August 14, 2003.

129. Ibid.

130. Jewish Virtual Library, "Israel's Security Fence."

131. Barbara Opall-Rome, "Israel Swaps Soldiers for Civilians," *Defense News*, February 20, 2006, 30.

132. Ibid.

133. Barbra Opall-Rome, "US May Allow Israel To Defer Arms Payments," *Defense News*, January 16, 2006, 1.

134. Vivek Raghuvanshi, "India, Israel Team to Develop 3 UAVs," *Defense News*, February 28, 2005, 14.

135. Alon Ben-David, "Extensive Cuts to Hit Israeli Ground Forces the Most," *Jane's Defence Weekly*, July 16, 2003, 16.

136. Opall-Rome, "Israel Security Experts Seek Strategy," 6.

137. Alon Ben-David, "IDF Branches Sparring for Share of US Funding," *Jane's Defence Weekly*, January 28, 2004, http://jdw.janes.com (accessed January 27, 2004).

138. Barbara Opall-Rome, "Israeli QDR Emphasizes Multirole, Linked Force," *Defense News*, February 13, 2006, 38.

139. Ibid., 38.

140. Ibid., 38.

141. Ibid., 38.

142. Ibid.,. 38.

143. Alex Fishman, "The Chaing Face of the IDF; The Security Agenda and the Ballot Box," *Strategic Assessment* 8, no. 4 (February 2006).

144. The data in this section draw heavily from a number of basic source documents on the balance. IISS, *Military Balance,* various editions; Jaffee Center for Strategic Studies, *Military Balance in the Middle East,* various editions; *Jane's Sentinel Security Assessments,* "Israel," various editions.

145. Barbara Opall-Rome, "Israeli Revamp to Strengthen Ground Forces," *Defense News,* October 3, 2005, 46.

146. Barbara Opall-Rome, "Israel Eyes 'Big Brother' Approach for Security," *Defense News,* October 31, 2005, 22.

147. Alon Ben-David, "Top Israeli Commanders Get Real-Time C4I System," *Jane's Defence Weekly,* October 3, 2005, http://jdw.janes.com (accessed October 20, 2005).

148. Ibid.

149. Associated Press, "Israel Deploys New Weapon," *Bell Globemedia Publishing Inc.,* July 22, 2004, www.globetechnology.com (accessed July 26, 2004).

150. Barbara Opall-Rome, "Israel Builds Precision Arsenal for Ground War," *Defense News,* April 18, 2005, 14.

151. "Israel Decides Not to Develop Merkava Mk5," *Jane's Defence Weekly,* October 2, 2003, http://jdw.janes.com (accessed January 8, 2004). Labeled as 2.

152. Opall-Rome, "Israel Builds Precision Arsenal for Ground War," 14.

153. Barbara Opall-Rome, "Israel Eyes Merkava MBT Replacement," *Defense News,* November 10, 2003, 34.

154. Barbara Opall-Rome, "IMI Proposes Buy of Merkava Production Line," *Defense News,* January 12, 2004, 6.

155. Alon Ben-David, "Israel Adjusts Acquisition Plan," *Jane's Defence Weekly,* June 30, 2004, www4.janes.com (accessed January 14, 2004).

156. *Jane's Sentinel Security Assessment,* Eastern Mediterranean, Israel, Procurement, November 6, 2002, http://jdw.janes.com (accessed January 28, 2003). Labeled 4.

157. Clifford Beal, "Israel's Spike Weapon Goes Network-Centric," *Jane's Defence Weekly,* October 1, 2003, http://jdw.janes.com (accessed January 8, 2004). Labeled 7.

158. Christopher Foss, "IDF to Integrate SADS into Humvees," *Jane's Defence Weekly,* September 28, 2005, http://jdw.janes.com (accessed September 28, 2005).

159. "Eastern Mediterranean, Israel, Procurement," *Jane's Sentinel Security Assessment,* November 6, 2002, http://jdw.janes.com (accessed January 28, 2003). Labeled 5.

160. Barbara Opall-Rome, "LORA Missile Called No Threat," *Defense News,* November 24, 2003, 6. Labeled 6. There is some concern that the LORA could be altered in such a way as to be in violation of arms control limits. The Israeli Missile Defense Organization vehemently denies this.

161. Barbara Opall-Rome, "Israel Seeks to Extend Precise Ground Strike," *Defense News,* September 12, 2005, 42.

162. Robin Hughes, "Israel Orders Surveillance Coverage," *Jane's Defence Weekly,* September 3, 2003, http://jdw.janes.com (accessed January 8, 2004). Labeled 8.

163. Barbara Opall-Rome, "Israel Army Taps Elbit UAV for Over-the-Hill Missions," *Defense News,* February 4, 2004, http://www.defensenews.com (accessed February 5, 2004).

164. Clifford Beal, "New Radio Units Primed for Israeli Forces," *Jane's Defence Weekly,* September 19, 2003, http://jdw.janes.com (accessed January 8, 2004). Labeled Baetjer 9.

165. Barbara Opall-Rome, "Israel Plans $550M JSTARS-Like Flier," *Defense News,* November 3, 2003, 14. Labeled 15.

166. Ibid., 14. Labeled 16.

167. "Special Forces, Israel," *Jane's Amphibious and Special Forces,* November 6, 2002; "Internal Affairs—Israel," *Jane's Sentinel Security Assessment,* October 3, 2005.

168. Robin Hughes, "Israel Extols 'Solid Mirror,'" *Jane's Defence Weekly,* October 3, 2003, http://jdw.janes.com (accessed January 8, 2004). Labeled 17.

169. Opall-Rome, "Israel Seeks to Extend Precise Ground Strike," 42.

170. Barbara Opall-Rome, "From Foot Soldier to Network Node," *Defense News,* October 20, 2003, 30.

171. The data in this section draw heavily from a number of basic source documents on the balance. IISS, *Military Balance,* various editions; Jaffee Center for Strategic Studies, *Military Balance in the Middle East,* various editions; *Jane's Sentinel Security Assessments,* "Israel," various editions.

172. Arieh O'Sullivan, "No Plans to Purchase More Apache Longbows," *The Jerusalem Post,* April 11, 2005.

173. Barbara Opall-Rome, "Israel Air Force to Buy More Apache Longbows," *Defense News,* October 6, 2003, 44. Labeled 11. One retired general insisted that the helicopter had mostly failed its missions in Iraq.

174. "Boeing Wins Israeli JDAM Contract," *Jane's Defence Weekly,* October 8, 2003, http://jdw.janes.com (accessed January 8, 2004). Labeled 10.

175. Robin Hughes, "Israel Orders Gulfstream to Fulfill Early-Warning Need," *Jane's Defence Weekly,* September 10, 2003, http://jdw.janes.com (accessed January 8, 2004). Labeled 12.

176. Barbara Opall-Rome, "C4ISR Dominates Israeli Investment Focus," *Defense News,* September 12, 2005, 26, 28.

177. Barbara Opall-Rome, "Israel's Air Force Looks Beyond FLIRS to Multispectral Sensors," *Defense News,* January 19, 2004, http://www.defensenews.com (accessed February 5, 2004).

178. Barbara Opall-Rome, "Israeli Aerospace Firms Join Forces," *Defense News,* October 3, 2005, 102.

179. "Special Forces, Israel," *Jane's Amphibious and Special Forces,* November 6, 2002; "Internal Affairs—Israel," *Jane's Sentinel Security Assessment,* October 3, 2005.

180. The defecting pilot was on maneuver near the Golan, suddenly turned towards Israel, and flew very low and fast over the Golan and the central Galilee. He landed in a remote civil strip near Megido. This led to a great deal of media comment in Israel, but such incidents are almost unavoidable. Although he flew for seven minutes without being intercepted, he flew at a time when IAF E-2Cs were not in the air and now nearby aircraft were scrambled, when the IAF was in a state of low alert, and flew without using any radar or communications emissions. He also stated later that he did receive warning he was being tracked by Israeli radar. Israel later used the MiG-23ML (G) for training and test and evaluation purposes. *Washington Post,* October 13, 1989, A-35; *Washington Post,* October 14, 1989, A-18; *New York Times,* October 12, 1989, A-10; *New York Times,* October 14, 1989, A-2; *Philadelphia Inquirer,* October 12, 1989, 18A; *Philadelphia Inquirer,* October 13, 1989, 17A; *Washington Times,* October 12, 1989, A-8; *Jane's Defence Weekly,* February 10, 1990, 221.

181. Christian Lowe and Barbara Opall-Rome, "Israel Air Force Seeks Expanded Anti-Terror Role," *Defense News,* March 28, 2005, 14.

182. Dan Williams, "Eyeing Iran Reactors, Israel Seeks U.S. Bunker Bombs," *Reuters,* September 21, 2004.

183. Aluf Ben, "US to Sell Israel 5,000 Smart Bombs," *Ha'aretz,* September 21, 2004, http://haaretz.com (accessed September 21, 2004).

184. Aluf Ben, "US Keeps Israel Out of New Fighter-Jet Development Program," *Ha'aretz,* October 12, 2005, http://haaretz.com.

185. Bill Gertz, "US to Restart Arms Technology Transfers to Israel," *Washington Times,* August 17, 2005, 3.

186. Nathan Guttman, "Israeli-Venezuelan Arms Deal on Hold," *The Jerusalem Post,* October 21, 2005.

187. Barbara Opall-Rome, "Israeli Experts Urge Slow, Steady Move to UCAVs," *Defense News,* November 7, 2005, 21.

188. This section draws heavily on a number of basic source documents on the balance. IISS, *Military Balance,* various editions; Jaffee Center for Strategic Studies, *Military Balance in the Middle East,* various editions; *Jane's Sentinel Security Assessments,* "Israel," various editions.

189. This analysis draws heavily on reporting by Global Security. See http://www.globalsecurity.org/space/systems/patriot-ac-3.htm and http://www.globalsecurity.org/space/systems/patriot-specs.htm.

190. The Arrow is a joint project between the United States and Israel. The Arrow had successfully intercepted target missiles during several tests. Concerns over Israel's ability to mass-produce Arrow parts have been alleviated by the construction of a parallel plant in the United States. See Barbara Opall-Rome, "Israel Boosts Arrow Arsenal As War Looms," *Defense News,* November 25–December 1, 2002, 14, for additional information. Labeled 13.

191. This analysis draws heavily on reporting by Global Security. See http://www.globalsecurity.org/space/systems/arrow.htm.

192. Alon Ben-David, "Rafael, IAI Unveil Surface-to-Air Missile Combo," *Jane's Defence Weekly,* January 21, 2004, http://jdw.janes.com (accessed January 27, 2004).

193. "Israel, US to Pursue Mobile Laser Concept," *Jane's Defence Weekly,* September 3, 2003, http://jdw.janes.com (accessed January 8, 2004). Labeled 14.

194. The data in this section draw heavily from a number of basic source documents on the balance. *Jane's Fighting Ships,* various editions; IISS, *Military Balance,* various editions; Jaffee Center for Strategic Studies, *Military Balance in the Middle East,* various editions; *Jane's Sentinel Security Assessments,* "Israel," various editions.

195. *Jane's International Defense Review,* April 1998, 29.

196. Barbara Opall-Rome, "Israel Reaches for New Combat Ships," *Defense News,* December 22, 2003, http://www.defensenews.com (accessed January 8, 2004). Labeled 19.

197. *Jane's Fighting Ships,* various editions.

198. Alon Ben-David, "Israeli Navy Opts for Fewer, but Flexible Vessels," *Jane's Defence Weekly,* September 17, 2003, http://jdw.janes.com (accessed January 8, 2004). Labeled 18.

199. Barbara Opall Rome, "Israel Reaches for New Combat Ships," *Defense News,* December 22, 2003, 15.

200. See Barbara Opall-Rome, "Israel Navy Boosts Layers of Anti-Terror Defenses," *Defense News,* January 23, 2006, 10.

201. Alon Ben-David, "Israel Seeks More Dolphins," *Jane's Defence Weekly,* January 21, 2004, http://jdw.janes.com (accessed January 27, 2004).

202. Barbara Opall-Rome, "Surgical Strike to the Highest Bidder," *Defense News,* May 15, 2006, 11:22.

203. Barbara Opall-Rome, "Israel's Naval Power Play," *Defense News,* May 24, 2004.

204. Areih O'Sullivan, "Navy's Plans To Procure New Vessels Frozen," *Jerusalem Post,* January 2, 2005.

205. "Special Forces, Israel," *Jane's Amphibious and Special Forces,* November 6, 2002.

206. Israel Ministry of Foreign Affairs, "Seizing if the Palestinian Weapons Ship Karine A," January 4, 2002, www.mfa.gov.il (accessed November 17, 2005).

207. Barbara Opall-Rome, "Israel Preserves Its Grip on Gaza Coast by Remote Control," *Defense News,* March 20, 2004.

208. Ibid.

209. "Israel on Alert over Port Security," *Jane's Intelligence Digest,* May 19, 2006.

210. IISS, *Military Balance,* "Israel," various editions; *Jane's Fighting Ships;* "Israel," various editions; *Jane's Sentinel Security Assessment—Eastern Mediterranean;* "Israel," various editions.

211. The data in this section draw heavily from a number of basic source documents on the balance. IISS, *Military Balance,* various editions; Jaffee Center for Strategic Studies, *Military Balance in the Middle East,* various editions; *Jane's Sentinel Security Assessments,* "Israel," various editions.

212. "Special Forces, Israel," *Jane's Amphibious and Special Forces,* November 6, 2002; "Internal Affairs—Israel," *Jane's Sentinel Security Assessment,* October 3, 2005.

213. Security and Foreign Forces, Israel," *Jane's Sentinel Security Assessment—Eastern Mediterranean,* September 19, 2005.

214. "Special Forces, Israel," *Jane's Amphibious and Special Forces,* November 6, 2002; "Internal Affairs—Israel," *Jane's Sentinel Security Assessment,* October 3, 2005.

215. "Security and Foreign Forces, Israel," *Jane's Sentinel Security Assessment—Eastern Mediterranean,* September 19, 2005.

216. Ibid.

217. Ibid.

218. Barbara Opall-Rome, "Shadow Warriors," *Defense News,* January 9, 2006, 22.

219. *Ha'aretz,* January 22, 2006.

220. U.S. State Department, *Country Reports on Terrorism,* Office of the Coordinator for Counterterrorism, April 27, 2005, http://www.state.gov/s/ct/rls/45394.htm.

221. http://www.state.gov/g/drl/rls/hrrpt/2004/41720.htm and http://www.state.gov/g/drl/rls/shrd/2005/.

222. Some reports give the range as 500 kilometers; *Jane's Defence Weekly,* March 10, 1999, 50–64.

223. *Baltimore Sun,* November 23, 1988; *Washington Post,* September 16, 1989.

224. *Tass International,* 1216 GMT, September 15, 1989; *Washington Post,* September 16, 1989; *Jane's Defence Weekly,* November 19, 1988; *Jane's Defence Weekly,* September 23, 1989, 549; *Washington Times,* July 22, 1987, D-4; *International Defense Review* 7 (1987): 857; *New York Times,* July 22, 1987, A-6; *New York Times,* July 29, 1987; *Mideast Markets,* November 23, 1987, 11; in Harold Hough, "Israel's Nuclear Infrastructure," *Jane's Intelligence Weekly,* November 1994, 505–511.

225. BBC and ITV reporting efforts seem to give more credibility to the idea that Israel has some form of relatively short-range nuclear armed missile. Ranges of anywhere from 750–930 NM have been reported, with accuracies of anywhere from 0.1 Km to radar correlator guidance packages capable of CEPs of 10 meters. *Bulletin of Atomic Scientists* 46 (January/February 1998): 48; *Washington Post,* September 16, 1989, A-17; *Washington Post,* November 15, 1989, A-14; *Economist,* August 1, 1987, 41; *Washington Times,* July 22, 1987, D-4;

Washington Times, July 24, 1987, A-9; *Washington Times,* April 4, 1988, 17; *International Defense Review* 7 (1987): 857; and *New York Times,* July 29, 1987, A-10.

226. Tass International, 1216 GMT, September 15, 1989; *Washington Post,* September 16, 1989; *Jane's Defence Weekly,* November 19, 1988; *Jane's Defence Weekly,* September 23, 1989, 549; *Washington Times,* July 22, 1987, D-4; *International Defense Review* 7 (1987): 857; *New York Times,* July 22, 1987, A-6; *New York Times,* July 29, 1987; *Mideast Markets,* November 23, 1987, 11; in Harold Hough, "Israel's Nuclear Infrastructure," *Jane's Intelligence Weekly,* November, 1994, 505–511.

227. *Washington Post,* October 26, 1989, A-36; *Boston Globe,* October 30, 1989, 2; *Newsweek,* November 6, 1989, 52.

228. *Jane's Intelligence Review,* September 1997, 407–410; *Jane's Defence Weekly,* March 10, 1999, 50–64; *International Defence Review, Extra,* 2/1997, 2.

229. It is also possible that Israel may have deployed nuclear warheads for its MGM-55C Lance missiles. Israel has 12 Lance transporter-erector-launchers, and at least 36 missiles. The Lance is a stored liquid fueled missile with inertial guidance and a range of 5–125 kilometers. It has a warhead weight of 251 kilograms, and a CEP of 375 meters. It was deployed in U.S. forces with the W-70 nuclear warhead. *International Defense Review* 7 (1987): 857; *Economist,* May 4, 1968, 67–68; *New York Times,* July 22, 1987, A-6; *Washington Times,* July 22, 1987, D-4; *Defense and Foreign Affairs,* June 1985, 1; *Aerospace Daily,* May 1, 1985, 5; *Aerospace Daily,* May 17, 1985, 100; *Aerospace Daily,* May 1, 1985; *Aerospace Daily,* May 7, 1985; Shuey et al., Missile Proliferation: Survey of Emerging Missile Forces, 56; CIA, "Prospects for Further Proliferation of Nuclear Weapons, " DCI NIO 1945/74, September 4, 1974; *NBC Nightly News,* July 30, 1985; *New York Times,* April 1, 1986; U.S. Arms Control and Disarmament Agency, *World Military Expenditures and Arms Transfers* (Washington: GPO, 1989), 18; Michael A. Ottenberg, "Israel and the Atom," *American Sentinel,* August 16, 1992, 1.

230. Harold Hough, "Could Israel's Nuclear Assets Survive a First Strike?," *Jane's Intelligence Review,* September 1997, 407–410.

231. Ibid.

232. Ibid.

233. Uzi Mahnaimi and Matthew Campbell, "Israel Makes Nuclear Waves With Submarine Missile Test," *Sunday Times* (London), June 18, 2000; Walter Pincus, "Israel Has Sub-Based Atomic Arms Capability," *Washington Post,* June 15, 2002, A1.

234. Associated Press, October 5, 1998, 0316; October 8, 1998, 1350; *Philadelphia Inquirer,* November 1, 1998, A-7.

235. Uzi Mahnaimi, "Israeli Jets Equipped for Chemical Warfare," *Sunday Times* (London), October 4, 1998.

236. This information is unconfirmed and based on only one source. Israel does, however, have excellent research facilities; laboratory production of poison gas is essential to test protection devices as is the production of biological weapons to test countermeasures and antidotes.

237. *Philadelphia Inquirer,* November 1, 1998, A-7; Associated Press, October 8, 1998, 1350.

238. *Washington Times,* October 7, 1998, A-14.

239. Hough, "Could Israel's Nuclear Assets Survive a First Strike?," 407–410.

240. T. Orszaq-Land, "Iran Threatens to Abandon the NPT," *Jane's Islamic Affairs Analyst,* October 1, 2004.

241. Abraham Rabinovich, "Iran boasts Dimona now 'within range,'" *The Washington Times,* August 24, 2004.

242. Kenneth R. Timmerman, "The Crisis Has Begun," *The Washington Times,* January 7, 2006.

243. "Iran Report," *RFE/RL,* 9, no. 2, January 23, 2006.

244. Shlomo Brom, "Is the Begin Doctrine Still a Viable Option for Israel?," in *Getting Ready for A Nuclear Iran,* ed. Henry Sokolski and Patrick Clawson (Carlisle, PA: Strategic Studies Institute, October 2005).

245. For further discussion, see Michael Knights, "Iran's Conventional Forces Remain Key to Deterring Potential Threats," *Jane's Intelligence Review,* February 1, 2006; Paul Rogers, "Iran: Consequences of a War," Oxford Research Group, Briefing Paper, February 2006.

246. http://www.globalsecurity.org/wmd/world/israel/popeye-t.htm.

247. http://www.globalsecurity.org/wmd/world/israel/popeye-t.htm.

248. http://www.globalsecurity.org/military/systems/munitions/blu-109-specs.htm.

249. http://www.globalsecurity.org/military/systems/munitions/jdam.htm.

250. http://www.globalsecurity.org/military/systems/munitions/blu-116.htm.

251. Jim VandeHei, "Cheney Warns of Iran As a Nuclear Threat," *The Washington Post,* January 21, 2005, A02.

252. Ewen MacAskill and Simon Tisdall, "Iran's Message to the West: Back off or We Retaliate," *The Guardian,* February 2, 2006, http://www.guardian.co.uk/iran/story/0,,1700266,00.html.

253. Tom Carter, "Tehran Nukes A Global Threat, Israeli Wars," *The Washington Times,* December 7, 2004.

254. Peter Brookes, "Iran: Our Military Options," *The New York Post,* January 23, 2006.

255. http://www.globalsecurity.org/wmd/world/israel/popeye-t.htm.

256. Barbara Opall-Rome, "Israel Fortifies Options in Face of Iran's Nuclear Work," *Defense News,* May 29, 2006, 6.

257. David R. Sands, "Israelis Urge US to Stop Iran's Nuke Goals," *Washington Times,* September 30, 2005, 1.

CHAPTER 5

1. These data are extrapolated from the CIA, *World Factbook, 2006,* http://www.odci.gov/cia/publications/factbook/geos/eg.html.

2. These totals are extrapolated from the IISS, *Military Balance,* 2005–2006. Other sources show significant variations in these numbers.

3. The data in this section draw heavily from a number of basic source documents on the balance. IISS, *Military Balance,* various editions; Jaffee Center for Strategic Studies, *Military Balance in the Middle East,* various editions; *Jane's Sentinel Security Assessments,* "Egypt," various editions.

4. "Egypt to Augment M1A1 Fleet," *Jane's Defence Weekly,* January 7, 2004, http://jdw.janes.com (accessed January 8, 2004). Labeled 21.

5. "Egypt Expands Armored Recovery Vehicle Lineup," *Jane's Defence Weekly,* July 14, 2004, http://jdw.janes.com (accessed January 19, 2005). Labeled 20.

6. Nikolai Novichkov, "Belarus to Upgrade Egyptian BTR-50PKs," *Jane's Defence Weekly,* September 18, 2002, http://jdw.janes.com (accessed January 9, 2004). Labeled 22.

7. Robin Hughes, "Egypt Seeks All-Terrain Vehicles," *Jane's Defence Weekly,* September 17, 2003, http://jdw.janes.com (accessed January 8, 2004). Labeled 23.

8. The data in this section draw heavily from a number of basic source documents on the balance. IISS, *Military Balance,* various editions; Jaffee Center for Strategic Studies, *Military Balance in the Middle East,* various editions; *Jane's Sentinel Security Assessments,* "Egypt," various editions.

9. Robin Hughes, "Egypt Receives First Upgraded Hawkeye," *Jane's Defence Weekly,* March 12, 2003, http://jdw.janes.com (accessed January 8, 2004). Labeled 25.

10. Robin Hughes, "Egypt Seeks Foreign Military Sales," *Jane's Defence Weekly,* July 30, 2003, http://jdw.janes.com (accessed January 8, 2004). Labeled 26; and Robin Hughes, "Egypt's Apaches to Receive Mission-Planning Systems," *Jane's Defence Weekly,* July 2, 2003, 19.

11. Hughes, "Egypt's Apaches to Receive Mission-Planning Systems," 19.

12. "BAE Systems Wins Egyptian F-16 Contract," *Jane's Defence Weekly,* January 15, 2003, http://jdw.janes.com (accessed January 8, 2004). Labeled 24.

13. The data in this section draw heavily from a number of basic source documents on the balance. IISS, *Military Balance,* various editions; Jaffee Center for Strategic Studies, *Military Balance in the Middle East,* various editions; *Jane's Sentinel Security Assessments,* "Israel," various editions.

14. The data in this section draw heavily from a number of basic source documents on the balance. *Jane's Fighting Ships,* various editions; IISS, *Military Balance,* various editions; Jaffee Center for Strategic Studies, *Military Balance in the Middle East,* various editions; *Jane's Sentinel Security Assessments,* "Egypt," various editions.

15. *Jane's Fighting Ships;* "Egypt," various editions; *Jane's Sentinel, Eastern Mediterranean;* "Egypt," various editions.

16. Much of the readiness, operational status, and modernization data used throughout this section on the Egyptian Navy is drawn from *Jane's Fighting Ships;* "Egypt," various editions; *Jane's Sentinel, Eastern Mediterranean;* "Egypt," various editions.

17. *Jane's Defence Weekly,* August 6, 2003, http://jdw.janes.com (accessed January 8, 2004). Labeled 28.

18. *Jane's Defence Weekly,* November 20, 2003, http://jdw.janes.com (accessed January 8, 2004). Labeled 29.

19. The data in this section draw heavily from a number of basic source documents on the balance. IISS, *Military Balance,* various editions; Jaffee Center for Strategic Studies, *Military Balance in the Middle East,* various editions; *Jane's Sentinel Security Assessments,* "Egypt," various editions.

20. Interviews and Lt. Col. Ewen Southby-Tailyour, "Special Forces: Egypt," *Jane's Amphibious and Special Forces,* November 13, 2002.

21. IISS, *Military Balance,* "Egypt," various editions.

22. U.S. State Department, *Country Reports on Terrorism,* Office of the Coordinator for Counterterrorism, April 27, 2005, http://www.state.gov/s/ct/rls/45394.htm. The description in the updated report issued on April 28, 2006, is virtually identical.

23. Ibid.

24. www.state.gov/s/ct/rls/crt/2005/64344.htm.

25. "Egypt's Bombs," *The Economist,* April 29, 2005, 49–50; Daniel Williams, "Sinai Bombers Linked to Gaza," *The Washington Post,* May 24, 2006, A14.

26. http://www.state.gov/g/drl/rls/hrrpt/2004/41720.htm.

27. http://www.state.gov/g/drl/rls/hrrpt/2005/61687.htm.

28. "Egypt: Forwards, Backwards," *The Economist,* May 27, 2006, 46; CIA, *World Factbook, 2006,* "Egypt."

29. Center for Nonproliferation Studies, Monterey Institute of International Studies, "North Korean Missile Exports and Technical Assistance to Egypt," http://www.nti.org/db/profiles/dprk/msl/ie/NKM_EeegptGO.html (accessed March 2003).

30. "Egypt's Budding Nuclear Program," *The Risk Report,* September–October 1996, http://www.wisconsinproject.org/countries/egypt/nuke.html.

31. *Jane's Defence Weekly,* October 14, 1998.

32. U.S. State Department, *Country Reports on Terrorism,* Office of the Coordinator for Counterterrorism, April 27, 2005, http://www.state.gov/s/ct/rls/45392.htm.

33. Michael Herzog and Brooke Neuman, *A New Reality on the Egypt-Gaza Border, Analysis of the New Israel-Egypt Agreement (Parts I & II),* Washington Institute for Near East Policy, October 2005.

34. Much of the following analysis is based on the work by Herzog and Neuman, in *A New Reality on the Egypt-Gaza Border, Analysis of the New Israel-Egypt Agreement (Parts I & II).*

CHAPTER 6

1. "Regional Round Up," *Jane's Terrorism and Security Monitor,* September 14, 2005, http://jtsm.janes.com (accessed October 26, 2005).

2. Ashraf Khalil, Ranya Kadri, and Josh Meyer, "Suicide Attacks Kill at least 57 at 3 Hotels in Jordan's Capital," *Los Angeles Times,* November 10, 2005, A1.

3. "Interview with General Khalid Al-Sarayrah, Chairman, Jordanian Force's Joint Chiefs of Staff," *Defense News,* May 15, 2006.

4. CIA, *World Factbook, 2006,* "Jordan," http://www.odci.gov/cia/publications/factbook/geos/jo.html.

5. The data in this section draw heavily from a number of basic source documents on the balance. IISS, *Military Balance,* various editions; Jaffee Center for Strategic Studies, *Military Balance in the Middle East,* various editions; *Jane's Sentinel Security Assessments,* "Jordan," various editions.

6. "Interview with Prince Feisal bin Al-Hussein, Special Assistant to the Chief of Staff, Jordanian Military," *Defense News,* March 20, 2006, 38.

7. "Jordan-Defense Production and R&D," *Jane's Sentinel Security Assessment,* June 1, 2005.

8. IISS, *Military Balance,* "Jordan," various editions.

9. Christopher Foss, "UK Design to Make Jordan's Tanks More Lethal," *Jane's Defence Weekly,* September 19, 2003, http://jdw.janes.com (accessed January 8, 2004). Labeled 33.

10. Rupert Pengelley, "Jordan Studies Interim 'Hybrid Turret' Upgrade for Challenger 1 Fleet," *Jane's Defence Weekly,* August 20, 2003, http://jdw.janes.com (accessed January 8, 2004). Labeled 34.

11. Robin Hughes, "Jordan Awards Contract for M60 Tank Upgrade," *Jane's Defence Weekly,* December 17, 2003, http://jdw.janes.com (accessed January 8, 2004). Labeled 32.

12. Lale Sariibrahimoglu, "Jordan Signs for Turkish Armored Combat Vehicles," *Jane's Defence Weekly,* July 16, 2003, http://jdw.janes.com (accessed January 8, 2004). Labeled 31.

13. Robin Hughes, "Jordan Orders Al-Jawad Armored Troop Carrier," *Jane's Defence Weekly,* October 18, 2002, http://jdw.janes.com (accessed January 9, 2004). Labeled 30.

14. Robin Hughes, "Jordan First with Dutch Gun," *Jane's Defence Weekly,* February 5, 2003, http://jdw.janes.com (accessed January 8, 2004). Labeled 35.

15. Christopher Foss, "BAE Pointing System Wins Orders in the Middle East," *Jane's Defence Weekly,* August 27, 2003, http://jdw.janes.com (accessed January 8, 2004). Labeled 36.

16. IISS, *Military Balance,* "Jordan," various editions.

17. The data in this section draw heavily from a number of basic source documents on the balance. IISS, *Military Balance,* various editions; Jaffee Center for Strategic Studies, *Military Balance in the Middle East,* various editions; *Jane's Sentinel Security Assessments,* "Jordan," various editions.

18. Much of this detail is taken from an interview entitled, "Prince Feisal Bin Al-Hussein, Special Assistant to the Chief of Staff, Jordanian Military," *Defense News*. March 20, 2006, 38.

19. Robin Hughes, "Amman Increases Air Force Assets," *Jane's Defence Weekly,* September 24, 2003, http://jdw.janes.com (accessed January 8, 2004). Labeled 37.

20. "Jordan Set to Buy F-16s," *Agence France-Press,* April 20, 2006, 10:47.

21. The data in this section draw heavily from a number of basic source documents on the balance. IISS, *Military Balance,* various editions; Jaffee Center for Strategic Studies, *Military Balance in the Middle East,* various editions; *Jane's Sentinel Security Assessments,* "Jordan," various editions.

22. "Jordan Receives Patriot Batteries," *Jane's Defence Weekly,* February 12, 2003, http://jdw.janes.com (accessed January 8, 2004). Labeled 38.

23. The data in this section draw heavily from a number of basic source documents on the balance. *Jane's Fighting Ships,* various editions; IISS, *Military Balance,* various editions; Jaffee Center for Strategic Studies, *Military Balance in the Middle East,* various editions; *Jane's Sentinel Security Assessments,* "Jordan," various editions.

24. IISS, *Military Balance,* "Jordan," various editions; *Jane's Fighting Ships,* "Jordan," various editions; *Jane's Sentinel,* "Jordan," various editions.

25. IISS, *Military Balance,* "Jordan," various editions.

26. "Special Forces—Jordan," *Jane's Amphibious and Special Forces* (accessed November 8, 2005).

27. The data in this section draw heavily from a number of basic source documents on the balance. IISS, *Military Balance,* various editions; Jaffee Center for Strategic Studies, *Military Balance in the Middle East,* various editions; *Jane's Sentinel Security Assessments,* "Jordan," various editions.

28. This analysis draws heavily on the declassified intelligence analysis of terrorist and extremist movements in the U.S. State Department country reports on terrorism, specifically on the revised edition issued in April 2005, chaps. 5 and 6, http://www.state.gov/s/ct/rls/c14813.htm, and April 28, 2006, www.state.gov/s/ct/rls/crt/2005/64344.htm.

29. U.S. State Department, *Country Reports on Terrorism,* Office of the Coordinator for Counterterrorism, April 28, 2006, Chapter 5—"Country Reports: Middle East and North Africa Overview," "Jordan," http://www.state.gov/s/ct/rls/crt/2005/64344.htm.

30. See "Israel Fears for Jordan's Future," *Jane's Intelligence Digest,* March 10, 2006.

31. http://www.state.gov/g/drl/rls/hrrpt/2004/41723.htm.

32. http://www.state.gov/g/drl/rls/hrrpt/2004/41723.htm.

33. *Washington Post,* August 16, 1995, A-26.

CHAPTER 7

1. CIA, *World Factbook, 2006,* http://www.odci.gov/cia/publications/factbook/geos/le.html.

2. "UN: Terrorists in Lebanon Won't be Allowed to Jeopardize Calm," *The Associated Press,* September 29, 2005, http://www.haaretz.com/hasen/spages/630509.html (accessed September 29, 2005).

3. Detlev Mehlis, "Report of the International Independent Investigation Commission, established pursuant to Security Council Resolution 1595 (2005)," Beirut, October 19, 2005, 53.

4. Riad Kahwaji, "Lebanon Seeks New Aid Source," *Defense News,* August 15, 2005, 6.

5. The election was held in four rounds on May 29, June 5, 12, 19, 2005 (next to be held 2009). Election results in seats by group—Future Movement Bloc 36; Democratic Gathering 15; Development and Resistance Bloc 15; Loyalty to the Resistance 14; Free Patriotic Movement 14; Lebanese Forces 6; Qornet Shewan 5; Popular Bloc 4; Tripoli Independent Bloc 3; Syrian National Socialist Party 2; Kataeb Reform Movement 2; Tachnaq Party 2; Democratic Renewal Movement 1; Democratic Left 1; Nasserite Popular Movement 1; Ba'th Party 1; Kataeb Party 1; independent 5. Source: CIA, *World Factbook, 2006,* http://www.odci.gov/cia/publications/factbook/geos/le.html.

6. Colum Lynch, "US Urges Continuation of UN Probe," *The Washington Post,* December 2, 2005, A20.

7. Associated Press, "Lebanon Tightens Syrian Border," *Baltimore Sun,* October 28, 2005.

8. John Kifner, "UN Reports Rising Flow of Arms from Syria into Lebanon," *The New York Times,* October 27, 2005, A6.

9. Warren Hoge and Steven R. Weisman, "UN Is Expected To Pass Measure Pressuring Syria," *The New York Times,* October 31, 2005, A1.

10. The data in this section draw heavily from a number of basic source documents on the balance. IISS, *Military Balance,* various editions; Jaffee Center for Strategic Studies, *Military Balance in the Middle East,* various editions; *Jane's Sentinel Security Assessments,* "Lebanon," various editions.

11. Kifner, "UN Reports Rising Flow of Arms from Syria into Lebanon," A6.

12. Hoge and Weisman, "UN is Expected to Pass Measure Pressuring Syria," A1.

13. The data in this section draw heavily from a number of basic source documents on the balance. *Jane's Fighting Ships,* various editions; IISS, *Military Balance,* various editions; Jaffee Center for Strategic Studies, *Military Balance in the Middle East,* various editions; *Jane's Sentinel Security Assessments,* "Lebanon," various editions.

14. *Jane's Fighting Ships,* various editions; IISS, *Military Balance,* various editions.

15. The data in this section draw heavily from a number of basic source documents on the balance. IISS, *Military Balance,* various editions; Jaffee Center for Strategic Studies, *Military Balance in the Middle East,* various editions; *Jane's Sentinel Security Assessments,* "Lebanon," various editions.

16. This analysis draws heavily on the declassified intelligence analysis of country efforts to deal with terrorists and extremist movements, and the nature of terrorist and extremist movements, provided in the U.S. State Department country reports on terrorism, specifically on the revised edition issued in April 2005, chaps. 5 and 6, http://www.state.gov/s/ct/rls/c14813.htm.

17. U.S. State Department, *Country Reports on Terrorism,* Office of the Coordinator for Counterterrorism, April 2005, Chapter 5—Country Reports: Middle East and North Africa Overview, http://www.state.gov/s/ct/rls/c14813.htm.

18. Office of the Coordinator for Counterterrorism, *Country Reports on Terrorism,* April 28, 2006, Chapter 8—Foreign Terrorist Organizations, www.state.gov/s/ct/rls/crt/2005/64344.htm.

19. International Crisis Group, "Hezbollah: Rebel without a Cause?," Middle East Briefing, July 30, 2003, 2.

20. Ibid., 2.

21. United Press International, September 28, 2000.

22. John Kifner, "Whose Holy Land? Lebanon," *New York Times,* October 15, 2000, 13.

23. *New York Times,* October 15, 2000, A-11.

24. Dalal Saoud, "Hezbollah Chief Seeks Soldiers-Detainees Swap," United Press International, October 7, 2000.

25. United Press International, October 20, 2000.

26. Sam F. Ghattas, "Hezbollah Threatens Israel," *Associated Press Online,* January 28, 2001.

27. Gareth Smyth, "Prepare to Assist Palestinians, Hezbollah Told," *Financial Times,* August 13, 2001, 5.

28. Hussein Dakroub, "Red Cross Envoy Discusses Hezbollah Offer for Trading Captured Israeli for Sparing Palestinian Lives in Jenin Refugee Camp," *Associated Press Worldstream,* April 11, 2002; and Bassem Mroue, "Hezbollah Offers to Trade Israeli Prisoners Besieged in West Bank," *Associated Press Worldstream,* April 28, 2002.

29. Kifner, "Whose Holy Land? Lebanon," 13.

30. *Associated Press Worldstream,* February 12, 2002.

31. Harvey Morris, "Israel Seizes Boat Loaded with Arms," *Financial Times,* May 23, 2003, 13.

32. Sudarsan Raghavan, "Hezbollah Acknowledges Teaching Guerrilla Warfare to Palestinians," Knight-Ridder/Tribune News Service, April 21, 2002.

33. Prime Minister's Media Adviser, "ISA and Israel Police Uncover Hezbollah-Financed and Guided Israeli Arab Terrorist Infrastructure," Israeli Ministry of Foreign Affairs Web site, February 8, 2004, http://www.israel-mfa.gov.il/mfa/go.asp?MFAH0ob90 (accessed March 12, 2004).

34. Matthew Kalman, "Hezbollah Confirms Backing 'Brothers in Occupied Palestine,'" *Globe and Mail,* July 22, 2004, A10.

35. Ibid., A10.

36. Ewen MacAskill, "Hezbollah Is Involved in West Bank, says Israel," *The Guardian,* October 15, 2004.

37. Kalman, "Hezbollah Confirms Backing 'Brothers in Occupied Palestine,'" A10.

38. Ibid., A10.

39. Dalal Saoud, "Hezbollah Women Protest, Chief Speaks of 'Factor of Terror,'" *United Press International,* October 29, 2000.

40. Tarek Al-Issawi, "Lebanese on Israeli Border Prepare," Associated Press, October 16, 2000.

41. Saoud, "Hezbollah Chief Seeks Soldiers-Detainees Swap."

42. "Statement by Prime Minister Ehud Barak, Jerusalem, October 7, 2000," available at the Israeli Ministry of Foreign Affairs' Web site, http://www.mfa.gov.il/.

43. Jack Katzenell, "Israel to Consider Leader's Release," *Associated Press Online,* April 6, 2001.

44. Joshua Brilliant, "Israeli: Any Price for Hostage Info," *United Press International,* May 10, 2001.

45. Tracy Wilkinson, "Israel Has New Idea of Trio's Fate," *Los Angeles Times,* Home Edition, October 30, 2001, pt. A, pt. 1, 14.

46. Zeina Karam, "Hezbollah Leader Threatens to Capture More Israelis over Prisoner Issue," *Associated Press,* July 27, 2003.

47. Communication by the IDF Spokesman, "The Release of Security Prisoners and Administrative Detainees," Israel Ministry of Foreign Affairs, January 29, 2004, http://www.mfa.gov.il/MFA/Government/Communiques/2004/-The+release+of+security+prisoners+and+administrati.htm (accessed June 16, 2004).

48. "Hezbollah's Risky Strategy," *Jane's Intelligence Digest,* February 6, 2004.

49. Ghattas, "Hezbollah Threatens Israel"; and Butros Wanna, "Hezbollah Puts Message on Billboard," *Associated Press Online,* June 9, 2001.

50. Daniel Williams, "Israeli Jets Attack Southern Lebanon," *Washington Post,* April 15, 2001, A16.

51. Dalal Saoud, "Lebanon-Israel-Hezbollah," *United Press International,* April 15, 2001.

52. *Associated Press Online,* April 16, 2001.

53. Saoud, "Lebanon-Israel-Hezbollah."

54. "Terrorist Attacks from Lebanon Against Israeli Targets Since the Israeli Pullout in May 2000," Israel Defense Forces Official Web site, posted June 8, 2004, http://www1.idf.il/DOVER/site/mainpage.asp?clr=1&sl=EN&id=7&docid=31840 (accessed June 16, 2004).

55. Sambar Kassbli, "Syria Steps up Criticism of Israel," *Associated Press,* April 17, 2001.

56. Ralph Atkins and Avi Machlis, "Israel Bombs Syrian Position in Lebanon," *Financial Times,* July 2, 2001, 8.

57. Harvey Morris, "Israel Launches Missile Attack on Hezbollah in Lebanon," *Financial Times,* October 23, 2001, 12.

58. Reuters, "Hezbollah Member Killed by Car Bomb," *Los Angeles Times,* August 3, 2003, 18.

59. Hussein Dakroub, "Hezbollah Shells Lebanon Border Area," *Associated Press Online,* August 9, 2003.

60. Samuel M. Katz, "Hezbollah: the Lebanese Shiite Party of God," *Special Operations Report,* 2004, 11.

61. Gareth Smyth, "Powder Keg Claims Threaten Lebanese Idyll: Rumours of Missile Build-up on Borders with Israel Suit Hezbollah's Mental Warfare," *Financial Times,* February 19, 2002.

62. John Ward Anderson, "Clashes on Border Drive Israeli Fears; Wider Conflict Predicted with Hezbollah," *Washington Post,* November 2, 2002, A19.

63. Michael R. Gordon, "Threats and Responses: Military Risks; Militants Are Said to Amass Missiles in South Lebanon," *New York Times,* September 27, 2002, 1.

64. Itamar Inbari, "Nasrallah: Hezbollah Seeking Stronger Weapons," *Maariv,* October 25, 2004.

65. Greg Myre, "Putin Visits Israel and Tries to Allay Its Security Worries," *New York Times,* April 29, 2005, 3.

66. "Israeli Planes Drop Leaflets over Beirut Denouncing Hezbollah after Clashes," The Associated Press, November 23, 2005.

67. Riad Kahwaji and Barbara Opall-Rome, "Hezbollah: Iran's Battle Lab," *Defense News,* December 13, 2004, 1.

68. IISS, *Military Balance,* "Syria-Lebanon-Israel," 2005/6 editions, 178.

69. Barbara Opall-Rome, "Mosquito Through a Net, UAV Finds Flaw in Israeli Air Defenses," *Defense News,* April 18, 2005, 1, 8.

70. David Ignatius, "Muslim Radicals in Power," *Washington Post,* February 3, 2006, A15, A19.

71. Emily Hunt, "Can Al-Qaeda's Lebanese Expansion Be Stopped?" *Policy Watch #1076,* Washington Institute for Near East Policy, February 6, 2006.

72. Office of the Coordinator for Counterterrorism, *Country Reports on Terrorism,* April 28, 2006, Chapter 8—Foreign Terrorist Organizations, www.state.gov/s/ct/rls/crt/2005/64344.htm.

73. http://www.state.gov/g/drl/rls/hrrpt/2004/41723.htm.

74. U.S. State Department, *Country Reports on Human Rights Practices—2005,* "Lebanon," Bureau of Democracy, Human Rights, and Labor, March 8, 2006, http://www.state.gov/g/drl/rls/hrrpt/2005/61693.htm.

CHAPTER 8

1. For an analysis of Israeli fears and concerns over this issue, see Bennett Zimmerman, Roberta Seid, and Michel L. Wise, "The Million Person Gap: The Arab Population in the West Bank and Gaza," Ramat Gan, Begin-Sadat Center for Strategic Studies, Midest Security and Policy Studies, No. 65, February 2005.

2. "Security and Foreign Forces, Israel," *Jane's Sentinel Security Assessment—Eastern Mediterranean,* September 19, 2005.

3. "Greater Jerusalem" has no fixed definition and is steadily being expanded eastwards. From Israel's perspective, it clear includes Mt. Scopus, East Jerusalem, and the Jerusalem No Man's Land.

4. "The Hamas Dilemma," *The Economist,* January 28, 2006, 43.

5. Rhonda Roumani and Scott Wilson, "Hamas is Resolute in Fighting Israel," *The Washington Post,* January 29, 2006.

6. For a discussion of the impact of the fighting, and options for action, see Robert E. Hunter and Seth G. Jones, *Building a Successful Palestinian State: Security* (Santa Monica: RAND, 2006).

7. Gal Luft, "Palestinian Security Services: Between Police and Army," Research Memorandum No. 36, Washington Institute for Near-East Policy.

8. Ibid.

9. Ephraim Kam and Yiftah Shapir, eds., "Chapter 13: Palestinian Authority," *The Middle East Strategic Balance: 2002–2003,* online ed. (Tel Aviv: Jaffee Center for Strategic Studies, Tel Aviv University, updated January 19, 2004).

10. Karin Laub, "Palestinian Security Force in Ruins," *Associated Press Online,* April 25, 2002.

11. Megan K. Stack and Rebecca Trounson, "Peace Plan May Hinge on Security Force in Disarray," *Los Angeles Times,* June 3, 2003.

12. Gal Luft, "From Clandestine Army to Guardians of Terror: The Palestinian Security Forces and the Second Intifada" (presentation given at the National Press Club, Washington, D.C., July 24, 2003).

13. IISS, *Military Balance,* "Palestinian Autonomous Areas of Gaza and Jericho," 2005/6 editions.

14. Ibid.

15. Jaffee Center Middle East Military Balance, Palestinian Authority, http://www.tau.ac.il/jcss/balance/toc.html (accessed December 6, 2005).

16. U.S. Department of State, *Country Reports on Terrorism 2004,* posted on Nexis April 2005.

17. Robin Oakley and John Vause, "Abbas Pledges to Unify Security," *Cnn.com,* March 1, 2005, http://www.cnn.com/2005/WORLD/meast/03/01/london.conference.

18. Agence France Presse, "Palestinian Parliament Demands Immediate Action on Security," March 24, 2005.

19. Ibid.

20. Ibid.

21. Mohamed Daraghmeh, "Abbas Orders Crackdown on Militants in Ramallah After they Attacked his Headquarters," *Associated Press,* March 31, 2005.

22. Molly Moore and John Ward Anderson, "For Abbas, a Crisis of Perception; Reform Plans Stymied by Difference in Palestinian, Israeli Views of Security Forces," *Washington Post,* Section A12, May 4, 2005.

23. Ibid.

24. Ibid.

25. Ibid.

26. Mohamed Daraghmeh, "Abbas Dismisses Key Security Chief in Step Toward Reform of Palestinian Security Forces," *Associated Press,* April 2, 2005.

27. Moore and Anderson, "For Abbas, a Crisis of Perception."

28. For additional details, see "Jane's Country Profile, Gaza and the West Bank," *Jane's Sentinel Security Assessment,* online (accessed April 10, 2006).

29. http://www.state.gov/g/drl/rls/hrrpt/2004/41723.htm.

30. http://www.state.gov/g/drl/rls/hrrpt/2005/61690.htm.

31. http://www.state.gov/s/ct/rls/crt/2005/64344.htm.

32. This section draws heavily on U.S. sources and interviews, and "Jane's Country Profile, Gaza and the West Bank."

33. U.S. State Department, *Country Reports on Terrorism,* Office of the Coordinator for Counterterrorism, April 27, 2005, http://www.state.gov/s/ct/rls/45394.htm.

34. Ze'ev Schiff, "IDF Cracks Down in West Bank; PA Arrests Jihad Men," *Ha'aretz,* December 6, 2005.

35. Aluf Benn, "Netanya Bombing/Analysis: Leave Hamas Alone," *Ha'aretz,* December 6, 2005.

36. See "The Charter of the Hamas" Articles One to Thirty-Six; and U.S. Department of State, "Patterns of Global Terrorism, 1998," Washington, GPO, April 1999, Appendix B, "Syria," and "Iran." For further summary historical details, see "Hamas: Origins, Development, and Prospects," *Jane's Islamic Affairs Analyst,* May 8. 2006.

37. Australian Government, "Hamas' Izz al-Din al-Qassam Brigades," National Security Australia, November 9, 2003, http://www.nationalsecurity.gov.au/www/nationalsecurity-Home.nsf/0/EFB123797285BD04CA256DDB00069E0F?OpenDocument (accessed June 13, 2004).

38. http://www.tkb.org/Group.jsp?groupID=49.

39. International Policy Institute for Counter-Terrorism, "Hamas (Islamic Resistance Movement)," Herzliya, Israel, www.ict.org.il/ (accessed August 6, 2003).

40. *Los Angeles Times,* June 19, 1998.

41. Reuters, June 25, 1998.

42. *Washington Post,* November 2, 1998, A-1.

43. *Washington Post,* October 17, 1995, A-1; *Washington Times,* September 4, 1995, A-9.

44. The poll was undertaken by the Palestinian Center for Public Opinion; see "76% of Palestinians Support Suicide Attacks," *Jerusalem Post,* June 4, 2001, 1.

45. International Policy Institute for Counter-Terrorism, "Hamas (Islamic Resistance Movement)."

46. Keith B. Richburg, *Washington Post,* November 14, 2000, A30.

47. Saud Abu Ramadan, United Press International, October 5, 2000.

48. Mary Curtius and Marjorie Miller, *Los Angeles Times,* October 8, 2000, A1; and Marjorie Miller and Robin Wright, *Los Angeles Times,* October 7, 2000, A1.

49. Lee Hockstader, *Washington Post,* October 7, 2000, A1.

50. Mary Curtius, *Los Angeles Times,* October 13, 2000, A1.

51. Keith B. Richburg, *Washington Post,* October 25, 2000.

52. Barry Schweid, *Associated Press Online,* October 26, 2000.

53. Barry Schweid, *Associated Press Online,* October 27, 2000.

54. Barry Schweid, *Associated Press Online,* November 22, 2000.

55. Jamie Tarabay, *Associated Press,* November 25, 2000.

56. For a full chronology of major Israeli targeted killings, including all those of prominent Hamas members, please see Chapter 6.

57. GPO, "Hamas Terrorist Attacks," Israel Ministry of Foreign Affairs, March 22, 2004, http://www.mfa.gov.il (accessed June 14, 2004).

58. Ibrahim Barzak, A*ssociated Press Online,* April 17, 2001.

59. Barbara Demick and Nomi Morris, Knight-Ridder/Tribune News Service, May 19, 2001.

60. Associated Press Online, January 24, 2002.

61. Associated Press, May 9, 2003.

62. Jamie Tarabay, *Associated Press Online,* March 2, 2001.

63. Jack Kelley, *USA Today,* October 18, 2000, 14A.

64. Hamza Hendawi, *Associated Press Online,* June 16, 2001.

65. Soraya Sarhaddi Nelson, Knight-Ridder/Tribune News Service, June 3, 2002.

66. John Pike, "Hamas (Islamic Resistance Movement)," http://www.globalsecurity.org/military/world/para/hamas.htm, last modified April 18, 2004 (accessed June 13, 2004).

67. Mark Lavie, "Hamas Will Continue...," *Associated Press Online,* June 5, 2001.

68. United Press International, August 23, 2001.

69. Saud Abu Ramadan, *United Press International,* October 21, 2001.

70. Saud Abu Ramadan, *United Press International,* December 5, 2001, A1.

71. Associated Press, December 5, 2001.

72. Mary Curtius, *Los Angeles Times,* December 13, 2001, A1.

73. Tracy Wilkinson, *Los Angeles Times,* December 22, 2001.

74. Tracy Wilkinson, *Los Angeles Times,* January 23, 2002, A3.

75. Associated Press, June 3, 2002.

76. Mark Lavie, *Associated Press Online,* June 20, 2002.

77. *Los Angeles Times,* June 23, 2002, A5.

78. Peter Hermann, *Baltimore Sun,* October 10, 2002, 1A.

79. James Bennett, *New York Times,* February 8, 2003, A9.

80. Karin Laub, *Associated Press Online,* May 5, 2003.

81. Text of the Hamas-Islamic Jihad Declaration, *Associated Press,* June 29, 2003.

82. Timothy Heritage and Barry Moody, "Hamas Leader Sees Mideast Cease-fire Failing," *MSNBC Online News,* July 3, 2003.

83. "Hamas Declares End to Ceasefire," *The Weekend Australian,* August 30, 2003, http://www.theaustralian.news.com.au/common/story_page/0,5744,7026241%255E1702,00.html.

84. John Ward Anderson and Molly Moore, "Hamas Won Power in West Bank Vote Local Elections May Prove to Be Harbinger," *The Washington Post,* January 6, 2005, A15.

85. Ibid., A15.

86. Ibid., A15.

87. Khalil Shikaki, "Willing to Compromise, Palestinian Public Opinion and the Peace Process," Washington, USIP, Report 158, January 2006.

88. Nidal al-Mughrabi, "Palestinian Police Link Hamas Men to Iran," *Reuters,* February 4, 1999.

89. For a detailed discussion of this issue, see Elie Rekhess, "The Terrorist Connection—Iran, the Islamic Jihad, and Hamas," *Justice* 5 (May 1995).

90. "Hamas Chief Meets Iran's Supreme Leader," *Iran Focus,* February 20, 2006.

91. Dr. Reuven Ehrlich (Avi-Ran), "Terrorism as a Preferred Instrument of Syrian Policy," ICT Research Fellow, www.ict.org.il/ (accessed October 16, 1999).

92. Robin Wright and David Lamb, "Syria Puts New Curbs on Militants," *Los Angeles Times,* May 4, 2003, 1.

93. Reported in Dexter Filkins, "Hamas Still Going Strong in Syria, Some Say," *International Herald Tribune Online,* www.iht.com (accessed July 16, 2003).

94. E-mail dated February 1, 2006.

95. Mahmoud al-Zahar (text from CNN Web site 29.01.06).

96. Ismail Haniyeh, press conference 26.1.06 (text from al-Jazeera translated by BBC Monitoring).

97. CIA, *World Factbook, 2006,* http://www.odci.gov/cia/publications/factbook/geos/le.html.

98. Scott Wilson, "Middle East Envoy Wars of Palestinian Authority Collapse," *The Washington Post,* February 27, 2006.

99. Ibid.

100. For a summary of Palestinian economic dependence on Israel, see Elizabeth Young, "Palestinian Economic Dependence on Israel," *Policywatch,* No. 1088, Washington Institute, March 23, 2006.

101. Interviews with Israeli officers and officials. Also see Scott Wilson, "Israeli General: Sanctions Won't Topple Hamas," *Washington Post,* May 24, 2006, A14; Steven Erlanger, "US and Israelis Are Said to Talk of Hamas Ouster," *New York Times,* February 14, 2006; Steven R. Wiesman, "US and Israel Deny Plans to Drive Hamas from Power," *New York Times,* February 15, 2006.

102. Joshua Brilliant, "Hamas, Fatah Pull Back from the Brink," *UPI,* May 23, 2006; Ibrahim Barzak, "Hamas Forces Clash with Abbas Loyalists," *ABC News,* May 26, 2006; "Palestinian Power Struggle," *Jane's Intelligence Digest,* May 24, 2006; "Palestinian Commander Killed in Gaza Blast, Hamas Blamed," *Israel Insider,* May 24, 2006; "Hamas Waskes Up to the Palestinian Security Nightmare," *Foreign Report,* April 13, 2006; "Reversing Roles: Hamas and Its Rivals," *Jane's Terrorism and Security Monitor,* March 15, 2006; "Head of New 3,000-strong Hamas Security Force Is Wanted Terrorist," *Associated Press,* May 18, 2006; Agencies, "Hamas Security Force Deployed in Gaza," *Guardian,* May 17, 2006; "Haniyeh Says May Increase

Hamas Security Force," *Reuters,* May 19, 2006; John Murphy, "Uncertain Moments for Gaza's Security," *Baltimore Sun,* May 25, 2006; and Khaled Abu Toameh, "New Hamas Security Force Operational," *Jerusalem Post,* May 17, 2006.

103. "Competing Palestinian Security Forces Face Off in Hamas-Abbas Clash," *Associated Press,* May 19, 2006; "Rival Palestinian Security Forces Clash," *CBC News,* May 19, 2006, 07:44:55 EDT; Brilliant, "Hamas, Fatah Pull Back from the Brink"; "Palestinian Commander Killed in Gaza Blast, Hamas Blamed"; Scott Wilson, "Bomb Blast Wounds Kery Palestinian Official," *Washington Post,* May 21, 2006, A23; Joshua Mitnick, "Hamas Security Force in Actions," *Washington Times,* April 25, 2006.

104. "Palestinian Power Struggle," *Jane's Intelligence Digest,* May 24, 2006; Ali Waked, "Israel to Transfer Arms to Abbas's Forces," *Ynet news.com,* May 26, 2006. For a broader discussion, see Aaron D. Pina, "Fatah and Hamas: The New Palestinian Factional Reality," Washington, Congressional Research Service, RS22395, March 3, 2006.

105. For additional sources, see "Palestinian Islamic Jihad and the new political landscape," *Jane's Intelligence Review,* April 1, 2006; and "Jane's Country Profile, Gaza and the West Bank."

106. http://www.tkb.org/Group.jsp?groupID=82.

107. See U.S. Department of State, "Patterns of Global Terrorism, 1998," Washington, GPO, April 1999, Appendix B, "Syria," and "Iran."

108. Information Division, Israel Foreign Ministry, "The Islamic Jihad Movement," January 1995; Jewish Virtual Library, "Fathi Shiqaqi," http://www.us-israel.org/jsource/biography/shiqaqi.html (accessed June 14, 2004).

109. For a detailed discussion of this issue, see Rekhess, "The Terrorist Connection—Iran, the Islamic Jihad, and Hamas."

110. Ibid.

111. *Al-Hayat,* December 12, 1994; *Al-Wassat,* December 12, 1994.

112. Sergei Shargorodsky, "4 Palestinians Die on 'Day of Rage,'" *Associated Press Online,* October 28, 2000.

113. "Suicide and Car Bomb Attacks in Israel Since the Declaration of Principles," Israeli Ministry of Foreign Affairs, http://www.mfa.gov.il/.

114. "Two Car Bombs Shake Central Jerusalem," *Ha'aretz,* May 29, 2001.

115. Soraya Sarhaddi Nelson, "Islamic Jihad Finding No Shortage of Young Troops Ready to Die," *Knight-Ridder,* January 25, 2003.

116. Ibid.

117. Mohammed Daraghmeh, "In Search of Stealthier Suicide Attackers, Islamic Jihad Encourages Women," *Associated Press,* May 31, 2003.

118. Ibid.

119. Ehud Ya'ari, "Terror Update," *The Jerusalem Report,* April 23, 2001, 28.

120. Keith B. Richburg, *Washington Post,* October 25, 2000.

121. Ibid.

122. Ibrahim Barzak, "Palestinians Arrest Leading Militant," *Associated Press Online,* June 23, 2001.

123. Mark Lavie, "Palestinian Police Arrest Top Islamic Jihad Activist, Setting off Violent Protest," *Associated Press,* November 14, 2001.

124. Ibrahim Hazboun, "Israeli Tanks Surround Arafat Office after Suicide Bomber Kills 17 Bus Passengers," *Associated Press,* June 6, 2002.

125. Saud Abu Ramadan, "Islamic Jihad Leader Detained in Gaza," *United Press International,* June 9, 2002.

126. Soraya Sarhaddi Nelson, "Diverse Palestinian Factions Form Coalition that Could One Day Eclipse Arafat," *Knight-Ridder,* January 28, 2003.

127. Saud Abu Ramadan, "Hamas, Islamic Jihad Dismiss Premier Post," *United Press International,* March 11, 2003.

128. Mark Lavie, "Hamas Agrees to Halt Attacks on Israelis," *Associated Press,* June 25, 2003.

129. Ibid.

130. Afshin Valinejad, "Hezbollah Gives Warning to Israel," *Associated Press Online,* April 24, 2001.

131. U.S. Newswire, Inc., "AJC Report Examines Deadly Role of Palestinian Islamic Jihad Group," July 18, 2002.

132. Reuters, September 27, 1999, 1223.

133. "Security and Foreign Forces, Israel," *Jane's Sentinel Security Assessment—Eastern Mediterranean,* September 19, 2005.

134. International Policy Institute for Counter-Terrorism, "Fatah Tanzim," http://www.ict.org.il/inter_ter/orgdet.cfm?orgid=82 (accessed July 24, 2003).

135. Ibid.

136. Ibid.

137. Ibid.

138. Israeli Ministry of Foreign Affairs, "The Tanzim: Fatah's Fighters on the Ground," www.mfa.gov.il/mfa/go.asp?MFAH0i0p0 (accessed July 25, 2003).

139. Derk Kinnane Roelfsma, "Analysis: Arafat Has the Numbers to Fight," *United Press International,* December 11, 2001.

140. Ibid.

141. Gal Luft, "The Mirage of a Demilitarized Palestine," *The Middle East Quarterly,* VIII, no. 3 (Summer 2001).

142. International Policy Institute for Counter-Terrorism, "Fatah Tanzim."

143. Mary Curtius and Marjorie Miller, "Hamas Threatens New Bombings in Israel," *Los Angeles Times,* A1, October 8, 2000.

144. Larry Kaplow, "Mideast Clashes out of Control? Arafat's Grip on Palestinians May Be Slipping," *Atlanta Journal-Constitution,* October 10, 2000, A4, and Nomi Morris, "Palestinian Leaders Say They Are United but Don't Coordinate Attacks," Knight-Ridder News Service, November 23, 2000.

145. International Policy Institute for Counter-Terrorism, "Fatah Tanzim Attacks from 1988 to the Present," http://www.ict.org.il (accessed June 12, 2004).

146. http://palestinefacts.org/pf_current_marwan_barghouti.php (accessed June 13, 2004).

147. Fatah Tanzim, "Profiles of International Terrorist Organizations," The Institute for Counter-Terrorism, http://www.ict.org.il (accessed October 25, 2005).

148. International Policy Institute for Counter-Terrorism, "Martyrs of Al-Aqsa," http://www.ict.org.il/organizations/orgdet.cfm?orgid=83 (accessed July 25, 2003).

149. Ibid. (accessed August 11, 2004).

150. Ibid. (accessed July 25, 2003).

151. Khaled Abu Toameh, "Arafat Invites Aksa Brigade to Join Security Services," *Jerusalem Post,* June 12, 2004.

152. Ibid.

153. Khaled Abu Toameh, "Fatah Acknowledges Aksa Brigades Link," *Jerusalem Post,* June 15, 2004, http://www.jpost.com/servlet/Satellite?pagename=JPost/JPArticle/ShowFull&-cid=1087182010628 (accessed June 15, 2004).

154. Molly Moore and John Ward Anderson, "Militants Make Unprecedented Push to Gain a Voice in Palestinian Affairs," *Washington Post,* July 8, 2004, A1.

155. Ibid., A1.

156. Molly Moore, "Guns Turned on Arafat's Authority," *Washington Post,* July 22, 2004, A1.

157. Khaled Abu Toameh, "Arafat Invites Aksa Brigade to Join Security Services."

158. Molly Moore and John Ward Anderson, "Suicide Bombers Change Mideast's Military Balance," *Washington Post,* August 18, 2002, A1.

159. John Ward Anderson, "Israelis Begin to Pull out of Gaza," *Washington Post,* June 30, 2003, A1.

160. John Ward Anderson, "Bombing Points to Palestinian Fissure," *Washington Post,* July 9, 2003, A22.

161. John Ward Anderson, "Northern Gaza Emerges after Israeli Occupation," *Washington Post.com,* http://www.washingtonpost.com/ac2/wp-dyn?pagename=article&node=&contentI-d=A52413-2003Jun30&notFound=true (accessed July 31, 2003).

162. International Policy Institute for Counter-Terrorism, Casualties Database, http://www.ict.org.il (accessed June 12, 2004).

163. Ibid.

164. Michele K. Esposito, "Chronology: 16 February–15 May 2004," *Journal of Palestine Studies* 23, no. 4 (Summer 2004).

165. David Rudge, "IAF Hits Al-Aqsa Leader in Nablus," *Jerusalem Post,* June 15, 2004, http://www.jpost.com/servlet/Satellite?pagename=JPost/JPArticle/ShowFull&-cid=1087290134721 (accessed June 15, 2004).

166. Arnon Regular, "IDF Kills 7 Militants in Nablus Operation," *Haaretz.com,* June 27, 2004.

167. Khaled Abu Toameh, "Fatah Acknowledges Aksa Brigades Link."

168. U.S. State Department, *Country Reports on Terrorism,* Office of the Coordinator for Counterterrorism, April 27, 2005, http://www.state.gov/s/ct/rls/45394.htm, and April 2006, http://www.state.gov/s/ct/rls/crt/2005/65275.htm.

169. "Suicide and Car Bomb Attacks in Israel since the Declaration of Principles," Israeli Ministry of Foreign Affairs Web site, http://www.mfa.gov.il/.

170. Ibid.

171. Voice of Israel Radio, Jerusalem, October 10, 2000, supplied by BBC Worldwide Monitoring.

172. "Shells Fired at Northern IDF Base," *Ha'aretz,* January 4, 2001.

173. Tracy Wilkinson, "Palestinians' Mortar Fire May Signal a Deadlier Conflict; Fighters Claim Success at Unnerving their Enemy. But Retaliation by Israel Exacts a Heavy Price," *Los Angeles Times,* April 10, 2001, 9.

174. Ibid., 9.

175. Steve Rodan, "Israel Claims PA is Producing Rockets," *Jane's Defence Weekly,* November 14, 2001; Doug Richardson, "IDF Hunts Qassam-II Rocket Workshops," *Jane's Missiles and Rockets,* April 1, 2002.

176. Doug Richardson, "IDF Hunts Qassam-II Rocket Workshops," *Jane's Missiles and Rockets,* April 1, 2002; Ed Blanche, "Hamas Boosts the Range of Qassam Rockets," *Jane's Missiles and Rockets,* September 1, 2003.

177. Mara Karlin, "Palestinian Qassam Rockets Pose New Threat to Israel," *Jewish Virtual Library,* http://www.jewishvirtuallibrary.org/jsource/Terrorism/Qassam.html (accessed July 20, 2004); Alon Ben-David, "IDF Wary After Qassam 2 Strike," *Jane's Defence Weekly,* September 10, 2003.

178. Blanche, "Hamas Boosts the Range of Qassam Rockets"; Ed Blanche, "Hamas' Qassam Rockets Claim First Fatalities," *Jane's Missiles and Rockets,* August 1, 2004.

179. Richardson, "IDF Hunts Qassam-II Rocket Workshops."

180. Blanche, "Hamas Boosts the Range of Qassam Rockets."

181. Nir Hasson, Aluf Benn, and Arnon Regular, "Qassam Claims First Fatalities in Sderot," *Haaretz.com,* June 29, 2004; Peter Enav, "Palestinian Rocket Kills 2 Israeli Youths," *The Associated Press,* September 29, 2004.

182. Kifner, "3 Are Left Dead By Suicide Blasts In Tel Aviv Street."

183. Matthew Levitt, "Assessing Arafat's Performance in the Fight Against Terror," *Peacewatch,* December 21, 2001.

184. Dan Williams, "Arafat Calls for End to All Attacks: After His Address, a Skeptical Israel Says, 'Start Making Arrests,'" *International Herald Tribune,* December 17, 2001.

185. "The Palestinians: Arafat's Choice," *The Economist,* December 15, 2001.

186. Levitt, "Assessing Arafat's Performance in the Fight Against Terror."

187. Ibid.

188. Ibid.

189. Howard Schneider, "Bomb's Fallout Sets Back Goals of Palestinians: Arafat's Cease-Fire is Seen as Result of Shifting Opinion," *Washington Post,* June 7, 2001, A26.

CHAPTER 9

1. CIA, *World Factbook, 2006,* "Syria," http://www.odci.gov/cia/publications/factbook/geos/sy.html.

2. CIA, *World Factbook, 2006,* "Syria," http://www.odci.gov/cia/publications/factbook/geos/sy.html.

3. Gary C. Gambill, "Hooked on Lebanon," *Middle East Quarterly,* 7, no. 4 (Fall 2005): 36–38.

4. Lee Kass, "The Growing Syrian Missile Threat," *Middle East Quarterly,* 7, no. 4 (Fall 2005): 32–33.

5. Riad Kahwaji, "Syria Ups Border Security Measures," *Defense News,* August 1, 2005, 14.

6. Kass, "Syria After Lebanon: The Growing Syrian Missile Threat," *Middle East Quarterly,* 7, no. 4 (Fall 2005): 28–29, http://www.meforum.org/article/755.

7. Riad Kahwaji, "Analysts: Syria May Broaden Proxy Wars Into Golan Heights," *Defense News,* December 1, 2003, 14.

8. Robin Hughes, "Iran Aides Syria's CW Program," *Jane's Defence Weekly,* October 26, 2005.

9. Table on Syrian Force Structure by Force, produced from the IISS, *Military Balance,* "Syria," 2005/6 editions.

10. Ibid.

11. Ibid.

12. Alon Ben-David, "Syria Upgrades T-72 Tanks," *Jane's Defence Weekly*, August 6, 2003, http://jdw.janes.com (accessed January 8, 2004). Labeled 39.

13. Elizabeth Konstantinova, "Bulgarian Arms Exports Investigated," *Jane's Intelligence Review*, February 1, 2003, http://jir.janes.com (accessed January 8, 2004). Labeled 40.

14. *Jane's Defence Weekly*, November 2, 1999, 20.

15. "Syria Plans Russian Arms Purchase," United Press International, February 17, 1999.

16. Ed Blanche, "Syria Discusses Buying Advanced Russian Systems," *Jane's Defence Weekly*, May 19, 1999, 17.

17. Simon Saradzhyan, "Bombing Spurs Interest in Russian Craft, Defenses," *Defense News*, July 19, 1999, 11.

18. Sharon LaFraniere, "Russia, Syria Hint at Weapons Deal," *The Washington Post*, July 7, 1999, A6.

19. Damian Kemp, "Russia Pushes Defense Sales as Exports Hit Highest for Years," *Jane's Defence Weekly*, July 14, 1999, 17.

20. *Jane's Defence Weekly*, November 2, 1999, 20.

21. Robin Hughes, "Country Briefing: Syria—Syria's Dilemma," *Jane's Defence Weekly*, September 7, 2005, http://jdw.janes.com (accessed September 28, 2005).

22. Riad Kahwaji, "Russia, Syria Revive Ties with Debt Reduction, *Defense News*, January 31, 2005, 10.

23. "Russia Halts Plans to Sell Igla to Syria," *Jane's Defence Weekly*, November 6, 2002, http://jdw.janes.com (accessed January 9, 2004). Labeled 41.

24. "Russia Confirms Missile Deal with Iran," *UPI*, December 6, 2005.

25. "Israel Anger and Russian Arms Deal," *BBC News*, January 12, 2005, www.bbc.co.uk (accessed January 21, 2005).

26. Hughes, "Country Briefing: Syria—Syria's Dilemma."

27. Ibid.

28. Ibid.

29. Ibid.

30. The data in this section draw heavily from a number of basic source documents on the balance. IISS, *Military Balance*, various editions; Jaffee Center for Strategic Studies, *Military Balance in the Middle East*, various editions; *Jane's Sentinel Security Assessments*, "Syria," various editions.

31. Hughes, "Country Briefing: Syria—Syria's Dilemma."

32. Interviews and IISS, *Military Balance*, various editions.

33. The data in this section draw heavily from a number of basic source documents on the balance. IISS, *Military Balance*, various editions; Jaffee Center for Strategic Studies, *Military Balance in the Middle East*, various editions; *Jane's Sentinel Security Assessments*, "Syria," various editions.

34. *Defense News*, June 30, 1997, 4.

35. *Flight International*, August 24, 1993, 12.

36. Based on interviews with British, U.S., and Israeli experts. For earlier source material see *Washington Times*, January 16, 1992, G-4; *Washington Post*, February 1, 1992, A1; *Washington Post*, February 2, 1992, A1 and A25; *Washington Post*, February 5, 1992, A-19; *Financial Times*, February 6, 1992, 4; *Christian Science Monitor*, February 6, 1992, 19; *Defense News*, February 17, 1992, 1.

37. Hughes, "Country Briefing: Syria—Syria's Dilemma."

38. The data in this section draw heavily from a number of basic source documents on the balance. *Jane's Fighting Ships,* various editions; IISS, *Military Balance,* various editions; Jaffee Center for Strategic Studies, *Military Balance in the Middle East,* various editions; Jane's Sentinel Security Assessments, "Syria," various editions.

39. *Jane's Fighting Ships,* various editions; IISS, *Military Balance,* various editions.

40. Interviews and *Jane's Sentinel,* "Syria."

41. Interviews and various editions of *Jane's Sentinel,* "Syria."

42. *Jane's Fighting Ships,* and IISS, *Military Balance,* various editions.

43. The data in this section draw heavily from a number of basic source documents on the balance. IISS, *Military Balance,* various editions; Jaffee Center for Strategic Studies, *Military Balance in the Middle East,* various editions; *Jane's Sentinel Security Assessments,* "Syria," various editions.

44. Office of the Coordinator for Counterterrorism, *Country Reports on Terrorism,* Chapter 5B, U.S. State Department, Washington, April 27, 2005, http://www.state.gov/s/ct/rls/45392.htm.

45. http://www.state.gov/s/ct/rls/crt/2005/64337.htm.

46. U.S. State Department, *Country Reports on Terrorism,* Office of the Coordinator for Counterterrorism, April 28, 2006. Chapter 6—"State Sponsors of Terror," http://www.state.gov/g/drl/rls/hrrpt/2004/41720.htm.

47. U.S. State Department, *Country Reports on Human Rights Practices—2005,* "Syria," Bureau of Democracy, Human Rights, and Labor, March 8, 2006, http://www.state.gov/g/drl/rls/hrrpt/2005/61699.htm.

48. Hughes, "Iran Aides Syria's CW Program."

49. Ibid.

50. See Kass, "Syria After Lebanon: The Growing Syrian Missile Threat."

51. http://www.fas.org/nuke/guide/russia/theater/ss-26.htm.

52. Center for Nonproliferation Studies, Monterey Institute of International Studies, "Syria Weapons of Mass Destruction Profile," May 1998, http://www.cns.miis.edu/research/wmdme/syria.html (accessed March 2003).

53. Michael Eisenstadt, "Syria's Strategic Weapons," *Jane's Intelligence Review,* April 1993, 168–173.

54. Dani Shoham, "Poisoned Missiles: Syria's Doomsday Deterrent," *Middle East Quarterly* (Fall 2002).

55. *Jane's Defence Weekly,* June 19, 2002, 40.

56. Sid Balman Jr., *UPI,* July 23, 1996; in *Executive News Service,* July 24, 1996.

57. *Far Eastern Economic Review,* August 22, 1991, 6.

58. Eisenstadt, "Syria's Strategic Weapons."

59. Elaine Sciolino with Eric Schmitt, "China Said to Sell Parts for Missiles," *New York Times,* January 31, 1992, A1, A2.

60. Shoham, "Poisoned Missiles: Syria's Doomsday Deterrent."

61. Steven Rodan and Andrew Koch, "Syria Preparing to Build Extended-Range 'Scud,'" *Jane's Defence Weekly,* June 19, 2002, 40.

62. *Jane's Sentinel Security Assessment,* posted June 28, 2001.

63. Center for Nonproliferation Studies, Monterey Institute of International Studies, "North Korean Missile Exports and Technical Assistance to Syria," http://www.nti.org/db/profiles/dprk/msl/ie/NKM_EesyriGO.html (accessed March 2003).

64. Numbers of aircraft are from various editions of IISS, *The Military Balance.*

65. *Jane's Sentinel Security Assessment,* posted June 28, 2001.

66. Bill Gertz and Rowan Scarborough, "Syrian Gas Practice," *The Washington Times,* November 26, 1999, A10.

67. *Jane's Defence Weekly,* September 3, 1997, 3.

68. Central Intelligence Agency, "Unclassified Report to Congress on the Acquisition of Technology Relating to Weapons of Mass Destruction and Advanced Conventional Munitions, 1 July Through 31 December 2001."

69. Eisenstadt, "Syria's Strategic Weapons"; in Center for Nonproliferation Studies, Monterey Institute of International Studies, "Country Overviews: Syria (Nuclear)," http://www.nti.org (accessed March 2003).

70. Central Intelligence Agency, "Unclassified Report to Congress on the Acquisition of Technology Relating to Weapons of Mass Destruction and Advanced Conventional Munitions, 1 July Through 31 December 2001."

71. "Russian Nuclear Assistance to Syria: Scam or Scandal?," *Middle East Intelligence Bulletin* 5, no. 1 (January 2003).

72. Washington Institute, *Supporting Peace* (Washington: Washington Institute, 1994), 83.

73. *UPI,* August 3, 1993.

74. United Nations Peacekeeping Operations, "Current Peacekeeping Operations, Syrian Golan Heights, United Nations Disengagement Observer Force," UNDOF Mission Profile, July 14, 1999. The budget for the force is roughly $33.66 million per year.

75. Kenneth S. Brower, "The Middle East Military Balance: Israel versus the Rest," *International Defense Review* 7 (1986): 910–911.

76. "The IDF's Security Principles," Office of the IDF Spokesman, April 1995; and Scotty Fisher, "Country Briefing Israel," *Jane's Defence Weekly,* February 18, 1995, 29–38.

77. For a good summary of events, see "Syria Under Seige, Bashar's Greatest Test," IISS, online strategic notes, Vol. 11, Issue 9, November 200501, November 2005.

78. For an analysis of Syria's economic profits from its past position in Lebanon, see Gary C. Gambill, "Syria After Lebanon: Hooked on Lebanon," *Middle East Quarterly* (Fall 2005), http://www.meforum.org/article/769.

79. Michael Slackman, "As Syria's Influence in Lebanon Wanes, Iran Moves In," *New York Times,* March 13, 2006.

80. See Kass, "Syria After Lebanon: The Growing Syrian Missile Threat."

81. "The Syrian Reshuffle: Consolidating the Hardline," *The Estimate,* February 27, 2006, 9–10.

CHAPTER 10

1. Kenneth R. Timmerman, "The Crisis Has Begun," *The Washington Times,* January 7, 2006.

2. Ali Akbar Dareini, "Iran Says It Will Resist 'Bully' Nations," *Associated Press,* February 1, 2006.

About the Author

ANTHONY H. CORDESMAN is Senior Fellow at the Center for Strategic and International Studies and a military analyst for ABC News. A frequent commentator on National Public Radio, he is the author of numerous books on security issues and has served in a number of senior positions in the U.S. government.

Recent Titles by Anthony H. Cordesman

2006

Arab-Israeli Military Forces in an Era of Asymmetric Wars
The Changing Dynamics of Energy in the Middle East, with Khalid R. Al-Rodhan
Gulf Military Forces in an Era of Asymmetric Wars, with Khalid R. Al-Rodhan

2005

The Israeli-Palestinian War: Escalating to Nowhere, with Jennifer Moravitz
National Security in Saudi Arabia: Threats, Responses, and Challenges, with Nawaf Obaid
Iraqi Security Forces: A Strategy for Success, with Patrick Baetjer

2004

The Military Balance in the Middle East
Energy and Development in the Middle East

2003

The Iraq War: Strategy, Tactics, and Military Lessons
Saudi Arabia Enters the Twenty-First Century: The Political, Foreign Policy, Economic, and Energy Dimensions
Saudi Arabia Enters the Twenty-First Century: The Military and International Security Dimensions

2001

Peace and War: The Arab-Israeli Military Balance Enters the 21st Century
A Tragedy of Arms: Military and Security Developments in the Maghreb
The Lessons and Non-Lessons of the Air and Missile Campaign in Kosovo

Cyber-threats, Information Warfare, and Critical Infrastructure Protection: Defending the U.S. Homeland, with Justin G. Cordesman

Terrorism, Asymmetric Warfare, and Weapons of Mass Destruction: Defending the U.S. Homeland

Strategic Threats and National Missile Defenses: Defending the U.S. Homeland

2000

Iran's Military Forces in Transition: Conventional Threats and Weapons of Mass Destruction